KISSINGER

KISSINGER

by Marvin Kalb and Bernard Kalb

LITTLE, BROWN AND COMPANY — BOSTON–TORONTO

FIRST EDITION

Library of Congress Catalog No. 74-5892

T 08/74

The authors gratefully acknowledge permission to quote from the following previously published materials:

"Twelve Professors Visit Capitol Hill Along Their Road to Damascus" by Michael E. Kinsley, published in the *Harvard Crimson*, May 15, 1970, Vol. 150, No. 78.

"I Think We Have a Very Unhappy Colleague-on-Leave Tonight" by Michael E. Kinsley, published in the *Harvard Crimson*, May 19, 1970, Vol. 150, No. 80.

"Kissinger's Pre-Nixon Peace Efforts; Sounded Ho Out Through Intermediary" by Jack Anderson, published in "Washington Merry-Go-Round," June 16, 1972. Copyright © 1972 by United Feature Syndicate, Inc.

Published simultaneously in Canada
by Little, Brown & Company (Canada) Limited

PRINTED IN THE UNITED STATES OF AMERICA

To Bella and in memory of Max,
To Madeleine and Phyllis,
And to Tanah, Marina, Deborah,
Claudia, Judith, and Sarinah

Acknowledgments

OUR THANKS GO FIRST to Henry A. Kissinger, who, as an historian as well as a statesman, understands the critical importance of primary sourcing. He has been generous with his time and his knowledge. He has never asked to read the manuscript. He appreciates the difference between journalism and history, as we do. Journalism is the raw data of history. This has been an attempt by two journalists to report on one man and his central role in the history of our time.

In the course of researching this book, over a number of years, we have conducted long interviews with scores of American and foreign officials in cities all over the world. Most of them retain positions of high responsibility in their governments. They deal with Kissinger, directly and indirectly, on a regular basis. They prefer to remain anonymous. We are respecting their wish, but we want all of them to know that we are indebted to them.

Madeleine Green Kalb conceived the idea for this joint project. She quarterbacked and edited the entire book, from first to final draft, with her usual devotion to clarity and substance. Her contribution has been prodigious, and our gratitude to her is deep and heartfelt.

Phyllis Bernstein Kalb also made a significant contribution to the book. She pursued facts, helped edit, and added style to the manuscript. Her commitment was total; and we are grateful for her encouragement.

Not for the first time, we offer our thanks to William J. Small, Senior Vice-President of CBS News, for his generosity and understanding. We also offer our thanks to Richard Salant, President, CBS News; Gordon

Manning, Vice-President, CBS News; and Sanford Socolow, Vice-President and Washington bureau chief, CBS News. Together, they have created an environment of professionalism, of which we are proud.

We are grateful to Larned G. Bradford, Senior Editor of Little, Brown and Company, for his encouragement and cooperation, especially during the final phase of the book's preparation.

Morton Janklow deserves a special note of appreciation. He is our friend and lawyer, and his help was invaluable. He provided the spark.

Harriet Moidel of CBS News typed and retyped the manuscript. We thank her not only for the skill and speed of her work but also for her loyalty, intelligence and friendship.

We are grateful to hundreds of colleagues around the world. They helped with the research, too, sharing their impressions, observations and knowledge with us.

We are also grateful to members of our family for their patience and understanding: Estelle Kalb Levine, Rose Bell Green, William P. Green, Sue Bernstein; and our daughters, who can now go back to making noise at home.

Needless to say, all errors are my brother's.

MARVIN KALB   BERNARD KALB

April 9, 1974
Washington, D.C.

Contents

The Summits of 1972

Negotiating the Final Pullout

From Scandal to War

Illustrations

With the advance American party in Peking, October, 1971. (Official White House Photo)

Touring the Great Wall of China, October, 1971. (Official White House Photo)

With Chinese Foreign Minister Chi Peng-fei, October, 1971. (Official White House Photo)

Briefing the press after the second China visit, October, 1971. (Official White House Photo)

The summit in China, February, 1972. (Hsinhua photo via the White House)

Toasting Chou En-Lai, February, 1972. (Official White House Photo)

With Anatoly Dobrynin, March, 1972. (Official White House Photo)

Kissinger and Nixon brief Senators Scott and Mansfield on China, April, 1972. (Official White House Photo)

At Kremlin signing ceremony, May, 1972. (Official White House Photo)

Kissinger and Nixon in Moscow, May, 1972. (Official White House Photo)

Between pages 360 and 361

With his brother Walter and their children, August, 1972. (Wide World Photo)

With Nguyen Van Thieu, August, 1972. (United Press International Photo)

At the Republican convention at Miami Beach, August, 1972. (Wide World Photo)

Kissinger at "Peace is at hand" news conference, October, 1972. (Official White House Photo)

With General Alexander Haig, Jr., at the Pentagon, November, 1972. (Official White House Photo)

With North Vietnam's Le Duc Tho, November, 1972. (Photo by Steve Northup, © Time Inc.)

With aides in the U.S. Embassy in Paris, December, 1972. (Photo by Harry Benson, © Time Inc.)

At the signing of the Vietnam peace agreement, January 23, 1973. (United Press International Photo)

Boar hunting with Brezhnev at Zavidovo, May, 1973. (Tass from Sovfoto)

The day's catch at Zavidovo. (Tass from Sovfoto)

At San Clemente party for Brezhnev, June, 1973. (Copyright by J. P. Laffont-Sygma)

With family after being sworn in as Secretary of State, September 22, 1973. (United Press International Photo)

Reviewing honor guard in Rabat, Morocco, November, 1973. (United Press International Photo)

With King Faisal in Saudi Arabia, November, 1973. (Photo by Jerrold L. Schecter, © Time Inc.)

Kissinger in Egypt, November, 1973. (Abbas Photo)

With Mao Tse-tung in China, November, 1973. (Wide World Photo)

President Anwar Sadat embraces Kissinger, January, 1974. (Wide World Photo)

Mr. and Mrs. Henry Kissinger, April, 1974. (Photo by David Hume Kennerly, *Time* Magazine © Time Inc.)

With the authors, March, 1974. (Photo by Dennis Brack)

KISSINGER

ONE

An Introduction

HENRY ALFRED KISSINGER is an extravaganza — all by himself. At fifty-one, after only five years in Washington, this energetic balancer of power has emerged from the relative obscurity of a Harvard professorship to become the most celebrated and controversial diplomat of our time. He has come to be recognized as the very portrait of American diplomacy, the way George Washington is identified with the dollar bill. A legend in half a decade, he has been described as, among other things, the "second most powerful man in the world," "conscience of the Administration," "official apologist," "compassionate hawk," "vigilant dove," "Dr. Strangelove," "household word," "the playboy of the Western Wing," "Nixon's Metternich," "Nixon's secret agent," "the Professident of the United States," "Jackie Onassis of the Nixon Administration," "Nobel warrior," "Mideast cyclone," "reluctant wiretapper," and "Secretary of the world" — a long list, especially in Washington, where praise of any sort is the only thing that never exceeds its budget.

From the beginning, Kissinger outraged the gray men who guarded the corridors of Richard Nixon's White House. His accent, his brilliance, his flair for self-promotion labeled him a heretic, destined for banishment. Yet it turned out that *they* — the Haldemans, the Ehrlichmans, those caught up in the torrent of Watergate — were to go, and *he* was to go on to even greater heights. From his start in the basement of the West Wing of the White House, as Assistant to the President for National Security Affairs, he would vault to the seventh floor of the State Department as Secretary of State, a position once held by Thomas Jefferson, Daniel

Webster, and John Foster Dulles. It was an unprecedented leap for someone of his origins — a refugee from Nazi Germany, a Jew. En route,
Kissinger acquired such a formidable reputation that, by the beginning of
1974, he would be viewed by many of Nixon's critics as the sole legiti-
mizer of a President discredited by Watergate. Whereas Kissinger had
once needed Nixon as a channel to power, Nixon now needed Kissinger
to help him remain in power. Their relationship had become so topsy-
turvy that the academic aide at Nixon's side was seen as perhaps the last
fortress against the unmaking of a President.

Henry Kissinger arrived in Washington at a ripe moment interna-
tionally. The United States and the world, he recognized, were in a fluid,
transitional period. For the first time, the nuclear superpowers were beginning to appreciate the limits of their own power and the need to find some
way of reducing tensions. And the other fellow's increasingly bigger bomb
wasn't the only convincing reason; wherever Kissinger looked, he saw
significant changes taking place within countries and among countries.

The United States no longer regarded itself as the policeman of the
world; those long, frustrating years of war in Indochina had altered
America's image of itself, but, even more important, the lopsided strategic
advantage that America had once enjoyed was lost. The Soviet Union
and China were now more hostile to each other than to the United
States; what was once thought by many analysts to be pure gospel — a
monolithic unity among the Communist countries, with Moscow calling
the signals — had proved to be a misreading of history. What is more, the
conflict between Moscow and Peking, coupled with their domestic problems, had prodded Russia into softening its policy of blunt confrontation
with the West, and China into reexamining its policy of lofty isolation.
Europe and Japan had more than regained their economic vitality; they
were now capable of playing a greater role in international affairs. Some
Arab leaders were beginning to recognize that war with Israel was not
the only policy option open to them. The new countries had emerged
from their first outbursts of nationalism and now seemed eager for more
profitable dealings with the rest of the world. There were tensions, but
not all were threatening. The world seemed to be rumbling its way
toward new relationships.

To Kissinger, these changing facts of international life added up to a
unique moment in history. He regarded timing as critical. "Opportunities
can not be hoarded; once past, they are usually irretrievable," he once

wrote. *When* to act, not only what to do, became a cardinal feature of his diplomatic style. He shuttled to and from everywhere, tenaciously trying to exploit the moment of opportunity. And, operating in the dangerous but potentially productive area between new hopes for peace and old fears of extinction, he helped promote policies that would be widely regarded as an effort to create a more relaxed, if still well-armed, world.

Foreign policy was the Administration's forte, with Kissinger its peripatetic negotiator. He would sip champagne with Kremlin leaders, humanizing them for a whole generation of Americans raised on the Cold War. He would try to establish a new, more rational and responsible dialogue with them, making détente — still one more try at détente — a worthy goal of American policy and putting limits, if possible, on the production and deployment of deadly nuclear weapons. He would journey to Peking, replacing two decades of hostility with a new effort to communicate with a quarter of the human race. He would fly the Atlantic at least a dozen times secretly, many more times publicly, to negotiate a compromise settlement of the Vietnam war, fighting off the hawks with one hand, the doves with the other, until, finally, in January, 1973, he was able to arrange a deal with Hanoi for the return of American prisoners from North Vietnam and the withdrawal of American troops from South Vietnam. In the Middle East, he would introduce "shuttle diplomacy" — flying back and forth between Jerusalem and Aswan, or Jerusalem and Damascus — in a major effort to substitute a pattern of negotiations for the endless conflicts of the region, achieving at least the start of disengagement by Arab and Israeli armies from the war zone. Altogether, his extraordinary efforts to recruit the nations of the world, big and small, to new rules of behavior became the stuff of international drama. They reached a climax in late 1973 when he was awarded the Nobel Prize for Peace for his role in the Vietnam cease-fire negotiations.

Not that everything he touched turned to gold.

More than one of his heralded agreements, when scrutinized in the cold light of dawn, appeared to lose some of their glow. His penchant for secrecy and surprise kept a number of America's allies out in the cold. His virtuoso style of diplomacy during the first Nixon term left the State Department demoralized and Congress just another spectator. Even his Nobel Prize was challenged by some critics as premature, a bad joke, particularly since Vietnam was still at war.

There were other criticisms too, more specific in nature.

From the left there was a chorus of indictments accusing him of having failed to justify, in moral or political terms, those extra four years of U.S. war in Vietnam and divisiveness at home. From the right came the accusation that he had given away too much to the Russians during the SALT negotiations, compromising American security in his quest for détente. And from his friends, right and left, there was deep disappointment that he had "tilted" in favor of Pakistan against India in 1971, while the soldiers from Islamabad were conducting what was described as mass murder of the Bengalis of East Pakistan.

Nor was that all.

He came under increasing suspicion as to the exact extent of his involvement in the wiretapping of his own National Security Council staff and of the press. His attempts to explain his relationship with the "plumbers" and to play down reports of military spying within the NSC left many with the uneasy feeling that he was being less than candid. His defense of his role was regarded by his admirers as plain realism and by his critics as plain deception.

Kissinger's route to power was created by the presidential election of 1968: Nixon won, and Kissinger was available. Though he had been anti-Nixon, Kissinger found the invitation to join the White House irresistible; it was a question of opportunity over doubt. He had been shuttling from Cambridge to Washington ever since the Eisenhower Administration, offering his opinions about foreign policy as a consultant on the outskirts of power. The new President-elect wanted to bring him into the center of power. Nixon was seeking a foreign policy specialist who shared his perception of how to manipulate America's dwindling power to achieve a new balance of power — what he would later call "a structure of peace." The fact that Kissinger's crossing over to Nixon was seen as a defection from the skeptical Eastern Establishment only heightened Nixon's conviction that he had made the right choice.

They converged from different starting points: Nixon, via hard-nosed politics, a Californian, chauvinistically conservative; Kissinger, via intellectual achievement, an immigrant, a hard-liner with an international bent. Yet they ended up with reasonably similar views on policy and the uses of power. Moreover, Kissinger would provide a coherent conceptual framework for Nixon's sudden diplomatic maneuvers. In their new role as gravediggers of ideology, both shared a global *realpolitik* that placed a higher priority on pragmatism than on morality. Both, almost as if they saw the planet as an unsafe place to inhabit, shared a compulsion for secrecy, a distrust of bureaucracy, an elitist approach to diplomacy; both preferred to present the world with a fait accompli rather than to reveal their intentions in advance.

True, their personalities are different, and both men are undoubtedly relieved that this is so widely recognized. Kissinger is warm, friendly, sensitive; Nixon's aloofness can never be mistaken. Kissinger can be a connoisseur of nuance, with a talent for subtle explanations and, when necessary, for elegant double-talk; Nixon specializes in the hard hyperbole, the sentence painted in black and white. Indeed, there are times when one catches a glimpse of pained self-control as Kissinger listens to a presidential oration. Both men are loners, at the summit yet still dogged by insecurities; but one prefers to hide away at crowded social gatherings, often with interchangeable celebrities, while the other hides away in more traditional hideaways.

Indeed, they are an odd couple. After more than five years of constant contact, their personal relationship remains more correct than close — even though Kissinger no longer has to worry about proving his loyalty or being undercut by the President's praetorians. For all practical purposes, Kissinger's dealings with Nixon have been business, not social. Occasionally, the President will invite his foreign policy adviser to a private dinner at the White House, but as a companion to the President, Kissinger has always been outdistanced by Charles "Bebe" Rebozo. Formality, the tone set by the President, has always characterized the Nixon-Kissinger relationship. Despite their differences in temperament, the man whom Nixon named as Secretary of State in August, 1973, wholeheartedly supports his chief's foreign policy. "You can assume," Kissinger once said, "that if I could not support a major policy I would resign."

It can be said of Henry Kissinger that the government saves money by paying him at a flat rate instead of by the hour. He puts in one of Washington's longest days. Up early — six hours of uninterrupted sleep means that the world has enjoyed a restful night, too — he's quickly on his way out of his six-room townhouse overlooking Rock Creek Park, often with his laundry in one hand and his attaché case in the other. In his early NSC days, he used to drive a white Mercedes through the two miles of rush-hour traffic to the White House but, both because of the pressures of work and the requirements of security, he soon capitulated to a chauffeur-driven limousine. He usually has breakfast at his office. While the decor in his home has been described as Midwestern Holiday Inn, his office is more a mix of Early American and Contemporary Bureaucratic. Since 1970, his NSC office has been on street level, just down the hallway from the Oval Office. It has tall French windows, and he's often framed in one of them, foot on the sill, while he talks on the phone. He'll wave to reporters passing by on their way to the White House Press Room, just a few yards away.

The walls, shelves, and tabletops are decorated with a variety of paintings, bric-a-brac, and mementos of his world travels. The most striking painting hangs just over a couch; it is a huge canvas in subtle tones of purple undulating out of a central reddish circle. Kissinger finds it relaxing. The painting, on loan from a friend in Cambridge, is the work of Jules Olitski, an abstract colorist of the New York school. "Don't tell Olitski where it is," the friend once said during the days of heavy U.S. involvement in Vietnam. "He's against the war, and he wouldn't like the idea of it hanging in Henry's office in the White House." Other paintings are souvenirs of his journeys to Moscow and Peking. Leonid Brezhnev presented him with a large still life, a bouquet of flowers painted by P. Kongolovsky, a socialist realist artist, in 1952. The Chinese gave him a scroll copy of a horse painted by Hsü Pei-hung, who achieved international fame before his death in 1953. The shelves are filled with books, including some he wrote himself. On a table behind his desk is a framed photograph of the President. "To Henry Kissinger," says the inscription, "for whose wise counsel and dedicated services far beyond the call of duty I shall always remain grateful. From his friend, Richard Nixon." On the desk, a direct telephone to the President.

When he was named Secretary of State, he inherited a second, more commodious suite of offices on the seventh floor of the huge governmental building in Foggy Bottom that he once did his best to avoid. He quickly introduced a more contemporary decor into the main sitting room, with abstract art, including paintings by Rothko and Pousette-Dart, illuminated by floor lights, replacing some of the portraits from the pages of American history that were on display during the tenure of his predecessor, William P. Rogers. A glance through his office window offers a panoramic view of the Washington Monument, the Lincoln Memorial, and, on a clear day, the Lee Mansion on the other side of the Potomac. He now spends more time here than he does at his NSC office, not only because of the requirements of being Secretary but perhaps because he wants to put a bit of distance between himself and the stricken leader in the White House.

Toward dusk, Kissinger will be reminded by his secretary about what's on the calendar for the second half of his working day. It could be a diplomatic reception at one of the embassies on Massachusetts Avenue, a cocktail party in Georgetown, an opening of a new play at the Kennedy Center, or sometimes all three. His very appearance at any affair proclaims it a triumph; most hostesses would rather have, say, twenty-three minutes of Henry than a full evening of all the other members of the Cabinet and Congress combined. Depending on the ambience, he will turn up as either an intellectual besieged by the problems of the world or a swinger tossing off surefire one-liners from his growing repertoire. The party over, Kissinger will begin working again. Often he waves a breezy farewell to his hostess, steps into his limousine, and promptly settles down to study a sheaf of documents handed him by an aide waiting out in the cold.

Yet for all the long hours he puts in, he has never looked better. Since his arrival in Washington, he's been wearing his hair and his waistline a little thicker. His contours seem to change with each overseas trip. In November, 1973, he came back from a ten-country, twenty-five-thousand-mile journey that took him to the Middle East and China looking as though Chou En-lai had fattened him up on shark's fin in three shreds and spongy bamboo shoots with egg-white consommé. "When I negoti-ate," he confessed, "I get nervous. When I get nervous, I eat. By the time this Arab-Israeli affair is over, I'll probably weigh three hundred twenty pounds." In Washington, he usually can be found lunching at the fash-ionable and expensive Sans Souci, where other diners will spend more time studying Kissinger than their checks. His fluctuating waistline has been good business for one of the local formal attire rental establishments. Since he can never be sure what he will weigh in at for any White House state dinner, he generally ends up renting white tie and tails at seventeen dollars a night. During Nixon's first term, Kissinger was outfitted no less than thirty-three times. Before dinner, his size is forty-two regular.

Along with the change from campus tweeds at Harvard to diplomatic uniform in Washington came, perhaps surprisingly to Kissinger himself, a new reputation as the nation's reigning "swinger." "I'm baffled and stunned," confessed a professor friend in Cambridge. "It is not the Henry we knew here."

"His swinging?" says another old friend. "Why not? It humanizes him."

Kissinger had his own assessment of his appeal. "They are women attracted only to my power," he used to say. "But what happens when my power is gone? They're not going to sit around and play chess with me." His most celebrated diagnosis of his success: "Power is the ultimate aphrodisiac."

Before he became Secretary of State, he cultivated his swinger image; but many people suspected he was really a swinger by photograph. He would pop up next to one charmer or another at one function or another and a lurking cameraman would film them side by side; the publication of the photo in the morning newspaper would further enhance his image as a swinger. As for Kissinger himself on this subject, he used to play it cool. There's a story that once when Peter Peterson, then Commerce Secretary and one of Kissinger's closer friends in town, asked him, "Tell me, Henry, when you go out with the girls . . ." Kissinger interrupted, grinning broadly. "Eat your heart out, Peterson," he chortled. That implied question might better be answered by the girls themselves, or at least by one who perhaps knows him best. "Henry," she says, definitively, "is very old-fashioned. He has old-fashioned virtues, and a strong belief in family life. He is a very moral man. The 'swinger' is as square as he can be."

After Kissinger became Secretary of State, the "swinger" became a "square." The Hollywood starlets vanished from his side and, on March 30, 1974, he married Nancy Sharon Maginnes, a tall, attractive New Yorker whom he had known since the early 1960s. With the same sort of secrecy that had marked his early trips to Peking and Moscow, he slipped out of the State Department and crossed the Potomac to Arlington, Virginia, where the civil ceremony took place. The newlyweds were already airborne for a ten-day honeymoon in Acapulco, Mexico, when the State Department made the announcement. This was one society note that was front-page news around the world.

The genius of Kissinger, a columnist once remarked, is that he tells you what he is *not* but never what he is. The result has been that the search for Henry's true personality has become an amusing Washington parlor game.

"Are you shy, by any chance?" he was once asked by an Italian journalist.

"Yes, I am rather," he replied, although there is no record of the expression on his face as he spoke. "On the other hand, however," he went on, "I believe I'm fairly well balanced. You see, there are those who describe me as a mysterious, tormented character, and others who see me as a merry guy, smiling, always laughing. Both these images are untrue. I'm neither one nor the other. I'm . . . no, I won't tell you what I am. I'll never tell anyone."

It may be that for a man who reigns wherever he goes, who cannot possibly live up to all the demands on his time, who has had the rare pleasure of discovering that there is a shortage of Kissinger, mystery is more spellbinding than autobiography. It is as if the details of his life, as refugee, immigrant, and professor, were too unexotic for the world of power and glamour in which he now lives. Hence, the gamesmanship, the enhancing of the social image he most exults in: the charming hieroglyphic.

But someone who has been out there in the floodlights as often as he has cannot remain wholly undecipherable. Quite often, in recent years, he has revealed some of the layers beneath the surface.

"When you think of my life," he confided early in 1974, "who could possibly have imagined that I'd wind up as Secretary of State of the greatest country in the world? I mean, when I couldn't even go to German schools . . . when I think I was a delivery boy in New York." The feeling of vulnerability that he acquired in his youth has never been totally eradicated. He is forever on the lookout for enemies — much more so than most Washington officials and Harvard professors are as a matter of course. Naturally he has turned this into a joke. "The first question I ask myself just before retiring every night, as I look under my bed: 'Is someone trying to get me?' "

When he catches a glimpse of a potential antagonist, Kissinger's instinct is to win him over with charm and humor. When he has a difference of opinion with a friend, someone whose allegiance is beyond question, he can be blunt and candid. When the friend is also a subordinate, Kissinger can be brusque and impatient. He is a demanding taskmaster, expecting, and for the most part getting, total loyalty and dedication. He knows he represents action, and he knows that everyone wants a part of it.

The same blend of humor and charm, toughness and candor, topped by no small amount of guile, characterizes his style with Congressmen and foreign leaders. He has the remarkable ability to convince two people with opposing viewpoints that he agrees with both of them — without in any way compromising his own position. One case in point was the reaction of Senators Henry Jackson and J. William Fulbright to separate briefings by Kissinger about the Brezhnev letter on the Middle East war that led to the U.S. military alert in October, 1973. Jackson, who is skeptical of détente, found it encouraging that the letter was assessed as "brutal." Fulbright, who is for even more détente, found it reassuring that the letter was assessed as "reasonable." Kissinger would later deny that he had spoken to either one of them.

Today, the prominence of Henry Kissinger is a matter of fact, but when the Nixon Administration first came to Washington, he was not even permitted to be "Henry Kissinger." Although he was always the "background" briefer on foreign policy issues, he could never be identified as anything other than "White House officials" or "a high Administration source." There were a couple of reasons for keeping Kissinger a top secret. For one thing, the Nixon people wanted no one to compete with the President as *the* voice of the Administration. For another, because of his accent Kissinger himself was not keen on having his voice recorded. "And there was also some concern about Henry's 'Dr. Strangelove' image," an ex–White House aide recalls. "Henry was quite sensitive about all this." But as Kissinger quickly demonstrated that he was the best briefer in recent Washington history, a virtuoso in explaining the President's foreign policy, and as his own confidence grew, he was liberated from the depths of the White House to appear "on the record" before the White House press corps. He made his official debut at the end of October, 1971, after one secret and one public trip to China.

Though he has been described as everything from "resident genius" to "con man," Kissinger prefers to avoid the flamboyant in describing his own role. Once, early in 1974, while driving along the San Diego Freeway from San Clemente to Los Angeles, he was asked to reflect on his hopes and ambitions.

"I'd like to leave behind a world that seemed to be more peaceful than the one we entered," he said softly. "More creative in the sense of fulfilling human aspirations. And of course, it's been my dream, which for many reasons has not been fully realizable, to have contributed in some sense to unity in the American people. That was my approach in Vietnam. And, you know, we couldn't foresee Watergate then." He looked out the window, watching California go by at fifty-five miles an hour. "No, I have my vanity and ego and everything else that people allege, and I'm sure it's true. But my policy is really more geared to what people will think in 1980 than to what the newspapers say tomorrow."

Yet when he is out there on the stage, being cheered as a global lion-tamer, he cannot resist the temptation to join in the applause. Once at a large Washington dinner a man walked up to him and said, "Dr. Kissinger, I want to thank you for saving the world." "You're welcome," he replied.

TWO

The Hiring of Henry

I T WAS MY IDEA," Clare Boothe Luce would reminisce years later, long after Richard Nixon had become President and Henry Kissinger a diplomatic phenomenon. "I wanted to introduce Henry to Nixon, and I more or less arranged it. I knew that Henry was not a Nixon man, that he didn't like him or trust him. He was a Rockefeller man through and through. But I thought they would hit it off. I told Nixon, 'I think you'll admire Henry.' I knew that if Henry spent an hour talking with Nixon the two men would get along famously."

It was dicey matchmaking by Mrs. Luce, who, throughout her various careers as playwright, Congresswoman from Connecticut, and Ambassador to Italy, had always believed that the Republic was safe only in Republican hands. The scene: her elegant New York apartment at 993 Fifth Avenue; the date: December 10, 1967, a pre-Christmas cocktail party. Henry Kissinger was among the first to arrive — a punctuality that was not to survive his later White House days of power and glamour. He knew very few of the guests, and vice versa, and with his limited talent for small talk, the "objective conditions," to use a favorite phrase of his, indicated a hasty disengagement.

He was just about to leave when Richard Nixon appeared. Mrs. Luce promptly shepherded them out of the crowded living room and into the privacy of the library — her personal attempt at linkage. Nixon and Kissinger talked for no more than five minutes, at a significant moment in their careers: Nixon, who had lost the 1960 election to John Kennedy and had seen Barry Goldwater win the 1964 Republican nomination, was attempting still another political reincarnation, hoping he could outwit his adversaries and win the Republican presidential nomination the following summer; Kissinger, a Harvard Professor of Government with widely recognized ability, was doubling as a consultant on foreign policy to the most challenging and persistent of those adversaries, Governor Nelson Rockefeller of New York.

But the two men did not touch on the sensitive subject of presidential politics. Instead, they talked about Kissinger's writings. The former Vice-President recalled his admiration for Kissinger's first major book, *Nuclear Weapons and Foreign Policy,* a best-seller in 1957. This controversial work had alarmed academicians and intrigued generals by focusing on the possibility of limited nuclear war. Kissinger recalled that Nixon had sent him a note of congratulations about the book. Kissinger had appreciated it.

Their first meeting never warmed beyond simple correctness. "Neither of us is very good at cocktail-party conversation," Kissinger recalled years later. He remembered Nixon as being stiff, himself as being aloof. Was Rockefeller the third man, an invisible presence that hovered between them? Or was it simply that Kissinger, though he had never met Nixon before, shared all the "academic prejudices" against him? In their brief conversation, Nixon said nothing to confirm those prejudices; on the contrary, Kissinger was forced to modify his caricature of the man. He was surprised to discover that Nixon "talked in a gentler way, a more thoughtful way" than he had expected.

As for Nixon, he left Mrs. Luce with the impression that he had enjoyed his first personal contact with Kissinger. He admired a Harvard intellectual with Republican ties who could stand on his own among the Bundys and Schlesingers of the suspect Eastern Establishment.

Kissinger did not meet Nixon again until November 25, 1968, a few weeks after Nixon's narrow victory over Hubert Humphrey and more than three months after Nixon had crushed Rockefeller and swept to a first-ballot victory at the Republican convention in Miami Beach. If this was a time of triumph for Nixon, it was a painful period for Kissinger.

Although his first encounter with Nixon had been pleasant enough, Kissinger, like so many other intellectuals, was depressed by the idea of a Nixon presidency. To them, Nixon seemed shallow, power-mad, unscrupulous, so compulsively anti-Communist that he would lead the United States into nuclear confrontations with Moscow and Peking. "That man

Nixon is not fit to be President," Kissinger would say to his anti-Nixon friends. On the eve of the convention in 1968, Kissinger was quoted as saying, "Richard Nixon is the most dangerous, of all the men running, to have as President."

Kissinger believed that America, in 1968, was a country in search of a unifying leader with an appreciation of national priorities and of the distinctions among international challenges. He looked to Rockefeller to fill this role. The only other politician in early 1968 who aroused a comparable sense of confidence in Kissinger was Robert Kennedy. "Bobby had a fire in his gut," Kissinger once said. "He could lead."

Kissinger had worked for Rockefeller for more than a decade, starting in the mid-1950s as the director of a series of foreign policy studies produced by the Rockefeller Brothers Fund. But there was more than detached academic study to the assignment; Kissinger became involved in Rockefeller's political world as well. As foreign policy consultant to the Republican Platform Committee, he witnessed the 1964 convention, heard the right wing cheering Barry Goldwater and jeering at the Governor of New York.

Four years later, after Vietnam had added President Lyndon Johnson to its list of casualties, Rockefeller reached out still one more time for the presidency. In May, he challenged front-runner Nixon for the GOP nomination. All of Kissinger's physical and intellectual stamina went into the Rockefeller campaign. He put in long days, engaging Rockefeller in a foreign policy seminar in the morning and his graduate students at Harvard in a similar exercise in the afternoon, and then returning to New York on the last flight from Boston.

Kissinger played a unique role. Often, when reporters interviewed the Governor about Vietnam or NATO or strategic arms and emerged feeling confused about the candidate's views, they were directed to Kissinger's office. "Go see Henry," Rockefeller's aides would say. "He's the only one around here who can explain what our position is and make it come out sounding right."

These routing directions were the result of an interplay between Kissinger's knowledge and Kissinger's style. His grasp of the broad sweep of policy was conceded, if at times grudgingly, by everyone on the staff. Equally important, though, was his bureaucratic technique. If he had a policy idea for Rockefeller, he would present it himself, not through a third party. Even then, Kissinger appreciated the critical importance in any bureaucracy of an intimate relationship between the adviser and the advised.

A number of Rockefeller's other advisers objected to this monopolistic approach. Among them was Emmet John Hughes, columnist, Eisenhower speechwriter, and Rockefeller's trusted counselor and spokesman. "Henry was in charge of foreign policy matters for the Governor and he was supposed to be subordinate to me," Hughes later said. "But it was impossible to get a statement I wanted Rockefeller to make on Vietnam past Henry. We finally got a policy statement out, but it was not nearly as tough as I wanted it. One of the most adroit things Kissinger was able to do was to convince people that he was always against the war. . . ."

Out of the smoke of Hughes's running skirmishes with Kissinger emerged the stories about how "difficult" it was to "work with Henry." Even if the stories were accurate, they missed the central point. It was never difficult for *Rockefeller* to work with Henry. The Governor had Kissinger's complete commitment and loyalty. This sense of dedication to the man above him was a characteristic that another man above him would later find indispensable.

In August, Kissinger accompanied Rockefeller to the GOP convention in Miami. The Governor's staff was still hoping that, by some quirk of fortune, their man could win the nomination, although all the pros had already given it to Nixon. Kissinger occupied a large suite on the fourteenth floor of the Americana Hotel, just down the hall from Rockefeller's. He was fascinated by the political process — the wheeling and dealing of presidential politics, the manipulating, releasing and leaking of news, the public and private talks between candidates and politicians, politicians and staffs, staffs and moneymen, moneymen and reporters, reporters and the public — in hotel lobbies, in back and front rooms, on national television. For a professor on summer leave, it was an extraordinary seminar, a lesson in government that Harvard could never duplicate.

"He really loved Miami Beach," a Rockefeller aide later recalled. "He was the expert working with the politicians, and they respected him. He seemed to thrive on the intrigue. But he always recognized what was essential and what was trivial in the conspiratorial give-and-take over small breakfasts and postmidnight bargaining."

What was essential, in Kissinger's view, was a Rockefeller victory — or, at a minimum, a victory for Rockefeller's views on Vietnam. A few weeks before, in a full-page ad in the *New York Times*, the Governor had proposed a specific plan for withdrawal that was regarded as rather advanced, especially coming from a Republican. Largely the result of Kissinger's thinking, it called for a four-stage operation starting with a

unilateral withdrawal of seventy-five thousand American troops and leading to an international peacekeeping force and ultimately to a political
reconciliation between the two warring parties.

Nixon had reacted with strategic silence. He ignored Rockefeller's
specific proposal, implying that he had a better idea — but that he was
not about to divulge it. Nixon was seeking to project the image of a
cautious and reasonable conservative who knew what was best for party
and country, implying that Rockefeller's public airing of his Vietnam plan
might be very good for the Governor in his pursuit of votes — but not
very good for the country in its pursuit of peace.

Now, at the convention, the confrontation between the two candidates
was further sharpened by the circulation of a semiofficial draft of a hard-
line Vietnam plank that reflected the views of Nixon's people rather than
Rockefeller's. It was on this divisive issue that Kissinger, with his candidate's go-ahead, quietly established contact with the enemy camp —
Nixon headquarters.

His probe came under the heading of policy, not politics; Kissinger
had no interest in switching candidates. During the convention, and even
before, a number of Nixon operatives — they were not "serious" men,
Kissinger later observed — tried to entice him away from Rockefeller
with, of all things, money. According to one account, they tripled their
original offer to Kissinger in an attempt to buy his defection, but he was
"outraged and offended by the idea that he could be bought."

All Kissinger was interested in was winning the support of the Nixon
camp for a Vietnam plank more in keeping with Rockefeller's thinking.
It was, at first, a discouraging exercise. Few of his opposite numbers
seemed to be educated in the complexities of Vietnam, and most of them
— public relations men from southern California — treated the issue as a
purely political one. Eventually, however, a plank emerged that put the
GOP's emphasis on talks rather than bombs. The bombing would come
later.

But the compromise in the Platform Committee was quickly overshadowed by the political arithmetic on the convention floor. The Nixon
machine proved unstoppable after all, and Rockefeller went down to a
692–277 defeat on the first ballot. The televised face of Richard Nixon
filled the land.

Kissinger was so devastated by Rockefeller's defeat that, according to
one account, he wept. He returned to his one-bedroom apartment at 400
East Fifty-fifth Street in Manhattan and slept deep into the morning. A

reporter friend who telephoned and woke him recalled that he sounded "more shaken, more disappointed, more genuinely depressed than I had ever known him." Again and again he referred disparagingly to "that man Nixon," who, he said, "doesn't have the right to rule."

But if Kissinger was anti-Nixon, Nixon was not anti-Kissinger. The telephone rang again later that day after it was all over in Miami, and on the line was a Nixon aide inquiring about Dr. Kissinger's availability to work with the Republican presidential nominee.

Kissinger's reply was conditional. In his "capacity as an expert," he said, he would be prepared to answer substantive questions about foreign policy. But he would not take part in formal meetings. He would not write position papers. In other words, he was not ready to join the Nixon team but, if they wanted to call him from time to time, his expertise would be available.

Why such an extraordinary leap, literally overnight, from overt antagonism to qualified accessibility? His critics later called it the height of opportunism — "I wonder who's Kissinger now?" His admirers argued that he had always felt that public duty transcended his own personal preferences; he had already contributed his thinking on United States foreign policy to the two previous Presidents as well as to the incumbent. Being available to a *candidate* for the presidency was just a flexible extension of his own foreign policy credo. Moreover, there were widespread rumors that Rockefeller would be offered an important post in a Nixon Cabinet. Kissinger felt reasonably certain that where Nelson went, *if* he went, so would Henry. It appeared that he was practicing on a personal level what he would later practice on a global level — keeping his options open.

Throughout August and September there was a steady stream of calls from the Nixon camp — a buzzing reminder of the winner's interest in the professor who was still faithful to the loser.

Occasionally, Democrats — Hubert Humphrey's people — would call Kissinger about one aspect of foreign policy or another, but these Democratic approaches never got very far. He was regarded as a Republican by just about everybody, even though he has always thought of himself as an "Independent."

Once, John Mitchell, then serving as Nixon's campaign manager, called for Kissinger's opinion about the Vietnam negotiations in Paris. Other

Nixon staffers called to ask Kissinger's views on Europe, NATO, the Soviet invasion of Czechoslovakia. Kissinger filled the callers in, keeping partisanship out.

Another time, a Nixon aide called and asked Kissinger how he would reorganize the State Department. It was not a subject that would normally leave him tongue-tied. He had many reservations about the proliferating State Department bureaucracy. That very year, in a paper for a seminar at the University of California, he had observed, "On the whole, if we could get rid of the bottom half of the Foreign Service we might be better off." But, in an unusual show of self-restraint, Kissinger suggested that it was much too complicated a subject to discuss on the telephone and, besides, it was hardly relevant to the immediate needs of the campaign or the country's foreign policy.

Only once during the campaign was there an inquiry that seemed to transcend the simple quest for expertise. Would Dr. Kissinger like to meet with the Republican candidate? The meeting never took place. "We just never made contact," Kissinger explained. But he was obviously intrigued by the signals from the Nixon camp. Just a few weeks after the convention, he was discussing the political situation with his old friend Helmut Sonnenfeldt, who had also come to the United States as a young refugee from Germany, and who had met Kissinger during World War II. Kissinger indicated to Sonnenfeldt, a career policy analyst at the State Department, that there had been emanations from Nixon circles. The two men speculated about working for a Nixon Administration, running through a variety of jobs — among them Assistant Secretary of State for European Affairs, Director of the Policy Planning Staff at the State Department, Assistant Secretary of Defense, possibly an ambassadorship. Sonnenfeldt urged Kissinger to hold out for "the Rostow job" — Special Assistant to the President for National Security Affairs, then held in the Johnson Administration by another professor, Walt W. Rostow. "After all," counseled Sonnenfeldt, "you're the only Republican I know with the proper academic credentials." Kissinger demurred. Such an offer, he said, was highly unlikely. But as long as they were engaged in such fanciful speculation, he asked Sonnenfeldt to join his White House staff if the job ever materialized.

Despite this sort of speculation, Kissinger spent most of his time in the period between the convention and the election shuttling between two worlds that were emphatically anti-Nixon — the political world of Rockefeller and the academic world of Harvard. He continued to maintain his close relationship with Rockefeller, flying to New York regularly to lunch with the Governor, whose feud with Nixon remained bitter, if muted in the temporary interests of party unity. His other world was even more strongly opposed to the GOP candidate. To many of Kissinger's Harvard friends, Nixon personified the least attractive qualities of American politics. They did not share the view of a "new Nixon"; they saw him as a calculating political creature who played to the lower instincts, as a demagogic trafficker in the technique of anti-Communism, as a throwback to an earlier, discredited period of American history — to McCarthyism. Worst of all, they saw Nixon as a hawk on Vietnam, the issue splitting America.

Kissinger's feelings about Nixon were well known to his colleagues, some of whom were already planning to staff a Humphrey Administration in the event the Democratic candidate won an election that was being forecast as very close. In October, just a few weeks before the election, Kissinger spoke at the Naval War College in Newport, Rhode Island. Afterward, over lunch, the conversation turned to the campaign. One participant remembers that the visiting professor diagnosed Nixon as "paranoic" and speculated about whether he would be able to withstand the pressures of the White House.

Even Nixon's victory in November could not stifle Kissinger on the subject of the President-elect. Kissinger's candid comments during a visit that month to the Rand Corporation at Santa Monica, California, surprised some of his listeners, among them, Daniel Ellsberg. Ellsberg — those were the days before the leaking of the "Pentagon Papers" — recalled that Kissinger was "very, very critical" of Nixon. "Everybody was quite amazed that a man connected with these political people would be so frank about the man who had just been elected," said Ellsberg. "Put it down to his relationship with Rockefeller."

Later, after he joined Nixon, Kissinger would say that he could not recall having made such ungracious remarks — but that he could not "exclude" the possibility. For a man whose powers of retention have been described as elephantine, his uncertainty has struck his critics and even his admirers as an understandable, if timely, lapse of memory. Kissinger prefers his own remembrance of things past. "My dominant recollection of my feelings about the President," he says, "was not that I didn't think he was fit but that he made me uneasy, and I didn't know anything good about him and I believed the bad things. But I had no independent knowledge. I hadn't ever really seen him before."

On November 22, a Friday, Kissinger flew down to New York for his standing lunch date with Rockefeller. They talked about the growing speculation that the Governor would be offered the post of Secretary of Defense in a Nixon Cabinet — and about whether he should accept the offer. "The idea that I would be offered something never crossed anybody's mind," Kissinger says, "or we would have discussed it." Midway in their conversation, the telephone rang. For Kissinger. The voice at the other end was unfamiliar, and so was the name that went with it. It was Dwight Chapin, a young aide of Nixon's. Could Dr. Kissinger see the President-elect the following Monday at the Pierre Hotel? At 10 A.M.?

Yes, Kissinger could make it; the only commitment he had for Monday was a seminar at Harvard at four o'clock that afternoon, his "Government 259: National Security Policy," which he had been conducting for more than eight years. In any case, he had been planning to remain in New York for the weekend, so it was only a matter of staying an extra morning — Monday, the twenty-fifth.

The call lent itself to a broad range of speculation. Kissinger insists to this day that he thought Nixon was summoning him merely "to talk about foreign policy."

Monday morning found Kissinger being ushered into Nixon's suite on the thirty-ninth floor of the Pierre — his impressive credentials preceding him: the five books, the dozens of articles, the expertise about foreign affairs and acquaintanceship with foreign leaders. For more than three hours Kissinger and Nixon were together, discussing their field of common interest: United States foreign policy. The substantive exchange of views nicely disguised what was taking place on another level: two cautious men sizing each other up. It was, for Kissinger, a curious experience. Behind the mutual appraisal, the obvious question lurked: was Nixon offering him a job?

Nixon certainly sounded him out in general terms about working in the new Administration. The slow approach may have reflected Nixon's own guardedness, or his sensitivity to Kissinger's avowed anti-Nixon sentiments, or his recognition of Kissinger's special relationship with Rockefeller. Kissinger's reply to the nonoffer was noncommittal. It depended on the nature of the job and on what happened to the Governor; if Rockefeller were to join the Administration, he would have first call on Kissinger's services. In the meantime, he agreed to Nixon's specific request to help find other specialists to fill key positions in the field of foreign affairs.

At one point in their discussion, Nixon summoned H. R. Haldeman into the room. It was Kissinger's first look at the crew-cut California PR executive who would be the President's indispensable man until April 30, 1973, when he was toppled by Watergate. The President-elect instructed him to arrange a telephone link with Dr. Kissinger at Harvard so that they could communicate more easily. But in a relationship without a major assignment, a hot line struck Kissinger as somewhat excessive, and he suggested that he could be reached quite easily through the Harvard switchboard.

Kissinger hurried from the Pierre to the airport to Harvard Square to keep his four o'clock appointment with his class.

The next day, when he called Rockefeller to tell him about his three-hour meeting with the President-elect, he learned that the Governor had just heard from Nixon that he would not be invited to take a Cabinet post in the incoming Administration after all. To the best of Rockefeller's recollection, Nixon had said nothing to him about the possibility of hiring Kissinger.

There wasn't much time for Kissinger to mourn Rockefeller's exclusion. The telephone rang; Chapin was on the line again — a commercial call from New York to Cambridge. Would Dr. Kissinger be free to return to the Pierre on Wednesday for a meeting with John Mitchell? "That's when I knew," Kissinger recalls. "Maybe now they were going to talk about *me*." He quickly got in touch with his old Harvard friend, McGeorge Bundy, president of the Ford Foundation, who had served Presidents Kennedy and Johnson as National Security Adviser. "It is possible I will be offered something," Kissinger confided. "What do you recommend that I consider?" Bundy suggested he try for the job of Director of the Policy Planning Staff.

It was in this state of anticipation that Kissinger, on Wednesday, November 27, flew from Harvard to the Pierre. He stepped out of the elevator on the thirty-ninth floor in search of the denouement, only to find himself confronted by Mitchell and a brief comedy of errors.

MITCHELL (*Businesslike*): Well, are you going to take the NSC job?
KISSINGER (*Suppressing elation*): It hasn't been offered — as far as I know.
MITCHELL (*Mitchell*): Oh, Jesus Christ! (*Stomps offstage. Returns a few minutes later, smiling*) The President-elect will see you in fifteen minutes.

The formal offer took place in the President-elect's suite. Nixon proposed that Kissinger become his Assistant for National Security Affairs.

Kissinger paused. He was extremely flattered, he explained, but he needed some time.

"Fine," said the President-elect. "Take a week."

This business completed, Nixon and Kissinger then moved into a lengthy discussion about the basic direction of the incoming President's foreign policy. Noontime came and went; Nixon, who rarely had lunch, and Kissinger, who rarely missed it, skipped the meal and went right on talking for almost four hours. They talked about Vietnam. The President-elect wanted to involve the Soviet Union in a solution to the war. Kissinger worried about the domestic disharmony caused by the war. They talked about China, triangular diplomacy, SALT, nuclear equilibrium. Kissinger felt that Western Europe had been ignored for too long, primarily because of Washington's preoccupation with Indochina. Nixon analyzed Soviet intentions in the Middle East and noted that he was dispatching former Pennsylvania Governor William Scranton on a fact-finding tour of the area. Kissinger thought that the United States should reorder its diplomatic as well as domestic priorities. Much to their mutual satisfaction, the two men found that they "tracked" well together.

By now, Kissinger was becoming a familiar face at the Pierre, even though he was still an unknown quantity to Nixon's aides. His writings were not exactly their bedtime reading. "Inappropriately unimpressed" was the way Ronald Ziegler, the President's loyal spokesman and a former PR man from California, would later describe his first reaction to Kissinger. That view was echoed by John Ehrlichman, a former zoning lawyer from Seattle who would be a key member of the palace guard until April 30, 1973, when he too was toppled by Watergate. "I had expected to see somebody much more imposing," Ehrlichman would later confess. "I'd never read anything Henry had written so I didn't have a real feel for his mental strength. I had heard that he was brilliant, that he was probably very temperamental, that he was going to be very tough to work with, that we were going to find ourselves in an adversary relationship."

In the next day or two, as Kissinger was making up his mind about Nixon's firm offer of the ideal job, he suddenly found himself dumping a good many of his academic prejudices against Nixon. His starting point can be found in a revealing comment he once made to columnist Joseph Kraft. "For people of my generation," he said, "Nixon had a certain reputation. I needed to assure myself that reputation was not deserved."

Characteristically, Kissinger relied greatly on his own reaction to

Nixon. "I was very impressed with him," he later recalled. In the field of foreign policy, he found Nixon better equipped than any of the presidential candidates he had met dating back to 1956, and he had met them all except Barry Goldwater. His estimates of them were no secret: even those whom he described as highly intelligent struck him as essentially ignorant about foreign policy. Eisenhower was a wartime hero — a great soldier but a mediocre President. Stevenson was eloquent and elegant — but soft, especially on the Russians. Kennedy left Kissinger feeling somewhat ambivalent. JFK was very attractive — but indecisive as well. At the time of Kennedy's assassination, Kissinger felt that a second term would have led either to greatness or to disaster. From a distance, Goldwater seemed essentially to believe that military power, unrestrained by diplomatic subtlety, was fully applicable in the nuclear age — a view which Kissinger regarded as simplistic and dangerous. Johnson's understanding of global politics was demonstrably minuscule. Humphrey (who revealed years later that he too would have named Kissinger as his foreign policy adviser) might have made an excellent President — except that his association with LBJ had tarnished his image and affected adversely his capacity for leadership. Rockefeller, though he had a "second-rate mind," had a "first-rate intuition about people," but while he could inspire those around him, he had been unable to inspire a presidential victory.

Which brought Kissinger back to square one — Nixon, the only President there would be, come January 20, 1969. The man who had made the offer.

Kissinger checked his own judgment with Rockefeller. His advice was instant and unhesitating: he urged Kissinger to accept. "I'm intuitive by nature," says the Governor, "and so I just felt it was right. I felt it was good and I was for it." Rockefeller did not allow his defeat by Nixon to affect his recommendation to Kissinger. "I had always been for Henry working with whoever was President," he says, "to help him in any way he could. He had done it with Kennedy and he had done it with Johnson, and I always encouraged him and urged him to make any of his talents and ideas available to whoever was President." A pause. "I feel the presidency is a very lonely job and that anyone who has a contribution should make it, regardless of party."

Next, Kissinger canvassed his Harvard colleagues: McGeorge Bundy, Arthur M. Schlesinger, Jr., Stanley Hoffmann, John Kenneth Galbraith, Adam Yarmolinsky, Richard Neustadt, Thomas Schelling, Guido Goldman, and others. Almost without exception, they advised him to take the job. They saw him as their man in Nixon's court, their entrée to the new world of Republican power.

His World War II friend, Fritz Kraemer, the man who has sometimes been described as Kissinger's mentor, had mixed feelings. "As your friend," he told Kissinger, "I can only say this will be an ordeal. The 'right' will call you the Jew who lost Southeast Asia; the 'left' will call you a traitor to the cause. But as a citizen, of course, you have to take it because no one is better qualified and your personal happiness is of no importance."

On Friday of that same week — November 29 — Kissinger called Nixon's office and requested an appointment with the President-elect. The round trip from Nixon to Nixon had taken less than forty-eight hours. "I've thought about it and we can make a treaty with each other," Kissinger told Nixon. "I'm going to take it, and I'm going to stop talking to people about it."

The formal announcement of the hiring of Henry was scheduled for the following Monday, December 2. But if Nixon thought he would have the pleasure of making the surprise announcement, he was to be disappointed. The thirty-ninth floor at the Pierre proved to be porous. The November 30 edition of the *New York Times* carried a front-page story by Robert B. Semple, Jr., headlined: "KISSINGER CALLED NIXON CHOICE FOR ADVISER ON FOREIGN POLICY." Carefully written, it reported that while Nixon sources would not confirm the offer, the President-elect was seeking "the full-time services" of Governor Rockefeller's adviser on foreign affairs. "Mr. Kissinger could not be reached for comment," Semple noted. Even then, Kissinger was displaying his talent for graceful disappearance.

When, on December 2, the President-elect finally introduced his new adviser to a crowded news conference at the Pierre, it came not as a Nixon revelation but rather as a confirmation of the *Times* story. Nixon was smiling; Kissinger smiling even more broadly. The President-elect made it clear that Kissinger was under orders to do away with crisis diplomacy "so that we may not just react to events when they occur."

Kissinger was properly self-confident, remarking at one point that he planned to bring foreign nongovernmental experts into the White House often for consultation, adding that he had "a very wide acquaintance all over the world of intellectuals of all points of view."

"I am one who likes to get a broad range of viewpoints expressed,"

Nixon added, "and Dr. Kissinger has set up what I believe — or is setting up at the present time — a very exciting new procedure for seeing to it that the President of the United States does not just hear what he wants to hear, which is always a temptation for White House staffers."

To those in the press corps and elsewhere who might have been surprised by the appointment of Kissinger before the appointment of a Secretary of State, Nixon explained, "Dr. Kissinger is keenly aware of the necessity not to set himself up as a wall between the President and the Secretary of State and the Secretary of Defense. I intend to have a very strong Secretary of State."

Praise came from all sides of the political spectrum. On the left, the *New Republic* cheered. On the right, William Buckley wrote, "Not since Florence Nightingale has any public figure received such public acclamation." In between, James Reston of the *Times* described the appointment as a "reassuring sign" that the incoming Administration was going to undertake "a serious and objective reappraisal of its security problems and priorities." And with his keen awareness of power relationships in Washington, Reston refused to accept Nixon's disclaimer about the limits of Kissinger's influence. "It is odd, in a way," he wrote, "that Dr. Kissinger should have been chosen by Mr. Nixon before the Secretary of State was selected, and this may lead to some friction. For Dr. Kissinger will be closer to the center of power . . . and he is a more forceful advocate than the normal run of State Department officials."

Overseas, divided Europe turned in a divided reaction. The western half, where Kissinger had many friends in high office, sighed with relief. The eastern half gasped. The Polish newspaper *Zycie Warszawy* saw him as a leading exponent of the "Cold War philosophy."

From the academic community, the response was generally enthusiastic. There were those who were still hostile to the very notion of a widely respected intellectual identifying himself with a man they considered a tricky and deceitful politician. More widespread was the view that the choice of Kissinger was an act of objective maturity — a plus for the new President. That Democrats regularly raided the campuses in search of creative talent was hardly a news bulletin, but here was a Republican, a Nixon, demonstrating the same sort of good sense. Kissinger's intellectual credentials helped reassure some scholars who were stunned by the realization that Richard Nixon, after all these years, was actually going to move into the White House.

Kissinger immediately took up his designated role as ambassador to the skeptical intellectual community. Within a few days — on December 6 — he drove to Princeton University for a dinner meeting of the International Association for Cultural Freedom. After expelling the press, Kissinger assured the assembled writers and intellectuals that henceforth the doors of the White House would always be open to them. He could not foresee then that they would pick up his invitation repeatedly, as other Administration doors slammed shut, first to denounce Nixon's policy in Vietnam and then, after Watergate had raised the most profound questions about the integrity of the Administration, to raise the ultimate question: why did he not disengage, choosing country over president?

In simpler times, before Watergate, when Nixon's stock was riding high, Kissinger would often joke about his initial qualms concerning the President-elect's offer. "It was really an unbelievable act of insolence on my part," he said. "The President-elect had a hell of a lot more to lose than I did by offering me the job. And if he had confidence enough to offer it to me, I could not say, 'I'll take a week and put you through a test to see whether my friends think it is immoral to work for you.' He was taking the chance."

The President-elect really did not know a great deal about him. He had read some of Kissinger's works — but not all. As for personal references, Kissinger went on, "My friends — I'd say almost all my friends — were liberal Democrats. I mean, with whom could he really check? If I had given him a list of ten people to recommend me, eight of them would have been people whose judgment he wouldn't rely on. I would have given him McGeorge Bundy, Arthur Schlesinger, Ken Galbraith, maybe Jerry Wiesner. If I was either disloyal or incompetent, it could affect his presidency, and he knew not a goddamn thing about me."

It was precisely Kissinger's friendship with such "liberals" that troubled the zealous conservatives who had given their lives to the Nixon cause. Political hatcheteers, with victory their only guiding principle, they had been through it all at Nixon's side — the bruising battles, the humiliations of the defeat for the presidency in 1960 and for the governorship of California in 1962, through the empty mid-1960s — until at last, in 1968, they were able to savor the sweet taste of triumph. Here, suddenly, was this Henry-come-lately, an intruder in their midst, foreign-born, with an accent and a Harvard education, joining Nixon only in victory. Kissinger was not their image of the Nixon White House. They were suspicious and resentful of him, and they distrusted many of the intellectuals from the Johnson Administration whom Kissinger was thinking about recruiting for his staff.

But their suspicions of Kissinger, known to Nixon, did not diminish the President-elect's satisfaction at having been able to lure the professor away from Harvard. For Nixon, the Kissinger connection had obvious dividends. He was able to outsmart the political analysts by suddenly unveiling a major adviser who was not a Nixon regular, and, for the first time in his political career, he was able to attract a widely respected intellectual to his service. "You've got to remember," cautioned William Safire, then a presidential speechwriter, "that Nixon was not always sought after by intellectuals, to put it mildly. He'd heard about Kissinger — one of the crown jewels in the Rockefeller diadem. He knew that he needed intellectual content in his Administration. And he was rich — rich in power. He could offer a Kissinger something Kissinger couldn't refuse, to use 'Godfather' terminology. He could offer him the action, the power, the center, and there was nothing he could offer before that could get a Kissinger away from a Rockefeller. He took a certain delight in that."

For Kissinger, accepting Nixon's offer did not seem to be much of a gamble. "All I had to lose was that I'd wind up like Rostow," he says. Rostow, LBJ's National Security Adviser, who was identified with escalation in Vietnam, wound up at the University of Texas because MIT, his original academic base, would not welcome him back. Later, whenever Kissinger ran into a salvo of criticism because of Nixon's Vietnam policies, he would fall back on what he hoped would be a defusing jest. "Ah," he'd chuckle, "I wonder how it will be at Arizona State."

Kissinger accepted the opportunity to work at the White House because his misgivings about Nixon were overcome by the prospect of exerting that much power. For years, Kissinger had been worrying about the problems of war and peace, about America's role in shaping a world that could avoid nuclear disaster. Though he had grappled with these problems, his ideas had not yet been tested. Harvard, despite its own estimate of itself, was ultimately an academic haven where an error of interpretation could result only in loss of face, not in extinction. The distance between Cambridge and the final seat of power was the distance between theory and reality.

Kissinger had offered his advice to three presidents even while maintaining his academic link at Harvard. Now he had an extraordinary opportunity to work full-time with a president, who, surprisingly, shared many of his basic views about the world. What Harvard professor could resist a chance to help shape American foreign policy at a critical juncture in history?

THREE

The Greening of a Greenhorn

HEINZ ALFRED KISSINGER — Heinz became Henry only in America — did not volunteer for his first lessons in diplomacy. Nazi persecution made him a reluctant student long before he reached his teens; he himself would have preferred to play soccer. By the time Heinz was seven, the streets of his Bavarian village of Fürth were overrun by Hitler's young bullies, and to be Jewish was to be a target. Heinz and his Jewish classmates were beaten up regularly. Years later, he was to tell an interviewer that in those first years as a refugee in New York, he would cross the street whenever he saw a group of boys walking in his direction.

The world into which Heinz was born was destined to be destroyed by the greatest horror in Jewish history. Middle-class, educated, comfortable, it had come into being some five hundred years earlier — as a result of the very hostility that was to destroy much of it during Hitler's heyday. Anti-Semitism in Nuremberg in the fourteenth century banned Jews from living within the city limits, so those who were expelled migrated to the outlying areas and helped create new villages — among them, the Fürth of young Kissinger. By the twentieth century, Fürth was widely known for its apparent religious harmony. It boasted a variety of churches, as well as a "magnificent synagogue," according to the authoritative eleventh edition of the *Encyclopaedia Britannica* (1910–1911). "The Jews also have a high school, which enjoys a great reputation," it added. Fürth "owes its rise to prosperity to the tolerance it meted out to the Jews, who found here an asylum from . . . oppression."

Heinz was born in Fürth on May 27, 1923. It was a year that Germany and Jews would remember — but for another reason. 1923 was the year that Adolf Hitler, in Munich, one hundred miles to the south, staged his provocative "beer-hall putsch," an attempt to seize power that wasn't so much unsuccessful as it was premature.

Heinz's parents had been married the previous year. Louis, his father, then thirty-five, was a respected *Studienrat*, or teacher-adviser, at the *Mädchenlyzeum*, a high school for privileged girls. Louis's father had been a schoolteacher, too. The traditions of Judaism were handed down from father to son; Papa Kissinger observed the Sabbath and the High Holy Days of Rosh Hashanah and Yom Kippur. "He was really a good teacher, very open-minded and too good-tempered to be a harsh disciplinarian" is the way he is remembered by a contemporary of Heinz's parents, Frau Emmy Wittenmayer, now an employee at the Fürth archives. "He was very polite and always gave advice willingly," she recalled. Heinz's mother was twenty-one when he was born; Paula Stern Kissinger was the daughter of a middle-class German-Jewish family, a master of traditional Jewish cooking, and the "practical" member of the family. The Kissingers' second son, Walter Bernhard, was born a year later. Home was a five-room second-floor flat on Matildenstrasse. In the apartment were books that young Heinz read and a piano he avoided.

The Kissinger sons started out in a close-knit, cozy world. They went to school with the other children of Fürth. They joined in the local soccer matches. Young Heinz was always available for a toss-up game, but it wasn't as an athlete that his father remembers him. "Henry was always the thinker," Louis Kissinger recalled many years later. "He was more inhibited than Wally, his brother. Wally was more the doer, more the extrovert." The brothers were close. "I'm sure as children we had the normal amount of sibling rivalry," Walter Kissinger once confided, "but there was never the element of great competitiveness in our relationship." (Walter, who has the same deep voice and engaging smile as his brother, went on to become a well-to-do businessman, and now lives on Long Island.)

Another portrait of Henry as a young boy — playful, exuberant, fond of flirting with the girls even then — is drawn by the handful of survivors from Fürth who built a new life for themselves in Israel after World War II. They remember Heinz in an affectionate way, the way most people remember youngsters who have come up in the world.

"He was a joyful and mischievous child," recalls Mrs. Else Esther Leon, who now lives in a home for the aged in Tel Aviv. She remembers Kissinger in his crib, the day he was born. "My son, Heinz Leon, was his best friend from the time they were infants. The two of them attended the same kindergarten and they continued to study together. Heinz Kissinger was full of the joy of life. Together with my son, he would constantly be thinking up new ways to play tricks, new ideas for mischief to enjoy themselves at school — at the teachers' expense."

It wasn't only the teachers, either. "He loved to associate with the girls," Mrs. Leon goes on. "He used to pull pigtails, according to my son, and when he grew up a bit, he loved walking the streets of the city accompanied by young girls and he would always collect the prettiest among them. I hear that even today he goes out with flashy women."

Young Heinz was "slender, of medium height, and neatly dressed, like the rest of the youngsters, and he did not wear glasses yet," says Mrs. Leon. The Kissinger family was very religious. "We used to go to the synagogue together. Heinz would attend services willingly and would be totally engulfed in the atmosphere of piety. He would pray with devotion."

Another vignette in the portrait of young Kissinger comes from Hetty Heipert, whose mother ran a grocery store. "Heinz," she recalls, "was a regular visitor. He would pass through on his way back from school, always in a rush, barging into the shop like a whirlwind. He would toss his book satchel into a corner and say, 'My mother will come to pick it up.' And he would immediately disappear, rushing off to play. Sometimes he would stay longer in the shop and even come in quietly and ask for sweets. My mother used to give him candy and cookies. He was very polite. He would thank her and run outside."

Eldad Shimon was Heinz's English and French teacher for two years at the Jewish school in Fürth. "Heinz did not distinguish himself as a student," he remembers. "He was very active in class. He would participate and express his views and answer questions — when he knew the answers. But he was not a brilliant student."

And finally, a Mrs. Pollack, who was Louis Kissinger's student between 1929 and 1931. "Heinz?" she says, wonderingly. "He was a child like any child. Who thought he would become so important and famous?"

As the Kissinger boys were growing up, the Nazis were growing stronger. In fact, the Bavarian environment was so charged with Nazi sentiment throughout the 1920s that Hitler's storm troopers goose-stepped into power in Fürth in 1930 — three years before the house painter who wrote, "The extermination of the jews is not a necessary evil . . . it is just necessary!" was to march into Berlin as Chancellor.

Altogether, the Jewish population of Germany was about half a million when Hitler began to implement his obsession. Fürth was home to about three thousand Jews out of a local population of eighty thousand. To Hitler, Fürth, with its long history of tolerance toward Jews, was an unacceptable challenge to Aryan purity; he scorned the city as a *Judenstadt*. Everywhere in Germany, the life of Jews became a hell, and the Kissingers were no exception. Indeed, even dead Jews were not exempt. The Jewish cemetery in Fürth was desecrated by the Nazis. The "magnificent synagogue" — and a smaller one, too — were razed on the same day. Jewish-owned shops were shut down. Swastikas replaced six-pointed stars. The walls of anti-Semitism were closing in.

The young boy who was later to write, "It is difficult for Americans to visualize national disaster" watched the Fürth he knew murdered by the Nazis. His father, a gentle man, was dismissed from his teaching post in 1933. For a while, he simply could not believe it; his hope was that the nightmare would pass. "He was a man of great goodness," Kissinger once told an interviewer, "in a world where goodness had no meaning."

For the Kissinger boys, there were fewer and fewer soccer games, and then there were none. Along with other Jewish students, they were expelled from their regular *Gymnasium* and were forced to attend an all-Jewish secular school. The streets became a battleground. Marauding gangs of German youngsters whose greatest ambition was to qualify for the Hitler Youth worked out their hostility on Heinz, Walter, and their Jewish classmates.

The spontaneity of youth often collided with the terrifying realities of the Nazi world in which they lived, and parents would be forced to remind their children that sudden impulses could be dangerous. "I remember that one Sabbath," Mrs. Leon said, "the two Heinzes, my son and Kissinger, went together to the municipal park near where we lived. There was a frozen lake where the children would slide and play. This was one of Heinz Kissinger's favorite pastimes. On that Sabbath, the two failed to return on time. They said afterward it was so pleasant and enjoyable in the park that they did not notice the passing of time until it was quite late. When they returned, they stood bashfully in the doorway, feeling guilty and worrying about what we would say. In Germany, in those days, it was one of the most sacred rules of behavior to return home on time and never to stay out after dark. And so my husband took off his belt and gave them a thrashing so that they would know and learn how one must behave. . . . They were just youngsters."

The anguish of those days is still vivid in the memory of Mrs. Kissinger, now in her seventies. "Our children weren't allowed to play with the others," she once said. "They stayed shut up in the garden. . . . The Hitler Youth, which included almost all the children in Fürth, sang in ranks in the street and paraded in uniform, and Henry and his brother would watch them, unable to understand why they didn't have the right to do what others did. . . . The two brothers stuck close together for protection."

By 1938, life for the Kissingers of Fürth consisted of being one step ahead of the next Nazi roundup of Jews. Twelve of their relatives were eventually to join the six million Jews killed by the Nazis throughout Europe. Of the three thousand Jews who lived in Fürth in 1933, the year Hitler formally assumed power, only seventy were counted at the first postwar religious service in 1945. The Kissingers fled in August, 1938, just three months before the infamous "Crystal Night" of November 9–10, when Hitler Youth and storm troopers went on a wild rampage against Jewish property and Jewish lives all over Germany.

"It was my wife who got us out of Germany," Louis Kissinger would later say about their escape. "Paula had an aunt in London. We took the boys there, and then after a few weeks came to America. . . . We have been back to Germany only twice since, in 1952 and in 1956, to visit the graves of our parents. Otherwise — well, you can understand, I am sure, how we feel."

Heinz was then fifteen, old enough to remember the abuse, the beatings, the degradation. Yet he has consistently minimized their impact on his life. "My life in Fürth," he once told a German reporter, "seems to have passed without leaving any lasting impressions. I can't remember any interesting or amusing moments." Almost word for word, he has relayed the same disclaimer to other interviewers. "That part of my childhood is *not* a key to anything," he says. "I was not consciously unhappy. I was not so acutely aware of what was going on. For children, these things are not that serious. It is fashionable now to explain everything psychoanalytically, but let me tell you, the political persecutions of my childhood are not what control my life."

This attitude has been described as anything from a "merciful loss of memory" to "escapist therapy." It has struck other Jewish refugees from Hitler's Germany as being a kind of exaggeration-in-reverse, as though Kissinger were somehow exempting himself from the psychological scars caused by Nazism in order that his diplomatic views might be accepted as pragmatic rather than personal. Still, if those were impressionable

years for young Heinz in a German world gone berserk, they have since
been superseded by the varied experiences and successes of his later
years.

For the Kissingers, home in America was an apartment in the developing German-refugee colony in the Washington Heights section at the
northern tip of Manhattan. It was, in those years, a solid, middle-class
neighborhood of assorted origins and religions, including many naturalized Jewish immigrants who had fled the pogroms of czarist Russia one
or two generations earlier and were now the parents of children born in
America. Yet even against so varied a local backdrop, the newly arrived
refugees could be spotted easily. The men wore somber clothes, the
women the mannish suits popular in Germany in the 1930s.

In a sense, they were aliens even to many of the immigrant Jews.
While their religion was the same, their culture was not. Those who had
fled the ghettos of prerevolutionary Russia were mostly working-class
Jews whose language was Yiddish, while the Jews of Germany could
boast some of the most distinguished intellects in a *Reich* they thought
had accepted them. Their first language was German. While profoundly
sympathetic to the plight of the refugees from Hitler, the earlier settlers
could not forget the condescension with which the German Jews already
established in America had greeted them at the turn of the century.

The Americanization of the Kissingers was not easy; everything was
new and challenging — language, work, school. The breadwinner of the
family discovered that his German academic credentials were not in
great demand in New York; he was reduced to taking a frustrating
clerical job. Mrs. Kissinger helped supplement the budget by putting
her culinary talents to work, turning out Jewish delicacies for Upper
West Side families on special occasions. She won a local reputation as
a first-rate cook, and gathered a clientele that kept her in great demand.
Years later, after her elder son's name had become well known in academic circles, she would sometimes do a nostalgic turn in the kitchen
for old customers — but she substituted a *nom de cuisine* for "Mrs.
Kissinger."

The boys were promptly enrolled in school; Heinz — about to become
Henry — joined the September, 1938, class at George Washington High
School. His school record noted that the new student had a "foreign
language handicap." It was a "handicap" that contributed to the shyness
of his GW days as well as to his sense of being a loner. His command

and use of the new language would later win the respect of diplomats throughout the world, but his accent — once described by a German-born friend of his as "ridiculously Bavarian rather than Prussian" — would stay with him into adulthood. "I was terribly self-conscious about it," he would say years later.

Still, Henry quickly began establishing academic records at high school. Whereas Nazism had made it difficult for him to concentrate on his studies, America freed him to make full use of his abilities. He became a straight-A student. Even when he switched to night school and found a job during the day so that he could contribute to the family income, his grades never sagged. He did better at math than at history. Indeed, he demonstrated such skill in tackling intermediate algebra and trigonometry that he decided to become an accountant. "For a refugee," he recalls, "it was the easiest profession to get into."

The job he found during his school days was in a shaving-brush factory in Manhattan. His initial responsibility was to squeeze acid out of the bristles. He was later promoted to delivery boy. "There are all these people who say that working my way through high school like that was also a traumatic experience and a great hardship," he later remarked. "But, I tell you, we had a very close family relationship and things did not seem that hard to me. I was not brought up to have a lot of leisure; there was no shame in that."

Once he received his high school diploma, the delivery boy was eager to begin studying for his profession. "Becoming an accountant," he recalled, "was then the height of my ambition." His superior grades at high school enabled him to enroll at the tuition-free College of the City of New York. Accountancy was taught at the Twenty-third Street branch of CCNY, a long subway ride from Washington Heights.

One evening, a few weeks before his twentieth birthday, Kissinger came home from a course in debits and credits to find an official letter that would change his life. "GREETINGS," it began; it was the U.S. Government's disarming way of announcing that one had just been drafted. Along with millions of other young men, Henry Alfred Kissinger exchanged blue serge for khaki and entered the United States Army. The greening of a greenhorn would be speeded up, too.

It was in North Carolina — beginning in February, 1943 — that Kissinger took sixteen weeks of basic training, a military cram course that had him crawling under barbed wire and learning how to fire a rifle. He became a naturalized U.S. citizen on June 19, 1943, in Spartanburg, North Carolina. Summer found him on a train bound for Easton, Pennsylvania, home of Lafayette College. A series of tests administered to the newest group of inductees had disclosed that Kissinger had a high enough IQ to qualify him to join three thousand other bright young men in a special program of college training. For half a year, Kissinger studied a variety of subjects, not including accountancy. But just as suddenly as the program began, it ended — a high-level decision resulting from public antagonism to the idea that while some GIs were dying on the battlefield, others were going to school. "One of the great snafus," ex–Private Kissinger would later say. "A great case of negative selection."

Once again, he was back on the rifle range — this time, at Camp Clairborne, Louisiana, as a foot soldier in the 84th Infantry Division. "Henry was very unhappy," his father once confided to an interviewer. "Acutely sorry for ourselves" was the way Kissinger himself has put it in recalling the mood among his group of soldiers. It was in the midst of such routine GI griping that a stranger in a jeep suddenly appeared. It was the beginning of a friendship that was to have an extraordinary impact on Kissinger's life.

"Out of this jeep driven by a lieutenant strides a private," Kissinger recalls. "He has an incredible air of authority. He yells in a terrible voice, 'Who is in command here?' Out comes a lieutenant colonel and confronts this incredible buck private. 'I am in charge here, Private,' the lieutenant colonel says. The private yells out, 'Sir, I am sent here by the General to speak to your company about why we are in this war.'"

The private was Fritz Kraemer, then thirty-five years old. He had left his established Protestant family on their estate near the Rhine and stormed out of an increasingly nazified Germany a decade earlier because, as he explained it, "I had to go." To the Ph.D. in law he had acquired at the Johann Wolfgang von Goethe University in Frankfurt, he added a second one — in political science — from the University of Rome. After Pearl Harbor, he enlisted in the U.S. Army and went on to organize a kind of military-government school for the officers and men of the 84th Division. He won a battlefield commission and eventually became a reserve colonel. Today, he occupies an office at the Pentagon as "the special adviser for politico-military affairs." His fiery, Old World style calls for a monocle, which he wears, and he is known to take walks in the countryside around Washington with a sheathed sword hidden in his

sleeve. He is still a man of strong opinions — in a variety of languages —
and his English retains the accent of his origin. "I have the voice of a
lion," he says.

But to get back to 1943 — to a Saturday morning in a cavernous GI
movie house, with the lion roaring onstage and twelve hundred cubs,
including Kissinger, in the audience. Kraemer spoke eloquently about
the moral necessity of fighting the Nazis. The impact of the extrovert
on the introvert was profound. Kissinger was stirred to do something he
had never done before — write a fan letter. "Dear Pvt. Kraemer," it read.
"I heard you speak yesterday. This is how it should be done. Can I help
you somehow?" It was signed: "Pvt. Kissinger."

Private Kraemer was impressed. "I saw him," he recalls, "because his
letter had no frills. None of that 'exhilarating,' 'wonderful,' et cetera, stuff
I dislike. 'This —' I said — 'This is a man of discipline and initiative.'"

The meeting between these two ex-Germans was one of the minor
events of World War II, yet it had a fallout that was to reach into future
decades. "After my first twenty minutes of conversation with Henry,"
Kraemer recalls, in a story he has been called upon to tell more than
once, "I had a most astounding experience. I met a twenty-year-old who
as yet knew nothing but understood everything. I said it to myself, of
course — not to Henry. This would be tactless. You don't tell a twenty-
year-old, 'You know nothing.' But his qualities were visible from the very
beginning. A natural phenomenon. I said to myself, 'This is amazing. He
is not the usual type. He has a sixth sense of musicality — historical musicality.' It was not his knowledge. He was so young. But he had the urgent
desire not to understand the superficial thing, but the underlying causes.
He wanted to grasp things."

Those were just Kraemer's first impressions of his meeting with "this
twenty-year-old Jewish refugee, whose people knew nothing really of
the great currents of history that were overcoming them." Years later, he
would often be described as Kissinger's "discoverer," a compliment that
sends the discoverer into a fury. "*Not* discovered," he roars proudly. "That
is too arrogant. What I was doing was — well, I evoked him to himself. I
would tell him, 'Henry, you are something absolutely unique, you are
unbelievably gifted.' I was only a psychological catalyst."

Kraemer promptly began agitating for his protégé to be chosen as the
German-speaking interpreter for the commanding general in the event
the 84th was ordered to Europe. Private Kissinger got the assignment
when his unit moved into Germany in the closing months of the war. He

had left Germany seven years earlier, a despised Jew running for his life; he returned an American with a conquering army.

The 84th moved into Krefeld — a devastated city in the state of North Rhine–Westphalia — with a population of two hundred thousand. Kissinger got the assignment of replacing chaos with order; Kraemer had sold the local U.S. general on Kissinger's "extraordinary intelligence and unparalleled objectivity," not to mention his fluency in German.

"I could only marvel," Kraemer has since recalled, "at the way this twenty-one-year-old did the job. In just two or three days, the government was again working, in a splendid fashion. Henry had planned things wonderfully. This was a prodigy. He had a fabulous innate sense of finding his way out of the most difficult situations. Here this little Kissinger had set up in three days a working municipal government in a large city where everything had been run by the Nazis just two days before."

Kissinger has even entered the postwar folklore of Krefeld. There is the birthday-cake story, for example. When the 84th commandeered a villa for division headquarters, the men found a birthday cake on the kitchen table. It was supposed to have been the high point in the celebration of the eighth birthday of Jochen Wirichs, but the Wirichs family had moved out in a hurry. The next day, Jochen's nursemaid, Frau Margerete Drink, summoned up her courage and returned to the villa on the chance that the cake had survived. It had, and it was returned by an American soldier who spoke German. "It was Kissinger," recalls Frau Drink. "He hasn't changed all that much. I saw him on television talking to the Chinese leaders. 'Mensh,' I said to myself, 'you spoke to that man yourself twenty-seven years ago." Frau Drink also remembers that Kissinger allowed her to visit the villa regularly to fetch provisions for the family — even though it was against regulations. "I found him very sympathetic," she says. "We often got American ration packages, with real coffee." It was a kindness that was remembered. Not too long ago, Jochen Wirichs, now in his thirties, sent Kissinger a case of *Alt Bier*, a dark beer that the Wirichs family has been brewing since 1838.

Kissinger demonstrated such skill at government administration that, within a year, as a member of the 970th Counter-Intelligence Corps, he was promoted to run the district of Bergstrasse, in the state of Hesse, with his headquarters in the hillside town at Bensheim, a hundred miles west of Fürth. His powers were extensive — including the power of arrest without questions. "When it came to Nazis," Kraemer recalls, "Kissinger showed human understanding, self-discipline. Unbelievable impartiality, really. This man is Jewish . . . iron-fisted . . . but without any harshness. He was guided in his everyday life by an unshakable conviction that moral values are absolute."

Bensheim, too, remembers Kissinger. He arrived with the panache of a victor — in a white 1938 Mercedes he had confiscated from a Nazi — and whisked past the medieval houses of the town until he came to a stop before the local tax office. "I'm Mr. Henry from the Counter-Intelligence Corps," he told the bewildered German sentry still on duty, "and I'm taking over. . . ." He carried out his administrative responsibilities in a way that won the grudging respect of the vanquished Germans, particularly of Mrs. Elizabeth Heid, who served as his secretary. She remembered, years later, that he used to say, " 'We have not come here for revenge.' You know," she added, "in those days right after the war, this sort of attitude was far from taken for granted."

He chose as his residence a villa in a suburb called "Adolf Hitler," and he would often spend his free time driving his Mercedes to the local sports field to watch the soccer matches. He was firm in enforcing the rules against any kind of fraternization with the Germans. "He was a master of keeping his distance," Mrs. Heid recalled. "He was completely self-assured, and he exuded so much authority that even his American friends would never dare to put their feet on the desk in his office."

Although the people of the Bergstrasse area pleaded with the American authorities to keep Mr. Henry in Bensheim, he was eventually transferred — by then, he was a sergeant — to the European Command Intelligence School at Oberammergau, not far from his birthplace. His own abilities, plus some behind-the-scenes promotion by Kraemer, by then a lieutenant, were responsible for the change. Kissinger's job involved, among other things, instructing field-grade officers in the art of rooting out Nazis who preferred to remain anonymous. He won a medal for the speed with which he had managed to round up the members of a local Gestapo unit. "It really wasn't too complicated for anyone who understands the German mentality," he told a friend years later. "I merely put an ad in the local newspaper saying all Germans with police experience who wanted jobs should show up at company headquarters, the next day, at a certain time, and sign up. The Gestapo people showed up and signed up by the dozen."

Although he was shy — "a lonely soldier who would not naturally talk to people and not naturally establish human contact," recalls a fellow GI — Kissinger was so effective in the classroom that, after his discharge from the Army, in May, 1946, he was retained by the command school as a civilian instructor in German history. His military career had earned him, among other mementos, a Bronze Star and two letters of commendation; his new civilian career started with a captain's rank in the Army's Military Intelligence Reserve — plus a salary of ten thousand dollars a year. For a young man with only a high school diploma to his academic credit, this was a lot of prestige and a lot of money — especially in Germany.

But it was not enough. "I want to go home and get a first-rate education," Kissinger confided to Kraemer. "I know only what I teach in school. Otherwise, I know nothing." Kraemer approved of Kissinger's attitude and encouraged his ambition. "You come from New York," Kraemer counseled Kissinger, "and the danger is that by geographical coincidence, you'll study at one of the local colleges in New York. When you go home, then at least go to one of the best schools in the country. Henry," he said, majestically, "a gentleman does not go to a local New York school."

Kissinger returned to the United States in the spring of 1947 and applied for admission to several colleges. The word came back that enrollment for the fall semester was closed. "But to its credit," he recalls, "Harvard agreed to take me, even though its enrollment was closed, too." In fact, Harvard granted him a scholarship.

Kissinger arrived in Cambridge as a twenty-three-year-old freshman, a little old for a beanie — but that wasn't his only distinction. He was accompanied by a cocker spaniel named Smoky, a souvenir of a trip to Paris during his GI service on the continent. Harvard took a dim view of pets in the dormitory but, for some reason, the rules were eased for Kissinger. "I think they thought they had a shell-shock case on their hands," he later said. But Smoky was a problem, and he was not universally appreciated. In the end, Smoky died while on a visit to Hyde Park with his master.

Financed by both the scholarship and the GI Bill, encouraged by various influential members of the faculty, driven by his eagerness to learn and his ambition, Kissinger took on Harvard with bulldog determination. Three years later, in 1950, he earned his Bachelor of Arts *summa cum laude*. His academic achievements produced an additional scholarship, and Kissinger earned his M.A. two years later, his Ph.D. two years after that. In the meantime, in February, 1949, while still an undergraduate, he married Ann Fleischer, like himself a Jewish refugee from Hitler's Germany.

Henry Kissinger has always been able to find a patron at significant turning points in his life; at Harvard he found William Yandell Elliott.

For his part, Elliott was delighted to find young Kissinger. When Kissinger enrolled at Harvard, Elliott, then about fifty, was already a legend, an irascible Professor of Government who, in Kissinger's words, "lived as a grand seigneur in a world where eminence has become a technical achievement." An All-America tackle at Vanderbilt, a graduate student at Oxford in the 1920s, a driving force in the Office of War Mobilization during World War II, Elliott of Tennessee was an eminent Cold Warrior in the 1940s, a passionate advocate of a tough anti-Communist approach in international affairs, a defender of the belief that America had a special role to play in a hostile world. In the opinion of some of his colleagues, he had never lived up to his earlier promise and was something of a pompous bore; but few would deny that he was a power at Harvard. Kissinger quickly struck him as being several cuts above even the brightest students. He seemed, said Elliott, "more like a mature colleague than a student."

Kissinger's first patron, Kraemer, pays tribute to Kissinger's second patron for helping to win recognition for their brilliant protégé. "Henry is a man of absolutely unbelievable fittedness," says Kraemer. "This word is not in Webster, but you'll understand. Elliott saw it at once. He's a man who's delighted to see a student of his be a man of excellence. Instead of pushing him down, it was Elliott who would say to people, 'Look, I can't make this panel, I can't accept such and such an invitation, but I have a student.' . . . Elliott created bases for Henry from which to do other things. What I did was to *evoke* Henry to himself. Elliott *helped* Henry. That's infinitely more."

For his part, Henry helped Elliott in a variety of administrative chores — an increasing number of them as the semesters went by. He did them conscientiously, too. It was a trait that pleased professors. Harvard in those Cold War days was expanding its research and academic facilities; hardly a term went by without a new institute, such as the Russian Research Center, being established, and a need developed for scholars who would not look down their noses at administrative responsibilities. Kissinger's career, along with his own horizons, widened.

Among Kissinger's contemporaries, there were some who found his style of operating a form of academic apple-polishing. "He was always aiming to cultivate relations upward rather than with his equals," says a Harvard classmate. "Everybody thought he was an extraordinarily able person, but what an SOB! A prima donna, self-serving, self-centered. I remember him as being thin, lean, hard, crew-cut, very military looking, and very close to Elliott. Elliott was already treating him as something special." Still, Kissinger managed to carry off the difficult feat of winning the support of Elliott's distinguished rival, Professor Carl Friedrich. "The atmosphere then was that you were either Elliott's protégé or Friedrich's," this classmate recalls. "Kissinger managed to be on excellent terms with both."

In Elliott, Kissinger found more than an academic patron; he found a friend and an inspiration. "We met every week for years," Kissinger recalled in a testimonial to Elliott on his retirement in 1963. "Bill Elliott made me discover Dostoevski and Hegel, Kant, Spinoza, and Homer. On many Sundays we took long walks in Concord. He spoke of the power of love, and said that the only truly unforgivable sin is to use people as if they were objects. He discussed greatness and excellence. And while I did not always follow his words, I knew that I was in the presence of a remarkable man."

It was easy for Elliott to return the compliment. "An unusual and original mind" was the way he described Kissinger. "He had a feeling for political philosophy. He was not like the stupid behaviorists who turn everything into an either-or proposition. He was not blind to the epic nature of history. He was not blind to the Bible. He understood the foundations of history."

This was a revealing choice of words: "a feeling for political philosophy," "stupid behaviorists," "epic nature of history," "the Bible." They delineate the nature of Elliott's input into Kissinger's intellectual growth; they also reflect a battle then taking place among the academicians at Harvard. In those days, there was a growing school of sociological thought vying for status with the long-established departments of history, government, and philosophy. For example, the Russian Research Institute on Dunster Street woke up one day to find, much to its amazement, that there were as many sociologists as historians on its faculty. The contempt of the established historians for their colleagues in "Soc Rel" was barely disguised. They regarded the sociologists as lightweight innovators who were analyzing the "behavior" of Stalin as if personal behavior could explain Soviet policy; conducting "interview projects" with refugees from Eastern Europe as if their conglomerate experiences could illuminate the nature of totalitarianism; and inventing a complicated new vocabulary as if pretentious terminology could disguise a lack of serious scholarship.

These behaviorists attracted money, though, and money begot more money; staffs, centers, ever more sociologically oriented projects proliferated. Every such inroad embittered the historians, who believed that real knowledge was the end product of a thorough study of the past. Study the Greeks and the Romans, they said. Read the philosophers. Analyze European history. But for heaven's sake, be "serious." Man can't be computerized, society can't be psychoanalyzed. It was the latest instance of the continuing battle between the traditional academic approach to learning and a new, unorthodox approach.

Many Harvard students found themselves drawn toward the *nouvelle vague*. Not Kissinger. Not this cautious, methodical, intense young academician. His instincts in such a situation were the instincts of conservatism. And so he joined his mentor Elliott at the barricades, defending the traditional approach to learning and attacking the forces of the behavioral scientists. Traditional Harvard became his citadel, its ivy-covered walls representing continuity, stability, and order.

Outside, beyond that reassuring world, another world was in convulsion. Intimidation was triumphing over courage at home, Communism was on the move abroad. The United States was in the grip of McCarthyism. Overseas, Stalin sent the Red Army into Eastern Europe, and the promise of democracy was quickly replaced by totalitarianism. Western Europe felt threatened, and George C. Marshall, who had helped lead the Allies to victory over the Nazis and had later been named Secretary of State, came to Harvard Yard to launch a massive economic program aimed at strengthening America's Atlantic allies. Ho Chi Minh was on the move in Vietnam in a war in which Communism and nationalism would provide the force that would defeat the French. Mao Tse-tung unfurled the red flag in the Square of Heavenly Peace in Peking. North Korea invaded South Korea. Even the most casual glance at the globe revealed a changing, revolutionary world.

To many students at Harvard, these developments seemed remote. Rarely were they perceived as a direct menace. To Kissinger, however, every convulsion, no matter how distant, seemed to take on the dimensions of a personal threat. His fears, his suspicions were easily aroused. He had little confidence in the ability of goodness to triumph on its own; he found little security in the high-sounding phrases about the "family of man" and the "indivisibility of peace" that emanated from the international gatherings of the day. In Kissinger's own experience, there was nothing to justify entrusting the question of survival to a string of slogans. The risk was too great, the odds too short. His own experience, instead, led him almost inevitably toward the strategy of *realpolitik*, a belief that power was the elemental force in history. The mere desire for peace would not bring it about. To Kissinger, the evidence was obvious. Against the Nazis, the Kissingers of Europe had no power, so death was dispensed to millions of Jews. Against the Russians, the East Europeans had no power, so dictatorship displaced their freedom. The list of tragedies was long.

But to think of power as inherently evil, he believed, was to miss the point of an age-old question. Power in itself was neutral; even if history was overloaded with examples of power being used wantonly and destructively, power could also be used to prevent catastrophe. The ultimate question was how power was to be used.

These thoughts shaped his academic output. His undergraduate thesis, presented in 1950 and modestly titled "The Meaning of History — Reflections on Spengler, Toynbee, and Kant," reflected Kissinger's view of the world as an imperfect experiment.

The thesis was heavy going. The writing style was ponderous. "The German was barely translated," one colleague remarked. What is more, Kissinger's reflections ran to more than three hundred and fifty pages — too many reflections even for Elliott's Government Department. A decree was handed down that, henceforth, theses would end before the hundred and fiftieth page. In Kissinger's case, the new ruling would have made little difference. "Elliott read only Henry's first hundred pages," a Harvard contemporary of Kissinger's recalls, "and gave him a *summa cum laude*."

But his undergraduate thesis was only a warm-up for his more ambitious doctoral dissertation. His original plan was to write a trilogy about an unusual period in European history — "the period of peace lasting almost one hundred years" from the Congress of Vienna in 1814–1815 to the beginning of World War I in 1914. It was to be a massive analysis of the construction and collapse of an international order. As it turned out, only the first part of the trilogy, dealing with the period between 1812 and 1822, was written; it was called *A World Restored: Castlereagh, Metternich, and the Restoration of Peace, 1812–1822.*

Kissinger's work focused on the diplomatic efforts in 1814–1815 to restore order to Europe after twenty-five years of war and revolution. Napoleon's attempt to impose his will on the entire Continent had been crushed in the terrible Russian winter of 1812. This was "the moment," Kissinger wrote, "when it became evident that Europe was not to be organized by force."

After Napoleon's defeat, the conservative victors met in Vienna. The settlement they reached was largely the work of two unusual diplomats — Lord Castlereagh, the British Foreign Secretary, and Prince Metternich, his Austrian host. "What is surprising is not how imperfect was the settlement that emerged," Kissinger wrote, "but how sane, not how 're-actionary,' according to the self-righteous doctrines of nineteenth century historiography, but how balanced. It may not have fulfilled all the hopes of an idealistic generation, but it gave this generation something perhaps more precious: a period of stability which permitted their hopes to be realized without a major war or a permanent revolution."

How was this accomplished? Kissinger credited these nineteenth-century statesmen with creating a balance of power — a framework in which it was in no country's interest to escalate a war to the point of toppling the carefully balanced structure; a framework in which each of the major countries had a vested interest in stability. This "stability" was as close as mankind could come to "peace." It might not be ideal, but it offered the best chance for survival.

To attain this state of balance, statesmen must use cunning and patience; they must be able to manipulate events and people. They must play the power game in total secrecy, unconstrained by parliaments, which lack the temperament for diplomacy. They must connive with "the largest possible number of allies." They must not be afraid to use force, when necessary, to maintain order. They must avoid ironclad rules of conduct; an occasional show of "credible irrationality" may be instructive. They must not shy away from duplicity, cynicism, or unscrupulousness, all of which are acceptable tools for statecraft. They must never burn their bridges behind them. And if possible they must always be charming, clever, and visible.

Metternich, until 1848, and then Bismarck, later in the century, played the game with extraordinary skill — avoiding major crises by their virtuoso balancing acts, never allowing sentimental attachments to interfere with the needs of policy, always ready to sacrifice the form of a settlement for the substance.

Later, when Kissinger became a presidential adviser and acquired a reputation as a master of secrecy and surprise in diplomacy, he would often be compared to Metternich by editorial writers around the world. Some observers even suggested that all of Kissinger's sophisticated theories about geopolitics added up to nothing more than a nostalgic yearning for the safe, conservative world of diplomacy in the early nineteenth century, when Europe was dominated by the Holy Alliance.

These comparisons are enough to drive Kissinger through the roof. Metternich is not his hero, he insists. "I don't believe he's the model for my current job, and I think there's a lot of second-rate psychological junk being produced," he says. "You can just as well say Castlereagh is my hero." Kissinger concedes that he found "one quality" of Metternich's particularly "impressive." When he was "faced with the massive collapse of a situation," Metternich "kept his head and focused on the day after tomorrow and didn't let himself be swept along. But," he hastens to add, "that doesn't mean that his kind of diplomacy — at a time when you had no telephone, no telegraph, no public opinion, when negotiators were out of touch with their governments — is repeatable. I can't even find the beginning of an analogy to the present period."

But as Kissinger talks about Metternich, it becomes clear that he feels the diplomats at the Congress of Vienna did have some lessons to teach the negotiators of today. This was not his view when he started out. Actually, he explains, he had intended to make Metternich the villain of his dissertation because he shared the accepted view of him as a "conservative reactionary." But in the process of research and writing, his view of Metternich changed. "In 1814 and 1815," he explains, "these people knew what they were doing. They weren't stumbling into a settlement. And therefore I tried to analyze how it was done."

In that analysis, he developed many of the ideas that would later become quickly identifiable as the hallmarks of Kissinger diplomacy. Given his view that the forces of conservatism and the forces of revolution were in constant conflict, with a high risk of violence, he concluded that the *aim* of foreign policy should be the establishment of a structure of peace; the strategy — the skillful use of a balance of competing powers; and the means — a mix of secret negotiations and the unabashed readiness to use military force if required.

It was during the time that Kissinger was writing the dissertation, in 1952, that Elliott put his protégé in charge of a new program that was to provide him with an extraordinary network of contacts in capitals throughout the world. It was called the Harvard International Seminar, and it brought together about thirty-five bright and influential foreigners to spend the summer along the banks of the Charles River discussing politics, philosophy, and history. For all concerned, it was a stimulating experience. After several summers, the program had brought Kissinger into personal contact with hundreds of up-and-coming politicians, scholars, and journalists, who would always be grateful to him for a stimulating July and August in Cambridge.

In its infancy, the seminar was a product of the Cold War. Like the National Student Association, it was partially subsidized by the Central Intelligence Agency, which channeled funds through foundations to avoid detection. It was the CIA's way of using scholars and universities in the fight against Communism. When the cover of the CIA's financial involvement was blown in 1967, Kissinger said he had not known of the agency's subsidy. He did know that no Communists were ever recruited for the seminar — he himself did the recruiting — and that Elliott, with his close Washington contacts, had no qualms about cooperating with the U.S. Government in what he and Kissinger accepted as a worldwide struggle against Communism. Moreover, as editor of the seminar's quarterly, *Confluence: An International Forum,* Kissinger shaped its anti-Communist outlook.

His activities at the seminar were only one example of Kissinger's entry into the world of power, politics, and diplomacy beyond Harvard. The fact that in the early 1950s Kissinger was emerging as a recognized hardliner made his admission to Washington's power center that much easier. With only a B.A. in hand, he became a consultant to the Army's Operations Research Office in Washington. In 1951, the Army sent Kissinger to South Korea to study the effect of military occupation upon the Korean people. "I knew absolutely nothing about Korea," Kissinger later reminisced. He also knew nothing about centuries of Korean-Japanese hostility, because he stopped in Japan to get letters of recommendation. "For the first two weeks in Korea," he said with a twinkle, "no one would see me." By the time he received his M.A. in 1952, he was making regular trips to the capital, and he had been named a consultant to the Psychological Strategy Board of the Joint Chiefs of Staff. Ability and ambition had placed him on the first rungs of the ascent to power.

FOUR

Ascent to Power

THE ASSORTED CAREERS of Henry Kissinger were coming along nicely at mid-century. He was a promising scholar with a widening circle of academic admirers even though, as one colleague at Harvard later said, "I can't recall that one thought of him as a giant in the field — not yet." His Ph.D. dissertation had won a Sumner Prize for distinguished scholarly achievement. He was getting good notices as an administrator of the Harvard International Seminar. His relations with Washington, while still in their infancy, showed promise of greater things to come. The graph line of Kissinger achievement had a vertical slant — until 1954, when he suffered his first major setback.

Harvard refused to grant him a position of tenure. It was an unexpected disappointment, for Kissinger had believed that his ascent to full-fledged membership on the faculty would be automatic upon the completion of his doctorate. Just why he was rejected is one of those academic secrets that will never be known, but a number of reasons have been suggested by colleagues who knew him at the time. First, he was described as "difficult," an aggressive young scholar who frequently curried favor with influential professors. Moreover, his widening interests outside the walls of Harvard convinced several faculty members that he was more interested in government service than in teaching or scholarship. The objection was not that "he wasn't brilliant," a Harvard contemporary of Kissinger's adds, "but that he would not serve Harvard. He would use Harvard."

At the time, the rejection was a devastating blow. When the news began making the academic rounds, the University of Chicago responded by offering Kissinger a professorship, but he rejected it. Several of his friends encouraged him to stay on at Harvard and accept temporary employment as an instructor in the hope that it would become permanent one day. He stayed. "Tenacity!" says Kraemer about Kissinger. "An important characteristic about him. He has the tenacity of three Sicilian mules, and with that tenacity he'll overcome everything."

Meantime, in New York, a job outside the strictly academic world suddenly opened up. *Foreign Affairs,* a quarterly published by the Council on Foreign Relations, an extremely influential private group that is sometimes called "the *real* State Department," needed a managing editor, and the magazine's editor, Hamilton Fish Armstrong, turned to Harvard. Kissinger's friends — among them a history professor by the name of Arthur M. Schlesinger, Jr. — promptly dashed off letters of recommendation. As it turned out, Kissinger did not get the job. Armstrong, who had been writing about foreign policy for decades, found his style too ponderous. But Kissinger did not leave the council's premises without making a strong impact. "Henry had great confidence in himself and he inspired confidence in the person he was talking to," recalled Armstrong's colleague, George Franklin, then the director of the council. Armstrong found the young scholar so intellectually stimulating that he asked him to consider another job.

The council needed a rapporteur, a study director for a high-powered, thirty-four-man panel that was to explore methods short of all-out war for coping with the Soviet challenge in a nuclear age. Kissinger's patron saint at Harvard, Professor Elliott, urged him to take the post, and sent the council an enthusiastic letter of recommendation. Other influential endorsements came from Schlesinger and from McGeorge Bundy, then Harvard's Dean of the Graduate School of Arts and Sciences. "The recommendations were extraordinarily good," Franklin says, "and also since these men represented different policies, it was perfectly obvious that it wasn't just because Henry happened to agree with them. I still remember our talk. Henry said, 'Well, if I'm going to come, you've got to let me do it exactly my way.'"

On March 8, 1955, Kissinger formally accepted the offer, with a letter that bore his assertive trademark. He was taking the job, he wrote the council, "not only because it seems directed in the main line of my own thought, but also because the council seems to furnish a human environment I find attractive." Henry and his wife moved to a New York apart-

ment, and Kissinger became absorbed in the study project that was to
mark another major turning point in his life.

The Eastern Establishment

The Council on Foreign Relations, with its headquarters in an old
mansion at Park Avenue at Sixty-eighth Street, was Kissinger's entrée
into the world of the Eastern Establishment; at its seminars on world
affairs and its black-tie dinners for visiting premiers and foreign ministers, he was introduced to men of influence and power, with broad
experience in government, diplomacy, the military, industry, and journalism. They accepted the established view that the goal of American foreign policy was to contain the Soviet Union through a worldwide system
of anti-Communist alliances led by NATO. But many of them were skeptical about the Eisenhower-Dulles strategic doctrine of massive retaliation. They felt that the threat to wage all-out nuclear war in response to
aggression anywhere and of any size lacked credibility. The dangers of
such an all-or-nothing strategy prompted the council to commission the
study group to come up with alternatives. Its members included Frank
Altschul, Robert Bowie, McGeorge Bundy, Gordon Dean (chairman),
Thomas K. Finletter, Lieutenant General James M. Gavin, Roswell L.
Gilpatric, Paul H. Nitze, Frank C. Pace, I. I. Rabi, David Rockefeller,
General Walter Bedell Smith, and more than a dozen others, all specialists
in relevant fields ranging from weapons production to the shaping of
policy.

The job as the panel's rapporteur was tailor-made for Kissinger; he had
been thinking along the same lines for some time. He was not the only
scholar who rejected the Administration approach, but he was among
the first to articulate these doubts, to advocate a basic change in strategy,
and to do so in the magazine that mattered — Foreign Affairs. The April,
1955, issue contained his article entitled "Military Policy and the Defense
of the 'Grey' Areas," which argued forcefully against massive retaliation.
Although he was a newcomer to the council, with only a Ph.D. to his
name, he felt no hesitancy in volunteering his thoughts about the best
strategy for safeguarding the Republic.

During council hours and after, Kissinger sought a middle road between nuclear holocaust and reluctant appeasement that would avoid what he later called "the dilemma of having to make a choice between . . . Armageddon and defeat without war." It was, in short, an attempt to find a way to learn to live with the bomb and survive. It was an eighteen-month project, and Kissinger devoted himself to it with characteristic energy and with a single-mindedness that excluded all interruptions to his train of thought. " 'Don't talk to me,' he would sometimes say to his wife," a friend of theirs recalls. " 'Henry,' I would tell him, 'this is inhuman. She has been waiting for you at home all day.' He was not even aware of that."

The result of that effort was his controversial study — *Nuclear Weapons and Foreign Policy,* published under council auspices in 1957. It marked a turning point in the debate on nuclear strategy.

"In Greek mythology," it began, "Nemesis, the goddess of fate, sometimes punished man by fulfilling his wishes too completely. It has remained for the nuclear age to experience the full irony of this penalty." At times eloquent, at times plodding, the book saw the world darkly, portraying the Soviet Union as a revolutionary, expansionist power seeking to undercut the stability of the Western world, led by the United States. This view reflected the Kissinger thesis in *A World Restored*: that there would always be a battle between the forces of conservatism and the forces of revolution.

Kissinger's innate strain of pessimism ran through the analysis — a "brooding melancholy," as Professor Stanley Hoffmann of Harvard has described it, a sense of pervading doom. In a reference to the illusions of pre-1914 Europe, Kissinger wrote, "In the long interval of peace, the sense of the tragic was lost; it was forgotten that states could die, that upheavals could be irretrievable. The dilemma of the nuclear period," Kissinger continued, "can . . . be defined as follows: the enormity of modern weapons makes the thought of war repugnant, but the refusal to run any risks would amount to giving the Soviet rulers a blank check."

How then could the United States respond to the Kremlin's unrelenting pressures — short of all-out nuclear war? Kissinger proposed a way out of the impasse: a policy of graduated deterrence that envisaged the possible use of tactical nuclear weapons from the very outset of a limited war. "Limited nuclear war," Kissinger wrote, "represents our most effective strategy against nuclear powers or against a major power which is capable of substituting manpower for technology."

Kissinger's unorthodox recommendation produced an uproar in Wash-

ington. The suggestion that a nuclear war could be limited clashed with
the basic assumption of the war-and-peace analysts, who believed that
once the button was pushed, the nuclear conflagration would become
total. The military establishment had been raised on that assumption, but
Kissinger pushed for a new school of thought. Discard World War II
notions about "unconditional surrender," he argued, and understand that
in the New World, where America's nuclear bombs are balanced against
the Soviet Union's, limited wars for specific political objectives are the
only plausible ones. As Kissinger put it, a limited war is "essentially a
political act . . . an attempt to affect the opponent's will, not to crush
it; to make the conditions to be imposed seem more attractive than continued resistance; to strive for specific goals and not for complete an-
nihilation."

Only by creating a "spectrum of capabilities with which to resist Soviet
challenges," wrote Kissinger, could Washington successfully hold off Soviet nuclear blackmail. The "spectrum" would obviously include a full
arsenal of strategic and tactical nuclear weapons — and a willingness to
use them. "In terms of deterrence," he wrote, "the ability to wage limited
nuclear war seems more suitable than conventional war because it poses
the maximum credible threat." Acceptance of this approach, he argued,
would provide the United States with a new military flexibility. The
Russians must be made to understand, by both word and deed, that an
all-out war — that is, extending a limited conflict into a global holocaust
— would threaten a "calamity far transcending the penalties of losing a
limited war."

For fourteen weeks, *Nuclear Weapons and Foreign Policy* was on the
best-seller list. "I am sure," Kissinger later told Franklin, "that it is the
most unread best-seller since Toynbee." It won Kissinger the Woodrow
Wilson Prize and a citation from the Overseas Press Club. The *Washington Post's* diplomatic correspondent at the time, Chalmers Roberts, described it as "undoubtedly the most important book of 1957, perhaps even
of the past several years." It prompted Vice-President Nixon to send
Kissinger a letter of congratulations. Secretary of State Dulles, whose
doctrine of "massive retaliation" was challenged by the book, accepted
the possibility of limited nuclear war. Influential Senators were seen with
the book. The Pentagon studied it, though entrenched generals strongly
disagreed with Kissinger's call for a merger of the Army and the Air
Force into a single service.

Many professors agreed with Kissinger on the need to find a strategic doctrine to translate nuclear power into policy, but some were aghast at his conclusions. They argued that Kissinger's "logical" explanation of how the U.S. and the USSR must "cooperate" to keep war limited was really the height of illogic. "IS 'LIMITED' WAR THE ROAD TO, OR FROM, THE UN-LIMITED KIND?" read a headline in the *New York Post*. August Heckscher, Director of the Twentieth Century Fund, asked whether a democracy could accept defeat in a limited war, knowing it possessed tremendous strategic nuclear power yet to be used. George Kennan and Dean Acheson questioned the capacity of Soviet leaders to deal rationally with a nuclear threat, be it limited or total. Do they think as we do? they asked. Why assume common responses to similar stimuli?

With the book, and the controversy it touched off, Kissinger moved to the very forefront of that segment of the academic community dealing with nuclear and national strategy, the new technocracy of scholarly experts in public affairs. When, in the summer of 1957, Kissinger returned to Harvard, he was not just another bright Ph.D. but rather a defense strategist with an international reputation. His absence from Harvard had proved to be an excursion to fame. The world outside Harvard Yard had given him something Harvard had denied him: confirmation of his own estimate of his ability. He was then thirty-four years old.

It was obvious that Harvard was pleased with Kissinger's return. He was granted tenure and named a Lecturer in the Department of Government, and he was promoted to Associate Professor in 1959 and full Professor in 1962. By then, he was the father of two children, Elizabeth and David.

But, even after returning to Harvard, Kissinger kept his ties with the world outside, serving as an adviser to the Rockefeller Brothers Fund. He had met Nelson Rockefeller in the early 1950s at a conference on military strategy in Quantico, Virginia. They met again during Kissinger's sabbatical at the Council on Foreign Relations. Their hard-line views harmonized nicely. Once Kissinger's book was completed, Rockefeller asked him to take on a part-time job as Director of the Special Studies Project — an eighteen-month Rockefeller-financed projection of the nation's major domestic and foreign problems over the coming years.

Once again, Kissinger was overseer of a highly influential group of Americans — among them Robert Anderson, Adolf Berle, Chester Bowles, Arthur Burns, Lucius Clay, James Dickey, John Gardner, James Killian, Charles Percy, Anna Rosenberg, Dean Rusk, David Sarnoff, and Edward Teller. Several panels were established. Kissinger sat in on all of them but apparently made an uneven contribution. One colleague, a member of the Economic and Social Panel, thought Kissinger had "nothing to say that was worth listening to. He was a dud, highly ineffective." Another participant, who heard Kissinger speak to the National Security Panel, thought he was "sensational, really brilliant."

The final report, written under Kissinger's direction, was released on January 6, 1958, and it was a front-page story. Titled "International Security: The Military Aspect" — and informally referred to as "the answer to Sputnik" — the report reflected the Kissinger view of a need for a strategy centered on tactical nuclear weapons (his controversial proposal was picking up some momentum). "The willingness to engage in nuclear war when necessary is part of the price of our freedom," it said. In keeping with Rockefeller's slogan of "a bomb shelter in every house," it called for the expansion of a nationwide civil defense system and a major increase in defense spending — three billion dollars annually over the next several years.

It was a tough report that met with approval at the Pentagon, which saw mortal Soviet threats lurking behind every Kremlin move. Capitol Hill responded with enthusiasm. "No amount is too high for defense," echoed Chairman Clarence Cannon of the House Appropriations Committee. Senator Henry Jackson said the Rockefeller report "should dispel all doubt about the halfway measures to meet the Soviet military threat." Senate Majority Leader Lyndon Johnson invited Rockefeller to appear "as soon as possible" before his Senate Preparedness Subcommittee.

Middle America, it turned out, was not far behind Congress in its eagerness to learn more about the report, which Rockefeller discussed on the "Today" show with host Dave Garroway on the very day of publication. Rockefeller was using its recommendations to launch his political campaign for the governorship of New York, but it was the report that produced most of the talk during the interview. When it was over, Garroway casually mentioned that anyone interested in a copy could get one by dropping a note to NBC. "You'll have to give away a Ford V-8 with every copy," one of his writers commented. "Who's going to write in for a book that will make people think?" A response of a thousand would have been regarded as remarkable, more than that as incredible. The next day, the mailman brought forty-five thousand requests. The day after that, another two hundred thousand requests arrived. The counting stopped as the mail piled up. It was either a tribute to the report or a symptom of national anxiety about whether a future was possible. Kissinger's name was turning up in letter boxes throughout the country.

He kept challenging what he regarded as the sloppy strategic thinking in Washington. Two months after the Rockefeller report came out, Kissinger was on the dais before the National Conference on Higher Education in Chicago, blasting policy-makers in the capital. Fresh from his observation over the previous few years of leaders in government, science and business, he was clearly pained by the fact that policy-making was in the hands not of professionals but of lawyers and businessmen. He argued that Soviet-American negotiations were generally a case of professionals taking on amateurs, and he concluded, "the professionals usually win."

Kissinger also kept up his attack against what he saw as an outmoded national defense policy. In the summer of 1958, appearing on CBS's "Face the Nation," he reverted to his principal theme — that policy based on massive retaliation had to be scrapped in the nuclear age. "This is too risky and, I think, too expensive," Kissinger warned. The United States had to develop a policy of flexible response, consistent with the challenges it faced. In a general discussion on the Middle East, he said that an American President in a crisis should not have to face the question of whether to risk thirty million American lives for the defense of, say, Beirut. (The crisis in Lebanon dominated the headlines that summer.) "In practice, I am afraid," Kissinger said, "the American President will have to decide that it is not worth it and it will therefore encourage the piecemeal taking over of the world by Soviet aggression." There was then no question in his mind that Russia intended to dominate the world and it was up to America to try to stop it — if possible, by means short of all-out nuclear war; hence, his emphasis upon the deterrent strategy of limited war, even limited nuclear war.

During these years, Kissinger was also branching out at Harvard. On the basis of a recommendation by his colleague, McGeorge Bundy, he was named Associate Director of Harvard's new Center for International Affairs. Later its Director, Robert Bowie, who had helped John Foster Dulles run the State Department, would say of the Kissinger appointment, "That's the worst mistake I ever made."

The Bowie-Kissinger confrontations were the result of clashes in personality and policy. Bowie found Kissinger too headstrong, his personality too abrasive. Bowie envisaged the center as a research operation, while his Associate Director thought it should teach as well. More important, Bowie ran into Kissinger's contempt for his MLF scheme, which called for a multilateral NATO naval force of twenty-five surface ships, each carrying eight nuclear weapons and run by crews of mixed nationalities. Kissinger found the scheme strategically inconsistent and an affront to European dignity. The MLF later became United States policy under President Kennedy, but it was abandoned by President Johnson. The uneasy truce between Bowie and Kissinger finally ended in 1960, when Kissinger resigned from his position at the center. But by then, he was well established in a directorship of his own, as head of the Defense Studies Program.

The professor who would later win the plaudits of the skeptical White House press corps for his articulate briefings on complicated issues displayed similar talents in the classroom. He was regarded as a first-rate, stimulating teacher. His course, the "Principles of International Politics," was one of *the* big courses on campus, and Kissinger lived up to its billing. His lectures were "meaty, invariably interesting and at times witty," according to the *Harvard Crimson*. But the undergraduate newspaper had a few reservations. Some students found his delivery "monotonic" and his reading list — sixteen pages — "savagely long." His description of modern policy-making was regarded as "grim."

As for his professorial colleagues, they still remember the Henry Kissinger of Harvard, although they confess that they have difficulty in finding *their* Henry Kissinger in the Henry Kissinger of Washington. "He was very sensitive about what his colleagues thought of him," says one faculty member who thinks very highly of him. Others found him arrogant. His reputation was that of an intellectual heavyweight with an extraordinary range of outside contacts. "Being at Harvard was — for any man who was really interested in power — not going to be enough," a Harvard colleague of Kissinger's says. "You're in the backwater of anything that has to do with power."

Kissinger overcame the limitations of geography by inviting power to Harvard. Just as he had, for his International Seminar, invited promising foreigners to spend the summer in intellectual discussion, he now, in his new job as head of the Defense Studies Program, kept a flow of invitations streaming toward Washington. Secretaries and assistant secretaries and deputy assistant secretaries of the Departments of Defense and of State would turn up before his Defense Policy Seminar. For them, it was a refreshing opportunity to swap the bureaucracy of Foggy Bottom and the Pentagon for the nonpartisan questions of the next generation of the country's elite. For Kissinger, it was an opportunity to present the practitioners of power to his students. He was, of course, not unaware that his invitations to these prominent personalities expanded his own ties with the power brokers of Washington. His guest-speaker approach prompted the suspicion among some Harvard professors that Kissinger did not really teach his own seminars but relied instead on imported talent. But the critical test of his approach rested with the students, and they loved it. So did the host, who thrived in his self-appointed role of devil's advocate, challenging the premises of his guests with a gusto that sometimes went beyond the call of professorial duty.

Throughout the late 1950s, Kissinger was absorbed with the question of nuclear strategy. A series of informal seminars on contemporary issues was then being conducted by Harvard and MIT, and Kissinger joined the seminar on arms control. Among the other participants were Bowie, Saville Davis, Max Millikan, Thomas Schelling, Arthur M. Schlesinger, Jr., Marshall Shulman, Jerome Wiesner, and Jerrold Zacharias. At the same time, he served as secretary of a similar panel sponsored by the Council on Foreign Relations. Here, in 1958–1959, he worked with, among others, Robert Amory, Major General Charles Bonesteel, John Fischer, James Fisk, William C. Foster, H. Rowan Gaither, Townsend Hoopes, Klaus Knorr, Hans Morgenthau, James Perkins, and Albert Wohlstetter. These were all substantial men, and not all of them shared Kissinger's views — in particular, his controversial attitude toward the employment of nuclear weapons.

His strategy came under increasing criticism as a contradiction in terms: a reliance on nuclear weapons to solve the dilemmas created by nuclear weapons. This criticism may have contributed to a major shift in his strategic thinking: the abandonment of limited nuclear war as "our most effective strategy." This shift was recorded in his second major book, *The Necessity for Choice: Prospects of American Foreign Policy.* Its publication in January, 1961, coincided with the inauguration of President Kennedy, then letting every nation know that the United States would pay any price to defend liberty. Kissinger was as troubled as ever about the Western capacity to resist Communist expansionism. He was still using "Sino-Soviet" as a hyphenated Communist threat, although other policy analysts were already beginning to detect a divergence between Moscow and Peking. "We are falling behind in the equation for all-out war," he warned. "We have insufficient strength for limited war. Our conventional forces are constantly shrinking."

But once having itemized his anxieties, he drew back from the brink.

> Some years ago, this author advocated a nuclear strategy. It seemed then
> that the most effective deterrent to any substantial Communist aggression
> was the knowledge that the United States would employ nuclear weapons
> from the very outset. A nuclear strategy appeared to offer the best prospect
> of offsetting Sino-Soviet manpower and of using our superior industrial
> capacity to best advantage. The need for forces capable of fighting limited
> nuclear war still remains. However, several developments have caused a
> shift in the view about the relative emphasis to be given conventional
> forces as against nuclear forces.

He still thought the Soviet Union ought to be made to believe that the
United States "might" use nuclear weapons, but he conceded that "the
years ahead must . . . see a substantial strengthening of the conventional forces of the free world." Disagreements within the American
military establishment about the nature of limited nuclear war, the
growth of the Soviet nuclear stockpile, the increasing significance of
long-range missiles, the impact on strategy of arms control negotiations
— all of these factors prompted Kissinger to "shift" away from the strategy
of limited nuclear war.

Kissinger distrusted the concept of détente with the Soviet Union — a
concept that had been winning widespread acceptance since President
Eisenhower's "Spirit of Camp David" meeting with Premier Khrushchev
in 1959. He felt the two societies approached negotiations in different
ways. "To us," he wrote, "a treaty has a legal and not only a utilitarian
significance, a moral and not only a practical force. In the Soviet view, a
concession is merely a phase in a continuing struggle." He also challenged
another prevailing notion at the time — that Russia was slowly evolving
into a more liberal, less intractable society. "It makes us overlook the
fact that we have to deal in the first instance with Soviet foreign and
not with its domestic policy." The book reflected Kissinger's impatience
with critics who were morally offended by a detailed discussion of
nuclear weapons, who sought to ascribe semialtruistic motivation to
either Moscow or Peking, who expressed a completely American faith in
the goodness of man and in the ability of the United States to repel an
aggressor in an all-out war. "Such attitudes — if they become generally
accepted —" wrote Kissinger, "would doom us as a nation. Far from
reducing tensions, they would reward Soviet intransigence."

Although Kissinger's main interest was Europe, he sought to strike a global note. In *The Necessity for Choice*, a virtual appeal to the new President to adopt a flexible security policy, he devoted an entire chapter to the "political evolution" of the newly independent nations. He called for increased aid — basically to offset Communist advances — and he concluded: "The best method of having a major impact on many countries will be to make a going concern of one country. India in Asia, Brazil in Latin America, Nigeria in Africa, could become magnets and examples for their regions if we acted with the boldness and on the comparative scale of the Marshall Plan." Otherwise, Kissinger recommended United States aid to regional groups of nations, seeking in this way to avoid individual commitments to small, unstable countries. And with uncharacteristic idealism, he urged the United States to "inspire" the new nations with its "national vitality . . . a dynamic American performance, an aura of confidence, a profound sense of purpose . . . a spiritual élan."

The Necessity for Choice closed with an intriguing chapter on the interrelationship between the intellectual and the policy-maker. Basically, Kissinger approved of the two working together to arrest "bureaucratic stagnation" and to liberate the forces of "creativity" before disaster struck America, but he could foresee problems in their relationship. The intellectual had to retain his independence, his sense of creativity, his belief in innovation, his quest for unorthodox solutions — or else, warned Kissinger, "he will turn into an administrator, distinguished from some of his colleagues only by having been recruited from the intellectual community." If the intellectual does not "from time to time return to his library or his laboratory to 'recharge his batteries,'" he might fall victim to the "pedantic application of administrative norms"; he might become a bureaucrat, "who condemns thousands without love and without hatred, simply in pursuance of an abstract duty." Years later, particularly during the U.S. bombing of North Vietnam, that judgment would be used against Kissinger by his critics, who would accuse him of not facing up to the "human" consequences of Administration policy.

John F. Kennedy's defeat of Richard Nixon in 1960 brought the New Frontier to Washington. It also brought a sizable contingent of luminaries from the new President's alma mater — among others, McGeorge Bundy, as Special Assistant for National Security Affairs; Arthur M. Schlesinger, Jr., as Special Assistant to the President; and Henry Kissinger, with only a foot in a door that he would try to push open. For academics who had found the eight years of President Eisenhower an uninspiring journey between Stand Pat and Status Quo, the start of the Kennedy period was intellectually exciting. The inaugural address set the tone, and the new Administration, at least rhetorically, began to push back the frontiers of the possible.

Kissinger's career in the new Washington began on a promising note. For one thing, President Kennedy, strongly influenced by the writings of Kissinger, General Gavin, and General Maxwell Taylor, dropped Dulles's doctrine of massive retaliation and adopted a policy of graduated military response to Communist challenges. For another, Kissinger, introduced to the new President by his old friend Schlesinger, was named a government consultant to three prestigious groups: the National Security Council, under McGeorge Bundy; the Arms Control and Disarmament Agency (ACDA); and the Rand Corporation.

It seemed a time of opportunity, both national and personal, but for Kissinger it turned out to be a frustrating experience. His foreign policy ideas fell on deaf ears, his style and Camelot's clashed, and his foray from Harvard as a full-fledged, though part-time, government consultant was short-lived.*

Kissinger was disappointed in the New Frontier and the new President. Kennedy was "fun," Kissinger recalls, but Kissinger was not much interested in fun in a President. *He* was interested in decisiveness, seriousness, a sense of purpose. He found few of these qualities in Kennedy, and he was put off by the "rich boy" style of the Kennedy crowd — the yachting and skiing parties, the swimming pool capers and the Georgetown set. In those days, he felt that "serious people" didn't behave that way.

But it was not just a question of style. While Kissinger appreciated the President's intellect, he had strong misgivings about the substance of Kennedy's foreign policy. The President struck him as too unsophisticated about the limitations of power, too easy in his promises of American help, too romantic in his vision of American omnipotence. To Kissinger, this was all a bad case of delusion replacing reality, of egotism riding roughshod over analysis.

One difference of opinion arose over the sensitive problem of Berlin.

---

* An indication of Kissinger's nonrole in the Kennedy Administration is the fact that he did not even make the indexes of the comprehensive books by Theodore C. Sorensen, Special Counsel to the President (*Kennedy*), Pierre Salinger, presidential Press Secretary (*With Kennedy*), or Roger Hilsman, Assistant Secretary of State for the Far East (*To Move a Nation — the Politics of Foreign Policy in the Administration of John F. Kennedy*). However, he did eke out almost three-quarters of an inch in the index of Schlesinger's *A Thousand Days*.

In August, 1961, when the Russians suddenly built a wall through the former German capital, Kissinger was deeply disturbed. He had consistently warned that the West should not "make concessions" that represented "a worsening of Berlin's position." He regarded the wall as an act of aggression which, if unchecked, could escalate into a world war. Kennedy took a different view: the wall, he privately told several of his associates, actually served to stabilize the situation in Eastern Europe. Publicly, the United States issued a formal protest and tried to intimidate the Russians with troop movements, but the wall did not come tumbling down. In sum, a minus for the West in Berlin, which Kissinger regarded as the touchstone of Allied European policy.

Kissinger disagreed with Kennedy's policy on other issues as well. Kennedy adopted the Bowie formula for an MLF — a multilateral nuclear force for NATO; Kissinger was still hostile to the scheme. Kennedy pressed for his "Grand Design" — urging Great Britain to join an embryonic European federation. Kissinger thought this was unrealistic on at least two grounds: it conflicted with de Gaulle's policy of asserting French interests and it ignored the rising tide of nationalism throughout Europe.

With Schlesinger's help, Kissinger, a believer in face-to-face exchanges, tried several times to make an end run around Bundy so that he could place his own views directly before the President. But most of the time, he failed; Bundy, as National Security Council quarterback, would block him, just as Kissinger himself, when he took over the NSC for Nixon, would block *his* aides from personally presenting differing views to his President. Some of the Kennedy people would later say that Kissinger became too much of an in-house critic. "A little harassing" is the way Kennedy once described the Kissinger style to Pierre Salinger, the presidential Press Secretary.

Kissinger created a series of minor diplomatic contretemps for the Kennedy Administration. In January, 1962, Kissinger, visiting India under a cultural exchange program, was asked for his opinion about whether Pakistan would enter into an alliance with China. "No," Kissinger responded, "Pakistan would never do anything so foolish." His remark produced black headlines in the Pakistan press and a diplomatic protest by Pakistan's Ambassador to Washington, who complained about Kissinger's "glib talk." After the furor died down, Kissinger visited the Khyber Pass. When he returned to India, he was asked for his opinion about the Baluchistan problem. Kissinger, much less inhibited in those days, replied: "I wouldn't recognize the Baluchistan problem if it hit me in the face." Again there were black headlines in the Pakistan press. "Kissinger does not recognize Baluchistan," one of them said. The Afghanistan Ambassador to Washington filed a formal complaint. Finally, Kissinger got a cable from Bundy. "If you don't keep your mouth shut," Bundy wrote, "I am going to hit the recall button."

A month later, the NSC and Kissinger parted company. The consultant had been encouraged to resign. "He left in a huff," a colleague of Kissinger's recalls. He did, however, retain the two other consultantships, with ACDA and Rand, neither of which called for day-to-day contact with the White House. He was to remain with ACDA through 1967, with Rand an additional year.

Years later, Kissinger admitted to friends that he had "blown it, messed up a good opportunity." Indeed, he was to look back on those days with nostalgia. "I first saw government at a high level in the early 1960s — at a time which is now occasionally debunked as overly brash, excessively optimistic, even somewhat arrogant," he recalled. "Some of these criticisms are justified. But a spirit prevailed then which was quintessentially American: that problems are a challenge, not an alibi; that men are measured not only by their success but also by their striving; that it is better to aim grandly than to wallow in mediocre comfort. Above all, government and opponents thought of themselves in a common enterprise — not in a permanent, irreconcilable contest."

Kissinger was back at Harvard full-time between 1962 and 1965. Except for a brief interlude in 1964, when he was at Rockefeller's side in his unsuccessful bid for the GOP presidential nomination, Kissinger was busy grappling with the intricate problems of Atlantic security. His convictions were spelled out in more than a dozen articles, appearing in such diverse periodicals as *Foreign Affairs, The Reporter, Harper's, Die Welt, Politique Etrangère,* and *Res Publica.* Between articles, he produced still another book, *The Troubled Partnership: A Reappraisal of the Atlantic Alliance,* published in April, 1965. His output was prodigious. His style had its own carefully plotted symmetry, but it struck some readers as a triumph of stamina over grace. "How a man who is unable to write will write so much and how by iron discipline make it at least half readable," says an old friend, "is one of his absolutely outstanding characteristics." By then, Kissinger was no longer concerned that his train of thought might be interrupted by family matters; he and Ann Kissinger were divorced in 1964, after fifteen years of what has been described as a stormy marriage.

Together, Kissinger's articles and the book added up to an indictment of American policy toward Western Europe during both the Kennedy and Johnson Administrations. There was far too little meaningful consultation between America and her allies, Kissinger charged, an accusation that would later be leveled against him when he was in a command position. He also felt there was far too much arrogance in the official American attitude toward the Europeans, especially toward French president Charles de Gaulle. Washington failed to understand that Europe had grown up since the days of the Marshall Plan, that she no longer appreciated American paternalism. The United States, he wrote, should not try to impose American solutions on European problems. "If we insist on remaining the sole trustee of policy everywhere, including Europe," he wrote, "the strain on our resources may be too great. The day will come when we will consider a measure of autonomy in Europe a blessing rather than an irritant."

Perhaps because he was European-born, perhaps because he was a student of global history, Kissinger could never comfortably accept the notion that the United States alone should be entrusted with the moral and political destiny of the world, or the idea, which grew out of the frontier experience, that nothing was beyond the power of America. For example, he could never share the faith of Dean Rusk in America's omnipotence. Once, in February, 1968, during a heated give-and-take with reporters on Vietnam, Rusk, then Secretary of State, pressed his forefinger against the top of a coffee table and asserted, "When the United States applies pressure on something, anything, it gives."

Kissinger worried about the possible consequences of such naïve Yankee exuberance. In June, 1966, he told Senator Frank Church, during an open session of the Senate Foreign Relations Committee, that he lamented the growing American tendency to play God "in every part of the globe." It is "clearly beyond our psychological resources," he said. The strain on American leadership might become too great. Kissinger expressed these views at a time when the United States was in the midst of its massive Vietnam commitment, but he did not openly challenge the Johnson Administration's Vietnam policy. He had learned a sobering lesson about going public with criticism during the Kennedy Administration. But he clearly had Vietnam in mind.

Vietnam Baptism

Vietnam was Henry Kissinger's entrée to the Johnson Administration, his third incarnation as a foreign policy consultant. This time, his government service came about through the good offices of Henry Cabot Lodge, Jr., who had been Nixon's running mate in the 1960 presidential race against John Kennedy and then served as Kennedy's Ambassador to South Vietnam. In July of 1965, Lodge had been appointed to a second tour as Ambassador in Saigon by President Johnson; once again, the choice was seen as an obvious political move to demonstrate bipartisan support for the expanding commitment of American power in a war that was becoming more controversial with every shipment of GIs. Lodge asked William Bundy, Assistant Secretary of State for East Asian and Pacific Affairs (and McGeorge's brother) to appoint Kissinger and Lodge's son, George Lodge, also teaching at Harvard, as consultants to the State Department during his ambassadorship. The request grew out of a suggestion by LBJ. "He suggested that I try to get some outside opinions, some new ideas," Lodge later recalled, "because he thought all he was getting from his regular advisers were the same old ideas, and he wanted to get some new ones. So I thought about it for a while and invited Kissinger. I knew him quite well, at the Harvard International Center, and I had great regard for his ability." Within a month, the appointment was cleared, and Kissinger, eager to get back into the center of things, entered the tormented world of Vietnam decision-making.

Vietnam was not Kissinger's specialty. His interests centered on nuclear strategy, Europe, the Atlantic alliance. The world he had traveled was the West, not the East. Thoroughly at home on the continent, he had never set foot in Southeast Asia. Still, it was not exactly an alien subject. Harvard was a hotbed of dissension on Vietnam. Kissinger was familiar with the thinking in official circles, which kept seeing "light at the end of the tunnel"; he read the press dispatches from Saigon, which regularly challenged the optimism of the Johnson White House; he was personally familiar with the French view that the war was a *guerre sale*.

The first of the many visits Kissinger would make to Vietnam took place in October, 1965. His companion on the journey was Clark Clifford, an influential Washington attorney and an adviser to Democratic presidents starting with Truman, who was to become Robert McNamara's successor as Secretary of Defense in early 1968. Their mission was to make an appraisal of the direction United States policy should take in Vietnam.

To be sure, Kissinger conferred with the obvious command points of power — on the American side, the Embassy and MACV (Military Assistance Command Vietnam); on the Vietnamese side, General Nguyen Cao Ky, General Nguyen Van Thieu, and other top military men. But since he was aware that the official version of reality was usually self-serving, he slipped out of the VIP rut and began soliciting the views of the non-establishmentarians. He talked with Buddhist leaders, local intellectuals, hamlet chiefs, newsmen. Recognizing that Saigon and the outlying villages were really two different Vietnams, he journeyed to the countryside and asked questions about Vietnamese history, society, and culture. What sort of people were these? What were their traditions? Did they have a political base? Could they cope with war? What about ARVN, the Army of South Vietnam? Could it be improved? How? How fast? Most important, could the United States help in any meaningful way other than by pouring in troops and the matériel of war?

When he had got it all together, as best he could on the basis of a fast-moving visit, Kissinger fell back on his old technique of reporting to no one but the boss — Ambassador Lodge, in this case. Just what one Henry told the other is classified. But a few days later, after Kissinger and Clifford had departed from Saigon, Jack Foisie, veteran Far East correspondent for the Los Angeles Times, filed a front-page story about their visit. He reported that they were "returning home dismayed by the almost total lack of political maturity or unselfish political motivation they found among current or potential leaders of the South Vietnamese government" despite the massive infusion of GIs and dollars.

En route to Washington, Kissinger stopped briefly at the Rand Corporation "think tank" in Santa Monica, California, to share his findings on Vietnam. The resident experts, all of whom either knew Kissinger or were familiar with his work, turned out en masse. "It was the most brilliant analysis of the war I'd ever heard," recalled a respected Southeast Asia scholar who was there. "He understood the military situation, the political situation. He had good judgment about which of the Vietnamese he'd talked to were worth listening to and which were worth discounting. His assessment was that we were pursuing a very erroneous military strategy, that we were not fighting a counterinsurgency operation but a conventional war against a nonconventional enemy, that we had nailed our flag to the mast of a bunch of worthless Saigon politicians and generals."

Once back in the capital, Kissinger began briefing officials at State and Defense. His style of operation was standard Kissinger procedure — individual private meetings. He talked about his Vietnam findings with Jonathan Moore, Bundy's Special Assistant, with Bundy, with McNamara, and with George Ball, among others. "And God knows, none of them ever knew what he said to the other ones," Moore recalls. "Presumably it was very similar or maybe identical, but no one ever knew and very little was written down." Since Kissinger's emphasis on private get-togethers could not be attributed to stage fright, it was generally attributed to a desire to make a maximum intellectual impact on an audience of one at a time.

As for his approach to understanding the puzzle of Vietnam, Kissinger was given high marks. "He was trying to figure out, really quite resourcefully and quite sensibly, how the whole societal context in which they think is different from ours," Moore recalls. "He really was very open about trying to find out what the hell was going on out there. He was very clean. His mind was open. He wasn't carrying a lot of ideological baggage around."

Even if Moore got the impression that Kissinger was unencumbered by "ideological baggage," the professor had in fact not given up his conceptual angle of vision; he still saw the world as a series of interrelated parts, with any shift in the balance producing a kind of ripple effect. His views were published in a guest column for *Look* in the summer of 1966. "The war in Vietnam," he began, "is dominated by two factors: withdrawal would be disastrous, and negotiations are inevitable." With that as an opener, he went on to spell out what he believed would happen around the world if the United States pulled out under conditions that could plausibly be presented as a Communist victory.

First, "a victory by a third-class Communist peasant state over the United States" would "strengthen the most bellicose factions in the internecine Communist struggle around the world." Second, a U.S. pullout would "demoralize" America's Southeast Asian friends, including Laos, Malaysia, the Philippines, and Thailand. Third, Japan and India might shift their "long-term orientation" away from Washington and toward Peking or Moscow if the United States failed to "honor its commitments."

And finally, he wrote, "a demonstration of American impotence in Asia cannot fail to lessen the credibility of American pledges in other fields." "We are no longer fighting in Vietnam only for the Vietnamese," he concluded; "we are also fighting for ourselves and for international stability."

To a remarkable degree, Kissinger's opposition to an American pullout was an uncritical reflection of the official wisdom of those days. Dean Rusk, who saw Peking Communists as hell-bent on Asian domination at a minimum, was then warning NATO that even countries as "far removed" as Iceland and Norway would be affected by a quick U.S. withdrawal from Vietnam. The Europeans discounted these warnings; they did not believe that the Soviet Union would suddenly engage in reckless expansionism the moment the last GI left Vietnam.

But his concurrence with Rusk went only so far: he did not share the Administration's visceral drive toward a military victory in Vietnam. Kissinger believed that such a victory was impossible: first, because neither Moscow nor Peking would allow North Vietnam, a fraternal Socialist state, to be beaten; and second, because there existed "a Communist 'shadow government' permeating every aspect of Vietnamese life." The "primary issue in Vietnam," he wrote, "is political and psychological, not military." For Kissinger, the best U.S. strategy would be the creation and expansion of "secure zones," containing "a maximum of population," which would "give us reliable negotiating counters at a conference."

A few months later, in October, 1966, Kissinger was back in Vietnam — this time, with Daniel Davidson, a young lawyer who was working for William Bundy. In contrast to his exploratory trip in 1965, Kissinger had a specific assignment: to help set up, if possible, an improved *chu hoi* program designed to instigate high-level defections from the Communist side. Afterward, he was to report his findings to the then traveling White House before President Johnson's summit meeting with his Asian allies later that month in Manila. Again, Vietnam was a discouraging experience. Kissinger's visit to a village was a case in point. As the story was later told, the local American adviser assured Kissinger that the village was "eighty-five percent pacified." A few hours later, he learned from the Vietnamese that, in fact, four out of five people in the village paid taxes to the Vietcong. Kissinger then had a private word with the adviser about those taxes to the enemy. How could he claim that the village was eighty-five percent pacified? "Ah," said the adviser, "the VC wouldn't dare to enter this village. The people pay their taxes *by mail*." It was a typical case of American wishful thinking and it served to compound Kissinger's skepticism about Vietnam.

From Saigon, Kissinger flew to Manila to report to Bundy and Lodge. It was an uneventful visit, except that it was to produce, a few years later, a minor *cause célèbre* on the antiwar Harvard campus. Since the side trip to the Philippines would mean missing one of his seminars, Kissinger asked Davidson to ask W. Averell Harriman, then an adviser to the President, to send along an explanatory cable to Dean Franklin Ford at Harvard. Harriman thought the intercession of the Government was a bit much, but he instructed Robert Miller, one of his aides, to comply. "The United States Government deeply appreciates Harvard's making Professor Kissinger available for his extremely successful mission to South Vietnam," the message read. "That mission was of great importance. Could only have been carried out by Kissinger and had to be complete prior to the Manila Conference." It was filed and forgotten. Later the cable was unearthed by a group of war-protesting Harvard students who had invaded the university President's office and ransacked his files, and it was used to portray Kissinger as having the closest ties to "Johnson's war." Actually, it was nothing more than the kind of "excuse" note a parent sends to the teacher when a child has been absent — except that this one was written in governmental English.

Kissinger's reputation as the world's most celebrated undercover operative would have to wait until the Nixon Administration, but he began his apprenticeship in secret diplomacy under President Johnson. He emerged as a pivotal figure in what came to be known as "Pennsylvania," the code name for an exchange of top secret messages between Washington and Hanoi through a French microbiologist whom Kissinger knew and who in turn knew another Frenchman who knew Ho Chi Minh. The three of them — Kissinger and his two partners in the undertaking — were all amateurs in the fine art of diplomatic negotiation, but they were highly motivated in the search for an end to the war. The objective, in its simplest form, was to swap a U.S. bombing halt for Hanoi's agreement to enter "promptly" into "productive" negotiations. The drama was played out between June and October of 1967, and though it did not get both sides to start talking, it was a forerunner of the secret diplomatic maneuvers that would bring the warring parties to Paris the following year.

The story begins over aperitifs. Kissinger, then a consultant to the

State Department, and Herbert Marcovich, the microbiologist, were among a small group of scholars who were meeting in Paris to discuss a variety of international problems. They had attended similar conferences over the years, their last such get-together having taken place the previous year at the Baltic resort of Sopot, Poland. While the two men were discussing Vietnam, Marcovich mentioned that a friend of his, Raymond Aubrac, a former underground Resistance fighter during World War II, now a Harvard- and MIT-trained engineer and administrator with the United Nations Food and Agricultural Organization in Rome, had gotten to know Ho Chi Minh twenty-one years earlier. Ho had journeyed to the Paris suburb of Fontainebleau, in 1946, to lead the Viet Minh's unsuccessful quest for independence from France, and he had spent some time at Aubrac's nearby villa. The visitor from Hanoi eventually became godfather to one of his host's children. Could Aubrac be used as a channel for peace? Kissinger, convinced of the "inevitability" of negotiations, checked with Bundy — privately. Bundy checked with Rusk, and Rusk checked with the President. Within a few weeks, the go-ahead signal came from Washington, with the caveat that Kissinger play the role of an interested party rather than an official of the United States Government. It was a predictable loophole in the event "Pennsylvania" was bungled.

Aubrac and Marcovich, with the approval of President de Gaulle, flew to Hanoi on July 21, 1967, and, three days later, met with Premier Pham Van Dong. To demonstrate that they were not simply acting on their own, they told the North Vietnamese Premier about their semiofficial link to Washington — Kissinger. Marcovich then outlined — "as a private idea" — a two-part proposal: an end to the U.S. bombing and a ceiling on North Vietnamese war supplies to the south.

Dong replied: "We want an unconditional end to the bombing and, if that happens, there will be no further obstacle to negotiations."

"Our view is thus," he continued. "U.S. power is enormous and the U.S. Government wants to win the war. President Johnson is suffering from a pain and this pain is called South Vietnam. We agree that the situation on the battlefield is decisive; the game is being played in South Vietnam. From the newspapers we see that some people want to confine the war to the South. However, the White House and the Pentagon seem determined to continue the war against the North. Therefore, we think that attacks on the North are likely to increase.

"We have made provisions for attacks on our dikes; we are ready to accept war on our soil. Our military potential is growing because of aid from the USSR and other Socialist countries. . . . We have been fighting for our independence for four thousand years. We have defeated the Mongols three times. The United States Army, strong as it is, is not as terrifying as Genghis Khan."

The North Vietnamese Premier insisted that American troops leave Vietnam but he said he was flexible about a timetable, realizing that some U.S. troops might have to remain in the south until a political settlement was reached. "We do not want to humiliate the U.S.," he added. North Vietnam would not try to impose a Communist regime on the south or press for an immediate unification of the country.

Later in the day, Aubrac, escorted by the Premier, met with Ho Chi Minh. When the meeting was over, Aubrac and Marcovich, using a pre-arranged code, signaled Kissinger, who met them in Paris within a few hours of their return from Hanoi. Kissinger filed the following report:

Aubrac said that what struck him immediately was how old Ho had become. He was dressed in a Chinese gown and walked with the aid of a cane. However, his intelligence was unimpaired, his eyes still had their old sparkle. He seemed to enjoy playing the role of a grandfather figure, not concerned with details.

Aubrac had brought as a gift a little colored stone egg. Ho gave three presents in return: silk for Aubrac's daughter, some books, and a ring made of metal from the 2,000th U.S. plane claimed to have been shot down over Vietnam. He remembered the first names of all of Aubrac's three children.

After speaking about Aubrac's family for about 15 minutes, Aubrac said: "Mr. President, do you know why I have come?"

Ho answered: "Yes."

Aubrac asked whether he had any comments. Ho replied by saying that he did not like the phrase "peace in Vietnam." It gave an impression of moral equivalence between the United States and North Vietnam; in fact, the U.S. is the aggressor and must be condemned. . . .

The details of the negotiations, said Ho, were in the hands of [Premier] Pham Van Dong. Ho then added: "Remember, many people have tried to fool me and have failed. I know you don't want to fool me."

He then turned the conversation back to family matters. He expressed regret that Aubrac had sold the house where he had stayed 21 years ago.

"Where shall I live when I next come to Paris?" He then asked whether he would be welcome in Paris, but avoided the question of whether he wanted an invitation.

He terminated the conversation after 50 minutes and was escorted from the room. Pham Van Dong walked with Aubrac to his car. He said that "we try to spare President Ho as many details as we can. He is an old man; we want him to live to see his country unified."

On August 3, a small group of American officials gathered in Washington to consider Kissinger's report — on the very same day that the President announced he was escalating the troop ceiling in South Vietnam to five hundred and twenty-five thousand, and five days before he ordered new air strikes against sixteen new sensitive targets, some near the center of Hanoi. It took these officials eight days to come up with an American response. Kissinger was asked to convey the following message to Pham Van Dong via the Marcovich-Aubrac channel: "The United States is willing to stop the aerial and naval bombardment of North Vietnam if this will lead promptly to productive discussions between representatives of the U.S. and the DRV [Democratic Republic of Vietnam] looking toward a resolution of the issues between them. We would assume that, while discussions proceed, either with public knowledge or secretly, the DRV would not take advantage of the bombing cessation or limitation. Any such move on their part would obviously be inconsistent with the movement toward resolution of the issues between the U.S. and the DRV which the negotiations are intended to achieve." This U.S. position was close to the so-called "San Antonio formula" for peace that was to be presented by LBJ a month later.

On August 17, Kissinger again met with Marcovich and Aubrac in Paris. He relayed the message. On instructions, he told them that the United States was prepared to negotiate secretly or publicly and that a partial cutback in the bombing might be preferable to a total halt so as to avoid focusing attention on the talks. The three men conferred for five hours. Kissinger was explicit about two points. The phrase "productive discussions" referred to the strong desire of the United States Government to avoid a protracted Korean-type negotiation while fighting continued. "Take advantage" referred to "any increase in the movement of men and supplies into the south." Marcovich told Kissinger he was worried about the heavy American bombing. Kissinger said that in the absence of meaningful negotiations, the intensity of violence was likely to continue to rise. He urged them to return to Hanoi to deliver the message to the North Vietnamese.

The two French intermediaries tried to obtain visas that very next day but these were denied. For the next two days, they met with Kissinger at a hotel on the Left Bank, rather than at Marcovich's house, to avoid detection. This time the trio became a quartet. Harriman's aide, Chester Cooper, accompanied Kissinger as a sign of American seriousness. Kissinger told his contacts that "effective August 24, there would be a noticeable change in the bombing pattern in the vicinity of Hanoi to guarantee their personal safety and as a token of our good will." This word came directly from Secretary of Defense McNamara. The restriction would hold "for ten days."

On August 21 and 22, United States warplanes carried out heavy raids in the Hanoi area. "Numerous lives" were lost, according to North Vietnamese authorities.

On August 25, the two Frenchmen met with Mai Van Bo, the North Vietnamese representative in Paris, and again requested visas. Bo replied that it was too dangerous to visit Hanoi during the bombing. The Frenchmen replied that they had assurances of safety in the Hanoi area through September 4. They gave Bo the text of the American message for transmission to Hanoi, described their contacts with Kissinger, and added several other points that had been made by Kissinger: that the United States wanted these exchanges to remain confidential, that bombing attacks on dikes in North Vietnam had been accidental, and that the United States was ready to send a representative to meet authorized North Vietnamese officials in Vientiane, Paris, Moscow, or anywhere else.

On August 31, Bo, noting the August 21 bombings, again rejected their visa requests. But on September 2, he summoned them to his mission and suggested rather mysteriously that they make certain nothing happened to Hanoi "in the next few days." They contacted Kissinger. He contacted Bundy. The bombing restrictions near Hanoi were extended for another three days, through September 7. But they still were not granted visas.

On September 10, at 6 P.M., the phone rang in Marcovich's laboratory. Bo had a message from Hanoi, an answer for Kissinger. It proved to be very disappointing.

"The essence of the American propositions is the stopping of the bombing under conditions. The American bombing of the Democratic Republic of Vietnam is illegal. The United States should put an end to the bombing and cannot pose conditions.

"The American message has been communicated after an escalation of the attacks against Hanoi and under the threat of continuation of the attacks against Hanoi. It is clear that this constitutes an ultimatum to the Vietnamese people.

"The Government of the Democratic Republic of Vietnam energetically rejects the American propositions. . . ."

On September 13, Kissinger, back in Paris once again, had breakfast with Marcovich. He was carrying a sealed message that contained Washington's reply to Hanoi's rejection. "We proposed a direct meeting between Hanoi's representative and Dr. Kissinger," President Johnson later disclosed in his account of his years in the White House. Kissinger wanted to deliver the message to Bo personally, but Bo informed his French contact that, because of the continued threat of air attacks on Hanoi, a direct meeting was out of the question. The next day, Marcovich delivered another sealed message from Kissinger expressing bafflement at Hanoi's attitude. "If we bomb near Hanoi," Kissinger wrote, "we're accused of bringing pressure. If we voluntarily and without any suggestion from Hanoi impose a restraint on our actions and keep this up without time limit we are accused of an ultimatum. In fact, the American proposal contained neither threats nor conditions and should not be rejected on these grounds." Both messages had been approved by Washington.

There were other sealed messages and contacts over the next few weeks, but Bo steadfastly refused to receive Kissinger or extend visas to the Frenchmen. "The Americans," he asserted, "are playing a double game — on one hand they are offering us a peace; on the other they increase their bombing." Finally, on September 24, Bo summoned Marcovich and read another Hanoi message to him. Bo rejected the "San Antonio formula" and for the benefit of the French intermediaries, added: "I accept your expression of confidence in Kissinger, but at the moment when the U.S. is increasing its escalation, it was not possible for me to see him. . . . We have no illusions about American policy."

Kissinger's reply was delivered to Bo by eight-thirty the following morning. The American envoy began by saying there was no point in trading charges and countercharges about "past activities." Clearly, he went on, Washington and Hanoi had great difficulty understanding each other's thought processes. This made direct contact essential. "Intermediaries, no matter how trustworthy," he wrote, "are not satisfactory substitutes." Kissinger stressed that all Washington required was the assurance that a bombing halt would lead to "prompt" and "productive" discussions. But the words "prompt" and "productive" were viewed by the North Vietnamese diplomat as camouflaged conditions.

Kissinger returned to Cambridge.

On October 10, Marcovich made a transatlantic telephone call to Kissinger and urged him to hurry back to Paris. Kissinger declined, saying the United States had made its overtures and it was now up to Hanoi to respond. Marcovich, indefatigable, was back at Bo's office by the end of the week, pleading with the North Vietnamese diplomat to keep the channel open. Bo's response was a written message, declaring that "at a time when the U.S. is pursuing a policy of escalation we cannot receive Kissinger. . . . It is only when the U.S. has ended without condition the bombardment that discussions can take place."

The reaction in the White House was to blame the impasse on Hanoi — but to keep trying, nevertheless. "With this statement, I became convinced again that Hanoi had no interest in serious talk about peace except, as always, on its own stiff terms," President Johnson wrote. "But we wanted to leave no stone unturned. On October 18 I met in the Cabinet Room with Secretaries Rusk and McNamara, Walt Rostow, and Dr. Kissinger. We reviewed the entire record of the talks in Paris, and on the strong recommendation of my advisers, I agreed that Kissinger should return to France and make one more attempt to get into serious discussion."

Kissinger shuttled across the Atlantic once again. His latest instructions noted: "It should be your objective from the start to indicate that the patience of your Washington friends is running out and that they feel that Hanoi has been unwilling to respond on any significant point." In Paris, his French contacts told Kissinger that it was most important that he try to see Bo straightaway. To demonstrate his own personal sense of urgency, Aubrac said he was willing to put his twenty-one-year-old friendship with Ho Chi Minh on the line to clarify the situation in the interests of peace. There were no objections from Kissinger, provided the North Vietnamese understood that there was nothing new to add to the U.S. position.

Aubrac dialed the North Vietnamese mission. Mai Van Bo accepted the call. With Marcovich listening on an extension, Aubrac said, "We would like to see you urgently."

Bo: "There is nothing new to say. The situation is worsening. There is no reason to talk again."

Aubrac: "There is something new and very important."

Bo: "There is nothing new to say. The situation is worsening. There is no reason to talk again."

Aubrac: "There is something very important — perhaps the most important juncture of our exchanges."

Bo: "What is the important matter?"

Aubrac said it related to Bo's last message and the sequence in which steps had to be taken to stop the bombing.

Bo: "Our position is perfectly clear." He then repeated his earlier statement that North Vietnam, for its part, had nothing new to say. There was no reason to meet.

Aubrac hung up. Disappointed, distressed, he telephoned Kissinger to say that Bo had refused to see them. Kissinger, equally disappointed, returned to Cambridge. "Pennsylvania" was dead.

According to some on the Washington end of "Pennsylvania," Kissinger, for a newcomer to the business, had turned in a surprisingly professional performance. He had been entrusted by LBJ to conduct a top secret negotiation, even though the President recognized that he was a close associate of Rockefeller and thereby a potential leak to the Republicans. In fact, his discretion was impeccable. He represented the U.S. position precisely. He stuck to his instructions. He reported conversations accurately. He was consistently candid — in both directions. Admittedly, he did not determine policy or control the negotiations; he was simply an intermediary between intermediaries. Still, these secret contacts with the North Vietnamese, though by proxy, provided his first experience in the difficulties of dealing with "the other side" and gave him a stark insight into the depth of the mutual distrust between Hanoi and Washington. This experience would prove invaluable when he served as Nixon's envoy to the North Vietnamese.

The goals of the two sides were completely contradictory, and so the war continued, and America's anguish over Vietnam led to the narrow election of a Republican President who campaigned on a pledge to "end the war and win the peace."

Kissinger was at Nixon's side when the new Administration entered the White House. In those last weeks before Inauguration Day, the newly appointed presidential adviser was already drafting the blueprint and the personnel for what would soon come to be known as "Henry's Wonderful Machine."

FIVE

Henry's Wonderful Machine

ONCE UPON A TIME, there wasn't a National Security Council. Still, the Republic flourished; wars, even world wars, were fought and won; and history was made, and often manipulated. Indeed, as venerable institutions go, the NSC is a tot, less than thirty years — or only five Presidents — old. Yet the NSC, because of the thirty-seventh President's style of decision-making, was throughout his first term the nation's most powerful foreign policy machine, with Henry Kissinger as the chief engineer.

The NSC of Richard Nixon began taking form during those busy pre-inaugural days at the Pierre. His first assignment to his newly appointed Assistant for National Security Affairs was to transform the loose structure of the NSC that was inherited from his predecessors into a model of centralized, calibrated policy-making.

The original NSC model was founded in 1947 "to advise the President with respect to the integration of domestic, foreign and military policies to the national security so as to enable the military services and the other departments and agencies of the government to cooperate more effectively in matters involving the national security." Its statutory members include the President, the Vice-President, the Secretary of State, the Secretary of Defense, and the Director of the Office of Emergency Planning. The Director of the Central Intelligence Agency and the Chairman of the Joint Chiefs of Staff sit in on meetings as designated advisers to the NSC. From time to time, depending on the issues under discussion, others may be invited. The language of the legislation establishing the NSC was so vague that the NSC has been used in different ways by each

President. In each case, it has been a question of who was in charge.

The NSC was created in reaction to the operating style of President Franklin Roosevelt during World War II; he ran foreign policy out of his vest pocket, so much so that one department or another would sometimes find itself left out in the shaping of a critical decision. When Harry Truman came to the White House, he asked James Forrestal, the country's first Secretary of Defense, to work out a system that would ensure that the opinions of Defense and of State would be taken into consideration. The result was the formation of the NSC, which in its earliest days was known as "Forrestal's Revenge."

Truman used the NSC in its Model T days as an instrument for coordinating the rapidly expanding role of the United States in confronting and containing the postwar rise of Soviet power. In practice, however, he found himself depending primarily on the advice of his strong secretaries of state, Marshall and later Dean Acheson.

The presidents after Truman shaped the NSC to reflect their own working style. Dwight Eisenhower chose to strengthen it by concentrating more power in the White House as a kind of military command center for national policy. But his general's habit of demanding a consensus on just about every issue turned the NSC into an arena for protracted negotiations that produced, in Dean Acheson's phrase, "agreement by exhaustion." In the final analysis, Eisenhower consulted himself on military matters and left the rest to another strong-willed Secretary of State, John Foster Dulles.

President Kennedy, with his absorbing interest in international affairs, dismantled much of Eisenhower's paper factory and ran foreign policy from his desk; the titular job of Secretary of State went to Dean Rusk and the job of running the NSC staff to McGeorge Bundy. During major crises, the task forces usually met at 1600 Pennsylvania Avenue. Foggy Bottom was no longer the fulcrum of decision-making.

President Johnson's obsession with Vietnam created a crisis atmosphere in the White House; the NSC became little more than a backdrop for ad hoc improvisation at Tuesday lunches in the Executive Mansion.

Nixon — anti–ad hoc, anticonsensus, at times even antilunch — wanted a leaner, leakproof NSC operation, with none of the freewheeling political give-and-take that characterized the Johnson-era NSC, when top advisers would come over to the White House to "reason together" with the President in an intensely personal way. He wanted total control and a clean break with the Democratic past.

"Nixon decided he wanted meetings held to a bare minimum," recalled General Alexander Haig, Jr., who served as Kissinger's deputy on the NSC staff before being promoted in late 1972 to be Vice Chief of Staff of the Army and in mid-1973, in the wake of the Watergate scandal, to be Haldeman's successor as Chief of Staff at the White House. "He wanted to avoid what he called 'waffle solutions,'" said Haig — the kind of bureaucratic distillations of policy designed to offend the least number of officials. Instead, Nixon wanted the NSC to provide "a series of options giving the President a spectrum of courses." Each department — State, Defense, the CIA — would be directly responsible for giving the NSC its most carefully considered and independent judgment, proposing specific courses of action.

In Kissinger, Nixon found an enthusiastic disciple, equally elitist in orientation, equally distrustful of the bureaucracy. Indeed, even before his Pierre days, Kissinger had given a good deal of thought to the urgent need to revamp the structure of NSC policy-making. The Johnson approach had been distinguished, in Kissinger's view, by a "constantly widening gap between the technical competence of the research staff" and "what hard-pressed political leaders were capable of absorbing." What was required, he argued, was the replacement of "crisis diplomacy" by an approach that anticipated problems before they became headlines, and explored possible solutions. The NSC, in his view, would be the ultimate clearinghouse for "options," as they came to be known, destined for the President.

Kissinger's and Nixon's thinking on the NSC coincided. The President-elect promptly approved his adviser's plan for the best utilization of the council. It incorporated their joint conviction that the NSC would be the *only* forum for reviewing and making policy at the highest level and would concentrate control over the execution of policy almost exclusively in the White House. What is more, the emphasis would be on replacing the conditioned reflex of patching up a crisis here, repairing a problem there, with a more conceptual approach, integrating U.S. responses and initiatives into a long-term global strategy. In his role as Assistant for National Security, as then envisaged, Kissinger would fill two roles: he would be a sort of traffic cop, routing options on to the Oval Office or back to the NSC staff for still another analytical once-over, and he would be the President's adviser on foreign policy matters whenever the President solicited his views.

To help him fulfill this dual role, Kissinger recruited an aggressive staff of foreign policy specialists. The staff, despite Kissinger's ties to a university with an abundance of available professors, was not imported en masse from Cambridge; rather, it was a mix of people with assorted professional backgrounds. He hired a number of young scholars from outside the Government, but mostly he stocked up on help from within the bureaucracy — politically oriented Pentagon officials and seasoned State Department regulars, theorists and technicians: carry-overs from previous Administrations.

Kissinger took them on for their ability, not their politics — a fact that disturbed Haldeman, who always felt ill at ease in the presence of intellectuals, and, in addition, was suspicious of anyone who was not totally committed to Nixon.

Within the NSC in those early months, staffers felt a sense of excitement about the opportunity to overhaul American foreign policy. Their intellectual élan was the envy of the eight-to-four-thirty ritualists throughout the Government. There was a kind of creative interaction between the boss and his staff. "The idea," Kissinger would later explain, "was to give them the sense that they were doing something uniquely important and to get a sort of monastic quality, dedication, which I think it's fair to say we succeeded in doing." After the break-in period, his collection of specialists turned into what Kissinger called "a very tight, devoted organization."

The compliment was returned by a number of his recruits. "You do things for Henry you didn't think you were capable of," said Winston Lord, a young fast-writing generalist, a graduate of Yale and the Fletcher School of Law and Diplomacy who had crossed over from Defense and who would eventually be at Kissinger's side during the secret trips to Peking and Moscow. "I think of Henry as a Vince Lombardi in pursuit of excellence."

It was quite a migration.

"I was the first to come over from State," Helmut Sonnenfeldt later recalled, a distinction that was later to be claimed by quite a few other early recruits. Sonnenfeldt, then chief of East European Intelligence and Research at the State Department, was attending a conference at West Point when he read the *New York Times* story about his friend's appointment. He telephoned to offer his congratulations, and they agreed to rendezvous later in the day in New York. Sonnenfeldt immediately assured Kissinger that he did not regard their conversation of a few months before, when they had speculated about Kissinger's possible appointment to "the Rostow job," as binding in any way; Kissinger was under no obligation to offer him a job on the NSC staff. But Kissinger made it clear that, just as he had wanted Sonnenfeldt to handle Europe in theory, he wanted him to in reality. They discussed the possibility of dividing Europe in two — eastern and western — but decided to keep Europe one. Sonnenfeldt then left for a winter holiday in Antigua. When he returned, he said "yes" to his friend Henry.

Colonel Alexander Haig, Jr., was intercepted at West Point. A member of the class of '47, he was visiting his alma mater in early December when he got a call from General Andrew Goodpaster, an old acquaintance of the President-elect's from the Eisenhower-Nixon days in the White House. Goodpaster, then helping draft the blueprint for a more formal NSC structure, invited Haig to the Pierre. He had been recommended, it turned out, by two old friends: Joseph Califano, a key LBJ aide, who had once been Haig's superior at the Pentagon under Robert McNamara, and by Dr. Kraemer, who had once worked with Haig at Defense in the early 1960s when Haig was the Army desk officer for Berlin and NATO. Haig was also a veteran of Korea and Vietnam and held a master's degree in international affairs from Georgetown University. "Kissinger," he says about their first meeting, "was looking for a military man who was not a classic military intellectual but rather a combat officer first — but with a political-military background." Haig met Kissinger's specifications. He thought he would be serving as military adviser to the NSC but found his initial responsibility centered chiefly on compiling the President's "morning situation report" — an approximately twenty-page political-military-intelligence update of the major overnight developments around the world. The colonel's discipline, diligence, and experience won him increasing responsibilities, not to mention stars on his epaulettes — four of them — by the time he left the NSC at the end of Nixon's first term. He soon got to be known as "Kissinger's Kissinger."

Roger Morris, a young Ph.D. from Harvard, came over from the Rostow NSC; he was hired by Kissinger in a limousine on a ride between the EOB and the Pentagon. An interview had been scheduled for the morning, but Kissinger was running late — a portent of things to come — so he suggested that Morris hop in and they'd talk on the way to Kissinger's next appointment with a platoon of generals. Morris, who took a very dim view of Nixon, recalled Kissinger's saying, "Look, I'd like to have good people around me and I don't consider that you're working for the President. As you know, I supported Nelson Rockefeller. I'm here because I'm working for the presidency, not for Richard Nixon personally. Whatever ideological feelings you may have about this man, I ask you to suspend them for the time being. Watch what we do." Kissinger impressed him by, among other things, "his serious nonpolitical demeanor." Before the car had rolled to a stop at the Pentagon, Morris was saying, "Well, why don't I give it a fling." He went directly from one NSC staff to the next, and he suspended his anti-Nixon sentiments — at least up until Cambodia in the spring of 1970.

For Morton Halperin, an appearance as guest speaker at Professor Kissinger's final seminar at Harvard immediately preceded the offer of a post on the NSC staff. It was December 16; Kissinger arrived twenty minutes late at his defense seminar. He introduced Halperin, then a thirty-year-old ex–Harvard professor who himself had regularly lectured at the seminar before going on to Washington as an Assistant Deputy Secretary of Defense for International Security. Halperin discussed Asian security after Vietnam. Kissinger sipped water, cleaned his eyeglasses, and jotted notes on a yellow pad. He then played adversary, challenging a number of Halperin's judgments. Once the graduate students had left, Kissinger asked his colleague to join him at the NSC. Halperin, though anti-Nixon and anti–Vietnam war, agreed; he switched from the Pentagon to the Pierre and began to work on Vietnam and strategic forces.

Lawrence Eagleburger, a career foreign service officer, got his job with Kissinger through a mutual friend, Francis Bator, who had once worked on Johnson's NSC staff and was now on the Harvard faculty. On Bator's recommendation, Kissinger invited Eagleburger to come for an interview. Eagleburger's credentials included a stint with Walt Rostow in the mid-1960s and experience overseas in such diverse posts as Belgrade and Tegucigalpa. Coincidentally, the President-elect's office had asked State for a career officer to be assigned to the Pierre to handle the flow of diplomatic messages; Eagleburger had been selected for the chore, and Haldeman, then Nixon's Chief of Staff, had concurred in the choice. Kissinger confirmed it — and promptly commandeered him. By mid-December, Eagleburger was at work, dealing with everything from the structure of the NSC to the handling of foreign VIPs eager to meet the President-elect.

Laurence Lynn, a Ph.D. from Yale in his early thirties, was asked to switch to the NSC staff from his post as a Deputy Assistant Secretary of Defense. On Halperin's recommendation, Kissinger and Lynn got together at the EOB. The ex-professor, tackling his job with characteristic dedication, said the incoming Administration wanted to carry out a comprehensive review of military-strategic-defense policy. Would Lynn head up the study? Kissinger also wanted Lynn to conduct "country-program studies" — detailed reviews of U.S. relations with many countries. Lynn asked for time to think it over. "Take a week," said Kissinger, echoing Nixon's suggestion to him of only a few weeks before. Lynn checked with about a dozen friends. Only one of them urged Lynn to accept the offer, all of the others putting him on notice that Kissinger would be "an impossible man to work for." The exception was McNamara, who referred to Kissinger as "an extraordinarily capable man, who might be an enormous asset to the Nixon Administration." Lynn joined the expanding staff at the EOB in late December.

Daniel Davidson, who had met Kissinger in 1966, was hired while he was in bed with a 103-degree fever. He had just returned to New York from Paris, where he had been serving as a member of Ambassador Harriman's team at the peace talks and he was looking for a new assignment. He telephoned Kissinger. It turned out to be an auspicious day, Friday, November 29: Kissinger confided that he would shortly be informing the President-elect of his decision to accept the NSC post. The next day, when the *New York Times* broke the story, Kissinger called back, and another staff position was filled. As soon as he recovered from the flu, Davidson was assigned a desk in the EOB.

Among others who flocked to the NSC staff those first months were Viron P. Vaky, then the acting Assistant Secretary of State for Latin American Affairs, with more than twenty years in the Foreign Service; John Holdridge, a Chinese-speaking career officer who had served in the United States Consulate General in Hong Kong and elsewhere in Southeast Asia; and Richard Sneider, also an old Asia hand, widely recognized as one of State's leading experts on Japan. Respectively, they headed up the Latin America, China, and Asia subsections of the NSC. Richard Moore, who had worked on Rostow's NSC staff, joined Kissinger's NSC to supervise the flow of paperwork. William Watts brought to the Kissinger team his knowledge as an ex–Foreign Service officer with experience in Moscow; he had been working on the Rockefeller staff in New York, specializing in urban affairs. W. Anthony Lake, then a young Foreign Service officer on leave from State, came down from Princeton to sign on as a Special Assistant to the Assistant to the President. It was a rallying to what they all regarded as a new opportunity for United States foreign policy, and they would have been startled if anyone had then suggested that a few of the original joiners would be leaving within a year or so — for reasons ranging from dislike of Kissinger's domineering and secretive style to disenchantment with the U.S. move into Cambodia.

Kissinger's NSC staff was broken into small subsections: the "front office," consisting of about a half-dozen close aides; a crisis center; a planning group; a research contingent; an analysis section; and the operations experts for Latin America, Europe, East Asia, Near East and South Asia, African and United Nations affairs, international economic affairs, and scientific affairs.

One of the staff's most important jobs was to supervise studies on a wide range of policy issues. A normal study would begin with an Interdepartmental Group (bureaucratically known as an IG). Chaired by the assistant secretary of State for the area under consideration — Europe, Africa, Latin America, etc. — an IG would consist of other assistant secretaries from Defense, Commerce, Treasury and other related departments, or their deputies, and one NSC staff member, who would make sure that all the options were reviewed and would then present the end product — the study — to Kissinger. The IG would never make a firm recommendation; its function was to produce a variety of "area" options for NSC consideration.

These options would then be clarified or refined by the NSC staff before they would be presented to the Senior Review Group, presided over by Kissinger, and consisting of the Under Secretary of State, the Deputy Secretary of Defense, the Director of the CIA and the Chairman of the Joint Chiefs of Staff, or their deputies, depending on the subject under review. The Senior Review Group's responsibility would be to ensure that "all realistic alternatives" were presented to the President. However, unless Kissinger considered an alternative to be realistic — a word that can be defined in an endless variety of ways — it would not get past the President's door.

At this point, these "alternatives" would be submitted formally to the President and the other statutory members of the NSC, with Kissinger presenting the various choices. "The whole thing is discussed in the National Security Council," explains Kissinger, "while the President is still deciding in his own mind. Everyone gets a crack at it. He likes to have the alternatives presented to him in writing. Then he stews about it and decides by himself."

Once a decision was made at the presidential level, it would be relayed back to Kissinger, who in turn would relay it to the Under Secretaries Committee — which was chaired by the Under Secretary of State, and included the Deputy Secretary of Defense, the Chairman of the JCS, the Director of the CIA — and Kissinger. This group's task would be to implement the decision, which was sometimes easier said than done. "The outsider believes a presidential order is consistently followed out," Kissinger once explained. "Nonsense. I have to spend considerable time seeing that it is carried out in the spirit the President intended."

From the very beginning Kissinger had far greater power than Bundy or Rostow ever had. Nixon's first administrative order, restructuring the NSC, placed all bureaucratic power in the field of foreign and defense policy in Kissinger's hands. This order stripped the State Department and the Secretary of State of prerogatives they had had in other Administrations; but at the beginning Secretary William P. Rogers made no fuss and later, when he did, it was too late. In addition to Kissinger's control over the flow of options to the President, he was put in charge of a number of key interagency committees; and as crises arose, powerful new committees were added to the list. Kissinger acted, as he once put it, "as administrative director and gadfly."

The Defense Program Review Committee tried to keep the annual defense budget in line with the Administration's foreign policy goals. The size of the defense budget — for example, eighty-five billion dollars for fiscal 1974 — provides a clue to the significance of the committee. Kissinger chairs it.

The Intelligence Committee sets general policy for the entire intelligence community — the CIA, NSA (National Security Agency), DIA (Defense Intelligence Agency), etc. It, too, is chaired by Kissinger.

The "40 Committee" (named after the presidential directive that set it up) deals exclusively with clandestine American intelligence operations. It, too, is chaired by Kissinger.

The Washington Special Actions Group (known as WSAG) is the top-level crisis group. It was formed in April, 1969, in the wake of a major crisis involving North Korea's downing of an American spy plane. Again, Kissinger chairs.

The Verification Panel, set up in July, 1969, is the White House "action center" for the meticulously detailed negotiations with the Soviet Union on limiting and controlling nuclear weapons. Once again, Kissinger chairs.

Often the membership of these various committees would be the same; only the name changed to suit the subject. But few foreign policy decisions could be made without going through this elaborate system. The upshot was that since Kissinger controlled the system, he controlled the decision-making process. "Everyone reports to Kissinger, and only Kissinger reports to the President" was the succinct summing-up of the way the NSC operation worked from the very beginning.

The new NSC approach — as envisioned by the President and executed by Kissinger — cut deeply into the territory of two traditional foreign policy shapers: the Department of State and the Pentagon. Their outcries were heard clear across town.

The first thing Henry Kissinger did when he arrived at his office in the White House basement on January 20, 1969, was to fire a list of fifty questions at a bureaucracy struggling to make the transition from Johnson to Nixon. Many questions were accompanied by impossible deadlines. Within a month, or sooner, Kissinger wanted detailed answers from the State and Defense departments, the CIA, Commerce and Treasury, and the Bureau of the Budget to such questions as: What is the state of American relations with China? With the Soviet Union? With India, both Vietnams, and Indonesia? Are the Soviet Union and China heading toward war? The list went on and on. The muttered complaint, "Who the hell does he think he is anyhow?" could be heard in the corridors of bureaucracy.

Kissinger recognized that the far-reaching list of demands might be a "heavy burden," but, as he told a group of White House reporters on February 6, "I think it will pay off over the months as we make decisions." The idea was not really his own, he went on; it came from the President. Nixon had decided that he "wanted to do an annual review of the international situation similar to the annual economic review which he makes to Congress," an overview of "where the United States is and where it is going." It had been planned originally as a year-end wrap-up to be released early in 1970, but then the President wondered whether it might not be a good idea to find out "what we took over when we started . . . what the international situation was like on January 20, 1969."

Kissinger took the President's suggestion as an order. He didn't want policy recommendations from the bureaucrats, he explained; he wanted raw data, "a benchmark . . . against which to test our recommendations."

The burden was shouldered most resentfully by the State Department. Officials there complained that Kissinger was merely "making work" for them. Their initial complaints soon became part of a pattern, as they realized that they were being elbowed out of the decision-making process by a small, tightly centralized White House staff. They decided to strike back.

The Foggy Bottom challenge to the Kissinger system was led by Under Secretary of State Elliot Richardson, the former Attorney General of Massachusetts, and by Jonathan Moore, a foreign policy specialist who was one of Richardson's deputies and an old friend of Kissinger's. Moore reminded Kissinger that only a few months earlier, at Harvard, he had talked sympathetically about quite a different NSC approach then being formulated by Moore in a study project at the Institute of Politics; it conceived of the State Department as *the* coordinator of foreign policy and the NSC as an open forum in which the various players would all get a fair crack at influencing the President's final decision. In Moore's view, the NSC was shaping up instead as a one-man band.

Richardson argued vigorously for the Moore approach, or at least a modest variation of it; he lost. He then tried to modify the Kissinger system to enhance the department's role, suggesting that he be placed in charge of the Senior Review Group. He lost that skirmish, too. In fact, Richardson would later tally his victories and defeats and discover that he had lost twice as many as he had won, and what he had won turned out to be minor victories. "There was some inclination on Kissinger's part to try to dominate the thing, but I think we worked out an agreement early in the situation and got along very well," Richardson later summed up, glossing over the realities with typical Brahmin understatement. With Moore's help, Richardson arranged a schedule of weekly luncheons with Kissinger, and they soon became the only meaningful link between the State Department and the White House. Richardson and Kissinger did a good deal of business over their chef's salads, and they developed a personal and professional bond, which Rogers came to resent. When Richardson was appointed Secretary of the Department of Health, Education, and Welfare in June, 1970, Rogers deliberately took his time about replacing him. Months passed. It was believed at the time that Rogers was trying to show Kissinger that Richardson was expendable. It was a counterproductive show of bravado. The department suffered; so did Rogers's already tattered relations with Kissinger. The two men barely exchanged a word. Kissinger privately ridiculed Rogers, but only among his closest aides. Rogers belittled Kissinger's accomplishments, but only among his closest aides. Appearances had to be maintained.

Rogers made the basic miscalculation of assuming that he could always depend upon his old friendship with Nixon to protect his prestige — and the department's — and to ward off any bureaucratic intrigue designed to undercut his power in the Administration. But that was apparently not what Nixon had in mind. Only in retrospect, when the heat of the battle was over, did Richardson and Moore fully appreciate that Kissinger was not issuing his own directives to create a personal power base but rather was carrying out the instructions of the President. "Once the President appointed Henry and Rogers," Moore explained, "you discover a certain imperative in the way Henry felt he had to operate. The President wanted to be his own Secretary of State; therefore he appointed the best front man he could find to run the State Department — an old friend, trustworthy, an amateur — and then appointed the finest mind in foreign policy that he could find anywhere to work exclusively for him. It was entirely logical."

Richardson echoed roughly the same thought. "The more I have seen of the President and Kissinger's handling of foreign policy issues," he said, "the more I have come to believe that it almost surely was at the President's initial directive that the structure is what it is — not because Henry engineered it that way, but because the President wanted it that way."

Kissinger's relations with Defense Secretary Laird were entirely different, even though they fought one another more often than any other two men in the Nixon Administration. They respected each other. They had met for the first time at the 1964 Republican convention, when Laird ran the Platform Committee and Kissinger was one of the committee's foreign policy advisers. Laird admired Kissinger's tough anti-Communism, and Kissinger admired Laird's pragmatic sense of politics. For sixteen years, Laird was a Congressman from Wisconsin, a force on Capitol Hill, who had given up seniority and a shot at the post of Minority Leader to accept Nixon's offer of the Pentagon job. Unlike Rogers, who fought Kissinger and lost, Laird fought Kissinger to a draw. They disagreed on Vietnam. They disagreed on the cost of weapons. They disagreed on aspects of the India-Pakistan war of 1971. They fought "like two tough tigers," according to Daniel Z. Henkin, then the Pentagon's spokesman; but neither bested the other, and they always withdrew from the battle with their honor and mutual respect intact. Once a month, sometimes twice, the presidential adviser would go to the Pentagon for breakfast with Laird. He would not willingly break bread with Rogers.

The generals at the Pentagon, who at first had complained to their congressional allies about Henry's system of controlling all information, came to the conclusion early in the Administration that this was the way the Commander in Chief wanted it, and Kissinger was merely his top sergeant. In "my experience with the military," Kissinger would later remark, "they are more likely to accept decisions they do not like than any other group." He apparently underestimated the Pentagon's capacity for ferreting out top secret information from the White House. Early in 1970, after a year of Nixon-Kissinger supersecrecy, Pentagon leaders allegedly planted a Navy yeoman in the military liaison unit of the NSC for the purpose of pilfering "eyes-only" documents, dealing with such sensitive subjects as Vietnam, China, and SALT, and then funneling these documents to the Pentagon. This clandestine system lasted until the end of 1971.

Kissinger defended the concentration of power in the NSC as the President's idea. The President, he explained, had "very strong views on organization." It was he — the President — who did not want the Under Secretary of State to chair the Senior Review Group. Leaving the job to Kissinger simplified matters, and cut down on the need to overrule decisions. The President wanted power in the hands of the foreign policy man directly under him, his adviser. "I," maintains Kissinger, who ended up on top, "was basically neutral about organization because I figured the President could run it either way."

Although Kissinger sprinkled his defense of the NSC operation with praise for the contributing departments, he in fact has always had a feeling bordering almost on contempt for the entire bureaucracy. That sentiment was clear from the start. "There are twenty thousand people in the State Department and fifty thousand in Defense," he said in 1972. "They all need each other's clearances in order to move . . . and they all want to do what I'm doing. So the problem becomes: how do you get them to push papers around, spin their wheels, so that you can get your work done?"

This condescending attitude worried many people who believed that foreign policy was the public's business, not the private property of an elite group of specialists. Senator J. William Fulbright, Chairman of the Senate Foreign Relations Committee, was disturbed back in 1969 by the idea that the trend toward an all-powerful NSC would take "very important matters out of the hands of the traditional agencies, most of which felt a responsibility to Congress," and by the fact that Congress could not hold Kissinger directly accountable. Later, in 1970, Senator Stuart Symington objected to Kissinger's plea of executive privilege every time he was asked to testify on Capitol Hill. He was the "Secretary of State in everything but name," Symington charged, and yet he was exempt from congressional scrutiny.

Kissinger tried to defuse the early criticism by playing down his own role and by poking fun at himself. "I cannot believe," he told a group of reporters, "that with seven people I am going to be able to take over both the State Department and the Defense Department."

On a more serious level, he consistently maintained that it was the President, not he, who made the decisions. Although, as head of the NSC system, he placed the final options before the President, he contended that he did not allow his own preferences to influence his presentation. "There is no 'Kissinger policy' on questions of substance," he says. "My task is to convey the full range of policy options to the President. If there were a 'Kissinger policy,' the whole new mechanism we have set up in the National Security Council — not to speak of relations between the governmental agencies — would be in a shambles."

While he believed that it would be "suicide" for someone in his position to champion his own policies without a presidential invitation, Kissinger did not see himself only in the role of Mr. In-Between. "When the President puts his feet up at the end of the day and says, 'OK, Henry, you've presented all the options, now what do you think?' of course I tell him what I think," he conceded. "But I try not to beat at him with my views. Anyway, he is not a man who encourages being beaten at."

There was no need to "beat at" Nixon. Kissinger's initial impression that he and the President shared a common world view was confirmed as they began to work together on a close and regular basis after the inauguration. Kissinger knew, almost instinctively, that he would be able to control the bureaucracy — and thus help reorder American diplomacy — only to the degree that he became indistinguishable from the President and his policies. He treated the President with total respect, as he tried to erase the image of a few months earlier, when he had been openly critical of Nixon. Subordinating his own well-advertised ego to Nixon's was no simple task. It required all the qualities that had propelled him into the White House in the first place — brains, contacts, toughness, and a steady stream of practical ideas.

Quite often, at the end of a cold January or February day, after most of the White House staffers had stuffed their papers into their attaché cases and gone home, Kissinger would head for the Oval Office, saying he had to check some late details with the President. The checking would be brief, and then the two men would talk about other things — sometimes for hours at a stretch. "After all," Kissinger later said, "I was one of the few people he could talk to that he could consider an equal in knowledge."

Occasionally, H. R. Haldeman or Ronald Ziegler, the new presidential spokesman, would amble into the Oval Office — and listen for a while. As the President and his adviser charted the future course of American diplomacy, they would swap stories about their travels and political experiences, their impressions about world leaders. Khrushchev. The kitchen debate. MLF. De Gaulle. Vietnam. NATO. China. SEATO. The missile gap. Brezhnev. The Cuban crisis.

They shared remarkably similar views about the world and America's changing role in it. Kissinger was always the more philosophical of the two, Nixon the more political. Kissinger brought his great theoretical knowledge to bear on a problem; Nixon's approach was instinctual — the attitude of a gut fighter who had survived some bruising political battles. But both were convinced by the turbulent events of the 1960s that the days of America's global responsibilities were over. "Whoever came in" to the White House in 1969, Kissinger told a group of the President's friends, "would have had to reassess the assumptions on which our policy was based." The Nixon Administration had "to preside over the beginning of a new phase of American policy at the precise moment when it had to liquidate the most outstanding vestige of the previous phase of American policy." This, of course, was a reference to Vietnam. "After all," he went on, "part of the reason why we got into the war . . . was the theory that aggression, wherever it occurred, was our job."

This view, both men agreed, was totally outdated; and Vietnam, while important, was not the only reason for the change. Western Europe had recovered its vitality — a fact that had been apparent to Kissinger eight years before and that he had sought to impress upon Kennedy. The same was true of Japan, and it was high time for the United States to abandon its old paternalistic attitude toward these areas and find a new basis for dealing with them. The Communist world, too, had changed profoundly:

the Soviet Union and China no longer represented one threat but two.

Still, for Kissinger, as a nuclear strategist, the most significant change in recent years was the radical shift in the balance of military power between the United States and the Soviet Union. He understood that the only reason the United States had been able to assume the burden of defending the entire non-Communist world between 1945 and the early 1960s was that it possessed overwhelming strategic superiority over the Soviet Union. It was this fact, not Kennedy's charm, that had forced Khrushchev to pull Soviet missiles out of Cuba in 1962. The historic importance of the missile crisis was that it propelled the Soviet Union into a massive catch-up program of missile and nuclear production. President Nixon, in 1969, was faced with a wholly new situation as he reexamined America's commitments and restructured the NSC.

The intricate NSC system was put to an early test. Shortly after midnight on April 15, 1969, word was flashed to the Pentagon that an American EC-121 spy plane, with thirty-one men aboard, had been downed, probably by the North Koreans, in the Sea of Japan. At 1:05 A.M., the Pentagon notified the NSC's Situation Room. At 1:07 A.M., the duty officer telephoned the news to Haig. Four minutes later, Haig called Kissinger. Under LBJ, Rostow's immediate reaction would have been to inform the President. Under Nixon, Kissinger waited — until he got a more detailed report. At 2:25 A.M., the Pentagon called to say that North Korea *claimed* it had shot down the plane. Kissinger still did not disturb the President. He asked for information on rescue operations and on military contingency plans. At 4 A.M., the Pentagon *confirmed* that the plane had been shot down by the North Koreans. Only then did Kissinger call the President to tell him about the incident.

"Is there anything I need to do now?" the President asked.

"No," Kissinger said, "we're getting all the facts together."

At 7 A.M., Kissinger again telephoned the President and arranged an 8 A.M. meeting in the Oval Office. Kissinger arrived with maps and initial reports from State and Defense. "There's only one thing I want to know," the President said. "Did it happen inside or outside the twelve-mile limit?"

"It happened about ninety miles offshore," Kissinger answered.

"Are you sure?" the President asked.

"Yes," Kissinger replied.

Nixon then told Kissinger that he did not want to examine the maps but he did want a full report on possible military and political responses. He also ordered that similar flights be stopped pending the outcome of his deliberations.

Anyone familiar with Nixon's previous record would have assumed that he would call for quick military retaliation. The previous year, in January, 1968, when the *Pueblo* spy ship was seized, Nixon had attacked Johnson's mild reaction to the North Korean attack. "Respect for the United States has fallen so low," Nixon charged, "that a fourth-rate military power like North Korea will hijack a United States naval vessel on the high seas." But as President, Nixon changed his angle of vision.

From six o'clock Tuesday evening until three o'clock Wednesday morning, Kissinger chaired an NSC review group and prepared a full report on alternative courses of action. This report was presented to the President and considered at two separate meetings on Wednesday. The Joint Chiefs recommended a retaliatory bombing strike against North Korea. Kissinger tended to agree with the JCS recommendation. The President seemed inclined to accept the recommendation, but Secretary Rogers urged him to give further consideration to the possibility that the Soviet Union or China or both might feel obliged to come to North Korea's defense.

All day Thursday Kissinger presided over another NSC study group, which prepared two highly detailed scenarios of what might happen if the United States bombed North Korea and what might happen if it did not. Defense Secretary Laird recommended that these ad hoc NSC groups, consisting of representatives of State, Defense, and the CIA, be established as a permanent body "to inject some order into crisis management." This was the beginning of the Washington Special Actions Group, later known as WSAG.

Again the President studied his options, but he still refused to order the bombing strike. Instead he called a news conference for noon Friday to announce that he had filed a protest with North Korea and that the EC-121 flights would be resumed – but with a military escort. He stressed that his decision was only a "preliminary one."

Nixon's statement was promptly denounced by Radio Pyongyang as "playing with fire." The North Koreans warned, "We will not sit with folded arms."

That afternoon the President discussed the crisis with Kissinger at great length. He asked him to poll the members of the NSC for their opinions. Kissinger reported, after an hour, that the majority of these top-ranking government officials opposed a retaliatory bombing strike. Kissinger, it is understood, was again asked for his opinion, and he replied that it was easier to get into a war than to get out of one. The EC-121 crisis was the first one, he told the President, that "we did not inherit," and he suggested that the U.S. response be systematic and deliberate. Kissinger sensed that Nixon seemed inclined to reject all recommendations for a swift retaliatory strike against North Korean bases, and he quickly shifted position. Kissinger began to pick up the Rogers theme of restraint in the face of the North Korean provocation. A retaliatory strike, he argued, could interfere with the larger goal of readjusting America's relations with China and Russia.

That night the President decided to drop the matter. Kissinger was pleased that he had reached his decision only after a full range of options had been examined.

By the time the first crisis was over, Kissinger had emerged as a public personality. He had an immediate impact on the press. Less than three weeks into the new Administration, he was on the cover of *Time* — quick work for an ex–Harvard professor with a constituency of one. In its February 14 issue, the newsweekly sent a valentine to Kissinger, a five-page tribute that carried him from Fürth to the White House, paying due respect to Metternich and Rockefeller en route. Kissinger had instructed his staff to cooperate fully with a team of *Time* reporters. He basked in his newfound fame. "He was eager for publicity," a former aide recalls. Before he took the job in the Nixon Administration, few working clairvoyants would have predicted so meteoric and controversial a career. "My mother, maybe," Kissinger once told a friend. "But me? No."

But while he enjoyed seeing his name in print, he was aghast at the idea that his staff might be leaking policy secrets to the press. One of the more famous in-house stories is that Kissinger, the day after some classified information turned up in a newspaper, opened a staff meeting by asking: "And who is here representing the *New York Times*?" His half-humorous question concealed a deep, almost paranoid concern about leaks, caused as much by his belief in elitist diplomacy as by the need to prove his staff's loyalty to the Haldemans of the White House. Kissinger worried about the need to prove his own loyalty, too. Before his first year in office ended, at least seven members of the NSC staff had been subjected to wiretaps on their home phones, without their knowledge, but with Kissinger's. For a number of staffers whose loyalty was to the country, not Nixon, the office atmosphere became so insufferable that they quit in disgust.

If this obsession with secrecy and loyalty made most of the staff reluctant to discuss the substance of policy issues, they could not always resist the temptation to provide impromptu profiles of their boss. It tended to make them the life of the party, provided, of course, Kissinger himself wasn't there.

A sampling of their comments provides an intimate portrait of Kissinger at work during those first months of the new Administration:

"I found him off and running from the day he stepped in here. From Day One, he had full confidence in his conceptions. He is a constant mentality in motion. There are very few times that he is really relaxed, even when he is relaxing."

"With him, it's a case of control or castrate."

"He is a highly complicated person. He thrives on adversity, even at the White House. He needs to feel challenged, admired, put upon, despised, loved; he needs to feel cornered so he can outperform everyone, almost as though he enjoys overcoming adversity and showing off his brilliance and subtlety."

"He hates to be disliked."

"He's a guy who's very intolerant of minutia. He can be extremely abrupt and discourteous, or even brutal with the people who bother him or things that bother him. On the other hand, when you really get a tough one, the guy's temperament becomes totally different. When he is confronted by a serious situation, when the heat is the toughest, he becomes extremely calming. . . . But he also has this well-timed sense of humor that he uses to break the 'tension spell,' and then in the next few moments to get the best out of people, their best thinking."

"He's a guy who doesn't like to leave his flanks unprotected."

"Henry recognizes quality and he recognizes mediocrity and inferiority. He really would like to get the best people, but, boy, he's got to get them on his own ground rules or he doesn't want them at all, and his ground rules are that they are anonymous and that they work only for him and they talk only to him and they don't goddamn well participate in any process except in terms that have been laid down. As a result, he doesn't always get those good men, and that's a defect in the process."

"He can be incredibly patient, willing to go back and rearticulate and reformulate proposals. But then he will fly off the handle if he hasn't the paper he wants maybe two hours after he's asked for it."

"I once was involved in writing a report, and it was the most bruising, intensely creative experience in my life. Henry would read a few pages. Hand it back. 'Wrong,' he'd say. 'Page two ought to be page four.' I'd leave frustrated. What the hell does he mean? Then I'd go back to the office and think hard and suddenly I'd seize hold of Henry's idea and write it and there it would be, right and clean. And then I'd see what he had in mind."

"Henry thinks in a constantly theoretical framework. Every time a wave occurs on the east end of the shore, he's got it tied into a relationship with the west bank."

"A brilliant mind but enormously insecure, intensely secretive. He is capable of the most extreme and sudden changes of personality."

"He's got a great memory. But when he has no fixed opinion of something, he regurgitates the best wisdom he's heard."

"I regard him with extraordinary admiration and respect and violently disagree with him on a number of things. That's the best kind of friend he can have."

"The things he would systematically conceal, I think, were the precise nature of the views held by the President and the interaction between the two. That was a very private matter, so far as we were concerned."

"There are times when I've wanted to go back to him and say, 'Where the hell is all that goddamned integrity you and I used to talk about? Where is it now? All you are is a goddamned brain operating with some reservations and qualifications for this brilliant and God-knows-what-else President."

"He's gotten such a bad press on how he's handled people. They complained and bitched and they made it appear as if Henry is impossible to work for. But I found working for him was very close to ideal. I learned more on that job, got more out of that experience than any other single experience I've ever had. He's a hard man to deal with, he's a complicated personality, and there are just many facets of the man that are hard to understand. So I think it's quite easy to get on a collision course with him."

"Henry had to make it on his own scrambling, out of pure talent. Nothing was given to him. He figured out that this was the ball game, and he was absolutely right. Figuring it out is one thing; carrying it out is another. But when he was beginning, the first year Henry was here, he was doing something he'd never done before in his life — working at the absolute pinnacle of power, as an operator instead of as a thinker. He had to deliver. He had to manage and run a bureaucracy. He had to be sure that the President not only was not influenced by anybody intellectually more than he influenced the President, he had to ensure that the President really and genuinely enjoyed working out the intellectual calculus of foreign policy with him — not alone, like he does with everything else I can think of. And lastly, he had to fight off all those people who resented him because of his intimacy with the President."

"You can see that it's his life's blood. He's more relaxed, tanned, happier, though heavier, his voice a little lower, since he's been in this job. Anybody else right now would be a wan, shaken wreck. *He* thrives on it. And I think he knew he'd thrive on it."

"It was a magnificent experience. Working at the absolute peak of your physical and mental ability, with somebody who is also working at his, who is incredibly intelligent, very serious and substantive. And it was also very exciting — having access to official planes, black limousines, the works. On the other hand, it was horrifying and very disillusioning to see how irrationally decisions can be made — well, that's too strong — rather, with what mixed motives decisions are made. And I think the thing that bothers me most of all, in retrospect, is the atmosphere, the style at that level of government . . . the incredible . . . well, elitism is the word. The secrecy, the arrogance, the feeling that the President and only the President is trying to accomplish something, and everybody else — well, the Congress and the public and the State Department and the bureaucracy — everybody is simply a barrier to be removed. And that is very dangerous."

Even in the early months of the Administration, the future Kissinger — as resident intellect, man-about-town, secret agent — was beginning to emerge. Competition from the highest Republican echelons was scant; the only possible entry was Martha Mitchell. Kissinger's sprint to super-stardom led John Mitchell in 1970 to brand him openly as an "egotistical maniac." Undaunted, at least publicly, Kissinger promptly turned this diagnosis into a compliment. "At Harvard," he declared, "it took me ten years to develop a relationship of total hostility to my environment. I want you to know that here I have done it in eighteen months."

SIX

SALT and Linkage
MAKING THE RUSSIANS PAY

A FTER A PERIOD OF CONFRONTATION, we are entering an era of negotiations." When Richard Nixon first uttered these words in his inaugural address on January 20, 1969, the Soviet Union reacted with a sud-
denness that caught Washington, including the President's Assistant for
National Security Affairs, off guard. Within a few hours, the Kremlin was
challenging the White House to live up to its promise. Foreign correspondents in Moscow were summoned to a rare news conference at the
Soviet Foreign Ministry, where they heard two senior Soviet spokesmen
make news, in contrast to the usual propaganda.

Leonid M. Zamyatin, Chief of the Press Department, and Kirill V.
Novikov, Chief of the Department of International Organizations, announced that the Soviet Union was ready to "start a serious exchange
of views" on limiting the nuclear arsenals of the two superpowers. "When
the representatives of the Nixon Administration are ready to sit down,"
Novikov stated, "we are ready."

The conciliatory tone in Washington and the conciliatory response
from Moscow sounded a hopeful note to many Americans who were
weary of a quarter-century of Cold War and Iron Curtain policies, of
confrontation and conflict, of billions going into a nuclear technology
that kept turning out more and more terrible weapons for mass death.
It was not forgotten that the new President himself was one of the
original cold warriors, but he now seemed to be talking in terms of
change. What better way to launch a new "era" in Soviet-American

relations than by launching the Strategic Arms Limitation Talks, known as SALT?

It made good sense to a number of influential Senators who were grappling with the problem of how to get out of the vicious, expensive cycle of newer and better weapons. The Democratic Chairman of the Senate Foreign Relations Committee, Senator J. William Fulbright of Arkansas, joined his Republican colleague Senator John Sherman Cooper of Kentucky in a bipartisan effort to encourage the day-old President to accept the Soviet bid.

It made good sense as well to the widely respected defense thinkers on the campuses, who were alarmed by the development of MIRV (Multiple Independently Targeted Reentry Vehicles), a technological breakthrough that would enable the United States to fire a cluster of warheads in the nose cone of a single missile and then have the capability to direct each warhead to an individual target. "We are in effect at a crossroads," warned Professor George Rathjens of MIT, who had once worked for the Arms Control and Disarmament Agency (ACDA). "We and the Soviet Union now have a better chance than we are likely to have for the foreseeable future to make decisions that may enable us to avoid or at least moderate another spiral in the strategic arms race."

The pro-SALT lobby exerted heavy pressure on the new Administration to snap up the Soviet initiative; in effect, to pick up where the Johnson Administration had left off. LBJ had been prepared to start SALT with the Soviet leaders at a summit meeting scheduled for early autumn, 1968 — a meeting designed to cap his presidency with a solid foreign policy achievement and to boost the presidential campaign of Senator Hubert Humphrey; but he was forced to cancel the meeting after Soviet tanks and troops moved into Czechoslovakia. He was so eager to start the arms limitation talks that, even after Nixon was elected, he tried to reschedule the summit and hold it before Inauguration Day; but the President-elect advised him that he could not endorse such a move and would not assume responsibility for such talks until after January 20.

On January 18, at a farewell press conference, Clark Clifford, the outgoing Secretary of Defense, urged the incoming Republican Administration not to delay the opening of SALT. By the middle of the year, he warned, the Soviet Union would overtake the United States in the number of land-based strategic missiles, the result of a massive Soviet effort beginning in the mid-1960s, after the Cuban fiasco, to achieve at least parity and possibly superiority in nuclear weapons.

Nixon easily could have won the support of normally anti-Nixon people by agreeing to immediate talks with the Russians. But the idea of taking the untested negotiating formulas of the Johnson Administration and rushing into SALT did not appeal to either Nixon or Kissinger. Pressure or no pressure, they decided to stall on SALT. Unlike the Senators, the scholars, or the Johnson men, who put the highest priority on starting arms limitation talks, the new strategists in the White House had an entirely different perception of SALT. Although they considered the limitation of nuclear weapons vitally important, they did not regard it as an isolated issue, but rather as one key element in a broader negotiation with the Soviet Union. Their strategy was based on an idea they christened "linkage."

"Linkage" was an up-to-date application of Kissinger's theories about the balance of power. His views on this subject had barely changed since he finished his doctoral dissertation at Harvard in 1954. "Could a power achieve all of its wishes," he wrote then, in his convoluted style, "it would strive for absolute security, a world order free from the consciousness of foreign danger and where all problems have the manageability of domestic issues. But since absolute security for one power means absolute insecurity for all others, it is never obtainable as part of a 'legitimate' settlement and can be achieved only through conquest." In the nuclear age, such conquest, one big power over another, becomes unthinkable, except by madmen. Thus, the only possible aim of a rational policy is "relative security" — or, as Kissinger put it, "the foundation of a stable order is the *relative* security — and therefore the *relative* insecurity — of its members."

Such a world order obviously survives on a balancing of rival claims, not the imposition of one over the other. For Kissinger, the Soviet Union had always been the potential upsetter of this balance. It was the only country with the manpower and nuclear muscle to pose a mortal threat to the United States — and it had consistently led the forces of disorder in a world struggling for order. It was time for the Soviet leadership to be educated in the fine art of balancing their country's interests with those of the other great powers. Consequently, every problem between the United States and the Soviet Union was linked with every other problem; and progress on one would affect progress on all.

Kissinger's approach to linkage was broad and somewhat philosophical; Nixon's was practical and specific. He had come to the conclusion, sometime before he took office, that the Russians held the key to peace in Vietnam and tranquillity in the Middle East. In his mind there was an obvious link between the Kremlin and those two turbulent areas.

Therefore, if the Soviet leaders wanted American credits, trade, and technology in their stalled drive toward modernization, and if they wanted SALT as a way of slashing arms expenditures that could be diverted to consumer goods, then they would have to pay. Nixon had in mind a form of diplomatic barter. The Russians had to be persuaded that it was in their own national interest to contain local wars rather than to inflame them. Then it might be possible for the Soviet Union and the United States to embark on a new stage in their relationship, to move from confrontation to cooperation.

Kissinger's ideas about maintaining the balance of power and Nixon's instinct for implicating Moscow in a Vietnam settlement combined to establish linkage as the basis of United States policy toward the Soviet Union. Moscow's January 20 invitation to begin strategic arms limitation talks was their first opportunity to test that policy.

"I wanted to move on a broad front," Kissinger would later explain. His objective was to achieve "the right balance of interests" to tempt and motivate Moscow toward cooperation in resolving a variety of issues. "I didn't want to play the game of atmospherics," he said, underscoring his well-known distaste at the time for "climates of goodwill." And Kissinger hoped to engage the Russians at the proper time in "concrete, precise negotiations" — each, in his mind, a kind of "hedge" against the temptation to renege on the whole package, or against the possibility that a sudden world crisis might disrupt the overall move toward accommodation. "This was the reason," he emphasized, "why we pushed so hard on linkage."

Their first job was to educate the NSC about their novel approach to international problems.

They began the very day after inauguration. Joining the President in the Cabinet Room of the White House were Vice-President Agnew, Secretary of State Rogers, Secretary of Defense Laird, Chairman of the Joint Chiefs General Earle Wheeler, CIA Director Richard Helms, Deputy Commander of United States forces in Vietnam General Andrew Goodpaster, Chief of the Office of Emergency Planning General George Lincoln and, of course, Kissinger. The issue on the table was the Soviet bid on SALT. The discussions were top secret; no decisions were announced. That afternoon, the only official reaction to the Kremlin's urgent proposal came from Robert J. McCloskey, the veteran spokesman at the State Department. SALT, he told reporters, would be getting "priority consideration" from the new Administration. There was no amplification.

Two days later, a second session was held at the White House with the same cast on the same subject. A third meeting was held two days after that. The President's verdict was quick in coming.

Nixon used his first news conference, on television — live, from the East Room — on January 27, to announce his decision on the Soviet SALT initiative. The word *linkage* never crossed his lips but the idea was implicit in many of his comments. Kissinger was in the audience, listening. Just up the street from the White House, at Sixteenth and L, Soviet Ambassador Anatoly Dobrynin's staff gathered around the television set to catch every word and every nuance.

"Ladies and gentlemen," Nixon began, "since this is my first press conference since the inauguration, I can imagine there are a number of questions. Consequently, I shall make no opening statement and will go directly to your questions."

Not until question number five was SALT raised; the first queries had dealt with the new President's legislative program, his "plan" for peace in Vietnam, his bleak forecast on improving relations with Peking, and his "major problems."

"Mr. President," began that fifth question, "on foreign policy, nuclear policy particularly, could you give us your position . . . on the starting of missile talks with the Soviet Union?"

"I favor strategic arms talks," Nixon replied, adding, "it's a question of not only when but" — it was to prove a very strategic "but" — "the context of those talks."

In an exposition that clearly reflected Kissinger's input, the President explained that there were two schools of thought about SALT: those, on the one hand, who wanted to proceed, regardless of "any progress on a political settlement"; and those, on the other hand, who opposed "any reduction of our strategic arms," unless it was preceded by "progress on political settlements."

Nixon refused to join either school. He struck a middle position.

"What I want to do is to see to it," he stressed, "that we have strategic arms talks in a way and at a time that will promote, if possible, progress on outstanding political problems *at the same time* — for example, on the problem of the Middle East and on other outstanding problems in which the United States and the Soviet Union, acting together, can serve the cause of peace."

"Linkage" had just made its debut as a cornerstone of a new U.S. negotiating strategy. While the President rejected the Soviet bid to deal with SALT as an isolated issue, he dangled the possibility of such talks before the Russians if they were ready to join in achieving "progress on outstanding political problems *at the same time.*" He listed the Middle East, he implied Vietnam. The challenge had now been thrown back at the Kremlin; on its reaction, Kissinger believed, would depend the possibility of détente.

But this important change in American strategy — linkage — was not fully understood at once. The focus of immediate attention was the President's refusal to begin SALT immediately. That was to be a great disappointment to many members of Congress, academicians, and editorial writers, and it came as a baffling surprise to most of the foreign diplomats in Washington, particularly the Russians. They sensed that a fundamental change in American policy had just been enunciated, but none of them, Dobrynin included, was quite sure how the alteration in American negotiating policy would affect Soviet-American relations. Dobrynin's cable to Moscow that night must have kept the Americanologists in the Kremlin burning the midnight oil.

Kissinger was disturbed by the President's apparently spur-of-the-moment decision to go public with even an intimation of linkage. He believed that linkage — if it were to be productive — should not be presented as a front-page challenge to the Russians. Instead, he would have preferred a more diplomatic approach, perhaps a private meeting with Dobrynin, so that he could explain the mutual advantages of linkage in detail. He felt, according to Laird, that "it could jeopardize the success of linkage to talk about it too much in public."

During the next few weeks, Kissinger became a faculty of one in explaining the concept to skeptical top-level bureaucrats. They were certain it would ensnare the big powers in thickets of controversy. He gave a seminar for members of Congress; they were equally skeptical, certain it would kill the chance for SALT. He also took on groups of newsmen. At a meeting with the White House press corps on February 6, 1969, he said there was "no attempt to blackmail" the Russians "into a disadvantageous settlement in one area in order to give something in another area."

His denial did not satisfy the Russians. One country's linkage was another country's blackmail. In a series of private and stormy meetings with Ambassador Dobrynin, Kissinger, in those early months of the Administration, tried to tutor the Soviet diplomat in the advantages of linkage. Dobrynin, a shrewd student of United States foreign policy who had been Ambassador in Washington since 1962, chose to flunk the course. To him, linkage was pressure, arm-twisting, extortion. The White House would not yield. For more than half a year, the United States stuck to its guns, insisting upon linkage. The Russians were as furious as they were puzzled by what they regarded as unrealistic obstinacy.

In standing fast on linkage, Kissinger had to withstand a good deal of criticism and pressure from his own side, too. "Henry took a lot of flak in those days," one of his aides said. "State wanted to extend credits to the Russians and sign an airline agreement. The arms control people wanted him to accept the SALT offer. Our European allies wanted Henry to accept the Russian proposal for convening a European Security Conference. There was even political pressure from Republicans to have a quick summit meeting with the Russians. After all, Kennedy had one."

But Kissinger, according to one close aide, "quite deliberately stalled" the impetus for an East-West accommodation until he was persuaded that the soil of détente had been properly seeded. Reorganizing relations between two superpowers was not an overnight proposition; it required meticulous preparation.

There was, in Kissinger's mind, another good reason to stall. The United States was not ready for that kind of complicated negotiation. He put it simply. "We did not want to engage in negotiations on a subject of this magnitude until we knew what we were talking about."

"We inherited a book this thin," Kissinger once remarked, bringing the palms of his hands together, almost touching, "the entire SALT deliberations of the Johnson Administration." Even before the Nixon entourage checked into Washington — on December 28, 1968, during a long Key Biscayne weekend — the President-elect ordered Kissinger to prepare a wide range of studies, including two specifically related to the general subject of strategic arms: one on the nation's "strategic posture," and another on the "consequences of a nonproliferation treaty."

Kissinger assigned the "strategic posture" job to a talented staff, led by Halperin and Lynn. They compiled a balance sheet of the strategic might of both superpowers: how many missiles, of all kinds, both countries possessed; the number of planes, tanks, submarines, troops; the force each country could mobilize in various time frames; detectable changes in the pattern of production by the other side; which weapons were being stressed, which weapons were secondary. Nor did the research stop with technology. The economic and political systems were also analyzed, not in overwhelming detail but in sufficient depth to determine whether the superpowers could sustain a substantial boost in weapons production.

The study, completed by late January, was reviewed briefly by State and Defense experts, more exactingly by Kissinger. He was searching for an answer to a question that Nixon had repeatedly raised in the heat of the campaign. As a candidate, Nixon had stressed the need for "clear-cut military superiority" over the Soviet Union, sharply criticizing the Democrats for settling for anything short of that. From the various charts attached to the study, Kissinger could confirm what he had instinctively felt: such "superiority" was unattainable in the 1970s. Now that the Russians were building Polaris-type submarines and ICBMs that were larger than any in the American arsenal, the old five- and six-to-one superiority that the United States had once enjoyed over the Soviet Union was simply beyond the President's reach in the 1970s. "It was impossible to escape the conclusion," Halperin noted, "that no conceivable American strategic program would give you the kind of superiority that you had in the 1950s."

Indeed, an inventory of the strategic balance as of January, 1969, showed that the Russians had made great strides in their determined effort to overtake the United States. The listing showed the U.S. with 1,054 ICBMs, 656 submarine-launched missiles, and 540 long-range bombers; the Russians with 1,200 ICBMs, 200 submarine-launched missiles, and about 200 big bombers.

The statistics and the study prompted a Kissinger recommendation to the President: "sufficiency" should be substituted for "superiority" as the goal of U.S. military policy. Nixon bought the idea, but he sought to camouflage his strategic retreat by suggesting that it would be a mistake to concentrate on semantics. "Our objective," he said on January 29, 1969, "is to be sure that the United States has sufficient military power to defend our interests and to maintain the commitments which this Administration determines are in the interest of the United States around the world. I think *sufficiency* is a better term, actually, than either *superiority* or *parity*."

Kissinger's other "strategic" study strongly endorsed the nuclear nonproliferation treaty that had been negotiated by the Johnson Administration. It concluded that the treaty contained no stipulations that could adversely affect U.S. interests. Kissinger urged presidential approval. On February 5, Nixon sent the treaty to Capitol Hill, requesting prompt Senate action.

After four days of debate, the Senate approved the treaty, 83 to 15, but not before attacking the Administration for delaying the start of SALT. Even Senator Fulbright could not fully appreciate the virtues that Kissinger had attributed to linkage.

A suspicion that hardened into a conviction began spreading throughout the capital. A number of Senators on the Foreign Relations Committee suspected that linkage was only a cover — hifalutin academic jargon to launch new weapons programs. Kissinger fought strongly against so cynical a reading of Administration intentions, but his arguments fell on deaf ears — especially since the President waited only one day after Senate approval of the nonproliferation treaty to announce a new kind of antiballistic missile program (ABM, as it came to be known) for the United States. Nixon called it "Safeguard," and he endowed it with four rationales, though he cited only three. One was to protect the United States "against any attack by the Chinese Communists." A second rationale was to guard "our deterrent system" — long-range missile sites — against Soviet attack. Third — to guard "against any irrational or accidental attack" from any source. Uncited by the President, but perhaps most significant of all, was the "bargaining chip" rationale. The ABM, in the President's view, would give the United States some negotiating currency in any forthcoming SALT dealings with the Russians.

In the early Administration deliberations on an ABM, Kissinger, according to Laird, was not a "strong supporter" of the system. Like Halperin and many academic critics, he tended to see Safeguard as a "weapons system in search of a rationale." But after the President made up his mind, finally, to go for the ABM, Kissinger apparently "got on board" — persuaded, it seems, by the President's argument that the United States needed an ongoing weapons system to trade off during SALT. With Lynn's help, Kissinger supervised an NSC study of the ABM. While he did not believe the United States should go barging into SALT, he did believe that a SALT agreement with the Russians would eventually be reached; if the President insisted upon ABM before SALT, Kissinger could see no advantage in resisting.

Besides, as Kissinger later confided to friends, it could have been much worse. The President was under considerable pressure from the Joint Chiefs of Staff to expand the country's strategic arsenal. They recommended that the United States resume the construction of ICBMs — frozen for several years at the level of 1,054 — and that the United States step up its production of nuclear-powered submarines and long-range bombers. Kissinger realized that the Soviet strategic arsenal was growing every day but, during an NSC meeting on March 5 devoted exclusively to a review of the ABM system, he argued strenuously against the JCS recommendations on the ground that they would escalate the arms race, thereby jeopardizing the long-range prospects for SALT and unnecessarily antagonizing the Russians.

A few years later, after Moscow and Washington had reached agreement on freezing ABM deployment in both countries, Kissinger took a decidedly more charitable view of this defensive weapons system. "Quite honestly," he said, "I don't know where we would have been without the ABM, since we had no programs at all that were moving."

While Congress openly debated the pros and cons of the Administration's proposal to build a limited ABM system, the JCS quietly won the President's endorsement to push for the development of the hydra-headed MIRV. MIRV would represent a quantum leap in weaponry; the switch from one-missile-one-bang to one-missile-multiple-bang had once struck McNamara as comparable to the switch from conventional to nuclear warfare. To stir up support and justify additional funds, Laird revived the Pentagon's annual "Red Peril" threat, leaking alarming information about the new Soviet offensive missile, the SS-9. "The Soviets are going for a first-strike capability," he claimed in an appearance on Capitol Hill.

Kissinger's precise position on MIRV is not easy to determine. He supported the President's decision, once it was taken; but it is a measure of Kissinger's style of operating that not even his closest advisers — those he worked with day after day up the ladder to SALT — are certain of his innermost feelings about MIRV. "Henry must have favored MIRV," says one of these advisers. "I've never known him to be squeamish about weapons. But if you're asking me, 'Do you know that Henry supported MIRV?' my answer is no, I don't know."

Kissinger recognized that MIRV would be a complicating factor in dealing with the Russians on arms control; there was no way to check on the number of warheads tucked inside the nose cone of such an ICBM without on-the-spot inspection — a concept consistently rejected by Moscow. Moreover, he recognized that the Russians could not realistically be asked to forego the development of their own MIRVs once they perceived that the United States was taking a commanding lead in this area of arms competition. On the personal level, it may be that his ambiguity grew out of an awareness that to be identified too closely with this new, dreaded weapon could undermine his relations with Harvard colleagues, many of whom denounced the MIRV decision as a big step toward a new arms race.

Still, there is reason to suspect that Kissinger raised no fundamental objections to the President's go-ahead on MIRV — that indeed, in the end, he favored it. For one thing, he had never believed that weapons alone cause wars. Men, politics, diplomacy are the culprits; weapons by themselves are neutral. For another, Kissinger could not shake the lesson of Czechoslovakia — the crushing of Dubček-style liberalism by Soviet tanks and troops less than one year before the MIRV deliberations. On August 20, 1968, Kissinger told a friend that the Russians, in the wake of the Czech invasion, were apt to "turn a more benign face toward the West." Their strategy, he told another friend, would be to "engage in arms talks to lull the Americans into a 'false sense of security.'" Kissinger's suspicions of the Russians were common knowledge, and it was likely that the continuing Soviet buildup of the SS-9s, coupled with their appeal for new arms talks, persuaded him to support the MIRV decision. In any case, once MIRV was blessed by the President, the question became academic; Kissinger rushed to its defense, often reminding reporters that research and development for MIRV had begun under McNamara.

Against this background of presidential deliberations and decisions on ABM and MIRV, Kissinger undertook an exhausting, often frustrating effort to prepare the U.S. negotiating position for SALT. No other issue — except Vietnam — so absorbed his attention during the first year of the Nixon presidency.

There was a seemingly never-ending run of NSC studies — more detailed than the first two studies about strategic arms — and Kissinger presided over them all. The day after the inauguration, Kissinger, on presidential instructions, began a detailed study project relating to American military power. It was subdivided into two parts: strategic nuclear power and general purpose forces. The idea was that this study project would serve as the basis for the SALT proposals that, one day, would be presented by the Nixon Administration to the Russians. After all, Kissinger would explain, "general meaningless principles" about disarmament were no substitute for "massive studies."

Over the next six months, many specific "massive studies" were ordered and produced — each assembled into a black loose-leaf book stamped "top secret." It was Kissinger's post-facto judgment that these studies were "one of the best investments we made." On February 3, he ordered a study on "U.S. Military Forces." Nine days later, a study on disarmament was commissioned. Eleven days after that, three more studies were ordered: on the defense budget, on the nation's military posture, and on the possibility of expanding the nuclear test ban to include underground tests. A few weeks later, Kissinger launched another study — this key one devoted exclusively to preparing negotiating "options" for SALT. A president, he felt, must enjoy a wide range of realistic options — not, as he was later to tell an audience in Hartford, Connecticut, "two absurd ones and the preferred one," which, he added facetiously, was "almost always choice two."

The first three or four months of SALT preparation, a Kissinger associate later recalled, were a "waste of time." Kissinger and the bureaucracy were at loggerheads. "The bureaucracy simply refused to knuckle under to Henry's wishes," and Kissinger apparently refused to knuckle under to its stubbornness. His attempts to force the bureaucracy to come up with carefully reasoned options proved to be a frustrating task.

Kissinger once explained:

> Most of the governmental process in Washington is geared to adversary proceedings. Most of the discussions within the bureaucracy crystallize [into] a policy, by having various departments come up with specific proposals for specific situations, and then have the policy emerge either as a compromise or as a specific decision of the President . . . .
>
> Most of the debates in the bureaucracy concern disagreements between departments about specific tactical responses to specific tactical issues, and, therefore, with respect to disarmament, there were those who said, "Disarmament is necessary," and there were those who said, "You can't trust the Russians." And usually in the past what happened was one negotiating position developed growing out of all of these, which was then put to the other side. Since the other side almost never came up with a similar proposal, that process had to be repeated over and over again with the result that we were spending more time negotiating with ourselves than with the Russians.

During the ascent to SALT, most of Kissinger's "debates" were with Laird's Pentagon and Rogers's State Department, more specifically with State's Arms Control and Disarmament Agency, for which Kissinger had once been a consultant.

It was impossible for Kissinger's comparatively small staff to prepare all of the detailed studies required to launch SALT. Most of the work was farmed out to a special Pentagon committee, run by Laird, or, to a much lesser extent, to the ACDA people in Foggy Bottom — the "arms controllers," as Kissinger referred to them with almost total derision. Laird was very proud of his committee's efforts. Often, he would praise John Foster, then his chief for research and development, and Gardner Tucker, his expert on systems analysis, for their contribution to the success of SALT. "We did most of the position work here," Laird explained, "then we sent it over to Henry at the NSC." Laird and Kissinger argued constantly about SALT: Laird more inclined to toughen the U.S. bargaining position — he never quite abandoned his earlier belief in "superiority"; Kissinger more inclined to strike a deal in his search for global balance. "We argued more about SALT than about Vietnamization," said Laird, "if that's possible!"

While Kissinger's SALT sessions with Laird were spirited and constructive, his sessions with Rogers were marked by animosity and distrust. Kissinger's unflattering estimate of the Secretary as an international affairs specialist was gleefully echoed by NSC staffers. "The only time Rogers opens his mouth is to change feet" was a typical comment at the NSC. Several of Rogers's aides retaliated by poking fun at Kissinger's accent and his caricature as a power-mad Dr. Strangelove. "What country is Herr Doktor nuking today?" they would ask.

The "arms controllers," Rogers among them, could not really comprehend Kissinger's stalling on SALT. No matter how often he set forth the particulars of linkage, no matter how often he called for detailed studies and considered options before entering into SALT, Rogers kept after him. It was precisely because he wasn't a foreign affairs expert, Rogers once said, that he felt he could challenge the prevailing wisdom. "Henry took a hell of a beating" from State, Laird says. And in recalling those heated discussions between the President's Assistant and the Secretary of State, one of Kissinger's aides says, "Henry and Rogers had a bitch of a battle every other day about SALT, Rogers saying, 'Let's go,' and Henry saying, 'Not yet.' " Rogers kept firing off one memo after another to the NSC, repeating his "let's go" on SALT. Kissinger was unbudgeable. "We could have made proposals to the Russians, but that was not what Henry had in mind. He did not want just proposals, which was all he was getting from State. He wanted to debate the issues, to narrow them down to realistic choices, options, for both countries. This was a totally new approach, and Rogers just didn't understand it."

Finally, on June 19, 1969, Rogers sought to take command. Even though some of the Kissinger studies were incomplete, the options still being refined, and the bureaucracy still sullen, Rogers, exasperated by the delay, summoned Soviet Ambassador Dobrynin to his office and told him that the United States was ready to open SALT negotiations on July 31. Whether Rogers acted on his own, or at the President's direction, is still being debated. To this day, NSC insiders maintain that Rogers had no authority to commit the United States to such talks because, in their view, the United States simply was not prepared. "Henry was furious," one of them recalls. "He did not think the time was ripe. The situation had not quite jelled, and so Henry kept stalling, waiting or hoping for the Russians to be more cooperative about Vietnam and the Middle East." One high official at State insists that Rogers acted on Nixon's instructions. "Rogers is not an egomaniac," he said, implying that Kissinger was. "He wouldn't act on his own."

Either way, Rogers's statement turned out to be more to Kissinger's advantage than to his own. July 31 came and went without the Kremlin picking up the Rogers proposal. Either the Russians, for all their posturing of impatience, were themselves not ready to open SALT, perhaps because of their preoccupation with the Chinese (border disputes earlier in the year had led to bloody clashes along the Ussuri River) or, even more humiliating for Rogers, they concluded that his word wasn't the final word.

Kissinger promptly exploited Rogers's statement for his own purposes. First, it gave him a ready-made excuse whenever disgruntled Congressmen and "arms controllers" taunted him about stalling on SALT. "We're ready," he'd say innocently. "The Secretary said so. It's the Russians who are stalling." "We used that Rogers statement shamelessly," one of Kissinger's aides says, "to fight off our critics. And you know, it worked." Second, it gave Kissinger a club to beat more comprehensive options out of a sluggish bureaucracy. By early July, options began rolling into the NSC shop, but Kissinger kept saying he was dissatisfied with the product. He kept going back to the bureaucracy to ask: "How can we be sure the Russians won't cheat?" The bureaucracy kept coming back with analyses that Kissinger kept finding unsatisfactory.

The CIA tried to bridge this intelligence dispute. Under Director Richard Helms's guidance, it began to produce a quarterly report for the NSC, showing almost exactly what the Russians had and then drawing a comparison, with only a claimed five or ten percent margin of error, with what they had had three months earlier. Like Kissinger, Helms felt that a SALT agreement would be meaningful only if it could be adequately monitored. Therefore, he helped the options process by pinpointing the Soviet weapons systems that could be monitored and those that could not be. One CIA official, who claimed to know the shape of Helms's thinking on SALT, cautioned: "If you're going to negotiate SALT, be sure that the things you negotiate are the verifiable ones. Don't get into anything that isn't."

This warning weighed on Kissinger's mind. Throughout the exacting process of readying the United States for SALT, he had concentrated on those weapons systems that could be checked. Those that could not were generally put aside. For this reason, MIRV was never seriously considered as a candidate for SALT negotiations. It required on-site inspection, and the Russians would certainly not allow foreign inspectors to wander around their top secret installations. Instead they insisted on "national means of inspection," diplomatic jargon for satellite reconnaissance. (In the end, as the art of high-altitude surveillance improved, the United States, in the final SALT agreement, yielded to stratospheric snooping as the means of monitoring Russian tests. At the time, it was the best the United States could get.)

Until July 21, 1969, Kissinger continued to encounter difficulties in refining the U.S. negotiating position on the problem of verification. Defense and State had their own ideas and the differences could not be bridged. Finally, with Rogers's SALT deadline only ten days away, Kissinger set up a verification procedure that, in the end, solved the problem and concentrated control in his hands. He established a new NSC group, the Verification Panel; very quickly, it began turning out alternatives on how to meet the critical problem of monitoring. Within a couple of months, Kissinger was able to narrow down the panel's output to about half a dozen realistic options, all of which accented verification and were therefore, in his mind, negotiable. At last Kissinger felt that the United States had a solid basis for proceeding with SALT. True, there had been no meaningful progress on the other outstanding issues between the United States and the Soviet Union, but Kissinger hoped that the start of SALT would stimulate Russian cooperation in these areas.

On October 20, 1969, the President and Kissinger met secretly with Ambassador Dobrynin. The U.S. was finally ready to begin SALT, they said; was the USSR ready? Dobrynin replied that the USSR was ready, too. It was clear that tensions on Russia's eastern front were relaxing as a result of border talks with the Chinese, begun that very day in Peking. The Russians, using a little reverse linkage of their own, might have felt that the prospect of a cooperative Moscow-Washington approach to SALT would have a chastening effect on the Chinese. Five days later, the U.S. and the USSR announced that SALT would begin in Helsinki on November 17.

At a news conference following the White House announcement, Rogers apparently tried once again to undercut Kissinger's policy of "linkage." SALT, he declared, is "not conditional in any sense of the word. We haven't laid down any conditions for those talks." When Kissinger learned of Rogers's comment, he was apoplectic, a condition that eyewitnesses talk about with awe. Rogers's remark was the wrong signal to send to the Russians. Kissinger recommended that linkage be resuscitated immediately. The next day, the President, coproprietor of linkage, instructed his spokesman, Ronald Ziegler, to do just that. "These talks cannot take place in a vacuum," Ziegler told reporters, who found keeping up with the Kissinger-Rogers feud one of the more diverting aspects of their job. "The President's feeling is that there is a certain relation between SALT and outstanding political problems."

The SALT announcement quickly produced strong congressional pressure for a Nixon proposal to freeze multiple-warhead testing in both countries. Many Senators hoped there was still time to force the MIRV genie back into its bottle. But the idea did not appeal to Kissinger. In his scenario for SALT, the time for such proposals would come much later — only after an initial period of probing the Russians in the actual negotiation. The President had another reason for resisting pressure to cut down MIRV; he wanted the United States to develop and perfect that technology before he was ready to freeze it. For all these reasons, Kissinger, on the eve of the first SALT talks, quietly informed Ambassador Dobrynin that the United States would be making no specific proposals — on MIRV or anything else; and he hoped Russia would be equally nonspecific.

On November 17, SALT began with the clinking of champagne glasses. The U.S. delegation was headed by Gerard C. Smith, a wealthy Washingtonian who was Nixon's Director of ACDA and had been John Foster Dulles's expert on nuclear matters during the Eisenhower years; the Soviet delegation, by Vladimir S. Semenov, a leading authority on Germany and a Deputy Foreign Minister since 1955. Smith read a Kissinger-drafted message from the President, which underscored the importance of linkage. "Wars and crises between nations," he cabled, "can arise not simply from the existence of arms but from clashing interests or the ambitious pursuit of unilateral interests. That is why we seek progress towards the solution of the dangerous political issues of our day."

In other words, the United States would follow a deliberate course. It would not rush into arms control agreements, welcome though they might be; it would wait and probe and watch for signs of progress on political problems, too. SALT was to be a test of Soviet intentions across the board.

Symptomatic of American policy and style was the negotiating package the U.S. delegation brought to Helsinki. There was no specific proposal. Instead, there were four illustrative proposals. All of them were to be considered talking points. They ranged from the idea of freezing offensive weapons to actually reducing their stockpiles. Kissinger presented the Russians with a choice, a series of options. In effect, he was asking: "Which is most appealing, or even more, which parts of all four illustrative proposals are most appealing? Maybe we can combine them." It was an unorthodox approach — based on what Kissinger called "building blocks."

At first glance, this approach seemed more complicated than it really was. Assume for a moment that one of the illustrative proposals focused on the ABM. Kissinger subdivided it into a half-dozen negotiating possibilities. At one extreme, no missile launchers would be sanctioned; at the other extreme, an unlimited number. In between, two hundred launchers, or five hundred, or even a thousand launchers, would be considered. So much for numbers. Then, assuming some rough agreement on, say, five hundred launchers for each side, consider next the question of geography. Should the ABM launchers be limited to the defense of national capitals, or ten major cities, or merely to the defense of land-based missiles? Let's talk about all of these possibilities. All are acceptable as a basis for negotiation. Which ones do you prefer? Which mix of numbers and locations? Let's not, at least at the beginning, get too specific. Instead, let's just narrow the range of options; let's play with our blocks.

This novel approach eliminated the old bureaucratic hang-up that accounted for the loss of so much time — the need, first, to agree in advance on a specific proposal (one acceptable to all departments of the U.S. Government) and then, if it should be rejected by the Russians, the need to crank up the whole process again on another specific proposal. Each time the entire bureaucracy had to be satisfied. Now, according to the new technique, all that was required was a rearrangement of the blocks, and a new formula for negotiation would emerge.

Kissinger is convinced that his building blocks saved valuable time. It took five years for the U.S. Government to hammer out and negotiate the Limited Test-Ban Treaty; more than four years to negotiate the Non-Proliferation Treaty — and that one, Kissinger is fond of noting, "didn't even concern us." Once it got under way on November 17, 1969, SALT I, as it came to be known, required only two and a half years to complete. For Kissinger, that was demonstrable proof of the value of his building-blocks approach to arms control negotiations.

The new approach succeeded not only in saving time but also in testing the seriousness of Soviet interest in SALT. No one really knew whether the Russian negotiators were going to operate in traditional Cold War fashion; whether, in effect, they were going to unroll a lengthy, stupefying proposal, pronounce it *the* basis for SALT negotiation, and proclaim their inability to change a single comma without Moscow's permission. After all, there never had been a detailed exchange of views about SALT, by its very nature an exceedingly complicated subject. A general set of political principles on SALT had been negotiated with the Russians in 1967 and 1968 by Llewellyn Thompson, then U.S. Ambassador to the Soviet Union, but the two sides had not yet jointly confronted such nuts and bolts problems as, say, missile vulnerability or trade-offs of old SS-13s for new submarine-launched ballistic missiles (SLBMs).

Much to Kissinger's satisfaction, the Russians very quickly got down to a serious discussion of all the technical aspects of SALT. By the time the negotiators adjourned for Christmas on December 22, 1969, agreeing to reconvene on April 16, 1970, in Vienna (thus establishing the pattern of alternating negotiating sessions between Finland and Austria), they had agreed, in their joint communiqué, that "each side is better able to understand the views of the other with respect to the problems under consideration." The phrase was not the usual diplomatic Pablum; it represented a genuine step toward mutual understanding of a devilishly difficult subject. But as Kissinger has so often pointed out, mutual understanding does not always ensure agreement; sometimes it merely serves to underscore differences.

On December 30, 1969, Kissinger sent the Verification Panel a secret memo that became the basis of the American negotiating position as it would unfold in 1970. When Smith and Semenov resumed their talks in April, the Americans for the first time fielded a range of specific proposals, but the Russians weren't buying — not then. The United States wondered if the Russians would accept a ban on MIRV, plus on-site inspection. The

Russians were not interested — either in on-site inspection or in depriving themselves of the chance to catch up with the United States in MIRV technology. The United States wondered if the Russians would accept a "zero ABM" proposal — no launchers, in effect no ABM, for either country. The Russians, who had their own *galosh* ABM system already dug in around Moscow, were not interested. The United States wondered if the Russians would accept a freeze on offensive missiles. Once again, the Russians were not interested. They pressed consistently for a limited agreement — limited to a defensive ABM freeze; only then, they said, would they be prepared to discuss a freeze on some offensive weapons systems. It was a proposition that appealed to Rogers and to Smith, but it did not appeal to either the President or Kissinger. Kissinger insisted that there had to be a simultaneous hookup between defensive and offensive weapons; one without the other was simply unacceptable.

By late July, 1970, the Kissinger view prevailed. The plan, as drawn up by Kissinger, dealt with both defensive missiles and offensive missiles. Option E, it was called by NSC insiders; it also got to be known, at the White House, as SWA, pronounced "sway," meaning "stop where we are." As presented to the Russians on August 4, it stipulated — on the offensive side — a ceiling on ICBM deployment, including SS-9s, at nineteen hundred for each nation and a total ban on land-mobile ICBMs; it excluded MIRV (Kissinger assumed the Russians would not buy a MIRV ban), and it made no mention of forward-based missile systems, the intermediate-range missiles based in central Europe. On the defensive side, it proposed a ceiling of a hundred ABMs for the defense of either Moscow or Washington, or no ABM system at all.

But SWA was unacceptable to the Russians. "They simply wouldn't hear about SWA or any other proposal involving the SS-9s," one of Kissinger's aides later said. "And we were totally hung up on the Soviet insistence on ABM alone." It was a frustrating situation.

Only once during that difficult summer did the Russians depart from their "ABM-only" script; and then it was to offer a proposal that was so outlandish that the United States rejected it out of hand. On July 10, the Russians interrupted their string of "nyets" to propose a Washington-Moscow alliance against "provocative attacks by third nuclear powers." Although China was not specified, there was little doubt that the Russians were aiming their proposal at China; and the United States dismissed it. Later, Kissinger would explain, "If the Russians were serious, they would have come to me with that kind of proposal — not to Smith."

By late summer, Kissinger knew that the President was eager to have a summit meeting with the Russians, preferably in Moscow, at some politically opportune moment before the 1972 elections. But until a formula could be contrived that would break the SALT deadlock, or until the Russians showed some interest in helping the President get out of Vietnam "with honor," he knew that the idea of a summit was a fantasy.

The linkage between SALT and Vietnam lay at the core of Administration strategy. Both problems had so far defied Kissinger's efforts at solution. At times, when he mentioned the word "Vietnam," Kissinger would seem to shrink in his armchair, looking half his size, biting his fingernails, muttering, barely audibly, "my nightmare."

SEVEN

Riding the Vietnam Roller Coaster

"Give Us Six Months"

For the first six months of 1969, President Nixon and Henry Kissinger were moderately optimistic about negotiating a speedy end to the war in Vietnam. Their timetable was measured in months, not years. They actually believed that the right formula, the right combination of force and diplomacy, could produce the miracle that had evaded LBJ's grasp for years.

"Nothing to worry about," Kissinger would say to his former Harvard colleagues. "We'll be out in a matter of months." To a visiting group of Quaker antiwar activists, he would confide that he was "quite optimistic" about the prospects for a rapid settlement. "Give us six months," he told them, "and if we haven't ended the war by then, you can come back and tear down the White House fence."

No one had to remind Kissinger that Vietnam had forced Johnson into premature retirement and his adviser Walt Rostow into academic exile. The previous Administration had failed, he felt, because it had stumbled planlessly from one disaster to another with no guiding strategy for either victory or extrication. These men deserved history's bitter judgment. But he reserved a better judgment for himself. He was positive he would succeed where all of the others had failed, because he had a plan. He had worked it out even before he moved into his White House office.

Kissinger's plan for American disengagement from Vietnam appeared in the January, 1969, issue of *Foreign Affairs*. Drafted at least five months earlier, the article, entitled "The Vietnam Negotiations," was released a month before official publication — in December, 1968, a few weeks after Kissinger was tapped to be Nixon's national security adviser. It commanded front-page attention. Although it was not an official document, it carried the Kissinger by-line; and the timing of its release suggested that it was the first installment of a new U.S. policy on Vietnam. It did, in fact, provide the new President with a theoretical framework for negotiating an American withdrawal from Indochina, and it became the starting point for all of the proposals originating in the White House for the next four years.

In no capital did its publication create more excitement than in Paris, where the United States and North Vietnam had just been joined by their allies — South Vietnam and the National Liberation Front, respectively — for a new four-cornered effort to negotiate an end to the war. It seemed at first that it was going to be no more successful than the bilateral effort of Washington and Hanoi that had been under way since May. Even before the opening gavel could be rapped, the two sides had become hopelessly bogged down in an argument over the shape of the negotiating table — a symbol of the political relationship among the four parties.

The question of the shape — should it be square, round, oval, rectangular, diamond, or some new, as yet uninvented, shape — was raised by the South Vietnamese in an obvious move to stall the negotiations until President-elect Nixon was inaugurated. They were hoping that the new Nixon would prove to be as hard-line anti-Communist as the old one. News of the Kissinger plan broke into this unseemly squabble about the furniture, touching off a new wave of speculation about an imminent breakthrough. It was flashed on the news tickers just as the South Vietnamese, led by their outspoken Vice-President Nguyen Cao Ky, were hosting a cocktail party at the fashionable Bristol Hotel on the Rue du Faubourg St. Honoré; and many of the negotiators, Americans as well as Vietnamese, buttonholed newsmen to ask if they had a copy of the Kissinger article.

For the negotiators in Paris, Kissinger's key point was a fresh approach to the deadlocked talks. He pointed out that "all the parties are aware . . . that the way negotiations are carried out is almost as important as what is negotiated." He proposed that the impasse could be broken by a new procedural formula, which came to be known as the "two-track" formula. On one track, Hanoi and Washington would focus exclusively on a *military* settlement of their conflict. On the second track, Saigon and the NLF would concentrate on a *political* solution for South Vietnam. It would be madness, Kissinger warned, for the United States to negotiate with North Vietnam concerning the terms of a political settlement for South Vietnam — a warning Kissinger himself began to ignore within his first year in office. Then, after settlements were reached on both tracks, an international conference would be convened to "work out guarantees and safeguards for the agreements arrived at . . . including international peacekeeping machinery."

Kissinger assumed that the North Vietnamese leaders would welcome this novel approach; he believed at that time that all they wanted was the total withdrawal of U.S. forces from South Vietnam. It was only later in 1971, when his original optimism began to fade, that he realized that they were really determined to get the U.S. to give them "total power."

In the event that Hanoi would not respond to his logic, Kissinger's article provided a fallback position. "If Hanoi proves intransigent and the war goes on," he wrote, "we should seek to achieve as many of our objectives as possible unilaterally. We should adopt a strategy which reduces casualties and concentrates on protecting the population. We should continue to strengthen the Vietnamese army to permit a gradual withdrawal of some American forces, and we should encourage Saigon to broaden its base so that it is stronger for the political contest with the Communists which sooner or later it must undertake." In other words, he was proposing a strategy reminiscent of General James Gavin's "enclave theory" — that would make Washington's war policy more palatable to the American public over the long twilight period of "honorable disengagement."

Kissinger, who based his judgment on his two visits to South Vietnam in 1965 and 1966, was still critical of LBJ's policies. He blasted the "end of the tunnel" psychology and the "kill ratio" approach of General William Westmoreland. "We fought a military war," he wrote; "our opponents fought a political one. We sought physical attrition; our opponents aimed for our psychological exhaustion. In the process, we lost sight of one of the cardinal maxims of guerrilla war: the guerrilla wins if he does not lose. The conventional army loses if it does not win." By such a yardstick, there could be little doubt that the U.S. Army had already lost the war in Vietnam.

Although Kissinger regarded the massive American escalation of the war in the mid-1960s as a "tragic blunder," he resisted all suggestions that the United States admit to an error and withdraw. Great nations, he believed, do not act impetuously; great nations must maintain the credibility of even a mistaken commitment. "The commitment of 500,000 Americans has settled the issue of the importance of Vietnam," he wrote. "However we got into Vietnam, whatever the judgment of our actions, ending the war honorably is essential for the peace of the world. Any other solution may unloose forces that would complicate prospects for international order."

For Kissinger, America's word and America's "honor" were at stake in the jungles of Vietnam; America's allies and adversaries were watching anxiously; the destiny of the world teetered on the barrels of the M-16. His flexible policy contained one essential point on which he would not compromise: "The United States," he wrote, "cannot accept a military defeat, or a change in the political structure of South Vietnam brought about by external military force."

Later, critics of his policy would denounce this point as a formula for "endless war," but in December, 1968, Kissinger's approach seemed promising. His explicit plan for ending the war was in such sharp contrast to the eternal Pentagon vision of military victory that it was greeted by a chorus of praise. "Remarkable analysis," editorialized the *Washington Post*. "There is no better illustration of the value of new men replacing old." Columnist Joseph Kraft wrote, "The best augury to date for the incoming Administration is the article on Vietnam by Kissinger," who "shows a powerful mind, rising above knowledge of the details to identify the way out."

During the campaign year of 1968, Nixon too had grappled with the challenge of Vietnam; but, whereas Kissinger had approached it as a professor seeking the light, Nixon had approached it as a politician seeking the presidency. Their perspectives differed, but their conclusions were remarkably similar.

Nixon's plan to end the war, unlike Kissinger's, had never been made public, although he permitted hints about the existence of such a plan to be given wide circulation during the campaign. Actually, Nixon had a

Vietnam speech all set for broadcast the night of March 31 — but the time was preempted by President Johnson, who announced a partial suspension of the air war over North Vietnam and a total suspension of his ambition to run for another term as President. Following Johnson's surprise announcement, Nixon decided not to deliver his speech; but the text, published later in *Catch the Falling Flag*, an insider book by Richard Whalen, a Nixon speechwriter at the time, reveals the outline of Nixon's Vietnam strategy.

"I've come to the conclusion that there's no way to win the war," he remarked to Whalen in the course of writing the speech. "But we can't say that, of course. In fact, we have to seem to say the opposite, just to keep some degree of bargaining leverage." If there was "no way to win the war" — a major change from his 1966 position, when he had campaigned as a hawk on behalf of Republican congressional candidates — there had to be some way to win the peace, or, at a minimum, to end a war that had become a national tragedy and a political liability.

Moscow was central in Nixon's diplomatic thinking. "If the Soviets were disposed to see the war ended and a compromise settlement negotiated," he wrote, in the speech that he never delivered, "they have the means to move Ho Chi Minh to the conference table." But, he went on, "The Soviets are not so disposed, and, in terms of their *immediate* self-interest, it is hard to see why they should be." The Russians, he said, "hold what could be decisive influence over the duration of the war, and yet they escape the normal hazards — and, more important, the responsibilities — of involvement." He was determined to alter this arrangement: the United States was making all the sacrifices, while, from a safe distance, the Soviet Union was encouraging its ally, North Vietnam, to new mischief. The trick was to persuade the Soviet leaders that it was in their own national interest to help the United States withdraw gracefully from Indochina. Vietnam could provide the first vital test of linkage — the concept that was to become the cornerstone of Nixon's foreign policy.

The adviser and the advised began working on Vietnam several weeks before Nixon's inauguration. In mid-December, 1968, only a few days after he had been hired, Kissinger called his old friend Henry Rowen, a former Assistant Secretary of Defense, and, at that time, president of the Rand Corporation. Could Rand compile a comprehensive, confidential analysis of Vietnam options? he asked. Rowen accepted the assignment. He appointed Daniel Ellsberg, who had lectured at Kissinger's defense policy seminars at Harvard in the 1960s, to head the project. Ellsberg pulled together a list of "A-to-Z" options — from all-out war to all-out withdrawal.

On Christmas Day, 1968, Rowen, Ellsberg and the options flew to New York. For four days, in a suite at the Pierre Hotel, Kissinger reviewed the options; he then left to join the President-elect at Key Biscayne, one of a number of posh resorts Kissinger was to come to consider homes away from home. One of the Ellsberg options called for "total and immediate withdrawal" of American troops from South Vietnam. Ellsberg did not favor it at the time — he then preferred testing in Paris the possibility of a negotiated mutual withdrawal by both U.S. and North Vietnamese forces — but he included the unilateral U.S. approach in his A-to-Z range. He has since claimed that Kissinger, or a top military aide to Nixon, drew a heavy black line through that option. "Nonsense," says Kissinger. "The President said, 'That's out,' and in the first go-around on Vietnam, it was."

In early January, Kissinger summoned Ellsberg to New York for another assignment that grew out of a presidential request for a government-wide study of both the political and the military aspects of the war. Kissinger asked Ellsberg to help prepare a list of probing questions, which were to be submitted to all relevant agencies of the government for their independent comments. On January 21, during his very first NSC meeting, the President reviewed the questions — twenty-eight of them, dubbed NSSM-1 (National Security Study Memorandum No. 1) — and ordered Kissinger to present them to the bureaucracy.

But long before the bureaucrats submitted their answers, Nixon had launched his own Vietnam policy. His first move was to change the "look" and the mandate of his negotiating team in Paris. He appointed Henry Cabot Lodge and Lawrence Walsh, a New York lawyer who once served in the Eisenhower Administration, to replace the Democratic team of W. Averell Harriman and Cyrus Vance. War critics charged that the switch caused the loss of vital momentum, but, in fact, the new Nixon-Kissinger duo moved quickly.

On the evening of January 22, three days before the expanded peace talks were finally to open, Nixon was at the theater in the East Wing of the White House watching *Shoes of the Fisherman*, a G-rated film starring Anthony Quinn. When the lights went on at 11 P.M. a message from Kissinger was waiting. Could the President see him for a moment? While

Nixon had been enjoying his first at-home feature film, Kissinger had been drafting new instructions for Lodge. He wanted to check the final details with the President.

The new proposal that Lodge was to present to the North Vietnamese represented the distillation of both Nixon's and Kissinger's thinking on Vietnam. It was in essence the two-track approach, separating the political and military elements of a settlement; and, as a first step on the military side, it called for a "mutual withdrawal" of American and North Vietnamese troops from South Vietnam.

This was a substantive change from the previous American position: in October, 1966, LBJ had pledged that the United States would withdraw its troops from South Vietnam six months *after* the North Vietnamese had withdrawn their troops, and after the "level of violence" had subsided.

For over an hour, the President and Kissinger huddled over a small writing table finishing the new instructions. Kissinger then cabled them to Paris without even pausing to check with the State Department. He was convinced that the time for serious negotiations had finally come. It was almost dawn on January 23 when Kissinger left his office. He felt a sense of accomplishment. The new Administration was calling the signals at last.

When William Bundy, a Johnson holdover as Assistant Secretary of State for East Asian Affairs, learned about the Kissinger cable, he "practically climbed a wall," according to one official. "It'll wreck SEATO," he exclaimed. In theory, it was under the auspices of the Southeast Asia Treaty Organization that the United States was fighting in Vietnam. Kissinger cavalierly brushed aside the State Department protest; it would be the first of many occasions when he would choose to ignore Foggy Bottom. In those early days, he was not yet sure of his power, but he proceeded anyway — knowing he had the President's backing for this early shift in policy.

The second Nixon-Kissinger move on Vietnam was aimed at the Soviet Union, the "key to peace" in Southeast Asia. It was clear from the President's first news conferences that he was trying to woo the Russians into a new and cooperative approach to a Vietnam compromise by dangling attractive bait before them — SALT, trade, an easing of tensions around Berlin, a European Security Conference. On January 27 and again on February 6, Nixon referred to the theory of linkage — though he did not use the word. It was not until his March 4 news conference that Nixon implied that he might be making progress in winning Soviet cooperation on a Vietnam compromise.

"It is well known that the Soviet Union was helpful in terms of getting the Paris peace talks started," the President began, "and I think I could say that based on the conversations that the Secretary of State and I have had with the Soviet Ambassador, I believe at this time that the Soviet Union shares the concern of many other nations . . . about the extension of the war in Vietnam. . . . They recognize that if it continues over a long period of time, the possibility of escalation increases." Then he came to the key point: "I believe," he stated, "the Soviet Union would like to use what influence it could appropriately to help bring the war to a conclusion. What it can do, however, is something that only the Soviet Union would be able to answer to, and it would probably have to answer privately, not publicly."

Later in the same news conference, a reporter asked if the President had asked the Russians to "cut off their supplies to Hanoi." Nixon avoided a direct response. "I am sure that the Soviet Union is keenly aware of the fact that we would be greatly gratified by anything that they can do that could pull some of the support away from the Government of North Vietnam." The signal could not be any clearer.

The third Nixon-Kissinger move was even more significant. While Lodge was tabling the new proposal in Paris for a "mutual withdrawal" of "foreign forces" from South Vietnam, Nixon had already decided on a more far-reaching step. Even before his inauguration he had decided to launch a program of gradual, unilateral U.S. troop withdrawals from Vietnam. He shared his thinking with Kissinger — but with no one else. "He did not communicate this to the bureaucracy," Kissinger later told us, "until about the middle of March because he wanted to get on top of things. He wanted to know what the pressures were."

The President used the early NSC meetings as a sounding board to try out some of his ideas, hoping to achieve a government-wide consensus on Vietnam policy. He asked Kissinger to present five Vietnam scenarios to his top advisers. The scenarios were based in part on the options drawn up by Ellsberg. They ranged from an extremely hawkish position to a comparatively dovish one.

As Kissinger explained it, the President could, first, decide to go for a "military victory." This would mean the destruction of North Vietnam through a program of heavy bombing and a blockade of North Vietnamese ports, accompanied by stiff warnings to Moscow and Peking not to interfere.

Second, he could limit most American military action to the south, and concentrate on defeating the Communist opposition there. This option would still involve air attacks against infiltration routes from North Vietnam through Laos and on into South Vietnam.

Third, the President could opt for a program of gradual withdrawal of American troops from South Vietnam and a gradual strengthening of the Saigon regime, whose military force, ARVN, would be expected to take up the slack.

Fourth, he could speed up American troop withdrawals, lean hard on the South Vietnamese to develop more military muscle, and pressure Saigon to move toward a political compromise in Paris.

Fifth, the President could call for an immediate end to the U.S. combat role in Vietnam and push for a quick deal in Paris, which would amount to capitulating to Hanoi's basic demands.

As Nixon and Kissinger expected, there was considerable agreement among the members of the NSC. The last choice — a quick American pullout — was rejected out of hand. The first choice — increased American involvement — was also rejected. None of the President's advisers had any interest in a military victory or a political defeat. The second option — continued American military involvement in the south without any change — was dropped as well; Defense Secretary Laird reinforced Nixon's conviction that the American people could not be asked to support an unpopular and unwinnable war any longer unless there was a marked decline in American casualties and costs.

That left the third and fourth options, and the difference between them was primarily one of degree. Laird argued for a comparatively quick American pullout, coupled with a major effort — later dubbed "Vietnamization" — to equip and train the South Vietnamese to fight their own war. Secretary of State Rogers went along with Laird's general approach but preferred to emphasize the Paris peace talks; Vietnamization, he thought, was too chancy, too time-consuming; negotiation, a better gamble for quick extrication from an impossible situation.

In broad terms, Kissinger agreed with Rogers. The diplomatic route seemed to him the only practical way out. He, too, favored an American troop pullout, but since he had little faith in Saigon's military capacity and was deeply skeptical about Saigon's political stability, he regarded Vietnamization as unrealistic. "I saw it as a bargaining ploy, a negotiating tool," Kissinger says, "but really I never thought it would work."

In a sense, Kissinger's presentation of the five options at these early top secret NSC meetings was a charade. The NSC was not called into session to debate and help decide on a broad range of policy choices; it was there, basically, to confirm the President's earlier decision to withdraw from South Vietnam. Additional confirmation for this decision came in February, when the bureaucracy turned in its answers to Kissinger's NSSM-1 questions. The two-inch-thick top secret report, running to more than a thousand pages, showed a government in disarray over the war. It revealed that, while the JCS considered B-52 strikes very effective, the State Department and the CIA did not. While the Pentagon generals believed in the "domino theory," the Pentagon civilians did not. The JCS and the U.S. Embassy in Saigon believed that bombing and blockading North Vietnam could cut off "enough war supplies" to force Hanoi to its knees, while the CIA, supported by a number of Pentagon civilians, thought "overland routes from China alone" could supply North Vietnam with sufficient weapons to carry on the struggle, "even if there were an unlimited bombing campaign." No one polled was very optimistic about Saigon's political or military capacity to "pacify the countryside." Optimists thought Saigon could do the job in "8.3 years"; pessimists thought it would take "13.4 years."

From all this confusion, only one fact emerged clearly: the Vietnam situation was a mess, and the United States had to find a way out without capitulating.*

In those early months of 1969, Kissinger's official optimism seldom flagged. On March 27, Chairman J. William Fulbright of the Senate Foreign Relations Committee, long a critic of the Vietnam war, was invited to the White House for a private discussion with Nixon and Kissinger about America and the world. The Arkansas Democrat told the President that if he ended the Vietnam war "soon," he would become a national hero — "just as Charles de Gaulle was after he ended France's

---

*Three years later, on April 25, 1972, the massive study — NSSM-1 — was leaked to influential members of the Washington press corps in what was apparently a dovish effort to embarrass the Administration, then in the midst of countering Hanoi's Easter offensive. In a quick counterattack, the White House played down the importance of the study. Kissinger said NSSM-1 was never seen as a "systematic study," merely as one way of "informing ourselves" about the war. Remember, he told us, "we were dealing with a shell-shocked, essentially Democratic bureaucracy that was reenacting all of its traumas over the last four years." His deputy, General Haig, told a reporter that NSSM-1 had "no real effect on policy," because by the time it reached the White House, it had already been "outdated and outdistanced" by events. This statement was essentially true.

war in Algeria." Fulbright recalled, "I left the meeting with the belief
that the President and Dr. Kissinger were in accord with my views
about the war." Kissinger escorted the Senator to the door, assuring
him "the new Administration would not follow the Johnson Administration's policy in Indochina." "I took this to mean," Fulbright later said,
"that the war would be ended forthwith in accordance with the President's plan." That was Kissinger's belief at the time.

There were a number of reasons for his optimistic approach — but
none so important as his belief that, through linkage, the Russians could
be persuaded to help end the war. During this period, Kissinger met
secretly with Soviet Ambassador Anatoly Dobrynin a number of times.
Neither has ever openly discussed these meetings; but according to a
few knowledgeable sources, Dobrynin kept emphasizing Moscow's interest in a peaceful solution to the war, and Kissinger kept emphasizing
Moscow's responsibility to reduce the flow of Soviet military supplies to
North Vietnam. Neither diplomat had to be reminded that eighty to
eighty-five percent of Hanoi's sophisticated hardware came from the
Soviet Union. Dobrynin implied that the Russians might help on this
score, but he made no promises. Occasionally, when Kissinger would
issue veiled threats about a resumption of full-scale U.S. bombing of
North Vietnam, and possibly even worse measures, unless Hanoi agreed
to a compromise settlement, Dobrynin would respond with exasperation
that the Soviet Union simply did not have the clout to deliver North
Vietnam — an independent, sovereign Socialist republic, after all.

Although this was all standard Soviet fare, Kissinger, in those early
days, chose to give it an upbeat interpretation; and he even tried to re-
ciprocate with appropriate moderation. For example, when the North
Vietnamese launched a fairly large-scale offensive in late February, 1969,
and there was immediate speculation in Washington that Nixon would
resume the bombing of the north, Kissinger successfully pushed for a
policy of no bombing — a deliberate signal of flexibility to the Russians
and to the North Vietnamese. Dobrynin caught the signal, and he implied to Kissinger that Hanoi had probably caught it, too.

Another important reason for Kissinger's optimism was his reading
of the mood in Paris. He believed that the opening, ritualistic phase of
the four-sided peace talks was ending and, with some new American
ideas on the table, a serious phase was beginning. Lodge was under
strict instructions to avoid propaganda about the past and to stress hope
for the future. After a month of meetings, Kissinger proclaimed, "We

have every hope that progress . . . can be made in a reasonable period of time."

Meantime, however, as the two sides continued to meet, Lodge found it difficult to get some of Kissinger's ideas across to the North Vietnamese. He would explain the advantages of the two-track formula; they would insist on a single-track negotiation, maintaining that the military and political elements of a settlement were inseparable. He would propose mutual withdrawal; they would insist on American withdrawal — and they would not even deign to discuss that idea until the United States had agreed to get rid of the Thieu regime and set up a coalition government, including the National Liberation Front.

Kissinger later told us that if the North Vietnamese had been daring enough to accept his two-track approach in 1969, they probably would have gained control over South Vietnam within a "brief period of time. The risk to us," he conceded, "would have been phenomenal."

Still another reason for Kissinger's optimism was the intelligence he had been getting from South Vietnam. The Communist offensive in the south seemed to be sputtering. The CIA reported that a number of North Vietnamese units were withdrawing from South Vietnam, although no one was sure whether this was an indication of North Vietnamese exhaustion or a signal of Hanoi's desire for serious talks. Kissinger was intrigued. On April 30 there was a hopeful political gesture from Tran Buu Kiem, then the senior NLF emissary to the Paris talks; a southern-born Vietnamese, he was one of the founders of the NLF in 1960. The NLF, he stated, was ready for "discussions with the other parties to make the conference move forward." Since this was the first time that Saigon was not explicitly excluded by the other side, Kissinger was encouraged. Finally on May 3, Le Duc Tho, a Politburo member who was to become Hanoi's senior negotiator in Paris, arrived in the French capital, and then even the pessimists began to think Kissinger might have been right after all in believing that serious negotiations were just around the corner.

A final reason for Kissinger's optimism at the time was "Operation Menu," the military code name for the secret bombing of Cambodia, or, more exactly, of North Vietnamese troop concentrations and staging areas along a ten-mile-wide strip of Cambodia bordering on South Vietnam. Kissinger, one of a handful of officials privy to this secret, believed that the bombing would not only prevent the fifty thousand North Vietnamese soldiers from shuttling back and forth across the Cambodian border and inflicting heavy casualties on American forces, but would also encourage the North Vietnamese to come up with a more flexible negotiating package in Paris. Kissinger was always a believer in the persuasive power of bombs.

"Operation Menu" was no small effort. Starting on March 18, 1969, about thirty-six hundred B-52 sorties were flown against enemy positions along the border; more than a hundred thousand tons of explosives were dropped on Cambodia, whose neutrality Washington then professed to respect. On some combat days, these raids made up as much as sixty percent of all B-52 operations in Southeast Asia.

The bombing was not officially acknowledged until May, 1970. Before that, the raids were wrapped in extraordinary secrecy. Vietnam specialists on Kissinger's own NSC staff and at the State and Defense departments were kept in the dark. So were the appropriate committees of Congress. An elaborate "double entry" bookkeeping system was devised so that those in the know at the Pentagon could keep a true record of what was dropped on Cambodia — that record was "eyes-only," top secret — while they provided a doctored record to the Senate Armed Services Committee, claiming that all the bombs in their report were dropped on targets in South Vietnam.

Kissinger had no trouble justifying the deception. He felt that if it became known that the United States was widening the war geographically, extending the bombing into Cambodia, this would prompt a wave of angry denunciations from an increasingly disillusioned Congress and from antiwar critics across the country. This kind of nationwide uproar would only complicate the Administration's plans for peace in Vietnam. Moreover, Kissinger did not want to embarrass Cambodia's Prince Sihanouk, who was, at that time, moving toward the reestablishment of diplomatic relations with the United States after a break of almost four years. If the Administration were to reveal the bombing, Sihanouk would have to take a stand. If he denounced the bombing, the United States might have to stop; if he acquiesced openly, he would antagonize Hanoi. So, the bombing remained "secret"; although it was known to the North Vietnamese who were being bombed; known to Sihanouk, who chose to look the other way; known to the South Vietnamese authorities. Only the American people were told nothing.

The first information they received about the secret raids in Cambodia came from the press. On May 9, 1969, William Beecher, then the Pentagon correspondent of the *New York Times,* reported that B-52s were carrying out "secret raids against North Vietnamese sanctuaries along the Cambodian border" and that Cambodian authorities had not only avoided any protest but were increasingly "cooperating" with U.S. and ARVN military units, "often giving them information on Vietcong and North Vietnamese movements into South Vietnam." The bombing, Beecher went on, represented a desire "to signal Hanoi that the Nixon Administration, while pressing for peace in Paris," was "willing to take some military risks avoided by the previous Administration."

Curiously, the story did not stir up the great outcry that Kissinger had feared. In the White House, however, it landed with the impact of a bomb. Nixon and Kissinger, already angered by earlier leaks of classified information, were infuriated by this latest one. It cast them in the role of hypocrites, who were talking peace while they were expanding the war; and it heightened their fears that sensitive diplomatic initiatives might be adversely affected.

Kissinger had additional reason for concern. Nixon's trusted palace guard suspected that the leaks had originated with members of Kissinger's newly recruited NSC staff, and he found himself on the defensive. He was, in fact, outraged by the leaks; and, in an attempt to demonstrate his own loyalty, he joined the search for the leakers. He knew that FBI wiretaps were quickly placed on thirteen government officials, including seven members of his own NSC staff, and four newsmen.* The taps went on in May, 1969, after the Beecher story appeared, and the Administration says the last ones came off in February, 1971.

By early May, Kissinger was sure the time had come for a major American initiative designed to have a solid "impact on the negotiations." A presidential Vietnam speech was set for mid-May, explaining publicly for the first time the principles on which the President and Kissinger felt a negotiated settlement of the war could be based. Kissinger wrote the first few drafts of the speech.

The speech was ready for delivery on May 14, at 10 P.M. One hour before the President was to speak, Kissinger asked Dobrynin to come to

---

*Helmut Sonnenfeldt, Richard L. Sneider, Morton Halperin, Winston Lord, Daniel I. Davidson, Anthony Lake, and Richard Moose, of the National Security Council staff; Lieutenant General Robert E. Pursley, military aide to former Defense Secretary Melvin R. Laird; William H. Sullivan and Richard G. Pedersen, both of the State Department; James W. McClane, John P. Sears and William Safire, of the White House staff; William Beecher and Hedrick L. Smith of the *New York Times*; Henry Brandon of the *Sunday Times* of London; and Marvin Kalb of CBS News, according to published accounts.

his office at the White House. He gave the Soviet Ambassador an advance copy of the speech, stressed its fresh possibilities, and then called his attention to a few key sentences:

> No greater mistake could be made than to confuse flexibility with weakness or of being reasonable with lack of resolution. I must also make clear, in all candor, that if the needless suffering continues, this will affect other decisions. Nobody has anything to gain by delay.

Kissinger translated these sentences into simple English. If the Russians "didn't produce a settlement," the United States would "escalate the war." Dobrynin promised to convey Kissinger's message to the Kremlin.

In his speech, Nixon ruled out a "purely military solution" to the war. He also rejected the advice of the antiwar critics who were urging him to dump President Thieu and settle for a coalition government in South Vietnam. "We do know the difference between an honorable settlement and a disguised defeat," Kissinger told newsmen shortly before the President spoke.

Nixon listed seven principles governing U.S. policy:

1. The U.S. seeks no bases in Vietnam.
2. The U.S. seeks no military ties.
3. If the South Vietnamese people wish to be "neutral," that is acceptable to the U.S.
4. "All political elements" in South Vietnam should be able to enjoy "full participation in the political life" of the country, if they are ready to drop the use of force or intimidation.
5. The U.S. is ready to accept "any government in South Vietnam" resulting from the "free choice" of the people.
6. The U.S. will not "impose" any government on South Vietnam, "nor will we be a party to such coercion."
7. The U.S. has no objections to "reunification," if that is what the people choose.

The President then advanced eight proposals for settling the military aspects of the war. They bore a striking resemblance to Rockefeller's 1968 plan, conceived by Kissinger:

1. All non–South Vietnamese troops would begin to withdraw.
2. Within twelve months, the bulk of these troops would be out of

South Vietnam; the rest would be withdrawn from combat and assigned to base camps.

3. All foreign non-Communist troops would be withdrawn, as all North Vietnamese troops left.

4. An international supervisory body, acceptable to all sides, would check on withdrawals.

5. The supervisory body would then help arrange ceasefires throughout the country.

6. The supervisory body would also help set up "elections under agreed procedures."

7. An early release of all prisoners of war would be arranged.

8. Finally, all parties to the settlement would agree to abide by the Geneva Accords of 1954 and 1962.

Kissinger did not expect the President's address to produce an instant miracle, but he was pleased that at last the United States had clearly spelled out its goals and aspirations in Vietnam. He hoped that Hanoi would consider the statement as carefully as he had helped compose it.

The next major U.S. initiative came only a few weeks later. After four months of careful preparation, Nixon and Kissinger were at last ready to announce the decision that they had made even before the inauguration — the decision to start the U.S. troop withdrawal from South Vietnam. They realized that it was a controversial decision; while it would be popular with the American people, it would run into serious objections from the JCS and from the Saigon regime of President Thieu. The first installment would be modest — twenty-five thousand combat troops out by the end of August. But Kissinger and the President believed that if the announcement of this first withdrawal were properly stage-managed, it could serve as the critical signal to Hanoi of Washington's determination to leave Indochina. They decided to make the announcement on June 8, a little more than three weeks after the President's May 14 speech. (It was Kissinger's belief that Hanoi needed at least three weeks to digest any major American pronouncement.)

In their eagerness to deal with the North Vietnamese, Nixon and Kissinger did not lose sight of the fact that their ally in this war was in the south; Kissinger had strong views about allies. He felt the United States should not undercut the Saigon regime. He had often deplored the American tendency to "play God" in Vietnam, and he had denounced the assassination of President Diem by U.S.-encouraged coup-makers in 1963 as a dreadful blunder. Soon after Kissinger came into office, he confided to Harriman that in his opinion one of LBJ's worst mistakes was to allow Clifford, then Secretary of Defense, to castigate Thieu publicly for his refusal to proceed to Paris in early November, 1968, to negotiate with the National Liberation Front. "That's no way to treat an ally," Kissinger told Harriman. It was to provide a show of togetherness that Nixon decided to meet with Thieu on Midway Island, a Pacific haven for gooney birds (and a U.S. naval station) located halfway between Washington and Saigon, for the announcement of the first U.S. troop withdrawal. It was an attempt not only to boost Thieu's prestige but also to use his presence as a way of reassuring the conservatives on Capitol Hill that South Vietnam supported the President's decision. The hawks in Saigon, of course, did not; Thieu's public concurrence was simply a way of making a virtue of the inevitable.

En route to Midway, the President, Kissinger, Rogers, and the others in the White House party stopped in Hawaii to touch base with the American military command — specifically, to inform General Creighton Abrams, commander of U.S. forces in Vietnam, of the dimensions of the withdrawal decision. Abrams and his JCS colleagues balked. The General was no innocent. He understood the domestic political need to begin the withdrawal program, but he thought it was the height of folly to pull out combat troops when the same numerical purpose could be served by pulling out supply troops, or at least a mix of the two. Abrams's problem was that he was only a general — not a signal-sender. He did not appreciate the meaning of Kissinger's signal to Ho Chi Minh. Kissinger wanted the ailing North Vietnamese leader to grasp the fact that the President was deliberately reducing his war-making machine in Indochina. A pullout of supply troops could have been interpreted in Hanoi as a sham.

Kissinger believed that the withdrawal of twenty-five thousand troops out of a total of over half a million would have little effect on actual U.S. power in Indochina, but it would constitute a meaningful signal of America's readiness for a solution. At this point, Kissinger actually believed that the President's first withdrawal announcement could persuade Hanoi to engage in serious negotiations. It wasn't the first time that Kissinger would be wrong on Vietnam.

After the Midway announcement, Kissinger struck an even more hopeful note. "We are now at the stage where serious negotiations should start," he said. Once again there was intriguing intelligence from Viet-

nam. A battlefield lull settled over the country. A number of North Vietnamese troop units were being withdrawn from South Vietnam in addition to those pulled out earlier in the spring. Communist forces in the
south were being broken down into small, guerrilla-size groups. Casualties dropped dramatically. Once again, Kissinger speculated — were these
return signals? He toyed with the idea that perhaps the North Vietnamese were beginning to respond to the American troop withdrawals.
Few of his aides agreed. Most of them felt the Communists were merely
regrouping for another attack. Nevertheless, Kissinger believed the withdrawals were preludes not to attack but to negotiation — despite the
fact that on July 10 Le Duc Tho abruptly left Paris for Hanoi without
explanation.

Kissinger, unlike many of his White House colleagues, wanted to believe in negotiations. Because of his close and continuing ties to the academic community, he was more actuely conscious of the surge of antiwar
sentiment sweeping across the nation's campuses. Just before he left for
Midway Island, Kissinger personally was bruised by the growing power
of this movement. He journeyed to Brown University in Providence,
Rhode Island, to receive an honorary degree. Instead, he received a
public humiliation. More than half of the nine hundred graduating seniors turned their backs on him. Kissinger realized that for these students
he was no longer a symbol of learning but a symbol of an Administration
pursuing a "senseless" and "immoral" war. It was the first time university
students were hostile to Kissinger; it was the last time he accepted an
honorary degree.

A challenge was written on the backs of those Brown seniors. Kissinger
returned to the White House tenaciously committed to the restoration
of trust between government and the campus. He believed that only a
quick, negotiated end to the war could prevent the students' antiwar
sentiments from exploding one day into mass violence or, just as de-
structive, into a feeling of mass alienation from society. Trust — so clearly
lacking in Kissinger's dialogue with the students — was also lacking in
his dialogue with "the other side." Somehow, he felt, if he could establish a sense of personal trust between American and North Vietnamese
negotiators, he could break the deadlock at the Paris talks and end the
war.

It was, in part, to create this bond of trust that Kissinger proposed
an unorthodox initiative. In mid-July, shortly before Nixon departed on
a round-the-world trip that was to include another meeting with Thieu,

in Saigon, and a groundbreaking presidential visit to Rumania, Kissinger persuaded him to open a personal line to Ho Chi Minh by sending the North Vietnamese leader a secret letter proposing serious negotiations and, if possible, the start of secret contacts in Paris between Kissinger and the North Vietnamese.

Kissinger proposed that the letter be delivered by a rather unusual postman: Jean Sainteny, a French banker and former official in Indo-china who had been on excellent personal terms with Ho since 1945. A man of goodwill and impeccable discretion, Sainteny happened to be in Washington visiting friends — among them, Kissinger, who arranged for him to see the President. Sainteny agreed to transmit to the North Viet-namese a letter from Nixon to Ho, dated July 15, proposing contacts. In this letter, the President acknowledged the difficulty of communicating "across the gulf of four years of war," but he promised that the United States would be "forthcoming and open-minded in a common effort to bring the blessings of peace to the brave people of Vietnam." And he repeated his now familiar warning: "There is nothing to be gained by waiting. Delay can only increase the dangers and multiply the suffering."

Sainteny delivered Nixon's letter to Xuan Thuy, head of the North Vietnamese peace delegation in Paris. Within a week, a reply came back from Hanoi, approving a secret meeting between Xuan Thuy and Kis-singer. Sainteny was informed, and so was Kissinger, who was then traveling with the President on his global journey. It was decided that on August 4, Kissinger would discreetly peel off from the homeward-bound presidential cavalcade and stop in Paris and Brussels — ostensibly to brief top French and NATO officials on the Nixon trip; actually to have a cover for his first secret meeting with the North Vietnamese.

Reporters kept a close check on Kissinger's whereabouts in Paris. They saw him at the U.S. Embassy, where he chatted with Lodge. They saw him at the Hotel Matignon, where he met with Premier Jacques Chaban-Delmas. They saw him at the Elysée Palace, where he conferred with President Pompidou. And yet, despite the journalistic sleuthing, Kissinger managed to slip through their net and to meet with Xuan Thuy.

The secret rendezvous took place in Sainteny's Paris apartment, with Sainteny staying only long enough to make the introductions and to show his guests where the drinks were kept. Xuan Thuy and Kissinger talked for almost three hours. Their exchange took place in French; Xuan Thuy, who is fluent in the language, brought along an interpreter, and Kis-singer, who reads French better than he speaks it, was accompanied by

General Vernon Walters, an accomplished linguist then serving as military attaché at the U.S. Embassy in Paris. There were no breakthroughs; the two men did little more than exchange well-known positions. But it was a start.

There were moments that day when it seemed that Kissinger's new career as a kind of diplomatic "007" would be exposed even before it got off the ground. Marilyn Berger, diplomatic correspondent for *Newsday* at the time, cornered Kissinger as he was leaving the U.S. Embassy. "Are you going to see Sainteny?" she asked, aware that Kissinger and Sainteny were old friends with more than a passing interest in Vietnam. Kissinger smiled but did not reply. He sped off in a chauffered limousine, unfollowed.

That afternoon, Hal Sonnenfeldt, one of Kissinger's closest aides, telephoned Berger and suggested they meet for a drink. Sonnenfeldt was trying to distract her. It did not work. "Is Henry seeing Sainteny?" she persisted. Sonnenfeldt tried to change the subject.

That evening, Berger again managed to corner Kissinger — this time at Orly Airport, just before he left for Brussels to brief NATO about the President's trip. "Did you see Sainteny?" she asked again. "No," Kissinger replied. A few moments later, as Kissinger entered the VIP lounge to meet briefly with the press, he apparently reconsidered his reply. He caught Berger's eye. "Yes, I did meet Sainteny," he confessed, but it was nothing more than "a ten-minute walk with an old friend." He then urged her not to report the story. However, a reporter from Agence France-Presse overheard the Kissinger-Berger conversation and said he intended to file the Sainteny item. Berger had little choice professionally but to do the same. The August 5 edition of *Newsday* carried her Paris-datelined story with the intriguing headline: "KISSINGER TAKES A DIPLOMATIC STROLL."

That very morning, Berger got a call from NATO Ambassador Robert Ellsworth in Brussels. "Don't publish that story!" he pleaded. It was too late, she told him; the story was already on the newsstands. She could not figure out why he was so overwrought, and he would not say. Only years later — after Kissinger's secret agentry had become the stuff of magazine covers — did she learn the reason for Kissinger's odd behavior. He feared that the Sainteny clue might lead her to Xuan Thuy and the first such secret negotiation between the two adversaries.

About three weeks after the Xuan Thuy–Kissinger meeting, the White House received word that Vietnam's legendary Communist leader, Ho

Chi Minh, had died. No one was certain what impact his death would have on Hanoi's policy. Ho's last communication to the United States, his reply to Nixon's message, reached Washington just a few days before his death. Although a number of American officials trained in deciphering Communist verbiage found hints of flexibility in Ho's response, the President found none. "It simply reiterated the public positions North Vietnam had taken in the Paris talks," Nixon later asserted, "and flatly rejected my initiative."

Kissinger was acutely disappointed. His friends found him suddenly pessimistic about the prospect of ending the war on "honorable" terms. His scenario was not working, and his enemies in the bureaucracy were gloating. He had really believed that the start of U.S. troop withdrawals from South Vietnam would encourage Hanoi to bargain seriously. Equally important, he had left a trail of hints in various foreign capitals that the United States no longer considered a coalition government that included Communists to be harmful to American national interests — so long as the coalition was not imposed. Surely, he thought, Ho's successors would understand Nixon's readiness to withdraw "with honor." Before them lay a great opportunity. If they waited, deferring substantive negotiations, then they would only have to face a stronger Saigon regime. That was the line he deliberately leaked to influence Hanoi's judgment.

Hanoi's leaders took a totally different view of the situation. They assumed that the beginning of American troop withdrawals would weaken rather than strengthen the American bargaining position, and they further assumed that it signaled the beginning of an irreversible pattern: the United States was on the run.

Neither side saw the logic of the other's position, and the deadlock deepened.

Kissinger appreciated the irony of the Vietnam problem. One day he met with a group of visiting Asian diplomats, and one of them asked politely, "Dr. Kissinger, how do we know that you will not repeat the mistakes of the Johnson Administration?" Kissinger smiled sadly. "No, we will not repeat their mistakes," he replied, in his best Chekhovian manner. "We will not send five hundred thousand men to Vietnam." There was an appreciative pause. "We will make our mistakes, and they will be completely our own."

In mid-September, the North Vietnamese in Paris dismissed the President's second troop withdrawal announcement — thirty-five thousand over the next three months — as "tokenism." A new military pattern emerged — not in South Vietnam, where the lull in the fighting continued, but in neighboring Cambodia. The Communists were clogging the infiltration routes of the Ho Chi Minh trail with new men and matériel, most of it destined for the expanding sanctuaries along the Cambodian border with South Vietnam. The heaviest concentrations of North Vietnamese power were only fifty miles west of Saigon. Kissinger and his top aides considered a "real slaughter blow" at the South Vietnamese capital sometime early in 1970 a distinct possibility. And, finally, antiwar groups all over the country began to prepare for a nationwide protest against the war on October 15.

Fall had come to the capital. The spring and summertime bloom had succumbed to the sobering realities of approaching winter.

Appeal to the Silent Majority

On October 13, two days before the scheduled antiwar moratorium, the President's Press Secretary, Ronald Ziegler, announced that Nixon would deliver a "major address" on November 3. The subject: Vietnam.

From campuses around the country, from columnists and commentators, from Republicans and Democrats on Capitol Hill, and even from his own official family, had come an increasingly insistent outcry against the war. It seemed as if the majority of the American people wanted "out," and the price was beside the point. To Nixon, though, the price *was* the point, and he refused to be swayed by the mounting criticism. He was convinced that the protests could undercut his efforts to achieve an "honorable" peace, and he decided to undercut the protest movement by launching a counterattack.

Nixon's political instincts, sharpened by years of cross-country campaigning in victory and defeat, convinced him that a calculated patriotic appeal to the American people could get him what he needed most: time to end the war his way. Americans always rallied round the President in a time of crisis; the trick now was to reach beyond the outspoken skeptics to the silent majority of Americans, who, he believed, represented an elemental, chauvinistic popular force that didn't like the idea of "losing" in Vietnam, that distrusted the "Eastern Establishment" as too liberal, too soft, too cosmopolitan. Nixon decided that the time had come to appeal to their jingoism.

Nixon had six full-time speechwriters. He called upon none of them. This speech was to be a Nixon original. He asked Kissinger to prepare raw data. Memos were quickly dispatched from the White House to the Secretaries of State and Defense and to Ambassadors Bunker in Saigon and Lodge in Paris, asking for a quick reading on the political, military, and diplomatic situation. In addition, Kissinger instructed two members of his NSC staff to compose a list of "talking points" for the President. Only when all of these facts, figures, and analyses had been assembled did the President retreat to Camp David in the Catoctin Mountains of Maryland to consider his options.

The October 15 moratorium — backed by college presidents, religious leaders, and a long list of Democratic Senators — even those who had not been in the forefront of the antiwar movement — was a dramatic portrait of opposition to America's participation in an endless and un-popular war. All across the country, the day was marked by silent vigils, prayer meetings, and peaceful protest marches. In Washington, tens of thousands of demonstrators — students, housewives, professional people, many of them wearing black armbands — gathered at the Washington Monument to hear antiwar speeches and then marched peacefully to the White House. In a number of cities, municipal flags were at half-mast. Classes were canceled at hundreds of colleges and universities.

Three days later, Kissinger, who had recognized back in the 1950s that "the acid test of a policy is its ability to obtain domestic support," paid a private visit to Harvard Square. He wanted to solicit the advice of some of his old colleagues and, perhaps just as important, he wanted them to feel that their judgments were meaningful to the White House. The visit proved to be a painful one for Kissinger. His professor friends had given the Administration "six months" and more, as Kissinger had requested, to end the war, but the killing continued with no end in sight. Their disappointment in Kissinger was unmistakable. A few of them said that they could see no difference between his policy and Rostow's — an assessment that cut to the bone. One of his dinner hostesses wore a blue and white moratorium button. A former colleague denounced the war as "immoral" — prompting Kissinger, in a controlled flash of temper, to advise his friends "not to oppose the technicians of power by becoming technicians of morality." Almost without exception, they strongly urged Kissinger to persuade the President to come up with a new and concrete proposal for peace and, at a minimum, to disclose a timetable for the withdrawal of all U.S. troops from Vietnam.

There is little doubt that, on his return to the White House, Kissinger offered Harvard's advice to the President. There is also little doubt that the President totally ignored it. From Nixon's point of view, Harvard was enemy terrain, and Kissinger's excursions were merely intelligence-gathering probes: preludes, in a way, to battle.

On October 21, Nixon began to draft his speech, interrupting his lonely effort every now and then to ask for the advice of his senior aides. Rogers and Laird recommended that the President concentrate on his hopes for peace and his plans for achieving it. Laird emphasized Vietnamization; Rogers, the Paris peace talks. Kissinger's recommendations ranged over some of the same ground but tended to accent a hard line more in keeping with the President's views. The drift of Nixon's thinking was indicated by one of his requests for information: "What are the exact figures on enemy massacres at Hue?"

Kissinger believed, at that time, that the North Vietnamese were seeking a "cheap victory" over the United States. They were clearly unable to defeat the more than half-million American troops in the field, or even South Vietnamese troops supported by U.S. air and naval power. But the reverse was equally true; the battlefield was a stalemate. The "other side" was hoping that the rising antiwar protest in the United States might make a difference, causing Congress to cut off war funds and forcing an American exodus from Vietnam. Peace, Kissinger felt, could come more rapidly by taking a hard line. If the North Vietnamese "want a reasonable compromise," he said, "we will meet them halfway. If they insist on American humiliation, we will resist." Kissinger thought the President was right when he told a few close advisers: "I don't intend to be the first President to lose a war."

Over the next week, Nixon worked on his speech, mostly in solitude. Finally, on October 29, he summoned Kissinger to his office and read it aloud to him.

"I must tell you in all candor," Kissinger told the President, "that I have no way of knowing whether this speech has any chance of being listened to."

"What this speech will tell," Nixon replied, "is whether the American people can be led in the direction we have to go."

On October 30, Nixon broadened the circle of his in-house critics. He read the speech to Rogers, Laird and Attorney General Mitchell. They gave it their complete approval. Late that afternoon, Nixon reread the speech to Kissinger, all but the ending. That he saved for the next day, when he read the speech to Kissinger still once more, adding his punch-line close: "And so, tonight, to you, the great silent majority of Americans, I ask for your support."

November 1 was a Saturday. Nixon and Kissinger went to Camp David, where again they reviewed the entire speech line by line. Kissinger, who was still uncertain about whether "it would fly," warmly congratulated the President.

On Monday, November 3, at 9:30 P.M., the President addressed the nation. Two hours earlier, Kissinger briefed radio and television reporters in the Roosevelt Room of the White House. The reporters, who had all been given advance copies of the speech, thought Kissinger looked nervous and distracted. The fact is, he had expected a wave of angry questions because the speech contained none of the peace initiatives that newsmen had forecast. But he got very few. At 8:30 P.M., Kissinger briefed dozens of newspaper and agency reporters in the East Room. Again, he seemed nervous. But again, there were few angry questions. The briefings over, Kissinger went to his basement office, closed the door, and watched the President on television.

Nixon spoke to a national audience estimated at more than fifty million people. He appealed for mass support for his plan to bring home all U.S. ground combat forces on an orderly but secret timetable, but he set no deadline for total troop withdrawal. He disclosed a pattern of secret contacts, direct and indirect, with the North Vietnamese. "I recognized," he said, "that a long and bitter war like this cannot be settled in a public forum." He alluded to personal appeals he had made through French President de Gaulle and the French Ambassador to Peking, Etienne M. Manac'h, who enjoyed a close rapport with the North Vietnamese. He referred to the Sainteny contact with Ho Chi Minh, without mentioning Sainteny's name. He disclosed his exchange of letters with Ho. He spoke of frequent overtures to Soviet officials, "to enlist their assistance" in getting meaningful negotiations started. And he revealed that Ambassador Lodge had held eleven private meetings in Paris with Xuan Thuy.

Most significantly, he said nothing about Kissinger's one secret exchange with Xuan Thuy. In his session with reporters, Kissinger had sought to preempt that sensitive area by noting, "We have released only those initiatives which we believe are clearly shut off and which offer no further prospect of success. We have deliberately not released anything else that might still have the slightest possibility of success."

Nixon's speech was one of his greatest gambles of 1969. If his reading of the "silent majority" was correct, then he would have bought more time to pursue his course in Vietnam. If his reading was wrong, then he would have fueled the very antiwar movement he wanted to contain.

The gamble apparently paid off. The White House reported the receipt of thousands of telegrams expressing support for the President's policy and denouncing his critics. There was some suspicion even at the time that this avalanche of telegrams was secretly arranged by the GOP. Ten days later, on November 13, Vice-President Agnew went on the attack. In a speech at Des Moines, at once aimed at impugning the credibility of journalistic coverage of the war and portraying the President as the unimpeachable source of wisdom, he blasted unnamed television commentators for their "instant analysis" of the President's speech. Once again, there was an apparently vigorous response from the "silent majority." Newsrooms were suddenly deluged by telegrams condemning broadcast journalists who had pointed out that there might be other ways of interpreting Vietnam developments. Once again, there was the suspicion that not all of the telegrams were spontaneous. The two speeches — Nixon's on November 3 and Agnew's on November 13 — were a premeditated, double-barreled effort to silence dissenters. There is no evidence that Kissinger opposed this strategy.

Elliot Richardson, who was then Under Secretary of State, was among the millions watching the President. "Nixon is the most audacious riverboat gambler there has been in the White House for some time," he said a few weeks later. "He could have taken the advice of many of his friends and quickly cut our losses in Vietnam and gotten out. But he didn't. He believes in what we are doing in Vietnam, and he chose the Vietnamization path. He knows that Vietnamization may not work, that Vietnam together with inflation can reverse the current five-to-three odds on his reelection, if neither can be brought under control. He knows all of that. But he is still gambling. He is gambling because he believes."

Kissinger also believed in the cause, but his public reaction to the November 3 speech was more calculated; it varied depending on his audience. Kissinger has always been a political chameleon, able to take on the coloration of his environment. Hawks and doves alike thought that they had found a kindred spirit in Henry.

"Brilliant," Kissinger told one Republican conservative, commenting on the President's speech. "Absolutely brilliant. He gambled and he won and we are all better off for it." Kissinger went even further, suggesting a plan for a six-month moratorium on congressional debate about the war.

A few years later, when the proposal surfaced, Kissinger insisted that it was never meant to be taken seriously.

With Georgetown doves, however, Kissinger projected a different image, reserved and troubled. He would nod sympathetically — looking uncomfortable, even pained — whenever he was subjected to a bitter critique of the Nixon speech. He would confide with disarming candor that he was uneasy about the Vice-President's salvos against television news or the President's use of hyperbole.

But behind all these carefully modulated reactions, Kissinger was actually pleased by the impact of the President's speech on millions of Americans. It "turned public opinion around completely," he told us, "and the North Vietnamese softened their line." Extra time had been won to give diplomacy — and bombs — another opportunity to untangle Vietnam.

It was in the fall of 1969, amidst all the talk about Vietnam, that Kissinger made the jump from the news columns to the society page. One evening, he dropped in at a fashionable cocktail party given by Georgetown hostess Barbara Howar in honor of women's libber Gloria Steinem. Overweight and over forty, sans sideburns, Kissinger was chatting with a number of guests when a young lady invited him to be photographed with Ms. Steinem and Senator George McGovern. In those days, it was a toss-up as to who was less well-known — the Senator or the Assistant.

The young lady was Sally Quinn, a society reporter for the *Washington Post*. "You really are a swinger underneath it all, aren't you?" she asked.

"Well," Kissinger replied shyly, giving her one of his famous options, "you couldn't call me a swinger because of my job. Why don't you just assume I'm a secret swinger."

Quinn quoted Kissinger in her story — the photograph, by the way, was cropped so that Kissinger and Ms. Steinem appeared as a twosome, McGovern ending up on the cutting room floor — and, *mirabile dictu*, what had started out as a joke escalated into a legend. Kissinger quickly began to light up the Nixon landscape — "linked" to a cast of dolls from coast to coast.

But Kissinger's talent for turning himself into good newspaper copy antagonized his senior colleagues at the White House. According to one ex-official, who had watched the strained interplay between Kissinger, on the one side, and Haldeman, Ziegler and Ehrlichman, on the other, "Kissinger's independent identity was a source of enormous irritation and envy to people like Haldeman and Ehrlichman." They were concerned "about Henry's competing with Nixon, and their objective was to keep Henry off-balance, on edge, unsure of his position, hit him at his weak points. You know, Kissinger didn't have to be very paranoic there to be concerned about being stabbed in the back. I'm sure he had to go along on certain things. A critic might call Henry a hypocrite. Friends would say, 'He is wise enough to know what to do to survive.' "

One day, Kissinger found himself walking side by side with Haldeman — both of them behind the President. They were all returning from a speech and Nixon decided at the last moment to make a detour by way of the Jefferson Memorial. It was the sort of extracurricular loyalty expected of the staff, but Kissinger was overheard to say, "If I'd known you planned *this*, I'd have walked back to the White House and got some work done." The quip turned up in the afternoon newspapers, and Haldeman was on the phone, complaining about Kissinger's failure to respect the White House law of silent devotion. Kissinger took it in stride, pointing out to the President's alter ego that the published comment was less damaging than the unpublished one. "What's that?" asked Haldeman. "Seen one President, you've seen them all," Kissinger confessed, with a laugh that was not reciprocated.

Yet if the White House inner-circle men did not join in the Kissinger boom, they were professional enough to recognize its political usefulness. An appearance by Kissinger at a Hollywood party might soften the stark image of the Nixon Administration; his sociability might temper the resentment against the White House's arrogant style of government. Though he worked for an Administration that regarded the press and the opposition party with suspicion, he had an open line to some of Nixon's most powerful critics, even to those on what would later become known as the "enemies" list.

On balance, the response to Kissinger's publicity by the President's minions was a mix — a grudging recognition of his effectiveness coupled with resentment at the way he would often outheadline the President. "Henry's relationship with the White House staff is as intimate as the one between Caesar and Brutus," was the way Peter Peterson once put it. "The only person I need to worry about is the President," was the way Kissinger, the loner in the White House, put it. "I go my own way."

From Moscow, early in December, 1969, came word that Hanoi might once again be interested in a serious dialogue. A week later, American industrialist Cyrus Eaton left a meeting with Hanoi's top leaders, including Le Duc Tho, with the clear impression that the North Vietnamese government had recovered sufficiently from the death of Ho Chi Minh, in September, to make another try at negotiations.

On December 15, during a briefing for newsmen to explain the President's third troop-withdrawal announcement (fifty thousand more U.S. troops would leave by April 15, 1970), Kissinger once again spoke about "straws in the wind" and "phrases dropped here and there," suggesting that Hanoi might be signaling a new willingness to talk. "I would think," he said, "that in the next two months or so it ought to become apparent whether the North Vietnamese leadership is in a position now to negotiate with somewhat greater flexibility."

The signs were not all favorable. The CIA reported that the infiltration corridors were more jammed than ever with fresh North Vietnamese troops — the rate, Kissinger said, was "five to ten times as large as it was a few months ago" — and Hanoi's official radio and newspapers attacked the President's Vietnamization program as "a policy to prolong the war and use Vietnamese to fight over Vietnamese for the selfish interests of the U.S. warmongers."

But these reports did not necessarily mean that negotiations were out of the question. Kissinger himself had long believed that Hanoi's tactics included "the use of unbridled ferocity until just before they are ready to settle."

The "straws" kept accumulating, and Kissinger grew more and more eager to renew negotiations. He tried in a number of subtle ways to signal the Administration's readiness to reach an accommodation. U.S. air sorties over Communist positions were reduced by twenty percent. MACV terminated virtually all search-and-destroy missions by the steadily dwindling number of U.S. troops. And Kissinger quietly spread the word that the retirement of Ambassador Lodge on December 8 and his replacement by a lesser-known career diplomat, Philip C. Habib, represented no downgrading of American interest in secret talks. The fact that this was a weak argument did not prevent Kissinger from spreading it.

Finally, in late January, 1970, the succession of signals got a bounce back from Hanoi. Habib learned that Le Duc Tho was returning to Paris, ostensibly to attend a meeting of the French Communist Party, actually to be available for secret negotiations on Vietnam. At Le Bourget Airport on January 31, the silver-haired North Vietnamese revolutionary-turned-*apparatchik*-turned-diplomat emerged from a Soviet airliner and announced his readiness for "serious negotiations," while at the same time accusing the President of speaking out of both sides of his mouth. "On the one hand," Le Duc Tho charged, "he speaks of peace, but on the other hand he is pushing so-called Vietnamization and trying to prolong the war."

Kissinger dismissed these accusations as "posturing" — a description the President accepted — and he quickly won Nixon's approval for an attempt at secret talks with Le Duc Tho. A few weeks later Kissinger was on his way to Paris for his first meeting with Hanoi's top negotiator.

Between late February and early April, 1970, Kissinger flew to Paris four times to meet with Le Duc Tho in a villa near the French capital. The meetings sometimes lasted as long as eight hours, but Kissinger was never absent from Washington for longer than forty hours at a time.

He developed an effective technique to cover his absences: he would be highly visible, almost incandescent, just before his departure for a secret rendezvous. He would be seen at a cocktail party where many reporters were present; at a fashionable French restaurant, lunching with a well-known columnist; at an elegant dinner, accompanied by an attractive companion; at a state occasion, surrounded by newsmen, bureaucrats, and diplomats.

Sometimes, even the President became a prop in a diversion. He and Kissinger would depart from the White House for Camp David — not unusual, after all — and Ziegler would routinely announce their travel plans. What he would not announce was that Kissinger, after getting his last-minute instructions from the President, would then leave by helicopter from Camp David for Andrews Air Force Base, outside of Washington, and board a jet flight to Paris via out-of-the-way military bases in West Germany and France.

Kissinger would often nap on the eastbound flight; on the way home, he and his aides, generally four members of the NSC staff, would prepare a detailed report for the President. Crewmen on the Kissinger flights found his energy remarkable; he seemed to be in constant motion — racing from one typing secretary to another, shouting orders to aides, occasionally pausing long enough to wolf down an airplane dinner, and then going on to edit and read and compile more notes. When he was particularly keyed up, he would pop one piece of chocolate after another into his mouth.

Although Kissinger seemed to be enjoying the entire process immensely, he preferred to create a different impression. The clandestine trips to Paris were, Kissinger told us, a "tremendous physical strain" and a "pain in the neck. I got no particular kick out of doing it secretly."

Despite the exhaustion, Kissinger had no serious complaints. For a time, in fact, during that early round of secret talks, he actually felt that he was making some progress. He negotiated with both Xuan Thuy and Le Duc Tho. Thuy struck him as "very precise, with encyclopedic knowledge," but he lacked Tho's charm and political clout. Tho was clearly the senior man, a member of the Politburo, a top-ranking official in Hanoi's hierarchy. Kissinger, who would get to know him well over three years of negotiations, considered him uncompromising, rigid, and a stern articulator of Hanoi's ideology. From the beginning of the secret talks Kissinger found himself sitting through lengthy Marxist lectures, listening to blistering attacks against the Saigon regime of President Thieu, and hearing endless repetitions of what he half-ironically called the "epic poem of the Vietnamese struggle for independence" — the story of hundreds of years of Vietnamese resistance to foreign aggression. Like many other Vietnamese from both the north and the south, Tho seemed to Kissinger almost totally absorbed with his own country — "monomaniacally" so.

In 1965, when Tho was opposed to negotiations with the Americans, he was quoted as saying, "The Americans are bandits. They are in our home. There is no point in talking to them. We have to chase them away." When he met for the first time with Kissinger, echoes of this attitude were apparent in his negotiating style. He listed his demands, showing no interest in compromise; all he wanted was Kissinger's capitulation. Kissinger found the experience "maddening."

Yet whenever he was asked for his opinion of the North Vietnamese negotiator, the diplomat in Kissinger usually came up with a sympathetic thumbnail biography. "Le Duc Tho is an impressive man," Kissinger once said, "who joined the Communist Party as a very young man — a man therefore driven, in the context of this time, by a certain missionary zeal; spent seven years at extreme hard labor in a French prison; organized guerrilla movements; and finally, after long struggle, wound up in the Politburo of a country that found itself at war almost immediately. He's a man who has never known tranquillity. And where we fight in order to end the war, he fights in order to achieve certain objectives he's held all his life. He holds values quite contrary to ours, and I never had any illusions about that. I didn't convert him to our point of view."

Although the differences between them remained fundamental, the tenor of their meetings was usually polite. "One thing you can say about us," Le Duc Tho once remarked to Kissinger, "whenever we part, we part with a smile."

All the smiles helped create a more congenial negotiating atmosphere, but in the spring of 1970 they contributed nothing to progress on the issues. Kissinger tried, in these first sustained dealings with the North Vietnamese, to avoid the problems on which agreement was impossible and to create instead a basis of mutual understanding. Behind the uncompromising rhetoric, Kissinger kept seeing the promise of serious negotiations. But it turned out that the two sides were totally opposed to one another on the basic issues of war and peace. Le Duc Tho continued to repeat his old demands for the ouster of the Thieu regime and the total withdrawal of U.S. forces from South Vietnam. He dismissed the President's May 14 and November 3 speeches, and he denounced the Vietnamization program.

Even on the less explosive issues, there was no progress. At one point, Kissinger and Le Duc Tho discussed an improvement in the living conditions of the American prisoners of war held by Hanoi, and in early March Kissinger was led to believe that the North Vietnamese might soon release a list of American POWs and allow them to communicate regularly with their families. But even that one flicker of promise died all too quickly. By early April, Kissinger thought it was pointless to continue. The President agreed.

Kissinger had given negotiations a good try, even though there were some officials back in Washington who looked at the deployment of North Vietnamese troops in Cambodia and felt he had wasted his time. William Sullivan, then Deputy Assistant Secretary of State in charge of Vietnamese affairs, believed that the North Vietnamese had already decided "to take another military crack and the hell with the negotiations." The Joint Chiefs of Staff, of course, took the same view. In retrospect, so too did Kissinger.

The fact is that in April, 1970, the situation was not ripe for a political settlement. The deadlock had been further complicated by a new source of conflict — a pro-American coup d'etat in Cambodia, that was to have a far-reaching impact on American actions in Southeast Asia, and it was to delay the resumption of negotiations between Kissinger and Le Duc Tho for over a year.

Cambodia: The Doctrine of Force

"I'd never seen him do that before, and that's why I remember it so vividly," a diplomat in Phnom Penh would later recall about Prince Sihanouk that fateful morning of January 7, 1970. "He was on his way to Europe, his annual taking-the-cure, mind you; he was already inside the plane, a commercial jet bound for Paris. Anyway, the Cambodians were still cheering, we — the diplomatic corps — had already wished him an official Godspeed. We'd all been through it dozens of times before. But then, suddenly, he reappeared, standing up there in the frame of the doorway, as though he were taking one last look."

In the retrospective analysis of the ouster of His Highness Prince Norodom Sihanouk, there would be other remembered vignettes. Such as his confession, later recalled by a Western ambassador, "I am tired, I am tired." Such as the reminiscence by another diplomat: "He was walking down the line of dignitaries, Cambodian officials and diplomats who'd come to see him off, laughing, joking, the usual banter, and then he came up to this particular fellow, a Cambodian, and he said loud enough for everyone to hear, 'Well, here's one man who wouldn't like to see me come back.' I forget whom he said it to, but it got a big laugh."

The last laugh, of course, wasn't the Prince's.

Within the next two months, Sihanouk — a godlike figure to the Cambodian peasants, an insufferable megalomaniac to the Cambodian elite — would be overthrown, and his Kingdom of Cambodia would finally be caught up in the war he had tried to avoid. The opening round of skirmishing — first, between South Vietnamese troops and the VC and North Vietnamese troops along the Cambodian border, and then between Cambodian troops and VC and NVA forces striking west from their border sanctuaries — would pave the way for an American invasion that Nixon would later regard as one of his greatest triumphs and Kissinger would uneasily justify as an "incursion." It would traumatize an already angry and divided America, producing an outcry on Capitol Hill, death at Kent State University, and a massive antiwar demonstration within hearing distance of the Oval Office.

But all of this was future tense in March, 1970, when the upheaval began. Sihanouk was still in France when a group of organized Cambodians, led by squads of military police in civilian clothes, suddenly began demonstrating in front of the NLF and North Vietnamese missions in Phnom Penh, demanding that their troops pull out of Cambodia. From Paris, the Prince denounced the demonstrations; he went on French television to charge that there had been contacts between the CIA and Cambodian rightists who "would like us to enter the American camp." Still, he had such a reputation for political guile that he was suspected of having himself masterminded the demonstrations as a dramatic way of prodding Moscow and Peking into prodding Hanoi to "respect" Cambodia's neutrality. In any case, he did not rush home, but flew instead to the Soviet capital. His detour proved fatal; even his well-known charisma did not extend that far.

On March 18, Sihanouk, ruler of Cambodia from the time the country won its independence from the French in the mid-1950s, was betrayed by his longtime aide, Marshal Lon Nol, an ailing, highly superstitious officer who had always done the Prince's bidding. Sihanouk got the bad news in Moscow and then flew on to Peking, where he charged that the CIA had engineered his downfall. In Phnom Penh, Lon Nol, supported by a small minority of aristocrats, army officers, and businessmen, assumed control. "It was an upper-class coup," a journalist reported at the time, "not a revolution." The coup brought to an abrupt end Sihanouk's agile neutralist policies.

Sihanouk had played an extraordinarily risky game of balancing two powerful opponents. He knew that his ill-equipped army of about thirty thousand was no match for the well-armed forty to sixty thousand NVA and VC troops along the Cambodian border. So he "officially winked" at their use of a strip of the Cambodian border, from which they could strike almost at will into neighboring South Vietnam. For a year he had winked at the unpublicized B-52 bombing of this border area by the United States. By walking the tightrope between Communism and the West, he had succeeded in keeping the war in Vietnam from inundating Cambodia.

But Sihanouk was now out, setting up a government-in-exile in Peking; and Lon Nol was in — and in a fix. To survive, he did precisely what Sihanouk had always said the military would do if it took power; he turned Cambodia's neutrality into anti-Communism. The effect was startling: Cambodia suddenly found herself trapped in an expanding war — both civil and foreign. The Cambodian volunteers who jauntily went off to fight under Lon Nol's banner in commandeered Pepsi-Cola trucks were no match for their opponents — an odd mixture of Cambodian Communist and non-Communist guerrillas, supported by the VC and the NVA. Lon Nol did what everyone knew he would do the moment he launched the coup: he appealed for U.S. help, for no less than five hundred million dollars' worth of weapons, planes, and other aid.

The sudden upheaval in Cambodia was regarded by the U.S. military as both a danger and an opportunity. The danger was that a Communist take-over of the entire country would turn Cambodia into an enemy redoubt and give the NVA and VC complete freedom of action along the Cambodian border, thereby threatening the strategy of Vietnamization — the turning of the war over to ARVN (Army of the Republic of South Vietnam). The opportunity was that the JCS could at last try to implement its long-held dream of "hot-pursuit," of "cleaning out" those Communist hideaways that had survived more than a year of secret B-52 bombing. Under LBJ, the military had been restrained; under RMN, a massive drive might be permitted. State Department officials advised caution. At the White House, Kissinger's staff began to study various courses of action.

On April 1, with the White House striking a public image of concern but not alarm, General Creighton Abrams, U.S. commander in Vietnam, presented three options to Kissinger's NSC for handling the increasingly dangerous situation in Cambodia: first, permit the South Vietnamese to make more cross-border raids into enemy sanctuaries; second, encourage the South Vietnamese to launch larger and more effective operations by providing American artillery and air support; third, help the South Vietnamese to stage a full-scale attack on enemy base-and-supply depots in the sanctuaries — and send American ground advisers along.

Kissinger presented these options to the President. Nixon delayed a decision. A few days later, the President took his family to see *Patton*, a movie about the swashbuckling commander who triumphed over challenge and crisis to emerge as one of the most daring, if tragic, generals of World War II. George Patton's greatest feat was to overcome all odds in rescuing the GIs trapped in the Battle of the Bulge. Nixon was smitten with *Patton*; Secretary of State Rogers later told Darryl Zanuck of Twentieth Century–Fox that the President was a walking ad for the movie. "It comes up in every conversation," said Rogers. Nixon felt that, like Patton, he was confronted by challenge and crisis; but he was uncertain about how to respond. It was clear from Kissinger's last round of talks with Le Duc Tho that Hanoi was not interested in negotiations — at least not in the terms then being offered by the United States.

By mid-April, the situation in Cambodia had become desperate. Thousands of Communist troops were roaming the countryside, cutting roads, closing a ring around Phnom Penh. They clearly outgeneraled and outgunned Lon Nol's army, which quickly discovered that enthusiasm and sacred amulets were no match for motivation and ambush. American officials in Saigon, already worried, grew frantic.

The President shared their anxiety — not only about the situation in Cambodia but also about his credibility in the Communist world. His record of relative restraint was part of a larger strategy, but he feared that it could be misunderstood by the other side. When the Communists had shelled Saigon shortly after his inauguration, thus violating their "understanding" with President Johnson, Nixon had done nothing. When the North Koreans shot down an American spy plane, Nixon again had done nothing. He began to feel besieged, haunted by the fear that he would be seen by the Communists as a powerless dove, unable to counter Communist-backed thrusts anywhere. Though he had no desire to take on any new military obligations in Southeast Asia, he felt that he could not let the Communists "get away with murder," as he confided to a friend at the White House. He was clearly leaning toward strong action. But what action? And where? And when?

April 20, 1970, a Monday, turned out to be the start of a ten-day countdown, although no one, not even the President, realized it at the time. Nixon began the day at San Clemente by announcing a fourth troop withdrawal — an additional one hundred and fifty thousand U.S. troops out of Vietnam by May 1, 1971. The number was increased to satisfy the growing demand in the country for an end to involvement in Vietnam; the time-span was extended to allay the anxiety of the U.S. military in Saigon about any accelerated withdrawals. Nixon coupled his announcement with a clear warning to Hanoi. "If increased enemy action jeopardizes our remaining forces in Vietnam," he said, "I shall not hesitate to take strong and effective measures to deal with that situation." He then flew to Washington.

On Tuesday, April 21, the White House launched the intensive deliberations that led to the controversial decision to move into Cambodia. Richard Helms, the CIA chief, accompanied Kissinger to his daily morning meeting with the President. Nixon wanted more information about Communist troop movements in Cambodia. Helms said the NVA was surrounding Phnom Penh. Kissinger felt that Helms's report lent "new poignancy" to Lon Nol's urgent requests for American aid. Nixon ordered a meeting of the NSC for the next day. That afternoon, Kissinger and Laird met with the President. The three men discussed Hanoi's "new aggressiveness"; their immediate focus of concern was what impact it might have on the Vietnamization program.

Early Wednesday morning, Kissinger invited Ray S. Cline, then Director of Intelligence and Research for the State Department, to his White House office. Did Cline have any fresh information, new insights? He didn't. Once again, Kissinger and Helms conferred with the President. At 10 A.M., Kissinger met with Lieutenant General John Vogt, Director J-3 (Operations) for the Joint Staff of the JCS. Kissinger wanted another Pentagon view, one below the Laird level. Vogt had no new information either; it all meshed with the single view expressed by Laird, Helms and Cline.

At 2:30 P.M., Nixon called his meeting of the National Security Council to order in the Cabinet Room. The Vice-President was there, so were the Secretaries of State and Defense, and the Director of the Office of Emergency Preparedness, Brigadier General George A. Lincoln. Admiral Thomas Moorer, then Acting Chairman of the JCS, and Attorney General John Mitchell were there. Helms was there. Kissinger delivered a detailed report on military and political developments in Cambodia. His point was that Lon Nol's government was in difficult straits. It was not yet clear whether the Communists wished to occupy all of Cambodia or merely to position themselves to set up a provisional coalition government. In either case, Kissinger argued, the expanding sanctuaries gave the NVA the capability to inflict increased casualties on U.S. forces in South Vietnam, and the resulting situation would almost certainly endanger the Vietnamization program, thereby threatening a slowdown in the withdrawal of American troops.

Kissinger's presentation was meticulous; no one in the room questioned its facts or assumptions. A consensus seemed to emerge: in order to protect American lives in South Vietnam, the United States should take some sort of military action to prevent a Communist victory in Cambodia. Some sentiment was voiced for using U.S. troops in Cambodia, but the stronger feeling at that time was that ARVN should handle the ground fighting and the U.S. role should be limited to air support.

That night, Nixon told Kissinger to direct the planning for a South Vietnamese attack against the Communist sanctuary in the Parrot's Beak, a jutting protrusion of Cambodia only thirty-five miles west of Saigon. There was still no action order; but Kissinger caught the drift of the President's thinking, and he had no objections.

On Thursday, April 23, WSAG met — the Washington Special Actions Group, formed a year earlier to handle the EC-121 crisis with North Korea. Kissinger chaired the meeting. Those attending were Under Secretary of State for Political Affairs U. Alexis Johnson, Deputy Secretary of Defense David Packard, Admiral Moorer, Helms, and Assistant Secretary of State Marshall Green. They discussed the military and political implications of a U.S.-backed attack into Cambodia — specifically, who was to do what, with whom, when. After the meeting, Kissinger met separately with Green, Packard, and Moorer. He then reported to the President.

In the late afternoon, Kissinger went to the home of Senator Fulbright to brief him and seven other Senators about the worsening situation in Cambodia. He was there from 5:30 to 7 P.M. His briefing was interrupted four or five times by calls from the President. Kissinger never revealed what the President had on his mind: a ground attack into Cambodia.

Kissinger and the other members of WSAG met again that evening — all of them in formal attire. They were on their way to a black-tie dinner at the embassy of the Republic of China for the visiting Vice-Premier, Chiang Ching-kuo, the son of Chiang Kai-shek. They discussed the planned attack against the Parrot's Beak.

After the meeting, the President retired to the Lincoln Sitting Room. Kissinger went to his office in the West Wing of the White House. They spoke on the telephone several times. Nixon raised a number of questions. If it made sense to attack the Parrot's Beak, why not all of the other sanctuaries? Could the U.S. mission in Phnom Penh, then consisting of only a handful of people, handle the extra burden of coordinating a massive attack? Kissinger inferred from these questions that the President was considering a broader assault into Cambodia, *using United States troops.*

In a final telephone call, well after midnight, Nixon told Kissinger that he wanted to see plans for attacks into all the Communist sanctuaries in Cambodia, and that he wanted to see Kissinger, Moorer, Helms, and Lieutenant General Robert Cushing, Deputy Director of the CIA, at seven-fifteen the next morning.

The five men met early Friday as scheduled; they explored the problems of sending GIs into the Fishhook, another protruding part of Cambodia north of the Parrot's Beak. Later, Kissinger met separately with each of the participants and then with the President. Nixon told Kissinger to call Laird and tell him American troops *might* be used against the Communist sanctuaries in Cambodia. Nixon knew Laird had grave reservations about such a move. So had Rogers. Both Secretaries feared an American attack into Cambodia would further inflame the antiwar movement on college campuses and on Capitol Hill. Both preferred a limited American role.

Kissinger, who had never had much faith in the South Vietnamese army, agreed with the President. If it was important to stop a Communist victory in Cambodia, thus protecting the withdrawal program in South Vietnam while demonstrating U.S. strength and determination to the Communist world, especially Moscow and Peking, then it was at least equally important that the mission succeed. Kissinger envisaged a massive, sudden attack into Cambodia, one that would be limited in duration and keyed to the single objective of denying Cambodia to the Communists for the period of the American withdrawal from South Vietnam.

Laird suggested that Kissinger sound out Capitol Hill. Nixon recommended John Stennis of Mississippi, Chairman of the Senate Armed Services Committee. Stennis was one of the few people who had been informed the year before that there had been B-52 raids against Cambodia. Kissinger and Stennis met for an hour, after which Stennis gave his reluctant endorsement to the plan to use American troops against the Parrot's Beak and the Fishhook.

That afternoon, Kissinger chaired another WSAG meeting, but he revealed few of the President's thoughts about using U.S. forces in Cambodia. Most of the discussion focused on the Parrot's Beak operation, in which ARVN was to play the major role.

That evening, Kissinger invited five members of his NSC staff into his office for a sort of devil's advocate discussion of various options dealing with Cambodia. "I suppose we were the house doves," one of them later recalled. The five were Anthony Lake, Winston Lord, Laurence Lynn, Roger Morris, and William Watts. The discussion, as Kissinger remembered it, was "stormy and emotional."

It centered on what actions the United States might consider to counter the Communist threat in Cambodia. Lake, who worked most closely with Kissinger as his Special Assistant, argued against an invasion. "It would be an extension of the war," he said, "and the President would be unable to get off that course, once he got into it, no matter what was said." Besides, it would lead to real problems in Cambodia in the future. The cost in domestic and foreign reaction was not worth it.

Morris echoed the same arguments. "We simply made the foreign policy argument that this was another exercise in futility," he recalled, "which was going to cause a loss of life and destruction and devastation to no real avail. In any case, we argued that all of the evidence was murky — very, very murky — as to what the other side was up to, whether the fall of Phnom Penh or the fall of Cambodia, as they conceived it, was as imminent as they said it was. We were arguing that this was business as usual in Southeast Asia. We also were trying to cast it in terms of what would happen here. We said, in effect, you're going to have — without trying to be dramatic about it in retrospect — blood in the streets if you go into Cambodia."

Watts expressed his deepest reservations. If it was Cambodia this year, he felt, it would be Laos next year and the bombing of Haiphong in two years.

Lynn was worried.

Lord did not disclose his views.

The meeting lasted about an hour. By the time the five had walked out the door, Lake had decided he could not go along with this latest escalation; Morris had reached the same conclusion; and Watts went home depressed, feeling very helpless and considering resignation.

For Kissinger, Saturday, April 25, started with an early morning meeting with Ehrlichman. He gave the President's Chief Domestic Adviser a detailed briefing on the Cambodian operation — "more," Ehrlichman remembered, "than was really meaningful for me." The "go" decision seemed clear to Ehrlichman "right then and there." Go — after both the Parrot's Beak *and* the Fishhook.

Kissinger then met with Lynn, privately. "He was the least emotionally against it," Kissinger recalled, "but he had the best reasons for not doing it." They related to cost effectiveness, Lynn's specialty. He argued that with an equal expenditure of resources in South Vietnam, the President could accomplish more, in terms of his long-range political goals in Southeast Asia, than by crossing a national border into Cambodia. Kissinger asked Lynn "on a very, very confidential basis" to examine the Cambodian plan and then systematically to raise questions about it. That night, Lynn sat in the Situation Room, jotting down one question after another on a yellow lined pad. After a few hours, there were eighteen questions. "The more questions I raised," Lynn later remembered, "the more really worried I got about this whole business." He gave the questions to Kissinger, who passed them on to the Pentagon "for study."

The Kissinger-Lynn talk was interrupted by a phone call from Camp David. The President wanted Laird's plans for the Fishhook operation. Kissinger got them and helicoptered to Camp David — in time for a hamburger with the President and his friend, "Bebe" Rebozo. Then, for two hours, Nixon and Kissinger studied the maps and charts and plans for an American ground attack into Cambodia. They discussed probable reactions in Moscow and Peking. They both agreed the outcry would be loud but manageable.

That evening, Nixon, Kissinger and Rebozo flew by helicopter to the Washington Navy Yard, where they met Mitchell. They boarded the presidential yacht, *Sequoia*, for a four-hour cruise on the Potomac, during which time they watched *Patton* once again. "If I have to see that movie once more," Kissinger told a friend, much later, "I'll shoot myself."

On Sunday, April 26, the President called an urgent meeting of the NSC. This time, Agnew and Lincoln were not invited. Kissinger led a discussion of the pros and cons of a U.S. attack into Cambodia. Would the gains from a successful military attack be worth the loss of domestic support? Could Saigon survive side by side with a Communist Cambodia? The President announced no decision. After the meeting, he asked Kissinger to join him in the family quarters of the White House. They reviewed the pros and cons all over again.

Monday morning, April 27, the inner circle met once again. There was a marked increase in tension. One adviser told Nixon, "Mr. President, I don't know much about domestic affairs, but if you do it, in my opinion the campuses will go up in flames." Nixon listened, and then said, "I want to hear that now, but if I decide to do it, I don't want to hear of it again. If I decide to do it, it will be because I have decided to pay the price." Laird, the dove in hawk's feathers, reluctantly endorsed Abrams's recommendation that American troops had to be used; if not, the General said he could not ensure success. Rogers wondered aloud whether Abrams and the other military chiefs were merely telling the President what they thought he wanted to hear. The thought troubled Nixon. He sat down and immediately drafted an "out-of-channels" cable to Abrams demanding the "unvarnished truth."

When the meeting ended, Nixon asked Kissinger to get the Pentagon to produce final plans and "any other recommendations" for U.S. and ARVN attacks against the Parrot's Beak and the Fishhook — and to produce them by nightfall.

He also asked Kissinger to confer with another Senator — John Williams of Delaware, a conservative Republican on the Senate Foreign Relations Committee. Unlike Stennis, Williams opposed the Cambodian attack. He was the second and last legislator to be consulted before the final decision.

That night, Kissinger went to dinner at the Brookings Institution, where leading American and Japanese academicians raised the question of Cambodia. They wanted to know whether it was true that the United States was considering a large-scale American aid program to Phnom Penh. Kissinger did not disclose that what the United States was really considering was a large-scale American attack.

That night, Nixon sat alone in his office, a yellow lined pad on his lap. According to columnist Stewart Alsop's intimate account, he jotted down a list of the pluses and minuses. He had clearly decided on some kind of military action. "Time running out," he noted. He wanted to avoid an "ambiguous situation — if we don't move and they don't either." He realized the "deep divisions" in the country were likely to become deeper as a result of American action in Cambodia.

Later that night, Nixon heard from Abrams. The "unvarnished truth" was that in his opinion American troops were necessary.

Very early Tuesday morning, April 28, Nixon called Kissinger to say that American troops would be used against the Fishhook area. Kissinger immediately produced his own yellow lined pad; he, too, had ticked off the pluses and minuses. Nixon glanced at Kissinger's list, Kissinger at Nixon's. The lists were almost identical. Kissinger told the President that it was his duty to warn him of all the hazards the Cambodian action might entail. Nixon replied that he had made up his mind: American troops would be used in Cambodia. He understood the hazards but now he did not wish to look back or to hear recriminations if the mission turned sour.

The President then notified Haldeman and Mitchell, later Laird and Rogers.

The South Vietnamese would begin the attack on the Parrot's Beak Tuesday night, Washington time; the Americans would begin the attack on the Fishhook Thursday night, Washington time. The President would address the nation at nine o'clock Thursday night.

Kissinger asked Watts to coordinate the Cambodian announcement. Watts declined. He told Kissinger he disapproved of the Cambodian operation, then went to his office and wrote a letter of resignation. When General Haig, Kissinger's deputy, learned of Watts's rebellion, he angrily confronted him in the Situation Room. "You have an order from your Commander in Chief," Haig declared, implying that Watts could not possibly resign. Watts countered with: "Oh yes, I can — and I have."

Haig called a meeting of several NSC staffers and asked Morris and Lake to write a first draft of the President's speech. Haig said, "We'll involve a couple of sizable American strike forces, and we'll want to lay out the reasons and all that." Morris listened and then, as he recalls it, "I just pulled Al Haig aside and said, 'Look, I just can't do it. I just can't. I'm not going to write this. I've done this sort of thing repeatedly in the last three or four years. Just for personal reasons alone, I've really had it.'"

Morris and Lake went back to their offices; instead of drafting a presidential address to the nation justifying the U.S. strike into Cambodia, they drafted a joint letter of resignation. It was delivered to Haig later the same day. "We know Henry's very upset and very tense now," Morris told Haig. "Will you pick a time to give him this? But it's very important to us that we deliver it today prior to what's going to happen. If you want to give it to him after it happens, when things have calmed down, that's fine too." The letter was delivered Saturday, forty-eight hours after the United States invaded Cambodia.

On Wednesday, April 29, Kissinger lunched with Thomas Dewey, a Republican elder statesman who was occasionally consulted on foreign policy. Dewey approved of the attack plans. The phone rang during lunch. It was Senator Robert Griffin of Michigan, the Republican whip. There were reports, Griffin said, of a South Vietnamese attack against the Parrot's Beak in Cambodia. Were they true? Yes, Kissinger replied, stressing the limited nature of U.S. involvement in that attack. He said nothing about the planned attack by U.S. forces against the Fishhook. Griffin found it shocking that the Senate GOP leadership had to learn about the South Vietnamese attack from newsmen, not from the White House.

That evening, Kissinger and Haldeman briefed the senior White House staff about the Parrot's Beak operation. They revealed nothing about the Fishhook operation.

Kissinger and Nixon conferred several times on the phone Wednesday night. Both were keyed up for Thursday.

Early Thursday afternoon, Kissinger and Haldeman were invited into the President's small private office just off the big Oval Office. Nixon wanted to read his speech to them. According to one account, they offered "only small comments."

At 3:50 P.M., Kissinger chaired the last WSAG meeting on Cambodia — basically a wrapping up of loose ends. He then briefed another hawk on the war, AFL-CIO President George Meany; Meany approved of the attack.

A few hours before the speech, Kissinger summoned his staff for an unusual meeting in the Executive Office Building. "It took place in the old Indian Treaty Room," recalled one participant, "and I thought it had a certain ironic twist about it because most of those treaties were later broken." Kissinger informed the staff on a confidential basis that the President had decided to send American troops into Cambodia. "This is a time we have to stand together," he said, according to another account. "We have to be behind the President. We've had an airing of views; this is the most carefully wrought decision we have made — very agonizing. No one has a monopoly on anguish. But I want to caution you that we're talking here about the integrity of the presidency. We're not talking about a man. For those of you who feel you cannot be behind the President, it's extremely important that at this point we have no public outcry of any sort. If you feel you must do that, then you should leave." He did not know at that point that Morris and Lake had already turned in their letter of resignation.

By the time Kissinger returned to his office in the White House, there was a call from Laird. The Secretary of Defense was startled by some of the President's language, especially his reference to COSVN — Central Office for South Vietnam — which directed the war in the south under Hanoi's supervision. Nixon seemed to be saying that "the headquarters for the entire Communist military operation in South Vietnam" would soon come under direct American attack, thus conveying a totally inaccurate impression. Laird knew, Kissinger knew, and many reporters knew that COSVN was no Pentagon in a jungle, no fortified command center, but rather was a kind of floating headquarters that kept shifting location. For a time, Laird and Kissinger tried to persuade the President to drop all reference to COSVN. They even tried to persuade him to allow General Abrams to announce the invasion. Nixon would have none of it. He was listening to the sound of a distant trumpet. He saw himself walking down the boulevards of history arm in arm with Churchill during the "blood, sweat, and tears" days of World War II, or with Kennedy during the Cuban missile crisis. This was to be his finest hour.

Within an hour, Kissinger was briefing a group of radio and television newsmen; their questions regarding the unfolding military operations dealt with immediate crises, not historical perspectives. Kissinger, on his own, warned the reporters not to expect the capture of COSVN. He offered a more modest objective. "We have no expectation of capturing the actual headquarters personnel, nor do we know that they are precisely in that area in any one given period," he said. "The strong possibility is that the personnel will have left by the time we move in there but we have expectation of destroying their communication facilities and, above all, their supply dumps."

The President finally appeared before the television cameras at 9 P.M. on April 30, his speech awaited by millions from coast to coast. His combative spirit sparked each sentence; his rhetoric was belligerent, challenging Communist forces everywhere. "If, when the chips are down, the world's most powerful nation . . . acts like a pitiful, helpless giant, the forces of totalitarianism and anarchy will threaten free nations and free institutions throughout the world," he said. "If we fail to meet this challenge, all other nations will be on notice that despite its overwhelming power, the United States, when a real crisis comes, will be found wanting."

It was only *after* the GIs had crossed into Cambodia that Lon Nol was officially informed of the "incursion" by Lloyd Rives, the U.S. Chargé d'Affaires in Phnom Penh. The "delay" was blamed on faulty communications.

The announcement of the Cambodian invasion hit the country like a bombshell. On dozens of campuses, students began marching, protesting, planning a mass demonstration in Washington for the following week. The National Student Association called for Nixon's impeachment, and Nixon reacted by referring to students, "you know, blowing up the campuses," as "bums." His comment triggered more demonstrations.

Kissinger spent the weekend receiving, pursuing, questioning, checking, then double-checking every report from Cambodia. He was in constant touch with the President. He also answered reporters' questions, met with selected Congressmen, set up appointments with ex-colleagues who wished to protest the expanding war, and took telephone calls from dozens of war critics who thought "Henry has gone out of his mind."

By Monday, May 4, hundreds of campuses were in a state of anguished upheaval. At Ohio's Kent State University, hardly a hotbed of radicals, National Guardsmen, attempting to clear an area of rock-throwing students, opened fire. Four students were killed, eleven others wounded.

The tragedy at Kent State grieved Kissinger deeply — not just because of the loss of life and the extension of violence but because of the bloody evidence of a nation tearing itself apart over a war no one could really understand. To a friend that night, he mourned, "I'm dead. Every war has its casualties. I am a casualty of this one." His confession implied no real doubts about the wisdom of the President's course. If he had disapproved of Nixon's policy, he could have argued against the Cambodian attack. But there is no sign that he ever mustered his considerable influence to persuade the President to hold his fire. Or that he ever considered resigning in protest. Quite the contrary, Kissinger supported the policy.

Tom Lehrer, an old colleague from Cambridge, sent him an angry telegram, summing up a widespread academic feeling. "If your influence with the President is as great as reputed," wrote Lehrer, a Professor of Statistical Mathematics at MIT, "your resignation now with a statement disassociating yourself from the Indochina policy might change the course of history for the better. If, on the other hand, you approve of that policy, you will have to face the opprobrium which will follow you for the rest of your life."

Kissinger explained to a few of his former colleagues from Harvard why calls for his resignation, while well meaning, were shortsighted. "Suppose I went in and told the President I was resigning," they remember his saying. "He could have a heart attack and you'd have Spiro Agnew as President. Do you want that? No? So don't keep telling me to resign."

But if Kissinger still had any illusions about his standing among his former associates, any lingering hope that their predictable outrage might be tempered by an understanding of either the reasons for the President's decision or his own role in the formulation of that decision, they were to evaporate completely on May 8. That day thirteen senior Harvard faculty members, all on a first-name basis with Henry for many years, stormed into his basement office at the White House to denounce the Cambodian operation and to appeal to Kissinger's conscience "to stop that madman."

Of course, Kissinger could have shut them out; a simple call to the Secret Service would have kept them off the White House grounds. But, in fact, Kissinger tried to maintain communication, consistent with a pledge he had made to his academic colleagues on December 4, 1968, shortly after accepting the President's offer. "The doors of my office are open to your ideas," he had promised, and "I invite you to share them with me. . . . If I cannot maintain the dialogue with my friends over all these years, I will not have done my job."

Kissinger knew them all: Thomas Schelling, Professor of Economics, author of *The Strategy of Conflict,* organizer of the group; Richard Neustadt, author of *Presidential Power;* Francis Bator, former Deputy Special Assistant to President Johnson for National Security; Ernest May, Professor of History and former military historian for the Department of Defense; Seymour Martin Lipset, Professor of Government and Social Relations; George Kistiakowsky, Professor of Chemistry and chief science adviser to President Eisenhower; William Capron, Associate Dean of the Kennedy School of Public Affairs and former Assistant Director of the Bureau of the Budget; Adam Yarmolinsky, Professor of Law, adviser to Presidents Kennedy and Johnson; Paul Doty, Professor of Biochemistry; Konrad Bloch, Professor of Biochemistry and Nobel laureate; Frank Westheimer, Professor of Chemistry; Gerald Holton, Professor of Physics; and Michael Walzer, Professor of Government.

The meeting glinted with tension, a tightly controlled tension.

"We made it clear to Henry from the beginning," Schelling later recalled, "that we weren't here lunching with him as old friends, but were talking to him solely in his capacity to communicate to the President that we regarded the invasion of Cambodia as a disastrously bad foreign policy decision, even on its own terms. Ernest [May] told Henry, 'You're tearing the country apart domestically.' He said this would have longtime consequences for foreign policy, as tomorrow's foreign policy is based on today's domestic situation. Then Bator and Westheimer chimed in with an explanation of how difficult it was for us to have Henry read in the newspapers beforehand of our coming. Bator said it was especially painful for him since he had held part of the same portfolio Kissinger now handles. But we felt that the only way we could shock him into realizing how we felt was not just to give him marginal advice. We wanted to shock him into realizing that this latest decision was appallingly bad foreign policy in the short run."

A phone call from the President interrupted the tirade — mercifully, from Kissinger's viewpoint. He disappeared for fifteen minutes. When he returned, he asked Schelling what "short-run" error had been made.

"It's one of those problems where you look out of the window," Schelling began, "and you see a monster. And you turn to the guy standing next to you at the very same window, and say, 'Look, there's a monster.' He then looks out of the window — and doesn't see the monster at all. How do you explain to him that there really is a monster?"

Schelling continued: "As we see it, there are two possibilities. Either, one, the President didn't understand when he went into Cambodia that he was invading another country; or, two, he did understand. We just don't know which one is scarier. And he seems to have done this without consultation with the Secretary of Defense or the Secretary of State, or with leaders of the Senate and House. We are deeply worried about the scale of the operation, as compared with the process of decision."

Neustadt added: "What this is going to signal to senior American military officers — and the Saigon government — is that if you put enough pressure on Nixon by emphasizing that American boys are dying, you can get the President to do very discontinuous things. And this makes his whole promise of withdrawal open to question."

Everyone spoke at least once. Only when it seemed that their collective spleen had been vented did Kissinger begin to respond. "Can I go off the record?" he asked softly. "No," Schelling replied. Kissinger said in that case he could not offer a detailed explanation but, according to Schelling, he did offer some solace to his old colleagues.

"First, he told us that he understood what we were saying, and the gravity of our concern. Second, he said that if he could go off the record he could explain the President's action to our satisfaction. And third he said that since we wouldn't let him go off the record, all he could do was assure us that the President had not lost sight of his original objective or gone off his timetable for withdrawal."

Bator interjected a note of skepticism. If Johnson and Rostow couldn't control the process of escalation, he wondered, then, even with the best of intentions, how could Nixon and Kissinger? Schelling told Bator to be quiet so Kissinger could continue, but Kissinger had little else to say. There was a brief moment when it seemed as though the room had lost oxygen; the meeting, purpose. Everyone rose, dispirited, overcome by a feeling of helplessness. Kissinger shook hands with each of his Harvard colleagues. When the door closed on the last of them, he slumped into a soft chair and stared vacantly out the window.

Michael E. Kinsley, an editor of the *Harvard Crimson*, interviewed many of the professors shortly after their hour-and-a-half session with Kissinger. Holton said: "It was not exactly what I would call a love feast. He said that he was moved by our visit, that he felt it's all a tragic situation. . . ." Bloch said: "He doesn't understand that the end-justifies-the-means philosophy is exactly the problem and what is antagonizing the large part of the population." Schelling said: "He refused to reply on the record, therefore he had our sentiments heaped upon him, he sat in pained silence and just listened." Lipset said: "I think we have a very unhappy colleague-on-leave." Schelling added: "I hope so."

The protests against the Administration's policy in Indochina continued to mount. To Kissinger, it seemed that every institution of government was under siege. Congress erupted in angry debate over legislation to remove U.S. troops from Cambodia and to restrict the President's warmaking powers. On May 9, over seventy-five thousand demonstrators, most of them college students, gathered in Washington to protest the invasion of Cambodia. Their demonstration was peaceful, but their mood was more angry than it had been the previous fall. Just before dawn, the President surprised his own Secret Service and drove to the Lincoln Memorial to mingle with the demonstrators, hoping to convert their hostility to support. He talked first about football, then about the war. Neither side budged.

Even among Nixon's own people, there were mutterings of doubt, second-guessing, the very "recrimination" he had told Kissinger he would not tolerate. "He knew he was swimming against the tide of the bureaucracy," Haig later said, "but he was confident he had made the right decision in spite of protest from a lot of the public and even his own Cabinet." Oddly enough, it was not Haldeman, or Ehrlichman, or even Nixon himself, who undertook to inspire confidence in the policy and trust in the President's leadership; it was Kissinger. Time and again, during this period of despair, Kissinger rose at the morning get-together of top White House staffers to deliver an old-fashioned peptalk. Keep the faith. Back the President. Maintain confidence in the policy. Hang tough. Ehrlichman recalled that "at those times," Henry was "a fighter, a real inspiring leader."

Indeed, it was Kissinger's unabashed demonstration of loyalty to the President at a time when others were wavering that finally solidified his relationship with the occupant of the Oval Office. He had been moving in that direction ever since Inauguration Day, but it was his unstinting support for the President through the Cambodian crisis, when Nixon was being portrayed by his critics as having taken leave of his senses, that established the real bond between them.

But Kissinger still could not dissuade Lake and Morris and Watts, and soon Lynn, from quitting. One Saturday morning late in May, Lake discussed his resignation with his former boss. Kissinger seemed "personally disappointed," Lake recalls, almost as though "I had flunked the seminar. It was as though I had rejected everything he'd taught me. He knew I understood it, but I think he saw it in terms of the stability of societies, and that Roger and I were evidence that people like us were not doing everything we could to hold society together but were falling prey to those same impulses that were driving society apart. He feels strongly that you don't walk out on the President at times of difficulty . . . walk out on the *presidency*."

It was in these moments of crisis, of challenge to society, that Kissinger's innate conservatism surfaced. His old fear of America's going the way of the Weimar Republic, lurching in frustration toward extremism, toward a modern-day Fascism, obsessed him. With Lake and with others, too, he would often turn bitter and sarcastic, calling them "bleeding hearts," suggesting that they were pandering to the left, giving free reign to their old anti-Nixon bias, retreating from responsibility. "We are the President's men," he would exclaim, "and we must behave accordingly." He believed that his Harvard colleagues were losing their perspective in their agony over Cambodia. This nation, Kissinger felt, was distinguished from others by its fidelity to commitments, its trust and generosity, its bipartisan devotion to international order, its opposition to tyranny and aggression. There was a difference between *us* and *them,* in Kissinger's mind, between the forces of order and the forces of revolution. Vietnam might be a tragedy, one into which the United States should never have intruded; but a great power must extricate itself from tragedy not in a moment of blind exhaustion but with honor and dignity. Here was a beleaguered President, trying to do what was right; and the Establishment was deserting him, as once the Establishment deserted democracy in Germany. The professors, writers and intellectuals were out in the streets with the kids. They had lost their objectivity and, more than that, their guts. The society had to be held together, he believed, until a new period of reconciliation could begin. Then America could again find her true spirit. But until then, damn it, "hang tough!"

Months later, Kissinger, briefing a group of editors in Hartford, Connecticut, would analyze the key problem, as he saw it: "It has been our conviction that if political decisions were to be made in the streets the victors would not be upper-middle-class college kids, but some real tough guys. . . . The society which makes its decision in this manner will sooner or later be driven towards some form of Caesarism in which the most brutal forces in the society take over. Therefore, we believe that what really was at stake here was not this President. What was at stake here was the problem of authority in this society altogether. If you look at the history of the last Presidents, one has been assassinated, another has had a complete collapse of his credibility. This country cannot afford to destroy another President in this manner, no matter what his political convictions are."

Kissinger hung tough. He met with one student and teacher delegation after another, always the very model of the charming, embattled professor doing his best against terrible odds to keep body, soul, and country together. And, in addition to his regular responsibilities, he met at least seven times with large groups of reporters — between April 30, when U.S. ground troops were ordered into Cambodia, and June 30, when they were out — rationalizing policy, fending off hostile critics and, of course, interpreting the President's position. "What the President meant to convey . . . ," or, "That would be my interpretation of what the President said, yes . . ."

In tense and hostile situations, Kissinger's humor served him particularly well. He could use it to ingratiate himself with his audience, to deflect attack and, when possible, to lower the level of criticism. He opened his May 9 "backgrounder" with the press by saying, "I was in the Situation Room plotting the war." Laughter. Kissinger quickly added, "Mr. Ziegler says, 'Put that off the record.' (Pause.) It sounds even better in German." More laughter. May 16 found Kissinger at Key Biscayne. His opening remark: "Does anyone have a question for my answers?" The first question, which focused on an apparent contradiction in official explanations of the Cambodian operation, concluded with these words: "I would ask you, who has been lying to us and through us to the American people?" Kissinger paused for only a second. "I like the constructive spirit in which the question has been put." More laughter still.

In all of these backgrounders, Kissinger generally made four points.

First, he tried to scotch speculation that a new American commitment to Cambodia would develop, similar to the one that had evolved in South Vietnam. U.S. forces, he assured everyone, would be withdrawn from Cambodia by the end of June.

Second, he portrayed the Cambodian operation as having bought at least six months of additional time for the orderly pullout of American troops from Indochina, and for the strengthening of South Vietnamese forces, too.

Third, he identified himself with student torment across the country. "These are my students," he said. "I have been teaching them. These are my colleagues. . . . This is not a very joyous occasion. . . . We recognize the anguish and concern of the people who are protesting and we hope that they will recognize at some point that no group in this country

— certainly those who are in responsibility must be included — has a monopoly of anguish on this conflict. . . . We are not eager for a confrontation. In a confrontation there aren't going to be any victors. There are only going to be victims."

And fourth, Kissinger suggested that the ending of American ground operations in Cambodia would provide a new opportunity to negotiate an honorable settlement of the war. Noting that the North Vietnamese had summoned home "several of their ambassadors" and that a meeting of the North Vietnamese parliament had been convened, he speculated that Hanoi was going through "a period of considerable reexamination," from which might emerge a Politburo decision to engage in "serious negotiations."

The President's assessment of the Cambodian operation was even more upbeat. The JCS had assured him that the invasion had disrupted enemy calculations in South Vietnam, that Communist military activity in the rich delta area and in the region around Saigon had dropped sharply. The JCS predictably pulled out all official stops in describing ARVN's performance in Cambodia. ARVN, they maintained, had acquired a new dimension of combat experience, and with it, a sense of pride and cohesion.

In fact, American air support had been critical to ARVN's performance: there were also nonmilitary reasons for ARVN's new aggressiveness, the sort the JCS did not discuss. For the first time, ARVN was fighting outside its own borders, and compared to the ill-equipped Cambodian troops — who were really instant soldiers, civilians in khaki — the South Vietnamese were tigers. For the first time, they had someone to look down on, just as Americans in South Vietnam looked down on ARVN. The South Vietnamese adopted a military swagger that was rarely seen when they were fighting in their own country. Their sense of being the savior of Cambodia only compounded their hatred of Cambodians, and there were continuing reports of plunder, rape, and murder of Cambodian civilians. For their part, the Cambodians began persecuting helpless Vietnamese civilians who had lived in Cambodia for generations, justifying these crackdowns on the grounds that the Vietnamese communities harbored VC and NVA; there were massacres of innocent Vietnamese, their bloated bodies floating down the waters of the Mekong.

The invasion was a long-term calamity for Cambodia — a cynical strategy that made a mockery of the sovereignty of a small, helpless country. It did not wind down the war, it widened it. The invasion was headlined by the White House as a sixty-day ground operation, no more, with the Americans kept to within twenty-one miles of the border, no more – but by the time the thirty-two thousand GIs who went into Cambodia were out, one-half of the country was in the hands of "the other side," and three years later the B-52s would still be bombing those same sanctuaries. In mid-August, 1973, after dropping half a million tons of bombs – more than twice the amount dropped on North Vietnam during the entire Nixon Administration – the President was forced by Congress to stop the bombing. If there was any trace of integrity in the operation, it was that very few people in Washington ever pretended that all the killing and bombing were for the good of the Cambodian people. Cambodia was just real estate for a war that overwhelmed her.

For Kissinger, the use of American power in Cambodia was not a moral question. It was only a logical extension of his doctrine that force – a deliberately shocking use of force – was required on occasion to advance the cause of diplomacy – in this case, the negotiation of a dignified American withdrawal from Indochina.

During most of 1969, Kissinger had tried to be logical with Hanoi, but America's logic didn't travel well. In November, 1969, he had applauded the President's address to the "silent majority" because he believed that by temporarily silencing the Administration's critics, it bought more time for the policy of gradual withdrawal. Now, in Cambodia, in May, 1970, he watched the United States demonstrate to Hanoi – and to Moscow and Peking, too – that it would use its military muscle in an effort to compel North Vietnam to abandon its dream of conquering South Vietnam by force.

It was time, Kissinger believed, for another try at serious negotiations.

Frustration in Paris

On July 1, 1970, the day after the last GI left Cambodia, President Nixon publicly signaled Hanoi that he was ready to resume negotiations by appointing one of the country's most respected and experienced diplomats, David Bruce, to head the American negotiating team in Paris.

Bruce, who had served as U.S. Ambassador to West Germany, France and Great Britain, arrived in the French capital in early August.

While Bruce was being briefed on the substantive distinction between a one-track and a two-track negotiating approach, Nixon and Kissinger were privately preparing a new proposal for breaking the deadlock. For several months a Vietnam Special Studies Group (VSSG), chaired by Kissinger, had been working on one key element of the proposal — a cease-fire. VSSG — consisting of the Under Secretary of State and the Deputy Secretary of Defense, high-ranking representatives of the CIA and the JCS, and other government experts — supervised a detailed examination (similar to the early SALT studies) of three different kinds of cease-fire in twenty of South Vietnam's forty-four provinces.

The first kind of cease-fire called for the withdrawal of all North Vietnamese troops from South Vietnam; this was the goal the United States had been seeking for years, without success. The second kind of cease-fire faced up to the fact that the North Vietnamese could not be totally dislodged from South Vietnam; a major American concession to Hanoi, it focused on the idea of regrouping the North Vietnamese troops in certain designated areas of South Vietnam. The third kind of cease-fire went from concession to capitulation; it in effect accepted Hanoi's claim that North Vietnamese troops could operate throughout South Vietnam, regardless of Saigon's counterclaim that Hanoi had no such right. That was dubbed a "cease-fire-in-place," and it called upon the North Vietnamese to do no more than stop fighting — thereby allowing them to retain political control over all the territory then under their military control.

Kissinger urged the President to test the third alternative — the cease-fire-in-place. He believed it was the most realistic of the three plans; and he hoped it might be sufficiently enticing to win Hanoi's eventual agreement. Two key State Department aides, Sullivan and Habib, backed Kissinger's belief that any successful negotiated settlement of the war would have to reflect the existing battlefield situation. General Abrams and President Thieu were bitterly opposed to the idea of a cease-fire-in-place; they were supported by Ambassador Bunker. From their vantage point in Saigon, they regarded such a proposal as "too risky" — as "militarily unbearable."

Before the Cambodian invasion, Nixon agreed with the Abrams-Bunker view that a cease-fire-in-place would pose too great a threat to the Thieu regime. But after that sixty-day spectacular, he developed considerable respect for ARVN's capabilities, and changed his mind. By midsummer the Kissinger proposal for a cease-fire-in-place moved center stage in Nixon's plans.

After winning the President's endorsement, Kissinger plotted a new approach to Hanoi. He urged Bruce to arrange another round of secret talks with the North Vietnamese. Hanoi signaled its readiness to talk by sending Xuan Thuy back to Paris after an absence of several months. In September, 1970, Kissinger crisscrossed the Atlantic twice for secret meetings with the North Vietnamese negotiator. He told Xuan Thuy that the United States did not wish to "humiliate" North Vietnam, occupy any of its territory, deprive it of political rewards already gained in twenty-five years of nonstop warfare — or even preserve American military bases in South Vietnam. In fact, he explained, the United States was willing to give the VC a "reasonable chance" at acquiring political power in South Vietnam through nonviolent means. Although the new American proposal for a cease-fire-in-place was not to be made public until October, it is quite likely that Kissinger informed Xuan Thuy of this departure in American policy.

None of this reassuring talk seemed to make any impression on the emissary from Hanoi. It soon became apparent that Xuan Thuy had no mandate to negotiate any new initiatives; all he could do was to restate Hanoi's familiar positions. Kissinger decided after these two September sessions that he would "never again" meet Xuan Thuy alone. "It's just a total waste of my time," Kissinger said. "He has no authority except to deliver messages. I sort of like Xuan Thuy. I have nothing against him personally. I am not saying he is a hard-liner. But he has no flexibility. All he can do is read his speech. Le Duc Tho has the authority to negotiate. Xuan Thuy does not."

Kissinger was back in Washington when Ambassador Bruce formally laid the new American peace plan on the negotiating table in Paris on October 8. In addition to its unprecedented call for a cease-fire-in-place, it contained four other major points, the most significant of which was a presidential commitment, for the first time, to a total withdrawal of American troops from South Vietnam. The other three points provided for what the United States regarded as a fair and reasonable political settlement, an international peace conference, and the immediate and unconditional release of all prisoners of war.

Kissinger trusted no one but himself to put the right sheen on this new program. In a series of briefings for newsmen, he stressed the fact that this was the first comprehensive U.S. plan to end the war — a plan that went well beyond the statement of principles enunciated by the President in his May, 1969, speech. Significantly, he said nothing about the key switch in American policy — the retreat from the previous negotiating proposal of "mutual withdrawal" to the proposal for a cease-fire-in-place. In fact, when reporters peppered him with questions about it, he was deliberately evasive.

One reporter asked point-blank, "Are we abandoning the previous requirement for 'mutual withdrawal'?" Kissinger replied, "No," adding, "of course, a lot depends on how you define 'mutuality.' But we are not abandoning this general principle."

Another reporter tried to force Kissinger to be more precise. "In other words, you are saying that the North Vietnamese have to withdraw their forces as we have been insisting all along when we withdraw ours?" he asked. "That is essentially correct, yes," Kissinger answered, "that is, as part of the negotiations."

The President's adviser usually tried to preserve his reputation for credibility with the press, but this was obviously one time when he felt the need to shave the truth for the sake of policy.

While Kissinger was deftly camouflaging this major U.S. concession from the American people, he made certain that the North Vietnamese caught the full implication of the change. They got the message — not only directly, from Bruce in Paris, but also indirectly, from Soviet Ambassador Dobrynin and Polish Ambassador Jerzy Michalowski in Washington. Both Communist diplomats spotted the significance of the change, checked with key State and White House officials, and then urgently cabled their discovery to Hanoi.

The North Vietnamese were unimpressed. They wanted no part of the new U.S. approach, even though it provided for the pullout of American troops from South Vietnam while their own troops would be permitted to remain. This major American concession was not enough for them. They continued to insist that Washington guarantee their political victory in the south before they would allow the Americans to withdraw "with honor." Despite all the time he had spent grappling with the Vietnam problem, Kissinger still did not fully appreciate this central feature of Hanoi's policy.

By the end of 1970, the situation looked even more bleak than it had a year before. On Christmas Eve, in a year-end review of foreign policy, Kissinger admitted to reporters, "We have been disappointed that negotiations have not been more rapid. And we had higher hopes for the peace initiative in October than have so far been realized." The depressing stalemate on the diplomatic front led inexorably to another turn of the military screw.

Laos — the southeastern sliver, where the Ho Chi Minh network of trails snaked through the forests for hundreds and hundreds of miles — was what the military was fond of calling a "lucrative" target. The trails had been bombed for years by U.S. aircraft, but there had never been an effort to cut them on the ground. No President had ever been willing to authorize any massive ground-troop action against the trails, although the military had been urging such action against the NVA's critical supply route for many years. Beginning in the summer of 1970, Nixon had been receiving enthusiastic reports about ARVN's new fighting spirit. ARVN had been tested in Cambodia and, Abrams maintained, had "hacked it." Now, in the first days of 1971, Nixon decided it was time to allow ARVN to hack its way into Laos.

Kissinger had little initial enthusiasm for the Laos operation, but he did nothing to block it. In mid-January, the strategy for the attack was approved by the President. Lam Son 619, as the South Vietnamese termed the operation, had a variety of objectives: to cut the Ho Chi Minh supply trails, to destroy NVA caches, to prevent the NVA from stabbing into the northern provinces of South Vietnam, to buy still more time for Vietnamization. Spilling North Vietnamese blood on the trails in Laos would save ARVN and GI blood in South Vietnam. Nixon realized that he could not send American troops across the border to fight alongside ARVN as he had done in Cambodia. The Cooper-Church amendment barred any such military involvement. But the amendment did not prevent massive U.S. air support for the twenty-thousand-man ARVN force when it struck into Laos on February 8. Once again, as in the case of Cambodia, this air support was critical; without it — without U.S. planes bombing, strafing, ferrying ARVN troops, hauling heavy artillery, transporting supplies and food — the operation could not have moved one foot across the border.

The Laos operation never lived up to expectations. While ARVN troops occasionally got in their military licks, many units were chewed up by superior Communist firepower. Thousands of ARVN troops fled in terror. One survivor, Sergeant Nguyen Van Duc, chose to attribute NVA aggressiveness to more than simple motivation. "The enemy was doped," he later said, in a state of shock. "I heard they were given 'no fear' medicine that made them fanatical and insensible to our fire. They kept coming in, running in on us, over the dead bodies of their friends."

What stunned millions of Americans, watching fragmentary reports of the operation on television, was the sight of ARVN soldiers clinging to the landing skids of American helicopters as they returned to Vietnam from the battleground. Some ill-fated soldiers fell to their deaths before the choppers landed. Others were pushed off while the choppers were still on the ground. "We have to think about ourselves, too," one American pilot said. "You just cannot lift this bird with fifteen guys clinging to it."

Forty-four days after it began, it was over — ahead of schedule. ARVN pulled out hastily. American correspondents described it as a rout. It was not a rout, Thieu retorted angrily, it was good strategy. "The object," he insisted, "is to surprise the enemy when ready to withdraw." He described the operation as ARVN's "biggest victory ever," and ARVN officers turned in statistical reports of enemy killed, caches taken, and trails cut that defied simple arithmetic. Their reports recalled the testimony of Lieutenant William Calley at the My Lai trial. "It was very important to tell the people back home we're killing more of the enemy than they were killing us," Calley said. "You just made a body count off the top of your head. Anything went into the body count: VC, buffalo, pigs, cows. Something was dead. You put it into your body count."

The Pentagon predictably supported Thieu's claims. The fact that Hanoi emerged from Lam Son 619 with a psychological victory did not prevent the JCS from hailing the operation enthusiastically as another success for the South Vietnamese. Kissinger, who had previously been dubious about ARVN, was beginning to accept the Pentagon's estimate. In a private report to the President, he struck a new upbeat note. "Our assessment is that the balance in the Indochina peninsula has swung in favor of the South Vietnamese," he wrote, soon after the Laos operation ended.

> Three years ago, ARVN units were engaged against enemy units in and close to South Vietnam's own population centers. Now ARVN units have shown themselves able to deal with the enemy threat in sanctuary areas without the support of U.S. ground combat forces or advisers while keeping their won territory pacified as well.
>
> They have demonstrated the ability to mount a complex multi-division operation in conditions of a difficult and unfamiliar terrain, adverse

weather and against a well-prepared enemy. Moreover, this is being achieved with a U.S. presence which has diminished by some 260,000 men since 1969.

Kissinger even seemed to enjoy the whimsical thought that one day a "fighting ARVN" would be unleashed against North Vietnam. In the middle of the Laos operation, Kissinger appeared with us on the "CBS Morning News," his first spot-news television interview. Quite pointedly, he declined to scotch a budding rumor that ARVN might soon direct its fury north of the seventeenth parallel. Kissinger would say no more than, "It's not the dominant probability at this moment." In fact, ARVN had no such plans, and Kissinger knew it, but he enjoyed this exercise in psychological warfare. It was designed to keep Hanoi offstride.

In early March, Kissinger, in the words of Washington columnist Mary McGrory, opened a "little spring offensive of his own." On a quiet Saturday afternoon he invited a trio of peace militants into the Situation Room of the White House. The Justice Department had just named them as co-conspirators in the Berrigan brothers' alleged plot to kidnap him. They talked for over an hour — Tom Davidson, twenty-five-year-old son of an Episcopal minister; William Davidon, a forty-four-year-old Quaker and Professor of Physics at Haverford College; and Sister Beverly Bell, a forty-four-year-old Sister of Notre Dame de Namur. After apologizing for an unfortunate remark he had made about "sex-starved nuns," Kissinger explained that he had wanted to see them in order to discuss the issues underlying the Berrigan case.

Afterward, Davidson told McGrory, "The scary part of it is he really is a nice man. He's got this weird thing for us who operate out of the morality bag. He sees himself as the conscience of the Administration. Of course our feelings about what conscience is are quite different." Davidon described the meeting as having an eerie quality. "There we were," he said, "accused of wanting to bomb, sitting with a man whose policies had brought about a bombing that was actually going on as we talked. I was talking to a man who considers mass murder, in certain circumstances, justified. I told him I thought war had no legitimacy."

The following week Kissinger issued a breakfast invitation to Senator George McGovern, who was a declared candidate for the Democratic presidential nomination. The two men talked for an hour and a half. McGovern told Kissinger that the Vietnam war was "almost one hundred percent wrong from beginning to end." Kissinger did not deny that American intervention had been a mistake, but he did point out that the President was limited by his constituency, by the overall world picture, and by other "outside" factors. McGovern later informed reporters that he was surprised by the extent of Kissinger's concern about the public reaction to the war and by his seeming lack of concern about the cost of the war in Asian lives.

A few days later Kissinger invited Eugene McCarthy, the 1968 peace candidate, to lunch at the White House. Just a few weeks before, McCarthy had told an antiwar teach-in at Harvard that there was "something to be said for the medieval practice of executing or exiling counselors who give bad advice. While I do not advocate this course," McCarthy said, "I have reservations about certain people, after giving bad advice, being welcomed back to the academic community." Kissinger had always been extremely sensitive on this subject, but it did not come up at the luncheon meeting. Kissinger and McCarthy talked instead about Michel de Ceteau, a French intellectual, about Zionism, the Dreyfus case, and other things mostly unrelated to Vietnam. "Each of us," McCarthy later recalled, "was using his best generalizations and his best quotes."

On March 25, Kissinger invited his old Harvard colleague, John Kenneth Galbraith, a longtime opponent of the war, to a White House breakfast. They, too, discussed a wide range of subjects — including Vietnam.

Kissinger hoped that these exchanges would help create more popular understanding for the Administration's unpopular policy — and buy more time, in effect, for the United States to wriggle its way out of Indochina. He consistently rejected a clean break.

Kissinger regarded every spasm of military activity as a prelude to negotiations. He had given diplomacy a chance after the Cambodian invasion; now, after Laos, he was ready to give it another chance. In the spring of 1971, he encouraged the President to compose still another peace plan. It was, for the most part, an elaboration of the one Bruce had tabled on October 8, 1970, but it advanced two new and significant concessions that, he felt, might finally bridge the gap between Washington and Hanoi.

First, it pledged a total American troop withdrawal "within six months" after the signing of an agreement — a major move toward meeting Hanoi's demand for a definite date for U.S. withdrawal. Second, it promised the resignation of President Thieu one month before nationwide elections in South Vietnam — a bow in the direction of Hanoi's requirement that Thieu be dumped. In addition there were the familiar proposals for an Indochina-wide cease-fire-in-place, an immediate and unconditional release of all POWs, international supervision of the cease-fire and the elections, and an international conference to "guarantee" the implementation of the new agreement.

This peace plan, which was not made public until January, 1972, not only launched the United States into a new round of secret negotiations with the North Vietnamese, it also confirmed Henry Kissinger as the undisputed master of the art of clandestine diplomacy. In August, 1969, he had met secretly with Xuan Thuy. In early 1970 he had made four secret trips to Paris to confer with Le Duc Tho. In September, 1970, he had met twice with Xuan Thuy. Now, in 1971, he would fly the Atlantic six times to meet the top North Vietnamese negotiator. Not once, after the first close call in 1969, did an army of pursuing journalists trap him into disclosing his mission.

At each of these six negotiating sessions in the spring and summer of 1971, the secret drama kept building, until Kissinger could, as he once put it, "almost taste peace." The first of these 1971 Paris exchanges took place on May 31, the Monday of the long Memorial Day weekend. The President had flown by helicopter to Camp David, diverting the attention of the White House press corps. Kissinger did his part, too: he turned up at a party and tossed off a few of his latest witticisms. While the guests were still laughing, he slipped away, departing for Paris Sunday night.

With some pride of authorship, Kissinger presented the new American proposal to Le Duc Tho. In an attempt to create an atmosphere of frankness, he explained that the United States Government knew — "we are not children" — that when the war in South Vietnam was over and the peace treaty was signed, the Americans would be ten thousand miles away and the North Vietnamese only three hundred miles away. It was therefore in America's interest that the settlement be fair — not only to Washington but also to Hanoi. The United States, he stressed, wanted a settlement that North Vietnam would "want to keep."

Kissinger placed special emphasis on the cease-fire-in-place, explaining that by its terms the North Vietnamese troops would *not* have to withdraw from South Vietnam. Kissinger's presentation was no more persuasive than Bruce's the previous October. Le Duc Tho rejected it. "The North Vietnamese," Kissinger later recalled, "insisted that any proposal that did not include political elements could not even be negotiated." It

1934: Henry Kissinger, eleven, with his arm around his brother, Walter, ten, in Fürth, four years before the Kissinger family escaped from Nazi Germany and fled to the United States. "The other children would beat us up," Kissinger once recalled, with understatement, about his youth during the heyday of Hitler. The Kissingers settled in upper Manhattan's Washington Heights section, then a haven for Jewish refugees from Germany.

From the Harvard yearbook, 1950:
"HENRY ALFRED KISSINGER. Born May 27, 1923 in Fuerth, Germany. Prepared at George Washington High School, New York, New York. Attended Lafayette College. Home address: 615 Fort Washington Avenue, New York, New York. College address: Adams House. PBH. National Veterans Scholarship, Detur 1948, Phi Beta Kappa, Senior Sixteen. Served in Army. Field of concentration: Government. Married Anne Fleischer on February 6, 1949."

March, 1967: At Harvard, as a professor in the Department of Government. It was at Harvard that he received his B.A. degree *summa cum laude* in 1950, his M.A. in 1952, and his Ph.D. in 1954. Prior to his appointment by President-elect Richard Nixon as Assistant for National Security Affairs on December 2, 1968, Kissinger had won widespread recognition as a foreign policy specialist and had served the Government in various consultancies dating back to 1950.

February 23, 1969: Aboard *Air Force One*, on President Nixon's first visit to Europe, only a month after inauguration, Henry Kissinger setting the pattern of personally briefing reporters – and taking their questions — on the objectives of U.S. foreign policy. It was a practice he would follow at home and abroad; no other senior adviser to the President was more available to newsmen. Listening, over Kissinger's shoulder, presidential spokesman Ronald Ziegler.

May 23, 1969: During his first months as the President's adviser, in his first office, in the basement of the West Wing of the White House. He later moved up to more comfortable quarters at street level. Beginning in the fall of 1973, he would spend most of his time at the elaborate suite, on the seventh floor of the Department of State, that went with the post of Secretary of State.

October 25, 1970: With Soviet Ambassador Anatoly Dobrynin, Soviet Foreign Minister Andrei Gromyko, President Nixon, and Secretary of State William Rogers, at the White House, discussing Soviet-American relations, with special emphasis on a strategic arms limitation agreement.

February 10, 1971: With his employer, at the White House. The wintry sun
streaming between President Nixon and Henry Kissinger suggests the question
that has been put more than once to the President's adviser: whether any "daylight" ever developed between them on certain controversial aspects of U.S. policy.
"I have one absolute rule which is that I never discuss publicly what I recommend
to the President" is his standard response.

July 13, 1971: Henry Kissinger being welcomed home by President Nixon, at San Clemente, on his return from his secret visit to China. It wasn't until two days later that the President, in a dramatic television announcement, disclosed that his adviser had held talks in Peking with Premier Chou En-lai from July 9 to 11, returning with an invitation for the President to visit China.

September 26, 1971: At Walla Walla, Washington. His autograph in demand, two months after his secret visit to China, when Henry Kissinger's reputation as President Nixon's "secret agent" made him front-page and magazine-cover news. Even critics of his Vietnam policy joined in celebrating the opening to Peking after more than two decades of mutual hostility between the United States and the People's Republic of China.

October 12, 1971: A candid portrait of harmony — at least outward — among the President's senior advisers. "The loner in the White House," as Henry Kissinger has often been described, had his differences of diplomatic opinion with Secretary of State Rogers (at Kissinger's left); Kissinger's intellectual independence and sophisticated life-style were viewed dimly by his coequals on the President's staff — H. R. Haldeman, White House Chief of Staff (with hand camera) and John Erlichman, Chief Domestic Adviser (in doorway, back to camera). Standing in the doorway is Charles Colson, an attorney and a Nixon loyalist, who was one of those always suspicious of Kissinger.

October 16, 1971: Chatting with reporters at Andrews Air Force Base, Maryland, prior to his departure on his second trip to China, to set up the presidential visit of February, 1972. This time, unlike the occasion of his first mission to Peking in July, 1971, there was no secrecy about his destination.

October 20, 1971: Arriving in Peking on his second trip and being welcomed (left to right) by acting Defense Minister Yeh Chien-ying, Chi Chao-chu (who had once studied at Harvard) of the Ministry of Foreign Affairs, and Foreign Minister Chi Peng-fei.

October, 1971: With the advance American party in Peking. The purpose of this trip was to arrange the details of President Nixon's itinerary for his February, 1972, visit.

October 26, 1971: Touring the Great Wall of China while, at the United Nations, the General Assembly voted to admit Peking and expel Taiwan. The Administration's effort to keep Taiwan in the UN along with the admission of Peking was badly undercut by the U.S. decision to keep Henry Kissinger in Peking two days longer than originally scheduled. It prompted many analysts to regard the U.S. fight on behalf of Taiwan as a charade.

October 26, 1971: With Chinese Foreign Minister Chi Peng-fei, pausing on the famous Avenue of Animals along the Sacred Way leading to the tombs of the emperors of the Ming Dynasty. From a selection of huge stone creatures, Henry Kissinger chose to pose with an elephant.

October 27, 1971: It was at this briefing in the Press Room of the White House — he had just returned from his second visit to China — that the Administration for the first time permitted Henry Kissinger to be identified as Henry Kissinger rather than as "a White House source." By then, he had so established his diplomatic credentials that the Administration's image-makers, originally determined to preserve the spotlight only for the President, finally allowed Kissinger to emerge from anonymity.

February 21, 1972: At the summit during President Nixon's visit to China — a one-hour meeting, shortly after his arrival in Peking, with Chairman Mao Tse-tung, at his villa at Chung Nan Hai in the Forbidden City. Their meeting had not been announced in advance; it was later given prominent display both by *Jenmin Jih Pao*, the Communist Party newspaper, and by Chinese television. Premier Chou En-lai, Tan Wen-sheng (interpreter), Chairman Mao, President Nixon, and Henry Kissinger.

February 26, 1972: With Premier Chou En-lai, in the Great Hall of the People, in Peking, during President Nixon's visit to China. With a toast of *mao tai*, a fiery sorghum liquor, they drank to the success of the Sino-American summit.

March 17, 1972: With Anatoly Dobrynin, Soviet Ambassador to the United States since 1962, in the Map Room of the White House, two months before President Nixon's departure for his first summit with Communist Party Chief Leonid Brezhnev, in Moscow. Dobrynin and Henry Kissinger — the "Big Two" one notch below the top — met frequently and privately over the years, each championing his own country's objectives within the framework of a realistic détente.

April 11, 1972: With President Nixon, less than two months after the summit visit to China, briefing the Senate Majority and Minority Leaders prior to their departure on a visit to the Chinese mainland. Montana Democrat Mike Mansfield had served as a Marine in China in the early 1920s; Pennsylvania Republican Hugh Scott is a noted collector of and authority on Chinese antiquities.

May 24, 1972: With President Nixon, Secretary of State Rogers (center) and Leonid Brezhnev (center right) in the Kremlin, during one of the many signing ceremonies in the course of the U.S.-Soviet summit in May, 1972. The Moscow summit took place on schedule, two weeks after the President had ordered the mining of the harbors of North Vietnam in the wake of Hanoi's April offensive.

May 29, 1972: With President Nixon, strolling within the Kremlin walls in Moscow, during the first of the summit meetings between the United States and the Soviet Union. It was the first visit ever by a United States president to the Soviet capital.

was not enough for the Americans to pull out; they had to deliver an acceptable political arrangement before leaving.

The second time Nixon's peripatetic adviser flew off for a secret rendezvous with the North Vietnamese, he recruited no less than the city of London as a decoy. He arrived in the British capital Thursday, June 24, lunched on Friday with Prime Minister Edward Heath, and then engaged in a series of meetings with Sir Burke Trend, known as the "Kissinger of Great Britain," on the functioning of the NSC and its London counterpart. As the sun came up on Saturday morning, Kissinger flew off to Paris, conferred with the North Vietnamese, and returned to London by nightfall. A handful of British officials knew he had been to Paris, but just what he was doing there was something else again. He spent a pleasant, highly visible Sunday in London and was back at his desk in the White House on Monday morning.

It was at this second secret session in 1971 that Le Duc Tho unveiled a nine-point peace plan. For the first time Kissinger could see the shape of a possible compromise. Each point was vague enough to embrace the views of both sides, and none was specific enough to offend the Americans. Kissinger surprised the North Vietnamese negotiator by quickly accepting Hanoi's plan as the "basis" for negotiating a settlement of the war. "From then on," Kissinger later explained, "every American proposal followed the sequence and the subject matter of the nine points."

But it was still rough going. Four days later, when Kissinger was back in Washington, the North Vietnamese in Paris publicly proposed a totally different peace plan — an old-fashioned, hard-line document that called for nothing less than Thieu's immediate removal and a date for total U.S. withdrawal. Kissinger immediately cabled Paris: was Le Duc Tho backing away from his secret June 26 plan? No, the North Vietnamese envoy assured him, he still stood behind his plan. Kissinger then grasped the essence of North Vietnamese strategy: while they remained willing to negotiate seriously in private, they would continue to engage in public propaganda clearly intended to inflame antiwar sentiment in the United States.

July was a doubleheader; Kissinger met twice with the North Vietnamese — once on the twelfth, the second time on the twenty-sixth. The fact that he was in Paris on July 12 was no secret. The U.S. Embassy announced that he was there to confer with Ambassador Bruce. What the press did not know was that Kissinger was on his way back from a trailblazing excursion to Peking — a top secret stopover on an otherwise highly publicized round-the-world trip that had taken him to South Vietnam, India and Pakistan. A large group of newsmen, spurred by rumors from Karachi that he might meet in Paris with a high-ranking North Vietnamese official, tried to keep up with him in the French capital. Kissinger managed to give all of them the slip. He later remarked that it was easier to get into Peking unobserved than into Choisy-le-Roi.

That evening, much to his delight, Kissinger was spotted dining at a two-star restaurant, Chez Garin, with Margaret Osmer, a television producer who was vacationing in Paris. The next morning photographs of them appeared in newspapers throughout the world. "Henry," observed Mel Elfin, Washington bureau chief of *Newsweek*, "is the only man I know who uses his private life to conceal his professional activities."

For four hours that afternoon, Kissinger had reviewed Hanoi's nine-point proposal, point by point. There was not enough time to complete the job, and the two sides agreed to resume the process two weeks later. On July 26, as the Apollo astronauts were blasting off for the moon, Kissinger was preparing to meet with the North Vietnamese. The lift-off at Cape Kennedy provided a sensational distraction.

By day's end on July 26, Kissinger and Le Duc Tho could actually measure progress — the scarcest commodity in their long negotiation. They had narrowed their differences on all but two of Hanoi's nine points. Kissinger could hardly suppress his excitement. He began to visualize "the shape of a deal." He believed he was on the threshold of a breakthrough — and well before the 1972 presidential election year, too, so that no one could accuse him of adjusting diplomacy to domestic politics.

For the next few weeks, Kissinger and the President worked on a revamped American peace plan that they hoped would accommodate the differences between Hanoi and Washington on the two remaining points: the terms of the American pullout and the political future of South Vietnam. On August 15, their plan was ready. While the President was announcing a radical change in his monetary and trade policy, Kissinger was quietly packing his bags for a fifth journey to Paris. The following day, Kissinger met with Le Duc Tho and presented an eight-point plan which, in his view, not only closely paralleled Hanoi's nine-point plan,* but also attempted to solve the two outstanding problems.

---

* The missing point was Hanoi's claim to war reparations. Kissinger later explained, "We took the position that we could not in honor make a peace settlement in which we would be obligated . . . to pay reparations." But, with specific presidential

To meet the first North Vietnamese objection, the United States proposed a hard date for total American troop withdrawal — August 1, 1972, provided an agreement in principle on the entire package could be reached by November 1, 1971. On the second point, the United States offered, first, a pledge of neutrality in the upcoming October 3 presidential election, in which Thieu was pitted against Vice-President Nguyen Cao Ky and General Duong Van (Big) Minh; next, a declaration of American willingness to limit aid to South Vietnam if Russian and Chinese aid to North Vietnam were limited too; and, finally, a statement of U.S. adherence to the principle of nonalignment for all the countries of Indochina. Kissinger felt that he was bending over backward to meet Hanoi's objections. He remained highly optimistic.

It took the North Vietnamese three weeks to consider the eight-point plan — a critical period during which they saw Ky and Minh pull out of the presidential race, leaving Thieu in the absurd position of running against himself. On September 13, after an additional week of intensive preparations, the sixth and last in this series of secret Kissinger–Le Duc Tho sessions took place in Choisy-le-Roi, a working-class suburb of Paris.

The North Vietnamese welcomed Kissinger by immediately turning thumbs down on the latest American plan, claiming that it did not begin to meet their objections on the two key unresolved issues. They complained that the proposed American withdrawal date was too far in the future, and that, since Thieu was now running unopposed, an American pledge of neutrality in the October 3 election was meaningless.

Kissinger realized that his optimism had been totally unjustified. It was clear that he was not going to get his peace settlement before 1972.

He now fully realized, for the first time, that when Le Duc Tho insisted time and again that the United States had to deliver South Vietnam to the Communists before the Communists would allow the United States to leave South Vietnam, he meant what he was saying. It was only in the third year of his official negotiations with the North Vietnamese that Kissinger finally stripped away the veil of illusion and grasped the central factor in Hanoi's calculation: the North Vietnamese really expected the United States to join them in displacing Thieu.

---

authorization, he did offer "a massive reconstruction program for all of Indochina in which North Vietnam could share to the extent of several billion dollars." An early estimate at the White House was that Hanoi would get one-third of a 7.5 billion-dollar aid program over a five-year period.

There had clearly been miscalculations on both sides. Kissinger had expected Hanoi to appreciate the logic of his position and the flexibility of his offer. The North Vietnamese, on the other hand, had assumed that Kissinger shared their cynical view of Thieu's uncontested campaign for reelection. They had witnessed the erosion of the original American negotiating position and concluded that the United States was angling to dump Thieu during the campaign — "generously leaving the methods to us," as Kissinger later remarked with a rueful smile. In fact, Kissinger had never intended to join Le Duc Tho in the decapitation of the Thieu regime. He had consistently proposed the opening of a "political process" that would not be "loaded in any direction," but it was not until the September 13 meeting that the North Vietnamese finally realized that he too meant what he was saying — that he was not seeking a cover for total surrender but a genuine compromise settlement. When they realized that this was the true American position, the North Vietnamese broke off the negotiations. They were not willing to settle for a mere crack at power; they wanted a sure thing.

On October 11, eight days after Thieu's embarrassing reelection, the United States secretly transmitted a slightly revised peace plan to Hanoi, proposing a meeting between Kissinger and Le Duc Tho for November 1. An accompanying note pointed out that this was "one last attempt to negotiate a just settlement before the end of 1971."

Two weeks later, Hanoi replied that Le Duc Tho could not meet Kissinger on November 1, and suggested November 20 instead. The United States accepted the date. But on November 17, Hanoi informed Kissinger that Le Duc Tho was "ill" and suggested a meeting with Xuan Thuy instead. Kissinger stuck to his guns. "No point would be served," he responded, by a meeting with Xuan Thuy alone. He would meet with Le Duc Tho or no one. Hanoi did not respond. The result, once again, was deadlock.

By Christmas 1971, Kissinger was again deeply discouraged about Vietnam. The records at MACV in Saigon showed that in the nearly three years since Inauguration Day, while Nixon and Kissinger and Le Duc Tho and Xuan Thuy were pursuing a policy of talking and fighting, more than fourteen thousand GIs had been killed and more than one hundred thousand wounded. Vietnamese casualties on both sides were much higher. Increasingly, the antiwar forces had been demanding that the Administration set a date for American troop withdrawal and negotiate a compromise settlement of the war. Kissinger had attempted to do both — but his efforts had been secret, and they had failed. After three years on the Vietnam roller coaster — riding to the peak of optimism one day, plunging to the depths of depression the next — Kissinger felt that he was as far away from a deal on Vietnam as he had ever been.

Every now and then, through the frustration and fog of Vietnam, an engineering scheme would cross his mind. If we could build a dam across the mouth of the Mekong River, he would wonder aloud, thereby flooding the entire country up to at least twelve feet, then maybe . . .

EIGHT

On the Brink in Jordan and Cienfuegos

K ISSINGER WAS NO EXPERT on the Middle East — before he became Nixon's adviser in December, 1968, he had never set foot in an Arab country and he had been to Israel only twice — but he was an expert on Soviet-American relations. Instinctively, he sought solutions for most international problems in a big-power context. The Middle East was no exception. He believed that Russia and the United States had an obligation to foster an accommodation between Israel and the Arab states.

This had been his view for many years. In July, 1958, when the Cold War was still a way of life, even at Harvard, he had recommended that the U.S. propose "big-power recognition" of "all frontiers" there against "outside forcible change" — and do so at a summit meeting. Normally Kissinger opposed summits, except for the specific purpose of ratifying important decisions; but he viewed developments in the Middle East with such alarm that he was prepared to make an exception. He believed there was a good chance that President Nasser of Egypt would soon try to extend his control over Jordan and Lebanon, thus creating a giant United Arab Republic; and he feared that such a sweeping extension of Nasserite control would almost surely trigger a preemptive Israeli strike against Cairo. He assumed that Russia would rush to Egypt's support, America would feel obliged to support Israel — and the upshot would be a big-power confrontation in the area.

Almost a decade later, in early June, 1967, such a confrontation seemed a distinct possibility. Nasser tried to block the Israeli port of Elath, after evicting the UN supervisors in the Sinai. Israel did not wait. General Yitzhak Rabin, the Israeli Chief of Staff, ordered the Israeli air force to attack Egypt. In less than a day, the Egyptian air force was destroyed; in less than a week, the Arabs surrendered. In the Six Day War, Israel gained control over all of the Sinai, the Old City of Jerusalem, the West Bank, the Gaza Strip, and the Golan Heights — a staggering humiliation for the Arabs, and for their Soviet patrons as well. Only extraordinary restraint and a mutually reassuring "hot line" conversation between President Johnson and Soviet Premier Alexei Kosygin kept the big powers from becoming embroiled in the war.

When Nixon became President twenty months later, the Middle East was still an acutely troubled area. At his first news conference, on January 27, 1969, Nixon sounded a note of alarm. "We need new initiatives and new leadership on the part of the United States," he proclaimed, "in order to cool off the situation in the Mideast. I consider it a powder keg, very explosive. . . . The next explosion in the Mideast, I think, could involve very well a confrontation between the nuclear powers, which we want to avoid."

If Vietnam was Nixon's most constant problem, the Middle East was his most dangerous. He was determined to strike an activist posture. Even before his inauguration, he had dispatched William Scranton to spread his diplomatic message of "evenhandedness" throughout the area, quickening pulses in Arab capitals and creating anxiety in Tel Aviv. And he had appointed Joseph Sisco, a skillful and energetic career officer, to be Assistant Secretary of State for Near Eastern and South Asian Affairs.

Sisco quickly formulated a policy paper on the Middle East that became the basis for an all-day NSC discussion of the problem on February 1, 1969. It also became the basis for Nixon's Middle East policy until the late spring of 1970, when it became clear that it had not worked.

As Sisco explained his policy, it had several objectives. Russia's rising influence in the area had to be contained. The Arab states had to be persuaded that Nixon intended to be strictly objective, detached and "evenhanded." Israel had to be coaxed into withdrawing from occupied Arab lands — with only "insubstantial" border changes. The United States had to take a direct hand in arranging a "genuine" peace, and Russia had to be made to join in this constructive effort.

Nixon, Rogers, Richardson, Laird, Helms — most of the top officials applauded Sisco's presentation, which was, as usual, clear and knowledgeable. "It is high time," one of them said, "that the United States stop acting as Israel's attorney in the Middle East." Kissinger shared little of this enthusiasm. He was present at the February 1 NSC meeting, just as he was to be present at most NSC deliberations on the Middle East; but he harbored doubts about the policy. In his view, the success of the Sisco policy would depend first, on a high degree of Soviet cooperation — and he wondered whether the Kremlin was ready to provide it — and second, on the willingness of the Arabs and the Israelis to vault over their wide differences — after all, they had yet to exchange one word with each other — and accept, grudgingly, an "imposed" solution.

"My view has always been," Kissinger told us, "that you have to know when to be active and when not to be active. I always thought there had to be a period of stalemate in which the various parties recognize the limits of what they could achieve. That didn't mean one shouldn't make an effort to defuse it. But I was always less optimistic about the possibilities of a real breakthrough than some others."

It was never Kissinger's style to be a wallflower during NSC debates on major policies, but on Nixon's orders he yielded the Middle East to Rogers and Sisco, thus sidestepping a bureaucratic hassle. "You have to give the bureaucracy something they can call their own," Kissinger later quipped. He also, quite consciously, struck a very low profile on the Middle East to avoid becoming a target of Arab extremist propaganda — the kind of venomous anti-Semitic propaganda that Egypt, Syria, Iraq, and some Palestinian groups had hurled at Arthur Goldberg and Eugene and Walt Rostow.

Still, if Kissinger, for various reasons, was forced into an uncharacteristically retiring role in these vital deliberations, he never hesitated to maintain that the United States had "an historical commitment" to Israel and that the preservation of Israel was in the national interest of the United States. He never concealed his strong concern about the Jewish state. As he told one close friend, "Look, anyone who has been through what I've been through has some very special feeling for the survival of the state of Israel." He never forgot that he had lost "many of his relatives in concentration camps," and he told friends that he viewed Israel as "a place of refuge for those who survived." One of those who survived was Kissinger's boyhood chum Kurt Fleischmann. When Kissinger learned in 1971 that Fleischmann had died in England, without ever having achieved his lifelong dream of visiting Israel, he sent a check to the Jewish National Fund to plant a grove of three hundred trees on the Jordan Hills near Jerusalem in memory of his friend from Fürth.

While Kissinger was kept busy in those early months of the Administration restructuring the National Security Council, drafting a new Vietnam policy, and coordinating overall relations with the Soviet Union — including careful preparations for SALT — Rogers and Sisco were meeting with Soviet Ambassador Dobrynin to try to win Kremlin approval of joint Soviet-American guidelines for peace in the Middle East. Concurrently, UN Ambassador Charles Yost met with his French, British and Soviet colleagues in pursuit of similar ends.

In Washington, by late October, 1969, the two sides had reached partial agreement on the guidelines. Rogers accepted the Soviet view that Israel could keep none of the Sinai Peninsula in the ultimate settlement; Dobrynin accepted the American view that demilitarized zones might be established to accommodate Israeli security concerns; and they both agreed that there could be "no rights bestowed by conquest." Nixon was not prepared to barter Israel's very existence for an agreement, but it must have been clear to the Russians that he was apparently ready to yield on many other points. He badly wanted a deal — not only for the sake of tranquillity in the Middle East but also for the chance to set a glowing precedent for other Soviet-American agreements on Indochina and SALT. But the negotiations foundered on such questions as the timing of Israeli withdrawals, guarantees for Israel's security, and the status of the Palestinians and Jerusalem. Russia rejected Rogers's proposals on these issues, even though they went a long way toward meeting Soviet objections. Nixon, disappointed by Soviet intransigence, decided to make the "Rogers Plan" public, and he instructed the Secretary of State to reveal the proposals in a December 9 speech.

Kissinger was not surprised by Russia's rejection, and he made no effort to rush to Rogers's rescue.

The Israelis were not surprised either. They used the Soviet rejection to press for the purchase of an additional fifty Phantom jet fighter planes.

Nixon turned a cold shoulder to the Israeli request. He pledged to maintain a balance of power in the Middle East, but he refused to sell any more planes to Israel.

Kissinger warned Nixon that Israel might begin to feel desperate, watching a steady buildup of Soviet antiaircraft missile sites on the west bank of the Suez Canal that could be used as a cover for launching a cross-canal operation. Israel might take strong unilateral action. Kissinger's warning was prescient. In January, 1970, Israeli planes began to stage a series of lightning attacks against missile sites and other military targets deep in the Egyptian heartland, bombing the very outskirts of Cairo.

Nasser felt humiliated. The Egyptian leader flew secretly to Moscow and pleaded for more military help. The Russians responded in dramatic fashion. They not only sent more military equipment — SAMs, tanks and supersonic jets — but also assumed a direct operational role in the defense of Egypt. They began to fly planes, and they began to man SAM sites, and they began to staff Egyptian army units down to the company level.

The Israelis were forced to stop their deep penetration raids, and they renewed their requests for more American Phantom jets. General Rabin, the dynamic military hero who had become Israel's Ambassador to Washington in 1968, opened a direct and secret channel to the White House, appealing for the President's help over the head of the State Department.

Nixon still refused to sell the jets. Instead, in early April, 1970, he ordered one more complete review of Mideast policy, concentrating on the new Soviet operational role in Egypt, the growing Soviet naval presence in the Mediterranean, and the possibility of coming up with another diplomatic initiative to stop the spiraling cycle of violence in the area. But this time, instead of sitting mutely at the table taking notes, Kissinger began to play a more creative and operational role in the unfolding of American policy. The new Russian involvement provided the context for his first official assignment on the Middle East. "Not without some bloodletting," as he later explained. Rogers and Sisco tried to hold on to their mandate, but Kissinger snapped it away. He ran the new NSC study for only a couple of weeks, when suddenly his attention, and Nixon's, and Rogers's were diverted by Cambodia. The new initiative was not really launched until after the crisis in Southeast Asia and on the college campuses had subsided.

For Kissinger, the Middle East always posed a split-level problem. The Arab-Israeli dispute festered on one level; and the possibility of a Soviet-American confrontation loomed over the other. State Department specialists have never missed a chance to point out that "Kissinger knows next to nothing" about the political and historical conflicts in the area — the irreconcilable Arab-Israeli confrontation superimposed on the bitter and bloody squabbles among the Arabs themselves. And Kissinger would not have argued the point. He often admitted his limitations in this respect, but he usually added, with a touch of sarcasm, that all of the specialists' knowledge, insight and experience had done little to improve the nasty climate in the area.

Kissinger focused on the "big picture" — superpower strategy, Kremlin intentions, the balance of forces, the chances of a general war being sparked by the embers of the local clashes. He believed that neither Russia nor America wanted war in the Middle East; but since both were aligned with the local contestants, they could be drawn into a general war even against their will.

He detailed his views in a briefing for a group of editors on June 26 in San Clemente — part of a post-Cambodia public relations drive by the Administration to woo the regional press. There would be other such briefings on August 14 in New Orleans, August 24 in San Clemente again, September 16 in Chicago, and October 12 in Hartford. Often, in explaining the geopolitical framework of the Middle East problem, Kissinger would fall back on the Balkan analogy. "The nightmare is that no one caused World War I," Kissinger told the editors; "no one wanted it at that particular moment, except Austria and Serbia. All the leaders of major countries actually went on vacation during July, 1914, then came back from vacation and a week later they were in a general war."

The situation in the Middle East was tense — and extremely complicated. It was not, he said, a simple case in which "right confronts wrong." Israel had a population of about two million five hundred thousand, and was surrounded by Arab states with a population of roughly eighty million. Israel had trained manpower, but the Arabs had overwhelming manpower that could be trained. Israel's survival depended, in Kissinger's view, on its "capacity to launch a rapid knockout blow." Under normal conditions, he explained, "if these were two opponents with roughly equal strength, you would say you want to bring about a military balance; but a military balance is death for Israel, because a war of attrition means mathematically that Israel will be destroyed." So, he concluded, "the Israelis have to aim for superiority."

This created an "insoluble dilemma." The Arabs could not accept the idea of Israeli military superiority. They had never accepted the existence of the state of Israel. Now, almost three years after the Israeli victory in the Six Day War, Kissinger went on, the Arabs had begun to feel that they were "living at the mercy" of the Israelis and thereby losing their "sense of dignity." They were becoming irrational and desperate. New radical Arab movements, spawned in this rising tide of frustration – such as Al Fatah and other extremist Palestinian groups – were pledged to overthrow moderate Arab regimes and then to destroy Israel. They sought political and military support from abroad, mostly from Communist countries that sympathized with their anti-Western, antiimperialist tendencies.

Actually, the Russians had been in the business of helping radical Arabs since 1955, when they began to supply Nasser with military and economic aid. But for Kissinger, the disturbing new factor in the situation was the Soviet decision to "inject their own combat manpower into the area," in March, 1970, "literally from one month to the other" changing the balance of forces in the Middle East. This was a critical decision that, Kissinger acknowledged, "no one counted on," implying that it came as a complete surprise to Nixon, to the Israelis, and even to himself. It created the danger that "the eastern Mediterranean might become a Soviet lake."

This danger dawned on Nixon just as he was ordering American troops into Cambodia. Kissinger drew the parallel himself. "It is, of course, nonsense to say that we did what we did in Cambodia in order to impress the Russians in the Middle East," he said. "It was not as simple as that. But we certainly have to keep in mind that the Russians will judge us by the general purposefulness of our performance everywhere. *What they are doing in the Middle East, whatever their intentions, poses the gravest threats in the long run for Western Europe and Japan and therefore for us.*"

Coming from a presidential adviser with Kissinger's power, these were strong words. Kissinger was brooding about a possible change in the strategic balance of power and a loss of oil to run the industrial machine of Western Europe, Japan and, to a lesser extent, the United States. He had an apocalyptic vision, similar to his 1958 vision of doom. If the radical Arabs, encouraged by the Russians, succeeded in taking over Lebanon and Jordan, a distinct possibility in the summer of 1970, then the huge oil reserves of Saudi Arabia would be vulnerable to leftist seizure and control. And then so too would be the oil-rich sheikdoms of the Persian Gulf – and ultimately Iran. Israel would be washed into the sea after a frightful battle. The wealth and strategic value of the Middle East would be denied to the West, and the global balance of power would shift, perhaps irrevocably, in Russia's favor. This explained the crucial importance of Jordan and Lebanon in Kissinger's strategic thinking.

Kissinger concluded the June 26 briefing on a startling note: "We are trying to get a settlement in such a way that the moderate regimes are strengthened, and not the radical regimes," he said. "We are trying to *expel* the Soviet military presence, not so much the advisers, but the combat pilots and the combat personnel, before they become so firmly established."

"*Expel.*"

The next morning, Kissinger used the word again. He told reporters, at still another marathon briefing, that during World War I there had been a theory about how to eliminate the German U-boat menace. Boil up the ocean, he said dramatically, and then the U-boats would have to come to the surface. In this way, they would be "expelled" from the ocean. Murrey Marder, diplomatic reporter for the *Washington Post*, quickly spotted the significance of the comment and, in a long front-page story from San Clemente on June 28, he quoted "high Administration officials" as endeavoring to "expel" the Russians from the Middle East. Most of Marder's colleagues received urgent "rockets" from their home offices, demanding a denial or confirmation. Ziegler issued no denial, and he could offer no confirmation. Kissinger was furious at Marder. For almost a year afterward, he refused to talk to one of Washington's most objective reporters — basically because the "expel" story had produced a rash of editorials criticizing Kissinger for having used such a strong word.

The word "expel" ricocheted off Foreign Ministry desks around the world, as though it were an errant missile. But was it errant, or aimed? Was Kissinger hinting, in the final hours of the Cambodian adventure, that the United States might move militarily against Soviet personnel in Egypt? Or that Israel might move? Surely not. But if not, why had he used the word?

High State Department officials quickly spread their own word — "inadvertent." To Soviet and Egyptian diplomats, and to newsmen, they said, "Henry made a mistake. It was inadvertent, completely inadvertent." The White House, less eagerly, signaled the same message. "Henry did not mean," one spokesman explained, "that the U.S. is going to use force to get the Russians out."

And, in fact, Kissinger did not mean that the United States was going to use force to "expel" the Russians from Egypt, even though he did not mind one bit injecting that possibility into the diplomatic puzzle. It made the Russians wonder and worry. It was an unorthodox diplomatic tactic that delighted Ambassador Rabin but shocked Rogers and Sisco and other State Department officials because it violated their sense of diplomatic decorum.

Kissinger's point was that he could visualize a time when the Egyptians would read certain signals in the international atmosphere and decide on their own to "expel" the Russians. In fact, two years later, at the time of the Moscow summit, the atmosphere did change dramatically. A mood of Soviet-American détente replaced the earlier mood of confrontation. The Egyptians felt betrayed. They came to the conclusion that the Soviet military advisers in Egypt must be pursuing their own selfish national interests rather than preparing for a war against Israel that could expand into a major confrontation with the United States. Within a few months after the summit, President Anwar Sadat, who had become President after Nasser's death in late September, 1970, astonished most observers by ordering Soviet combat personnel out of Egypt — and expelling a large number of Soviet advisers, too. Kissinger's attitude was one of quiet satisfaction. The Russians, in fact, had been "expelled."

Kissinger set off his verbal bombshell just as the United States was in the final phase of preparing a new diplomatic initiative. This initiative, worked out by Sisco while Kissinger was busy with Cambodia but cleared by his NSC staff, came to be called the "stop shooting, start talking" proposal. It was proposed to Israel, Egypt and Jordan in June. It differed from all previous initiatives in that it ignored Russia and the UN. It was a purely American action.

The "stop shooting" part of the proposal focused on a ninety-day cease-fire along the Suez Canal. The "start talking" part called for negotiations among Israel, Egypt and Jordan based on two "concrete commitments," to quote Sisco. One obliged Egypt and Jordan to recognize Israel's right to exist within "secure and recognized boundaries," and to make peace with Israel; the other obliged Israel to commit itself to the principle of withdrawal, with the understanding that the questions of new boundaries and real security would be settled through negotiation.

For nations locked in a condition of almost nonstop war for twenty-odd years, these were steep conditions. And yet, largely as a result of Sisco's dogged efforts, Jordan agreed; and then, on July 23, Egypt agreed; and finally, on July 31, Israel agreed. The fragile cease-fire along the Suez Canal formally began on August 7, 1970 — but not before an outbreak of temper and tension between Sisco and Kissinger.

On August 5, Kissinger called Sisco to raise a few questions about the terms of the cease-fire. Neither Kissinger nor Sisco chooses to recall the questions, but there were reports at the time that Kissinger was dissatisfied with some of the procedures for checking on whether the cease-fire was being observed. Sisco, who ran a one-man negotiating effort, resented Kissinger's late intercession. He made the point that only one man could run the negotiations, and that man was Joe Sisco. If he succeeded, then the Administration succeeded. If he failed, then, he said, "I get egg all over my face, and you get a new Assistant Secretary." Kissinger admired Sisco's determination, and he dropped his complaints. The two men have had their differences, but they have learned to respect one another.*

One provision of the August, 1970, cease-fire was that there was to be no military movement or buildup within a range of fifty kilometers on either side of the canal. In other words, it was to be a standstill cease-fire. Sisco has insisted that the Egyptians understood this provision very clearly, and that the Russians did, too. But in conversation with Kissinger, Sisco was very reluctant to produce "proof" that the Russians really understood; and Kissinger remained skeptical about the degree to which Dobrynin ever committed himself to the standstill part of the cease-fire. In fact, when Rogers negotiated the cease-fire terms with the Russians, he was very casual in describing this provision to Dobrynin, and there is a good chance the Russians really did not understand it.

As it turned out, both Russia and Egypt violated the standstill provision almost from the moment the cease-fire went into effect. They built new missile sites and moved others much closer to the canal.

The Israelis spotted these violations immediately, and they complained bitterly to the Americans. Within a few days, Rabin brought photographic proof to Kissinger, but it took almost four weeks before Rogers

---

* In January, 1971, they had another run-in. After a long and complicated negotiation, Sisco and Rabin had reached a written understanding on the terms of "proximity talks" between Egypt and Israel. Before giving his final approval, however, Rabin wanted Israel to be in a position of clearing any proposal Sisco might offer the parties. "No self-respecting sovereign government can give you a veto over its negotiations," Sisco asserted. Rabin balked. Sisco called Kissinger and urged him to tell Rabin that the Sisco position was the American Government's position. Kissinger asked, "What *are* Rabin's concerns?"
"I have two or three formulas for handling his concerns," Sisco responded.
"Are you going to clear those formulas with me?" Kissinger wanted to know.
"No," Sisco answered.
"You want me to intervene with Rabin — blind?"
"That's exactly what I want you to do," Sisco said. "It's too complicated for me to explain, and I am not asking you to get in the middle of my negotiation. You either have confidence in your negotiator or you don't. Now will you intervene with Rabin or won't you?"
Kissinger thought for only a second. "Okay, you sonovabitch, I'll do it." The next day, Rabin called Sisco with Israel's approval.

and Sisco would confirm the violations. Even though Sisco had at least a twenty-four-hour lead time on the start of the cease-fire on August 7, it was not until August 9 that he ordered a U-2 spy plane into the skies over the canal to take pictures of military emplacements and thereby to have a baseline from which violations could be measured. This complicated the confirmation process. Rabin told Kissinger that it appeared that the Israelis had been taken to the cleaners by the Americans, and the Americans by the Russians. Nixon seemed to agree. He was angry at the Egyptians and reserved a special fury for the Russians. They had rejected the "Rogers Plan" of December, 1969. They had moved operational combat personnel into Egypt. And they had violated the standstill cease-fire. He wondered if they thought he was a pushover.

Indeed, for a time, in September, 1970, it seemed that the Russians were not taking Kissinger or Nixon very seriously. They were stalling on SALT. They were belligerently uncooperative about Indochina. And they were instigating trouble in the Middle East. They began to challenge Western interests in Jordan, touching off a brinkmanship crisis that, for a time, took priority over Vietnam. Cambodia had upset everybody, but there was little chance of a big-power confrontation in Indochina. Jordan, on the other hand, aroused some of Kissinger's bleakest fears. Could it become the Balkans of 1970?

Jordan's problems are, in part, geographic. A small desert kingdom with a mixed population of Bedouins and Palestinians — many of them refugees from the wars of 1948 and 1967 — Jordan is surrounded by four states — Israel, Syria, Iraq, and Saudi Arabia — each of which poses a different degree of danger for King Hussein's regime. During the summer of 1970, a low-grade civil war that had been simmering for a number of years came to a head. The Palestinian commando organizations, led by Al Fatah, were determined to destroy Hussein's pro-Western regime, so that they could use Jordan, as they had been using Lebanon and Syria, as a base for raiding Israel. Hussein was determined to maintain the tranquillity that existed along the Israeli-Jordanian border. The commandos, increasingly frustrated and bitter, stepped up their attacks against the Arab Legion, Hussein's British-trained army. One cease-fire after another collapsed.

At last, on September 6, the crisis burst into the headlines when one of the commando groups — the Popular Front for the Liberation of Palestine — hijacked three commercial airliners in Western Europe and forced them to land at an abandoned British airstrip near Zerqa, twenty-five miles northeast of Amman. The PFLP held four hundred and seventy-five hostages, most of them Americans returning from European vacations. The terrorists threatened to kill them and blow up the planes unless all Palestinians held prisoner in West Germany, Switzerland, and Israel were released.

Hussein tried to fight back, but he seemed powerless to cope with this frontal challenge to his sovereignty. The PFLP accelerated its terrorist attacks against the King's forces, and the civil war spread throughout Jordan. While the hostages baked in the cruel desert heat, not knowing from one minute to the next whether their captors would break under the pressure and shoot them all, the UN met in urgent conference — but was unable to settle the crisis. At last, on September 12, the PFLP removed the hostages to Palestinian camps near Zerqa and then blew up the three planes. Within the next few days, most of the hostages were released, although fifty-five Jewish passengers remained in PFLP hands until September 29, a few days after Hussein crushed the commando movement in Jordan, aided to no small degree by an extraordinary mix of American pressure and Israeli military threat.

On September 15, a number of top officials, including Kissinger, Packard, Helms, Sisco and Moorer were attending a black-tie dinner honoring Laird at Airlie House in Warrenton, Virginia. At 8:30 P.M., there was a call for Kissinger from the White House. Directly from 10 Downing Street, London, had come the word that Hussein had just placed Jordan under martial law and replaced his civilian government with generals, signaling a royal decision to destroy the commando insurrection. The British felt that the situation was critical. Kissinger commandeered a White House helicopter and, with a few of his colleagues, flew back to the White House, arriving there by 9:30 P.M.

Kissinger quickly convened an *ad hoc* WSAG meeting in his office. It lasted about an hour. There was a general consensus, according to one participant, that this "looked like the denouement for Jordan"; according to another participant, that this was "clearly Hussein's most critical, decisive challenge," and that the exploding civil war could soon begin to affect American interests in the Middle East. After the formal meeting, Kissinger and Sisco continued their discussions until past midnight, when the President joined them. There was sketchy CIA intelligence that Syrian tanks with Soviet advisers were moving toward the Jordanian border. Nixon took a call from London. Kissinger called Rabin. It began to look bad, but no one knew how bad.

On September 16, Nixon, Kissinger and Sisco flew to Chicago to brief a group of midwestern editors. Jordan was very much on the officials' minds.

Nixon spoke "off the record," meaning he could not be quoted, but the *Chicago Sun-Times* broke the ground rules and later, much to everyone's surprise, received a White House commendation for the violation. The reason was simple: Nixon had said that the United States might have to intervene in Jordan if Syria or Iraq threatened Hussein's regime, and he wanted that implied warning to be heard in Moscow, Damascus and Baghdad.

Sisco and Kissinger spoke on "background," meaning their comments could be attributed to "Administration officials." Sisco was asked specifically at one point whether the United States had plans to intervene in Jordan. He replied carefully, "There are no plans to intervene." However, he added this intriguing afterthought: "Obviously, it is normal, routine planning to cover every contingency and to weigh what the pros and cons are."

Sisco betrayed none of his private anxieties about Jordan, calling the overall situation "reparable"; instead, for the public, he focused on the Russian role in violating the standstill cease-fire along the Suez Canal. His month-long hesitation about fingering Soviet "complicity" in the violations vanished.

"The Soviets are right on the ground," he said. "The Soviets are heavily involved in the UAR. They have got technicians, they have got advisers, they have got people there in an operational capacity. These violations could not have taken place without their knowledge and without their complicity."

In his talk, Kissinger speculated about Soviet intentions. "One of the things that I find so puzzling in the Soviet performance on the cease-fire in the Middle East," he said, "is to try to figure out a motive for it. . . . Why the Egyptians and the Russians violated the cease-fire literally, practically from the first day onward in a way that was so flagrant, I have really found it very hard to explain to myself."

Not a single editor asked why, if the violations were in fact "so flagrant," the State Department and the White House had taken almost a month to acknowledge them.

On September 17, the Jordan civil war became more serious. Hussein's new military regime opened a massive drive against the Palestinian extremists, in Amman and in some of the northern cities, in a bid to reassert royal authority. Syrian tanks moved closer to the Jordanian frontier. Nixon met with his top advisers — Kissinger, Rogers, Laird, Helms, Sisco, Moorer, and Haig — to consider the next possible step. The question was: if the Syrian tanks cross the line, does the United States move? And, if so, in what way?

Laird was concerned about the use of American troops in the Middle East so soon after they were used in Cambodia; Kissinger was also concerned, but not to the same extent. He felt that the United States had to prevent Hussein's collapse — if necessary, by direct American military intervention. There was no question in his mind that if the commandos, backed by the Syrians, Iraqis and Russians, succeeded in overthrowing the King, there would be a major Israeli strike against the Arabs and there would be an immediate threat to the balance of power in the area. Moorer made the obvious point that there was a limit to the forces that the United States could muster for an intervention. Sisco underscored one central irony: an American intervention might save Hussein in the short run, but it could so undermine him in the long run, so undercut his credibility among other Arabs, that it might be better to consider using Israeli rather than American forces to rescue him.

That night, Nixon met with Kissinger and Sisco to prepare for the visit of Golda Meir the next day. The seventy-two-year-old Premier had just flown into New York, touching off an avalanche of speculative stories about Israeli disenchantment with the Nixon Administration. Tempers on both sides were said to be short, confidence shaken. If the United States was ever going to ask Israel to rescue Hussein, Nixon realized he would have to woo Mrs. Meir. He decided to approve an Israeli aid request for five hundred million dollars and to dispatch eighteen Phantom jet fighters ahead of schedule.

On September 18, Mrs. Meir met in Washington with Nixon and Kissinger and twice with Rogers and Sisco. They discussed the Jordan crisis in great detail, but Nixon did not propose Israeli intervention. He informed the Israeli leader of his decision about the aid and the planes, and urged her not to lose sight of the advantages of diplomatic discourse with Egypt. Mrs. Meir pledged Israel to respect the cease-fire along the Suez Canal, but she categorically refused to engage in peace talks with Cairo until the Egyptian and Soviet missile sites, stealthily and illegally slipped closer to the canal, were dismantled and withdrawn.

It was in the course of these Washington discussions that Kissinger got the first word from Rabin and from Abdul Hamid Sharaf, Jordan's youthful and effective Ambassador, that a number of Syrian tanks had actually crossed the Jordanian frontier and that they were advancing on Irbid, in northwestern Jordan.

Kissinger and Rabin were on the phone several times that night, discussing different aspects of the unfolding crisis.

Kissinger had Sisco call the Russians. Were the reports accurate? he asked. Had Syria invaded Jordan? The Russians assured Sisco that, rumors to the contrary, Syria had not invaded Jordan.

On September 19, Rabin and Sharaf separately called Kissinger with the news that at least a hundred Syrian tanks had crossed into Jordan.

It was Saturday, but the White House was never busier. Kissinger presided over a nonstop WSAG meeting in the Situation Room — the SitRoom — a soundproof basement room with a rectangular table seating about fourteen people, sound-absorbing carpets, paneling and wall maps, indirect lighting, and, most important, electronic contact with the CIA, the Pentagon's National Military Command Center (which tracks troop movements around the world) and the National Security Agency. Kissinger coordinated all military, diplomatic and political moves in this complicated and extremely serious war-gaming.

By nightfall, there were reports of more Syrian tanks crossing into Jordan. Kissinger was furious at the Russians. They had given their word: it meant nothing. He recommended an alert of American forces. The President agreed. It was a selective alert, rather than the kind of across-the-board alert that so alarmed Americans in October, 1973. First the 82nd Airborne Division was alerted, and the news was deliberately leaked. Then airborne units in West Germany were moved to airfields, crossing the Autobahn in so conspicuous a fashion that the Russians could not fail to pick up the signals. "We wanted to get picked up," Kissinger told us. Throughout this studied muscle-flexing exercise, the Sixth Fleet was augmented, and its ships steamed slowly toward Lebanon and Israel.

Nixon backed up these military moves with a stern warning to the Russians to restrain the Syrians and with a private assurance to Hussein not to worry about the Israelis.

The public and private signals were not lost on the Russians. The Soviet Chargé d'Affaires in Washington, Yuli M. Vorontsov, filling in for the vacationing Anatoly Dobrynin, called on Sisco to criticize the military alerts and the reports of new American military aid to Israel. His tone was propagandistic, or so it seemed to Sisco. The American diplomat told Vorontsov that prudence would be more beneficial than propaganda. The problem, Sisco stressed, was "outside involvement" in Jordan. It had better cease, because the United States would not tolerate the change in the balance of power that could result from the toppling of Hussein.

Sunday, September 20 — a long and crucial day — brought an Israeli report to Kissinger that Syrian armor and infantry forces were "pouring" into Jordan. Another hundred or more Syrian tanks had crossed the border along with a "division" of Syrian infantry troops. Hussein threw everything he had against the Syrians and, for a few hours, stymied their advance.

Rogers issued a statement denouncing the Syrian "invasion" as an "irresponsible and imprudent" action. He demanded a Syrian withdrawal.

Sisco summoned Vorontsov to the State Department. What value had Soviet assurances? Sisco asked sarcastically. He warned that if Syria continued its attacks, Israel would probably be forced to intervene — although he had no authority from Israel to make that statement. He also warned that the United States might be forced to intervene. These warnings were carefully designed to pressure the Russians into restraining the Syrians. Sisco knew at the time that Soviet military advisers had accompanied the Syrian forces as far as the Jordanian frontier but had not crossed it. This meant that the Russians were involved at least in the planning of the Syrian attack. "Remember," Sisco told Vorontsov, "you are to report very carefully to the Kremlin that we cannot give you any assurance whatever on the question of Israeli intervention, or American intervention, directly in this situation."

Kissinger stayed in the SitRoom, overseeing the operation under close presidential direction. One observer said later, "This was his real baptism of fire in a crucial crisis management situation. . . . He felt this was a serious and direct challenge to the balance of power in the area, and to the West in general. He knew the Russians were involved, and he knew therefore that we had to be involved. He did well. He did very well, coordinating the diplomatic and the military sides of the problem."

Did Kissinger "enjoy" the manipulation of American power? another top official was asked. "Enjoy?" the official exclaimed, a look of astonishment on his face. "Henry adores power, absolutely adores it. To Henry, diplomacy is nothing without it." A Pentagon aide related how Kissinger leaned over large maps, moving toy battleships and aircraft carriers from one end of the Mediterranean to the other, arguing with admirals, expounding on military tactics and then picking up the phone to order the JCS to change the deployment of the Sixth Fleet. The World War II sergeant had become all at once a general and an admiral and, during that crisis, a kind of deputy Commander in Chief.

There were two points of view in these fast-paced deliberations. Rogers represented the cautious group, pressing diplomacy over military feinting or action. He demonstrated common sense and, as one of his deputies put it, "no real propensity for trigger-happiness." Kissinger led the power-oriented group, believing that the United States would never become "credible" to the Kremlin, in the Middle East or anywhere, for that matter, unless it was prepared to show power — and use it — in defense of its interests. In most debates of this sort, Nixon tended to side with Kissinger.

In New York, that Sunday evening, Golda Meir was the star attraction at an Israeli Bond dinner for three thousand invited guests in the Grand Ballroom of the New York Hilton Hotel. She spoke without text or notes, warning everyone it would be a long speech if her feet didn't hurt, a short one if they did. She spoke for an hour and five minutes. Her feet didn't hurt. "If we will not fight for our freedom and safety," she asserted, "then nobody will." The audience gave her a solid round of applause.

Rabin, a few seats away, glanced at his Prime Minister with admiration. An aide handed him a note. "Call Kissinger at the White House urgently," it read. It was past 10 P.M.

Rabin went to a small anteroom, the clattering of dishes and the occasional bursts of applause still audible as he dialed the White House on a hotel phone. Kissinger's voice seemed tense. He said the Jordanians had asked him to pass on an urgent message: would Israel provide Jordan with air support against the advancing Syrian tanks?

Rabin made two quick points. First, he said, he had no up-to-date intelligence, but he had ways of getting it; and second, since he would never treat Kissinger as a "mailman," a "simple messenger boy," he wanted to know the American attitude toward this extraordinary Jordanian request. Did Kissinger mean to imply that he supported the idea of an Israeli strike against the Syrian tanks? And, if he did, what would the United States do if the war escalated?

Kissinger told Rabin the situation was "critical, an emergency"; he conveyed an impression of imminent disaster. But he admitted these were valid questions. He and Rabin agreed to talk again in forty-five minutes. Kissinger jotted down the number.

Rabin caught Mrs. Meir's attention when he reentered the ballroom. At an inconspicuous moment, the two Israelis slipped into the anteroom. Rabin told her about the Kissinger call. She quickly decided that she would have to call Israeli Deputy Premier Yigal Allon, who was running the country in her absence. She wanted him to confer urgently with other Israeli leaders about the Jordanian request, and to send a small photo-reconnaissance plane over the battle zone. Dawn was breaking over the Middle East, and the plane could have its pictures within a few hours.

Kissinger called again, on schedule. He did not have "considered replies" to Rabin's questions, but he stressed the urgency of the situation and recommended that Rabin fly to Washington immediately. The last shuttle had already left. Kissinger said a Jetstar would be at the MATS (Military Air Transport Service) terminal at LaGuardia Airport at about 1 A.M. Rabin would be flown to Andrews Air Force Base in Maryland. A White House car would be waiting. Kissinger again repeated the "critical" nature of Hussein's request, and he asked for a quick Israeli reply.

Rabin conferred again with Mrs. Meir; she conferred with Israeli Foreign Minister Abba Eban, who was also at the dinner. At 1 A.M., as Rabin was speeding out to LaGuardia Airport, Mrs. Meir was speeding out to JFK Airport, where an El Al airliner was waiting to fly her back to Israel.

It was almost 3 A.M., Monday, September 21, when Rabin arrived at his home in the Forest Hills section of Washington. Kissinger was still in the SitRoom at the White House. Sisco was in the Operations Center at the State Department. All three men were hooked into a "secure" conference call. Rabin told them the Israeli Cabinet would be meeting in emergency session at any minute. The Israeli air force was ready to strike at the Syrian tanks. Rabin had no doubt that the Israeli jets could destroy the tanks, if Jerusalem flashed the green light. Kissinger again stressed the "urgency" of the situation. So did Sisco. Rabin said he understood, but he still wanted to know what the United States would do if, for example, the Egyptians began to attack Israel — with Soviet assistance. Kissinger and Sisco said they understood his concern. They would be in touch later in the morning. Rabin then called Jerusalem to report on his latest talk with the Americans, and then he took a nap. Kissinger and Sisco did not sleep that night.

Hussein had sent another message. Irbid had fallen to the Syrians. Benjamin Welles reported in the *New York Times* that Hussein seemed "panicky" when, on an open line from his palace to the American chancery in Amman, then ringed with commandos, he issued another appeal for help — this time, from the Americans and the British. He resorted to code: "I'm OK up above but in bad trouble down below" — meaning that his air force was still intact but his armored forces were badly battered.

The latest intelligence said Syria now had three hundred tanks in Jordan. In the northeast, Iraq had twenty thousand troops restlessly priming for intervention. Hussein was in desperate trouble, and the Palestinian extremists, still holding the fifty-five airline hostages, seemed ready to take drastic action. Five U.S. divisions, based in West Germany, were put on full, ostentatious alert. The Sixth Fleet was expanded from two to five carrier task forces.

The British, remembering the British, French and Israeli intervention against Egypt in 1956, became alarmed. Ambassador John Freeman told Rogers that Britain would not intervene militarily. He expressed the hope that the United States would not, either. It was clear that most of Western Europe opposed American intervention. It was equally clear that Nixon had made up his mind that Hussein would not be toppled, that the balance of forces in the Middle East would not be changed. He realized that he was facing a critical challenge. He could have gone to the people, as Kennedy had done during the Cuban missile crisis, but he chose, four months after Cambodia, to keep this crisis as muted as possible. When Rogers recommended a new diplomatic approach to the Russians, possibly a joint Soviet-American effort to cool passions in the area, Nixon, with Kissinger's strong support, vetoed the proposal. Instead, Vorontsov was again told that there would be an acute danger to peace unless the Syrian tanks retreated. No option would be ruled out. "Call your boys back" was Nixon's unambiguous message.

It was clear that in this venture the United States had only one ally, Israel. Nixon ordered Kissinger to become the key American in coordinating U.S.-Israeli actions with Rabin. The public spotlight was still to be directed at Rogers and Sisco, but quietly, out of the glare of publicity, without the full knowledge of the State Department, the burden of negotiating an unprecedented and secret American-Israeli understanding for joint military action in the Jordan crisis was placed on the shoulders of Kissinger and Rabin.

Kissinger immediately called Rabin, and the two men got down to work. (Rabin was later to joke rather proudly that he knew more secret ways in and out of the Executive Mansion than the Secret Service.)

Rabin, with Dayan's permission, briefed Kissinger on the full range of Israeli military planning, and twice a day, he delivered a rundown on the latest Israeli intelligence. In essence, Israel was planning a pincer attack against Syrian forces concentrated in the Irbid area. Armored units stationed near the Golan Heights — two hundred tanks, to be exact — would move east and then south toward Irbid. Similar units near Nablus, in the occupied west bank, would strike due east toward Irbid. Israel would then count on Jordanian armor moving north from Amman. The Israeli air force would soften up the Syrian positions around Irbid. Coordination between Israeli and Jordanian forces would be necessary, and Hussein would be assured that Israeli forces would be withdrawn from Jordan the moment the operation was completed. There would be no extension of the post-1967 borders in Jordan. Syria would be another matter, but that was not discussed in detail.

Rabin told Kissinger that several dozen Israeli tanks were being moved during the day from the southern part of the country toward the west bank. A number of marked reconnaissance planes were flying over Syrian positions.

Rabin's basic question remained: if Israel, at Hussein's request, were to decide to strike, what was the United States prepared to do? Kissinger still had no answer.

Late that Monday afternoon, Vorontsov called on Sisco and signaled a possible change in the Soviet attitude. He warned against "all" outside intervention, and he disclosed that Russia was urging restraint on Syria and he hoped the United States would urge similar restraint on Israel. Rabin was convinced the Russians were genuinely concerned about Nixon's next step. They seemed to feel that since he had behaved so outrageously in Cambodia, he might act outrageously in the Middle East too.

There was evidence by nightfall that Jordan had stopped the Syrian advance. Hussein's tanks had performed better than anyone, including the King, thought possible.

The Israeli Cabinet met once again. The new question was, would Syria now commit fresh forces to her stymied invasion of Jordan? There were at least two hundred additional tanks on the Syrian side of the border, another five hundred deeper inside Syria. Another question: would Soviet advisers who had not crossed the border with the advancing Syrians get new orders — and march south?

The Israeli Cabinet reached a decision. If the additional Syrian tanks moved, with or without the Russians, then Israel would intervene. Rabin had part of his answer for Kissinger, but he did not have all of it —

because the Israelis attached a very significant condition that could have involved the United States in a Middle East war. Rabin delineated his government's attitude in a White House meeting with Kissinger. Sisco joined some of the critical deliberations that night — but not all.

Rabin told Kissinger solemnly that if Syria sent fresh reinforcements into Jordan and if, as expected, the Jordanian army began to collapse, Israel would agree to Hussein's request, as transmitted by the Americans. The Israeli air force would be ordered into action against Syrian tanks. But Israel reserved the right to send combat troops into Jordan if such additional action were considered necessary. Moreover, Israel would not limit her military action to Jordan. Air and ground attacks into Syria might also be required to secure the "political goal" of saving Hussein's pro-Western regime. Finally, Rabin stressed that Israel needed an "American umbrella" against any possible Soviet countermoves. He did not define "umbrella," but he made it clear that Israel would not save Hussein unless Kissinger could offer solid presidential assurances of an American determination to use force, if necessary, against any Soviet move against Israel from the Suez Canal or from the Mediterranean. Kissinger could not offer such assurances.

Later that night, the battlefield situation began to force a presidential decision, potentially one of the most critical decisions Nixon had to make. Syria moved a small number of additional tanks across the border, and it appeared that a mass movement could be under way. The Jordanian army could not dislodge the Syrians from Irbid. The commandos were staging more daring attacks against the King's troops. Hussein sent another appeal for "urgent help." The United States decided to act.

Kissinger and Rabin met once again. The Israeli Ambassador again stressed his government's desire to keep the United States out of military action in the Middle East, but repeated that Israel wanted Nixon's word that the U.S. would either deter or prevent any Soviet intervention resulting from an Israeli move into Jordan or Syria. Kissinger checked once more with the President.

This time Nixon gave his approval. Their understanding was stark and historic: Israel would move against Syrian forces in Jordan; and if Egyptian *or Soviet* forces then moved against Israel, the United States would intervene against *both*. The situation seemed so critical that there was no time to put this extraordinary understanding into writing. Both acted — each in its own way.

Israeli tanks, in great number, moved toward the Jordan River. The

Golan Heights came alive with visible preparation for war. At military airfields throughout Israel jet engines were revved up and missile racks and bomb bays were loaded. An American aircraft carrier eased to within sixty nautical miles of the Israeli coastline. A Russian trawler was watching as a small military transport plane with American markings flew into Tel Aviv. The Russians presumably tracked the flight. After a few hours, the plane flew back to the carrier. Kissinger was particularly proud of this innocent signal of coordinated American-Israeli action. Sisco told Vorontsov that there was no question about Israel's capacity to move, and no question either about America's determination to rescue Hussein from Syrian and commando attacks.

Suddenly, on Tuesday, September 22, the tension snapped. Reassured by the American-Israeli coordination, Hussein launched an all-out attack against the Syrians. His tanks moved north toward Irbid, and his Hawker Hunter jet fighters cracked hard at Syrian armor surrounding Irbid. And, to Kissinger's relief, there were reports by nightfall (midday in Washington) that a few dozen Syrian tanks had begun to swing around and head north toward the border. There were other reports that Russian diplomats had rushed to Damascus on Monday evening to turn off the invasion.

A clear hint of this switch in Soviet policy emerged at a dinner party that evening at the Washington home of Dr. Ashraf Ghorbal, then head of the Egyptian Interests Section at the Indian Embassy. Kissinger went to the party so that he could be available for a brief chat with Vorontsov in the event the Russians had anything meaningful to say. When the Soviet diplomat spotted Kissinger, he seemed ill at ease, as though he weren't sure whether to approach him or not. Finally, over coffee, Vorontsov took Kissinger aside and urgently emphasized that Russia was doing everything in its power to stop Syria. Kissinger looked skeptically at the Russian envoy. "The last time we talked, you told me the Syrians would send no more troops." Vorontsov answered defensively: "We didn't know the Syrians would cross the border; our own military advisers stopped at the border and went no further." Kissinger snapped, "You and your client started it, and you have to end it." He did not reveal that by then he had information that the Syrians were beginning to turn around toward their own border.

By Wednesday, September 23, the Russians were reappearing at Washington cocktail parties, wondering why everyone had been making such a fuss about Jordan. The last of the Syrian tanks were, by that time, withdrawing from Jordan. American and Israeli military movements ceased, just as quickly as they had been geared up for action. Kissinger and Rabin shook hands. Along with the Jordan crisis itself, their unheralded but major understanding lapsed into history, even though both men realized that a precedent had been established. If the United States, in 1970, could undertake joint military planning with Israel, a country with which the United States had no formal defense pact, even to the point of promising an "umbrella" of U.S. protection against any Soviet move against Israel, then such a binding arrangement could be repeated.

Because of the special Kissinger-Rabin relationship, many Israelis came to regard Kissinger as a "good friend," even though Kissinger regards Israel as only a special part of a larger strategic contest with the Soviet Union. When, in mid-1971, Rogers leaned on Rabin to make "unilateral concessions" in the ongoing negotiations about an interim solution to reopen the Suez Canal, even threatening for a brief time to hold up jet plane deliveries, Kissinger interceded. Later in the year, when the Rogers-Rabin dispute began to make headlines in the press and problems for the Republican National Committee, Kissinger got the President's permission to assure Rabin that plane deliveries would continue and State Department pressure would stop. That intercession paved the way for Mrs. Meir to visit the President in early December and set the stage for Israel's sympathetic view of his candidacy in 1972. Rabin spoke undiplomatically about his admiration for Nixon and Kissinger and his fear of McGovern, and he helped swing many traditionally Democratic Jewish votes into the GOP column.

Those were the days when Kissinger chose not to publicize his association with the Middle East. Although he met with Rabin on dozens of occasions, discussing or debating the most sensitive questions of war and peace, there was only one public occasion at which he gave Rabin more than a passing nod. It took place in the fall of 1972, when the presidential election was only a few weeks away. The Israeli Philharmonic Symphony Orchestra was celebrating the twenty-fifth anniversary of Israeli independence with a special concert at the Kennedy Center in Washington. McGovern showed up. Nixon did not. He sent Kissinger and Rogers instead. All of the bigwigs — Republican, Democratic, and Israeli — shared the central boxes overlooking the decorous crowd in the orchestra — a mix of prominent Congressmen, journalists, lawyers, officials, and security men. At intermission, McGovern rose and received a spirited round of applause. Later, when the concert was over, everyone began filing out of the auditorium, except for two men standing conspicuously, face to face, in earnest conversation, in the presidential box. They were Henry Kissinger and Yitzhak Rabin, and no one in the concert hall missed this public display of a special Israeli-American relationship.

Kissinger's major theme in those days was not new; he merely struck it with new force. The existence of nuclear weapons, he insisted, should impose special restraints on the superpowers. It was too dangerous for them to continue to push heedlessly in pursuit of marginal political advantage in different parts of the world. It was obviously a hard lesson for both superpowers to learn. American war critics suggested that the United States had not learned this lesson either and Kissinger could, in a sense, see the logic of their argument. But he was more concerned about the Russians.

"Our relations with the Soviet Union have reached the point," he told newsmen on September 16, "where some important decisions have to be made, especially in Moscow. . . . Events in the Middle East and *in other parts of the world* have raised questions of whether Soviet leaders as of now are prepared to pursue the principles that I outlined earlier; specifically, whether the Soviet leaders are prepared to forego tactical advantages they can derive from certain situations for the sake of the larger interest of peace."

The Russians had obviously not learned Kissinger's lesson. At the same time that they were playing with fire in Syria and Jordan, half a world away they appeared to be on the verge of upsetting the 1962 Kennedy-Khrushchev understanding on Cuba.

In early September, 1970, a U-2 spy plane, flying its lackadaisical once-a-month pattern over Cuba, happened to snap a picture of a soccer field near a new military barracks in the vicinity of Cienfuegos, a naval base on the south coast of Cuba. The picture raised a few eyebrows at the CIA. Baseball is the Cuban national sport; soccer is the Russian national sport. The number of U-2 flights increased sharply over the next few days. The new pictures only deepened official concern. They showed new communications towers, new barracks and new antiaircraft sites — some completed, others under construction. They also showed, in the harbor of Cienfuegos, a nine-thousand-ton Ugra-class submarine tender and two barges that normally store radioactive wastes from nuclear-powered submarines. Intelligence had it that a nuclear submarine was in the waters off Cienfuegos, and that many Russian ships were docked in the harbor, unloading cargo and personnel.

Why all the new bustle and construction? Officials began to suspect the Russians might be building a nuclear submarine base — a clear violation of the 1962 understanding. According to its terms, the Russians could protect Cuba. They could build defensive military installations, but they surely could not build a base for nuclear-powered submarines. By no stretch of the imagination, Kissinger figured, could such subs be categorized as "defensive."

When Kissinger brought the photo intelligence, embroidered by his own hard-line analysis, to Nixon, the President saw red. The Russians were not only encouraging the commandos and the Syrians to move against Hussein; they were also, it seemed, extending the rules of the game beyond reasonable limits in Cuba. Nixon decided to take a firm stance on the Cuba problem — but to do so in an unprovocative manner. He would make few public proclamations, but he would allow Kissinger to drive home the point that the Russians were playing with fire if they thought he would yield to the proposition that they could use Cuba for offensive military purposes. Nixon had lost to Kennedy in 1960; he was not going to lose to Kennedy's ghost in 1970. He ordered Kissinger to get busy.

At the Chicago briefing for editors on September 16, a briefing devoted largely to the Middle East crisis, Kissinger sounded a muted alarm: "If they start operating strategic forces out of Cuba," Kissinger noted pointedly, "say, Polaris-type submarines, and use that as a depot, that would be a matter we would study very carefully." He then helped the Russians draw a somber analogy. "If we put the Polaris submarine into the Black Sea, we have every right to do it.* There are many newspapers who would say that is a provocative thing to do. Why operate so close to the Soviet border? If one significantly changes the deployment of one's strategic forces," he went on, "that is something the other side is bound to notice. Therefore, both sides have to decide whether they want to restrain measures which they have a legal right to take. We are watching these events in Cuba and it isn't yet clear what, exactly, the Soviet Union is doing there. The fleet is rotating in and out, and we are watching events very carefully."

---

* Kissinger was wrong. The Montreux Convention of 1936 provided that no warships could go through the Dardanelles into the Black Sea.

Privately, Kissinger summoned Dobrynin, who had just returned from Moscow, to his White House office and sounded an alarm. First he described the American intelligence findings and then he charged that the Russians were violating the terms of the 1962 understanding by building an *offensive* base in Cuba. Dobrynin expressed surprise. Kissinger then outlined the full consequences of such continued Soviet activity for the broad range of Washington-Moscow relationships. The Russian envoy, according to Kissinger, "turned ashen." He understood the deeper meaning of Kissinger's warning. Not only would progress toward Soviet-American détente be halted, but an updated "missile crisis" could easily result. Dobrynin promised Kissinger that he would report to Moscow and try to obtain "clarifications." Kissinger stressed that he was not really interested in "clarifications" so much as in "assurances" that the Russians would immediately stop their construction of a submarine base in Cuba.

A week passed before Dobrynin called for an appointment. The silence seemed ominous. At Cienfuegos, the construction continued. Nixon and Kissinger grappled with the problem of presenting this new challenge to the American people. Cambodia, Jordan, and now Cuba might come through as too rich a menu of crises; some critics were already beginning to suggest that the President was "manufacturing" confrontations with the Russians merely to demonstrate his machismo. Selectively Kissinger briefed a handful of Congressmen and columnists, warning of a "grave confrontation" with Russia unless the base construction ceased. On September 25, C. L. Sulzberger, the foreign affairs columnist for the *New York Times*, broke the story. At noon, the Pentagon confirmed it and, late in the afternoon, during a backgrounder for reporters, Kissinger solemnly warned the Russians that the President would regard the construction of a nuclear submarine base in Cuba as a "hostile act."

Rogers was baffled by Kissinger's warning and criticized him for "engaging in Cold War rhetoric." The Secretary of State had the same information about the Cienfuegos base as Kissinger, but he refused to draw apocalyptic conclusions about Soviet intentions. He did not think a sub base at Cienfuegos would upset the balance of forces in the Caribbean; he did not even believe the Russians were eager to make trouble. State Department experts had their eye on the Middle East and on SALT, and they simply could not share Kissinger's vision of Soviet intrigue. So, not for the first time, the Rogers clique in Foggy Bottom sniped at Kissinger's "intervention" in their bailiwick; some of the Soviet specialists blasted his unorthodox approach to the Kremlin, convinced that Kissinger could not "lecture" to the Russians as once he had lectured to Harvard undergraduates. Kissinger recalls that he and Rogers had quite a "blowup" about the Cuban incident.

Finally, on September 27, a quiet Sunday reserved for final preparations for a presidential trip to the Mediterranean, Kissinger heard from Dobrynin. The Soviet Union was not violating the 1962 understanding on Cuba, the Russian envoy assured Kissinger. No offensive military installation was being built at Cienfuegos.

Kissinger and Nixon left for the Mediterranean, relieved but less than fully reassured. Several times, on their swing through Naples, Belgrade, Madrid and Dublin (the President could not resist a stopover in Ireland), Kissinger mentioned "the Cuban incident" to reporters. He still had no evidence that the construction had actually stopped.

Shortly after the President returned to Washington, on the evening of October 5, Dobrynin called on Kissinger once more and confirmed the validity of the 1962 understanding on Cuba. A week later, Rogers got the same message from Soviet Foreign Minister Gromyko during a UN dinner in New York. On October 13, the Russians responded publicly to Washington's pressure. The official Soviet news agency, Tass, published a special communiqué, stressing that the Soviet Union "has not been and is not building its own military base" in Cuba. On October 22, Gromyko told the President, during a private chat at the White House, that the 1962 understanding on Cuba would be "upheld." It was in this time frame that the first proof of Gromyko's assurance was developed in a CIA darkroom: a series of photographs showing a slowdown in the construction of a Soviet submarine base in Cuba. Soon the construction was to stop completely.

The "Cuban incident" could have developed into a full-fledged crisis between the two superpowers, but preventive diplomacy aborted it. Kissinger learned from the Jordan and Cuban experiences that sometimes the Russians could be encouraged to see the light if the dangers inherent in their policies in different parts of the world could be pointed out to them *before* national ego became so enmeshed in the policies that a detached judgment became impossible. These were not the only times that Kissinger lectured to the Russians, and with good effect. But even Kissinger wouldn't conclude that his special brand of tough talk alone could persuade the Russians to shift the fundamental direction of their policy.

Other factors would have to be brought into play. One was the disastrous shape of the Soviet economy after more than fifty years of Communist rule; another was China. Kissinger had felt for a long time that the Soviet system badly needed an overhaul; but it was surely not for him to propose it, nor was any Kremlin leader eager to undertake so massive a job. It was the sudden outburst of labor discontent in Poland in December, 1970, which toppled Wladyslaw Gomulka from power, that forced Brezhnev to act. The Polish proletariat, led by the workers of Gdansk, rioted against the Socialist system, which, so far as they were concerned, had produced very few of the glories envisaged by Marx. Not the liberals but the laborers were in a state of mini-rebellion against the system, and their actions, if unchecked, could have set a disruptive example for the rest of Eastern Europe. The Russians insisted that the Polish rebellion be suppressed. The post-Gomulka leadership of Edward Gierek then moved quickly to satisfy some of the economic complaints that had driven the workers to violence.

"After the Polish rioting," one of Kissinger's aides explained, "Brezhnev realized that his hold on power had suddenly become vulnerable; that he too could lose power, as Gomulka had, unless he drastically overhauled Soviet society — most especially the economy." The abacus would have to be replaced by the computer, and foreign trade and capital would have to be stimulated. There appeared to be no other alternative.

The critical need for Western technology and credits compelled Brezhnev to think about experimenting with a policy of détente with the West. Only through an easing of political relationships could Brezhnev create an environment for a major expansion of trade. Politics provided the link to economics.

Kissinger, the old professor of linkage, quickly spotted the new opportunities opened by the Polish uprising. He proposed that the President set up a direct channel of communication to the suddenly vulnerable Brezhnev. The first message left the White House on January 9, 1971. Many others followed. Although no one has divulged their precise contents, their theme is no secret. Nixon suggested that the United States might be ready to help Brezhnev modernize the Soviet economy — if Brezhnev was ready to ease his position on a broad range of stalled political issues, such as SALT. In other words, "by becoming more flexible, more sensible, more willing to engage in meaningful discussions with us," to quote an NSC staffer, Brezhnev could be assured of getting American economic help. "That sort of linkage Brezhnev understood very well."

The test of the new relationship was SALT. Nixon and Brezhnev quickly authorized another Kissinger-Dobrynin effort to break the dead-lock on strategic arms negotiations. For the next four months, the two envoys conducted a series of top secret talks, mostly in Kissinger's office but sometimes at the Soviet Embassy. The official SALT negotiator, Gerard Smith, knew nothing about these huddles. Semenov, his Soviet counterpart in the Helsinki-Vienna exchanges, was kept informed about the Washington talks by his Foreign Ministry. Smith's exclusion did not particularly upset Kissinger. He had a mandate from Nixon to reach a SALT compromise with Dobrynin, and he couldn't be bothered with bureaucratic details or personal feelings.

Brezhnev could not afford the luxury of being disdainful to his col-leagues. He needed Politburo support for his new policy switch to détente with the United States. Some hard-liners balked, and there must have been a few rip-roaring political battles in the Kremlin. But by late March, Brezhnev was able to rally sufficient political support from the ranks of the Central Committee to convene the Twenty-fourth Congress of the Soviet Communist Party and to proclaim the victory of his policy of détente.

Free for a time of political problems, Brezhnev finally felt strong enough to compromise on SALT. The earlier Soviet position had stressed the importance of reaching an agreement first on defensive weapons — particularly the ABM. The American position linked defensive to offen-sive weapons in any prospective SALT agreement. During the fourth round of SALT, and after numerous secret exchanges between Brezhnev and Nixon, the Russians changed their position, and Kissinger and Do-brynin were able to strike a compromise. The Russians accepted the American linkage between offensive and defensive weapons, and the Americans agreed to give priority to an ABM deal in a broad negotiation that would also include some categories of offensive weapons.

It had been a rough four months of bargaining for both negotiators, but it was especially rough on Dobrynin. He was five thousand miles away from his leader; Kissinger's leader was just down the hall. At one point, Dobrynin actually complained about the "excessive secrecy" that Kissinger kept demanding. The White House, obsessed by the need to prevent leaks, insisted that both sides work off a single draft of the negotiating points. No carbons were allowed. Kissinger responded by telling Dobrynin that the Russians had been easier to negotiate with in the nineteenth century, when the basic haggling between the two countries had only been about the price of Alaska. Dobrynin quickly retorted that those Russians did not have to contend with Henry Kissinger! Kissinger felt that, this once, Dobrynin deserved the last word.

On May 20, 1971, shortly after noon, Washington time, Nixon went on television to read a short joint announcement, drafted by Kissinger and Dobrynin, underscoring the link between offensive and defensive weapons in any SALT agreement that would be reached between the two superpowers. It was a "breakthrough" of historic proportions, Nixon insisted.

The "breakthrough" was a big step in the direction of the Moscow summit of May, 1972. It had political spin-offs for both leaders. Brezhnev could then face his two critical problems — economic backwardness and confrontation with China — with the assurance that, to some degree anyway, Nixon was ready to do business. The President, for his part, could approach the year of his reelection campaign with the prospect of a major improvement in Soviet-American relations looming on the near horizon and with the secret joy of knowing that he had a fantastic surprise that he would soon be able to spring on everyone — an historic opening to China. In Nixon's mind, China was the key to Russia — and to much else, too.

NINE

The China Breakthrough

The Making of a New China Hand

When Henry Kissinger descended upon Washington in early 1969, China was clearly not one of his pet subjects. "I can't recall anyone ever inviting me to dinner to hear my views about *China*," he once told an aide. The China specialists agreed. "Henry's knowledge — substantial knowledge and appreciation of nuances — about China was *zilch*," said one noted scholar. Kissinger could not even use chopsticks.

In his 1957 best-seller *Nuclear Weapons and Foreign Policy*, he did devote one chapter to an analysis of "Sino-Soviet Strategic Thought," but it was a classic Cold War analysis, filled with the assumptions that were fashionable in the 1950s about the "unity" of the Sino-Soviet bloc. He studded it with catchy quotations from the works of Mao Tse-tung. "Enemy advances, we retreat; enemy halts, we harass; enemy tires, we attack; enemy retreats, we pursue." These sixteen words, Kissinger concluded, defined Mao's strategy of "protracted limited war."

Kissinger made little effort to get behind the wall of Mao's thoughts into the crisscrossing byways of Chinese history and culture. While he became more aware in the 1960s of the emerging rift between Moscow and Peking, his vision of China retained its Cold War grimness, unchanged since the days of John Foster Dulles.

He was alarmed by China's first atomic blast in October, 1964. He was disturbed by the publication a year later of a manifesto by then Defense Minister Lin Piao — one of China's greatest revolutionary military leaders,

who had been with the Red Army since its formation in 1927. The manifesto portrayed Asia, Africa, and Latin America as the revolutionary
"world countryside," surging to "final victory" over the "world cities" of
North America and Western Europe. Many sophisticated China-watchers
saw Lin's exhortation as simply a militantly phrased do-it-yourself pre-
scription for revolution for the Vietcong and other insurgent forces, but
it struck some analysts, including Kissinger, as a radical blueprint for
Chinese aggression on a world scale. And the unleashing in 1966 of the
Great Proletarian Cultural Revolution — which sent millions of Red
Guards rampaging through the countryside, closed down universities,
pitted soldier against worker in an effort to purify the Chinese revolution — seemed to Kissinger to be unchecked madness.

Although he was a vintage anti-Soviet hard-liner, he began to sympathize with the Russians in the deepening Sino-Soviet rift. Kissinger
described the Peking regime as a threat not only to Russia but also to the
new Asian order that he hoped would follow an "honorable" end to the
Vietnam war. "When I came into this job, we still considered China the
most hostile nation we faced," Kissinger later admitted. "I didn't know
what they were like."

Richard Nixon, from the beginning of his political career, had taken a
similar view of the Chinese Communists. He was a conservative young
Congressman from California in 1949, when Mao Tse-tung established
his regime and Chiang Kai-shek fled in defeat to the island of Formosa.
In his campaign for a Senate seat a year later, Nixon declared: "All that
we have to do is to take a look at the map and we can see that if Formosa
falls the next frontier is the coast of California." While running for Vice-
President in 1952, Nixon charged, "China wouldn't have gone Communist
— if the Truman Administration had had backbone." The search for
scapegoats was under way, the question being "Who lost China?" — as
though China were America's to lose.

Despite his antagonism toward Mao's Communist regime, Nixon was
a shrewd enough politician to see China as a fact of international life
that could be used for his own political profit — as far back as 1960.
At that time, according to the late columnist George Dixon, Nixon made
an attempt to get into China. He was so delighted with the political
impact of his "kitchen debate" with Soviet Premier Nikita Khrushchev
the year before that he wanted to duplicate the feat in China. "Mr. Nixon
subscribes to the theory," Dixon wrote, "that if it worked once it can

work twice and that if he can achieve a 'breakthrough' into the forbidden country that holds one-fourth of the earth's people his 'image' will be so gigantic he'll overshadow any stay-at-home Democratic opponent." His trip was aborted when two Democratic Senators — Warren Magnuson of Washington and Clair Engle of California — threatened to "tear the roof off" if the State Department helped the Vice-President get into China but declined to help them.

Still, Nixon's interest in visiting China did not prevent him from taking a sharply anti-Peking position during the 1960 campaign against John F. Kennedy. In October, during a television debate with the Democratic candidate, Nixon asked, "Now, what do the Chinese Communists want? They don't want just Quemoy and Matsu. They don't want just Formosa. They want the world."

But by the mid-1960s, with the Democrats caught in the quagmire of a Southeast Asian war, Nixon addressed himself to the subject of "Asia after Vietnam," focusing on the challenge of China. "Any American policy toward Asia," he wrote in *Foreign Affairs*, in October, 1967,

> must come urgently to grips with the reality of China. . . . Taking the long view, we simply cannot afford to leave China forever outside the family of nations, there to nurture its fantasies, cherish its hates and threaten its neighbors. There is no place on this small planet for a billion of its potentially most able people to live in angry isolation. But we could go disastrously wrong if, in pursuing this long-range goal, we failed in the short range to read the lessons of history.
>
> The world cannot be safe until China changes. Thus our aim, to the extent that we can influence events, should be to induce change. The way to do this is to persuade China that it must change: that it cannot satisfy its imperial ambitions, and that its own national interest requires a turning away from foreign adventuring and a turning inward toward the solution of its own domestic problems.

Though Nixon was still a staunch anti-Communist, he was aware of America's changing mood, and he recognized the political advantages of proclaiming a new era of reconciliation with the Communist world. He continued to view Moscow as his major adversary; but, given the sharp tension in Sino-Soviet relations, he began to see Peking as his major weapon in the diplomatic game of exploiting the tension to gain leverage over the Kremlin. "The Russians have a definite thing about the Chinese — an obsession," one of Nixon's closest aides later explained. "So here was a piece of leverage that simply could not be overlooked. Any sensible man would use it. That's the name of the game." Ironically, many analysts believed that Nixon was then the only prominent American politician with a shot at the presidency who could even talk about overhauling America's outdated policy toward China without fear of a right-wing backlash. His anti-Communist credentials were impeccable.

Nixon was to play the China game with the skill and cynicism it required. During the 1968 campaign, he began to sketch the outline of his new policy. Hints emerged in various ways. One day, British journalist Henry Brandon asked the GOP candidate if he might at some point consider making "common cause" with Russia against China. Nixon retorted that he was opposed to any tactic that suggested the white world was "ganging up" against the nonwhite. Our policy, he insisted, must be "untainted" by any "suspicion of racism." On another occasion, he told one of his political associates that he might travel to Peking — "if they would give me a visa."

By the time Nixon changed his status from candidate to President, he had already pieced together the elements of a new policy toward China. He would try to open a simple dialogue with the Chinese leaders, aimed at bringing them into a more rational discourse with the United States, and he would start by cooling official American rhetoric, including his own. Another step would be to ease trade and visa restrictions. Still another step would be to reduce American troop levels at bases ringing China and eliminate unnecessary military maneuvers near or over China. Next, he would indicate a willingness to revise the U.S. view of Taiwan — the Chinese name for Formosa. And, finally, he would begin to pull U.S. forces out of Indochina, the immediate focus of Peking's concern about American intentions. Throughout this evolving process of accommodation, Nixon and all of his top lieutenants were to deny publicly that their opening toward China had anything to do with exerting leverage on Russia.

Kissinger not only denied this aim of Nixonian policy; he looked hurt when anyone dared to suggest it. "I think that's a very dangerous game," he would say, becoming deadly serious, "a very dangerous game." Only rarely has he come close to an admission. "They are competitors," he once said, "and that is a fact of life." But he quickly added, "We don't play the game of pitting Russia against China."

February 1, 1969, was a Saturday, and Kissinger arrived early at his office in the White House basement. In those first few weeks of their relationship, Kissinger and Nixon did some of their communicating by memo.

Neither yet felt totally at ease with the other. Nixon had spent part of the weekend alone, dictating staff memos into a small tape recorder. One of the memos, unsigned, was on Kissinger's desk. "I think we should give every encouragement to the attitude that this Administration is exploring possibilities of rapprochement with the Chinese," it read. "This, of course, should be done privately and should under no circumstances get into the public print from this direction."

Kissinger, who thrived in an atmosphere of secrecy, conferred with a few staff men and later discussed China at lunch with Under Secretary of State Richardson. They were intrigued by a Chinese Foreign Ministry statement broadcast by Peking Radio on November 26 proposing an early resumption of Sino-American ambassadorial talks in Warsaw, which had been suspended since January 8, 1968, and they were particularly struck by Peking's allusion to the five principles of "peaceful coexistence," the specific language of the 1955 Bandung Conference of nonaligned countries, a moment of maximum Chinese contact with the non-Chinese world. They concluded that China's emergence from the Cultural Revolution and her anxieties about Russia could explain the tone of the message.

China specialists on Kissinger's staff and at the State Department were jubilant about the possibility of resuming the Chinese-American talks in late February; and they were deeply disappointed when the meeting scheduled for February 20 was abruptly canceled by the Chinese after the U.S. granted asylum to Liao Ho-shu, a Chinese diplomat who had defected in the Netherlands. Some of the specialists believed that this was just a pretext, and that the real reason for the cancellation was Peking's preoccupation with policy disputes at home and with rising tensions along the border with the Soviet Union.

Kissinger had shared little of his staff's excitement about the resumption of talks, and he shared little of their disappointment when the February meeting was canceled. He favored the effort to improve relations with China, but he was skeptical about any quick openings.

Kissinger's approach, at least at the beginning, was more long-range, more global. He envisaged a new, five-cornered world — consisting of the United States (economically and militarily powerful), Western Europe (an expanding economic power but militarily a dependency of Washington), Russia (economically vulnerable but militarily a colossus), China (demographically and geographically gigantic but in every other way living only on its potential), and finally Japan (an economic giant but a military dwarf, disarmed by constitutional fiat). In such an expanded world, an approach to China could be very useful. It could influence Russia to adopt a more flexible position, thereby easing the Moscow-Washington stalemate that had dominated the postwar era. The possible combinations for diplomatic change seemed endless.

In February, 1969, he was preoccupied with immediate problems — Vietnam, SALT, the upcoming presidential swing through Western Europe — and he considered China back-burner stuff, unlikely to become an urgent matter for several years. Indeed, for the first six months of 1969, Kissinger was a mere passenger on the Administration's China train. The President was clearly its sole engineer.

While Nixon was privately "exploring the possibilities of rapprochement with the Chinese," he was publicly playing it cool. At his first news conference, on January 27, just five days before the China memo appeared on Kissinger's desk, Nixon was asked whether he had any plans for "improving relations with Communist China"; he responded by denying any "immediate prospect of any change in our policy until some changes occur on their side."

In early February, however, the President confided to Mike Mansfield of Montana, the Senate Majority Leader, who had served as a young Marine on gunboat duty in China in the early 1920s, that he was going to try to "open the door" to the Chinese mainland. Nixon reiterated his conviction that the Chinese had to be involved in "global responsibility" before Sino-Soviet hostility broke out into open warfare. "When the door is open, Mike," he told Mansfield, "I want you to be the first high-level American to visit China." Mansfield, who had long been interested in Asian affairs, was flattered. "I'd like to go myself," Nixon added, "but that doesn't seem quite feasible for the moment."

On February 18, the President instructed Secretary of State Rogers to declare that the United States wanted to engage in a broad program of cultural and scientific exchanges with China.

On February 21, while Kissinger was briefing newsmen about the upcoming European trip, the question arose: would the President discuss China with the European leaders?

"Yes," Kissinger answered. "Any review of the international situation must involve an assessment of the role of a country with a population of seven hundred million. Moreover, two of these countries, Britain and France, have diplomatic relations with mainland China. They have not been ostensively happy relations, but nevertheless, it will enable them to make their judgment of what they think the trends are and *the President has always indicated that he favors a policy of maximum contact* [italics added by the authors]."

In fact, Nixon had never — in public — indicated a policy of "maximum contact." Quite the contrary. Kissinger was obviously reflecting Nixon's private policy.

On March 1, in the Grand Trianon Palace near Versailles, Nixon internationalized his approach to China. He told French President Charles de Gaulle that "whatever the difficulties," he was determined to open a dialogue with Peking.

De Gaulle listened carefully, remembering, perhaps, the U.S. reaction to France's opening of relations with Peking in 1964. The State Department had deplored the French move, calling it "an unfortunate step, particularly at a time when the Chinese Communists are actively promoting aggression and subversion in Southeast Asia and elsewhere."

Nixon, five years later, was now trying to walk in de Gaulle's footsteps. Looking into the future, the American President told the French President that he envisaged the admission of Peking to the United Nations and then the "normalization of relations" between China and the United States. He acknowledged China's deep suspicions of the West, especially the United States, but said he would allay them by "putting an end to the American involvement in Vietnam" and by starting "step-by-step contacts" with China.

A few weeks later, when de Gaulle was in Washington to attend the funeral of former President Dwight D. Eisenhower, Nixon formally requested that the French President convey the spirit of America's new policy to the Chinese. De Gaulle agreed. One of his last diplomatic acts was to summon Etienne M. Manac'h, who had just been appointed Ambassador to Peking, to his office on April 23, 1969. He instructed Manac'h to transmit President Nixon's message to the Chinese leaders "at the highest level."

Manac'h arrived in Peking in early May and quickly carried out his assignment. At first most of the Chinese leaders, including Premier Chou En-lai, were skeptical. They remembered Nixon's past utterances on China, and they suspected a trap. But they listened, and they seemed to be cultivating a very special interest in the theme of improved Sino-American relations. For them, Taiwan was the crux of the problem.

The Chinese Communists had a clear memory of the changing American policy on Taiwan: Truman, in January, 1950, had said the United

States "would not provide military aid and advice to the Chinese forces" that had fled in defeat from the mainland to the island of Taiwan; his Secretary of State, Dean Acheson, a few days later pointed to the President's decision as proof that the United States would not meddle in the internal affairs of China. No one, neither Chiang Kai-shek's defeated Nationalists nor Mao's victorious Communists nor the pro-Chiang U.S. Government, then regarded Taiwan as anything but a province of China. But the outbreak of war in Korea in June of that year caused the United States to reverse its policy on the grounds, stated by Truman, that a Communist take-over of Taiwan would be "a direct threat to the security of the Pacific area and to the United States forces." The province suddenly became "free China." Truman ordered the Seventh Fleet to patrol the Taiwan Strait and prevent military operations in either direction. A new element had been added to the hostility between Peking and Washington.

In his talks with the Chinese, Manac'h, a talented diplomat and former schoolteacher with an extensive background in Asian affairs, tried to place Taiwan in historical perspective. It was not only a juridical problem — who owns Taiwan? — but a political one, emotional and intractable, unlikely to vanish with the mere wave of a magic wand. It was necessary to understand that any solution to the problem of Taiwan would lie at the end of the road, and not at the beginning. Of all the Chinese leaders, Chou seemed the first to grasp the message.

Other messages were soon to follow. For a few weeks in July and early August, the President traveled around the globe, stopping in South Vietnam, Guam, India, Pakistan, and Rumania. In Islamabad and in Bucharest, Nixon echoed his China-opening theme to General Agha Muhammad Yahya Khan and President Nicolae Ceauşescu. The United States is getting out of Vietnam, he said, and the United States wants to talk with China. Both Yahya Khan and Ceauşescu had cordial relations with Peking and cool relations with Moscow, and each promised to convey the President's sentiments to the Chinese leaders.

All during that summertime journey, Nixon saw China over the horizon. Hugh Sidey, Time-Life's perceptive President-watcher, recounted that while Nixon's jet soared over Asia, Haldeman told Kissinger that " 'the boss' seemed to have it in his mind that he might be visiting Peking before another year was out." Kissinger, whose admiration for Haldeman rivaled the Hatfields' for the McCoys, scoffed at the idea. The President, he responded, would be lucky if he got to China by the end of his second term.

But Nixon was clearly angling for a visa.

At his Guam stopover, Nixon enunciated a policy — dubbed by Mansfield the "Nixon Doctrine" — that contained an implied message for the Chinese: the days of American intervention in peripheral wars were over. The United States, Nixon said, was willing to honor its commitments with rhetoric, money, and matériel but not with men — unless the threat to an ally came from a nuclear power. If implemented, the doctrine would clearly mean a lowering of the U.S. profile throughout Asia.

The unprecedented stop in Rumania — no American President had ever before paid a formal visit to a Communist capital — was another signal. Nixon had visited Bucharest once before, as a private citizen with his eye on the GOP nomination. He had made an overseas trip in 1967 to brush up his image as a world statesman. The Rumanians had given him a warm reception, which he appreciated all the more after he was snubbed by the top-ranking officials in Moscow. Shortly after his inauguration, Nixon learned that Ceauşescu, who was in trouble with the Russians because of his ongoing friendship with the Chinese, would welcome a presidential visit. The idea appealed to Nixon and Kissinger, although it alarmed the State Department traditionalists. Llewellyn Thompson, twice Ambassador to Moscow and a respected Soviet specialist, and a number of his State Department colleagues warned the President that he could expect an outburst of Soviet indignation if he accepted Ceauşescu's invitation. Nixon's decision to ignore State's advice pleased Kissinger. On June 28 the Bucharest visit was announced. The Kremlin was stunned. On August 2 Nixon arrived in Bucharest and received a tumultuous reception from the Rumanian people, who apparently saw him as their hedge against total Soviet domination. For his part, Nixon wanted to signal Moscow that a new era in East-West relations had dawned — and Peking that he was ready to go anywhere.

The Nixon Administration did not rely solely on foreign intermediaries or foreign signals. In early June Kissinger posed a broad question to the State Department: what specific steps could the United States take toward "normalizing relations" with Peking that would not unduly disturb America's allies in the Pacific? Richardson brainstormed about China with a few of his close aides and then, in a memo that "broke the back" of the problem, to quote one participant, he listed five possibilities. These were all in the economic sphere, and they ranged from reducing controls on American subsidiaries trading with China to allowing American tourists to buy up to a hundred dollars in Chinese-made goods.

Within a week, Kissinger got back to Richardson. The President had reviewed the list and given the green light to two of the five recommendations. The Under Secretary was delighted. Soon there would be other recommendations and other green lights; and then, starting in midsummer, at regular intervals, the United States began announcing unilateral acts of reconciliation toward China. For example:

July 21, 1969. Scholars, journalists, students, scientists and members of Congress could now automatically have their passports validated for travel to China. In addition, American tourists could buy up to a hundred dollars' worth of goods originating in China.

August 8, 1969. Rogers expressed the Administration's desire to resume the Warsaw talks.

November 7, 1969. The United States suspended naval patrols in the Taiwan Strait, ending the nineteen-year legacy of the Korean War.

December 15, 1969. Washington announced that all nuclear weapons on Okinawa would be removed by the end of the year.

December 19, 1969. The hundred-dollar ceiling on the purchase of Chinese goods was lifted; such goods could now be purchased in unlimited amounts. In addition, the Commerce Department announced that foreign subsidiaries of American companies could trade in nonstrategic goods with China.

This tattoo of signals aimed at Peking coincided with the first publicly reported military clashes between the Chinese and the Russians along their long border, bringing the two countries dangerously close to war.

In early March, 1969, shooting broke out on what the Russians call Damansky Island and the Chinese call Chenpao Island, in the Ussuri River, which flows between the northeastern province of Heilungkiang in Manchuria and the Maritime Province of the Soviet Far East. Casualties were heavy. A few months later, during the summer, small-scale clashes were reported along the Amur River and at the boundary of the province of Sinkiang, more than two thousand miles west of the Ussuri. The clashes came as a stunning surprise to the world outside of Peking and Moscow; but, in fact, tensions — fired by propaganda and troop buildups on both sides — had been escalating for some time. The Russian-Chinese border had been in dispute for some three centuries, but the Chinese Communists had not raised the issue with their "fraternal ally," the Soviet Union, until the early 1960s, when ideological and policy differences drove a wedge between the two Communist powers. Now their alliance was shattered; what the U.S. Government had once regarded as the unshakable unity of Moscow and Peking had ended in pools of blood along the Ussuri and the Amur.

It was against this background that Kissinger, in late August, 1969, invited Allen S. Whiting, a former State Department specialist on China who had become a Professor of Political Science at the University of Michigan, to a freewheeling session on the Sino-Soviet confrontation. The setting was the sunny terrace just outside Kissinger's small office, a few doors away from Nixon's, at the presidential compound overlooking the Pacific at San Clemente. Joining them in the talk was Kissinger's NSC China specialist, John Holdridge.

Whiting quickly made it clear that he did not share Washington's comparatively casual reaction to the clashes along the Sino-Soviet border. U.S. intelligence knew that Soviet troop strength along the Chinese border had increased from thirteen "thin" divisions in 1965 to twenty-five "thick" divisions by the spring of 1969, and was still increasing, yet the prevailing Government view was that the Soviet buildup was defensive. Kissinger, like many other officials, tended to feel that China was more likely to attack Russia than Russia was to attack China. No alarm bells sounded at the White House, even after the recent clashes.

Whiting, by contrast, was alarmed, and he blamed the Russians for the increase in tensions along the border. He made two basic points. First, he argued, the Russians might very well be preparing a preemptive strike against China's nuclear force, hence their sizable buildup not only of troops but of missiles, planes and tanks along the Chinese border. After all, only a year earlier Brezhnev, invoking his doctrine of "limited sovereignty" for Socialist states other than Russia, had ordered his troops into Czechoslovakia to smash what he perceived as the threat of Prague liberalism. If Brezhnev considered Maoism to be a threat to Moscow's hegemony over the Communist world, then China's small but growing pile of nuclear weapons could be seen as reinforcing the threat. Indeed, during the summer a number of Soviet diplomats in different countries had begun to suggest that Russia might soon do everyone a favor by destroying China's atomic force. The word "blitzkrieg," so charged with memories of the Nazi attack on Russia, was often used.

Whiting's second point followed from his first. Whether Russia actually attacked or not, China felt threatened, living under the cloud of a Soviet "surgical strike." China could not count on Soviet restraint or rationality.

Suddenly, her former ally to the west was a greater threat than her enemy to the east. For Peking's politicians, this was a shattering realization. A lifetime of struggle had been invested in the comforting idea that Russia, despite her faults, was a friend and America, because of her faults, was an enemy. Now they decided it was time to revive the old Chinese tradition of playing one barbarian off against the other; China, for the time being, would make "common cause" with America against Russia.

To Whiting, this represented an historic opportunity. America, appreciating China's dilemma, could reach across the Pacific in friendship for the first time in twenty years; and China, reeling from the Cultural Revolution and alarmed by the Soviet border buildup, might very well welcome the gesture. A chance for a radical realignment of Pacific powers snapped into focus — for Kissinger, for the very first time.

Kissinger was clearly impressed by Whiting's analysis and, years later, was to admit its influence on the development of his thinking about China. Other scholars contributed, too — A. Doak Barnett, Edwin Reischauer, Jerome Cohen, Lucien Pye, Henry Rosovsky, George Taylor, James Thomson, and John King Fairbank — the dean of the China scholars — but none was apparently as influential as Whiting.

For the first time, Kissinger focused on the possibility that the Russians were much more likely to attack the Chinese than the other way around. He later admitted that he had been wrong in assuming that the Chinese were so irrational that they were planning an attack against the more powerful Soviet Union. He began to understand that there were "two sides" to the Sino-Soviet dispute. He realized the "subtlety" of China's messages, the gap between her hot rhetoric and her cool actions. He recognized the "absurdity" of dealing with China through intermediaries. This was all old hat to many China-watchers, the stuff of years of frustration during which they had tried to swing senior governmental policymakers toward a more realistic judgment of China, only to discover that the bureaucracy was really more comfortable with its dated, one-dimensional view.

Belatedly, Kissinger became a convert — a latter-day Marco Polo discovering the new China — and he plunged into his subject with all of the eagerness and occasional naïveté of the newcomer to Asia.

Nixon had been flashing his signals to Peking since the spring but there had been no positive response; significantly, there had not been any of the usual denunciations either. Then, as summer turned to fall, Kissinger heard from the Rumanians and then from the Pakistanis that the Chinese might soon be interested in resuming the Warsaw talks. He decided to try to speed up the Chinese timetable and make Peking aware of Nixon's desire to open a dialogue.

Since 1955 there had been a hundred and thirty-four meetings between Chinese and American diplomats in Warsaw and earlier in Prague, but there had been few genuine exchanges. Slogans were swapped, but not real negotiating proposals. Kissinger wanted to establish a channel for serious conversation — to end this pattern of "stupefying boredom."

In early October, the President's clearance in hand, Kissinger cabled Walter J. Stoessel, Jr., then U.S. Ambassador to Poland, and specifically instructed him to seek out the top-ranking Chinese envoy at the next convenient diplomatic function and to propose to him the resumption of the Warsaw talks. In the best of times, this would have been a highly unorthodox approach; but in these circumstances, with China and the United States barely exchanging glances across a crowded room, such an approach would be, in Kissinger's words, "an unbelievable event." And the Chinese would certainly report it back to Peking.

The idea was apparently so "unbelievable" that the first time around, Stoessel, though a career diplomat, completely ignored his cabled instructions.

Several weeks later, Kissinger again cabled the same instructions to Stoessel, and again Stoessel ignored them. The Ambassador, a specialist on Soviet affairs, did not query Kissinger about them, nor did he seek any clarification. Weeks passed. Kissinger was quickly discovering the ingenious way in which the bureaucracy could frustrate presidential directives; up until that moment, however, no ambassador had ever chosen to ignore two clear cables from the White House. Kissinger sent a third cable, but by late November, to his surprise, there was still no action. "Finally," Kissinger recalls, "we had to tell him, 'Either you do it, or we will get somebody who will.'"

Finally, on December 3, Stoessel, under duress, carried out his mission. His opportunity came at a Yugoslav reception, where he spotted Lei Yang, Chargé d'Affaires at the Chinese Embassy. Eyewitnesses report that Stoessel tried to approach the Chinese envoy several times, only to find that, each time, Lei would deliberately waltz away. At last, after whispering a hurried good-bye to his host, the Chinese diplomat darted toward the door. Stoessel, who prides himself on keeping in trim shape with tennis, swimming, and skiing, had to sprint after his quarry down a flight of stairs before he could "exchange a few words" with him, as John King, a State Department spokesman, described the scene the next day. The "few words" were an American invitation to begin "serious talks" with the Chinese.

Lei must have been shocked by Stoessel's unorthodox approach. A few years later, during one of Kissinger's trips to Peking, Chou En-lai recalled the incident. "If you want to give heart attacks to our diplomats," he joked, "approach them at social functions and propose serious talks."

Stoessel and Lei met formally at the Chinese Embassy on December 11. They talked for an hour and fifteen minutes. The result of their conversation was an agreement to resume the Warsaw talks. For the first time, the Chinese had responded — and favorably — to the long series of private and public American signals. "It was not love of America but fear of Russia that motivated Chinese policy," as one China specialist has put it. The new Chinese stance was directly traceable to the fact that border talks in Peking between China and the Soviet Union had reached an impasse in early December and Moscow had reacted with new denunciations that were read by the Chinese as threats of war.

On January 8, 1970, Peking and Washington announced that the Warsaw talks would be resumed on January 20. Robert J. McCloskey, the State Department spokesman, disclosed at the regular noontime briefing for newsmen that the talks would start at the "Chinese Communist Embassy." A few hours later, on precise White House orders, McCloskey amended his remarks. The talks, he declared, would start "at the Embassy of the People's Republic of China." Never before had any American spokesman referred to the Peking regime, founded in 1949, by its official name. Three times, McCloskey repeated "the People's Republic of China," just to make sure the signal bounced clearly across the Pacific.

As scheduled, American and Chinese diplomats met on January 20, at the Chinese Embassy. It was their first get-together in more than two years. The atmosphere was "businesslike." Both sides had fresh proposals for exchanges of journalists, students, and scientists. The United States also expressed the hope that China, "as a gesture of goodwill," would release the few Americans who had been detained by Peking since the Korean War. They reached only one agreement — to meet again on February 20. Kissinger was pleased with this modest but positive result. A channel of sorts had been reestablished.

On February 18, there was another signal — this one from the President himself. Nixon sent a special report to the Congress entitled "U.S. Foreign Policy for the 1970s, a New Strategy for Peace." The section on China was loaded with flattering references to the "great and vital people," the "gifted and cultured people" of China, and it underscored the "historic ties of friendship with the Chinese people." This section, drafted and redrafted by Kissinger, pledged the U.S. to "take what steps we can towards improved practical relations with Peking." Nixon did not use the official name — the People's Republic of China. That was to come later in the year.

On February 20, American and Chinese diplomats — Stoessel on the one side, Lei on the other — met for the second time in two months. According to Kissinger, the Chinese arrived at the American Embassy with a big surprise for their hosts: they proposed that the talks be moved to Peking. And they hinted that they would welcome a high-ranking U.S. official to head the delegation.

There has been some controversy about who actually initiated this unusual proposal. State Department China experts contend that they went to the February 20 meeting with a surprise of their own — namely, a proposal that the United States send a high-ranking official to visit Peking. Kissinger, on the other hand, maintains that the United States made no such proposal at that time. He concedes that the State Department might have been considering it but that it was never cleared by the White House nor submitted to the Chinese — at least, not then.

The idea that an official American delegation would be welcome in Peking was intriguing. In the context of China's growing anxiety about Soviet intentions, a Chinese overture to the United States made sense. But Peking's phraseology was deliberately vague. The Chinese did not explicitly invite a high-level American to visit Peking; they seemed to be saying that the Americans could send anyone, high or low, at their own discretion. The Chinese, who can be exquisitely precise, did not even say whether the American should be dispatched secretly or whether his mission would be simply a continuation of the Warsaw talks in a new setting. In any event, the United States did not leap at the Chinese overture. Kissinger wasn't sure whether the proposal was merely an attempt to undermine Washington's relations with Taiwan or whether the Chinese had more serious discussions in mind. Nor was he certain that Peking would be the ideal location for the talks.

The State Department experts had their own concerns — whether the Chinese would grant "diplomatic immunity" to American negotiators in

Peking; whether the Chinese would allow the Americans to set up a "secure" channel of communications with Washington; whether the Japanese and the Taiwanese would interpret such a Peking journey as an American kowtow to the Chinese. After all, some of them argued, why should the Americans, like other tribute-bearing foreigners before them, journey to the Middle Kingdom? Why not the other way around?

For the next month or two, Kissinger focused on these concerns, and others. The Administration's effort to open a new dialogue with China had alarmed Soviet specialists at the State Department. Just as they had worried about the President's journey to Rumania, they now worried about this sudden coziness with the Chinese. They were convinced that the effort would yield skimpy diplomatic dividends in the near future and that it would antagonize the Russians to the point of jeopardizing chances for improved Soviet-American relations. Moreover, they argued that if the game was really to exploit the Sino-Soviet quarrel, it would have no effect. Kissinger listened to their arguments, but ultimately ignored them. The "big picture" required an opening to China.

A third Chinese-American meeting in the Warsaw series had been arranged for May 20, primarily to propose guidelines for a more serious exchange of views, perhaps even in Peking. But twenty-four hours before the envoys were to meet, Peking canceled the session in view of what it called the "increasingly grave situation" caused by the U.S. invasion of Cambodia on April 30.

Through several "third party" contacts, Nixon assured the Chinese that the strike into Cambodia did not represent a change in the privately conveyed Administration desire to get out of Vietnam and to improve relations with Peking. It was considered significant that the Chinese did not cancel the May 20 meeting until May 19, almost three weeks into the Cambodia operation. One explanation, favored by Kissinger, was that political in-fighting in Peking had produced divided counsel. In retrospect, it was seen that there were clearly two factions struggling for power: a pragmatic group, led by Chou En-lai, championing the new tactic of an opening to Washington to counter the Soviet threat, and a so-called "ultra-leftist" group, led by Marshal Lin Piao, clinging to the revolutionary line of resisting both Washington and Moscow. In early June, even before all the American troops had been withdrawn from Cambodia, Chou reportedly told Emil Bodnaraş, a visiting Deputy Premier of Rumania, that he still favored better relations with the

United States, but that he could not speak for the entire Chinese leadership.

In Peking, from August 23 until September 6, 1970, the political and military leadership of China met in a special secret plenum to resolve, once and for all, the bitter dispute between the Chou and Lin factions of the Communist Party. The Chou faction triumphed, principally because its policy of replacing extremism with moderation at home and abroad won the support of Mao Tse-tung. The hard-liners were gradually losing influence in Peking. Lin Piao remained as Defense Minister for the time being, but his grip was slipping. The outcome of this power struggle had a direct bearing on Peking's opening toward Washington.

The first signal of the new Chinese attitude was flashed on China's National Day, on October 1. High up on the reviewing stand atop the mammoth vermilion-pillared Gate of Heavenly Peace, before hundreds of thousands of Chinese parading in T'ien-An Men Square, stood a smiling Chairman Mao, seventy-six years old, surveying the revolution he had led for half a century. And next to him stood Edgar Snow, the American writer who had journeyed to the Communist Party's headquarters in the caves of Yenan in the mid-1930s to return with his classic report, *Red Star over China*. Official photographers focused on these two old friends, flashing a clear message: Mao was giving his blessing to a move toward Washington. Kissinger needed no interpreter.

Snow and Mao talked that day about many things. Mao said he was "not satisfied with the present situation," with the "official lying" and the "maltreatment" of Party members during the Cultural Revolution. He also expressed deep concern about the Russians. Sino-Soviet ideological differences were now irreconcilable, he emphasized. Polemics between Peking and Moscow might have to continue "for ten thousand years." When the Chinese leader spoke about America, he sounded a sympathetic note that Snow had not heard for many years. China might well follow America's lead in decentralizing wealth and responsibility, Mao remarked, suggesting that in some ways, China, the land of continuing revolution, could learn from America, the land of vibrant conservatism.

Nixon and Kissinger had heard about the August-September plenum, and its presumed results, and they had seen the Mao-Snow picture in the morning newspapers. Both realized that it was time to step forth with a bold initiative. Nothing had come of the Chinese proposal, made back in February, to move the Warsaw talks to Peking. Now Nixon and

Kissinger, operating in total secrecy, decided to up the ante with an equally intriguing counterproposal — that the talks in Peking be conducted "at a high level." They did not specify how high.

In late October, they found two eager couriers. Dozens of heads of state, including Rumania's Ceauşescu and Pakistan's Yahya Khan, had come to New York to celebrate the UN's twenty-fifth birthday. On October 24 these two leaders were among the thiry-one heads of state or government invited to a White House dinner, and the next day Nixon met for almost an hour with Yahya Khan, who would soon be visiting China. The President asked the Pakistani leader to convey the new American proposition to the Chinese, and it is not unreasonable to suppose that he also expressed his own desire to visit Peking at some unspecified time in the future.

On that same day, Ziegler hinted at a major change in American policy toward China's admission to the UN. "The U.S.," he stated, "opposes the admission of the Peking regime into the UN at the expense of the expulsion of the Republic of China." In other words, the United States had adopted a two-China formula. It represented a big step away from the official U.S. view that Taiwan alone should represent China in the UN.

On October 26, Ceauşescu was accorded a warm and colorful reception on the White House lawn — Marine band, national anthems, the Cabinet, high school students "bused" to the White House for the occasion. That afternoon, the two Presidents discussed China, according to their spokesmen; and, that evening, Nixon delivered a toast, pointing out the uniqueness of Rumania's good relations with "the United States . . . the Soviet Union . . . and the People's Republic of China." It was the first time an American Chief Executive had referred to China as "the People's Republic of China."

Most newsmen missed the significance of the phrasing, but Soviet Ambassador Dobrynin did not. After the White House dinner, he telephoned Kissinger and asked for an explanation. Kissinger replied coyly that it had no special meaning. Didn't the Russians call China the People's Republic of China?

Nixon and Ceauşescu apparently discussed many aspects of the China problem, including Taiwan. The Rumanians have privately claimed that Nixon told Ceauşescu that, so far as he was concerned, Taiwan was not an international but an internal problem, to be resolved by the Chinese themselves, preferably in a peaceful way. This had always been Peking's position — but not Washington's. For twenty years, the United States had insisted that Taiwan was not a province of China but an "independent" nation with which Washington maintained a defense treaty.

"Totally wrong," Kissinger told us, about the Rumanian story. He maintains that the President did not shift ground on the Taiwan issue until a year later. But, given Nixon's determination to start serious talks with the Chinese, it seems logical to assume that he conveyed some hint of a possible American shift on the sensitive Taiwan issue at this time.

The new American signals — some of them in the form of diplomatic notes — were all communicated to the leaders in Peking within a few weeks. Yahya Khan, in China from November 9 through 14, was the principal courier. Much to his surprise, he was received by Mao on November 13. Gheorghe Rădulescu, a Deputy Premier from Rumania, visited China at roughly the same time. He was received by Chou.

During the next two months — December, 1970, and January, 1971 — the Americans and the Chinese conducted a completely secret exchange of messages, via Pakistan. This exchange, Kissinger later explained, was "the first serious, nonsparring exchange" between the two countries in more than twenty years. "The mail was read," he pointed out — a reference to the mailmen, whose curiosity may have got the better of them — so, naturally, "both sides left themselves escape hatches." The American messages were extremely vague, while the Chinese were "highly ambiguous." Kissinger, who drafted the American notes, and who was first to read the Chinese replies, was often struck by the difference between Russian and Chinese diplomatic communications. The Chinese, he recalled, "were always much more civilized and elegant . . . much more delicate in style and drafting" than the Russians. In effect, Washington and Peking were playing mood music to one another, deliberately avoiding strident notes and crescendos of propaganda.

To preserve secrecy, and with it the option of denial in the event these seedlings did not take root, the Chinese notes never were signed. Nor was there any salutation, although the contents were clearly intended for the President. The notes were all handwritten on white paper with blue lines. For the most part, the Chinese said all they had to say at any one time on a single sheet of paper.

These messages, after a while, became "warmer and warmer," according to Kissinger. The two sides were edging toward an improvement of relations that in time could be capped by a high-level American visit to Peking, perhaps even a presidential visit. According to Snow's semi-official accounts of his conversations with Chou and Mao during this period, the prospect of a Nixon visit was openly discussed. Snow quoted Mao as saying in December, 1970:

> The Foreign Ministry was studying the matter of admitting Americans from the left, middle and right to visit China. Should rightists, like Nixon, who represented the monopoly capitalists, be permitted to come? He should be welcome because, Mao explained, at present the problems between China and the USA would have to be solved with Nixon. Mao would be happy to talk with him, either as a tourist, or as President.

Snow continued:

> Yes, he said to me, he preferred men like Nixon to social democrats and revisionists, those who professed to be one thing, but in power behaved quite otherwise.
>
> Nixon might be deceitful, he went on, but perhaps a little bit less so than some others. Nixon resorted to tough tactics but he also used some soft tactics. Yes, Nixon could just get on a plane and come. It would not matter whether the talks would be successful. If he were willing to come, the Chairman would be willing to talk to him and it would be all right. It would be all right, whether or not they quarreled, or whether Nixon came as a tourist or as President. He believed they would not quarrel. . . . Discussing Nixon's possible visit to China, the Chairman casually remarked that the presidential election would be in 1972, would it not? Therefore, he added, *Mr. Nixon might send an envoy first, but was not himself likely to come to Peking before early 1972.*

In fact, Snow reported that "several urgent and authentically documented inquiries" had reached Peking indicating that "the President wished to know whether he or his representative would be received" in China.

Kissinger has flatly denied this report, claiming that the United States never formally proposed a presidential visit. However, he has allowed for the possibility that one of his many intermediaries might have conveyed to Peking's leaders the President's "private feelings" about visiting China. The distinction may appear artificial, but diplomats place great emphasis upon such distinctions. In this particular case, it would have allowed Nixon to communicate a personal desire to travel to China without it appearing that the President of the United States of America was petitioning Peking for a visa.

In February, 1971, Nixon allowed Indochina to break the rhythm of forward movement in his secret dealings with China. His approval of the invasion of Laos by South Vietnamese forces, supported by U.S. air power, alarmed the Chinese. The secret exchanges between Washington and Peking, by way of Islamabad, abruptly stopped: for six weeks, no direct messages were exchanged. According to one report, the Chinese alerted thirty divisions in Yunnan, the province bordering on Laos and North Vietnam. The Chinese were clearly anxious, despite American assurances, that the U.S. had limited aims in Laos and that China was not being threatened.

Ole Aalgaard, then the Norwegian Ambassador to Peking, an occasional intermediary, was puzzled by the Chinese alert. Surely China did not consider the Laotian operation a "direct threat," he remarked to Chiao Kuan-hua, a Vice Foreign Minister and, with Mao and Chou, one of the architects of the Chinese opening to the United States. Chiao recalled a moment during the Korean War when President Truman was insisting on the "limited" nature of American aims while General Mac-Arthur was unleashing the American Army toward the Yalu River. We are "fairly confident of Nixon's limited intentions in Laos," he told Aalgaard, "but not sure some general wouldn't take it into his head to provoke China, or cover failure with a drastic escalation."

The Chinese military alert finally produced assurances from Washington on the highest level. On February 17, the President told newsmen that the Laotian operation "should not be interpreted by the Communist Chinese as being a threat to them." On February 25, in his second foreign policy report to Congress, Nixon repeated in writing his earlier reference to the Peking regime as the "People's Republic of China." And on February 26 Kissinger told us, during a televised interview, "We consider it highly unlikely that Communist China will come in under the circumstances that now exist . . . *despite the temporary flare-ups that are inseparable from the disengagement process. . . .*" (Italics added by the authors.) Kissinger then reiterated Nixon's pledge that the United States was getting out of Indochina.

The Chinese had seen many "barbarians" come and go throughout history. The Americans were no exception. By Chinese standards, "America's burst of global imperialism was," to quote Professor Ross Terrill, a Harvard specialist on China, "an affair of a single evening. It ran only from the quivering sense of power of 1945 until the lesson of the powerlessness of power in Vietnam." Ironically, the failure of the Laotian operation ensured the success of the China opening.

By March 5, 1971, Mao, convinced finally that America represented a receding tide in Asian affairs while the Russians represented a rising threat, sent Chou to Hanoi with an important message: China would not intervene in Vietnam, despite the Laos invasion, because Peking believed that the United States was withdrawing from Indochina.

On March 14 Chou told a European diplomat in Peking, during the course of a wide-ranging all-night discussion about Indochina and Sino-American relations, that China had made a fateful decision: to open a high-level dialogue with the leaders of the United States. Another Chinese official said, "The opening up is going to go far. It is going to be a big thing."

Almost immediately, the indirect exchange between the two capitals resumed. The tone of the messages — transmitted through a Pakistan suddenly rent by civil war — changed. Before, they had been deliberately vague, almost philosophical. Now they became specific. Nixon and Kissinger, disheartened by another wave of antiwar criticism, found the change exhilarating. More and more, the messages suggested the imminence of a breakthrough. "Seventy percent," judged Kissinger by late March. There was "a seventy percent chance" that some high-ranking American would soon be traveling to China.

Over the Himalayas — and Beyond

One evening in the early spring of 1971, as the cherry trees around the Tidal Basin began to blossom, a handwritten note was delivered to Henry Kissinger at the White House by Pakistan's Ambassador to the United States, Agha Hilaly. For Hilaly, an experienced diplomat, dropping off the sealed envelope was nothing more than carrying out an errand at the request of President Yahya Khan in Islamabad. For Kissinger, it represented a turning point in Chinese-American relations.

The note — no salutation, no signature, on the customary white paper with blue lines — was from Peking; it was the latest and by far the most important in the secret exchange of correspondence between the two capitals. It extended an invitation for an "American envoy" to come to Peking for high-level talks with Chinese leaders. Two names were suggested: Rogers and Kissinger.

Kissinger glanced at his watch; it was seven-fifteen. He immediately tried to inform the President, but the President was then entertaining guests in the State Dining Room. Kissinger got in touch with one of the military aides and told him to ask Nixon to get back to him as soon as possible. "Don't let the President go to bed," Kissinger instructed the aide. "I must see him."

After saying good night to the last of his guests, the President met with Kissinger in the Lincoln Sitting Room. The significance of the message was obvious. The two men talked well past midnight. "It seems to me," Nixon mused, "they may want a summit meeting."

The sensitive question of who would go to Peking was not decided that night.

For their part, the Chinese anticipated from the very outset that Kissinger would be the envoy. It was clear from comments they had made to foreign diplomats in Peking that they respected the former Harvard professor; they had read his books and undoubtedly had acquired a more intimate portrait of him through the North Vietnamese who had been secretly negotiating with him in Paris. Once, during the winter, Vice Foreign Minister Chiao Kuan-hua had told Norwegian Ambassador Aalgaard that he would like to meet Kissinger. And one of Chou En-lai's close aides told Edgar Snow that he looked forward to "crossing verbal swords with such a worthy adversary." "Kissinger!" he exclaimed. "There is a man who knows the language of both worlds — his own and ours. He is the first American we have seen in his position. With him it should be possible to talk."

Nixon decided on Kissinger. "I've thought about it," he said. "I will send you."

Kissinger was delighted. It took "a fantastic amount of guts," he later joked. "Richard Nixon sends me alone, cut off from communications. For all he knew, I was going to sell Alaska."

Nixon and Kissinger, a pair of elitists in foreign affairs who shared a distrust of bureaucracy, began quietly to orchestrate a series of actions that would alert the American people to the possibility of an historic breakthrough while at the same time would reveal little of substance. It was the Chinese who dramatically went public.

On April 6, toward the finale of an international Ping-Pong competition in Nagoya, Japan, the Chinese team invited the American team to tour China. The invitation had the appearance of sheer sportsmanship, but it was actually a major political gesture toward the United States. It was, as *Time* magazine put it, "the ping heard round the world." The U.S. Embassy in Tokyo queried Washington about whether the team's passports could be validated. The reply came rocketing back: Yes.

That very night, Nixon summoned the National Security Council into extraordinary session. He called on Kissinger to review the broad outlines of the Administration's new China policy, but he did not inform any of the members of the NSC, except for Secretary of State Rogers, about the secret Chinese invitation or the tentative American response. Nixon, operating on a "need to know" basis, had decided that the others did not need to know. Most of the NSC members applauded the President's China initiative; Vice-President Agnew criticized it. He thought that an opening to China would be dangerous to American interests; certainly it would poison U.S. relations with Taiwan. Agnew was overruled, but a few days later, he invited nine reporters into his hotel room in Williamsburg, Virginia, well after midnight, and repeated his objections to the approach to Peking. Agnew's comments were supposed to be off the record, but some reporters who were not included in the nocturnal bull session broke the story. The President was reported to be "steaming mad."

On April 10, nine Ping-Pong players, four officials, two wives, and three journalists who were given visas at the last moment, crossed the Lo Wu Bridge connecting Hong Kong with China. They represented the first official American delegation to set foot in the ancient land since the Communist victory in 1949.

The American party was treated to carefully rehearsed yet captivating Chinese hospitality. And since they had come at China's invitation to fulfill a special sort of prediplomatic mission, they were received by Chou En-lai.

On April 14, in the Great Hall of the People, the Chinese Premier, in a message that clearly was meant to sound beyond the huge reception room, told them: "You have opened a new page in the relations of the Chinese and American people. I am confident that this beginning again of our friendship will certainly meet with majority support of our two peoples." There was a pause. "Don't you agree with me?" he asked. The Americans burst into applause, and they reciprocated by inviting a Chinese Ping-Pong team to tour the United States. The invitation was quickly accepted.

Nixon and Kissinger, surprised at the speed with which the Chinese had begun implementing their opening to the United States, tried to keep the momentum going. Within a few hours of Chou's remarks, the White House announced a package of liberalizing measures designed to narrow the gap between the two countries. The twenty-one-year-old embargo on U.S. trade with China was relaxed. Visas for Chinese wishing to visit the United States would be expedited. Currency controls were loosened to enable China to use U.S. dollars to pay for imports. American oil companies would be allowed to sell fuel to ships and planes going in and out of China. American-owned foreign ships would be permitted to dock, in Chinese ports.

In the next two weeks, Nixon kept piling on the signals of American readiness for rapprochement with Peking. On April 21, he assured Graham B. Steenhoven, who, as president of the U.S. Table Tennis Association, had led the delegation to China, that he "certainly would cooperate" with the projected visit of the Chinese team to the United States. On April 26, a presidential panel recommended that Peking be admitted to the UN but that Taiwan not be expelled. On April 29, Nixon talked with reporters about "our new China policy." "What we have done," he noted, "has broken the ice. Now we have to test the water to see how deep it is." He then volunteered a comment that was meant to be studied by those sending him unsigned notes from Peking. "I hope," the President said, "and as a matter of fact, I expect to visit mainland China sometime in some capacity — I don't know what capacity."

At the time Nixon dropped that tantalizing aside, both he and Kissinger, extrapolating on the basis of the secret Chinese note of a few weeks earlier, now viewed a presidential visit to China as "a possible outcome" of the Ping-Pong visit. Indeed, there was no longer much doubt that, barring an unpredictable turn of developments, the President, as Mao had forecast, would embark on a journey to China in early 1972, the start of a presidential election year.

Many evenings during May and June, after the secretaries had gone home, Nixon and Kissinger would retire to the Lincoln Sitting Room, a Victorian parlor in the southeast corner of the White House. Haldeman would occasionally join them, sometimes Rogers — but no one else. They would read and reread the secret notes from China. The President would raise questions, Kissinger would try to answer them.

Together, Nixon and Kissinger reviewed the issues that were certain to come up during the secret negotiations in China: U.S. policy toward

Taiwan, the seating of Peking in the UN, the withdrawal of GIs from Indochina, and the degree of normalization in relations between Washington and Peking. Together, they wrote the opening statement that Kissinger was to read to Chou En-lai — as well as ten hypothetical communiqués that Kissinger, on behalf of the President, could accept. A voluminous briefing book was prepared on Chinese history, culture, and current events.

Kissinger, a scholar once again, did his secret boning up on China mostly in the privacy of his home, late at night. The student of Metternich, Bismarck, and Castlereagh asked the CIA to send him a detailed biography of Chou; in a quick afterthought, he broadened his request to include all the world leaders — "for my files," he added protectively. He discreetly elicited the views of various Sinologists, but he was always careful not to reveal his true purpose. They appreciated his intellectual curiosity and thought he was simply shopping for the latest insights on China. He led a double life — in public, he would talk about Vietnam, Russia, and Europe; in private, he was becoming a new China hand. He was quick to use self-deprecating humor to throw anyone off the scent. One day, the *New York Times* ran a brief item speculating that Kissinger would go to China if diplomatic relations were reestablished. An NSC staffer, in the dark about the China connection, kidded Kissinger about the report. "One of my admirers" at the State Department, replied Kissinger, figured out that Peking was "just about as far away from Washington as he could think of sending me."

In Peking, influential Chinese kept bringing up Kissinger's name in conversations with foreigners in China. On June 19, two Chinese diplomats asked Professor Ross Terrill about the views of McGovern, Kennedy, and Fairbank on Sino-American relations, about the 1972 presidential campaign, and about Kissinger. How much power does Kissinger have? Is he more "open-minded" about China than officials at the State and Defense departments? Would he be ready to offend the Russians if strategy required it? The fascination with Kissinger became even more intense during the first days of July. On one occasion, Terrill, who is fluent in Chinese, found himself chatting with Kuo Mo-jo, one of China's best-known authors and propagandists. Terrill wanted to talk about culture. Kuo wanted to talk about Kissinger. "We don't know enough about the thinking of this man," he said.

In the midst of these secret preparations on both sides, the *New York*

Times, working just as secretly with official documents that had come into its possession, published a front-page story on June 13 that rocked the White House. It was the first installment of the "Pentagon Papers," a massive, classified history of the U.S. role in Indochina through May of 1968. Kissinger learned about the *Times* exclusive when he got off a plane in California and saw the newspaper headlines. His first reaction was to blame Laird for the leak. He called to check with Haig. "How many papers do you think the *Times* has?" Haig asked. "Oh, I don't know," Kissinger replied. "Seven? Ten?" "Would you believe ten thousand?" Haig said.

Kissinger believed that these leaks posed an unprecedented threat to the three sensitive negotiations then under way: with China, in connection with his secret trip; with the Soviet Union, on limiting strategic arms; and with North Vietnam, on finding a way to end the war. He was concerned that the Chinese might reconsider their invitation to him because they felt they could not rely on American discretion. Moreover, Kissinger felt personally embarrassed because he was the only high-ranking White House official who knew Daniel Ellsberg, then being identified as the source of the leak.

The President quickly decided to try to stop the publication of the "Pentagon Papers" on the grounds that "the national defense interests of the United States and the nation's security" would suffer "immediate and irreparable harm." The Justice Department obtained an injunction against further publication, but after various legal proceedings, the Supreme Court ruled that the right to a free press under the First Amendment overrode any other considerations. The *Times* resumed publication of its series and, shortly thereafter, published two other stories — one on India and Pakistan and the other on the top secret U.S. negotiating position on SALT — which led the President and Kissinger to believe there was a hemorrhage of leaks that could damage national security. Nixon at that point ordered Ehrlichman to set up a secret special investigation unit within the White House that came to be known as the "plumbers." Its original assignment was to plug the leaks. Although Kissinger eagerly encouraged the general effort to plug all leaks — he was constantly appalled at the frequency with which classified information appeared in the press — he has consistently maintained that he knew nothing about the existence of a "plumbers" unit, or about any of its activities.

Kissinger's concern about Peking's reaction to the "Pentagon Papers" leak was excessive. The Chinese, more fearful of the Russian threat along their border than of a possible disclosure of their contacts with the Americans, did nothing to interrupt the schedule of Kissinger's secret visit to China. The dates were set — July 9 to 11 — forty-nine hours to turn two decades of Sino-American hostility into a new start in relations. A round-the-world trip was arranged to serve as a decoy.

Kissinger left Andrews Air Force Base, near Washington, on July 1, in a presidential jet. Two days later, he was in Saigon, talking with President Thieu and Ambassador Bunker. The press corps was large and eager, stalking Kissinger's every move. He was front page in the *New York Times,* a major television story on the "CBS Evening News" with Walter Cronkite. On July 4, he arrived in Bangkok, where the press corps was smaller. The story was smaller, too, and Kissinger dropped off the front page. He smiled at newsmen but said not a word. On July 6, he flew into New Delhi. There was a moment of excitement; the presence of one hundred antiwar demonstrators forced Kissinger to slip out of the airport through a side exit. The moment made page 42 of the *Times.* On July 7, the dwindling and frustrated band of newsmen covering Kissinger trapped the American envoy as he was leaving Prime Minister Indira Gandhi's office. They wanted to know if he would see Le Duc Tho when he got to Paris, reasoning that a Kissinger link to Vietnam was their only story. No, Kissinger fibbed. The fib inspired the AP to file only a four-paragraph story, which managed to get on page 8 of the *Times.* News interest was falling rapidly. Normally the fact that the press was ignoring him would have sent Kissinger into a daylong fit of depression — this time, he was delighted. On July 8, a Thursday, Kissinger flew into the hot, new city of Islamabad, capital of Pakistan, and no one seemed to care any more.

"I had brought the press to tears," Kissinger recalled, "having six appointments a day, every day, and never saying a word. They had to stand there in that heat watching me go in, come out, go in, come out, and never saying anything. By the time I hit Islamabad, there were only three newsmen left."

That afternoon, the greatest disappearing act in modern diplomatic history was to unfold. It had all been worked out meticulously in advance between the White House and Pakistan's President Yahya Khan. As the indispensable middleman, routing the secret exchange of notes between Washington and Peking, he was in on the scheme from its inception. His discretion and cooperation were to help "tilt" Nixon toward Pakistan in the war that would erupt on the Indian subcontinent later in the year.

The plan worked smoothly. First, Kissinger paid a ninety-minute courtesy call on the President. Next, the word went out, as previously arranged, that the visiting American, exhausted by the long journey, would have to cancel a formal dinner in his honor (which had in fact been set up for the sole purpose of being canceled) and would be driven to the eighty-five-hundred-foot-high hill station of Nathia Gali for a brief rest. The next day, July 9, the Pakistan government announced that Kissinger would be forced to extend his stay in Nathia Gali because of a "slight indisposition" — "Delhi belly," some reporters called it, a common enough problem for fast-moving travelers. Other reporters were skeptical; they speculated that Kissinger had slipped off to East Pakistan to lend a hand in settling the crisis developing between Yahya Khan and the insurgent Bengali leaders in Dacca. No one suspected China.

As part of the cover, the trip to Nathia Gali was to be as conspicuous as possible. So a decoy caravan of limousines, flying the flags of the United States and Pakistan and accompanied by a motorcycle escort, rolled through the streets of Islamabad and up into the mountains. It was led by the U.S. Ambassador to Pakistan, Joseph S. Farland. He was later joined by Sultan Mohammed Khan, the Secretary of the Ministry of Foreign Affairs, who had twice before served in Peking and was now in charge of the grand deception.

Nathia Gali, a cluster of hilltop bungalows with private, winding driveways, played its assigned role to perfection. A Pakistani doctor had been summoned there to treat a patient — only after a careful advance interrogation had convinced Khan that the doctor could not distinguish between Kissinger and any other Caucasian. "Have you ever laid eyes on Dr. Kissinger?" he had been asked. "No." "Surely you must have seen his pictures in the newspapers?" "No." So, the doctor, thinking he was treating Kissinger, treated a grateful Secret Service man who actually had a case of "Delhi belly."

To preserve the fiction, the government kept a steady stream of visitors driving from Islamabad to Nathia Gali to pay their respects to the indisposed traveler. The Chief of Staff of the Pakistan army, the Minister of Defense, and a score of other officials dropped in to inquire about Kissinger's health. All were intercepted by Khan. He'd serve them a cup of coffee and tell them that Kissinger was resting and could not be disturbed.

Actually, Kissinger had never gone to Nathia Gali. After his meeting with Yahya Khan on the evening of his arrival, he retired to the President's guesthouse. He stayed there until two-thirty in the morning, when Sultan Mohammed Khan arrived to escort him to Islamabad International Airport for the flight to Peking. The unusual time had been dictated not only by the need for secrecy, but by the schedule set down by the Chinese; they wanted Kissinger to arrive in Peking at noon. Kissinger joined the Khan in his 1971 Toyota Corona, and they sped off. "I remember that Kissinger was very quiet in the car, very much absorbed in his own thoughts," the Khan later recalled. "I could see that he wanted to be left alone and I respected that."

They arrived at the airport shortly after 3 A.M. The plane — a Pakistan International Airlines 707 — was waiting at the far end of the tarmac; Kissinger's own 707 was parked in a more conspicuous position in an effort to convince the curious that he was still in Nathia Gali. A few minutes before Kissinger boarded the aircraft, four senior Chinese officials entered the plane. They were Chou's welcoming party; they had been in the capital for three days, but had remained in seclusion. One of Kissinger's two security men had no idea where his boss was going; when he got on the plane and "saw four Chinese sitting there," Kissinger recalled, "he nearly dropped his teeth." Kissinger was joined by three of his aides — Winston Lord, a personal assistant, and John Holdridge and Richard Smyser, both specialists on Asia.

The plane and its cargo attracted almost no attention. PIA flew many flights into Peking, scheduled and unscheduled. Kissinger could have been a British businessman, and the four Chinese officials could have been representatives of the Chinese textile industry. That was how they must have struck everyone at the airport — except M. F. H. Beg, a former Pakistani Foreign Office type who had given up diplomacy for journalism years before and who happened to be at the airport when Kissinger arrived to board the special PIA plane. Beg, who was a stringer for the *Daily Telegraph*, spotted him.

"Isn't that Kissinger?" he is supposed to have asked a Pakistani official.

"Yes," the official replied, casually unloading one of the White House's biggest state secrets.

"Where's he going?" Beg wanted to know.

"China," came the answer.

"Why's he going there?"

"I don't know."

Beg quickly returned to his office and filed an urgent story to his newspaper in London, little realizing that he was about to become part of a new journalistic legend on Fleet Street. The editor on duty read the story — once, then twice, and then a third time. And then he spiked it! "Damn fool Beg," he said, according to the legend. "That bloke must be drunk. Really, Kissinger going off to China! Ridiculous!"

Shortly after 3 A.M. on July 9, Kissinger's plane was on its way to China. It did not fly the usual commercial route. Instead of arcing southward, around the rim of China, it cut northeast, over the most spectacular mountaintops in the world, directly for Peking.

Kissinger's mood was almost giddy. "I got a tremendous kick out of it," he later recalled. "I was going into a country I had never known or seen. I was the first to go in. It was . . . adventurous!"

The mood was clearly contagious. "Fantastic!" Winston Lord exclaimed. "Fantastic and in a way intoxicating. It was just so big, it was hard to take it all in."

For Lord, the trip to China had an extra dimension of excitement. His wife, Bette, is a Shanghai-born Chinese who left China at the age of eight, and whose book, *Eighth Moon*, tells of her sister Sansan's life in China under the Communists. Lord has always enjoyed claiming that it was actually he, and not Kissinger, who was the first American official in China. Just before they flew over the Pakistan-China border, Kissinger called Smyser to the back of the plane for a brief conference. That left Lord closer to the front of the plane than any other American on board. "I beat everybody in by about five yards," he boasted. "I felt great."

Kissinger was reading his thick briefing book on China — the one he and Nixon had prepared so meticulously — when dawn touched the snow-covered mountain peaks. He had pored over the book every night of this trip, after completing his daily chores. K-2, the second tallest mountain in the world, a magnet for intrepid climbers, loomed in intriguing silhouette outside his window.

At high noon, the PIA plane landed at an almost deserted military airfield near Peking. Kissinger was met by Marshal Yeh Chien-ying, one of the venerable leaders of the Chinese revolution, who had replaced Lin Piao as China's number one military figure; Ambassador Huang Hua, a skillful English-speaking diplomat who was soon to be dispatched to Canada and then to the United Nations; and two Foreign Office officials. The introductions were brief. The Chinese and American officials then drove to a handsome guesthouse on a small lake just outside Peking. The windows in Kissinger's car were veiled by thin silk curtains. Kissinger could see out, but no one could see in. The secrecy was absolute. He was now on his own, with no means of communication with Nixon.

Shortly after their arrival at the guesthouse, the American party joined their Chinese hosts for a sumptuous feast. Lord, Smyser, and Holdridge used chopsticks; Kissinger used a knife and fork, but apparently that was no insurmountable handicap. By the time he left China, two short days later, he had gained five pounds. "A guest of the state must have starved to death three thousand years ago," Kissinger jested, "and the Chinese are determined that it will not happen again."

At 4 P.M., Chou En-lai arrived at the Kissinger guesthouse. This was highly unusual protocol. Normally a head of government would not pay a call on a visitor, especially one without any state rank. This visitor was flattered and impressed. Chou, who was born in 1898, had played a giant role in modern Chinese history. He was one of the earliest members of the Chinese Communist Party. In the late 1930s and early 1940s, Chou entertained many Americans in Yenan and Chungking; he led the Communist negotiating team to the unsuccessful truce talks with the Nationalists and the Americans in the immediate post–World War II period. As Foreign Minister and Premier, he maintained China's links with the outside world; he was China's most widely traveled senior diplomat.

Chou and Kissinger, their staffs at their side, sat on opposite sides of a rectangular table covered with green felt. They talked for almost eight hours, through dinner and well into the night. There was no fixed agenda. Kissinger had his briefing book, his "Bible," as it came to be known, and he often consulted it. In fact, Kissinger read a formal opening statement. It had taken him and Nixon six hours to compose it. It took only ten minutes to read it. It was a clear and unemotional exposition of the President's reasons for wishing to begin a Chinese-American dialogue. Toward the end of Kissinger's exposition he used an adjective which caught Chou's fancy. "So here we are," Kissinger said, "after twenty-two years of separation, in this, for us, *mysterious* land."

"Mysterious?" Chou asked in astonishment. "Why mysterious?" Chou's question astounded Kissinger. He had dealt mostly with Russian Communists; Chinese Communists were a new breed. He had expected a sharp opening thrust on Vietnam or Taiwan, but not an inquiry into the nature of mystery.

For the next ten minutes, Kissinger and Chou drifted off into an exchange about national images — why *did* China appear mysterious, and America restless and slightly naïve? Their initial formality began to melt. Humor replaced protocol. Kissinger and Chou ranged away from their briefs into rambling reflections on their societies and political systems. They covered the nineteenth-century foreign intervention in China, Mao's Long March in the mid-1930s, the French and American revolutions. They dipped into the history of Sino-American relations since 1949.

That first Kissinger-Chou exchange set the tone for an extraordinary new relationship. "Just damned exciting," one White House aide later remarked, after reading Kissinger's forty packed pages of firsthand impressions. "If there are two more interesting people in foreign policy anywhere in the world, I don't know who the hell they are."

Chou came through to Kissinger as subtle, brilliant, indirect; a politician of vision who refused to get bogged down in petty detail. Kissinger appreciated his style and he particularly remembered a remark of Chou's. "There is turmoil under the heavens, and we have the opportunity to end this." He often wondered later what would have happened if Chou had taken a North Vietnamese approach to the Sino-American détente — if he had pounded the table and demanded that the Americans cut off military aid to Taiwan, and break relations with Chiang Kai-shek, before he would agree to talk to them.

It was almost midnight when Chou suggested that their talks be recessed until the next day. Before leaving, though, he expressed curiosity about a speech Nixon had made in Kansas City on July 6. The President had described a future dominated by "five great economic superpowers: the United States, Western Europe, the Soviet Union, mainland China, and, of course, Japan." This pentagonal vision fascinated Chou. Kissinger, of course, was familiar with the concept, but he declined to amplify on the President's statement, since he had not read the text.

Early the next morning — Saturday, July 10 — a full transcript of the President's speech was delivered to Kissinger's guesthouse. In the margins were many of Chou's handwritten notes. There was a covering message. "Please return," it said. "Our only copy." Kissinger was charmed.

Before they were treated to another twelve-course lunch, Kissinger and his small group of aides toured the Forbidden City, where the Chinese emperors had once lived in lofty splendor. It was his only tourist stop on the entire trip.

In the afternoon, again at 4 P.M., the Kissinger-Chou talks resumed, this time at Chou's office in the Great Hall of the People. They were to follow this alternating pattern — a touch of delicate Chinese protocol — during all of Kissinger's subsequent visits to Peking. This second session, like the first, lasted about eight hours. Once again, their exchange was marked by stimulating repartee and personal rapport.

Kissinger and Chou reached no specific agreements. That was not the purpose of the Kissinger mission. But in his thick briefing book there was enough latitude for Kissinger to explore the basis for future understandings.

One principle was that Taiwan should be considered a part of China and the political future of the island should be settled by the Chinese themselves. This represented a major concession by the United States, a reversal of a twenty-year policy of treating Taiwan as a more or less independent country. A second principle was that the political future of South Vietnam should be settled by the feuding Vietnamese parties — after a cease-fire, a return of prisoners, and a total withdrawal of American troops. This reflected Nixon's latest offer to the North Vietnamese, conveyed by Kissinger during one of his secret meetings with Le Duc Tho. And a final principle was that all Asian disputes should be settled by peaceful means. This referred not only to the division of Korea but also to the far more significant tensions along the Sino-Soviet frontier. Taiwan was vitally important to China; Vietnam was vitally important to the United States; and the Sino-Soviet quarrel was vitally important to both of them. These three principles were to guide the evolution of Sino-American relations.

The two sides broke for dinner — Kissinger and his group returning to the guesthouse. At 8:30 P.M., they reassembled at Chou's office, where the discussion suddenly shifted from general principles to one concrete proposal and one concrete response. Chou formally invited the President to visit China. Kissinger accepted on Nixon's behalf. He pointed out, however, that the visit would have to be carefully prepared — in terms of agenda, tours, newspaper and television coverage, even an advance trip for government officials and television technicians to make sure that security and coverage went smoothly. He added that the visit could not take place later than May, 1972.

"May was set as the outside date," Kissinger later explained, "because the President directed that a step of such importance for world peace and for long-term relationships between our country and the People's Republic of China should not get mixed up in any partisan considerations" — namely, the presidential campaign of 1972.

There had been a chance, before Kissinger's visit to China, that Chou and Mao might invite Senators McGovern and Kennedy to visit China sometime in 1971. Now that was out of the question. By inviting the President, Chou and Mao gambled that the political tide in America would be running strongly in Nixon's favor and that he would be overwhelmingly reelected.

On Sunday morning, July 11, there was a final meeting between Kissinger and Chou. This one, lasting two hours, took place in Kissinger's guesthouse. The two men had a practical problem to deal with: how would they communicate in the future? Would they continue to use the mailbox in Islamabad? No, they decided quickly and definitively — Kissinger on instructions from his "Bible," Chou on direct instructions from Mao. Yahya Khan, Ceauşescu, Manac'h, Aalgaard — they had all become obsolete in the glow of the new and promising Kissinger-Chou relationship. China and the United States would now communicate directly, through their embassies in Paris, Ottawa and a number of other capitals.

Kissinger and Chou also agreed on the wording of a final communiqué, to be released at 10 P.M., Eastern Daylight Time, on July 15. That would give Kissinger enough time to return to Islamabad, become visible once again, pick up his own airplane, proceed to Paris for another scheduled secret meeting with Le Duc Tho, and fly on to San Clemente for a jubilant report to the President.

Then the two negotiators, buoyed by success, plunged into another Chinese feast; they parted with broad smiles.

Marshal Yeh Chien-ying escorted Kissinger to the deserted military airport, where the PIA plane waited. On the way, the aging Chinese leader told Kissinger that when he had gone into the hills with Mao, several decades before, he had never thought he would live to see a *Communist* China. He was struggling then, he said, for future generations. Yet here he was, and here was Kissinger. A miracle, in its way. Kissinger said he would return to Peking in a few months to prepare for the President's trip.

For the return flight to Islamabad, it was wheels up at 1 P.M. Sultan Mohammed Khan was waiting for him at the airport. "Kissinger was happy, elated," the Khan later said. "Quite a difference from when he had left."

Kissinger had gone to China to break a pattern of more than two decades of isolation, to open a direct dialogue between the two countries, and he had succeeded. He had gone to China to encourage a new, flexible, and constructive attitude on the part of the Chinese leaders, and he thought he had succeeded. He had gone to China to worry the North Vietnamese, and to gain strategic leverage over the Soviet Union; he hoped he would succeed in these endeavors, too.

The Secret Service men had occupied the NBC studios in Los Angeles several hours before the President arrived. He had asked for network time for a brief announcement of "national importance." Nixon arrived shortly before 7 P.M. as buoyant and good-humored as reporters had ever seen him. "You fellows ready?" the President asked, as the second hand ticked away the final moments.

"Good evening," the President began.

"I have requested this television time tonight to announce a major development in our efforts to build a lasting peace in the world.

"As I have pointed out on a number of occasions over the past three years, there can be no stable or enduring peace without the participation of the People's Republic of China and its seven hundred and fifty million people. That is why I have undertaken initiatives in several areas to open the door for more normal relations between our two countries.

"In pursuance of that goal, I sent Dr. Kissinger, my Assistant for National Security Affairs, to Peking during his recent world tour for the purpose of having talks with Premier Chou En-lai.

"The announcement I shall now read is being issued simultaneously in Peking and in the United States:

> Premier Chou En-lai and Dr. Henry Kissinger, President Nixon's Assistant for National Security Affairs, held talks in Peking from July 9 to 11, 1971. Knowing of President Nixon's expressed desire to visit the People's Republic of China, Premier Chou En-lai on behalf of the Government of the People's Republic of China has extended an invitation to President Nixon to visit China at an appropriate date before May, 1972. President Nixon has accepted the invitation with pleasure.
>
> The meeting between the leaders of China and the United States is to seek the normalization of relations between the two countries and also to exchange views on questions of concern to the two sides."

The moment the President completed his surprise announcement, the cameras switched to studio commentators for reaction. They were all flabbergasted, and one anchor man was literally speechless as he looked out into the living rooms of America. The country was stunned and so was the world.

In the last hour or so before the President addressed the nation, Secretary Rogers had been frantically telephoning, trying to get the word out to the ambassadors of those countries that would be most affected by the new U.S. policy toward China. He managed to reach about twenty ambassadors — among them Shen of Nationalist China, Dobrynin of Russia, and Ushiba of Japan. Shen promptly and predictably denounced the President's decision. A "shabby deal," he labeled it. "We think that's not the kind of thing a friend and ally should do to another without prior consultation and notice." Dobrynin had no immediate comment, but Moscow soon erupted with angry charges of Chinese-American collusion. Ushiba had no comment either, but the surprising news was a blow to the Sato government. Statesmen and editorial writers in many parts of the world praised Nixon's thunderbolt action but, at the same time, it set off strong currents of anxiety. Europeans began to worry about other Nixon "surprises," Asians about other Nixon "shocks." Unpredictability became the hallmark of Nixonian diplomacy. In April, there was the "ping heard round the world." In July, the ping ponged.

For Nixon, the China announcement was sheer euphoria. Not even de Gaulle, his political model in many ways, could have carried off a more surprising coup. He had outmaneuvered Ted Kennedy, Leonid Brezhnev, and Le Duc Tho in one swoop; he had captured the headlines of the world; he had seized the political and diplomatic initiative.

For Kissinger, who spent a great deal of time over the next weeks and months smoothing the ruffled feathers of both allies and adversaries, the President's announcement had a very special meaning. He had already become something of a celebrity, even before China, but now he was catapulted into national and international stardom. On July 17 the *New York Times* dubbed Kissinger "the inscrutable Occidental." He manages "the development of presidential diplomacy," it wrote, "while creating the illusion that he is a fulltime permanent floating cocktail party guest of honor. That takes dazzling intellect, fancy footwork, beguiling aplomb and, it sometimes seems, mirrors."

Having returned from China in glory, Kissinger now set about preparing for the President's trip. One of his responsibilities was to brief newsmen, Congressmen, and columnists about China — seeding public opinion with a new perspective on an old controversy, and, in the process, enhancing his own increasingly central role in White House deliberations. Our reception in China, he would tell people, was "enormously gracious and polite"; we were treated "extraordinarily well"; the talks were "very businesslike, very precise, no rhetoric on either side." Clearly, China was no longer to be regarded as a "threat," nor Chou as a remote and ambiguous figure.

Kissinger also spent a considerable amount of time alerting the President to possible barriers to a smooth trip. He urged Nixon to stop all actions that might be regarded as hostile by China. Drone flights were suspended. Nixon did not have to be reminded that President Eisenhower's planned visit to the Soviet Union in 1960 had been aborted when a U-2 spy plane was shot down over Sverdlovsk. Kissinger also urged the President to restrain Chiang Kai-shek from taking any harassing action against the mainland. This was easier said than done; Chiang felt betrayed by Kissinger's visit to Peking, and he wasn't listening to Nixon any longer.

The relationship of the United States with the Nationalist regime on Taiwan was clearly the most sensitive issue facing Peking and Washington. Kissinger's concession to Chou — that Taiwan was a part of China — went a long way toward resolving the problem, but it stopped short of a formal U.S. commitment. After Kissinger's return, the United States took two steps consistent with this concession. First, it began to thin out the nine-thousand-man American garrison on Taiwan. If Taiwan was part of China, then there was no longer any justification for an American military presence there. Moreover, the thin-out was in harmony with the Nixon Doctrine, which Kissinger had explained to Chou at some length. And if any Congressmen objected to the withdrawal, there was a ready explanation for them. The main job of the Taiwan garrison, it could be argued, was to service the needs of the big American military machine in South Vietnam; and that machine was now being dismantled.

The second step concerned American policy toward Chinese representation in the United Nations. For twenty-two years, Taiwan had been China in the UN, chiefly through the efforts of the United States. Once Kissinger had agreed, in effect, that Taiwan was a province of China, that fiction lapsed. The switch required a new policy. Ever since the fall of 1970, the United States had been leaning toward a two-China policy. Now, on August 2, 1971, Rogers stepped out of the shadows at the State Department to announce the new policy. From now on, he said, the United States would support Peking's admission to the UN, even its claim to the Security Council seat, but it would oppose any effort to deprive Taiwan of its UN membership or its seat in the General Assembly.

Kissinger had given Chou a general preview of the new American policy while he was in Peking. Much was left unsaid, of course, but it was tacitly understood that the United States would try to retain a UN seat for Taiwan, Peking would fight this American effort and probably win, and both sides would then accept the UN's verdict.

However, before the UN could play its part in the unfolding Chinese-American drama, a major political crisis erupted in China. Defense Minister Lin Piao had not accepted his defeat by the moderates the year before, when Chou had swung China's foreign policy toward an opening to Washington. Mao's decision to receive Nixon apparently convinced Lin it was time to act. He launched a desperate bid for power that the Chinese were later to say included a "plot to assassinate" Mao himself. For a few weeks in September, 1971, the Nixon visit hung in the balance.

But with Mao's active support, Chou beat back Lin's challenge and the Defense Minister tried to escape. On September 12, so the Chinese story went, he commandeered a Trident jet, one of the few in the Chinese air force, and flew toward the Soviet Union. He never made it. The plane crashed in a sandstorm over the Gobi Desert of Mongolia.

Strange things happened in China before the full story of Lin's aborted coup made the diplomatic rounds in Peking. All flights were grounded. The traditional National Day October first parade was canceled. Chinese propagandists unfurled an alarming slogan — "Prepare for war" — presumably against the Soviet Union. Tensions escalated. But by early October the crisis vanished as mysteriously as it had surfaced; and a greatly relieved Kissinger prepared to leave for Peking on his second prepresidential journey.

The trip was announced on October 5, during the buildup for the China vote at the UN. Kissinger would be returning to China on October 20 for a "maximum of four days" in order "to make concrete arrangements" for the President's visit. In Kissinger's world of signals, none perhaps was more cleverly contrived than his decision to extend his China visit for an additional two days. Instead of leaving Peking on October 23 or 24, as planned, he left on October 26. The China vote at the UN took place on the afternoon of October 25, Kissinger's next-to-last day in China. His presence there was eloquent proof of the double-edged character of American policy: while Rogers was proclaiming a fight to the death for Taiwan's seat in the General Assembly, Kissinger, on precise presidential instructions, was proclaiming the birth of a new relationship with Peking.

After Peking won overwhelmingly, the President denounced the conduct of those anti-Taiwan delegates who danced in the aisles of the UN.

He could not have been surprised by the vote, which was accurately predicted by Assistant Secretary Samuel DePalma and other State Department experts. Nevertheless, Nixon used the vote to justify a cutback in the U.S. contribution to the UN, a cutback he had intended to order in any case, and he went ahead with his plans to visit Peking. On November 30, Kissinger announced the dates: Nixon would be in China from February 21 to 28, 1972. For the first time he stated publicly that it was Washington's position that "the ultimate relationship of Taiwan to the People's Republic of China should be settled by direct negotiations between Taiwan and the People's Republic of China."

In addition to the bilateral problems between Washington and Peking, there were four other diplomatic problems, involving other countries, which Kissinger had to juggle carefully to avoid endangering the President's upcoming journey to China.

1. *Impact on Japan.* The Land of the Rising Sun was a problem for both China and the United States, but for different reasons. In his talks with Kissinger, Chou En-lai had expressed concern about a "tide of militarism" running through Japanese life. He wanted American help in containing the tide. Nixon had his own reasons for distrusting the Japanese. In 1969 he had reached an important understanding with Prime Minister Eisaku Sato: the United States promised to return Okinawa, an American military base since World War II, to full Japanese control and sovereignty; in exchange, Sato promised to limit Japanese textile exports to the United States. Although Nixon delivered on his promise, Sato welched on his; and the President reacted vindictively. He began to ridicule the Japanese, treating one group of American businessmen to an imitation of a Japanese hissing and bowing, and repeating a current White House joke: "The definition of a man ahead of his time is Spiro Agnew talking about a 'fat Jap' in the 1968 campaign."

Kissinger offered no imitations, but he privately disparaged the Japanese, sometimes referring to them as "little Sony salesmen," or "small and petty bookkeepers" who confused their trading ledgers with diplomatic documents.

When Rogers raised a valid question about the impact on Japan of the secrecy surrounding the first Kissinger visit to Peking, neither Nixon nor Kissinger expressed any concern. In fact, the President seemed to enjoy the idea that Tokyo would be shocked.

One month later, on August 15, Nixon in effect devalued the dollar in a surprise move to strengthen the U.S. trading position, knowing his decision would have a disastrous effect on the Japanese yen and the entire Japanese economy. Once again, he proceeded without any prior notice or consultation.

These twin shocks — China and devaluation — combined to accelerate Sato's departure from power. Japanese-American relations were jolted out of their comfortable postwar mold — a turn of events that was not at all unwelcome in Peking.

2. *Moscow Summit.* On July 16, shortly after returning from his first visit to Peking, Kissinger echoed the official line: the United States would not play Russia and China off against each other. "Nothing that has been done in our relations with the People's Republic of China," he stressed publicly, "has any purpose or is in any way directed against any other countries, and *especially not against the Soviet Union.*" Actually, there were other reasons for trying to improve U.S. relations with China besides gaining leverage over the Kremlin; for example, there was the hope China could help end the Vietnam war, and there was the further hope China would soon cooperate in nuclear disarmament. But the essence of the Kissinger strategy toward China was to gain more room for maneuvering against Russia in the tight corners of the world.

A few weeks later, on August 4, Nixon revealed that in October, 1970, during one of his annual meetings with visiting Soviet Foreign Minister Andrei Gromyko, they had agreed that "a meeting at the highest level should take place" but that it "would be useful only when there was something substantive to discuss that could not be handled in other channels." Now the President was suggesting, in effect, that a more cooperative Soviet attitude toward Berlin and disarmament could lead to a Moscow summit. Nixon was using his new leverage, but he never stated this openly.

The tactic worked — more smoothly than anyone had expected. On September 29, during another Nixon-Gromyko meeting, the President noted "progress" on a number of issues bedeviling the two countries, and said he hoped a Moscow summit could be arranged. On September 30, Rogers and Gromyko signed two marginal agreements that served to warm up the atmosphere of Soviet-American relations. One agreement improved the hot line between Washington and Moscow; the other involved technical procedures for preventing nuclear accidents. And, on October 1, a significant breakthrough occurred in Berlin. East and West reached agreement on a preliminary Berlin settlement.

On October 12 the President announced that he had accepted an invitation to visit Moscow "in the latter part of May," 1972. Kissinger's move toward Peking had obviously encouraged a greater degree of Soviet cooperation in dealings with Washington.

"Neither trip is being taken," the President said soothingly, "for the purpose of exploiting what differences may exist between the two nations. Neither is being taken at the expense of any other nation." To the Russians, as well schooled as anybody in the language of diplomatic denial, it became increasingly obvious that the United States would use to its full advantage the Sino-Soviet split. They felt more and more powerless to break out of the new triangle and to reconstitute the old two-sided world.

Nixon was making the Russians feel very insecure. The more insecure the Russians felt, the less insecure the Chinese felt. This could not help but improve his reception in Peking.

3. *Tragedy on the Subcontinent.* Personal diplomacy, the trademark of the Nixon-Kissinger team, had its price. On the Asian subcontinent, a brutal war was brewing; but, for a good part of the year, Kissinger simply did not have the time to deal with it, and, of course, he did not trust the bureaucracy to manage it. The turn of developments was catastrophic for American policy in the area. The United States, having contributed ten billion dollars in aid to India over the years, found itself siding with a corrupt Pakistani military dictatorship against the world's most populous democracy. Moreover, the dictatorship lost and the democracy won.

On March 25, 1971, General Yahya Khan, the President's useful intermediary with China, had imposed martial rule on East Pakistan, separated from the West by one thousand miles of hostile Indian territory. He was hoping to nullify the results of an election that clearly expressed the desire of the local population — the Bengalis — for political autonomy and, by military means, to put an end to the rebelliousness of the more populous eastern half of Pakistan. The result was a bloodbath. Yahya's soldiers embarked on what the Bengalis and their Indian supporters described as a ruthless campaign of murder, rape, and other atrocities against unarmed civilians in villages and towns throughout East Pakistan. By autumn, over ten million terrified Bengalis had fled across the border to India, which was ill-equipped to handle the flood of refugees. Prime Minister Indira Gandhi threatened war, in support of the Bengalis, who had gone beyond talk of autonomy and now would settle for nothing less than independence.

While all this was going on, Kissinger was busy with other things. Occasionally, at the beginning of the crisis, he would run into the Indian Ambassador, Lakshmi Kant Jha, at a Washington cocktail party, and would imply that he personally favored autonomy for the Bengalis. The Indian Ambassador assumed that the United States would take some action to restrain Yahya Khan, but as spring turned to summer and summer to fall, Kissinger began to display an unmistakable pro-Pakistani bias.

There were a number of reasons for this — some simple, some complicated. The most obvious, of course, was that Kissinger did not want to alienate the Pakistanis; Yahya Khan had been invaluable during the secret contacts with the Chinese. Another simple reason was that Nixon liked Yahya Khan and disliked Mrs. Gandhi. The Pakistani leader struck the President as an Asian Tammany Hall type; Mrs. Gandhi struck him as "cold-blooded." Besides, even before becoming President, Nixon always seemed to get more of a kick out of his stops in Pakistan than his stops in India.

On another level, Kissinger recognized the shifting power alignments in Asia and concluded that America's long-range interests in that region would be best served by a policy that balanced the budding Indian-Soviet alliance with an informal Pakistan-China-America hookup. He believed that if Pakistan were to disintegrate under Indian economic and military pressure, then India would completely dominate the subcontinent, Soviet influence would skyrocket, the strategic balance would be disrupted, China would become alarmed, and a major war, involving the big powers, could erupt.

Not until late October, by Kissinger's own admission, did he devote much attention to the bloodshed in East Pakistan. By then, Mrs. Gandhi was preparing for the possibility of war. On November 4 she arrived in Washington, where Nixon, Kissinger, and Sisco tried desperately to persuade her to be patient. Kissinger's theme was: give political evolution a chance. Mrs. Gandhi made no promises. On December 3, soon after her return to New Delhi, persuaded that patience would not resolve the situation, she ordered the Indian army to cross the border into East Pakistan. Fighting also broke out along India's borders with West Pakistan.

Kissinger was furious. He had been trying to arrange secret talks between Yahya Khan and Bengali leaders in Calcutta — as well as the release of Bengali leader Sheik Mujibur Rahman, imprisoned in West Pakistan. Kissinger believed that he was making modest progress when the Indian invasion destroyed his efforts and produced a rip-roaring battle between Kissinger and Sisco over the direction of American policy. According to the "Anderson Papers," the supersecret minutes of White House meetings during the India-Pakistan war, Kissinger displayed a degree of rage rarely seen even by his personal aides. "I am getting hell every ten minutes from the President that we are not being tough enough on India," he fumed. Kissinger wanted the United States "to tilt in favor of Pakistan" primarily because he felt Pakistan was in great danger; he suspected that India intended to dismember West Pakistan as well as detach the eastern part.

Sisco disagreed. Forcefully expressing the State Department's best judgment, Sisco argued that India had limited ambitions in the war. India wanted a free and independent East Pakistan, which was to be called Bangladesh, but India did not want to extend the war into West Pakistan. Sisco predicted a short war, and he saw little chance of "foreign intervention," meaning Soviet or Chinese. Therefore, he argued for a policy of cool rhetoric and calm behavior. Sisco lost the battle.

On December 4, a chilly day, State Department spokesman Robert McCloskey summoned the Saturday morning contingent of reporters into his second-floor office. Sisco, looking uncomfortable, stalked into the room, carrying his White House instructions from Kissinger. "India bears the major responsibility," he charged, "for the broader hostilities which have ensued." Sisco, an excellent briefer, carried out his mission, placing the United States squarely on Pakistan's side, but his heart wasn't in it.

Three days later, faced with strong public disapproval and fierce editorial and congressional criticism of the Administration's policy, Kissinger felt obliged to justify the President's course. He convoked a "background" session for the White House press — which meant that he could not be quoted. It proved to be a pointless precaution. Passions were riding too high, and Barry Goldwater got hold of the Kissinger transcript and placed it in the Congressional Record, much to Kissinger's chagrin. Kissinger seemed defensive and, on several occasions, he clearly shaded the truth to satisfy the needs of policy. He claimed that the new American approach to China had nothing to do with the American attitude toward Pakistan and Yahya Khan; that the United States was not anti-India; that the United States had been busy all spring and summer trying to head off the war; and, most important, that the United States "favored political autonomy for East Bengal . . . as the inevitable outcome of a political evolution."

But Kissinger's real attitude came through clearly when he stated,

"We believe that what started as a tragedy in East Bengal is now becoming an attempt to dismember a sovereign state and a member of the United Nations." He endorsed a State Department charge of aggression by India. And he warned Russia that the improvement in Moscow-Washington relations might be "jeopardized" by a continuation of the war.

On December 9 the CIA produced a report that Kissinger found alarming. It claimed that the Indian Cabinet was discussing a major military effort "to straighten out the frontier of West Pakistan" and to destroy the Pakistani army. This confirmed Kissinger's suspicion that India had decided to dismember West Pakistan, and he communicated his sense of impending disaster to the President. Nixon resolved to do "anything" short of direct U.S. military intervention to save West Pakistan. East Pakistan was gone in any case. It was merely a matter of time. Twice Kissinger summoned Ambassador Jha to the White House, displayed the CIA intelligence, and demanded that India reconsider. Jha refused to comment. Kissinger's concern deepened, despite Sisco's judgment that the CIA report was unnecessarily alarmist. The White House, in a display of old-fashioned gunboat diplomacy aimed at India and Russia, ordered a naval task force of eight ships, led by the nuclear aircraft carrier *Enterprise,* and carrying two thousand Marines, to sail from the waters off Vietnam to the Bay of Bengal.

On Sunday, December 12, Nixon and Kissinger flew off to the Azores to meet French President Pompidou; this was to be the first in a series of brief meetings with allied leaders about the monetary crisis and the upcoming presidential trips to Peking and Moscow. On the long flight, they decided that the time had come to pressure the Russians into restraining the Indians. If indeed the opening to China had produced new leverage on the Kremlin, then this surely was the moment to test it. They composed careful instructions for Ambassador Jacob Beam in Moscow: he was to make it clear to the Russians that if they allowed India to dismember West Pakistan, they would be jeopardizing the President's plans to visit Moscow. The implied warning was that the President's trip to Peking would not be affected. Beam got his instructions on December 13, and he transmitted the message to the Soviet Foreign Ministry.

December 13 went by. There was no response from Moscow or New Delhi. The war continued. David Kraslow, who was then Washington bureau chief for the *Los Angeles Times,* noted in a dispatch from the

Azores that Kissinger seemed more preoccupied with the possibility of Pakistan's dismemberment than he was with the announced devaluation of the dollar, one result of the Nixon-Pompidou meeting. Kissinger was annoyed by the report.

On the afternoon of December 14, Nixon and Kissinger boarded *Air Force One* for the return flight to Washington, still having heard nothing from Moscow. New Delhi had sent word that India had no plans to dismember Pakistan. Kissinger remained skeptical. He thought the message might be a smoke screen for an Indian attack.

In the rear section of *Air Force One* were three reporters, the "pool" that represented the press corps accompanying the President. Kraslow was one of them; the two others were Helen Thomas of UPI and Frank Cormier of AP. Shortly after takeoff, Kissinger left the President and wandered back for a chat with the reporters. They talked about his breakfast meeting with Pompidou, about Treasury Secretary John Connally's erroneous remark the previous night denying that Nixon and Pompidou had reached a decision on devaluation, and about the possible effect of the India-Pakistan war on the President's plans to visit Moscow.

After Kissinger left them, the three reporters typed out a "pool report" — their impressions of his comments — which they would share with their colleagues once they had all regrouped at Andrews Air Force Base. What Kissinger had said was a bulletin: if the Russians did not restrain India within the next few days, the President might have to take a "new look" at his summit plans. Normally, the "pool" would not show Kissinger their report, but this time the three reporters believed the news was so sensitive and sensational that Kissinger ought to have the option of retracting or revising it.

While Kissinger was reviewing the pool report with the President, the reporters argued among themselves about whether Kissinger was deliberately "leaking" a bombshell or speaking out of turn. They examined and reexamined the relevant part of the report. It read:

> Asked if the U.S. has any cards left to play in this situation, Kissinger said the U.S. is working on many fronts to try to bring the war to a close. He said the Soviet Union has not played a very restraining role — to put it mildly. . . . Asked what the Soviet motive is in its behavior on the India-Pak war, Kissinger said it is apparently to humiliate China — to show the world that China cannot prevent what is happening to Pakistan.
>
> Asked if there is a danger of the south Asian situation deteriorating to the point that it might affect the President's plans to visit Moscow,

Kissinger said not yet but that we would have to wait to see what happened in the next few days.

Asked if we should infer from that statement that if the Russians didn't begin to exercise a restraining influence very soon, the plans for the President's trip might be changed, Kissinger said in such an event the entire matter might well be reexamined. He said the U.S. is definitely looking to the Soviets to become a restraining influence in the next few days. But if the Russians continue to deliberately encourage military actions, a new look might have to be taken at the President's summitry plans.

Kissinger returned the report to the three newsmen. In his own hand, he had crossed out the word "matter" and substituted the words "U.S.-Soviet relationship," hardening the meaning of the warning. The sentence now read: "Asked if we should infer from that statement that if the Russians didn't begin to exercise a restraining influence very soon, the plans for the President's trip might be changed, Kissinger said in such an event *the entire U.S.-Soviet relationship* might well be reexamined."

The moment *Air Force One* landed, Thomas and Cormier filed bulletins. They did not quote Kissinger; they merely said "it was understood" the President would reconsider his Moscow journey unless the Russians quickly exerted a restraining influence on India. The bulletin led all of the evening television news broadcasts. Later that night Ziegler issued a tepid and ritualistic denial. "The U.S.," he said, "is not considering canceling the U.S.-Russia summit and no U.S. Government official intended to suggest this." He privately confirmed, however, that Kissinger had discussed the pool report with the President. John Scali, a former newsman who had joined the White House staff, backed up Ziegler's official version; Kissinger, Scali told reporters, had absolutely no authority to issue the summit warning.

On December 16, the two-week war ended, with Pakistan split into two separate states. Kissinger claimed a share of the credit for having prevented Moscow and New Delhi from dismembering West Pakistan. There were many officials, Sisco among them, who strongly doubted that India had ever had any such plans. Kissinger stuck to his story that the warning from the plane had compelled the Russians to lean on India, and that the cease-fire was a result of this pressure. By claiming that he had "saved" West Pakistan, Kissinger could assert that he had rescued an ally of the United States and a friend of China, and that his new "leverage" magic had worked to advance American interests on the subcontinent; the balance, however tenuous, had been preserved, and Moscow had been taught still one more lesson about global responsibility.

In fact, the Administration's policy during this crisis resulted in severe damage to the moral influence of the United States and in diplomatic gains for Russia in a major confrontation with her big-power rivals, in Washington and Peking. For Kissinger, it was a personal disaster. His image as a candid articulator of U.S. policy was badly tarnished. His liberal friends in the press began to snipe at his judgment; his former Harvard colleagues once again reminded their students of Henry's "insensitivity" to the human factor in foreign policy equations. Moreover, he felt that Haldeman and Ehrlichman, always on the lookout for an anti-Kissinger opportunity, were then engaged in an intensive effort to undermine his position at the White House. The upshot was Kissinger's belief that he was losing presidential favor, that his constituency of one might be setting him up as the fall guy in the event the Moscow summit collapsed. It was his feeling, for example, that Goldwater would not have placed his backgrounder in the *Congressional Record* without White House approval; that Sisco would not have been in such open disagreement without at least a degree of White House backing; and that the records of the secret WSAG meetings would not have been leaked to columnist Jack Anderson unless the Nixon palace guard had deliberately arranged it. In December, 1971, Kissinger seriously considered quitting his job.

Kissinger's self-advertised paranoia might have been working overtime; because Nixon, far from encouraging the leak, was actually incensed that top secret deliberations were finding their way into the press. He ordered the "plumbers" to discover the source of the leak. They quickly traced part of the problem to a Navy yeoman, Charles E. Radford, a stenographer-typist who had been assigned to the military liaison unit of the NSC for more than a year. Radford denied that he had leaked reports of the WSAG deliberations to Anderson; but the "plumbers" reportedly came up with embarrassing evidence that linked Radford to a military snooping ring within the NSC. It was alleged that Radford pilfered batches of documents from the NSC and funneled them across the Potomac to the Pentagon.

The young yeoman insisted, at the time and since then, that he had merely been following the orders of Rear Admiral Robert O. Welander, his immediate superior. Welander denied this. David Young, a lawyer who had once been Kissinger's appointments secretary but was then working for Ehrlichman, interrogated Welander as part of the "plumbers' " investigation. Kissinger listened to the tape of that interrogation. He learned that among the documents pilfered was an "eyes-only" report that he had written for Nixon on his secret talks with Chou. Radford, who accompanied Kissinger on that round-the-world trip, had been left behind in Pakistan when Kissinger flew on to Peking; but he was back on board for the Islamabad-Teheran leg when the report on the secret China trip was actually written. It was only after listening to the tape that he learned that Radford had rifled documents from briefcases and burn bags — the sacks used to collect and destroy classified documents.

Those were dark and gloomy days for Kissinger. They began to brighten up a bit only after the India-Pakistan crisis had vanished from the front page, and the President presented him with new diplomatic challenges.

4. *Vietnam Stalemate.* When Kissinger was in Peking in July, he was surprised to learn that Chou En-lai considered Vietnam, and not Taiwan, to be the biggest obstacle on the road to a substantial improvement in Sino-American relations. Throughout the summer and fall, Kissinger repeatedly tried to convince the Chinese leader that the United States would continue to withdraw from Indochina — hopefully, in such a way that Hanoi would not be in a position to occupy the entire peninsula and turn it into a potentially pro-Soviet stronghold at China's doorstep.

Kissinger hoped that the U.S. opening to China would help end the war — indirectly — by exerting pressure on Moscow to exert pressure on Hanoi. But by late 1971, it was clear that, so far, this strategy was having no effect on North Vietnam's stubborn pursuit of victory. Kissinger had met with Le Duc Tho, both before and after his first trip to Peking, but their intensive secret negotiations failed to break the deadlock, basically because Nixon refused to dump Thieu during the October elections.

In December, an urgent meeting of the Politburo of the Lao-Dong (Workers') Party convened in Hanoi. Truong Chinh, a ranking ideologue, in a sharp attack on the Nixon-Kissinger strategy, accused the United States of trying to "create contradictions among the Socialist countries with a view to achieving conditions advantageous to the Americans." The United States, he said, was seeking "détente among the big powers" in order to continue "bullying the small countries." The leaders of North Vietnam realized that if Nixon and Kissinger were successful in creating a triangular détente among the "big powers," then Peking's and Moscow's support for Hanoi might be diminished, and their own plans for reunifying Vietnam could be frustrated. They deeply resented the fact that their allies had extended invitations to Nixon, "the world's bloodiest aggressor," and they were determined to resist all American efforts to force them into a compromise settlement.

But how could this be done? Could Nixon be defeated by military force? Or by diplomatic guile? The North Vietnamese opted for a mix of the two: they would continue their diplomatic stall, delaying another series of meetings with Kissinger, while preparing for a major invasion of South Vietnam.

The stalemate on the negotiating front continued into the new year, as the North Vietnamese increased the flow of men and supplies into the south. By January, 1972, Nixon and Kissinger thought they could see the direction of Hanoi's strategy, and they decided on a dramatic counterploy. In order to jolt Hanoi, and to undercut the critics who kept accusing the Administration of having no plan for ending the war and no desire to negotiate with the North Vietnamese, the President went on television on the evening of January 25, 1972, to disclose the details of Kissinger's six secret meetings with Le Duc Tho in 1971. As the campaign year began, Nixon wanted to be on record as a President who tried to go the extra mile for peace in Indochina.

Although the President's sensational revelations did little to advance peace, they did wonders for Kissinger's battered ego. The February 7 issues of *Time* and *Newsweek* featured Henry Kissinger on their covers. "I understand it's the kiss of death to be on both covers the same week," Kissinger, with a faint smile, remarked to presidential speechwriter Safire. "Yes," Safire reassured him, "but what a way to go."

TEN

"The Week That Changed the World"

T HE AIRPORT AT PEKING seemed deserted. A small group of American newsmen, who had arrived the evening before, waited restlessly in the biting cold of the north China morning. It was Monday, February 21, 1972, and Richard Nixon was about to achieve an authentic "first": a presidential visit to China. His plane, the *Spirit of '76*, was less than a half hour away, flying north from Shanghai; and yet the tarmac was almost empty, the atmosphere icy. "This is the best reception Nixon's had since he went to the AFL-CIO meeting," one reporter wisecracked. There were no Chinese leaders in sight. "Where's Chou?" another reporter asked his Chinese interpreter. "Around," he answered mysteriously.

Fifteen minutes later, the President's blue and white jet broke through the morning haze. The chief security agent on board routinely radioed another agent on the ground.

"What about the crowd?"

"There is no crowd," came the answer.

"Did you say, 'No crowd'?"

"That is an affirmative. No crowd."

By the time the *Spirit of '76* was making its final approach to the airport, there was a quick change in the scenery. A single American flag was run up a pole, to share the breeze with the red flag of China; an honor guard of some three hundred and fifty men in the khaki, green, and blue uniforms of the different branches of the People's Liberation

Army (PLA) suddenly appeared; and Premier Chou En-lai led a small reception committee across the tarmac toward the plane.

There was a faint ripple of applause when the President, hatless, and Mrs. Nixon, in a fur-lined red coat, emerged from their aircraft. "How was your flight?" Chou asked in English. "It was very pleasant," Nixon replied, his voice carrying across the tarmac. "We stopped in Hawaii and Guam to catch up on the time. It is easier that way. The Prime Minister knows about that. He is such a traveler." The handshake between the President and the Premier recalled a lost opportunity — when the outstretched hand of Chou En-lai had been spurned by Secretary of State John Foster Dulles at the Geneva Conference in 1954.

Among the arriving Americans, Chou spotted Kissinger. "Ah, old friend," he said, smiling and shaking Henry's hand. Kissinger, the old China hand, was making his third voyage to Peking in seven months.

There were no speeches, no foreign diplomats, no "ordinary" Chinese with paper flags and bouquets of flowers. This was to be an austere welcome, marking a midway point between hostility and détente. The PLA band played the national anthems of the two countries — "The Star-Spangled Banner" and "The March of the Volunteers." Chou and Nixon reviewed the honor guard and then disappeared into black limousines for the half hour ride to Taio Yu Tai — "The Fishing Terrace," a government guest compound near a lake in the Peking suburbs. Henry Kissinger had slept there before, in July and again in October. The President drove past a gray, wintry tableau. Few Chinese picked up their heads to look at the speeding caravan, and those who did reacted with silent indifference. The roads were lined with giant posters of Chairman Mao's thoughts, emblazoned in white Chinese ideographs on red backgrounds: "Make trouble, fail; make trouble again, fail again; make trouble until doom: that is the logic of the imperialists and reactionaries."

The President had prepared meticulously for his journey. "A trip to China," he had told *Time*, "is like going to the moon." He had boned up on everything — from table etiquette (he practiced using chopsticks) to Mao's poetry. Twice he had sent Kissinger to Peking, just to make certain that there would be no diplomatic ambushes. More than a month before the trip, he had sent a small army of communications experts to China — from White House signal corpsmen to network field producers — to arrange a clear television picture of his visit for the voters back home.

A miniature television city sprang up, almost overnight, just outside the airport. And for weeks before the journey, the President, late at night, had huddled with Kissinger to discuss the issues affecting his trip to Peking: Taiwan, the Sino-Soviet dispute, the internal political struggle in China. They realized that the only current problem that could seriously threaten the success of the summit was the ominous intelligence of a new Communist buildup in Vietnam. Hardly a day passed in January and February that Kissinger did not bring the President reports about the unusual concentrations of North Vietnamese artillery, heavy tanks and troops poised for an attack against the south. Officials speculated about a North Vietnamese offensive at a daily press briefing. "The offensive could start at any time," Kissinger said on February 9. "We expect that it may well start." Nixon was not eager to launch a massive bombing campaign on the eve of his departure for Peking; yet he was concerned that Hanoi was angling to embarrass him — and to embarrass Mao Tse-tung, too. It was clear that the North Vietnamese resented China's opening to the U.S.; they feared a sellout. David Boulton, a British television director in Hanoi during this period of obvious strain in Chinese–North Vietnamese relations, reported that busts and posters of Mao were vanishing from Hanoi stores while busts of Marx, Lenin, Stalin and Ho were still on the shelves; and that while books in some foreign languages were available — English, French and Russian among them — books in Chinese, even Mao's Little Red Book, were disappearing.

Although by mid-February the North Vietnamese offensive had not materialized, Nixon decided, just before he left for Peking, to protect his military and diplomatic flanks by unleashing the Air Force against Communist positions throughout Indochina. Saigon announced one thousand sorties by B-52s and fighter-bombers against North Vietnamese concentrations in the tri-state border area where Laos, Cambodia and South Vietnam meet, and an additional hundred and twenty-five sorties against long-range guns just north of the DMZ — although North Vietnam was technically off limits to American bombers.

Kissinger felt the massive bombing would strengthen the President's hand in China. It was the right kind of signal. "Everything seems to be in good shape," an NSC staffer remarked a few days before the President's trip to Peking. "Of course," Kissinger replied. "Why else do you think I'd be as relaxed as I am?"

At his briefings with newsmen, Kissinger repeatedly stressed two points: first, that the President's journey to China was *not* intended to be an anti-Soviet action; and second, that the journey would have a genuine long-term importance. "What we are attempting to do with the People's Republic of China is not to have a visit," Kissinger emphasized; "what we are attempting to do is start an historic evolution."

For Richard Nixon, landing on the moon might have been a warmer experience than landing in Peking. "A bit frosty," was the way one Nixon aide described the President's reception. "Chou had a faint come-to-me smile and I was afraid they were going to portray the President as a supplicant." Yet China was a land of constant surprises and shifting impressions. A few minutes after Nixon arrived at the guest compound, there was an unexpected phone call. Would it be convenient for the President and Dr. Kissinger to be received by Chairman Mao now? a voice asked. Nixon knew, from Kissinger's advance trips, that he would be meeting the legendary Chinese revolutionary, perhaps even more than once, but he had not imagined that a meeting would be arranged so quickly. Normally Mao would wait to meet a visiting foreign dignitary until a day or two before his departure from China. Nixon was pleased by the distinction but not overwhelmed. He decided to be a few minutes late.

Mao lived in the southwest corner of the old Forbidden City in a one-story house surrounded by vermilion walls topped by glistening yellow tiles. Nixon arrived through the West Gate. Two armed guards stood at attention. The car stopped at the entranceway to Mao's home, where two unarmed officers wearing no insignia welcomed the President and Kissinger. Secretary of State Rogers had specifically not been invited, a snub for which Chou later tried to make amends.

Mao greeted the Americans in his large study. Chou was there, of course, and so was Wang Hai-jung, a slight, bespectacled woman in her early thirties, who was identified as an assistant to the Foreign Minister, but who, as Mao's niece, wielded far greater power than her title would imply. Tang Wen-Sheng, who was born in Brooklyn, New York, and went to China as a young girl, was the interpreter. The study had a Spartan look. It was lined with books — most of them in Chinese, some half open, piled one on top of the other on small tables or on the floor. In one corner was Mao's large desk, also piled high with journals, scripts and books. A semicircle of easy chairs faced a round coffee table and a couple of wide windows through which Nixon could catch a glimpse of a garden, barren and cold in the winter.

Mao was dressed in the familiar haberdashery of Chinese Communism: an austere gray tunic and matching trousers. At seventy-eight years of age, he still radiated a sense of command. Yet his style was informal, surprisingly casual for a man who long ago won a reputation as one of the historic figures of the twentieth century.

Nixon and Kissinger were aware that they were in the presence of a legend who was still a leader: an authentic Chinese revolutionary who was completely unlike the Communist bureaucrats of Russia. He was still an adventurer, willing to disrupt China for the sake of a cultural and psychological revolution. They were the technicians of power, second- and third-generation leaders who equated Communism with their monopoly of state control and distrusted popular disorder as antithetical to the interests of the Party and the state. Mao was a first-generation original, who helped form the Chinese Communist Party in the early 1920s, when there wasn't a prayer of attaining power. He led the Long March in the 1930s — ninety thousand Communists when they left southern China, ten thousand Communists when they reached the caves of Yenan in the north. He commanded the Red Army against Chiang Kai-shek, then against the Japanese, then against the Americans; and now, in a strange twilight war against the Russians, he was again at the barricades.

In his brief exposure to China, Kissinger had acquired a new and sympathetic appreciation of Mao. He saw the Chinese leader as governing an ancient society that was essentially theological in nature — its beliefs and behavior bounded by Mao's "thoughts." He understood why the Maoists had disrupted China, during the tumultuous days of the Cultural Revolution, in a drive to revitalize a revolution that had lost some of its original zeal. Kissinger had become a Sinophile. What had seemed crazy to him only a few years earlier suddenly made sense.

Kissinger perceived Mao as a visionary, and Nixon as a pragmatist; yet these philosophical differences faded into insignificance. Political expediency — their separate concerns about Russia — had drawn them together in the Forbidden City.

The Mao-Nixon meeting lasted a little more than an hour, half of which was devoted to translation. Mao was alert, philosophical and humorous. He was clearly in charge. Chou, by contrast, seemed to freeze in his presence, never once flashing any of his own charm or originality of thought. He was, without doubt, the humble follower, the obedient subordinate. Mao ran China just as surely as he controlled the flow of conversation with Nixon.

Mao used no notes. He never seemed to emphasize any one point. He never ticked off his idea for an agenda. He conveyed the impression of meandering from one thought to another, in no particular order — Taiwan, Japan, Indochina, the struggle against "hegemony" (another way of saying Russia), the importance of expanded contacts between China and America. A few weeks later, however, after studying the transcript of the Mao-Nixon talks in the quiet of his White House office, Kissinger belatedly realized that Mao had in fact outlined the Shanghai communiqué, the only official declaration to emerge from the President's week in China. For every paragraph in the communiqué, he noticed, there was a sentence in the Mao-Nixon conversation. In retrospect, Kissinger felt that the talk with Mao had merely been "the overture to a Wagnerian opera."

Within a few hours, the Chinese government produced news photographs and film of a smiling Mao and a grinning Nixon for distribution to the foreign press, and officially described their meeting as "serious and frank." The message was clear: Mao had personally and quickly blessed the Nixon visit. The muted welcome at the airport could now be forgotten.

Nixon and Kissinger never met the Chairman again that week. His direction was sensed but not seen. Chou slipped gracefully into the director's chair. Only then did Chou begin to exhibit the qualities that had so captivated Kissinger: his sense of humor, his grasp of detail, his capacity for candor, and his sweeping sense of history and philosophy. Chou became the President's guide, host, and negotiating opponent.

Because of the visit to Mao, the plenary session scheduled for Monday afternoon began an hour and a half late. This initial meeting was devoted to speechmaking and picture-taking. The mood was good. Chou noticed that many of the President's aides and advisers were young. "We have too many elderly people in our government," the seventy-three-year-old Chinese leader commented politely, "so on this point we should learn from you."

For the next four days Nixon and Chou met in restricted sessions. Kissinger sat at the President's right. Only John Holdridge and Winston Lord accompanied them. Down the hall, parallel discussions took place between Rogers and Chi Peng-fei, the Chinese Foreign Minister. The pattern was obvious. Nixon and Chou would discuss matters of principle; Rogers

and Chi would discuss the implementation of specific agreements concerning travel, trade, and tourism. Late in the evening, after the banquets,
the concerts and the table tennis exhibitions, Kissinger would meet with
Chiao Kuan-hua, a Deputy Foreign Minister, to work on the drafting of
the final communiqué. These were the rough negotiating sessions.

On Monday evening, Chou hosted a banquet in the President's honor
in the Great Hall of the People. The dining room was cavernous, swallow-
ing up the eight hundred American and Chinese officials. National flags
added a touch of color to the drab setting. A Chinese military band
played "America the Beautiful," "Home on the Range," and other American songs. There was no head table, but Nixon and Chou sat at a round
table for twenty, and everyone else sat at tables for ten. The menu was
the best of China's cuisine: hors d'oeuvres (including aged eggs, small
carp in vinegar sauce, and other delicacies); spongy bamboo shoots and
egg-white consommé; shark's fin in three shreds; fried and stewed prawns;
mushrooms and mustard greens; steamed chicken with coconut; almond
junket; pastries and fruits, mostly north China tangerines. Nixon used
chopsticks; Kissinger tried.

Chou's toast was upbeat. The President's trip to China, he said, was a
"positive move." The "gates to friendly contact have finally been opened."
Nixon was expansive, almost impatient. "At this very moment, through
the wonder of telecommunications, more people are seeing and hearing
what we say than on any other such occasion in the whole history of the
world." He seemed eager to justify the occasion. One of Kissinger's young
China specialists had found a Mao poem that made the appropriate point.
"So many deeds cry out to be done, and always urgently," Nixon quoted
Mao. "The world rolls on. Time passes. Ten thousand years are too long.
Seize the day; seize the hour."

Nixon seized a small glass of mao tai, a fiery Chinese liquor, and toured
the banquet hall, clinking glasses with Chinese officials and toasting their
health, ending with a special toast to Mao. If this delighted the Chinese,
it infuriated William F. Buckley, Jr., one of the eighty-seven American
newsmen with Nixon. "When he toasted the bloodiest, most merciless
chief of state in the world," the conservative columnist wrote, "he did so
in accents most of us would reserve for Florence Nightingale." Buckley
was in a clear minority. The pollsters reported that the overwhelming
majority of Americans supported the President's opening to China.

The two architects of the opening — Chou En-lai and Henry Kissinger

— approached one another during the banquet and clinked glasses of *mao tai.* They knew that they had done their work well.

On Tuesday, February 22, Nixon, Kissinger, and Chou began their secret deliberations in the Great Hall of the People. This first substantive exchange lasted almost four hours. In midafternoon there was a stir around the kiosks on the streets of Peking. The most important propaganda organ in China, *People's Daily,* normally the source of venomous anti-American tirades, carried eight favorable stories about Nixon's visit to China, and three front-page pictures of the President, two of them with Mao, the other with Chou. Chou was responsible for the layout. During the banquet on Monday evening, he had left for five minutes to check out the picture and copy spread for the next day's paper. This was an indication of how closely Chou controlled every aspect of the President's journey. Kissinger regarded the February 22 edition of *People's Daily* as a collector's item. It sanctified the Nixon visit for the Communist Party cadres down the line from Peking to the smallest villages in Tibet or Sinkiang, thus accelerating Chou's drive toward accommodation with America. The paper had an almost magical effect upon the Chinese masses. With Mao's blessing, they began to smile at the Americans.

On Tuesday evening, the President's hostess at a performance of the *Red Detachment of Women* was Mao's wife, Chiang Ching, the radical high priestess of the Cultural Revolution. She chatted amiably with the President, showing no outward discomfiture at fraternizing with a man who could not have been on her list of favorite people. The Americans assumed "the old man made her do it." The ballet — created under Chiang Ching's direction in 1964, and one of the two "model" or "exemplary productions" approved by Chairman Mao in accordance with his axiom, "Art is to serve workers, peasants and soldiers" — made the point that a young peasant girl could find happiness leading a detachment of Communists to victory over Chiang Kai-shek's troops. The President gave this revolutionary ballet a rave. "While it was a powerful message and intended for that," he declared, "it was also very dramatic — excellent theater and excellent dancing and music and really superb acting."

On Wednesday the site of the talks shifted to Nixon's guesthouse. At exactly 2 P.M., Chou's large black Red Flag limousine pulled into the driveway. The President was waiting for the Premier. So was a pool of reporters. Nixon, with self-conscious courtesy, helped Chou remove his topcoat. They posed for pictures. "How are you all?" Chou asked the newsmen and photographers. "Better than they deserve," Nixon interjected, in an attempt at humor. As the photographers clicked away, Chou said, "Take more pictures of your President." That prompted another Nixon ad lib. "If they had them," he remarked, "they would burn them." Nixon and Chou walked briskly into the first-floor conference room and sat down on opposite sides of the green felt-covered table. Kissinger joined Nixon. Rogers vanished with Chi Peng-fei. The talks lasted four hours, twice as long as scheduled.

In the evening, the presidential party attended a sports spectacular of gymnastics, badminton and, of course, Ping-Pong. Nixon kept pointing and gesturing, obviously enjoying the skill of the Chinese performers. Kissinger, seated way down to the left of the President, stared intently at the Ping-Pong match, no doubt plotting strategy.

Columnist Joseph Kraft attended a reception at the Soviet Embassy. "A sadder party there never was," Kraft observed. A Russian diplomat pointed out that when Soviet Premier Alexei Kosygin met with Chou, the Chinese described their talk as "frank"; but when Nixon met with Mao, the Chinese described their talk as "frank and serious." The difference depressed the Russians. When Kraft met the Soviet Ambassador, Vassilly S. Tolstikov, and remarked that the Nixon trip to Peking should improve the climate for his trip to Moscow in May, Tolstikov stared at Kraft in utter incredulity. "We'll have to see about that," he said.

On Thursday, February 24, Nixon and Rogers were escorted to the Great Wall of China, a forty-minute ride northwest of Peking, while Kissinger remained at the guesthouse working on the communiqué. The Great Wall stretches some two thousand miles across northern China, and it is one of the country's most spectacular tourist attractions — the high point of the trip for most visitors. Nixon walked slowly along the ramparts, trailed by dozens of journalists. "What do you think of the Wall, Mr. President?" a reporter asked. "I think that you would have to conclude," Nixon concluded, "that this is a great wall." A rise in the ramparts loomed ahead. "We will not climb to the top today," the President remarked to his host, Marshal Yeh Chien-ying. "We are already meeting at the summit in Peking."

On the return ride to the capital, the President and Marshal Yeh stopped at the famous tombs of the Ming emperors. "It is worth coming sixteen thousand miles to see the Wall," Nixon observed, "and it is worth coming that far to see this, too." At one point, a reporter intercepted the President and asked if he would recommend that Americans apply for tourist visas to visit China. "I think it would be very valuable and worthwhile for Americans — and, for that matter, people in all countries — to be able to visit China," he responded, setting off a rush of speculation that the Americans and the Chinese had already reached agreement on a tourist exchange program. The speculation was premature.

That afternoon Nixon and Kissinger met with Chou and Chiao for four hours of hard bargaining. Then they broke for a modest meal of Peking duck. Everyone looked tired — "bushed," as Kissinger put it. Chou, for the first time that week, drained his glass of *mao tai* during his toast to the President. He told a story about the Long March — how, when Mao's depleted force reached the Yangtze River, he had written an inspirational poem, urging them to press on to the Great Wall. No man could truly be considered great, Mao had suggested, until he reached the Wall after a long and difficult journey. Chou added pointedly that, that very morning, the President had reached the Wall.

After dinner, the four key negotiators resumed their talks, which continued well into the night. There was, according to one aide, "no pulling of punches, no effort to cover up or paper over differences." Although in his earlier talks with the Chinese, Kissinger had found a number of general principles on which both sides could agree, he now ran into a number of specific differences on which agreement proved to be impossible. In these circumstances, how could Kissinger and Chiao draft a final communiqué?

Kissinger felt the Chinese needed a communiqué more than the Americans did, for two reasons: first, to justify Nixon's presence to the Chinese people, and, second, to present the Russians with a tangible example of Chinese-American cooperation. Therefore, he felt that it was up to the Chinese to break the deadlock. As it turned out, Chou and Nixon came up with a solution. They agreed to write separate sections into the communiqué, one expressing the American view of a particular problem — say, Vietnam — and the other expressing the Chinese view.

"This communiqué was unique," Nixon later claimed, "in honestly setting forth differences rather than trying to cover them up with diplomatic double-talk." In fact, it was not unique; but it was highly unusual.

When Nixon and Chou left that night, Kissinger and Chiao walked across a small wooden bridge from the President's guesthouse to another two-story gray brick building, where they worked almost until dawn, composing a mutually acceptable communiqué.

On Vietnam, the U.S. declared its support of the President's eight-point proposal of January 27, 1972, and of its long-range goal of self-determination for the people of Indochina; and the Chinese declared their support of the seven-point proposal of the Provisional Revolutionary Government.

On Korea, the U.S. expressed its support for South Korea, while the Chinese expressed their support for the April 12, 1971, proposal of North Korea on "peaceful unification."

On Japan, the U.S. placed "the highest value on its friendly relations" with its Asian ally, while the Chinese "firmly" opposed "the revival and outward expansion of Japanese militarism."

On the India-Pakistan war, the U.S. made a show of evenhandedness by supporting the cease-fire and "the right of the peoples of South Asia to shape their own future in peace, free of military threat"; while the Chinese "firmly" supported the Pakistan government.

This procedure — letting each side express its own view — had a certain utilitarian value. It overcame a particular hurdle in the negotiations, and it tended to soften language that could otherwise have been offensive. For example, the Chinese had some standard phraseology about Vietnam that, in a Peking-Hanoi context, was required rhetoric. "We are like lips to teeth," the Chinese would often declare; or, "we are the reliable rear area for the struggle of the fraternal Indochinese people." But in a Washington-Peking context, such language was unacceptable. Chiao had the grace to shift gears. In the final communiqué, he contented himself with a general expression of support for Hanoi's program for peace.

On Taiwan there was little grace and less give. This was the issue that posed the greatest challenge for Kissinger. Although each side would be permitted to state its own view, the issue was so sensitive, and so complicated, especially for the Chinese, that each side agreed to allow the other to check out its statement — an agreement that added an extra dimension of contention to the overall effort.

By dawn on Friday, February 25, Kissinger and Chiao had completed most of the Taiwan section of the communiqué. After a brief break, they resumed their drafting chores while the President and Marshal Yeh Chien-ying went sightseeing once again. This time it was the Forbidden City. During the night, a light snow had fallen, prompting Marshal Yeh to wax poetic. "The snow," he said, has "whitewashed the world."

When Nixon saw the jade burial suits of a prince who died in 113 B.C., he remarked, "Well, you wouldn't walk around in that." Rogers, who was with him, chuckled. When Nixon noticed a pair of earplugs that an emperor had used so he couldn't hear any criticism, he quipped, "Give me a pair of those."

Both the President and Marshal Yeh hinted at big doings. "How's the trip going, Mr. President?" a reporter called out. "I'll have something to say about that tonight," Nixon replied, smiling. Marshal Yeh added, "It is my hope that people of our two countries and people of the world can enjoy peace and good harmony." Once again speculation about a major breakthrough in the negotiations spread through the press corps. Vietnam? Diplomatic relations? No one knew, but they all sensed a "blockbuster," as one Nixon-watcher put it.

When Nixon and Rogers returned to the guesthouse, they conferred with Kissinger about the communiqué, particularly the sensitive section on Taiwan. Rogers raised one of his rare objections. Prompted by an aide, the Secretary argued that a few words in the draft language had to be changed to make it easier for the Chiang regime to accept. For example, in one sentence he wanted the word "stressed" to be changed to "stated." Kissinger felt that Rogers was quibbling, but the lawyer in Nixon supported the quibble of a fellow lawyer; and Kissinger had to reopen the negotiation with Chiao, who appeared to be annoyed at the need for a last-minute change.

On Friday evening, the President and Chou had still another restricted session, but they were not able to untangle the Taiwan knot. Now it was Nixon's turn to host a dinner for Chou. The setting was still the same cavernous chamber in the Great Hall of the People, but the mood had changed. Monday it had been expectant; by Friday it had begun to approach the anticlimactic. The meal was superb, and the Chinese military band still tried to strike an American theme. "She'll Be Comin' Round the Mountain" and "Billy Boy" were on the program. But there was a distinct sense of letdown. The toasts were flat. After the dinner, as Nixon and Chou walked out of the hall, reporters noticed that they were not talking to each other. The reporters sensed deadlock. Ziegler cautioned against that interpretation.

Kissinger has maintained that there was no deadlock. "I can assure you," he told a group of reporters the following week, "that Friday night was no different from any other night."

Nevertheless, the effort at breaking the nondeadlock lasted until 5 A.M. After the banquet, Nixon, Kissinger, Chou and Chiao drove back to the guesthouse. It was past 10 P.M. Chou bade the President good night before he retreated to the conference building with Kissinger and Chiao. They talked for almost an hour. Chou presented Kissinger with some new language on Taiwan. Kissinger, the shuttlecock in these negotiations, brought the Chinese offer to the President's guesthouse. Rogers joined them. The three Americans conferred until past midnight. At last Nixon gave his approval, conditional on several minor modifications. Rogers went to bed, and Kissinger returned to the negotiating effort with Chou and Chiao. After a while, Chou left, and Kissinger and Chiao settled most of the remaining problems, one by one. Three or four times in the course of the long night, Kissinger telephoned the President for guidance. Nixon got very little sleep; Kissinger got none. Shortly before dawn on Saturday, February 26, Kissinger and Chiao, weary but game, decided to take a break before submitting their common effort to their principals, who were scheduled to fly to Hangchow later in the morning. As far as they were concerned, they had reached agreement on the two Taiwan paragraphs.

The Chinese paragraph read:

> The Taiwan question is the crucial question obstructing the normalization of relations between China and the United States; the Government of the People's Republic of China is the sole, legal government of China; Taiwan is a province of China which has long been returned to the Motherland; the liberation of Taiwan is China's internal affair in which no other country has the right to intervene; and all U.S. forces and military installations must be withdrawn from Taiwan. The Chinese Government firmly opposes any activities which aim at the creation of "one China, one Taiwan," "one China, two governments," "two Chinas," and "independent Taiwan" or advocate that "the status of Taiwan remains to be determined."

The American paragraph read:

> The United States acknowledges that all Chinese on either side of the Taiwan Strait maintain there is but one China and that Taiwan is a part of China. The United States Government does not challenge that position. It reaffirms its interest in a peaceful settlement of the Taiwan question by the Chinese themselves. With this prospect in mind, it affirms the ultimate objective of the withdrawal of all U.S. forces and military installations from Taiwan. In the meantime, it will progressively reduce its forces and military installations on Taiwan as the tension in the area diminishes.

Clearly, these two key paragraphs in the final communiqué were artfully crafted, and each negotiator could interpret them in his own way without embarrassing the other. The Chinese could assert that Taiwan was an "internal matter" in which the United States could not intervene; and, more than that, that the United States had promised to withdraw "all" of its troops and installations there. On the other hand, the United States could assert that it would withdraw "all" of its forces and installations only when the issue of Taiwan had been settled peacefully — meaning only after Peking had renounced force as its means of "liberating" Taiwan. Meantime, the United States would gradually withdraw its forces, "as tension in the area diminishes" — meaning as the Vietnam war drew to a close. In this way the Americans implied that if China wanted to accelerate the U.S. pullout from Taiwan, it had only to pressure Hanoi into a compromise settlement.

Later in the morning, Nixon and Chou met at the airport to review the communiqué. There was enough discussion to delay their departure for over an hour. They then decided to continue their discussions on the plane, a Russian-built Ilyushin-18 turboprop. (Kissinger had urged the President to use Chinese planes on all internal flights so as not to offend the Chinese leaders.) The President's own jet followed a few minutes later, so that the White House communications system would be available once the party arrived in Hangchow.

The President and Chou reviewed the Peking honor guard, while Kissinger broke away from the ceremony and proceeded to the plane. At the ramp he shook hands warmly with a number of Chinese officials who would not be going on to Hangchow — among them Marshal Yeh, Kissinger's first official host in China. Kissinger and Yeh gripped each other's hands, absorbed in an animated conversation, until at last Kissinger boarded the plane. Mel Elfin of *Newsweek,* one of the pool reporters, greeted Kissinger. "What did he want, Henry?" Elfin asked in mock seriousness: "To be sure you'd come back as the first American ambassador?" "Ambassador?" exclaimed Kissinger, grinning. "Yeh was just checking to see whether I'd be willing to replace Chairman Mao."

The President was just then getting on board with Chou. Jokes over.

For a time during the two-and-a-half-hour flight, the President deserted Kissinger, Chou and Rogers. He went up front seeking quiet to jot down some thoughts on one of his familiar yellow lined pads for the final wording of the communiqué. By the time they reached Hangchow, Nixon and Chou had agreed to release the communiqué on Sunday in Shanghai.

Hangchow is a lovely lakeside city. In the thirteenth century, it inspired a young Italian visitor named Marco Polo to write, "So many pleasures may be found [in Hangchow] that one fancies himself to be in Paradise." Kissinger, as enthusiastic about China as Marco Polo, thought that one of Hangchow's pleasures would be a second, less hurried audience with Mao; but that was not to be. Kissinger was disappointed, and so was Nixon, though neither has admitted it.

Nixon was taken by boat to tour West Lake, bounded by walkways, temples and parks with names like "Listening to Orioles among the Willows." Another elaborate feast preceded his first restful night in a week. Then, on Sunday morning, Nixon and Chou motored to the new airport terminal in Hangchow, built in forty days by ten thousand laborers after it had become certain, in October, 1971, that the President would be visiting the city.

Shanghai, China's most Westernized city, was Nixon's last stop. While Kissinger prepared to hold an extraordinary news conference elaborating on the communiqué, the President visited an industrial exhibition. He was still reluctant to talk substance. As he told newsmen in Hangchow, "I had to do everything I could to assure that we did not jeopardize possible agreement in some areas. Here was a long road and it had to be traveled with discretion." As he gazed up at huge portraits of Communist leaders, Nixon noted, "That's Marx, and that's Engels, and that's Lenin, and that's Stalin."

"Yes," responded his host.

"All four."

"Yes."

"Four."

"Yes."

"That's Engels."

"Yes."

"We don't see many pictures of Engels in America."

The Chinese knew Kissinger would be briefing the press; they also knew he would be asked about the American defense commitment· to Taiwan and he would reaffirm it — on Chinese Communist soil. They were not happy about the arrangement, but they finally accepted Kissinger's explanation that domestic American politics required a ritualistic defense of the Taiwan regime.

It was 5:50 P.M. when Kissinger and Assistant Secretary of State Mar-

shall Green met with the American — and Chinese — press corps in the
Banquet Hall of the Industrial Exhibition Center. The Q-and-A session
lasted thirty-six minutes. For Kissinger, it must have seemed like thirty-
six hours. He struck reporters as nervous and cautious, and he spoke
slowly and deliberately. He began by describing the process of drafting
the communiqué, and then carefully explained that the purpose of the
trip was "an attempt by two countries to start a process by which . . .
they could . . . mitigate the consequences of [their] disagreements."
Green interjected the thought that the negotiations had been friendly
and candid, and that Rogers had played a major role, talking with Chou
for an hour and a half on the plane ride to Hangchow and for "almost
forty minutes" in the Secretary's hotel room that afternoon. (There was
a theory among newsmen that this was Chou's attempt to make up for
the earlier slight to Rogers.)

Kissinger then ticked off the following points:

- that the U.S. defense treaty with Taiwan had not changed during
  the China trip ("We stated our basic position with respect to this
  issue," he said, "in the President's State of the World report in
  which we say that this treaty will be maintained. Nothing has
  changed in that position.");
- that a "contact point" would soon be set up to handle the early
  negotiations on trade and exchanges;
- that a "senior U.S. representative" would go to Peking "as the
  need arises";
- that Nixon and Chou had discussed Taiwan and Vietnam "can-
  didly and seriously";
- that China had gone beyond the stage of "Ping-Pong diplomacy"
  by joining the United States in common opposition to "hegemony"
  by any other country over Asia and the Pacific region;
- that Mao had kept close tabs on the course of the negotiations;
- and, finally, that neither China's policy, nor America's, was "directed against the Soviet Union."

The news conference was unrevealing and studded with half-truths.
Later Kissinger explained that he had held back in order to avoid provok-
ing the Chinese into a counterblast while the President was still on Chinese soil.

At the final banquet on Sunday evening, Nixon was expansive. "This was the week that changed the world," he proclaimed. Then, after expressing confidence that "we will build . . . a bridge across sixteen thousand miles and twenty-two years of hostility which have divided us in the past," the President toasted the Premier and said, "Our two peoples tonight hold the future of the world in our hands."

Nixon presented a gift to Mao, and one to the Chinese people: for the Chairman, a group of porcelain swans by Boehm of Trenton, symbols of peace weighing two hundred and fifty pounds and valued at at least two hundred and fifty thousand dollars; for the Chinese people, two musk oxen named Milton and Mathilda. In return, the American people were given two rare black and white pandas named Hsing-Hsing and Ling-Ling.

The President left Shanghai on Monday morning for a one-stop flight back to Washington, where he landed at exactly 9 P.M. — prime time. He was welcomed home as a conquering hero. James Reston's column on February 29 was entitled "Mr. Nixon's Finest Hour." "His China policy," Reston wrote, "will stand out as a model of common sense and good diplomacy." Reston's was the predominant view. The Buckley brothers disagreed. Senator James L. Buckley of New York characterized the trip as a "disastrous adventure in American diplomacy." A private session with Kissinger on March 7 softened the tone of his criticism but not its substance. Columnist William F. Buckley, Jr., labeled America's Taiwan paragraph in the joint communiqué "a staggering capitulation."

In Taipei, there was sullen silence from Chiang Kai-shek's government, but inspired stories appeared in the Taipei press denouncing the communiqué and claiming that people all over the Pacific had now lost faith in Washington's word as an ally.

In Moscow, the Soviet government was bitter but restrained, while its controlled press opened a vicious attack on China and strongly implied that the Nixon visit was basically an anti-Soviet action.

In Tokyo, the Sato government collapsed and within seven months its successor, led by Kakuei Tanaka, reestablished formal diplomatic relations with China.

In Saigon, there was reluctant praise for the President's trip.

In Hanoi, there was silence. Within a few days, Chou flew to North Vietnam to reassure his allies. He was unsuccessful, and Hanoi began to assert a more independent policy of its own.

In Bangkok, the Thai government began to maneuver — away from Washington and toward Peking. An official spokesman said that Thailand was expecting an invitation to send a Ping-Pong team to China.

In Western Europe, there was approval, mixed with anxiety. What might this unpredictable man do next?

Around the globe, there was a strong feeling that the trip had created a new diplomatic world. It symbolized a breakthrough in Chinese-American relations, and Russia would have to adjust to this change. It made China "respectable" once again in American political life. If Nixon could go there, anyone could. In a private meeting with newsmen on March 1, Kissinger concluded that the trip not only opened an historic process whose shape could be only dimly perceived at the time, but also gave everyone "an option on the future." He and the President now began to look toward Moscow — and the crunch on Vietnam.

ELEVEN

Haiphong Harbor:
A Place for Jugular Diplomacy

O N MARCH 31, 1972, Good Friday for the Catholics of Vietnam, the
North Vietnamese burst across the DMZ — four full divisions,
backed by heavy Soviet tanks and covered by long-range artillery. Both
the timing and the scope of this invasion astonished most American
officials, including Henry Kissinger. He had expected a less ambitious
enemy offensive in late January or early February — before, or even during, the President's journey to Peking. But when, by mid-March, the
offensive had not materialized, Kissinger began to think that the North
Vietnamese might have changed their minds. Perhaps, he felt, the Peking
summit had gone so well that Hanoi had been forced to reconsider its
strategy. Or perhaps the enemy offensive had been stymied by increased
U.S. air strikes against Communist strongholds. In a moment of self-
delusion, he began to believe that there wouldn't be a Communist offensive after all.

For months, while the North Vietnamese were preparing their surprise
invasion, they had been dangling before Kissinger the possibility of more
serious talks. On January 26, the day after Nixon dramatically revealed
that Kissinger had been meeting secretly with Le Duc Tho for months,
and that their talks had ended in deadlock, he sent a private message to
Hanoi proposing a new try at secret negotiations. A few weeks later, the
North Vietnamese accepted the President's offer, suggesting any date
after March 15. Kissinger quickly proposed March 20, and Hanoi
accepted the date.

On March 6, however, the North Vietnamese began to delay, proposing that the meeting be postponed until April 15. Kissinger replied that he would be in Japan that day. What about April 24? For ten days there was no answer from Hanoi; as a demonstration of U.S. impatience, Ambassador William Porter, who had replaced Bruce in Paris, suspended the regular semipublic talks.

At last, on March 31, Kissinger received a message from Hanoi agreeing to the April 24 date on condition that the regular Paris talks be resumed as well. He immediately drafted a reply confirming April 24 for the secret meeting and April 13 for the resumption of the semipublic talks. But before his message could be coded and cabled, Hanoi launched its offensive. Kissinger later learned that Hanoi had "decided to go military" back in October of 1971, when Le Duc Tho had developed his diplomatic "illness." From that moment on, Kissinger told us, "their problem was to gear the negotiation in such a way that it would support" their military objectives. Their delays were carefully calculated. "It was very smart, tough bargaining on their part."

By Saturday, April 1, the Communist attacks widened, and Kissinger became more concerned. From the sanctuaries in Cambodia — they were still there, more threatening than ever, despite the U.S. "incursion" of 1970 and the continued bombing — several thousand NVA troops cracked across the border, cutting south toward the city of An Loc, while several thousand others smashed eastward from Svay Rieng, a sanctuary area farther south. An alarmed but not yet galvanized Saigon lay sixty miles away. Kissinger conferred several times with the President, Abrams and Bunker, but there were no command decisions.

By Sunday, April 2, as the NVA drove farther south into Quangtri Province, and elements of ARVN's untested 3rd Division reeled back under their pressure, Kissinger reluctantly concluded that the United States faced a full-scale invasion of South Vietnam. Once again he had miscalculated the enemy's intentions. Not since the Tet offensive, early in 1968, had the Communists moved so broadly and blatantly against South Vietnam. Twelve out of their thirteen ground combat divisions, almost their entire military force, had been thrown into battle. Hanoi's Defense Minister Vo Nguyen Giap, whose motto had always been "Strike only if success is certain," was going for broke. Clearly this offensive was to be his grand finale, the military spectacular preceding the American diplomatic cave-in; the attack that Thieu was shortly to dub "the decisive battle of the war." Giap's strategy: to seize a provincial city, proclaim it a provisional capital for the Provisional Revolutionary Government (PRG), attract diplomatic support, and then negotiate the formation of a coalition government to replace Thieu.

"The U.S. side has been showing great restraint in its response," Kissinger cabled the North Vietnamese on Sunday, "in order to give the negotiations every chance to succeed." Actually, the United States Government was so stunned by the North Vietnamese invasion that it didn't know what to do.

On Monday, April 3, Kissinger convened the Washington Special Actions Group (WSAG) — his vehicle for crisis management ever since the spring of 1969. For the next six weeks, WSAG was to meet almost every day, sometimes twice a day, collecting all of the raw data for Kissinger's recommendations and Nixon's decisions, and then converting the decisions into action.

No minutes were kept. After Jack Anderson obtained secret WSAG records relating to the India-Pakistan war, Kissinger streamlined the operation. Fewer officials; tighter security and discipline; less chance for leaks.

In this crisis, as in others, Kissinger played the central coordinating role. On most days, he would arrive at his White House office by 8 A.M. and have breakfast there while reading the overnight file of embassy dispatches and military intelligence collated by Haig or members of his staff. By eight-thirty Kissinger would be attending the regular White House staff meeting, and by nine sharp he would be conferring with the President in the Oval Office, reviewing what had been done and then helping Nixon decide what had to be done next. Often in the course of these discussions, the President would place calls to Rogers or Laird or Moorer and listen to their judgments before asking for Kissinger's. These sessions in the Oval Office could run an hour, sometimes two. By noon in Washington, midnight in Saigon, Kissinger would be issuing the President's latest instructions for the next day's war in Indochina or diplomacy in Paris.

Carefully orchestrated tidbits of information about this process of secret decision-making would then be released to the public by a small corps of press officers: Ziegler, who knew little about foreign policy at the beginning but learned a lot at the White House; Dan Henkin, who knew a great deal and cautiously rationed out his nuggets to newsmen at the Pentagon; and Robert McCloskey, who managed to retain his credibility while helping newsmen at the State Department understand the nuances of policy. These three men would get their briefing orders from Nixon, Kissinger, Haig, or WSAG, and they were the only ones who were permitted to talk to the press. Most other officials at the White House, the Pentagon, and the State Department refused to take calls from newsmen.

It was a streamlined, slick operation, so tightly controlled that the people generally learned only what the White House wanted to tell them. In addition to the official tidbits, the White House would occasionally leak information in a deliberate effort to enhance the President's image or further the ends of policy. According to one such leak, when a White House aide questioned a presidential decision on political grounds, Nixon is supposed to have snapped angrily, "The hell with politics. What is at stake is the viability of our foreign policy." Other such inspired leaks drew attention to the movement of American planes and ships, creating the impression that Nixon was determined to beat back the North Vietnamese invasion.

On April 4, two big decisions were made: the first was political, the second military. The first decision involved the Soviet Union. It was clear to Kissinger from the beginning of the offensive that the North Vietnamese could never have invaded South Vietnam without Soviet tanks and long-range artillery. For the second time in four months, he believed, the Russians were supporting a reckless military adventure. India first, now Vietnam. When would they learn? Nixon and Kissinger decided that they had no choice but to run the political risk of fingering the Russians for complicity in the invasion. But, in an effort to protect the summit, scheduled to begin on May 22, they decided that the initial accusation was not to come from Kissinger at the White House but from McCloskey at Foggy Bottom.

On Tuesday, April 4, the State Department spokesman was given precise instructions by Haig following the regular morning meeting of WSAG. McCloskey was to mention the fact that Soviet arms were supporting the North Vietnamese invasion of the south, but he was not to dwell on it. U. Alexis Johnson and William Sullivan, who had attended the WSAG meeting, later amplified Haig's instructions during a noontime fill-in for Rogers, at which McCloskey was present. They made the point that Haig's orders came from Kissinger. McCloskey then faced a briefing room crowded with reporters on tight deadlines, and he apparently performed his task so well that Ziegler later called with congratulations. "Exactly what we wanted!" he said.

Kissinger made the mistake of thinking the charge of Soviet complicity in the invasion could be fine-tuned. One careful State Department comment, one run of news stories, and no more. But the cumbersome bureaucracy upset his calculation. One official comment led to others — not only at the State Department, but at the Pentagon and the CIA, too; and the initial burst of headlines encouraged more journalistic digging, which produced a rash of stories about a developing crisis in Soviet-American relations that could destroy the summit.

Kissinger worried about the Russians getting the wrong signal, and he ordered Government spokesmen to play down the Russian angle. Later he told James Reston that he personally had opposed the idea of fingering the Russians and that the State Department had gone too far. These Kissinger thoughts eventually made their way into a Reston column. Those Administration officials who knew the truth were astonished. When the issue was raised at the White House, Kissinger, professing his own innocence, said he couldn't figure out where "Scotty" ever got that impression, adding that he hadn't seen Reston "for weeks."

Although Foggy Bottom quickly took its cue from Kissinger — Secretary Rogers even went so far as to deny, quite heatedly, that the Administration had ever intended to "finger" the Russians — the Pentagon remained loyal to Kissinger's original orders. On April 6, Admiral Moorer, at a luncheon meeting of the Overseas Writers, charged that the "new factor" in the Vietnam war was the presence of Soviet tanks and artillery in South Vietnam. On April 7, Secretary Laird hardened the criticism. Eighty percent of Hanoi's sophisticated hardware, he charged, came from Russia. Moscow's role was thus "critical" in furthering Hanoi's war aims.

Kissinger got word of Laird's charges during a lunch with a Washington columnist. "Godammit!" he exploded. "I told him to stop." Kissinger explained that McCloskey was to have blamed the Russians once, and that was to have been the extent of public criticism. "Laird forgets that he is no longer a Congressman," he muttered.

Three days later, however, the game plan changed, and no less a finger-pointer than Nixon took up the issue. On April 10, the President spoke at a State Department ceremony marking the signature of an international convention banning the use of biological weapons. His comments were drafted by Kissinger. As Soviet Ambassador Dobrynin listened impassively from the dais, Nixon first praised the Russians for cooperating in arms control agreements and then indirectly criticized them for encouraging the North Vietnamese invasion. "Every great power," he stressed, "must follow the principle that it should not encourage, directly or indirectly, any other nation to use force or armed aggression against one of its neighbors." Afterward, Dobrynin had no comment for reporters, as he walked briskly through the Diplomatic Lobby to his waiting Cadillac.

The second big decision of April 4 focused on the American military response to the North Vietnamese invasion. That morning, the Pentagon officially announced that the United States would "take whatever steps are necessary to protect remaining U.S. forces in South Vietnam." Unofficially, reporters were then informed that ten to twenty B-52 strategic bombers had just left their North Carolina air base for the long flight to Thailand.

This was the start of an extraordinary buildup of American air and naval power in Indochina. Within a month after the North Vietnamese offensive had begun, the United States had six aircraft carriers on station in the Gulf of Tonkin, plus five cruisers and forty destroyers. On Guam, the B-52 fleet rose to almost one hundred. At U-Tapao, in Thailand, there were fifty-three B-52s and two hundred and twenty-four fighter-bombers. At Danang, there were a hundred and thirteen fighter-bombers. All told, by the end of April, there were over one thousand American warplanes directing their firepower against Communist positions in Indochina.

When Pentagon experts first learned about White House plans for more intensive use of the B-52s, they demurred. This strategic bomber, in their view, was too old for bruising round-the-clock tactical missions. Moreover, there was an acute shortage of pilots, and those who were available to fly — some on second and third tours of duty in Vietnam — were simply too tired to be effective. Kissinger impatiently brushed aside their concerns. He was using the B-52s to send signals to Hanoi, Peking and especially Moscow, and he really did not want to be bothered at that point with Pentagon projections about pilot and plane weariness. He was busy *running* a war: leaning over huge maps of the battle area, moving fleets from one end of the Pacific to the other, barking out orders to admirals and generals. Observed one high Pentagon official who had almost daily contact with Kissinger during this time: "Henry's the biggest signal-sender in the world. Only trouble is, he keeps sending them to the Communists, but he never seems to get any of ours."

On April 6, for the first time, U.S. planes were sprung from their 1968 restraints, and fighter-bombers struck sixty miles north of the

DMZ without apology or contrived explanations about "protective re-action." That day, Admiral Moorer pointedly warned Hanoi that American attacks would "inch northward" unless the Communist offensive stopped. The warning had no effect. On April 7, Loc Ninh, northwest of Saigon, fell to the advancing North Vietnamese troops, and major battles broke out on the outskirts of An Loc and Quangtri City.

April 8 brought an alarming cable from Bunker and Abrams to Kissinger. It warned that the Communists were clearly engaged in an all-out effort to topple the Thieu regime, that the offensive could last "for several months" and that substantial American air and naval support was required to head off a Communist victory. Kissinger carried the bad news to Nixon, who immediately ordered B-52 raids against North Vietnam. For the first time since November, 1967, these big bombers hit military targets deep inside the country. On April 10 they bombed the port city of Vinh, a hundred and forty-five miles north of the DMZ. It was only the beginning.

For the next three days the President's top advisers urgently debated the wisdom of B-52 raids against Hanoi and Haiphong. Helms provided the WSAG meetings with the up-to-date intelligence. Laird was bearish on the bombing, fearing a congressional uproar that could jeopardize financial support for the war. Rogers was bearish too; he feared a rapid escalation of the fighting that could endanger the Moscow summit. Moorer and Kissinger were the strongest advocates of B-52 strikes against North Vietnam's capital and its major port; Moorer because he felt such strikes would soon cripple the Communist offensive in the south; Kissinger partly because he agreed that such strikes would hurt the Communists but, more important, because he desperately wanted to "signal" Moscow that the United States was determined to stop the North Vietnamese offensive, even at the risk of endangering the summit.

After listening to these arguments and counterarguments, Nixon retreated into his office for another one of those "painful" and "lonely" decisions. Kissinger had a feeling the President was going to flash the green light. "You could tell the old man had made up his mind he wouldn't be screwed," said one NSC staffer.

By April 15, Nixon had made his decision. He approved the plan, code-named "Freedom Porch Bravo," for a weekend of B-52 raids against Hanoi and Haiphong; he told Kissinger to put the plan into effect immediately. The idea was to destroy some of North Vietnam's oil depots and compel Hanoi to call off the offensive. A Kissinger aide explained,

"We consider it a tactical decision . . . partly political, partly military. We are trying to compress the amount of time the North Vietnamese have to decide whether the offensive is worth continuing and whether they have the means to continue it."

Four Soviet merchant ships in Haiphong Harbor were damaged during the air attacks. Moscow protested what it called "acts of aggression," but the protest contained no explicit warnings. China protested, but even more cautiously. U.S. spokesmen responded sharply to these protests. Stop the offensive in the south, they said, and the raids will stop. Continue the offensive, and the U.S. is, to quote one spokesman, "prepared to bomb anywhere in North Vietnam."

The new bombing produced the expected criticism on Capitol Hill and in editorials. On April 17 the *Washington Post* charged: "What President Johnson and his predecessors steadfastly tried not to do over fifteen years or more, President Nixon has managed to do almost overnight; he has brought the war in Indochina to the brink of a head-on confrontation with the Soviet Union by his decision to send American bombers over the suburbs of Hanoi and the port of Haiphong and to amass an American naval armada off the North Vietnamese coast." Members of the Senate Foreign Relations Committee condemned the bombing during testimony by Rogers and Laird on April 17 and 18. Both Cabinet officers concealed their own inner doubts behind a ringing endorsement of the bombing. Rogers refused to rule out any possible U.S. military action except the reintroduction of American ground troops and the use of nuclear weapons. "We're not going to make any announcement about what we're not going to do," he stated. Laird went further. He warned that the United States might mine the ports of North Vietnam.

Kissinger did not pay much attention to the criticism in the press or the Senate. He did not believe that the bombing was the sort of provocative action that would trigger a major confrontation with the Russians. What he knew, and the critics did not know, was that he was on his way to Moscow.

Although Administration officials had criticized the Russians, directly and indirectly, for their role in the invasion, and the Americans had launched major military action against Moscow's ally, North Vietnam, the Soviet Union and the United States still managed to do some important bilateral business in April. Dobrynin and Kissinger were engaged once again in a highly secret exchange about SALT. Some six weeks before the scheduled summit, Kissinger had given the Soviet envoy a carefully considered compromise designed to facilitate agreement. The heart of the compromise was his promise that if the Russians agreed to include submarine-launched missiles in the final package, then the Americans would allow them to have a substantial numerical advantage in this category of offensive weapons, subject only to a Soviet willingness to scrap their basically obsolescent land-based SS-7 and SS-8 long-range missiles and a certain number of their H-class submarines.

The compromise offer impressed Dobrynin. He felt, for a variety of reasons, that the time had come for Kissinger to pay a secret visit to Moscow. It might help break the deadlock on SALT, and it might ease the building tension created by Vietnam. Besides, if Kissinger could fly secretly to Peking to make arrangements for a presidential visit, then there was no reason why he could not fly to Moscow for the same purpose.

The Soviet Ambassador arranged for Brezhnev to extend an invitation. Kissinger accepted it, for reasons more closely linked to Vietnam than to the summit. He hoped to be able to persuade Brezhnev that a Communist military victory in Vietnam was a bad bet for Soviet policy. No great power could allow itself to be humiliated by a small country; therefore, in the tangle of Indochina, there lurked the danger of a major confrontation between Moscow and Washington over a prize that was unworthy of their efforts in other, more significant fields — such as SALT. If the President could propose a reasonable compromise on SALT, despite the North Vietnamese invasion, then perhaps Brezhnev could produce a compromise on Vietnam. Kissinger still had not given up hope of persuading Brezhnev to limit Soviet arms deliveries to North Vietnam.

On Wednesday evening, April 19, Kissinger left the White House at cocktail time and stopped in at a fashionable Georgetown party. Once again, he was playing his Kissinger-on-the-town role: a visible appearance before every secret departure. Later, his White House limousine sped through the darkness to Andrews Air Force Base, where he boarded one of the big presidential jets. Already on board were four NSC officials: Helmut Sonnenfeldt, his deputy for European affairs; John Negroponte, a Vietnam expert; and Peter Rodman and Winston Lord, his personal staff assistants. Also on board was Dobrynin, a rather unusual passenger. The Soviet Ambassador was to join the Kissinger-Brezhnev talks, and there really was no better way of slipping out of Washington without detection. Kissinger and Dobrynin did little talking during the flight. Kissinger slept and Dobrynin read.

Ten hours later, morning in Moscow, the special jet landed at the VIP area of Vnukovo Airport, normally reserved for domestic flights. Vassilly Kuznetsov, a Deputy Foreign Minister, greeted Kissinger, and then they all ducked into black limousines for the twenty-minute ride to a luxurious dacha in the Lenin Hills. The dacha was one of a half-dozen government residences on the outskirts of Moscow, where several of the top Kremlin leaders lived.

Kissinger's lease on the Lenin Hills dacha ran four days — for him, quite long enough. Unlike the trip to China, this Moscow assignment provided no thrills. It was a business trip. It was not that he had spent much time in the Soviet Union, or even knew the country well. In fact, the joke among Foggy Bottom Russian experts was that Kissinger's knowledge of the Soviet Union stopped at the Pripet Marshes. But Kissinger believed that he understood as much about Russia as he needed to know. After all, there was nothing exotic about the portrait of a solid, entrenched bureaucracy perpetuating a system of totalitarian controls. Russia's leaders were no longer revolutionaries or visionaries, like the leaders of China, but rather plodding functionaries who were important only because of the enormous power they wielded.

That first evening, Foreign Minister Andrei Gromyko came to Kissinger's dacha for a two-hour talk about the meetings with Brezhnev, which were to start at ten the next morning. For at least five hours a day, for the next three days, Brezhnev and Kissinger met at a nearby government dacha reserved for confidential talks. Kissinger later described him as a man of "concrete positions and concrete objectives" who excelled at "doing things rather than philosophizing about them," an "elemental" and "physical" person who knew what he wanted and how he could get it. He was earthy, tough, direct, and at the same time, Kissinger recalled, gracious, polite, even warm.

Brezhnev and Kissinger were meeting to prepare for the President's visit to Moscow, and yet they found that they spent at least half their time on Vietnam. Both of the superpowers shared a common desire to see the war ended, but they could not find the key to peace. Brezhnev implied that he was unhappy about the timing of the North Vietnamese offensive, but he stressed that Russia was not in the driver's seat in Hanoi.

Kissinger made his pitch about the Russians reducing arms deliveries to North Vietnam. It fell on deaf ears. Brezhnev made it clear that while he might consider the North Vietnamese foolish and headstrong, he had no choice but to continue supporting them. Hanoi was a "fraternal ally," and besides, there was China.

Kissinger also made his pitch about the responsibility of great powers to avoid encouraging any nation to use force against a neighbor. That too fell on deaf ears. Brezhnev asserted that Russia would continue to aid "progressive mankind" against the "forces of reaction."

Finally, Kissinger made his pitch about the President's strong desire to negotiate a fair and honorable end to the war, based on any reasonable proposal that would give all the South Vietnamese a chance for political expression and political power. He even gave the Soviet leader an advance look at the President's latest cease-fire proposals, which had not yet been presented formally to the North Vietnamese. Here Brezhnev indicated that there might be some give. He implied that the North Vietnamese were too stubborn, too rigid in their negotiating approach to Washington and Saigon. He seemed to be suggesting that he had recommended a more flexible stance. He told Kissinger that Le Duc Tho would be returning soon to Paris and that he was eager for another secret meeting with Kissinger. Brezhnev could offer no guarantees about a breakthrough, but he urged Kissinger to resume the secret talks.

Throughout their discussion about Vietnam, there was no shouting, no bluster. But there was really no meeting of the minds. Kissinger repeatedly stressed one chilling message. The United States, he said, could not accept a military defeat in South Vietnam, and would take "whatever steps are necessary" to prevent a Communist military victory. Both men were aware that the threat of major American military action might risk a Soviet-American confrontation and jeopardize the summit.

Although Kissinger and Brezhnev made little progress on Vietnam, they were more successful in dealing with SALT. In this case, arms control was a purely bilateral issue. The two superpowers were bargaining over the future of the world, and the exclusion of everyone else, from China to Luxembourg, was a luxury only the powerful could afford. Kissinger explained the President's compromise offer, which he had presented to Dobrynin in Washington, and he was pleased when Brezhnev accepted it the following day. Henceforth, submarine-launched missiles would be included in any SALT package. This was a giant step toward agreement. There were still a half-dozen unresolved problems, but they suddenly seemed manageable. Kissinger could see the distinct outline of an historic SALT agreement, embracing both offensive and defensive weapons.

In addition to Vietnam and SALT, Kissinger and Brezhnev discussed a wide range of other problems — from Berlin to trade. They were determined to lay the groundwork for a successful summit, at which a number of substantive agreements could be signed.

After each formal meeting, Kissinger and his staff compiled reports that were cabled to the White House from the closely guarded plane at Vnukovo Airport. One day the communications equipment on Kissinger's plane developed trouble. The staff asked if they should use the equipment on General Brent Scowcroft's plane. The President's military aide was in Moscow to prepare technical facilities for the summit. Kissinger said no. Scowcroft was not to know he was in Moscow. What about using the Embassy's communications? No, Kissinger repeated. Ambassador Jacob Beam was to be kept in the dark, too. Finally, after a day of puttering around with the equipment, Kissinger's crew repaired the gear, and communications with the White House were reestablished.

Security was absolute. Except for a small group of Soviet officials and his own staff, no one in Moscow knew Kissinger was in the Soviet capital; Beam was not informed until the last day of Kissinger's stay. There were no dinner parties, no press leaks, no Bolshoi Theater in the evening. Instead, the Bolshoi came to Kissinger — in the shape of long and painfully dull movies. Kissinger and his colleagues found a few hours of relaxation at the Dom Priyomov, a reception hall and sports center in the Lenin Hills compound reserved for Politburo members and their wives and friends. Negroponte did several laps in an Olympic-size swimming pool. Sonnenfeldt and Lord played tennis with a Russian pro, complaining constantly about the quality of the rackets. And, Kissinger, ever the signal-sender, decided that he would play Ping-Pong with the chief of Moscow security. The Russians knew all about Ping-Pong diplomacy.

On the last day of his visit, Kissinger spent six hours with Gromyko, working almost exclusively on preparations for the summit. There were last-minute details to be settled about the agreements on health research, environmental problems, space cooperation and "incidents at sea." And there were arrangements to be made for the press, hotel space to be set aside for officials, and a thoughtful itinerary to be organized for Mrs. Nixon. Before Kissinger left, Gromyko showed him through the Kremlin apartments where the President and his staff would be staying during the summit. Kissinger thought the setup was pretty impressive.

Early Monday afternoon, April 24, Kissinger left Moscow. The following day the White House announced that he had been in the Soviet capital for four days. Reporters wanted to know why the secrecy? "We are at the moment in a very delicate phase of international relations," Ziegler responded. "It was felt by both sides that there should be a minimum of speculation and a minimum of prior discussion until there was an opportunity to explore each other's views." There had been exchanges between Nixon and Brezhnev, he reminded the reporters, since early 1971. "It was felt in the last few weeks that a more direct exchange might be desirable."

The news of Kissinger's latest vanishing act set off a new round of applause in the press. "How he performs this delicate and dangerous role," Reston wrote, "is a *miracle* which defies physical and intellectual endurance." Kissinger explained it more disarmingly. "I'd do anything for caviar."

No sooner had Kissinger returned from Moscow than he began to help Nixon put the finishing touches on his latest Vietnam speech. On April 26, the President announced first that another twenty thousand American troops would be withdrawn from South Vietnam by July 1, leaving only forty-nine thousand there; second, that the regular Paris peace talks, suspended since March 23, would be resumed the next morning "with the firm expectation that productive talks leading to rapid progress will follow through all available channels"; and, finally, that American air and naval attacks against North Vietnam would continue until the Communists stopped their offensive.

Nixon used exceptionally strong language to denounce North Vietnam. He charged that its "brutally inflicted" invasion of South Vietnam was a "clear case of naked and unprovoked aggression across an international border." It was, he charged, "a desperate gamble to impose a Communist regime on South Vietnam." Never before had the President seemed so publicly concerned about the possibility of a Communist military victory — "with the inevitable bloodbath that would follow for hundreds of thousands who have dared to oppose Communist aggression." Nixon invoked the name of General Abrams five times to justify the Administration's claim that "the South Vietnamese have made great progress." Although White House officials quickly denied that the President was setting up Abrams as the fall guy in the event that Saigon collapsed, it was obvious that Nixon was worried that Vietnam could become an election year albatross, an embarrassment inconsistent with the "great role" he believed the United States was "destined" to play in the world. Once again he appealed to the American people to support his policy and to spurn the calls of critics and Congressmen for "immediate withdrawal."

Kissinger briefed newsmen twice before the President spoke. Like Nixon, he seemed unusually gloomy. Kontum and even Pleiku might be overrun, he conceded. No, he said, "we have accepted no restrictions" on bombing Hanoi and Haiphong. Yes, "we will insist on a restoration of the 1968 understandings." And yes, the "Communist forces which crossed the DMZ must be returned." But it was part of Kissinger's genius as a briefer that he could echo the President's sentiments faithfully and yet strike a different note. That night his theme was "negotiations," not the presidential theme of "invasion," which Kissinger described as a "six-week spasm." This "spasm," in Kissinger's view, held "the key to the outcome of the war," which was, he stressed, "at a very decisive juncture." He had found an alternating pattern of conflict and conversation in Hanoi's behavior, and he pointed out that Le Duc Tho was returning to Paris. "That doesn't mean he is traveling with acceptable baggage," Kissinger cautioned; but it did suggest that the offensive was "as much a political action as a military one." He expected a new round of secret talks to begin soon in Paris. "There is only one issue left," he explained. "Will they make a settlement that leaves the Government of Vietnam [Saigon] *as a legitimate political structure,* or will they seek to destroy it and set up a Communist government?"

For the next week, the news from South Vietnam continued to make grim reading. Kissinger met with the President every morning to review reports of continuing Communist attacks, some threatening to cut South Vietnam in half. There were ARVN units that fought well, but there were others that were decimated. Kissinger grumbled about Laird "overselling" Vietnamization. Abrams kept cabling the White House that American air and naval support was "essential." Without it, he implied, ARVN would crumble, and Thieu would be through. The news strongly suggested that, once again, the White House had badly misjudged Hanoi's capacity for sustained warfare. Rather than "run out of gas," as Kissinger had thought likely, North Vietnam's newly armored units kept rumbling forward, taking small towns and threatening big ones. ARVN desertion rates zoomed; Saigon's repression increased. A sense of foreboding began to permeate the American bureaucracy. Not even the news, known to very few, that Kissinger had arranged a secret rendezvous with Le Duc Tho for May 2 could lift the gloom around the White House.

On the evening of April 30, a number of John Connally's friends, who had gathered at his ranch for a sumptuous barbecue honoring Nixon, caught a glimpse of the President's somber mood. Several times during his toast, Nixon referred to the possibility of a Communist take-over of

South Vietnam. He repeated Abrams's assurance that the South Vietnamese could hold, "provided the United States continues to furnish the air and naval support." He underscored the global importance of Vietnam. "What is on the line," he stated flatly, "is not just peace in Vietnam, but peace in the Mideast, peace in Europe and peace not just for the five or six or seven years immediately ahead of us, but possibly for a long time in the future."

A question was raised by one of the guests — whether by prearrangement, the White House would not say. Had the President ever thought about bombing the dikes of North Vietnam? Nixon barely missed a beat. Yes, obviously, he had thought about the dikes, which he defined as a "strategic target and indirectly a military target." But, he said, if he were to bomb the dikes, he would be causing "an enormous number of civilian casualties." Then he warned, "We are prepared to use our military and naval strength against military targets throughout North Vietnam, and we believe that the North Vietnamese are taking a very great risk if they continue their offensive in the south. I will just leave it there, and they can make their own choice."

Connally led his guests in applauding the President's carefully chosen words.

On May 1, as news of Nixon's calculated dike warnings made headlines around the world, and as Red Army tanks rumbled through Red Square in the traditional May Day parade, other Soviet tanks rumbled into Quangtri City, the capital of South Vietnam's northernmost province. ARVN cracked under intensive North Vietnamese artillery bombardment, and the troops fled south along Highway 1 toward Hue, only twenty-four miles away. For Saigon, it was a debacle, an unseemly rout. South Vietnamese troops simply broke ranks and ran, leaving behind their tanks, guns, armored cars and artillery, an unexpected windfall for the Communists. Hanoi's troops entered Quangtri, fixed a red flag to a pole on top of the Citadel, and proclaimed a major victory, just as the last American advisers were being helicoptered out of the fallen city.

The loss of Quangtri was a staggering blow to Saigon — and to Administration faith in Vietnamization. A number of East European diplomats in Washington feared that the President might feel so trapped by Vietnam, so humiliated by Saigon's poor performance, that he would order drastic action, such as hitting the dikes, to vent his fury and frustration and, if possible, to frighten Hanoi and Moscow into reconsidering their course of action.

The news from the Connally ranch and Quangtri City provided an unsettling backdrop for Kissinger's secret May 2 meeting with Le Duc Tho which, like the others, took place in a Paris suburb. Kissinger arrived with a new Nixon offer that he thought could be the basis for a quick settlement of the war. If the North Vietnamese would agree to a cease-fire and a return of American POWs — that and nothing more — the United States would withdraw from Indochina within four months.

Kissinger believed the offer was so simple that Le Duc Tho would accept it, understanding what Kissinger could imply but never state: that the Communist offensive had driven Nixon to streamline his policy down to bare-bones requirements: the prisoners and a decent interval of time for withdrawal; that, in effect, Nixon wanted to get out of Vietnam so badly that all he was asking of Hanoi was an exit visa. In the process, he might be compelled to use bombastic rhetoric and rough bombing, but that would be only to cover his retreat. Nixon wanted out — if possible, by election day. Kissinger felt that from a North Vietnamese standpoint the offer could not have been more reasonable. Moreover, he thought Brezhnev had given him assurances that Hanoi would be flexible.

Once again, though, Kissinger had misread his opponent. Le Duc Tho disdainfully rejected Nixon's offer. As Kissinger recalled that three-hour session, the nadir of his long negotiations with the North Vietnamese, Le Duc Tho was "tough," "brutal," and "unyielding."

The North Vietnamese did not want to negotiate — not then. All they did was "read me their public statement," he said. "It had taken us six months to set up the meeting and innumerable exchanges and when we got there, what we heard could have been clipped from a newspaper and sent to us in the mail." After Le Duc Tho read the statement, Kissinger remembered, "I'd say, 'How about de-escalation and a cease-fire?' They'd say, 'Wars aren't fought to have a cease-fire. Wars are fought to have victory.' I'd say, 'How about de-escalation alone?' They'd say, 'We don't fight to de-escalate.'" Riding the crest of the Communist victory at Quangtri, Le Duc Tho was pushing for the maximum — American help in ousting the Thieu regime and in organizing a coalition government that would exclude Thieu — an arrangement which Kissinger described as "the imposition, under the thinnest veneer, of a Communist government." To Kissinger, this was totally unacceptable. Le Duc Tho was unwilling to compromise.

The meeting was a fiasco, and Kissinger wearily returned to Washington once again. He strongly suspected that the news of his failure in negotiation, coupled with Saigon's failure in battle, would compel the President to take sudden action that could torpedo the Moscow summit.

Kissinger's suspicions were well grounded. When he returned to the White House on the night of May 2, there was a message from the President asking Kissinger to join him on a cruise down the Potomac. Was it to be *Patton* all over again?

For three hours, Nixon and Kissinger reviewed the day's humiliating encounter with Le Duc Tho, the discouraging reports from South Vietnam, and the prospects for the Moscow summit. Nixon seemed particularly angry at the Russians. Brezhnev had led him to believe that a Kissinger–Le Duc Tho meeting would be fruitful; instead it had proved to be a disaster. Was Brezhnev deliberately playing him for a fool? And if so, for what reason? Kissinger had no bright answers, and Nixon began to suggest the need for dramatic action that would force the Russians to pay a high price for continuing to support the war.

They reviewed a range of military options. Hitting the dikes? It was the newest option. Nixon rejected it. What about landing South Vietnamese marines in North Vietnam, an Inchon-type landing designed to intersect Communist supply lines into the south? Nixon rejected that option, too. He had no faith in the military capability of the South Vietnamese, and he feared China might easily misconstrue such an approach as a basic switch in America's Indochina policy. Reintroduce American ground troops? Rejected. Nuclear weapons? Rejected. The President's options dwindled down to two: more unrestricted bombing; or, for the first time in the war, mining the ports of North Vietnam. Mining would amount to an open interference with international shipping in and out of Haiphong — a frontal challenge to the Soviet Union.

There were no presidential decisions that night; but Kissinger could see the direction of the President's thinking, and he felt decidedly uncomfortable about it.

Kissinger spent Wednesday and Thursday in nonstop conference with Nixon, discussing the mining option. LBJ had rejected it; and, in 1970, when the JCS had raised it, Nixon had rejected it, too. Now, the President was changing his mind. He felt that the mining idea made more military sense than at any other time because, for the first time in the war, the North Vietnamese urgently needed a daily flow of fuel for their tanks and armored vehicles on the battlefields of the south. A cut, or reduction, in the flow of fuel from their depots near the ports could seriously cripple their offensive — if not immediately, then soon. Moreover — again, for the first time in the war — the idea of mining seemed politically feasible; Nixon felt he could take this drastic action against North Vietnam without risk of strong Soviet or Chinese counteraction. Hanoi was becoming increasingly estranged from its two big Communist allies as they moved toward better relations with the United States. Nixon gambled that there was a good chance the U.S. could blockade North Vietnamese ports without damaging its relations with China and Russia.

Kissinger, on the other hand, had his doubts — not about the idea of mining as such but about its possible effect on the Moscow summit, which was vitally important to his scheme for a global balance of the major powers. Kissinger surprised his colleagues at a WSAG meeting one morning by implying that he opposed the mining and intended to tell Nixon that it might jeopardize the summit. No one knows whether he actually did convey his concern to the President. In Washington there has always been a vast difference between telling a colleague that you favor, or oppose, a line of policy, and telling the President. Dean Rusk used to get very upset when he heard cocktail chatter to the effect that Robert McNamara opposed the bombing of North Vietnam and told Johnson so, when he knew perfectly well that it was quite often McNamara's own recommendation that triggered the bombing. At another WSAG meeting that week, Kissinger repeated his belief that the mining of North Vietnamese ports would more than likely lead to a postponement of the summit. He remarked to an old friend that he feared Vietnam still had the capacity to distort the nation's diplomatic priorities.

Of course, it is possible that Kissinger, as one of his closest aides put it, was merely "agonizing about his image with the liberal community, about whether he would come to be associated with the hard line and be called the Walt Rostow of the Nixon Administration," and that was why he deliberately spread the word that he had "nagging doubts" about the mining. Kissinger, in moments of crisis, has often managed to convey the impression to congenial columnists that he really opposed some of the President's hard-line decisions and that he stayed at the White House after the most painstaking and agonizing reflection only to offset the influence of the Goldwater conservatives.

He was still the White House's ambassador to the liberal and academic communities — a responsibility he took very seriously, and a role he played very skillfully. Nothing was more important to Kissinger, as the country slowly withdrew from Indochina, than to reestablish a coherent conversation between the right and left wings of American political life. He often considered himself a link between these two hostile and uncommunicating worlds. Often he was the only link.

Although Nixon leaned very heavily on Kissinger's counsel during the days preceding the mining decision, he still seemed terribly alone. He needed another kind of listener, who could sympathize with him about his domestic political problems. In May, 1972, Kissinger could not fill that need, but one of Kissinger's least-loved colleagues could. John Connally, the bull in the china shop of international finance, was suddenly incorporated into Nixon's inner sanctum of advisers, even though, in Kissinger's view, his knowledge of foreign affairs on a good day couldn't fill a thimble. Kissinger respected Connally as a politician but not as a statesman. It seemed absurd for the President to lean on him for advice about a critical decision. When speculation arose that Connally might be appointed Secretary of State, replacing Rogers, Kissinger was shocked. He told some of his friends that if Connally became Secretary of State, he would quit. Months later, he denied that there was any "tension" between Connally and himself — a denial no one took seriously.

On Friday, May 5, Nixon conferred with all of his major advisers — Kissinger, Rogers, Laird, Moorer, Helms and Connally. He was strongly inclined to order the mining of North Vietnamese ports, but he had not yet made his final decision. He asked for their advice. With varying degrees of enthusiasm, they supported the idea of a blockade. Most of them shared the President's view that Russia had helped plan the North Vietnamese offensive to humiliate the President and to weaken his position during the summit. On this point, Kissinger expressed a minority view: he believed that while Russia had supplied the weapons for the offensive, the Soviet government had not encouraged the offensive and did not appreciate its timing. Although enthusiasm for the mining was in short supply, no one had a better idea for hurting Hanoi and helping Saigon. Kissinger argued for heavier B-52 bombing as an alternative; Nixon agreed to step up the bombing — not as a substitute for the mining but as a supplement to it. On another point there was no debate; everyone simply assumed that the President's summit journey to Moscow would probably have to be postponed. A few advisers — not including Kissinger — suggested that it might be a good idea for the President to seize the initiative and postpone it himself — on the grounds that it would be unwise for the President to be in Moscow while the allied military position continued to disintegrate in South Vietnam. A speech-writer was asked to draft a statement along these lines. It was written but never released. Nixon decided to test the Russians instead.

On Friday evening, the President took several yellow lined pads to Camp David, and there, over the weekend, he wrote the speech that was to become his biggest gamble of the year. He decided to mine the ports of North Vietnam. He would *warn* all ships, but he would not *stop* them. During the Cuban missile crisis of 1962, President Kennedy had ordered the Navy to stop and board all suspicious-looking Russian ships heading for Cuba. Nixon wanted to avoid a superpower confrontation with the Soviet Union, but he was determined to impose a price on continued Russian support of the war. He drew a distinction between quarantining North Vietnam, which would have ensured a confrontation, and merely mining its ports, which would at least give the Russians the option of finessing the confrontation. Either way, he knew he was challenging Moscow; it was a high-risk venture in international diplomacy.

Nixon returned to the White House on Sunday evening. He told Kissinger about his decision and asked him to tell the JCS to swing into action. Moorer assured Kissinger that everything was ready. Later in the evening the President called Kissinger for the latest intelligence from South Vietnam. Kissinger reported that North Vietnamese troops were in an excellent position to strike on three fronts — Hue in the north, Kontum in the central highlands, and An Loc on the approaches to Saigon. He added that they had been in position for more than two days, and they had not yet attacked. In fact, west and north of Hue, several North Vietnamese units had even withdrawn a few miles. The two men concluded that the North Vietnamese were regrouping for an attack. Nixon instructed Kissinger to convene an emergency meeting of the National Security Council for 9 A.M., Monday, May 8.

The NSC met for three hours. Nixon's decision to mine the ports and to bomb the rail lines from China surprised no one. There was really no debate. Nixon looked "determined" and "resolute," according to Ziegler, and he did not invite criticism or alternative suggestions. Kissinger offered none, despite his earlier reservations.

"If anyone had predicted," Kissinger later admitted to us, "that by May 8, we'd wind up in this position, I wouldn't have believed it." The mining was to be "an absolutely last resort."

After the meeting, when Kissinger and Connally returned to their offices, there was a message from Nixon, asking both of them to come to the Oval Office immediately. For ten minutes the President reviewed his decision with both advisers. It seemed that he needed last-minute reassurance, and Kissinger and Connally provided it — Connally with more conviction than Kissinger.

At 2 P.M., Nixon called Kissinger with the "execute order." Tell the JCS to proceed, he said.

Early in the evening, after putting the finishing touches on his seventeen-minute speech, Nixon met briefly with his Cabinet. He arrived to their applause, presented a cursory review of the problem and his decision, and then left to their applause. No one raised any questions. It was as if the Cabinet were a Stalinist Politburo, a meek and frightened group of courtiers willing to rubber-stamp any of the leader's decisions so long as they retained his grace.

At 8 P.M., Nixon briefed congressional leaders in the Roosevelt Room of the White House. He began: "Let me come directly to the point and tell you of a decision I have had to make." He then summarized his speech, listed the courses of action he had rejected, and explained why he believed the mining of North Vietnam's ports was the proper course. He asked for their support. There was no response — either positive or negative.

As Nixon met with the congressional leaders, Kissinger was meeting in his office with Dobrynin. He gave the Soviet envoy a copy of the President's speech and stressed that the United States was not seeking a confrontation with the Soviet Union and that the President was still hoping to proceed with his summit plans.

Kissinger did not hold his customary briefings for newsmen before the speech.

The President spoke at 9 P.M. He charged that the North Vietnamese invasion of South Vietnam, which, he said, was "made possible by tanks, artillery and other advanced offensive weapons supplied to Hanoi by the Soviet Union," had "increased the risk" of a Communist military victory and "gravely threatened the lives of sixty thousand American troops" who were still in Vietnam. While asserting that the South Vietnamese had "fought bravely to repel this brutal assault," he pointedly refrained from expressing confidence in ARVN, in Vietnamization, or in the judgment of General Abrams, as he had done only twelve days earlier.

Nixon listed three possible courses of action. The United States could immediately withdraw all troops; but this, he said, would jeopardize peace all over the world. He rejected this course. The United States could continue to try to negotiate an honorable compromise. This course he accepted — but with one proviso. "There is only one way to stop the killing," he stated, "and that is to keep the weapons of war out of the hands of the international outlaws of North Vietnam." That brought Nixon to the third course of action — the one he had felt obliged to choose: strong American military action against North Vietnam. He listed the measures he had ordered:

1. "All entrances to North Vietnamese ports will be mined to prevent access to these ports and North Vietnamese naval operations from these ports."

2. "United States forces have been directed to take appropriate measures within the internal and claimed territorial waters of North Vietnam to interdict the delivery of supplies."

3. "Rail and all other communications will be cut off to the maximum extent possible."

4. "Air and naval strikes against military targets in North Vietnam will continue."

Nixon then lifted the veil on his latest peace plan — the one Le Duc Tho had rejected on May 2. Nixon's military announcements were so dramatic that most observers missed the significance of his drastically curtailed political expectations in Vietnam.

At the end of his speech, Nixon addressed a special message to the Soviet Union. "Let us — let all great powers — help our allies only for the purpose of their defense," he said, "not for the purpose of launching invasions against their neighbors. Otherwise the cause of peace, the cause in which we both have so great a stake, will be seriously jeopardized.

"Our two nations have made significant progress in our negotiations in recent months. We are near major agreements on nuclear arms limitations, on trade, on a host of other issues. Let us not slide back towards the dark shadows of a previous age. . . . We are on the threshold of a new relationship. . . . We are prepared to continue to build this relationship. The responsibility is yours if we fail to do so."

The White House switchboard came alive, said Ziegler the next morning, "to a greater degree than I can recall." At least twenty-two thousand telegrams, running five or six to one in support of Nixon's decisions, poured into the White House. At the time, the public did not know that many of these telegrams had been sent by the Committee to Re-elect the President.

Clearly, Nixon was prepared to sacrifice his summit in Moscow for the sake of an "honorable" withdrawal from Vietnam. Months later he was still talking about the historic proportions of his May 8 decision. It was, he told a group of POW families, "the hardest decision I have ever made since becoming President of the United States." The United States, he explained, was "faced with the specter of defeat, and I had to make a choice, a choice of accepting that defeat and going to Moscow hat in hand, or of acting to prevent it. I acted."

At two dinner parties on the night of May 8, high-level Russian and American officials paused to watch the President's speech. Nikolai S. Patolichev, the Soviet Minister of Foreign Trade, who had arrived the day before to explore the prospects for Soviet-American trade, was dining with Peter Peterson, then Secretary of Commerce. Patolichev made no comment about the speech after it was over; he continued to talk about trade.

In Georgetown, at the home of Secretary of the Navy John Warner, Admiral Vladimir Kasatonov, Deputy Commander of the Soviet Navy, was dining with a small group of American officials, including Sonnenfeldt from the White House and Herbert Okun from the State Department. Kasatonov had led a high-level delegation of Soviet naval officers to Washington to work out the final details of the "incidents at sea" agreement, which was to be signed at the summit. As the President spoke, the Soviet Admiral stood silent and motionless, staring blankly at the television set. The Americans stared anxiously at him, waiting for his reaction. After an uncomfortable pause, Kasatonov managed to say, "This is a very serious matter. Let us leave it to the politicians to settle this one." He seemed to be implying that technical discussions on naval cooperation between the two countries should continue despite the President's action. Months later, Okun recalled that evening and, paraphrasing Dean Rusk during the Cuban missile crisis, quipped, "We were highball to highball, and they were the first to clink."

Tuesday, May 9, was the day of suspense. No one in Washington knew how the Communists would respond to Nixon's decision. In Moscow, Brezhnev summoned the Politburo into emergency session. The hardliners, led by Pyotr Shelest, the gruff Party boss of the Ukraine, argued that the Soviet government ought to cancel the summit and challenge the American blockade. Brezhnev opposed a showdown. But there was no official public comment about the mining. That night Tass ran a small item saying Defense Minister Grechko had left Moscow for

Damascus on a previously scheduled visit. Experts in Washington assumed that he would not have left if a major military crisis was foreseen.

In Peking, there were similar high-level deliberations; they produced an official, low-key protest. "The seven hundred million Chinese people," Peking said, "provide a powerful backing for the Vietnamese people; the vast expanse of China's territory is their reliable rear area."

In Hanoi, there were cries of outrage and preparations for extensive bombardment as the country's ports began to be seeded with deadly American mines.

In Saigon, there was jubilation.

In Washington, the reaction was mixed. The doves, especially Senator George McGovern, denounced the President's decision, but not all the hawks praised it. George Wallace took an odd position, supporting the Commander in Chief but suddenly appealing for a total pullout from Indochina. The corridors of Capitol Hill buzzed with speculation about the President's political prospects.

At the State Department, a group of Soviet experts gathered to ponder the Kremlin's possible reaction; they concluded that the Russians would *not* call off the summit. But, since Kissinger's NSC shop seldom paid any attention to Foggy Bottom, their opinion was ignored.

At the White House, Kissinger's closest advisers closed their briefing books on the Moscow summit. They figured that there would be no need for further preparation.

At 11:20 A.M., Kissinger appeared behind a small lectern in the East Room, an uneasy and unconvincing smile on his face, to explain the President's decision to newsmen. It was a remarkably persuasive performance, even though some of the reporters thought "Henry didn't have his heart in it."

Kissinger opened his presentation by noting that he "need hardly emphasize that this was a very painful and difficult decision," which was taken "only because it was believed that no other honorable alternative" existed. He then reviewed the negotiating impasse, starting with the President's revelation on January 26, 1972, of Kissinger's 1971 secret talks with Le Duc Tho, and concluding with the judgment that despite Brezhnev's private assurance in April that the North Vietnamese were ready for a "serious exchange of views," his meeting on May 2 with Le Duc Tho had produced nothing but total deadlock. The North Vietnamese, he said, were more determined than ever to impose their rule on

South Vietnam and to force the United States to help them to do so. This total deadlock, Kissinger explained, was one of the reasons the President had decided to mine the ports of North Vietnam and bomb the rail links coming down from China. He skimmed lightly over the more important reason — the need to counter the North Vietnamese invasion, which was shattering the Administration's Vietnamization strategy. At one point he openly acknowledged that American intelligence about the invasion had been faulty. "We perhaps . . . underestimated the massive influx of offensive weapons, particularly from the Soviet Union . . . that . . . tipped the balance in the North Vietnamese direction," he said. But his major purpose, after rationalizing the President's decision, was, if possible, to save the summit.

His technique was to describe the benefits of Soviet-American cooperation in so compelling a way that the Russians would lift their sights beyond Vietnam to see the wonders of a new era. Great powers, he said, ought to be able to "work out some principles of international conduct" so that confrontations over peripheral trouble spots could be finessed. The United States and the Soviet Union, he stressed, echoing the President's major theme, were on the threshold of a "new relationship" that transcended the normal pursuit of one successful negotiation after another — a "new relationship" that sought to establish common bonds of commitment to a peaceful world by implicating ever increasing numbers of Soviet and American bureaucrats in joint ventures. Then, if a crisis arose, Kissinger hoped that there would "be enough people who have a commitment to constructive programs so that they could exercise a restraining influence."

Although Kissinger hoped that point had already been reached, he was not sure it had. At the briefing, he refused to make any predictions. "I am not of course able to predict what the Soviet reaction will be," he said cautiously. He told a columnist later that afternoon, "You know, I've worked fifty times harder on Russia than on China. I don't want to ruin the summit."

That evening, he accepted a last-minute invitation to a Chevy Chase party honoring Indonesian Ambassador Sjarif Thajeb. Vietnam, he told several of the guests, "is a peripheral concern of both the United States and the Soviet Union." He acknowledged that because of the mining decision the summit would "probably" have to be "rescheduled"; but he added, "We certainly hope the Russians will not sacrifice everything we have gained between us for the sake of Vietnam." If that was the case, asked one reporter, "then why do we take action that could jeopardize everything?" Kissinger looked pained, as if the question was not an unfamiliar one at the White House. There was a long and awkward pause. "The President felt . . . ," Kissinger began, searching for the right words, "that the mining was necessary."

"The President felt . . ." The phrase was striking. Here was a presidential adviser who had learned to draw no distinction between "the President," "the United States," and "I," and who was accustomed to use only the royal "we" whenever he briefed the press. "We felt," "we decided," "we proposed," he would say — and suddenly, on the evening of May 9, he switched to "the President felt." Kissinger seemed to be trying to retain his standing with liberals and Democrats by suggesting that, while he was loyal to the President, there might be some difference of opinion on the issue of mining between himself and Nixon.

Months later, Kissinger said that at the time he had thought the odds were no better than fifty-fifty that the summit could be salvaged. "I thought they would try to save it," he explained, "but I wasn't sure they would know how."

On Wednesday, May 10, Kissinger suggested a way out for the Russians, and the odds on a summit began to rise slightly. He called Dobrynin and invited Patolichev to stop by at the White House the following morning for a chat with the President. After all, he said, Kosygin had received Maurice Stans when he was in Moscow as Secretary of Commerce, and Brezhnev had received Secretary of Agriculture Earl Butz even more recently. The President, Kissinger explained, thought a "courtesy visit" with the Soviet Foreign Trade Minister would be in order. Dobrynin indicated that he thought it was a good idea, but he made no firm commitment. He said he would check with Patolichev and call back later.

Patolichev and Kasatonov continued their negotiations all day Wednesday as though no crisis existed at all. Early in the evening, Dobrynin called Kissinger to confirm the Patolichev appointment with the President. "Nine o'clock tomorrow?" Dobrynin asked. "Nine o'clock," Kissinger replied. The pressure suddenly eased. Kissinger informed Nixon that his gamble on the summit was "looking good."

On Thursday, May 11, Patolichev and Dobrynin arrived at the White House shortly before the appointed hour. Kissinger, Peterson, and Peter M. Flanigan, a presidential adviser on international trade, greeted the Russian visitors; then they all joined the President in the Oval Office. Kissinger asked Dobrynin if he minded "publicity" about the meeting. Dobrynin said he had no objection, and White House reporters and photographers were invited in. The atmosphere was one of the usual contrived cordiality. Nixon and Patolichev chatted about languages. The President, who speaks none except English, said he thought Russian was easier than Polish and proved it by saying the Russian word for friendship — *druzhba* — but stumbling over it when he tried to say it in Polish. After a few minutes the newsmen and photographers were ushered out of the Oval Office, and the diplomats spent almost an hour discussing the prospects for increased Soviet-American trade. No one raised the issue of Haiphong Harbor or referred to the summit.

When Patolichev returned to the Soviet Embassy, an NBC News television reporter asked him if the President's trip to Moscow was "still on." "We never had any doubts about it," Patolichev answered through an interpreter. "I don't know why you asked this question. Have you any doubts?"

Patolichev's remark was a bulletin news story. It coincided with the first official reaction from Moscow to the President's speech. In a formal Kremlin statement, the Soviet government charged that Nixon's decision to mine the ports of North Vietnam was an "inadmissible" threat to Soviet shipping and a "gross violation of the generally recognized principle of freedom of navigation." The Russians "demanded" that the "blockade" be lifted "immediately"; but they issued no ultimatums, and they did not call off the summit. They seemed to be ducking the President's challenge. "Nixon's playing poker," a Soviet official explained, "but we're not going to play poker" with him. In fact, as the statement was being distributed by Tass, Foreign Ministry officials in Moscow were meeting with General Scowcroft, continuing their technical preparations for the summit.

Kissinger realized that the President's gamble had worked. Brezhnev had managed to hold his hawks at bay and to opt for continued détente with the United States. He needed tranquillity in his volatile East European backyard; he needed Western technology to transform and modernize Russia's backward economy; he needed a summit with Nixon to offset the American opening to China. In short, he needed so much that he swallowed the humiliation of the mining and prepared to welcome Nixon.

As soon as Moscow's reaction became clear and he was sure the

President could have his mining and his summit, too, Kissinger's tune changed. The old "we" returned to his speech. His optimism and self-confidence reappeared. With the summit secured, Kissinger turned his attention to the probable impact of the mining and bombing on Hanoi. He began to parrot the most optimistic JCS judgments about the effect of the American military moves on Hanoi's capacity to continue the fight. Moorer had told Kissinger that the mining would have an immediate and decisive impact on Hanoi's ability to sustain large-scale warfare in the south. Laird was dismayed by Kissinger's acceptance of the JCS appraisal. When he learned that Kissinger was describing the mining as "our knockout punch" and claiming the North Vietnamese would suffer a major setback by July 1, Laird snapped angrily at him, "Why the hell are you overselling the mining? There's nothing magical about July 1. The war will still be going on. The effect of the mining won't be felt until the fall, if then." Kissinger brushed aside Laird's caution. He preferred to listen to Moorer's optimism. As Laird later explained it, "Henry always enjoyed those military briefings, and he tended to believe them — especially when they fit into his strategy."

Kissinger believed Moorer on another crucial issue, and Moorer turned out to be right. Before the mining decision was announced, North Vietnamese troops and tanks had been poised for a major attack on Hue. But they had not moved. Now, after the summit scare had eased, Kissinger began to accept Moorer's explanation for their puzzling inaction. They had been forced to abandon their planned attack on Hue, Moorer said, because they had been badly punished by the bombing and the mining, and they had overextended their lines of supply.

This break in Hanoi's offensive proved to be crucial. Saigon gained time to regroup its shattered forces. Washington gained time to readjust its summit relations with Moscow. And the North Vietnamese never regained their offensive stride. Within a few months, their leaders were back in urgent conference, under renewed Russian and Chinese pressure to compromise with the Americans. Hanoi had come perilously close to disrupting the President's triangular strategy — but then paused when it might have persisted, and lost a unique opportunity.

Kissinger came away from the May 8 crisis with new respect for Nixon's instinct for jugular diplomacy.

TWELVE

The Moscow Summit

AMONG THE HUNDRED AND EIGHTY-TWO NEWSMEN flying into Moscow on May 22, 1972, on two TWA and Pan Am charter flights, there were several old-timers who had witnessed Nixon's famous "kitchen debate" with Nikita Khrushchev in the summer of '59. How could they ever forget it?

The Soviet leader, wearing a baggy white linen suit and a straw hat, was in Sokolniky Park at the official opening of the American National Exposition — a sparkling display of American economic and cultural life, the first of its kind to be sent to the Soviet Union. From cars and kitchens to records and refrigerators, all explained by Russian-speaking American guides, it was an instant success. Admission lines were unusually long, even by Russian standards, and tickets became collectors' items. Khrushchev was shepherded through the exhibition by Vice-President Richard Nixon, who was visiting Moscow for the first time. It was a wild scene. Scores of Soviet and American newsmen, officials and security police trailed Khrushchev and Nixon from one display to another. All the while, Khrushchev seemed to be getting more and more contentious, determined not to appear overawed by this show of American abundance. He began to argue with Nixon about the relative merits of their competing systems. Khrushchev lost his cool, and Nixon's voice kept rising. By the time they reached a model home, they were shouting at one another.

"We'll answer your threats with our threats," boasted Khrushchev in a small, crowded kitchen. "We have the means at our disposal that can have bad consequences for you."

"So have we," Nixon retorted, his jaw stiffening.

"Ours are better," snapped Khrushchev.

The kitchen drama became the keynote for Nixon's presidential campaign. Cameras recorded the debate, and Nixon's political stock zoomed. He struck many Americans as a leader who could stand up to the Russians. Standing near Khrushchev throughout this verbal battle was another Soviet official, who listened but added nothing. Five years later, in October, 1964, that official, Leonid Brezhnev, led a Kremlin coup against his boss. He branded Khrushchev a "harebrained schemer" and replaced him as First Secretary of the Soviet Communist Party. Less than eight years later, in May, 1972, during another presidential campaign, Brezhnev welcomed incumbent Nixon to the Kremlin. It was, for both of them, a long way from the kitchen.

Once the Haiphong Harbor crisis had eased, the United States and the Soviet Union resumed their intensive preparations for the summit. Kissinger's shop again took out its eleven thick briefing books, which covered everything from the trade of grain to the trade-in of missiles. At midnight on May 17, Kissinger and Dobrynin helicoptered to Camp David to confer with Nixon about the summit. Dobrynin spent the night at the presidential retreat, the only Communist ambassador ever to be so honored. On May 18, Dobrynin talked with Kissinger in the morning, mostly about SALT, and with Rogers in the afternoon, mostly about trade.

On May 19, the Central Committee of the Soviet Communist Party met again in Moscow, obviously to give final clearance for the Nixon visit. Brezhnev addressed the meeting, stressing the need for a "business-like and realistic approach to Soviet-American relations." Kissinger later told us that he thought Brezhnev was a "really big man" for having swallowed the May 8 embarrassment.

On May 20, Nixon left for Moscow, with a two-day intermediate stop in Austria. He said he was not seeking to "make headlines," but rather to engage in "very important substantive talks."

On May 21, Nixon lunched with Chancellor Bruno Kreisky in a hotel overlooking the fairytale turrets and towers of Salzburg, while the Chancellor's son led an anti-Vietnam demonstration near City Hall. On the eve of his Moscow summit, Nixon busied himself with his briefing books, and Kissinger divided his time between the President and the press.

For forty-five minutes, in an improvised press room, Kissinger lectured about summitry in the thermonuclear age. He traced the origins of the summit, diagnosed the differences between the two societies, and then projected an essentially grim (he would say "realistic") picture of the future. In his view, the two great powers could not avoid nuclear catastrophe — the "living would envy the dead," Khrushchev had once said — unless they learned to become equal partners in the preservation of peace. Their very strength, Kissinger insisted, imposed a responsibility on both of them to exercise restraint.

On SALT, Kissinger projected good odds that an agreement would be signed in Moscow; or, if not in Moscow, then shortly thereafter.

On trade, Kissinger hinted that there would be no agreement at the summit but that there would be enough progress to lead to an agreement sometime in the summer. The key to expanded trade, he explained, was a settlement of the Soviet World War II lend-lease debt.

On Vietnam, Kissinger admitted that the President's mining decision of May 8 (Kissinger stressed that it was Nixon's decision) was a calculated risk but that he did not believe it would interfere with efforts to improve Soviet-American relations. Vietnam, he conceded, would probably be an important part of the summit discussions, but it would not be allowed to overshadow other bilateral issues.

On two occasions, Kissinger's humor cut through the heavy atmosphere. A reporter asked politely if it was Kissinger or Nixon who had actually spoken with Brezhnev in late April. Kissinger answered: "I speak for the President when I speak with [Brezhnev]." The smiles began to spread around the room, and Kissinger self-mockingly added: "My megalomania hasn't reached *that* point yet. It is working up to it, but not yet." The smiles turned to laughter. Kissinger continued, glancing at Ziegler: "They have somebody on the staff who takes every joke out of the transcript." More laughter.

The second exchange of humor ended the briefing. Max Frankel of the *New York Times* asked what he called a "procedural question." "Do you plan to dribble out announcements through the week or is there going to be one big orgy of agreements?" Kissinger, who rarely misses a chance to needle the *Times*, replied: "I see that Max, with the dispassionate nature that we associate with his newspaper, has given us a choice between an orgy and dribbling it out, so whatever we do, we are doing very badly." A pause. "Our plan is to dribble out an orgy of announcements." It worked. "(Laughter)," said the transcript.

All day, a pale, spring sunlight bathed Moscow, lightly gilding the onion-domed churches of the capital; but by 4 P.M. on May 22, when the President's sleek blue and white jet landed at Vnukovo Airport and taxied to the VIP lounge, the sun had slipped behind some low-lying clouds. The kind of soft drizzle the Russian peasants call a "mushroom rain" had begun. And then, suddenly, it stopped; and the sun reappeared in time for an austere Russian welcome.

Nikolai Podgorny, President of the Soviet Union, and Alexei Kosygin, Prime Minister, led a contingent of high Soviet officials to the airport to welcome President Nixon. Leonid Brezhnev was conspicuously absent. The diplomatic corps waited patiently. One notable absentee was the Ambassador of the People's Republic of China. An impressive honor guard from the Moscow garrison stood at rigid attention. A large group of reporters and photographers lounged on improvised grandstands, taking pictures and comparing notes on the Peking and Moscow arrivals. Podgorny and Kosygin approached *Air Force One* as the front door opened and the President and Mrs. Nixon emerged. Long-range lenses caught the picture of the Podgorny-Nixon handshake, the reviewing of the honor guard, and the playing of the national anthems. While Hubert Humphrey and George McGovern battled for California's primary votes, their GOP opponent was ceremoniously conducting the nation's diplomatic business in full view of a coast-to-coast constituency.

Dobrynin greeted Kissinger with a warm handshake, the kind one proud impresario extends to another. They exchanged a private joke, and both broke into broad grins. Kissinger carried a bulging briefcase.

The motorcade from Vnukovo to the Kremlin was at least fifty cars long. Nixon, Podgorny and Kosygin drove in a long, black Zil, the Soviet equivalent of a Lincoln, past groves of birch trees and endless rows of identical new housing developments, until they reached the outer rim of Moscow and the start of Leninsky Prospekt, an eight-lane boulevard lined for the next few miles with about a hundred thousand curiously undemonstrative Russians. A few waved; many carried small paper Russian and American flags; most just stared. It was very un-Russian behavior; their normally pro-American sentiments seemed strangely subdued.

Leninsky Prospekt had been cleared of traffic. The President's Zil moved at a brisk fifty-five-mile-an-hour clip. In less than twenty minutes, the red-brick crenellated walls, gold-domed churches, and green and yellow palaces of the Kremlin came into view. The auto procession rolled over the bridge spanning the Moscow River and then through the Borovitsky Gate into the Kremlin, seventy acres on a hill blooming with May lilacs.

Nixon, Kissinger and a few other close aides were shown into ornate apartments within the Kremlin walls. Rogers was taken to the new Rossiya Hotel, a five-minute walk from the Kremlin. Within a few minutes, there was a call inviting the President to visit General Secretary Brezhnev's office. The protocol parallel with Peking was obvious but, this time, the summons from the top man was no surprise. Kissinger and Dobrynin had arranged every detail in advance. Kissinger was not invited to join the first two-hour Nixon-Brezhnev meeting in the Kremlin, but the President had been well briefed about the Soviet leader's style.

During his April meetings with Kissinger, Brezhnev had appeared nervous, constantly fidgeting with his cigarette holder; but, with Nixon, he appeared to be much more composed, exuding a sense of self-confidence and savoir faire. He was vain about his clothing and looks. To one high-ranking Western visitor he once said: "Look, people say I have thick eyebrows. Do I have thick eyebrows?" It was a rhetorical question; he had already begun to trim them. To another visitor, he remarked: "People say I have been brutal. Do I look brutal?" Ever since Russian tanks and troops had crushed the liberal Dubček regime in Czechoslovakia, in August, 1968, Brezhnev had been sensitive about Western cartoonists who turned him into a kind of beetle-browed villain. He seemed to take special pains with his appearance whenever he was conferring with West European and American dignitaries. During his tour of France, he seemed forever to be combing his hair; and during the President's tour of Russia, he seemed forever to be brushing nonexistent lint off his conservative business suits. He wanted to look the part of a serious peace-maker, a leader respected by his people. It was almost as if he were saying to Pompidou and Nixon that the three of them belonged to an exclusive men's club that did not admit outsiders. "For a European mind like mine," he is supposed to have remarked with some exasperation, "the Chinese are impossible to understand." The point was none too subtle: the Chinese were strange and somewhat untrustworthy; he was just one of the boys.

Brezhnev even tried humor, the kind he thought Nixon would appreciate. "Maybe we should send Gromyko and Rogers first to Mars to see what it's like up there," he joked, "and if they don't come back, we shouldn't go." Gromyko had often borne the brunt of Khrushchev's humor in the past. "I can tell Gromyko to drop his pants and sit down on a cake of ice for years," Khrushchev used to joke, "and, you know, the fool, he'd do it!" Now it was Brezhnev's turn to ridicule the Foreign Minister and Ministry. In some quarters of the Nixon White House, such humor was greatly appreciated. Brezhnev, in his talks with Nixon, rarely seemed to depend upon the expertise of the Foreign Ministry. Instead, he leaned for guidance on a Soviet Kissinger named Andrei Aleksandrov, a spare, bespectacled diplomat and linguist.

There was a formal Kremlin dinner on Nixon's first evening in the Soviet Union. Brezhnev designated Podgorny to deliver the major toast. The Soviet President, an ex-Party worker from the Ukraine, used such words as "practical" and "realistic" to describe the Kremlin's attitude toward the summit. Podgorny pledged his country to a "radical turn toward relaxation of existing tensions," although he said he did "not underestimate" the "serious complications" that existed in "certain parts" of the world. This was obviously an indirect reference to the Vietnam war. Nixon, in his toast, alluded to the war in a manner that was classically Kissingeresque. "Great nuclear powers," the President stressed, "have a solemn responsibility to exercise restraint in any crisis and to take positive action to avert direct confrontation." Such powers, Nixon added, echoing the main point of his May 8 speech, were obliged "to influence other nations in conflict or crisis to moderate their behavior."

When the dinner ended, Nixon and Kissinger conferred for almost an hour about Tuesday's agenda. It was to focus almost entirely on European security problems.

From Tuesday, May 23, through Friday, May 26, the summit was split-level. On the lower level, Rogers, Flanigan, Warner, and sometimes Nixon and Kissinger, conferred with Kosygin, Gromyko, and Patolichev, but never Brezhnev, about secondary issues, such as trade, environment, medicine and good conduct on the high seas. There was at least one Soviet-American agreement on these issues signed each day — apparently on the theory that an agreement a day kept the Chinese at bay. On the upper level, Nixon and Kissinger met with Brezhnev, Aleksandrov, and sometimes Podgorny and Kosygin, for long and secret deliberations about SALT and Vietnam. The result of their SALT negotiations became public on May 26; it took many months before the upshot of their Vietnam discussions became known.

Tuesday, May 23. Secretary Rogers and Boris V. Petrovsky, Minister of Public Health, started the series by signing a Medical Science and

Public Health Cooperation Agreement, which pledged both countries to cooperate in research on heart disease and cancer and in the new area of environmental ailments. The agreement provided the means for exchanging information, organizing scientific conferences, and facilitating contacts between individual scientists and institutions.

Presidents Nixon and Podgorny signed another bilateral agreement twenty minutes later. It was an extendable five-year U.S.-USSR Environmental Protection Agreement — the first comprehensive agreement of its kind between two major industrialized nations.

Wednesday, May 24. President Nixon and Prime Minister Kosygin signed a third bilateral agreement, which had been in the works since October, 1970, on Joint Scientific and Technological Endeavors. The agreement envisaged a joint test rendezvous and docking mission in 1975, using specially modified Apollo- and Soyuz-type spacecraft. This mission presupposed a trained corps of bilingual American and Soviet spacemen and technicians; it further presupposed extensive contact among the space scientists of both countries.

Thursday, May 25. Navy Secretary Warner and Fleet Admiral Sergei G. Gorshkov, Commander in Chief of the Soviet navy, signed that day's bilateral agreement. It bore a clumsy title — the Washington-Moscow Naval Agreement on the Prevention of Incidents on and over the High Seas — but it represented the first significant deal between the military establishments of both countries since World War II, when Russia and America were allies in the war against Hitler. The agreement established "rules of conduct" for the two biggest navies in the world. It was an unusual effort to reduce harassment and avoid collisions on the high seas that could lead to unintended tension between the two superpowers.

Friday, May 26. Rogers and Kosygin signed the penultimate bilateral agreement of the week — the one establishing a Joint U.S.-USSR Commercial Commission. Patolichev had discussed the idea with American officials when he was in Washington, and the two sides agreed to organize a permanent economic commission with responsibilities ranging from setting up credit arrangements and most-favored-nation treatment to joint exploitation of raw materials. In 1970, there was only a hundred-and-ninety-million-dollar trade turnover between the two countries; in 1971, it climbed to two hundred and twenty million dollars, and both sides hoped that it would zoom up after the summit meeting.

Although Kissinger was not intimately involved in the negotiation of all of these new joint ventures, he strongly encouraged them. He wanted the summit to look right. The "orgy of agreements" conveyed an impression of progressive détente, which helped further his goal of a new relationship between the superpowers by implicating ever larger segments of the bureaucracies of both countries in cooperative pursuits.

All of these agreements were preludes to SALT, the summit's ultimate prize. All along, everyone had assumed that Friday was to be the day SALT would be concluded. But before Nixon and Brezhnev could put their signatures to the pact, there was a rough period of intensive negotiation, during which the key negotiators — Kissinger for the American side, Gromyko for the Soviet side — thought for a time that the SALT prize might lie beyond their grasp.

When Nixon and Kissinger arrived in Moscow, the two sides were close to an agreement on SALT. Only four or five stubborn problems remained. The first attempt at solving them took place in Brezhnev's Kremlin office late Tuesday afternoon. The meeting, attended by the President and lasting well into the night, succeeded in clearing away two of the unresolved problems.

One concerned the ABM — the antiballistic missile system. A draft treaty limiting each country to two ABM sites (one protecting the capital, the other protecting an ICBM field) and two hundred interceptors had already been negotiated, but Kissinger and Dobrynin had not been able to handle the radar dilemma. It was an almost insoluble technical problem but it had to be solved because it had important security implications. Every modern military machine requires radar. But whereas space tracking, for example, requires only light radar, an ABM system, to be effective, requires heavy radar. At what point was light radar to be considered heavy? That was the technical problem. The security implication was related to the fear that Russia, or America, might take it into its head to cheat, claiming that it was building a radar complex for space tracking when actually it was building a radar complex for a new and clandestine ABM site. For better or for worse, Nixon and Brezhnev had to set an arbitrary line, separating heavy from light radars, and base an ABM treaty on their less than professional judgments. In the end, they agreed to set a ceiling of two heavy and eighteen light radars around an ICBM field in each country — and six MARCs, or Modern ABM Radar Complexes, within ninety miles of the capitals of each country.

The second problem concerned land-based mobile ICBMs, which in fact neither country yet possessed, but which were technically feasible and therefore a strategic concern. ICBMs were normally locked into hardened or, in any case, stationary sites. Each country's satellite detection system could keep check on the size and number of the other country's ICBM force. That knowledge was an essential ingredient of any arms control agreement. But if ICBMs could be made mobile and fired from heavy trucks or railroad cars, then there would be no sure way for either country to know the number and location of the other's ICBM force. That insecurity, in a thermonuclear world, could lead to catastrophe.

Nixon and Brezhnev recognized the complexity of the problem. After lengthy debate, they promised one another that they would not build land-based mobile ICBMs. But Brezhnev refused to write this promise into the interim agreement. Nixon stressed that the United States would state its own understanding of the prohibition in a separate declaration that would be submitted to Congress; and he warned that if the U.S. caught Russia cheating on this issue, it would immediately abrogate the entire SALT agreement. Brezhnev said that he understood and agreed. Kissinger assumed that Brezhnev had political problems with some of his hard-liners, who resented such sweeping Soviet commitments to abstain from building strategic arms.

At one briefing for newsmen, Kissinger acknowledged that the President and Brezhnev had discussed the problem of "mobile missiles," but he provided no details. He refused to confirm the fact that during the SALT discussions, Nixon, the supposedly tough lawyer who had frequently criticized LBJ for approving imprecise "understandings" with the North Vietnamese, had engaged in a few understandings of his own, on far more serious matters, with the Russians. After the briefing, Kissinger admitted to a few persistent reporters the existence of "oral stipulations" between Nixon and Brezhnev which, he insisted, would have to be submitted for congressional approval, along with the ABM treaty, the interim agreement on offensive weapons, and the protocol on nuclear submarines that together composed the arms control package.

Unfortunately, the Nixon-Brezhnev agreements and understandings about ABM radars and mobile missiles did not constitute any "open sesame" to a SALT deal. Some problems remained. There was still a deadlock on the critical question of ballistic missile submarines. How many missile-launching submarines could each side have? How many missile launchers? These were serious complications. If Russia or America wanted to "trade in" an old ICBM, or an old nuclear-powered submarine, how many missile launchers, or modern missile-launching submarines, could either country get in return?

The idea that diplomats and politicians could figure out a sensible exchange ratio between old ICBMs and new submarine-launched missiles was weird. Was one new missile worth ten old ones, or fifteen, or five? Judgments had to be fallible, almost by definition. The nuclear arsenals of the two superpowers were asymmetrical. How could one properly judge security? Russia had more megatonnage, but America had more warheads. Russia could produce more of a bang, but America could achieve greater accuracy. Negotiators for both sides were bargaining about their countries' survival; and yet it seemed that everything was being reduced to mathematics and political expediency.

It was left to two nocturnal negotiators — Kissinger and Gromyko — to break the submarine deadlock. It was almost midnight on Wednesday when Kissinger and Gromyko opened a do-or-die negotiation on the submarine hang-up in the Soviet Foreign Ministry in downtown Moscow. Kissinger was assisted by Sonnenfeldt, Lord, and William Hyland, a Soviet specialist on the NSC staff; Gromyko, by Dobrynin, Leonid Smirnov, a Deputy Prime Minister in charge of weapons production, and Georgy Kornienko, a Foreign Ministry expert on American politics. After four hours, the two sides succeeded in narrowing their differences but not in resolving them. One specific difference seemed so incapable of solution at 4 A.M. that Kissinger and Gromyko decided to defer their deliberations until the following night. The problem was to define the expression "under construction." That may sound simple, but it proved to be stubbornly complicated. They were seeking to set a ceiling on the number of missile-launching submarines each side would be allowed to have, and they needed to agree first how many each side already had, and how many were "under construction." Question: Was a submarine to be considered "under construction" when it left the drafting board? Or when its parts began to be manufactured? Or when its parts began to be assembled? Or when it was completely assembled, hull and all, but not yet tested? There was no obvious answer.

On Thursday, except for the time Nixon spent discussing trade and watching a performance of *Swan Lake* at the Bolshoi Theater — a must for any touring dignitary — the President and Kissinger spent most of the day trying to fashion a compromise that would satisfy the JCS, Barry Goldwater and Henry Jackson, and still permit agreement with the Russians. The Kremlin had argued for a long time that the ceiling for the U.S. side had to include the French and British missile-launching submarines, which theoretically were part of NATO. Nixon flatly rejected that argument. The Russians had also demanded not parity but superiority in the number of submarines and missiles, because they lagged so far behind the United States in the actual deployment of warheads and in the development of MIRVs. Nixon decided, even before the summit, that he might have to yield on this demand for several reasons: first, he wanted and needed a SALT agreement; second, he knew (because Brezhnev had strongly emphasized this point) that he could not achieve an agreement without this kind of fundamental compromise; and third, he realized that the Russians were on a crash building program for ICBMs and modern missile-launching submarines, whereas the United States had not added a single ICBM to its arsenal in years and had only just begun to think about a more advanced submarine called the Trident. In other words, Nixon realized that he did not have the strongest hand for bargaining, and he wanted to try to arrest the ongoing Soviet ICBM and submarine programs before the strategic balance between the two countries, which had been changing substantially in recent years, swung decisively in Russia's favor.

After a great deal of consideration Nixon instructed Kissinger to make the Russians a final offer. It was in fact close to the deal that finally emerged. The Russians, by its terms, could have an absolute ceiling of sixty-two modern missile-launching subs and nine hundred and fifty launchers. The United States, on the other hand, would accept a ceiling of forty-four subs and seven hundred and ten launchers. But the President insisted that if the Russians wished to reach that ceiling they would have to "trade in," or retire, approximately two hundred and forty old missiles of the SS-7, SS-8 and H-class submarine variety.

Nixon was reconciled to the idea that if the Russians rejected his compromise offer he would have to go home without a SALT agreement. Obviously, he would have been disappointed, but he figured he could go no further if he hoped to retain JCS support for SALT. He could always argue national security and survive the political backlash of failure, even in an election year.

On Thursday night, after the ballet, Kissinger returned to the Foreign Ministry to confront Gromyko. According to the presummit Kissinger-Dobrynin scenario, Friday was to be reserved for signing a SALT agreement. Kissinger quickly took the line that SALT was too important to be rushed. If more time for negotiation was needed, then more time should be taken. If SALT could not be completed by Friday, then Saturday, or Sunday, or even the following Sunday would do. Gromyko took a different line. Agreement had to be reached on Friday. Kissinger was puzzled by Gromyko's insistence on Friday. He didn't know whether it was rooted in Kremlin politics (perhaps Brezhnev had promised his colleagues a SALT agreement by Friday), or in a Byzantine commitment to form (an agreement a day meant an agreement a day); either way, it put the pressure on Gromyko, an advantage Kissinger enjoyed.

Both sides reviewed their positions, and then, happily, resolved the "under construction" dilemma. As Kissinger later explained, "some of the more profound minds in the bureaucracy, which is not necessarily saying a great deal," decided that the critical moment in submarine construction occurred when the parts were riveted to the hull. Still unresolved was the gut question of the number of submarines. At 1 A.M. Friday, Kissinger presented the President's revised offer. For two more hours, he and Gromyko debated its merits, but it quickly became clear Gromyko neither could nor would make the final decision. The offer would have to be presented to Brezhnev.

Frustration mounted, finally yielding to humor.

"Did you hear, Gromyko," Kissinger teased, "that they launched an SS-9 [Russia's giant missile] and nothing happened?"

"In this country," Gromyko shrugged, "nothing works."

On the table was a bowl of fruit. Kissinger wondered aloud whether he should speak closer to the apple or the orange, implying that one or the other probably contained a miniature microphone. He smiled. Gromyko glanced up at the ceiling — at a typical Soviet sculpture of a buxom woman. He pointed to one of her breasts. "No," he is supposed to have confided mischievously, "I believe it is in there."

By 3 A.M., the two comics decided that they had carried their college humor and negotiating mandates to the outer limits of mutual tolerance. Kissinger gave Gromyko the clear impression that although the President really wanted a SALT agreement, he could go no further.

Later Friday morning, Brezhnev summoned the Politburo into extraordinary session, presumably to discuss the latest Nixon offer. There was apparently little debate. The Soviet leader could argue, with solid justification, that Nixon had made the major concessions. Russia, by the terms of the proposed SALT agreement, would have more missiles and more submarines than the United States, and there would be no restrictions on its MIRVing those missiles or expanding its air and naval forces.

As the Politburo gave the go-ahead signal to Brezhnev, Nixon and Kissinger were meeting in the President's Kremlin apartment, prepared to accept a setback on SALT. At 11 A.M., there was a call from Gromyko. Could Kissinger and Sonnenfeldt meet him and Smirnov in St. Catherine's Hall? The location seemed a good omen. St. Catherine's was where the summit had begun and where, with SALT, it might end.

At 11:30 A.M., the meeting opened with a strong suggestion by Gromyko that the deadlock had been broken and that Brezhnev was ready to accept the President's compromise with a few minor modifications. At noon, Kissinger called Ziegler, alerting him to the possibility of a SALT announcement later in the day. "When?" Ziegler wanted to know. "I'll tell you later," replied Kissinger. By 1 P.M. the time had come for Gromyko to check with Brezhnev, and Kissinger with Nixon — the final check before the deal was confirmed. A few minutes later, the two negotiators shook hands. All SALT systems were go.

There was still a technical problem — the actual drafting of the final agreement. It was agreed that this would be done by the two SALT delegations in Helsinki. Kissinger thought that the tedious process would probably take a day, and that the signing ceremony could take place on Sunday. But Gromyko insisted that the signing had to take place that very night, and he suggested an unprecedented time-saver. Joint instructions were sent to Smith and Semenov, the chief American and Soviet SALT negotiators, so that there could be no misunderstandings. All afternoon there was unparalleled cooperation between the two delegations in Helsinki. By 6 P.M., the drafting had been completed — sloppily, as it turned out — but Kissinger and Gromyko had already agreed on an 11 P.M. signing in the Kremlin. Semenov joined Smith on the U.S. delegation plane, and both negotiators flew to Moscow for the grand event, arriving shortly before 9 P.M.

Ziegler had arranged a nine-thirty briefing for the White House press corps in the snack bar of the U.S. Embassy. Smith, exhausted but pleased, arrived for the big show. For the first time in years of secret negotiating, he could finally talk about *his* baby and, for a brief moment, bask in the publicity of a successful outcome. But he had not reckoned on Kissinger's ego or determination to capture the same publicity. Ziegler and Kissinger arrived ten minutes late, and then, for twenty-five embarrassing minutes, the three men argued in the pantry about who would do the briefing —

Kissinger or Smith. Finally, these negotiators, who had cracked the secret of SALT, cracked the secret of ego. They agreed to share the limelight.

Ziegler introduced Kissinger *and* Smith; but Kissinger got first call on the microphone. His eloquence and self-confidence overshadowed Smith. At last, with only a few minutes remaining in the briefing, Smith got a turn at the microphone. Reporters kept asking him how many submarines the Russians actually had, and he kept evading a specific response. The reporters became exasperated, and Kissinger grew restless. "Since I am not quite as constrained . . . as Ambassador Smith," Kissinger said, recapturing the microphone, "lest we build up a profound atmosphere of mystery about the submarine issue, I will straighten it out as best I can." Kissinger revealed that the base figure had always been in dispute, but that it ranged between forty-one and forty-three. Smith sat down.

Kissinger should have been exhausted, after five days of nonstop negotiations, but instead his fatigue was converted into energy. Kissinger had what Walter Lippmann once called "the indispensable quality — stamina." Negotiation, Lippmann told Ronald Steel in a *Washington Post* interview on April 1, 1973, "is a very tiring thing, and no physically weak man can make a good diplomat. . . . Kissinger is endowed physically with the attributes necessary for a good negotiator." For Kissinger, sleep would have been unproductive. That night, he needed to tell the world about SALT.

"It is foolish or shortsighted," he told the reporters in the snack bar, "to approach the negotiations from the point of view of gaining a unilateral advantage. Neither nation will possibly put its security and its survival at the hazard of its opponent and no agreement that brings disadvantage to either side can possibly last and can possibly bring about anything other than a new circle of insecurity. Therefore, the temptation that is ever present when agreements of this kind are analyzed as to who won is exceptionally inappropriate.

"We have approached these negotiations from the very beginning with the attitude that a wise proposal is one that is conceived by each side to be in the mutual interest and we believe that if this agreement does what we hope it will, that the future will record that both sides won."

So Kissinger certainly believed; and yet his motivation in striking this theme was more complex. He knew that close scrutiny of the SALT agreement would uncover its essential asymmetry. SALT bestowed a clear advantage in missiles and submarines on the Russians. Senator Jackson was not the only one who quickly spotted this flaw. But Kissinger's conviction, fully shared by Nixon, was that the negotiated freeze on ICBM production and the ceiling on submarines and submarine-launched missiles would save the United States from the threat of being substantially outdistanced by the Soviet Union in the strategic race for power. The race could not be allowed to become a rout.

At 10:50 P.M., Ziegler interrupted Kissinger's discourse. The signing ceremony in the Kremlin was to be at eleven, only minutes away. Reporters complained bitterly. They still had many questions. Ziegler advanced a proposal. A joint Soviet-American briefing was set for eleven-twenty, or thereabouts. How about another briefing, just for Americans, at 12:30 A.M., back here at the snack bar? Too much trouble, getting from the hotel to the Embassy, a reporter complained. "Can't we meet at the hotel?" Agreed.

While Kissinger and Smith were briefing the press at the snack bar, Nixon and Brezhnev were dining at Spaso House, once a beer baron's mansion and now the home of the American Ambassador to Moscow. Van Cliburn, the keyboard symbol of Soviet-American friendship, played Chopin, Scriabin and Debussy. Brezhnev marveled at the Baked Alaska dessert. "You've just been served hot ice cream," Brezhnev shouted across the banquet room to another Politburo member. "America is a country of miracles." Both leaders were in an expansive mood. In a short time, they would be signing the SALT agreement, a giant step toward international sanity.

"We look forward to the time when we shall be able to welcome you in our country," the President said in his toast, referring to the invitation he had extended earlier to all three Soviet leaders. "Every leader of a nation wonders at times how he will be remembered in history," Nixon continued. "We want to be remembered by our deeds, not by the fact that we brought war to the world, but by the fact that we made the world a more peaceful one for all peoples of the world."

At 11:07 P.M., Nixon and Brezhnev led an elite corps of Soviet and American officials into Vladimir Hall, an ornate white, green and gold room in the Great Kremlin Palace, for the signing of the SALT package. With minimum pomp and pageantry, the leaders of the two most powerful nations on earth signed unprecedented agreements that put modest limits on their strategic nuclear power. Nixon used his own fountain pen; Brezhnev chose one from a pen stand. They each signed two Russian- and two English-language sets of the agreements; and each leader then retained one Russian copy and one English copy.

Unreported at the time was the fact that both men realized that all four copies contained major errors and that, the following day, after the errors had been corrected, they would have to repeat this signing ceremony in total secrecy. So rushed was the final drafting in Helsinki on Friday afternoon that not even the figures were accurate. All day Saturday Philip Farley of ACDA and Smirnov prepared new sets of the final accords, after having cleaned up the errors.

Brezhnev had invited the entire Politburo to the signing ceremony, even Shelest, the hard-liner who had opposed the summit. That was his style. The presence of his top colleagues ensured a greater degree of shared responsibility — and ultimately political support — for important decisions. For example, he had brought most of the Politburo to Bratislava for a crucial meeting with Czech leader Dubček, just before his decision to send the Red Army into Prague.

It was 11:13 P.M., six minutes into the new age of nuclear restraint, when Nixon and Brezhnev rose to the arrival of trays of champagne. They toasted one another for a brief five minutes and then parted. By 11:18 P.M., the waiters were clearing the champagne glasses, and the lights were dimmed in a deserted Vladimir Hall.

For the first time, the two superpowers had reached a bilateral agreement to put ceilings on the development of weapons of mass destruction. They recognized the critical importance of man-made satellites to keep a clear check on compliance, and they won one another's agreement not to tamper with the satellites. For the first time, Brezhnev signed significant accords with a capitalist power, thus committing not only his personal prestige but the collective prestige of the Communist Party to the accords — and to the spirit of détente that they symbolized. And, for the first time, both sides flashed the signal to the rest of the world that nuclear weapons had gone a long way toward making ideology obsolete, and that differing views of political and economic theory would have to take second place to the urgent requirements of survival. At least, that was the hope.

It was a stage set for a Fellini movie. Kissinger, who had briefed newsmen everywhere from the White House to Shanghai, from the George V in Paris to an aircraft carrier in the Mediterranean, settled on a hotel nightclub in Moscow to inform the traveling American press corps about SALT — actually, to continue the snack bar briefing. The Starry Sky, located on the first floor of the Intourist Hotel, a few hundred yards from

Red Square, looked like the Roseland Ballroom, vintage 1935. Kissinger stood on the dance floor, the Frank Sinatra of diplomacy, occasionally clutching his only prop, a standing microphone. The bandstand was eerily empty, except for a few White House aides and Signal Corps experts who were recording the event. A Soviet Secret Service agent watched impassively from the side. A stained-glass skyline of skyscrapers was the barely perceived backdrop. Reporters sat around small tables, holding not highballs but ballpoint pens, and more in the dark than usual. The only illumination came from rotating, winking ceiling lights, which threw weird patterns of light on the walls, floors and tables. All eyes were on the star, enveloped in a soft yellow spotlight, crooning his melody of détente through SALT, and cracking a couple of jokes, as if he were the lead in a Hasty Pudding production called *Everything You Ever Wanted to Know About Diplomacy, But Never Dared to Ask.*

In this surrealistic setting, Kissinger explained the complicated arithmetic of SALT. It was 1 A.M., Saturday, May 27, the start of his forty-ninth birthday, and Kissinger showed no signs of strain. Everyone assumed the nightclub was bugged, and no one could shake the spooky feeling that, as Kissinger spoke, Gromyko was listening from a command post in the Kremlin, just down the block, shaking his head in disbelief at the vision of Kissinger revealing secrets of Soviet security in a Russian nightclub.

"The Soviet Union has been building missiles at the rate of something like two hundred and fifty a year," Kissinger disclosed, adding with a slight grin, "If I get arrested here for espionage, gentlemen, we will know who is to blame."

Asked how many warheads U.S. bombers carried, Kissinger could not resist providing the answer. "Since I have given out the Soviet figure," he said, "I might as well give out the American figures."

Forty minutes into this bizarre briefing, there was a sharp knock at the door behind Kissinger. All the doors had been locked. Reporters stopped writing; Kissinger paused. He waited for a moment. Nothing happened. He continued his briefing. A few minutes later, the knocking resumed. It was impossible to forget that in Russia midnight knocks at the door could have a sinister connotation. After a few seconds of silence, Kissinger smiled. "That must be a Harvard student," he remarked, "late for my lecture."

The lecture continued. No one ever learned who had done the knocking.

"Dr. Kissinger," one reporter asked, "how many of our submarine missiles are being MIRVed and how many of the Minutemen are being MIRVed?"

Kissinger: "I don't know exactly what the number of Minutemen is that is being MIRVed. Of the submarines, my trouble is I know the number but I don't know whether it is classified or not."

Q: "It is not."

Kissinger: "It is not? What is it then?" (Kissinger was playing one of his favorite games: testing the knowledge of his interrogator.)

Q: "You have deployed eight."

Kissinger: "But you don't know how many we are converting."

Q: "You are converting thirty-one." (Everyone burst into laughter.)

Kissinger: "I thought all my former staff members joined candidates." (Even more laughter. Kissinger, as usual, got the last word.)

At 2 A.M., this nightclub act ended, and Kissinger returned to the Kremlin, where he found Nixon working on his weekend plans. The two men conferred about the President's trip to Leningrad, where he would be going later in the day, and about his television speech to the Russian people scheduled for Sunday evening. Kissinger would not be accompanying Nixon to Leningrad, Peter the Great's "window on the west." He would be shifting gears once again. Vietnam, not tourism, was on his agenda.

All summit long, Kissinger had kept a special check on the still worrisome Communist offensive in Vietnam. An ARVN collapse could have demolished the summit by forcing the President to abandon Moscow for the Situation Room in the White House. But with each day that the South Vietnamese forces held the line, Kissinger gained a bit more confidence in ARVN. He realized that Thieu's army was still not out of the woods — and that it was more dependent than ever on U.S. air and naval support; but ever since the mysterious pause in the Communist advance on Hue, ARVN seemed slowly to be reacquiring the military initiative. It recaptured hamlets that had been lost to the North Vietnamese, and it loosened the Communist stranglehold around An Loc and Kontum. It even began to force the North Vietnamese to pull back from their strongpoints north of Hue. ARVN still lacked sustained aggressiveness; but, clearly, since the President's May 8 decision, the danger of a Communist military victory had been sharply diminished.

For Kissinger, the turn for the better in ARVN's fortunes provided another opportunity to plump for a negotiated compromise — one of his major goals in Moscow. In all his conversations with the Russians, Kissinger kept stressing that the President was determined to lead the United States out of Indochina. All he required of North Vietnam was a respectable exit.

On Wednesday evening, in the middle of the intensive SALT negotiations, Nixon and Kissinger had joined Brezhnev, Kosygin and Podgorny at a modern dacha situated in a grove of white birch trees on the banks of the Moscow River. It was one of Brezhnev's weekend hideaways. For more than five hours, they had ranged over every aspect of the Vietnam issue. The discussions were, to quote Kissinger, "long, sometimes difficult, and very detailed."

Nixon and Brezhnev apparently found themselves in sharp disagreement on a number of points. Brezhnev made the standard Soviet accusations, denouncing the American mining and bombing of North Vietnam, demanding an end to all "acts of war" against a "fraternal Socialist ally," and urging Nixon to withdraw all his troops and negotiate on the basis of Hanoi's peace program. For his part, the President responded by denouncing the Communist invasion of South Vietnam and lecturing the Russians about great-power responsibility and restraint. Nixon's main point was that Brezhnev should persuade the North Vietnamese to accept the American peace program and to take a chance on a favorable political evolution in South Vietnam.

On Saturday, May 27, while Nixon and Rogers went sightseeing in Leningrad, Kissinger continued the Vietnam dialogue with Gromyko. The Soviet Foreign Minister apparently restated his usual line about the importance of resuming secret negotiations with Le Duc Tho. Kissinger pointed out that the mere resumption of negotiations would not be enough. "That is not the issue," he told newsmen a few days later. "What we want is a negotiation that produces a prospect of an early end of the war." Gromyko was not in a position to promise anything on that score.

Like most Russians who were close to the summit negotiations, the Soviet Foreign Minister was worried about speculation that the Americans were drawing a tight link between trade with Russia and peace in Vietnam. Although the speculation was essentially correct — linkage was the cornerstone of Kissinger's diplomatic approach — the President's adviser assured Gromyko that American trade policy did not involve a strict quid pro quo arrangement. As he later explained, "I am denying that we ever said to the Soviet leaders, 'If you do this for us in Vietnam, we will do that for you on trade.' You have to recognize that these are serious people, and we didn't come here to buy them."

But Kissinger continued, coming much closer to the truth, "It has always been understood . . . that as our general relationships improve, we can accelerate progress in every area." No translation was required. Not for the newsmen listening to Kissinger, and certainly not for Gromyko. Kissinger was denying the use of "direct linkage" while affirming its general validity. He was having it both ways. Trade was the carrot part of his policy toward Russia; the stick was the mining action against Soviet ships in the ports of North Vietnam. Despite Kissinger's pressure, Gromyko kept insisting that the Kremlin didn't control North Vietnam, and that Kissinger was overestimating the degree of Soviet influence in Hanoi.

On Monday, May 29, just before the conclusion of the summit meeting, Nixon and Brezhnev discussed Vietnam again. Despite their differences on specific issues, they both agreed that the Vietnam issue had to be defused. Both men realized, after the May 8 crisis, how close Vietnam had come to disrupting the summit; they agreed that no small country should be allowed to interfere with the pattern of détente. The Russians were not unsympathetic to the American claim that the North Vietnamese were unreasonable and inflexible. Brezhnev did not like the idea that Hanoi had held its fire before the Peking summit and then had unleashed a sensational, go-for-broke offensive before the Moscow summit, especially since Hanoi's move had produced an American countermove, which, in turn, had caused a major Soviet humiliation. He seemed to resent Hanoi's move more than Washington's. Brezhnev had committed his prestige to a policy of détente with the West, particularly with the United States. He derived daily dividends from each new bilateral agreement, from SALT to desalinization, overwhelming his domestic political foes. A successful summit would prove his point that the United States and the Soviet Union shared an ever widening community of interests. Vietnam, in this context, paled into insignificance. Besides, when it came right down to it, Brezhnev was confident that once the Americans had withdrawn, the Communists would win the political struggle in South Vietnam. Kissinger never said anything to dissuade Brezhnev from this view.

Thus, by a process of subtle bargaining, in which more was implied than stated, there emerged between Nixon and Brezhnev an understanding that it was in the interest of both superpowers to end the war in Vietnam quickly. Kissinger hoped that in practical terms that meant both sides would start reducing arms deliveries to their respective clients, and that in this way Moscow could persuade Hanoi to see the advantages of adopting a more flexible negotiating policy.

Nixon and Brezhnev concluded their formal sessions on Monday morning. Kissinger conducted a briefing at midday — and then a final one in the evening. Nixon and Brezhnev signed the twelve-point Basic Principles of Relations between Russia and America, an unusual document that symbolized the closing of a two-decade period of "rather rigid hostility," according to Kissinger, and the cautious opening of a new era of "restraint" and "creativity." Then, after issuing a joint communiqué, Brezhnev hosted a glittering reception in St. George's Hall in the Kremlin. Although Nixon had ridiculed the customary "froth" at summits only a week before, and Brezhnev had stressed the "businesslike" character of this summit, both leaders were as buoyant as cheerleaders. The Kremlin orchestra struck up "Oh! Susanna" as Brezhnev practiced his new American vocabulary — "okay," he kept repeating — and Nixon his Russian word — "khorosho," meaning "good." The Russians had won a degree of political parity with the United States — and a shot at military superiority — and the Americans thought they had secured a promise of Soviet help on Vietnam. Not even a last-minute embarrassment could dampen the official enthusiasm.

Nixon was to fly to Kiev in a Russian plane. (It was a repeat of the Peking–Hangchow arrangement.) After the airport ceremonies, the President climbed up the steps of a sleek Soviet jet liner. Television viewers around the world saw pictures of the President waving, and then stepping into the plane. And then — nothing happened. There was no takeoff. The plane engines were cut off. Kosygin, Podgorny and other Kremlin leaders stood glumly under black umbrellas in the rain. Television reporters speculated about the cause of the delay. Suddenly, after about thirty minutes of waiting, the picture of the plane was replaced by a total blank; Moscow television, embarrassed by the delay, had pulled the plug.

Meantime, inside the plane, red-faced Soviet officials had begun to explain to the American President that one engine wouldn't start. For almost an hour, the crew tried to start the engine, but it was no use. The decision was made to switch to a backup plane. Podgorny and Kosygin boarded the plane and apologized to the President. Holding back a grin, Nixon commented that it was better to find out about faulty engines *before* takeoff. Kissinger, obviously eager to ease Soviet embarrassment, asked Podgorny if he had ever heard of the "Law of the Wickedness of Objects."

"No," Podgorny answered, looking puzzled.

"Well," Kissinger explained, "if you drop a piece of buttered bread on a new carpet, the chances of its falling with the buttered side down are in direct relationship to the cost of the carpet."

The Americans laughed, but Podgorny clearly didn't get the joke. His round, peasant face looked vacant. Kissinger thought he would provide another example of his "law."

"If you drop a coin on the floor," Kissinger said, staring right into Podgorny's eyes, "the chances of it rolling away from you, rather than toward you, are in direct relationship to the value of the coin."

Podgorny still looked blank. Finally, he said: "Whenever I drop coins, they roll toward me."

Kissinger, who had had C students before, briskly returned to essentials: "Maybe it's time for us to go to the other plane." The stewardesses, meantime, had taken all the flowers and candy from the defective plane and transferred them to the backup. That plane's engines started.

Another "mushroom rain" was falling on Moscow as the President's borrowed jet took off for Kiev, his next stop. Among Russian peasants, there has always been a superstition that a "mushroom rain" brings rich harvests. In Moscow, that week, Kissinger felt on top of the world, crowning his celebration with a running commentary on the results of the summit.

On the Basic Principles, which some reporters were beginning to interpret as a guide to joint action, Kissinger cautioned: "We have no illusions. We recognize that Soviet ideology still proclaims a considerable hostility to some of our most basic values. We also recognize that if any of these principles is flouted, we will not be able to wave a piece of paper and insist that the illegality of the procedure will, in itself, prevent its being carried out. . . . We have laid out a road map. Will we follow this road? I don't know. Is it automatic? Absolutely not. But it lays down a general rule of conduct which, if both sides act with wisdom, they can, perhaps, over a period of time, make a contribution. At this point, it is an aspiration. We would not have signed it if we did not believe there was a chance for implementing this aspiration."

On Vietnam: Q: Dr. Kissinger, do you plan to go back to Paris anytime soon?"

Kissinger: "I would start being one of the great bores in Washington if I stopped these secret trips."

Q: Dr. Kissinger, did either side advance proposals . . ."

Kissinger: "I just do not want to go into the details of the Vietnam negotiations or discussions because I do not think it would serve any useful purpose, except to say that the discussions were very extensive.

"Are we more optimistic about a rapid end of the war as a result of these discussions?" Kissinger asked rhetorically. "I just do not want to speculate about what the impact will be, how Hanoi will interpret this situation."

On the Sino-Soviet quarrel, which lay at the very heart of Kissinger's strategy: "Our basic position with respect to both of these large Communist countries is that we will not discuss one of them in the capital of the other. We recognize that they have serious differences with each other on a number of issues in which the United States is not primarily engaged, one of them being the border dispute, the other one being an ideological conflict over the interpretation of Leninist doctrine with respect to which our competence is not universally recognized." (Lots of laughter.)

On Nixon's approach to summitry: "The President has always approached these meetings . . . from a totally unsentimental point of view, and he has not had the illusion that he could charm leaders, who have been brought up on their belief of a superior understanding of objective factors, by his personality."

On summitry in general: "We're going to try to use the next summit as we used this one, to speed up things that might be in progress and reach solutions more quickly. . . .

"The Monday before we left there was a deadlock [on the incidents-at-sea agreement], and the President intervened and offered a suggestion on how to handle it. They accepted within twenty-four hours and it was settled. . . .

"We would expect the next summit will be as carefully prepared, but it won't take three years. . . .

"Where the hell else would you get so many hours with Brezhnev and Kosygin . . . ?"

On trade: "We never expected to get more than a joint U.S.-Soviet commission in Moscow. Anything else we would have gotten in Moscow would have been a nice extra. The settling of the lend-lease issue is tied to other issues. Lend-lease, credits and grain all belong together."

On whether the Cold War was then over: "That remains to be seen. If we form our relationships on the basis of the statement of principles, we will be in a different period. But there will still be competition and maybe even antagonism. But I don't think our relationships will ever be the same."

For Kissinger, Teheran, next stop on the presidential trip, was Nadina Parsa. For Nixon, Teheran was the Shah of Iran. Henry had a lot more fun.

It was almost midnight, May 30, the end of a long day that had begun in the Ukraine and concluded in old Persia with a belly dancer in the lap of a presidential adviser. The Shah had just hosted a formal white-tie dinner for the President — pleasant, but dull against the tapestry of Moscow summitry — and Kissinger was restless. Prime Minister Amir Abbas-Hoveida, aware of Kissinger's fabled reputation with women, invited him to a Parsa performance. Parsa? The name meant nothing to Kissinger. "Then come along," Hoveida whispered playfully. "You'll like it." His tone suggested an illicit experience Kissinger could never duplicate in the West Wing.

Parsa was Nadina Parsa, Teheran's most spectacular belly dancer, who was at that time entertaining the White House press corps in the ballroom of a luxurious hotel. Kissinger and Hoveida arrived, and newsmen turned their gaze from Nadina to Henry. Aides dropped soft cushions to the ballroom floor for the honored guests, and quickly newsmen swarmed around them. Parsa had every right to feel offended. She was not used to middle-aged men with bulging midriffs and horn-rimmed glasses stealing the spotlight from her. So, she performed. She wiggled and gyrated and pulsated and whirled her way from the stage to the grinning and appreciative stranger, who sat on his pillow, cross-legged, like a Persian potentate. She bumped and vibrated furiously. Kissinger's eyes widened. Photographers snapped a few pictures until Iranian plainclothesmen stopped them on Hoveida's orders. Suddenly, Parsa wiggled in front of Hoveida, kissed his cheek and plopped into Kissinger's lap. Kissinger did not even blush. He smiled broadly and chatted amiably with his newest Iranian connection. "I shall return," Kissinger proclaimed, striking a Douglas MacArthur pose, as he beat a strategic retreat, Parsaless.

The following day, a few "pool" reporters trapped Kissinger on board *Air Force One* on the flight to Warsaw, the last stop before Washington. "How did you like her?" one reporter asked.

"She was a charming girl," Kissinger replied seriously, "and very interested in foreign affairs."

"Really?"

"Yes, we discussed SALT. I spent some time explaining how you convert a SS-7 to a Y-class submarine."

"Is that right?"

"Yes, of course, what else?" bantered Kissinger. "I want to make the world safe for the Nadinas."

THIRTEEN

The Beginning of the End

THE NAMES OF THE SUMMER OF '72, as events unfolded, were Nikolai V. Podgorny, G. Gordon Liddy, Le Duc Tho, George McGovern, Chou En-lai, E. Howard Hunt, Leonid Brezhnev, James W. McCord, Jr., Ronald Ziegler, Nguyen Van Thieu, J. William Fulbright, Richard Nixon, and Henry Kissinger. And Frank Wills. Wills's name has survived as a footnote of the time because he was the private security guard who noticed something odd as he was making his rounds at the Watergate office building on the night of June 17. He discovered a strip of adhesive tape depressing the latch on a basement door. He removed it and locked the door. Twenty minutes later, he found that the tape had been replaced. He called the police, they arrested McCord and four others in the offices of the Democratic National Committee, and that led to Hunt and Liddy and ultimately to the White House.

Two days after the break-in, Ronald Ziegler dismissed it as a "third-rate burglary attempt . . . something that should not fall into the political process." Watergate, at that point in time, was overshadowed by a number of developments that once again aroused optimism in the White House about the chance for a diplomatic settlement in Vietnam before the election.

On June 15, President Podgorny flew to Hanoi. The North Vietnamese, feeling betrayed by Russia's hospitality to Nixon, were nevertheless dependent on Moscow as the chief supplier of their war matériel, and they listened carefully to Podgorny's message. It was simple but fundamental:

he suggested it was time to switch tactics, time for serious negotiations with the United States. The risk, he argued, would not be critical; after all, Nixon seemed serious about withdrawing, and the new U.S. position no longer demanded a North Vietnamese troop pullout from the south. Podgorny probably also conveyed Brezhnev's view that nothing could prevent a Communist victory in the south in any case. After leaving the Hanoi Politburo to ponder his advice, Podgorny flew back to Moscow, where he promised that the Soviet Union would "do everything possible for a de-escalation of the Vietnam war" and for the success of the talks in Paris that he said would resume shortly. It was a new vocabulary for the Russians — the first time they had so openly committed their prestige to a resumption of negotiations. It clearly reflected the Soviet conclusion that the advantages of dealing with Washington on such matters as trade, credits, and SALT were important enough for Moscow to lend Nixon a hand in settling the Vietnam war.

On the very day that Podgorny was using his persuasive powers in Hanoi, Kissinger was using his in the White House in an effort to win the support of nearly a hundred congressional leaders for the SALT agreement with the Soviet Union. Even before the President returned from Moscow, there had been some complaints that the agreement contained loopholes that permitted Russia important strategic advantages. For three hours, Kissinger and the President described the complex accords on controlling nuclear weaponry. Kissinger was particularly convincing; even Senator Fulbright, one of his severest critics in those days, remarked that his only regret was that the whole country had not had the opportunity to hear Kissinger's presentation. The applause for the Nixon-Kissinger policy of détente and summitry seemed for the moment to drown out congressional criticism of the Nixon-Kissinger policy on Vietnam; the President and his adviser hoped that the results of the Moscow summit might rally countrywide support for the Administration's initiatives to end the war on its own terms.

A few days later, on June 19, Kissinger popped up in Peking — his fourth visit in less than a year — to reinforce the triangulation of U.S. foreign policy. He was given a warm welcome by Chou En-lai, who indicated that the Chinese, because of their fear of the Soviet buildup along the border, were placing good relations with Washington ahead of their commitment to Hanoi. After he returned from his five-day visit, Kissinger suggested that China, like Russia, was urging Hanoi to negotiate a settlement with the United States that would allow the Americans to leave "with honor." "We do not believe there is any major country in the world today that wants the war to continue," he declared.

The results of Kissinger's interlocking diplomacy, coupled with American military pressure, prompted Hanoi to convene a special strategy session toward the end of June. All the top North Vietnamese diplomats, including Xuan Thuy, were recalled. Kissinger anticipated that as a result of the reassessment under way in Hanoi Le Duc Tho would soon be returning to Paris with new negotiating instructions. He hoped they would reflect a major change in Hanoi's position that would break the stalemate and lead to a negotiated end to the war.

"Where is Henry?"

It was a perfectly logical question on Tuesday, July 18. The presidential staff at San Clemente had just broken camp after eighteen days in the California sun, and Kissinger was missing from the usual Nixon entourage assembled at the Marine air base at El Toro to board the *Spirit of '76* for the flight to Washington. Across the tarmac reporters could spot the President, Haldeman, Ehrlichman, Colson, and Ziegler – but not Kissinger. For four hours and forty minutes – the time it took to fly across the country – the press corps speculated about Kissinger's latest disappearing act. The guess was that he had slipped off for another secret rendezvous with Le Duc Tho in Paris.

"All I can tell you," Ziegler said, in reply to repeated queries, "is he flew back to Washington Monday with his children. I have no comment on where Henry Kissinger is, period." Indeed, Kissinger's two children – Elizabeth and David – had spent some time with their father at San Clemente. But that was Monday. What about Tuesday?

The next morning's newspapers echoed the speculation that Kissinger had gone off to Paris. The sluggish stock market, looking for any hint of negotiating progress during still another summer of war, began to go up. "A Kissinger market," the analysts would soon begin calling it.

Back in Washington, a reporter checked with Kissinger's office.

"He in?" asked the reporter, testing the waters.

"No," replied one of his well-trained secretaries, "but I'll tell Dr. Kissinger you called just as soon as he comes in."

"Might that be this evening?" the reporter probed.

"It might."

It wasn't. That evening, Kissinger flew to Paris.

The next morning, at 10 A.M., the White House and the Foreign Ministry in Hanoi announced simultaneously that Kissinger and Le Duc Tho were meeting near the French capital. It was the first time the two antagonists stripped away the secrecy surrounding such sessions. At State and Defense, officials smiled knowingly, though they knew nothing. In New York, the market jumped eighteen points in three hours of heavy trading. Later in the day, the White House released still more information. The talks between Kissinger and Tho had lasted six and a half hours. The evening television newscasts, reporting these details, quickened the pulse of a country eager for an end to the war.

Kissinger flew back to Washington that night; this time, with his ETA made public in advance, he was met by a crowd of reporters. They got a wave but not a word, and Kissinger proceeded directly to the White House. He told the President that, though Hanoi's position had not changed in any concrete way, he could sense a change in the tone of the discussions. The poison seemed to have been drained out, certainly when compared to the hostile meeting of May 2, before the mining of Haiphong Harbor and the President's trip to Moscow. It was quite possible, Kissinger believed, that there might soon be a substantive change in the North Vietnamese position as well.

Kissinger and Le Duc Tho met again on August 1 and again on August 14 — three times in less than a month. This was an unusually brisk pace. Kissinger's impression that Hanoi's approach had changed was confirmed at these two August meetings; the strategy session in Hanoi seemed to have led to a softening of the North Vietnamese attitude toward the Thieu regime. All along they had been insisting that Thieu would have to resign before there could be any thought of a cease-fire. Suddenly they began to talk about the "reality" of "two administrations," "two armies," and "three political groupings" in South Vietnam.

These phrases were critically important; the very admission that there was more than just the *one* political organization in the south — the Communist Provisional Revolutionary Government — seemed to be implicit recognition that the Saigon regime existed on a level with the PRG. The phrase "three political groupings" referred to the possibility of a coalition composed of the PRG, the Thieu regime, and an undefined "middle" group.

Hanoi's stance now indicated some give. But he could not be sure how much importance to ascribe to the change. Most of Le Duc Tho's time — "eighty percent of his time," Kissinger would later say — was spent in denouncing "Thieu and his clique."

Hanoi, meantime, was accusing the United States of bombing the highly vulnerable dike system of North Vietnam and causing widespread flooding in the heavily populated Red River delta. The U.S. reiterated its denials that the dikes were deliberately targeted, although Government spokesmen conceded that there might have been some "inadvertent" damage from American bombs aimed at adjacent military targets. The controversy touched off a national and international uproar. At one point, Nixon indignantly declared that the war critics were being "taken in" by North Vietnamese propaganda. "If it were the policy of the United States to bomb the dikes," he declared at an impromptu news conference, "we could take them out, the significant part of them out, in a week. We don't do so . . . because we are trying to avoid civilian casualties, not cause them." He seemed determined to prevent these accusations about the U.S. bombing of the dikes from snowballing into a major challenge to his policy in the politically sensitive months ahead.

As the presidential campaign swung into high gear, Kissinger's comings and goings kept building an air of expectancy about Vietnam. Ziegler's announcements seemed programmed to suggest the imminence of a breakthrough, or, at the very least, an effort of such seriousness that it deserved the support of every voting American. Indeed, Ziegler rationed out news of Kissinger's itineraries as if each takeoff were bringing the world one step closer to the President's goal of "a generation of peace." His White House briefings were marked by such words as "sensitive," "delicate," and "careful"; his closing line was often one variation or another of "I wouldn't want to encourage any speculation" — which inevitably produced the opposite effect.

The appetite for peace whetted the appetite for Kissinger; he was pursued everywhere. The day after his August 14 meeting with Le Duc Tho in Paris, he flew off to the small Swiss resort town of Laax-Films for a family celebration of his parents' fiftieth wedding anniversary. He was followed by scores of reporters and cameramen. As they congregated around him, pressing for information, he was superbly reticent, which only compounded their suspicion that something was up. "No, really,· I can't say anything about the talks," he replied.

"But can you tell us whether there has been any progress?"

He smiled. "No, really, I can't." A pause. "You understand," he added, taking them into his confidence while the cameras were rolling.

Yet even these innocuous tidbits were featured on the evening television news broadcasts and in many newspapers. A reader of the *New York*

Times the next morning would find Kissinger and his daughter Elizabeth gliding across the front page in a cable car against a snow-covered background.

After the family party, he boarded a Swiss government helicopter and flew from Laax-Films to Zurich, where he waved to the press and got on a presidential jet bound for Saigon. "The President," the White House announced, "has asked Henry Kissinger to go to South Vietnam for a general review of all aspects of the Vietnam problem, including the negotiations in Paris."

Skeptics promptly charged that Kissinger's contrails were nothing more than a Nixon tactic for fending off criticism of his inability to end the war during his first term in office. Senator George McGovern, a month after winning his party's nomination for the presidency, accused Nixon of "manipulating" American public opinion by sending "his chief foreign policy specialist on a highly publicized global junket on the eve of the Republican National Convention." Not long before, McGovern had rejected Nixon's offer — the traditional tender of the incumbent to the opposition standard-bearer — to have his foreign policy adviser brief the South Dakota Democrat on national security issues. Instead, McGovern sent his own foreign policy adviser, Paul Warnke, a former Deputy Secretary of Defense under LBJ. Kissinger, miffed by McGovern's slight, shunted Warnke to his deputy, General Haig. Warnke, in turn, minimized Haig's fill-ins, saying there was "little new" in them.

On the long flight from Zurich to Saigon, Kissinger curled up with a book — not one of the heavy briefing tomes dealing with the negotiations but a new biography of Metternich. "What else would a modern Metternich choose to read?" observed the *Washington Post.*

On August 16, the day Kissinger arrived in Saigon, Le Duc Tho suddenly left Paris for Hanoi, with stopovers in Moscow and Peking. The North Vietnamese were suspicious of the overtures to the U.S. by their giant allies; their anger was clearly reflected in *Nhan Dan,* Hanoi's official newspaper, which rebuked Russia and China for "throwing a lifesaver to a drowning pirate" and "departing from the great, all-conquering revolutionary thoughts of the time and . . . bogging down on the dark, muddy road of compromise." This was all good news to Kissinger, whose spirits were further buoyed by intelligence reports that Peking and Moscow were slowing down on military supplies to North Vietnam.

President Thieu, in Saigon, was no less suspicious of *his* giant ally. Indeed, when Kissinger arrived in the South Vietnamese capital, the cafés along Tu Do — the Rue Catinat of French days — were buzzing with speculation that the United States and North Vietnam had already reached agreement on a compromise settlement that would force the anti-Communist leader of the south into a coalition with his Communist enemy.

The next morning, Kissinger met at Independence Palace with Thieu — a master of Saigon's politics, with a local reputation for being able to walk in four directions at the same time. Kissinger was accompanied by his aide Winston Lord and by Ambassador Ellsworth Bunker, who, after more than five years in South Vietnam, had earned the local nickname of "Mr. Refrigerator" because of his diplomatic cool. Thieu was accompanied by two close advisers, Nguyen Phu Duc and Hoang Duc Nha. Only one session had been planned, but it was agreed that another meeting would be held the following day to explore in greater detail the "two administrations, two armies" concept that Kissinger had discussed with Le Duc Tho in Paris only a few days earlier. "I really won't talk," Kissinger told the reporters who trailed him from the palace down the broad boulevard to the American Embassy. "There is really no sense in asking me questions." They kept on asking, he kept on smiling.

The second meeting, on August 18, ran for four hours. Again there were no details available. Saigon's establishment became increasingly anxious. "Kissinger must be here with a political solution in mind that includes the removal of Thieu," one Vietnamese Senator concluded. There were mutterings of despair at MACV. The fear of betrayal filled the palace. For Vietnamese whose destinies were linked with Thieu's survival, Kissinger became a symbol of sellout. Although Thieu did not trust Kissinger and Kissinger did not have unbounded confidence in Thieu, Kissinger did, according to one of his aides, admire the South Vietnamese leader "as someone who is defending the interests of his country as well as he could with a very uncertain ally." During their talks, Kissinger tried to explain to Thieu the pressures on American diplomacy during a presidential campaign while at the same time reassuring him of the firmness of Nixon's resolve on Vietnam.

That night, Kissinger departed for Camp David, stopping in Tokyo for a chat with Japan's new Premier, Kakuei Tanaka, about his upcoming visit to the United States. There was little time left before the GOP was to open its convention in Miami Beach and Nixon wanted to clear his foreign decks before concentrating on presidential politics. When Kissinger got back, he immediately provided Nixon with a detailed rundown of his talks with Le Duc Tho and Thieu. He indicated that a break-through by election time was a definite possibility.

The day after Kissinger's return, Secretary Rogers joined him and the President for dinner. The following day, the *Miami Herald* published an interview with Rogers in which he said he was "convinced" that "either we will have a negotiated settlement before the election, which I think is a possibility, or we will have one very soon after President Nixon's reelection." The Administration immediately backed away from Rogers's prediction. White House spokesman Gerald Warren said that Rogers "was not making a prediction based on any event or any exchange that may or may not have occurred." State Department spokesman Robert McCloskey added, more cautiously, "I have no authority to establish connections between the interview and the Kissinger briefing on Saturday night, or to discuss any conclusions that the Administration may have reached."

Kissinger was livid. He told a reporter that not only might the Secre-tary be wrong in his projection but, in addition, his comments could end up harming the negotiations. Actually, Rogers had merely echoed Kissinger's private judgment — and Nixon's, too. But Kissinger was con-cerned that the North Vietnamese might try to exploit this eagerness to try to wrest more concessions from the United States before the election or, failing that, to stall until after the election. "There won't be any more talk like that," Kissinger said angrily.

The convention opened on August 21 with extra hoopla making up for the lack of suspense. Nixon was "the one." His triumphs in Peking and Moscow were hailed as major steps toward "a generation of peace." He was portrayed as being on the verge of a settlement in Vietnam. No one contributed more to this image than Kissinger. The Harvard professor became a political asset as well as a diplomatic one.

On August 22, the second night of the convention, Kissinger starred in a GOP film extolling the virtues and achievements of the President. The house lights dimmed in the cavernous hall as Kissinger appeared on a giant screen, sharing with the electorate his own revised estimate of Nixon. "I, like most of my colleagues, had always been opposed to him," began Kissinger's soft-sell commercial, "and had formed certain images about him and I found that he was really, was totally different from the image intellectuals have of him. He's very analytical but quite gentle in his manner, and I always had quite a different view." Television carried his words to the nation. "There's a certain, you know, it's a big word, but it's a certain heroic quality about how he conducts his business. . . . I believe that his impact on foreign policy will be historic no matter what happens. He has provided one of the big watersheds in American international history." The President's adviser went on to say that what Nixon "is trying to do is pretty well what he's done, is to revitalize our alliances, to get into a new relationship with the Soviets, to begin to feel our way toward the Chinese and to end the war in Vietnam." It was pure show biz, and the Republican delegates cheered.

The Republican National Committee did not have to write Kissinger's script. It was an expression of his own deeply held views. He regarded a Nixon victory as essential, and McGovern as a disaster. Kissinger believed that a McGovern victory would give the North Vietnamese the triumph that had eluded them on the battlefield. "If McGovern wins in November," he later said, "then everything that we've worked for, everying we've been trying to do, becomes academic."

The convention film was not Kissinger's first appearance as a campaigner; he had been turning up at a number of lunches and dinners attended by Republican and Democratic contributors — many of them Jewish community leaders who were alarmed by McGovern's vacillating policy toward Israel. In early July, Taft Schreiber, a major Nixon fundraiser, invited Kissinger to one such luncheon in Beverly Hills, and later in the month, Wall Street financier Gustave Levy and retired Detroit industrialist Max Fisher, both Republicans who had helped bankroll more than one GOP campaign, invited Kissinger to similar gatherings in New York. Kissinger did not engage in fund-raising; he always left before there was any talk of money, insisting that his presentation was "nonpartisan." But his pitch was so transparently pro-Nixon and so implicitly pro-Israel that the message was not lost on his listeners. Ziegler, when questioned about these appearances, denied that Kissinger was "going around fund-raising." "He's too busy," Ziegler explained. "There are many others who do that. He's doing a great job in foreign policy."

At the convention, Kissinger was lionized not only as a foreign policy virtuoso but also as a one-of-a-kind celebrity. He was carefully trailed by five Secret Service agents and an army of admirers. A few women managed to slip through the net of security and implant a kiss on the face that had launched a thousand quips.

One evening, Betty Beale of the *Washington Evening Star and Daily*

News found Ruta Lee, an actress, sitting next to Kissinger in his box at Convention Hall. Miss Lee volunteered the opinion that Kissinger had "devastating charm." Who, Miss Beale asked, had arranged for her to sit next to Kissinger? "God," Miss Lee responded, pointing upward.

Dorothy McCardle of the *Washington Post* filed her report on Kissinger's lighthearted carryings-on at a party hosted by the Ronald Reagans on board the *Florida,* a rented, hundred-and-fifty-foot yacht moored in Pelican Bay. "As usual," she wrote, "Kissinger was kissed by women who spotted him and deluged him with questions. One of them told him she had felt sure that he would go on to Hanoi like some of those other Americans after he left Saigon. Kissinger, seldom at a loss for words, stopped, eyed the woman thoughtfully, and said with a serious air, 'Oh, I'm saving that for later.' 'Is he really going to Hanoi?' another woman asked. Any answer to that question was cut short when Kissinger was asked whether he will ever involve himself in elective politics. 'I have no plans for seeking public office,' he said."

At this point in his career, Kissinger was riding high. Even such critics as Mary McGrory had grudging praise for his "dazzling exploits in big-power diplomacy." Peter Lisagor, one of the most able reporters on the White House beat, wrote, "Henry Alfred Kissinger has ceased being a phenomenon. He has become a legend, and the word is not lightly used. Few presidential assistants have undertaken as many diverse roles and executed them with such skill, wit and aplomb." Lisagor continued, "He is the compleat cosmopolitan, urbane without swagger, self-centered without smugness. As a reputed ladies' man, he undoubtedly has given aid and comfort to every squat, owl-eyed, overweight and middle-aged bachelor in the land."

A few weeks after the convention was over, Kissinger was on the move again — flying to Moscow for a publicized meeting with Brezhnev, and then to Paris for a secret meeting with Le Duc Tho. Kissinger arrived in the Soviet capital on September 11, the same day the North Vietnamese negotiator arrived in the French capital to discuss a new peace plan just released by the PRG. Although State Department officials immediately dismissed the plan as "old wine in new bottles," Kissinger felt that it contained important indications of concessions by "the other side." It put in writing what Le Duc Tho had been hinting at in his talks with Kissinger in July and August. The text stated: "A solution to the internal problems of South Vietnam must proceed from the actual situation — that there exist in South Vietnam *two administrations, two armies and other political forces.* To achieve national concord," it went on, "the sides in South Vietnam must unite on the basis of equality, mutual respect, and *mutual non-elimination. . . . Neither a Communist nor a U.S. stooge regime shall be imposed on South Vietnam.*" (Italics added by the authors.) For the first time, the Communists were officially and publicly acknowledging the existence of the Thieu regime, despite their uncomplimentary language; they were refraining from demanding the ouster of the Thieu regime as an essential condition for a cease-fire; and they were implicitly pledging themselves to a political process in which neither side would try to "eliminate" the other or try to "impose" itself on the other.

Kissinger spent four days in Moscow discussing the link between Russia's need for grain and credits and America's desire to see the Vietnam war ended. When he arrived, he seemed to be in a particularly jolly mood. He bantered with Deputy Foreign Minister Kuznetsov about a controversial Soviet basketball victory over the United States at the recently concluded Olympic Games in Munich, and amused Ambassador Dobrynin with a tale of misadventure in Munich. "The Germans dropped me down an elevator today," he said. It seems that Kissinger and Rainer Barzel, West Germany's opposition leader, got into a Munich hotel elevator meant to hold four people; when six overprotective security agents piled in with them, the elevator fell from the ground floor to the basement. No one was hurt, but all eight men were stuck in the stuffy elevator for a half hour. The Russians loved that story.

Kissinger arrived in Moscow just as Brezhnev was trying to recover from two damaging blows: a critical shortage of grain, created by a dismal harvest; and the humiliating expulsion of Soviet military advisers from Egypt. Neither blow could have destroyed Brezhnev's position, but together they made him more vulnerable that ever before. Fortunately for Brezhnev, Nixon did not press his advantage. The President was grateful to the Soviet leader; he believed that the changes in Hanoi's negotiating posture were partly the result of Soviet pressure. Kissinger agreed; he preferred to think of Hanoi as a Soviet client than as a fiercely independent ally of the Soviet Union. There was disagreement within Kissinger's own shop on this key point; Haig and Negroponte, for example, maintained that the North Vietnamese were changing their policy and beginning to back down not because of Soviet pressure but because of the effect of the continued American mining and bombing.

Kissinger, more comfortable with his own "big-power" analysis, welcomed Brezhnev's assurance that North Vietnam would become even more flexible in the weeks ahead. Brezhnev's assessment was based on his recent talks with Le Duc Tho, who had stopped in Moscow again on his way to Paris. Kissinger liked to consider himself a tough, unsentimental negotiator, but these qualities were not reflected in the deal he negotiated with Brezhnev in Moscow. Once the Soviet leader agreed to settle the lend-lease debt, which dated back to World War II and had been a major stumbling block in all previous trade negotiations, Kissinger was ready to produce his own compromises. Within a few days, the United States and the Soviet Union had agreed on the terms of an extraordinary trade pact.

Easy credit terms were extended to Moscow under an agreement for the purchase of at least seven hundred and fifty million dollars' worth of U.S.-grown grains from private American exporting companies over the next three years. Kissinger was so eager to conclude the deal that he ignored or didn't see intelligence reports about the magnitude of the Russian crop failure; besides, he had no idea how much wheat various private American dealers were selling to the Soviet purchasing agents. The upshot was that the Russians got bread and the Americans got burned; the Communist bureaucrats turned out to be shrewd traders in the capitalist market. The Soviet Union managed to buy an immense amount of grain at guaranteed low prices, well below the market price at the time the grain would actually be delivered; the American taxpayer ended up subsidizing this Soviet purchase. In addition, the exports contributed to shortages of wheat in the United States; the price of bread and feed soared; milk and meat prices rose precipitously; the American consumer, and the entire American economy, suffered because neither Nixon nor Kissinger appreciated the economic ramifications of the deal. They were concentrating on linkage; to them, the sale of food grains was politically advantageous, and they never looked beyond that.

Next, the Administration promised to extend "most-favored-nation" status to Russia in its trade dealings. But many members of Congress balked at giving the Russians any special trade concessions until there was some liberalization of Moscow's restrictive emigration policy toward Jews and other minorities who wished to leave the Soviet Union.

A multibillion-dollar arrangement on exploiting Siberian natural gas was also concluded. This, too, was to touch off a major controversy in the United States. Critics asked how the U.S. could pour money into the economy of a country that was still building deadly missiles to threaten the U.S., and how the United States could consider becoming dependent upon the Soviet Union for so vital a need as energy?

Both nations expanded port facilities for each other's merchant ships, and Russia promised to allow more American businessmen to open offices in Moscow. The dimensions of the deal, distinguished by generous Yankee credits to the Communists, suggested not only Nixon's gratitude for Soviet help on Vietnam — presumed if not yet proven — but also his desire to create a web of international Soviet-American arrangements that would demonstrate to the Kremlin that cooperation was more productive than confrontation.

Kissinger, jubilant about this "major progress" in Soviet-American relations, left for Paris by way of London, in an attempt to keep his meeting with Le Duc Tho as secret as possible. After conferring quite visibly with British Prime Minister Edward Heath, Kissinger slipped out of London on the morning of September 15, after instructing his aides, who were staying at Claridge's, to leave "Do not disturb" signs on their doorknobs and duck out of the hotel without paying their bills. Eventually, the U.S. Embassy paid the bills, but Kissinger's passion for secrecy was beginning to wear on some of his aides.

Kissinger's party flew across the Channel in an old Convair and landed at Le Vésinet, a secret French military base near Paris. They were then chauffeured to Gif-sur-Yvette, where the French Communist Party had access to a handsome villa that had once been the home of the artist Fernand Léger. There, among some of the finest examples of twentieth-century cubism, the latest round of the Vietnam negotiations unfolded.

Le Duc Tho explained how Hanoi interpreted the PRG's September 11 proposals. He stressed that no government would be "imposed" on the South Vietnamese people. Kissinger argued that despite the modification in Hanoi's position, the new proposals would still involve the removal of the Thieu regime, and that President Nixon would never accept this. There was no point in Hanoi's hoping for a McGovern victory, he went on; Nixon would never be more generous than at the present moment — before the election; after the election, the President could be expected to enjoy the usual year-long "honeymoon," which would free his hands of most restraints; finally, he explained, Nixon had proved in the past that he was not afraid to take drastic military action to reach his diplomatic goals. All wars had to end sometime, Kissinger observed. Wasn't this the best time for the Vietnam war to end?

Kissinger and Le Duc Tho reached no substantive agreements. They set their next meeting for September 26. Kissinger slipped out of Gif-sur-Yvette and returned to Washington late that night, reporting to the President well past midnight. The next morning, Kissinger breakfasted with Rogers, and then he continued his deliberations with Nixon on the sunny South Portico of the White House. For a few minutes, cameramen were permitted to approach them and take a couple of pictures for the Sunday papers, which were filled with news about Nixon's approaching landslide.

Later in the morning, Kissinger briefed the White House press. He was upbeat about Russia and cautious about Vietnam. He revealed none of the new shifts in Hanoi's policy, and suggested instead that the September 11 proposals "leave something to be desired."

When Kissinger met Le Duc Tho again on September 26, the North Vietnamese negotiator produced still another innovation. Rather than establish a "provisional government" composed of "three equal segments," as provided by the September 11 plan, Tho proposed establishing a "National Council of Reconciliation and Concord," still composed of "three equal segments" but lacking governmental responsibility, and operating on the "principle of unanimity." This proposal indicated two major changes in Hanoi's policy. A "council" was clearly not a coalition government; and "unanimity" seemed to ensure a veto for Thieu over all council deliberations. For the first time, Hanoi was providing a formula by which Thieu could remain in power, while, at the same time, it could assert that a tripartite entity was being created. It was not a perfect formula, but it provided enough flexibility for Kissinger to propose a second straight day of discussions. Tho accepted the suggestion, and for the first time in almost thirty-eight months of secret negotiations, both sides really believed that they were approaching the beginning of the end.

The following morning, Kissinger and Tho examined Hanoi's "council" proposal in detail. How would it function? Who would be represented? It was clear who Thieu and the Communists were, but who belonged to the "third segment"? And who would decide? The two men agreed in principle on a cease-fire-in-place but disagreed about its territorial scope; Kissinger insisted that it extend to all of Indochina, Tho that it be limited to South Vietnam. Though there were still-unresolved issues, Kissinger, in late September, was again optimistic. In fact, he was so hopeful about the possibility of a breakthrough before election day that he tended to ignore the details, assuming that they could be taken care of later by the bureaucrats and technicians. Kissinger had a grand vision in mind — a late October announcement of an agreement in principle, followed, within ninety days, by a cease-fire, an international conference, and the start of a political process involving all the factions in South Vietnam.

Kissinger and Le Duc Tho agreed to meet again on October 8. When Kissinger got back to Washington, the President was in California; but the following evening, after Nixon returned to the capital, the two men met on board the presidential yacht, *Sequoia;* they were joined by Haig and Haldeman. As they cruised along the Potomac, they talked about the political implications of a preelection peace in Vietnam. Nixon apparently felt so confident of victory that he urged his aides to ignore the election date and plump for the best possible peace settlement. But all of them were aware of the relationship among the calendar, the negotiations, and the reelection of the President.

FOURTEEN

"Peace Is at Hand"

On OCTOBER 5, Richard Nixon invited reporters into the Oval Office and bounced a message off their notebooks to the policy-makers in Hanoi. He declared that the United States would not be stampeded into a Vietnam agreement simply because the presidential balloting was just a month away. "If we can make the right kind of settlement before the elections," he said, "we will make it. If we cannot, we are not going to make the wrong kind of settlement before the elections. We were around that track in 1968 when well-intentioned men made a very, very great mistake in stopping the bombing without adequate agreements from the other side. . . . The election, I repeat, will not in any way influence what we do at the negotiating table."

Kissinger believed that, despite Nixon's private and public disclaimers, he would be delighted to see a workable agreement reached before election day, November 7. In the 1968 campaign, Nixon, as the GOP candidate, had promised peace within four years; he had only four weeks left.

Moreover, Kissinger's own reading of peace prospects was extremely optimistic. He had just received a cable from Le Duc Tho, in which the North Vietnamese negotiator promised to make "a great effort to settle the war" at their next meeting. Kissinger felt "the constellation of forces was uniquely right," said one of his aides. "How many times in the future are we going to have the Soviet Union in a condition of near-famine, China absolutely terrified about what the Soviets might do along their border, and a conservative President so sure of his reelection that he can afford to be more receptive to a settlement?" the aide quoted Kissinger as saying. "Henry was hell-bent to get out before the election."

Kissinger's state of mind came through clearly in a long interview on the eve of his October 8 meeting with Le Duc Tho. Kissinger was asked to comment on criticism that he was putting his intellectual powers at the disposal of "a bankrupt policy."

"I don't think it's bankrupt," he responded. "It is a question of public morality." Kissinger objected to the fact that his critics acted as if they had a "monopoly of anguish and a monopoly of moral sensibility. I don't say that somebody who disagrees with us is immoral, wrong, a traitor, or any of the things they tend to call their opponents," he went on. "In fact, one of the tragedies of this war is that we have lost any capacity for understanding the moral complexity of these issues. It isn't a self-evident decision — that when fifty thousand mothers have sons who died there, that you tell them it was a horrible absurdity; and not only didn't we achieve what we wanted — that can happen — but we are now going to achieve the opposite of what we wanted; we are going to mock the very thing we started out to do by putting the opponents in, the people whose victory we were trying to prevent.

"The moral obligation we have," he continued, "is to give the South Vietnamese a chance; we have *no* moral obligation to stay there for all eternity, to prop them up against the vicissitudes that might befall them, because then we might be damned forever. But there's a big difference between saying one day, 'We're your allies,' and the next, 'We are now throwing you to the wolves.'

"What did de Gaulle do for France in Algeria?" Kissinger asked rhetorically. "He wanted to leave in such a way that the departure seemed an act of policy so that France could keep some of its dignity. . . . That was his great achievement, not the precise outcome of the war.

"Withdrawal," he continued, "isn't the problem. The problem is they won't let us. They want us there right now: they don't want us out."

"If there were an American withdrawal, wouldn't the other side give up the prisoners?" he was asked.

"No," he replied. "They would then use the prisoners to get us to stop economic and military aid. That would be the next round."

Kissinger hoped that the peace he was seeking in Vietnam could lead to a measure of peace in the United States as well. "Maybe we can bring a peace in Vietnam," he said, "that our critics can feel is reasonable and that others can feel is not dishonorable. That we haven't done yet. . . . If we succeed," he went on, we "will have restored a degree of public confidence . . . that the country is not led by criminals, fools, but by serious people. The difference between our debates now and in the forties and fifties, except for the McCarthy hearings, is that at that time we all thought we were part of a going concern. No matter how unhappy we were with Dulles, for example, we didn't really think he was out of our moral framework. We disagreed with him; we would have done it differently. But now we are in a conflict where victory is meaningless and defeat is unbearable. And that we have to transcend. And if we don't do it, somebody else has to do it, but it's got to be done.

"However it comes out," he said, "the war is going to be a misfortune for this country. All we've got left to get out of the war is a shred of dignity, and hopefully — if we settle it by an act of policy other than by just running — a chance of restoring some sense of unity to our discussion again, across the board."

The next morning, Kissinger, on his nineteenth transatlantic trip in search of a Vietnam accord, was welcomed by Le Duc Tho at the doorway of the Léger villa at Gif. After the usual small talk, they proceeded to the dining room to pick up the thread of their protracted negotiations. For the first few hours, their exchanges amounted to set pieces from earlier encounters. Tho attacked the Thieu regime and reiterated the NLF's September 11 proposal, demanding a political solution to the war prior to a military solution — an approach that the United States had consistently rejected. Tho seemed to be probing for a soft spot; Kissinger was unyielding. There was an awkward pause. Tho seemed to be hesitating about his next move; Kissinger wasn't sure why. Finally, the envoy from Hanoi suggested a two-hour break.

Kissinger used the time to explore the French countryside around Rambouillet, a village famous for its fourteenth-century château. For centuries, it had been linked with the royalty of Europe; Francis I, in the 1540s, and later, Charles IX and Catherine de Medici enjoyed strolling through the beautifully landscaped garden. In the summer of 1944, a war correspondent named Ernest Hemingway had paused at the château to write some memorable dispatches about the U.S. Army then on its way to liberate Paris, twenty-eight miles to the northeast. Now Kissinger paced these historic grounds, wondering why Tho had requested a recess.

The riddle was solved by the time he returned to Gif; Tho had needed final clearance from Hanoi before presenting Kissinger with a nine-point proposal "on ending the war and restoring peace in Vietnam." Even a quick reading of the details made it clear that the North Vietnamese proposal represented a significant breakthrough. For the first time, Hanoi seemed ready to separate the military from the political aspects of the war, thereby accepting Kissinger's two-track approach: the United States and North Vietnam would settle the military side of the war — through compromise, not conquest — by proclaiming a cease-fire, followed by a withdrawal of American troops and a return of American prisoners; and at a later time, a political accommodation would be worked out between the competing Vietnamese factions.

Equally important, perhaps, Tho's proposal came in the form of a *draft agreement* — in English. Clearly, the North Vietnamese wanted a deal. The dialogue of the deaf was ending. Kissinger read the draft once, then twice, then a third time, looking for the catch. He couldn't find it. Hanoi had unambiguously dropped its demand for Thieu's dismissal and his replacement by a coalition government.

As he studied the draft, Kissinger did detect a number of problems. First, the cease-fire would apply only to South Vietnam and would not include Cambodia and Laos. Next, the draft was vague on the prompt establishment of an "International Commission on Control and Supervision" to police the cease-fire; Kissinger felt it was imperative to have an adequately manned international force on hand immediately after the cease-fire to prevent both sides from going on a spree of land-grabbing during the uncertain first phases of a stand-down. Finally, the tone and the wording of the draft tended to denigrate the Saigon regime in a manner certain to infuriate President Thieu — and perhaps President Nixon, too. But in Kissinger's view, these were manageable problems. Overall, Hanoi had made major concessions, opening the door to a dignified American withdrawal from Indochina and a return of American POWs — perhaps by Christmas. A preelection deal suddenly became a realistic probability. Kissinger suggested another meeting for the next morning.

"This is it!" Kissinger exclaimed as he entered his black limousine for the hour-long drive back to the American Embassy in Paris. "We've got a deal." His enthusiasm was contagious. Haig, Lord, Negroponte, Rodman — they all sensed that the corner had been turned on the Vietnam negotiations.

At the Embassy, Kissinger immediately telephoned Haldeman; it had become his practice to telephone the President's Chief of Staff, rather than the President himself, in order to prevent foreign intelligence monitoring services from recording the President's voice in any sensitive negotiations. A summary of the new Hanoi proposal would soon be cabled to Washington, he advised; it deserved the President's "urgent consideration." Kissinger also sent the President a list of questions, such as: "Do we go for a deal now? Do we wait? What is my area of negotiating latitude?"

These were the nine points in Hanoi's draft:

1. The U.S. respects Vietnam's "independence, sovereignty, unity and territorial integrity," as defined by the 1954 Geneva Accords. At that time, there was, for Kissinger, no debate on this point.

2. A cease-fire will begin in South Vietnam within "twenty-four hours after the signing of the agreement." All U.S. troops will be withdrawn from South Vietnam "within sixty days." No debate.

3. "All captured and detained personnel" will be released "simultaneously with the U.S. troop withdrawal" — in other words, within sixty days. Again, no debate.

4. "An administrative structure called the National Council of Reconciliation and Concord, of three equal segments, will be set up to promote the implementation of the signed agreements by the Provisional Revolutionary Government of the Republic of South Vietnam and the Government of the Republic of Vietnam, and to organize the general elections." There was to be considerable debate about this point.

5. The reunification of Vietnam "will be carried out step by step through peaceful means." No debate.

6. "An International Commission on Control and Supervision will be established." Kissinger wanted to know when. "An international guarantee conference on Vietnam will be convened within thirty days of the signing of the agreement." No debate. It had been Kissinger's idea in the first place.

7. All sides pledge to "respect" the "independence, sovereignty, unity and territorial integrity" of Laos and Cambodia; and they further pledge to "refrain from using the territory of Cambodia and the territory of Laos to encroach on the sovereignty and security of other countries." Since the North Vietnamese regarded South Vietnam as part of their own country and did not include it with "other countries," this pledge had little practical meaning. Moreover, Hanoi said nothing about a cease-fire in Laos and Cambodia.

8. The U.S. "will contribute" to "postwar reconstruction in the Demo-

cratic Republic of Vietnam and throughout Indochina," and a "new, equal
and mutually beneficial relationship" will be established between Hanoi
and Washington. There was to be a great deal of discussion about how
much American aid would be funneled into North Vietnam — and under
what terms.

9. "This agreement will come into effect as soon as it is signed." This
sounded innocent enough, but it was to provoke a major argument about
who was to sign the agreement, how, and when.

Though Kissinger was eager to keep his scheduled appointment with
Le Duc Tho the next morning, Monday, October 9, he was forced to
postpone it twice; he was waiting for the President's response to his questions, and he also wanted to be certain that the American counterdraft,
composed by Haig during the night and containing few substantive
changes, had Nixon's backing. When, finally, the President's approval
was flashed by Haldeman, Kissinger and his entourage raced to Gif, and
the negotiations began to move swiftly. Sixteen hours Monday, sixteen
hours Tuesday. In this supercharged atmosphere, differences narrowed
so significantly that Kissinger and Tho actually worked out a tentative
timetable for implementation: October 18 — the U.S. would stop the
bombing and mining of North Vietnam; October 19 — Kissinger and
Tho would initial the draft agreement in Hanoi, after Kissinger had
cleared it with Thieu in Saigon; October 26 — the foreign ministers of
both countries — Rogers for the U.S., Trinh for North Vietnam — would
formally sign the agreement in Paris; and, on October 27, a standstill
cease-fire would roll across South Vietnam.

At this point, the pace of the negotiations and the timetable for implementation seemed almost breathless. Kissinger has never denied his
eagerness for a compromise settlement of the war, but he rejects the
theory that it was he who pushed for a preelection deal. He insists that
it was Le Duc Tho who wanted the negotiations to be completed by
the end of October — perhaps believing that Nixon would be more flexible on peace terms *before* his reelection.

Nevertheless, Kissinger was clearly elated about the imminence of an
agreement with North Vietnam — so elated that he cut diplomatic corners
in dealing with the South Vietnamese representative in Paris. Kissinger
briefed him in general terms on the course of the negotiations, but he
deliberately withheld the key fact: that the two sides had exchanged
draft agreements and established a timetable for implementation.

Kissinger assumed, from the beginning, that he could handle Saigon — the haughty professor handling the difficult pupil. Though his affection for both Vietnams was not exactly unbounded, Kissinger seemed to have more respect for Hanoi than for Saigon.

Haig and Negroponte were among those aides who cautioned Kissinger against rushing into a deal with Hanoi and ignoring Saigon. "Some people think a major mistake was made at that time," one official later said. "The smartest thing we could have done was fly back to Washington, get a good night's sleep, clear the fog out of our minds, check out the draft carefully, with ourselves and with the South Vietnamese, and then return to Paris for another hard look at the agreement with the North Vietnamese. But no, Henry would have none of that. He wanted the deal, and he wanted it then." Another official added: "The North Vietnamese calculation was that the U.S. was so eager that once they gave us a treaty, we would jump at it. And they were right."

In the grand rush toward the finale, there was simply not enough time to scrutinize the fine print of the nine points and the numerous appendices of the draft agreement. The Americans were careless and permitted ambiguities to slip into the draft. If Kissinger had been negotiating with the Russians or the Chinese, he no doubt would have been extremely meticulous about every syllable; but with the North Vietnamese, after more than three years of painful negotiations, and with only four weeks remaining before the presidential election, he seemed more concerned about nailing down the deal than about making sure that every detail was correct — an attitude that played right into Le Duc Tho's hands.

There were other kinds of problem, too. On October 11 — a day and night of bargaining, checking and double-checking that began at 9:30 A.M. and lasted until 2 A.M. — American bombers struck at Hanoi. The French diplomatic mission was wrecked and the French Ambassador, Pierre Susini, sustained fatal wounds. There was an international outcry. France protested, and American antiwar critics accused the President of negotiating with bombs. There was fear that the talks at Gif might be fatally wounded, too. Tho privately complained to Kissinger, who in turn succeeded in getting a temporary suspension of air strikes against the North Vietnamese capital. Still, through these dangerous moments, they both kept to their agenda of sorting out the diplomatic verbiage, hoping that the climax of a cease-fire was indeed within reach.

By nightfall, Haig implored Kissinger to ask for a few more days, just in case Saigon balked. Kissinger did not think Saigon could balk; after

all, here was a deal that kept Thieu in power. But he still proposed to
Tho that their original timetable be allowed to slip. Now, not on October
18, but on October 21, the bombing would stop; on October 22, the agreement would be initialed in Hanoi; and, on October 30, it would be
formally signed in Paris. Tho was suspicious — there was hardly a reser-
voir of trust between the two countries — but he agreed to the new timetable on condition that Kissinger "commit" the United States to keeping
it. Kissinger assured Tho that, while the draft agreement would have to
be checked with Saigon, he anticipated no problems. He knew that "there
were a lot of loose ends," but, assuming goodwill on both sides, he promised Tho that the U.S. would make every effort to meet the new timetable. "It's worth the gamble," he later told an aide.

At the concluding session, while their aides picked their way through
the draft agreement, Kissinger and Tho plunged into a long, philosophical
talk, each viewing history from his own vantage point. There were allu-
sions to the French, American, and Chinese revolutions. There was praise
of North Vietnam's courage and fortitude. There was a pledge of American help to rebuild Hanoi's wartime devastation. There was even a warm
compliment for Tho's endurance and his realism in accommodating to
the two-track approach. Tho seemed genuinely touched. He was, according to one eyewitness, close to tears as he embraced Kissinger,
French-style. Both diplomats promised to defend the principles of their
agreement and not to allow any of the "loose ends" to impede progress
toward a cease-fire and, afterward, toward the reconciliation of the Vietnamese people and the reconstruction of their battered homeland. They
said *au revoir*, promising to meet in Hanoi on October 22.

On October 12, after four consecutive days of talks — unprecedented
during their years of negotiations — Kissinger flew back to Washington,
landing at Andrews Air Force Base at 5:52 P.M. With only a wave at
newsmen, he got into a waiting car and drove off to the White House
to report to the President. "How are the girls in Paris?" inquired the
President. "Not enough time," replied the "swinger." They spent an hour
reviewing the Paris negotiations. The next morning, they were joined by
Haig and Rogers. Correspondents and photographers were given a
couple of minutes to eavesdrop on calculated banter and to film the
President and his aides. White House spokesmen were barraged with
questions; they divulged no facts but they did not discourage speculation
about a breakthrough.

The meeting at the White House coincided with Le Duc Tho's departure from Paris to Hanoi by way of Moscow and Peking. "There are still some difficult things to settle," the North Vietnamese negotiator told reporters at Orly Airport. He smiled and waved expansively, and reporters got the impression that their long vigil on the Vietnam story might be ending. "I shall return to Paris," Tho declared. "There is no problem about that."

Over the weekend, Kissinger scheduled his next moves, building toward a preelection settlement. On Monday night, October 16, he would fly to Paris. On October 17, he would confer with Xuan Thuy about a number of unresolved issues and then, late that evening, depart for Saigon. On October 19 and 20, he would obtain Thieu's approval of the draft agreement. On October 21, he would fly to Hanoi. On October 22, as he had promised Le Duc Tho, he would initial the agreement.

Kissinger was clearly on cloud nine. Though he himself was always outraged at the very notion of a "leak," his private euphoria could not be contained, and he shared a few choice impressions with friendly columnists: first, that he had encountered a new North Vietnamese attitude at the latest round of talks in Paris — serious, businesslike, stripped of propaganda; second, that Tho had concluded, perhaps with a bit of prodding by Kissinger, that the President would become even more intransigent on the subject of bombing after his reelection; third, that an interim peace agreement would be signed perhaps even before November 7; finally, that practical arrangements for a deal had been discussed.

It was in this frame of mind that Kissinger flew into Paris on the morning of October 17 for a meeting at Choisy-le-Roi with Xuan Thuy. Among Kissinger's papers was a two-page handwritten letter from the President. "Do what is right for an honorable peace, without regard to the election," it read. A settlement might be "a slight plus for the election," but "basically" it was "a mixed bag for a variety of reasons." The letter was leaked by the White House as evidence of the President's preelection statesmanship.

Included in Kissinger's party were two new faces: William Sullivan, a Deputy Assistant Secretary of State, serving as the department's top specialist on Vietnam and Indochina, and George Aldrich, a legal adviser for the Department of State. For the first time, Kissinger had broken out of his own tight NSC circle for bureaucratic help. Given his mania for secrecy, this departure could only be explained by Kissinger's conviction that he was then entering the mopping-up stage of the negotiations.

Kissinger and Xuan Thuy met from 10 A.M. to 10 P.M. — still another twelve hours of reviewing the draft agreement. As Hanoi's spokesman in Paris, Nguyen Thanh Le, would describe their secret meeting a week later, "They went over the texts again, chapter by chapter, article by article, phrase by phrase, word by word." Certain specifics were still in dispute; for example, Articles 7 and 8C.

Article 7 dealt with, among other things, the periodic replacement of armaments, munitions, and war matériel that had been "destroyed, damaged, worn out, or used up" after the cease-fire. Xuan Thuy argued for the loosest sort of control; Kissinger argued for the tightest form of control. Article 8C dealt with the release of political prisoners in the south. Saigon admitted that there were as many as eighty thousand political prisoners, though there were probably many more. Not all of them were Vietcong supporters, but their mass release would have strengthened the ranks of the Communist underground infrastructure in the south. Xuan Thuy insisted on this point, but he ran into Kissinger's opposition.

The American envoy emphasized that Thieu's concurrence was essential for a successful conclusion of the negotiations. If the North Vietnamese envoy persisted on maximizing his advantages, he would in the process maximize Thieu's resistance, and the whole agreement might be placed in jeopardy. But Xuan Thuy was unyielding; indeed, at one point he seemed to up the ante. He suggested that the release of the political prisoners in the south be linked to the release of the American POWs in Hanoi. Kissinger lost his cool. The POW release, he warned, could not be tied to any other issue, or there would be no deal at all. After a heated exchange, Xuan Thuy relented on the linkage, but he emphasized the critical importance that Hanoi attached to a quick release of all political prisoners. Apparently this was a key demand of the Provisional Revolutionary Government.

This hard bargaining was taking place against a deadline. Kissinger had already informed Xuan Thuy that he would be leaving for Saigon in the evening, and he hoped to resolve the remaining problems before his departure. The North Vietnamese diplomat kept stalling, either because he had no negotiating flexibility or because he was gambling that by letting the clock run out he might force Kissinger to make concessions. Instead of yielding, Kissinger became increasingly impatient. He demanded a quick resolution of the two major issues; Xuan Thuy refused to budge. Both negotiators knew that to keep to his timetable, Kissinger would have to be airborne for Saigon by 11 P.M., when Orly

August 15, 1972: With his brother Walter and their children at the Swiss Alps resort town of Laax-Films, where the Kissingers gathered to celebrate the golden wedding anniversary of their parents. Henry Kissinger flew here after a meeting with North Vietnam's Le Duc Tho in Paris; from here, Kissinger proceeded to Saigon for talks with South Vietnam's President Nguyen Van Thieu.

August 17, 1972: With South Vietnam's President Nguyen Van Thieu at Doc Lap (Independence) Palace, Saigon. Their relations were less than warm, stemming from the clash between Washington's desire for a compromise that would offer the United States "peace with honor" and Saigon's desire to avoid compromise and to fight on, preferably with U.S. military support.

August 23, 1972: Listening to President Nixon deliver his acceptance speech after his nomination for reelection at the Republican convention at Miami Beach. A political film shown from the floor featured Henry Kissinger saying that there was "a certain heroic quality about how he [Nixon] conducts his business. . . ." Four years earlier, Kissinger, then rooting for Nelson Rockefeller, was quoted as saying: "Richard Nixon is the most dangerous, of all the men running, to have as President."

October 26, 1972: Announcing "Peace is at hand" at a news conference in the Press Room of the White House. Henry Kissinger's appearance here was forced by the surprise disclosure by Hanoi only a few hours earlier that North Vietnam and the United States had already agreed to sign an accord "ending" the war on October 31; Hanoi demanded that the United States meet the timetable. The agreement was finally signed January 27, 1973, in Paris, but only after further negotiations, a massive arms lift to Saigon, and the most intensive U.S. raids of the war against the north in late December, 1972.

November 13, 1972: With General Alexander Haig, Jr., at the Pentagon, following Haig's return from a difficult round of talks in Saigon, where he had sought to persuade President Nguyen Van Thieu to concur in a U.S. determination as to what constituted an acceptable "peace" agreement. The General's visit to Saigon coincided with a massive air and sea lift of U.S. war matériel to South Vietnam.

November, 1972: With North Vietnam's Le Duc Tho, during the stalemated negotiations between Henry Kissinger's "Peace is at hand" on October 26 and the B-52
blitz against North Vietnam in the latter half of December. At Gif-sur-Yvette,
where many of the secret talks took place between the United States and North
Vietnam.

December, 1972: At his command post in the U.S. Embassy in Paris, during the crucial round of still-deadlocked negotiations with the North Vietnamese that preceded the B-52 raids against the heartland of North Vietnam a few days later. NSC aide Winston Lord leans over the desk of secretary Bonnie Long. In the background is NSC aide Peter Rodman.

January 23, 1973: With North Vietnam's Le Duc Tho, initialing the Agreement on Ending the War and Restoring Peace in Vietnam, a masterly set of compromises and ambiguities that did not end the war but did provide an exit for the United States from a decade of military involvement in Vietnam. The initialing climaxed more than three years of secret negotiations between the two sides. At the Hotel Majestic, in Paris.

May, 1973: In nondiplomatic dress, tagging along with Leonid Brezhnev and marksman, at the Volga River hideaway at Zavidovo, the Soviet equivalent of Camp David. It was during his stay here that Henry Kissinger negotiated the details of Summit II — the Brezhnev visit to the United States in June, 1973.

May, 1973: The day's catch at Zavidovo included a boar. Kissinger had declined Leonid Brezhnev's invitation to join in the hunt, saying: "I don't like to kill animals." Weeks later, a boar's head was presented to Kissinger in Washington by Soviet Ambassador Anatoly Dobrynin.

June 23, 1973: With actress Jill St. John and friends, at a poolside fiesta-style party with some two hundred guests, many of them Hollywood celebrities, honoring Leonid Brezhnev during his June 18–25 visit to the United States. At President Nixon's La Casa Pacifica villa, overlooking the Pacific, at San Clemente.

September 22, 1973: Just after being sworn in as the fifty-sixth Secretary of State — the first naturalized citizen in the nation's history to attain the post. Son David, twelve, and daughter Elizabeth, fourteen, join Kissinger's parents, Mr. and Mrs. Louis Kissinger of New York, on the platform in the East Room of the White House. His voice cracking with emotion at one point during his acceptance speech, Henry Kissinger declared: "There is no country in the world where it is conceivable that a man of my origin could be standing here next to the President of the United States."

November 6, 1973: Henry of Arabia! On his first visit to an Arab country – in Rabat, Morocco — reviewing his first honor guard as Secretary of State. Henry Kissinger subsequently became a frequent commuter to the Middle East and, in his negotiations with Egypt and Israel, added "shuttle diplomacy" to the annals of history.

November 8, 1973: With King Faisal of Saudi Arabia, the world's largest exporter of oil. Kissinger sought, on his first visit to Riyadh, to persuade Faisal to relent on using oil as a diplomatic weapon and to lift the oil embargo against the United States. He was unsuccessful then, but Faisal would join other Arab states in March, 1974, in lifting the embargo — only after Kissinger had negotiated an agreement stipulating that the Israelis as well as the Egyptians withdraw their forces along the Suez Canal.

November 8, 1973: On the first of his visits to Egypt, where he took time out from diplomacy to pose with the country's most celebrated heirloom, at Giza. "Which of us is the real Sphinx?" he joked.

November 12, 1973: With Chairman Mao Tse-tung, in his study at Chung Nan Hai, in the Forbidden City, during Henry Kissinger's sixth visit to Peking and his first as Secretary of State. It was their third get-together.

January 18, 1974: Being embraced by President Anwar Sadat of Egypt, after both Egypt and Israel had separately signed an agreement on the disengagement of their forces along the Suez Canal — the first diplomatic breakthrough between the two countries in a quarter of a century. "You are not only my friend," said Sadat. "You are my brother." At Aswan.

April 4, 1974: Mr. and Mrs. Henry Kissinger, on their wedding trip to Acapulco.

March 8, 1974: With the authors, in his office at the State Department.

Airport closed. This meant that he would have to leave Choisy-le-Roi no later than 10 P.M. Kissinger, according to one account, became "almost hysterical," pacing furiously from one end of the room to the other and imploring Xuan Thuy to be reasonable.

Shortly before ten, Kissinger abruptly announced: "I'm leaving. I must go to Saigon."

"Dr. Kissinger," Xuan Thuy replied, "if you go to Saigon, we'll never settle it. We'll never settle the problem."

"We'll solve it by cable," Kissinger countered, gathering his papers together.

"Why not leave it till we get to Hanoi?" Xuan Thuy persisted.

By then, Kissinger was on his way out of the villa.

Kissinger arrived at Tan Son Nhut Airport in Saigon Wednesday night, October 18, expecting to spend only two days in South Vietnam. He had complete confidence in his ability to win Thieu's support for the draft agreement. To sell his case to the anxious South Vietnamese President, Kissinger had assembled an impressive supporting cast. It included Ambassador Ellsworth Bunker; Army Chief of Staff General Creighton Abrams, who had once commanded U.S. forces in Vietnam and had been a driving force in upgrading the Vietnamization program; Admiral Noel Gaylor, the new Commander in Chief of the Pacific command, who had flown in from Hawaii; General Frederick Weyand, Abrams's successor in Vietnam; and Philip Habib, Ambassador to Korea, who had served in Saigon between 1965 and 1967 and later as acting head of the U.S. delegation to the Paris peace talks. Kissinger set up a command post at Bunker's official residence at 38 Phung Khac Khoan, a treelined Saigon street with more than its share of barbed wire, sandbags, and American MPs.

The arrival of this high-powered American delegation in Saigon intensified the gossip in the local cafés — at L'Amiral, Brodard, Aterbea, Ramuntcho, Givral, and La Pagode — that Vietnam was once again at a turning point in its turbulent history. People recalled the old Vietnamese superstition about the "law of nine." Something always seemed to happen in the years whose last two digits added up to nine. The Japanese occupation had ended in 1945. The war with the French ended in 1954. The overthrow of President Ngo Dinh Diem had taken place in 1963. What would 1972 bring?

Hanoi, more than seven hundred miles to the north, struck one American journalist on October 18 as a capital sprucing up for a celebration. Arnaud de Borchgrave, senior editor of *Newsweek*, who had arrived in Hanoi a few days earlier, saw thousands of North Vietnamese snake-dancing through the park, clanging cymbals and shaking tambourines. They were honoring the antiaircraft gunners who had shot down the "four-thousandth American warplane" of the war, but it seemed to de Borchgrave more like a rehearsal for a victory parade.

At ten o'clock that morning, de Borchgrave was escorted to the official residence of Premier Pham Van Dong for an exclusive two-hour interview. It started off casually; the Premier, clad in a white shirt and light gray slacks, welcomed his visitor with a friendly handshake. The Premier and his visitor began by reminiscing, in French, about de Borchgrave's visits to Hanoi in the early 1950s, and they had a good laugh about the stories the French had then been putting out about Ho Chi Minh's imminent demise from tuberculosis. But they soon got to the urgent issue of how the war might be settled. Dong knew all the still-secret details of what had taken place in Paris between Tho and Kissinger; de Borchgrave was probing for information.

"Negotiations," the Premier said, "are in an extremely important phase. . . . Our intentions are serious. . . . A peaceful settlement must be just for both sides — not to serve temporary political ends. We won't allow it, and we will fight against it. But we will do nothing to jeopardize a happy conclusion at this stage by talking out of turn."

It was then, apparently in an effort to enhance Hanoi's negotiating position, that Dong deviated from the agreed scenario worked out between Le Duc Tho and Kissinger, and made a comment that would have a disastrous impact on Kissinger's attempt at a *tour de force* in Saigon.

De Borchgrave asked the Premier if Thieu could be "part of the Saigon administration component in a three-sided coalition government . . . ?" Dong knew that there would be no coalition and that Thieu would remain in power. But he replied: "Thieu has been overtaken by events. And events are now following their own course." That statement suggested that the South Vietnamese President might not even be part of a coalition.

De Borchgrave: "What about the idea of two administrations in the south . . . ?"

Dong: "All your questions reflect the present evolution. One must accept that there are two administrations, each in control of their own zones. It's an undeniable fact. Everyone must respect this state of affairs."

De Borchgrave: "Then a cease-fire followed by American withdrawal will take place first and then direct negotiations between the PRG and the Saigon regime?"

Dong: "This is the present evolution, and it is a positive one. The situation will then be two armies and two administrations in the south and given that new situation they will have to work out their own arrangements for *a three-sided coalition of transition* and defuse the situation in the wake of the American withdrawal. . . ."

De Borchgrave, who did not know that Hanoi had dropped its demand for a "coalition" government in the secret talks on October 8, assumed naturally that a settlement was close and a "coalition" would be a key element in it. The following day, when he returned to the Premier's residence to review with him the transcript of the interview, Dong did not alter his reference to a "coalition." Eager to cable these first high-level disclosures about a breakthrough in Paris, de Borchgrave made plans to take the next of the biweekly flights linking Hanoi with Vientiane, in Laos.

On Thursday, October 19, the morning edition of *Dai Dan Toc,* a Saigon daily, carried an unusual picture of Henry Kissinger — not one of his arrival the previous night but a copy of the *Harvard Lampoon*'s centerfold — a photomontage showing the presidential adviser sprawled on a rug and wearing nothing but a smile, *à la* Burt Reynolds in *Cosmopolitan.* "Kissinger," the caption read, "has no more secrets." Kissinger, in fact, was still clothed in quite a few secrets, and he chose not to shed them all at once — a decision that would affect his face-to-face negotiations with Thieu as well as the calendar of "peace" he had negotiated with Tho.

The first of the crucial round of talks with the South Vietnamese opened on that morning at 9 A.M. at Independence Palace; both sides crowded into President Thieu's "situation room." The South Vietnamese delegation included, among others, his adviser, Hoang Duc Nha; Foreign Minister Tran Van Lam; Special Adviser on foreign policy Nguyen Phu Duc; and South Vietnam's Ambassador to the U.S., Tran Kim Phuong. Kissinger was accompanied by Bunker, Abrams, Sullivan, and several

NSC staffers. Their meeting lasted three and a half hours. It was, by all accounts, orderly and unabrasive, with Kissinger doing most of the talking.

Kissinger presented Thieu with an English-language copy of the draft agreement that he had negotiated with the North Vietnamese. He explained its terms in a detached manner, stressing several key points that he felt confident the South Vietnamese would recognize as being to their advantage: first, not only would Thieu retain power but, more important, he would have a veto over all decisions of the National Council of Reconciliation and Concord which, Kissinger suggested, was basically a fig leaf for Hanoi and "not a coalition"; second, the Communists were now committed to "a political process," meaning they had been forced to forsake military conquest in the foreseeable future; third, as added insurance, the United States would be maintaining air bases in Thailand, and the Seventh Fleet would remain in neighboring waters as a shield against any renewal of Communist aggression; fourth, U.S. economic and military aid to the Thieu government would be allowed to continue — and would continue; fifth, the United States was pretty well convinced that it could achieve an "understanding" with Russia and China to limit arms deliveries to their ally; finally, the draft agreement would permit the United States to withdraw it troops, recover its prisoners, and support its friends in Saigon in a dignified manner.

Kissinger also took pains to point out to Thieu that there was no time like the present for coming to terms with the North Vietnamese; the draft agreement, if signed now, would leave Thieu with a military force of one million men and control of about eighty-five percent of South Vietnam's nineteen million people. Even though the agreement would leave scattered parts of the thinly populated countryside in Communist hands and allow the PRG to have token representation in Saigon, Kissinger maintained that Thieu could survive and even prosper in the postwar period.

"This is a good agreement," Kissinger summed up, "worthy of our joint efforts." He did not go into detail about the still-unresolved portions of the agreement, and he told Thieu nothing about the timetable for initialing in Hanoi and signature in Paris.

Thieu, for his part, showed no outward emotion. He smiled courteously and promised Kissinger that he would study the draft agreement. A second meeting was scheduled for early evening.

Kissinger left the palace encouraged by Thieu's reaction. He failed to understand that the Vietnamese, like other Asians, prefer to avoid direct personal confrontation. Rather than say no, they will often respond with an ambiguous nod. Kissinger assumed that Thieu would consult with his advisers, with key members of the National Assembly, with his corps commanders, and ultimately concede the virtues of the agreement — all this, Kissinger hoped, within forty-eight hours. Kissinger smiled at the assembled newsmen standing in the torrid Saigon sun, but said nothing. He stepped into his waiting limousine and drove the few blocks down Duong Thong Nhat to the American Embassy. Foreign Service officers and secretaries applauded Kissinger as he entered the lobby. A few summoned up the courage to ask him to autograph their copies of his picture in *Dai Dan Toc*. Kissinger, in good humor, obliged.

At the palace, the mood was grim. Thieu was, to quote one of his closest aides, "ticked off." He felt that Kissinger had not dealt with him in good faith. True, he had been informed through his emissary in Paris that the Kissinger-Tho talks had reached a climactic stage on October 8, and the "high points" of the negotiations had been cabled to him from Paris. But not until the morning session, just concluded, had he ever seen the actual draft, and this offended him. He asked Nha to study the text and to convene a special meeting of Saigon's National Security Council for midafternoon.

Of all the Vietnamese close to Thieu, Nha was the closest. Thieu's cousin and adopted nephew, Nha represented, at thirty-one, a new generation of Vietnamese nationalists: American- rather than French-trained — a graduate of the University of Pittsburgh, class of 1966; Thieu's specialist on the United States, even though Nha's relations with local Americans were so limited and, at times, so strained that some officials in the U.S. Embassy referred to him privately as "that punk kid" — "a social climber who is making the most out of being Thieu's relative." Nha served as Thieu's Kissinger, keeping a wary lookout for anything that he suspected might imperil his homeland; his overriding obligation, he felt, was to the survival of South Vietnam at an agonizing moment when the Americans were exhausted with the war and the North Vietnamese were pressing their advantage.

While Thieu was meeting with members of the National Assembly and assuring them that he would not be pressured into a settlement, Nha began to go through the draft agreement that Kissinger had given Thieu earlier that morning.

"My God," Nha reacted, after he had read the draft several times, "this is not an agreement!" Several of the articles struck him as "very incomplete" and "very inconsistent," others as "downright very bad." He quickly reported his impressions to Thieu and the NSC. One point in particular aroused his curiosity and anxiety. Just what was meant by "administrative structure"? In English, the phrase sounded harmless enough, but in Vietnamese, it could take on a threatening significance. "I suspect," he said, "that the Communists must mean some kind of 'governmental' structure." In the palace's anticoalition view, it was only a short hop from "administrative" to "governmental." Thieu cut short the session. "We'll ask Dr. Kissinger," he said.

At seven o'clock that evening, Kissinger and Bunker returned to the palace. Thieu asked for a copy of the draft agreement in the *Vietnamese* language. There were some problems, he explained, but perhaps they were simply linguistic. Kissinger apologized; he promised the President that a Vietnamese-language draft would be delivered to the palace later that night. What about this "administrative structure"? Thieu asked. Meaningless, Kissinger replied; *it* has no power and, besides, *you* have the real power of the veto. Thieu nodded, noncommittally.

As Kissinger drove back to Bunker's residence, he still believed he could win Thieu's endorsement in time to keep his secret pledge to Tho. He had twenty-four hours left.

Friday morning's meeting opened with the usual polite handshakes and greetings. But the doubts and resentments that had built up during the night on the Vietnamese side quickly became apparent. "Dr. Kissinger," began President Thieu, "why did you not give us any advance word on the draft agreement?" Kissinger responded softly, his deep voice barely audible. He wanted to deliver it in person, he explained. It was too sensitive, too historic an agreement, to be entrusted to the regular diplomatic couriers or to be cabled through normal diplomatic channels. Thieu's implied accusation — that the United States and North Vietnam had negotiated behind Saigon's back — put Kissinger suddenly on the defensive.

Thieu forged on, both he and Kissinger tautly correct. During the next hour, Thieu focused on what he regarded as three major obstacles that had been uncovered in his reading of the Vietnamese text of the draft agreement.

To begin with, what was this "National Council of Reconciliation and Concord"? Was it an administrative structure, a governmental structure, or a coalition? In English, the words "national council" could not really be interpreted as a "coalition." But in Vietnamese, there was confusion. Was the proper Vietnamese term to be *co cau chinh quyen* — which meant, literally, *governmental structure:* power running from a central authority down to the local hamlets; or was the proper term *co cau hanh chinh* — which meant *administrative structure:* not power but a table of organization running from top to bottom? Actually, Kissinger and Tho had debated the distinction between these two Vietnamese terms, and Kissinger had insisted that the Vietnamese term closer to the English meaning was *co cau hanh chinh,* or administrative structure. Tho had seemed to agree, but Kissinger, in a hurry to complete the negotiations, had not painstakingly checked out the term that the North Vietnamese finally included in the Vietnamese text. "It just went flying past us, it was too fast," one of the American negotiators explained. The term Tho had inserted was fine for Tho, but not for Thieu and Kissinger. *Co cau chinh quyen* had been used in the Vietnamese text, and Thieu, Nha, and the other South Vietnamese immediately assumed that either Tho and Kissinger had conspired to deceive Saigon, or that Kissinger himself had been deceived by Tho. "There is no doubt about it," Thieu concluded. The agreement, in his view, called for a *"governmental* structure" — a coalition with the Communists: *co cau chinh quyen.* Unacceptable.

Second, the agreement referred to "three Vietnamese states": North Vietnam intact, and South Vietnam divided into two parts, with Saigon administering the areas under its control and the Vietcong the areas under its control. Thieu refused categorically to yield sovereignty over any part of South Vietnam. The occupation of South Vietnamese territory by North Vietnamese troops was illegal, he insisted; it had been achieved only at gunpoint. No legitimate agreement could sanction aggression. How could Kissinger have agreed to such a concession?

Finally, Thieu raised still another vital issue: there was no mention of a North Vietnamese military withdrawal from South Vietnam. Why not?

Kissinger took on the questions, one after the other. The "coalition" difficulty? That, he insisted, was a "misunderstanding" that could be easily cleared up in another session with Le Duc Tho. The "three Vietnamese states"? Another "misunderstanding"; but, in any case, what practical significance did the phrase have? President Thieu had a million-man army and American backing. The "pullout of North Vietnamese troops"? Yes, this was a problem — but not a new one; ever since the fall of 1970, the United States had given up its insistence on a with-drawal of Communist forces. Moreover, these in-country forces would tend to wither away since the agreement banned the introduction of replacement troops.

The Vietnamese later charged that Kissinger "put a smoke screen in front of us." Thieu was politely adamant. He demanded complete, satis-fying answers. "If we sign this agreement," Nha said, "we are going to look ridiculous. We are going to look as though we surrendered to the Communists." Kissinger, controlling his anger, conceded that Thieu had raised several valid questions, and he accepted Thieu's recommendation that the two sides compose a "study group" to try to resolve these problems. The group, under Foreign Minister Lam's direction, would meet the next day.

Kissinger returned to Bunker's residence, disappointed, agitated. Still, he felt, Thieu would eventually come around. "He probably has to con-sult with his corps commanders once again," Kissinger remarked to an aide.

Still, it was clear that Kissinger's timetable, so carefully negotiated with Tho, would have to be revised once more. In the name of the Presi-dent, Kissinger sent an apologetic cable to Hanoi, proposing still another delay. A few more days were required, he explained, to settle a number of problems. He anticipated no fundamental difficulty, he said, and he there-fore recommended a third timetable: October 23 for an end to the American bombing and mining, October 24 for the initialing in Hanoi, and October 31 for the signing in Paris. Much to Kissinger's relief, Hanoi reacted quickly and positively. The new timetable was accepted, but the North Vietnamese warned that the "U.S. side must not advance any pretext to change the schedule again."

The Vietnamese NSC met again in midafternoon on that Friday. This time Vietnamese texts of the draft agreement were analyzed. Nha, as rapporteur, went over the document point by point. After an hour and forty-five minutes, the NSC members had come up with no less than twenty-six changes. "And that," as one of them later said, "was just at first glance."

On Thursday, October 21, against the background of a series of VC and NVA attacks throughout the country, the top American and South Viet-namese negotiators, with the exception of Thieu, gathered at the residence of Foreign Minister Lam at 57 Hong Thap Tu, a busy, well-guarded thoroughfare not far from the presidential palace.

"Dr. Kissinger," the Foreign Minister began, "I suggest we start this meeting with a small prayer." Kissinger could not conceal a weary smile. "Lord," the Foreign Minister intoned, in his French-accented English, "bless this meeting between the representatives of the Republic of South Vietnam and Dr. Henry Kissinger." One of Kissinger's aides later recalled: "I knew we were heading for a blowup."

Nha was the first to speak. "Dr. Kissinger," he began, "here is our checklist. There are twenty-six changes we want to make in the draft agreement." Kissinger was stunned, but he controlled his temper. "Let's hear them," he said. One after the other, Nha ticked off the points in dispute, some minor, others significant. Kissinger, after a while, succeeded in explaining away most of their objections, but he had obvious difficulty with six points: the "administrative structure," the "three Indochinese states," the omission of any reference to a withdrawal of North Vietnamese forces from the south, the right to self-determination, the use of Cambodia and Laos for the routing of troops and supplies, and finally the reestablishment of a firm demilitarized zone between the two Vietnams.

Kissinger sought to play down the importance of these points. "Structure?" he asked rhetorically. "Remember, you have a veto."

"North Vietnamese troops in the country? Well, let's be realistic; they're there."

"The three Indochinese states? A typographical error."

"That's hard to believe," Nha retorted. "You had experts there, and interpreters, and you made the same mistake twice in the same text. No, Dr. Kissinger, that was no typographical error."

Tensions mounted. "We have fought this war for fifteen years – to accept this?" Nha was angry. "It would be like surrendering to the Communists. We cannot sign this agreement."

After three hours, it was clear that Kissinger and Nha were at loggerheads. The meeting was adjourned. One Vietnamese later described Kissinger and Nha as "two sparring partners." "Kissinger," he said, "is like Richelieu. He has brains, fantastic brains, but you wonder if he has a heart. When we pressed him on these points, he blew his fuse, and it revealed the weakness of the man – that he can be easily duped by the Communists." An American negotiator looking back on that period observed, "What we did to the South Vietnamese that October offended them in eighty-five different ways."

Kissinger returned to the Embassy in an angry mood. He paced from one room to the next, his jacket off, tie askew, snapping orders to his aides, popping candy into his mouth. His grand design for a preelection deal that he believed was in the best interest of both the United States and South Vietnam seemed out of reach. The grudging respect he once had for Thieu vanished. "Who the hell does he think he is?" Kissinger exclaimed. "When someone tries to thwart the will of Henry Kissinger, you become aware of the incredible size of his ego," one source close to the negotiations observed. Kissinger had made a promise to Tho and felt an obligation to deliver; Thieu could not be allowed to undercut his credibility or his strategy.

The biweekly flight from Hanoi to Vientiane was warming up, ready to take off. It was noontime at Gia Lam International Airport, across the old Daumier Bridge from the North Vietnamese capital. De Borchgrave, his interview with Premier Pham Van Dong tucked in his attaché case, was waiting for his old friend Mohammed Maklouf, the Egyptian Chargé d'Affaires, to join him for a farewell cup of coffee. At the last moment, Maklouf raced into the departure lounge. He apologized for being late, but explained that he, and all the other foreign diplomats in Hanoi, had been summoned to the Foreign Ministry at 6:30 A.M. They were informed that a cease-fire agreement between the United States and North Vietnam was ready for signature, and they were asked to advise their countries to exert pressure on President Nixon to sign before election day, November 7. Although the North Vietnamese had approved Kissinger's proposal for another delay, they assumed that the United States was stalling — using Thieu as a pretext for Nixon's own unwillingness to wrap up the deal before his reelection. Maklouf told de Borchgrave that he had radiotelephoned the news and the request to President Sadat via Peking. He then chuckled. "This shows you how out of touch the North Vietnamese really are. They think we have influence in Washington."

The arrival of the ICC plane from Hanoi, three hundred miles to the northeast, is one of the bigger social events in remote Vientiane; there is always the possibility of picking up some gossip or information from the North Vietnamese capital, and local diplomats often turn up at Wattay Airport to welcome the four-engine, propeller-driven Boeing 307. G. McMurtrie Godley, the U.S. Ambassador to the "Land of the Million Elephants," was there to welcome de Borchgrave. "How did it go?" he

asked, as the two men climbed into the Embassy limousine. "Fantastic,"
replied de Borchgrave. "Dong told me that American prisoners would
start being released before the withdrawal of American troops is completed, and that a three-sided coalition would be set up, probably without Thieu." Godley was astonished. "Let's call Bill Sullivan in Saigon,"
he said, reaching for the car's radiotelephone. Within a matter of minutes,
via back-channel routing through the Embassy, Sullivan was on the line.
From his limousine racing down a roadway skirting the northern bank
of the Mekong River, Godley gave his State Department colleague a
quick fill-in on de Borchgrave's report. "Do you think he should talk to
Henry?" Godley asked. "He's standing right here," replied Sullivan. De
Borchgrave then got on the hookup and told Kissinger the details of his
trip to Hanoi: how he had interviewed the Premier, how the North
Vietnamese leader had specified that about half the interview was off
the record, how de Borchgrave assessed its significance. Kissinger asked
for a "drop copy" of the entire interview to be rushed to the Embassy
in Saigon.

Two hours later, Kissinger and Sullivan were poring over both parts of
the interview — the off-the-record part and the on-the-record part; *Newsweek*, because of the urgency of the material, would release the on-the-
record part as a news story at 6 P.M., Washington time, October 21, one
full day before it was published in the magazine. What Kissinger read
sent him into a rage. Dong's reference to a "three-sided *coalition* of
transition," plus his statement that "Thieu has been overtaken by events,"
was *not* what he had negotiated with Le Duc Tho in Paris. Sullivan,
equally stunned, figured that either the North Vietnamese were "did-
dling" the Americans or else there was a "genuine misunderstanding."
Either way, Kissinger suddenly had the sinking feeling that he was
caught in an obstructionist cross fire — from Thieu, who was resisting the
agreement, and from Dong, who was giving it new dimensions. He felt
beleaguered, his timetable was threatened, his grand scheme in jeopardy.
But having traveled so far down the road toward a settlement, he persisted in searching for a new way out of the trap.
He decided that he would show Thieu the interview. He suggested that
Bunker telephone Nha and ask for an appointment. "The President is too
busy," Nha replied. "The Communists are attacking close to Saigon."
Kissinger took the phone. "I must speak with President Thieu," Kissinger
persisted. "This is very important. There has been a new development.
I must see him." Nha was immovable. There was no point to a meeting

unless Kissinger had the answers to Saigon's questions. Did he? Kissinger hesitated. Then there is no point to a meeting, Nha reiterated. In desperation, Kissinger proposed a meeting for the next morning — Sunday — at the presidential palace. Just the four of them — Kissinger, Bunker, Thieu, and Nha. Completely confidential. 8 A.M. Agreed? Agreed.

By now, Kissinger's protracted stay in Saigon had touched off feverish speculation that the talks were dealing with the most sensitive issue of the future of South Vietnam. Reporters besieged the U.S. Embassy, but the staff provided the sort of empty information that only intensified the curiosity of the press. "All I can tell you," one spokesman said, "is that these are the most important diplomatic negotiations of the last two decades." He also disclosed that Sullivan had slipped off to Vientiane and Bangkok, thereby implying that a "peace" agreement might apply to all of Indochina.

At dawn on October 22 — "damned early for me on a Sunday morning" — Nha was awakened by a telephone call from a South Vietnamese Embassy official in Washington. The de Borchgrave interview with Pham Van Dong had just been released, and the official wanted to inform President Thieu of its contents, particularly the Premier's references to the "positive evolution" of the negotiations and the setting up of a "three-sided coalition of transition." Nha immediately telephoned Thieu. "I knew it," Nha exploded. "Kissinger is trying to trick us." "Maybe," Thieu replied, "or maybe he is being duped."

At 8 A.M., Kissinger and Bunker entered the President's office. Thieu opened the session. "We don't think this agreement is acceptable to us," he began, "and we don't think we can sign it in its present form." Referring to the twenty-six objections raised by his government, he said, "Some of the points are minor, but several are major. To sign would be like surrendering to the Communists. It would make a mockery of the thousands of Americans and Vietnamese who died here."

Kissinger calmly repeated his arguments — about the veto that Thieu would enjoy, the million-man force under his command, the continuing American aid. Thieu just as calmly rejected them all.

There were three principal objections, the South Vietnamese leader emphasized. "First," he said, "we oppose the 'council' because it is now clear that it is really a 'coalition.' Second, we cannot agree to the continued presence of North Vietnamese troops in our country. Third, we cannot accept a demilitarized zone through which the North Vietnamese can move back and forth. We cannot sign the agreement."

Kissinger diplomatically disputed Thieu's logic and offered several formulas designed to overcome South Vietnamese objections. He showed Thieu a copy of the Dong interview and pointed to those segments in which the North Vietnamese Premier said, "We have done everything humanly possible for a successful conclusion. . . . Our intentions are serious. . . . A peaceful settlement must be just for both sides. . . ." Thieu read it, but his eye also hit on the word "coalition" and the sentence "Thieu has been overtaken by events." In them, Thieu found additional reason for refusing to sign the agreement.

But Thieu did not want to appear too negative. He agreed in principle to the idea of a cease-fire-in-place. In fact, he asserted that he was ready to entertain all formulas for "peace," but he wanted to examine them "on paper." Magazine and newspaper interviews were not what he wanted. "And don't tell us," he pointedly told Kissinger, "that you can work out a secret understanding with Tho. We want no secret understandings with the Communists. We know the Communists well. They violate everything they sign."

Thieu finally put the ultimate question to Kissinger: how could *he* have agreed to such a draft? Kissinger repeated his belief that he thought it was a good agreement.

By now, it was almost 10 A.M. Kissinger was scheduled to depart for Phnom Penh, a half-hour flight from Saigon, to confer with Cambodia's embattled President Lon Nol. Thieu requested that Kissinger return by 5 P.M., and he agreed. He shook hands with Thieu and Nha and left for the airport.

Accompanied by Sullivan and Negroponte, Kissinger flew to Pochentong Airport in Phnom Penh in an Air Force T-39, a small twin-engine jet courier. They helicoptered directly to Lon Nol's official residence, where for four hours Kissinger discussed Cambodia's role in the unfolding negotiations. The situation in that country was critical; about two-thirds of Cambodia was then in the hands of "the other side," not to mention the sanctuaries the NVA and the VC still maintained along the border with South Vietnam — the very same sanctuaries that U.S. troops had moved into in the spring of 1970. Lon Nol promised to proclaim a cease-fire in his country the moment one was proclaimed in South Vietnam. For his part, Kissinger promised that American military and economic aid to Lon Nol's regime would continue. A cease-fire in Cambodia would acquire significance, Kissinger knew, only if there was a cease-fire in neighboring South Vietnam — a prospect that was becoming increasingly elusive.

While Kissinger was in Phnom Penh, Thieu had conferred once again with key military and legislative leaders and assured them that he would not accept a "three-sided coalition" government that had been brought to Saigon as part of "a prefabricated package" — a contemptuous reference to the draft worked out between Kissinger and Tho.

Five o'clock found the four key men — Kissinger, Bunker, Thieu and Nha — in the President's office. Thieu began by making it clear to Kissinger that he could not sign this "unacceptable" agreement. "It is not a question of dragging our feet," Nha interjected, an allusion to accusations that Thieu had done just that in late 1968 by refusing to join the Americans at the Paris peace talks. "We want to be very cooperative, but you yourself have not given us adequate answers to these questions, so how can we accept?" "If necessary," Thieu added, "we will fight alone."

Kissinger was "apoplectic," according to one Vietnamese observer. "I've succeeded in Peking, Moscow, and Paris," Kissinger was quoted as saying. "How can I fail here?"

"You cannot be impatient, Dr. Kissinger," Thieu said, "or the Communists will blackmail you. This is not a good agreement. If I were to sign it, there would be bloodshed in Vietnam in six months." Kissinger implied that the United States might cut off aid. Thieu showed his contempt for Kissinger's argument by turning around to look at the maps on the wall, leaving Kissinger talking to the back of his head. "We still will not sign the agreement," Thieu repeated. Kissinger then raised the possibility that the United States might sign a separate peace with North Vietnam. Thieu was unyielding. "We had better fight for six more months, out of our remaining resources, and die — than sign this agreement and die now."

"You're a giant," Thieu then told Kissinger, according to Italian journalist Oriana Fallaci. "So you can probably afford the luxury of being easy in this agreement. I cannot. A bad agreement means nothing to you. What do those three hundred thousand North Vietnamese [in the south] mean to you? Nothing. What is the loss of South Vietnam if you look at it on the world's map? Just a speck. The loss of South Vietnam may even be good for you. . . . It may be good to contain China, good for your world strategy. But . . . a little Vietnamese doesn't play with a strategic map of the world. . . . For us, it isn't a question of choosing between Moscow and Peking. It's a question of choosing between life and death."

Kissinger could not afford to be moved by Thieu's lectures. He stared into the face of deadlock. "I'm not going to come back to South Vietnam," the Vietnamese remember him as saying. "This is the greatest diplomatic failure of my career!" Nha glanced at Kissinger. "I'm sorry about that, but we have a country to defend."

"I shall have to return to Washington for new instructions," Kissinger finally said.

"While there, please convey our concern to President Nixon about those three basic principles," Thieu emphasized, rendering his final, devastating judgment, "because if we don't get a satisfactory answer, then we do not accept or sign the agreement."

The meeting was over. Kissinger shook Thieu's hand — avoiding Nha — and stormed out of the room, Bunker bringing up the rear. He had Thieu's agreement, in principle, for a cease-fire-in-place, but he had nothing else.

Kissinger returned to Bunker's residence and immediately dispatched an urgent cable to Nixon, explaining the deadlock and, in effect, recommending a separate peace with Hanoi if Thieu's foot-dragging continued. To Kissinger's surprise, Nixon rejected the recommendation; he ruled out a separate peace — at least, for the time being — and instructed Kissinger to cool his confrontation with Thieu and to reassure him that the United States and South Vietnam would remain allies in common pursuit of peace. Kissinger, no longer freewheeling, experienced the constraint of a traditional diplomat on a short tether. What do we tell Hanoi? he asked. The President told him to send Tho still another message, which, while not explicitly reneging on the U.S. promise to sign the agreement by October 31, indicated that it was going to be difficult to meet the deadline. To sugarcoat Tho's anticipated disappointment and underscore U.S. determination to complete an agreement quickly, Kissinger was also to inform Tho that the United States would stop all military activities north of the twentieth parallel on October 25.

At 8 A.M. Monday morning, Kissinger returned to the presidential palace to say good-bye to Thieu. He hoped that Thieu might have changed his mind overnight. The two men reviewed their respective negotiating positions, but it was clear that the distance separating them had not narrowed. Thieu gave Kissinger a letter for Nixon, spelling out

South Vietnamese reservations about the draft. Thieu repeated that he was willing to strike a deal with North Vietnam, but only when the deal was right. Kissinger stressed that the United States still wanted to conclude the war on a note of allied harmony and on a basis of justice and fairness for all.

Kissinger then sped from the palace to the airport. Newsmen and photographers were kept about fifty yards from the blue and white jet. Kissinger arrived, glanced toward the cameras, and, after a slight pause, approached the press. His diplomatic radar warned him that a dejected expression might send discouraging signals to a world expecting a peace agreement. Smiling expansively, he shook the hand of a young woman reporter with long black hair. "I came over here," he said, "only to see you."

"Was it a good trip?" a reporter asked.

"Yes," he replied.

"Was it productive?"

"Yes. It always is when I come here."

"Are you coming back?"

Kissinger didn't answer. He just flashed his diplomatic smile.

By the time Kissinger's jet reached its cruising altitude for the long flight to Washington, the U.S. Embassy released a bland statement. "We have made progress. Talks will continue between us and the Government of Vietnam. It is not in the interest of negotiations to be more specific at this time." Kissinger had cleared every word. *Tin Song*, the Saigon daily financed by Nha, was more candid. "The general impression among observers," it observed editorially, "was that the negotiations between the Republic of Vietnam and the United States had been conducted in a very heated atmosphere in the face of unyielding Vietnamese determination to stand pat on its position."

Thieu's trump card in his dealings with Kissinger was the power of his weakness. He knew that the Americans feared that if they pushed the South Vietnamese too hard and too fast, the corrupt, undermotivated military and bureaucratic structure of South Vietnam might come tumbling down — with a crash that would endanger the withdrawal of U.S. forces. In that event, Nixon's repeated pledges of "peace with honor," would explode in his face. It was Thieu's awareness of his ability to create such a scenario of disaster that had emboldened him to thwart Kissinger's scheme for ending the war. The South Vietnamese President was angling for more arms, more aid, more time from the

United States. He felt he had to condition his own people to the idea of "peace." In a sense, war had become a way of life for the Vietnamese. For a quarter of a century, they had fought — but never alone, always at the side of the "white man" who they felt had nothing but contempt for them. Thieu, recognizing that the Americans were indeed leaving, wanted to protract their stay as long as possible — to give him more time to strengthen the country's infrastructure not only for the political war to come but the military war that he was certain would continue.

Later that very long Monday, on his way back to Washington, Kissinger sent another cable to Tho. This time he dropped all references — implicit and explicit — to the October 31 deadline. He emphasized the need for another negotiating session in Paris, citing three contributing factors: "difficulties in Saigon," "ambiguities" raised by the Pham Van Dong interview, and "signs" that the Communists might be preparing for a land-grabbing operation immediately after a cease-fire was proclaimed.

When Kissinger returned to Washington that night, he warned the President that Hanoi might develop second thoughts about the deal because of all the delays in the implementation timetable, but he pointed out that Dong and Thieu had each raised awkward questions about the agreement that would have to be clarified and resolved before it could be signed. He concluded that there was no way the deal could be completed before election day. Nixon did not seem disturbed. The polls were predicting a landslide. Most Americans, observing the diplomatic flurry of the past few weeks, assumed that the end of the war was near. Kissinger sensed that the President did not want a preelection deal if the price was an open rupture between Washington and Saigon, with the possibility of a disastrous aftermath.

On Tuesday, October 24, the morning after Kissinger's return to Washington, White House spokesman Ronald Ziegler announced that the President, Kissinger and Rogers had met for an hour to review the latest efforts in Saigon and Paris to achieve a negotiated settlement. "We are making some progress," Ziegler said; but he cautioned against "excessive speculation."

The reason for Ziegler's guarded remarks soon became apparent; President Thieu, in Saigon, had just gone on television to tell the South Vietnamese people about his bitter negotiations with Kissinger. In a two-hour television report, Thieu, tense and nervous, speaking at times from notes and at times extemporaneously, said that the proposals negotiated between the Americans and the North Vietnamese in Paris were unacceptable.

While he acknowledged that there might soon be a standstill cease-fire in South Vietnam, he stressed that his regime would never accept a coalition government, nor the presence of "three hundred thousand" North Vietnamese troops in the south. "If a coalition is created," he argued, "within less than one year, not five thousand nor fifty thousand nor five hundred thousand but five million people will be killed by the Communists." And he added: "As of now, no agreement has been reached or signed . . . and nobody can do anything on our behalf or force us to follow their decisions."

The North Vietnamese spokesman in Paris immediately issued a blanket denunciation of Thieu's report. He charged that Thieu "obstinately opposes peace and national concord." But he claimed that Thieu was not acting on his own. "The United States Government uses Nguyen Van Thieu as its zealous mouthpiece in its policy of prolonging the war and obstructing serious negotiations aimed at a rapid, peaceful settlement of the Vietnamese problem," he said. Kissinger sensed that Hanoi might be preparing a dramatic move but he was not quite sure what kind — military or diplomatic.

Since Kissinger's return to Washington, just about every diplomatic reporter in town had been trying to get through to him to find exactly what was going on. Among them was Max Frankel, then Washington bureau chief of the *New York Times*. On Tuesday, he had had no luck. Midmorning, Wednesday, October 25, there was suddenly a call from Kissinger's office.

"My lunch date just fell through," the presidential adviser said. "How about lunch today?" Frankel quickly accepted. Kissinger suggested twelve-thirty, at the Sans Souci, his favorite restaurant, a block away from the White House.

Over their small table, Kissinger conveyed to Frankel the impression that he was on the brink of a major achievement. On the immediate horizon, Kissinger implied, was a Vietnam peace, the objective that *Times* editorial writers and others who saw the war as a senseless tragedy had been advocating for years — a peace, in other words, that could unite both doves and hawks and reunify the country. The President, Kissinger said, deserved praise, not criticism, from the *Times*.

Frankel began to probe for specifics. Kissinger sketched the broad outline of a deal. A cease-fire was imminent. Troops out, prisoners back.

Thieu was to control most of the countryside and all of the population centers. The Communists were to get to keep pockets of territory that would be recognized as VC preserves, protected by the hundred and forty-five thousand North Vietnamese troops that the United States estimated Hanoi had in the south. Mixed political committees were to be established to come up with a new constitution and new elections. And much more.

Frankel walked Kissinger back to the White House. Later that afternoon, he telephoned to double-check the lunchtime details. Often in such circumstances Kissinger might claim that what he had revealed was "off the record" or "just for your guidance." This time, he confirmed the information, and it was soon in type, ready for the *Times*'s front page.

At 5:47 P.M., Washington time, Hanoi Radio interrupted its normal broadcasting to announce that there would soon be "an important statement" from the Government of North Vietnam. This alert was picked up by FBIS, the Foreign Broadcast Information Service, a monitoring system supervised by the CIA for the private information of government officials. Hanoi-watchers did not get overly excited. "Important statements," in their experience, related as often to agricultural policy as to foreign policy. Hours passed without amplification.

When Howard K. Smith, Washington anchor man for the "ABC Evening News," finished his broadcast that night, he went to the White House to talk with Kissinger. He, too, got a rundown on the negotiations — perhaps not every detail but enough to make a surefire opening for his newscast the following evening. As it turned out, Hanoi was to provide him with a better lead.

At 1:46 A.M., Thursday, October 26, Hanoi's propaganda bomb exploded on FBIS — a twenty-five-hundred-word government statement that revealed the terms of the nine-point Vietnam agreement, plus the details of the secret negotiations that led up to it. "At a private meeting on 8 October, 1972," Hanoi disclosed dramatically, "the DRVN side took a new, extremely important initiative: it put forward a draft Agreement on Ending the War and Restoring Peace in Vietnam." The "American side itself admitted that the draft agreement" was "an important and very fundamental document which opened the way to an early settlement." After summarizing the nine points, Hanoi further disclosed that "at the proposal of the U.S. side," the two sides had set up a timetable — twice postponed by the U.S. — calling for signature of the completed document on October 31.

In a reference to Kissinger's message of October 23, Hanoi charged that by deferring signature indefinitely, and claiming "difficulties in Saigon," the U.S. had "created a very serious situation." Everyone knew, Hanoi went on, that Thieu was a U.S. "tool for sabotaging all peace solutions to the Vietnam problem." Accusing the Nixon Administration of lacking "goodwill," Hanoi demanded that the agreement be signed, as agreed, on October 31.

With this stunning broadcast, the North Vietnamese ripped the veil of secrecy off the most secret of negotiations. They had pulled a trick out of Nixon's own repertoire. In January, 1972, the President had broken a pledge of secrecy by revealing Kissinger's secret meetings in Paris with Le Duc Tho, hoping with that disclosure to snap the deadlock in the negotiations and, if possible, to bolster sagging popularity polls at home. Now Hanoi, possibly worried that the United States had trapped them into concessions without any real intention of coming through with a pre-election signature, tried to seize the propaganda initiative and to force the President to sign the document that Kissinger and Tho, on October 12, had jointly hailed as all but complete. "Peace is at the end of a pen," a North Vietnamese spokesman declared. "All that remains is for the United States to grasp that pen."

At 2 A.M., a ringing telephone broke into Kissinger's sleep. It was Haig, relaying the news of the Hanoi broadcast that he had just received from the White House Situation Room. Kissinger quickly called Nixon, then Sullivan. Sullivan, as it turned out, did not have to be awakened. His son, a college student, had called from the West coast with the news only moments before. He had picked it up on the radio. "Don't stand anyone to a round of drinks just yet," Sullivan cautioned his son.

For the next three hours, Kissinger, Haig and Sullivan were hooked into a series of conference calls, trying to figure out how to respond to Hanoi's maneuver. These three veterans of the Vietnam negotiations believed at first that Hanoi's purpose was to torpedo the negotiations but quickly concluded that Hanoi meant simply to pressure the U.S. into signing the agreement by October 31. Sullivan recommended that Kissinger hold a news conference in the morning — basically to assure North Vietnam that the United States was still committed to the October 8 formula for peace, even though a little more time was required.

By 7:30 A.M., Nixon and Kissinger were discussing strategy over breakfast. The President endorsed the news conference format for responding to the North Vietnamese. Private communications could have served the needs of diplomacy, but not the needs of public relations two weeks before a presidential election. Kissinger realized that his appearance before the press would provoke awkward political questions. He was sure to be asked, for example, why this same agreement could not have been reached four years earlier and he knew that his explanations might be received with some skepticism. But he wished to reaffirm the American commitment to an end to the war that was not pegged to the calendar of politics.

Kissinger had one persistent fear — that the leaders in Hanoi "might conclude that we had sprung one gigantic swindle on them — to expose their forces in the south, so that they could be destroyed." He felt that the United States was "never going to get this agreement unless we nail ourselves to it, and tell Saigon that this is it."

Kissinger would have preferred to hold the news conference in the afternoon, in the event any additional information surfaced, but the President opted for the morning — the sooner the better. The two men agreed that Kissinger would emphasize one theme — that the United States would stick to the essentials of the original agreement but would not be stampeded into signing by October 31. He would point out that there were still several problems which, while not major, could not be ignored; these could probably be resolved in another negotiating session of three or four days in Paris. The President did not necessarily know that his aide would utter four words that were destined to send America's spirits soaring and be featured in banner headlines around the world.

From 8:30 to 10 A.M., Kissinger, Haig and Sullivan reviewed the situation from all angles — Washington's, Saigon's, Hanoi's. Ziegler was eager to know when Kissinger wanted to begin. The networks — radio and television — preferred "live" coverage. Kissinger threw the "live" decision back at Ziegler; Ziegler threw it to Haldeman; Haldeman ruled it out. Live cameras, he implied, were for the President, not for Kissinger. The "when" was Kissinger's decision. Shortly after 10 A.M., he notified Ziegler that he would be ready in about an hour.

Alone in his office, Kissinger jotted down his thoughts on a single sheet of paper. He then picked up some documents and, at 11:35 A.M., walked into the White House briefing room, followed by Ziegler, Sullivan, and Haig.

"Ladies and gentlemen," he began, speaking slowly and clearing his throat often, "we have now heard from both Vietnams and it is obvious that the war that has been raging for ten years is drawing to a conclusion. . . .

"We believe that *peace is at hand*. We believe that an agreement is within sight."

Occasionally glancing down at his briefing paper, but more often peering into the television cameras filming his comments for later broadcast, Kissinger launched into a careful, analytical dissection of the state of the Vietnam negotiations. "Hanoi Radio," he said, had "correctly stated" the main elements of the October 8 proposal — the nine points that composed the agreement. "We have no complaint with the general description of events," he stated. But citing "certain concerns and certain ambiguities," Kissinger put some distance between Washington and Hanoi on one contentious problem — *when* the agreement would be signed. Hanoi's target date was October 31; Kissinger stressed that though October 31 had been a realistic date at one point, the United States now needed an extension of the deadline.

"What remains to be done can be settled in one more negotiating session with the North Vietnamese negotiators lasting, I would think, no more than three or four days, so we are not talking of a delay of a very long period of time." Deeper into his presentation, the "concerns" and "ambiguities" became "six or seven very concrete issues."

Among them were:

— the problem of discouraging a land-grabbing operation by the North Vietnamese;
— the problem of defining the powers and prerogatives of the International Commission for Control and Supervision;
— the problem of linking cease-fires in Laos and Cambodia with the one in South Vietnam;
— the problem of clarifying the comments of the North Vietnamese Premier in his interview with de Borchgrave;
— "linguistic problems" — a reference to the question of whether the National Council of Reconciliation and Concord was a "coalition government" or an "administrative structure";
— "technical problems" related to the Geneva Accords of 1954 involving the demilitarized zone between North and South Vietnam;

— and, finally, the problem of who should sign the agreement: just the U.S. and North Vietnam, as proposed by Hanoi? Or all four parties, as proposed by Kissinger?

"We remain convinced that the issues that I have raised are soluble in a very brief period of time. . . .

"Peace is within reach in a matter of weeks, or less, depending on when the meeting takes place."

Kissinger concluded his statement by reinforcing his three main points: "We will not be stampeded into an agreement until its provisions are right." (Hanoi, take note.) "We will not be deflected from an agreement when its provisions are right." (Saigon, take note.) "And with this attitude and with some cooperation from the other side, we believe that we can restore both peace and unity to America very soon." (Electorate, take note.)

The first question was political. Kissinger was asked why "this program could not have been achieved four years ago." He replied that there was no such possibility because "the other side consistently refused to discuss the separation of the political and military issues." The U.S. position, he noted, had always been two-tracked: first, to end the war; second, to have the two South Vietnamese sides jointly solve their own internal problems. The North Vietnamese, he said, "never accepted [it] four years ago, three years ago, or two months ago. . . . The first time it was accepted was on October 8. As soon as it was accepted, we completed within four days a rough draft of an agreement from which we have since been operating."

In answer to another question, Kissinger denied that the negotiations had anything to do with the election: "The implication that this is all a gigantic maneuver which we will revoke as soon as this period is over is unworthy of what we have gone through." He reaffirmed the Administration's commitment to the October 8 agreement, with certain modifications. "We have given a commitment that a text that will be agreed to at the next session will be the final text and that no new changes will be proposed." And he emphasized that though there might have been "an honest misunderstanding" regarding the October 31 target date, "the most significant aspect cannot be whether one signs on one date or another. The significant aspect is that when one is so close to an agreement, whether one perfects it and then signs it regardless of the deadline. There is no magic about any one date."

The news conference concluded at 12:35 P.M. "Peace is at hand" was the bulletin that ricocheted around the world within a matter of seconds. A sense of relief surged across the country. The families of POWs and servicemen rejoiced. Congress cheered. The stock market soared. Lost in the sudden exultation was Kissinger's mention of "nuances," "differences," and "six or seven concrete issues." It was a moment to savor the bitter-sweet mood of not-quite-peace; a moment to forget the statistics of war-not-quite-over. During Nixon's presidency alone: more than 15,000 Americans killed, over 110,000 wounded, over $50,000,000,000 spent, over 3,600,000 tons of American bombs dropped, over 600,000 South Vietnamese civilian dead and wounded, not to mention much higher ARVN, NVA, and VC casualties.

Even on such a triumphant day, Kissinger could not relax. From 3 to 4 P.M., he briefed TV reporters, amplifying his news conference remarks. From four to five, he returned calls from columnists, accepting congratulations and dispensing additional insights. From five to six, he conferred with columnist Joseph Kraft. From six o'clock on, he took calls from reporters. Again, he doled out supplementary details — most of which appeared in the papers, ascribed to "a senior White House official," or "Government sources." The next day, Kissinger received Henry Brandon of the London Sunday Times, and then, in turn, representatives of the New York Times, AP, UPI, Time and Newsweek. The day after, he met with Eric Sevareid and other prominent commentators. Altogether, he sought to build up an extraordinary journalistic momentum behind the idea of "peace is at hand" in the hope that it would help heal the nation's Vietnam wounds and convince the country that those extra four years of war could not be blamed on the Administration.

No other official was allowed to brief, not even the handful who knew about the negotiations. "Call Henry," they would counsel. "He'll talk to you." There was no cross-reference on any of these stories, no double check, no named source. This singular exercise in diplomacy, politics and public relations was based upon a paucity of sources and an abundance of trust in the integrity of one official who, at the pinnacle of his power, could control the entire flow of news about one story.

Six hours after Kissinger left the White House Press Room, a cable arrived from Hanoi. Le Duc Tho proposed an early resumption of the Paris negotiations; but, according to Kissinger, he mentioned no specific date. "One more negotiating session," Kissinger had just promised, in public; such a session, lasting "three or four days," would still produce a final peace agreement by election day, which is what Hanoi wanted — and would redeem Kissinger's pledge and projection of events. Nixon rejected Tho's proposal.

Some observers felt that, since Kissinger's "peace is at hand" statement, the President no longer needed peace in a hurry. Others suspected that Nixon was not only misleading the North Vietnamese, he was also misleading Kissinger, allowing him to race from one world capital to another in breakneck pursuit of a preelection trophy, accumulating more political points with each passing day of suspense — knowing all the while that the promise of peace was more valuable politically than a hastily concluded peace agreement. Such an agreement might have given rise to accusations that Nixon was playing politics with peace, after he had gone on record as saying that "the right kind of settlement" took precedence over votes.

Kissinger found himself caught between the President's unhurried pace and Tho's obvious readiness to negotiate. Kissinger would have preferred to resolve those "six or seven concrete issues" and sign the agreement the moment "its provisions were right," regardless of any "arbitrary deadlines . . . established by our own domestic processes," as he had explained at the October 26 press conference. Whatever his personal preferences, he played his assigned role. It was to lead him into the worst three months of his life.

FIFTEEN

The Vietnam Finale

I'M UNITING VIETNAM and both sides are screaming at me."

Henry Kissinger had just arrived at the National Day reception at the South Vietnamese Embassy on November 1, six days after his famous "peace is at hand" news conference. Instantly, he became the center of attention in a salon crowded with diplomats, generals, Senators, Congressmen, and journalists — all asking: *When?* "Newspapermen keep calling me every fifteen minutes taking my temperature," he joked. "And here they are, all around me, and it looks like I'm holding a press conference." People kept thrusting forward, shaking his hand, shouting congratulations; cameras kept clicking through it all. An unidentified woman slipped up to Kissinger's side and murmured: "Are you the *real* Henry Kissinger?" "That's what I'm told," replied the real Henry Kissinger. One of the final pictures was taken with Chiang Kai-shek's Ambassador to Washington, James Shen. "You don't want to get your picture taken with me and ruin yourself," joked Kissinger. "Now they won't let you back into Taiwan." "And now they won't let you back into Peking," countered Shen. "Think on that."

Kissinger moved toward the hors d'oeuvres table, which featured such delicacies as *chao-tom*, a shrimp paste wrapped around sugar cane and flavored with a pungent fish sauce called *nuoc-mam*. "I love Vietnamese food," he murmured; but the crowd was so thick that Kissinger never made it to the *chao-tom*, and he left after a respectable twenty-five-minute appearance.

Kissinger drove down Massachusetts Avenue to the White House, where the President was putting the finishing touches on a political speech scheduled for broadcast the following night. Only the week before, Kissinger had sent a surge of optimism through the nation and the world by suggesting that the end of the war required just "one more negotiating session." The President, in his November 2 address, seemed to draw back from that heady projection.

His tone was cautious — strikingly different from Kissinger's. Nixon agreed that "a major breakthrough" had been achieved and that "peace with honor" would "soon" be proclaimed. But it was clear that he envisaged a timetable extending well beyond Kissinger's "three or four days." "We are going to sign the agreement when the agreement is right, not one day before," he said, "and when the agreement is right, we are going to sign, without one day's delay."

There were other differences between Nixon and Kissinger. The President said his goal was a cease-fire throughout Indochina even though he knew the Kissinger-Tho draft agreement did not call for a cease-fire in Cambodia and Laos along with the cease-fire in South Vietnam. Moreover, Nixon placed his emphasis on "ambiguities," "details" and "central points," never once suggesting that they could be speedily resolved. Nixon concentrated on what still had to be done; Kissinger on what had already been done.

These differences were more than rhetorical. Although they both sought an end to U.S. involvement in Indochina, it became increasingly clear in early November that the President was going to try to set a higher price on a settlement than Kissinger believed was negotiable with the North Vietnamese. Thieu's almost daily denunciations of the draft agreement as "a sellout" seemed to reignite the President's cold-warrior instincts; if Hanoi was so eager to sign the agreement, then there must be something wrong with it.

In Nixon's band of loyalists, it was easy to find enemies of Kissinger, who were only too eager to expand on the defects of the agreement. Kissinger, for a combination of reasons, had accumulated more than his share: bureaucrats who were jealous of his successes, offended by his brusque intolerance, or who quite simply despised him. They were not reluctant to undercut his reputation as the Merlin of American diplomacy and to damage his professional relationship with the President.

There were Pentagon officials, close to Laird, who gave the President what they labeled as *confirmed* intelligence of a North Vietnamese plan for a massive land-grabbing operation in the south after the proclamation of a cease-fire. Only an adequately manned international police force, in position at the moment the shooting stopped, they argued, could frustrate such a scheme; and there was no provision for such a force. The implication was clear: Kissinger had been reckless. Rogers advanced the State Department's brief that the negotiating and drafting had been too quick and too sloppy. Even Haig, who had recently opened an independent channel to the President, complained that Kissinger had been gentle with Tho and brutal toward Thieu. But the most intensely anti-Kissinger criticism came from Haldeman and Ehrlichman, who allegedly began to spread the rumor that Kissinger had overstepped his authority during the negotiations, reaching what amounted to a private deal with Tho behind the President's back. Should a cease-fire collapse and Thieu be jeopardized, Kissinger was the obvious scapegoat.

Hanoi, Moscow and Peking knew nothing about this sniping — the juicy stuff of Washington's back corridors — but Communist officials in all three capitals sensed the differences in tone and emphasis between Kissinger, on October 26, and Nixon, on November 2. Strong reactions were inevitable.

Hanoi Radio accused the Administration of "hatching a dark, vile scheme to deceive the American people and to undermine attempts to settle the war." *Pravda* charged that the U.S. was "reneging on its commitment" to sign the Vietnam peace accord, thus "complicating the entire international situation." *Jenmin Jih Pao*, speaking for the Chinese Communist Party, questioned U.S. "sincerity," adding that "such issues as international supervision and the relationship between ending the war in Vietnam and a cease-fire throughout Indochina, far from being insignificant, are important issues of substance."

Cavernous U.S. Air Force C-5 cargo planes flew into Tan Son Nhut Airport with thundering regularity, and U.S. military cargo ships kept Saigon's dockhands working around the clock — all part of an unprecedented air and sea lift designed to give South Vietnam a year's worth of military supplies during the first three weeks of November. It was at this same time that U.S. bases throughout South Vietnam were turned over to the Saigon regime. These twin actions were a presidential assignment that the Pentagon carried out with remarkable efficiency. Not only were Air Force planes put to work but commercial cargo planes were chartered for the rush delivery. Among the war matériel were some ten thousand tons of tanks, armored personnel carriers, artillery, jet engines, ammunition, and spare parts. Inventories in the United States, South Korea, Taiwan, and Iran were tapped for one hundred and twenty F-5 jet fighter planes, ninety A-27 light attack bombers, thirty A-1 propeller-driven bombers, thirty C-130 Hercules transport planes, twenty AC-119 gunships, and two hundred and seventy helicopters. Virtually overnight, Saigon emerged with the fourth largest air force in the world — more than two thousand aircraft — even though its pilots had not yet been checked out to fly some of the more sophisticated planes.

When the North Vietnamese became aware of the dimensions of this American airlift, they denounced Nixon and Kissinger for "strengthening the Nguyen Van Thieu clique to prepare for new aggressions." It was an obvious accusation, but the crash delivery program was motivated by three considerations that had nothing to do with "new aggressions." To begin with, stocking up Thieu's arsenals to overflowing was an attempt to persuade him to go along with the U.S.; it was also a demonstration that the U.S. was a reliable ally that was not about to collude with an enemy at the expense of a friend. Moreover, both the air and sea lift and the turning over of U.S. bases to Saigon were designed to beat the timetable of the Kissinger-Tho draft agreement; once it became effective, the supply of arms would be limited to a one-to-one replacement basis, and all U.S. military installations in the south would have to be dismantled within sixty days. The bases were therefore turned over to the South Vietnamese before the agreement became operative. Kissinger, who had always believed in the positive power of weapons in any negotiations, hoped that a well-supplied Thieu would be more flexible about a cease-fire agreement.

In the first week of November, the President spent many hours in his hideaway office in the EOB consulting with Kissinger and formulating policy for the "final" phase of the negotiations. Whether it was going to last "three or four days" or longer, both men agreed that the end was near. They also agreed that Thieu's consent to a deal, while highly desirable, was not to be the decisive factor. They would make, according to Kissinger, "a genuinely major effort" to fashion an accord that Thieu could accept; they would even submit some of South Vietnam's major objections for renegotiation, even though they anticipated in advance that Tho would reject them. But if they succeeded in negotiating an accord *they* could accept, they would sign it.

They divided the issues into two categories: major and minor.
Into the major category, these items:

— working toward recognition of the demilitarized zone, described
by the 1954 Geneva Accords as a "provisional demarcation line —
pending the general elections which will bring about the unification of Vietnam," as an inviolate border separating the two Vietnams;

— arguing for a token withdrawal of North Vietnamese troops (one
early proposal called for the withdrawal of thirty-five thousand
troops from the two northernmost provinces of South Vietnam in
return for a "proportional reduction" in the size of the South Vietnamese army);

— pushing for a cease-fire throughout Indochina rather than in South
Vietnam alone;

— arranging for an international peacekeeping force, in place at the
time of the cease-fire and in sufficient strength to discourage and
monitor any large-scale violations of the agreement.

In the minor category, these items:

— clearing up "linguistic problems" — a reference to the requirement
that the Vietnamese- and English-language texts be in absolute
conformity so that there would not be even the slightest hint of
"coalition";

— arranging for all four parties to be present at the concluding ceremony and to sign the final document.

Kissinger anticipated no great obstacles to solving these problems.

His negotiating priorities sorted out, Kissinger undertook a series of
exchanges with Hanoi, resulting in a private agreement on November 4,
three days before the election, to resume the Paris negotiations on November 20. He was hopeful about the possibility of a quick settlement. For
one thing, Hanoi talked as though it wanted to settle. For another, the
new round of negotiations would bring together two diplomats who only
a few weeks earlier believed they had "peace" in hand; since then, the
credibility of each negotiator had suffered — Kissinger's as a result of

Nixon's refusal to meet the October 31 deadline in the face of Saigon's resistance; Tho's as a result of his inability to deliver to Hanoi's Politburo the cease-fire he thought he had negotiated with the Americans. The opportunity to recoup "peace" was now just a few weeks away.

The election on November 7 lived up to the pollsters' forecast: a landslide for Nixon, the greatest triumph of his political career; he had won forty-nine states, with more than sixty percent of the popular vote, in contrast to the thin plurality of seven-tenths of one percent that had carried him into the White House four years earlier. That only fifty-five percent of America's eligible voters — the lowest turnout in a presidential election since 1940 — actually went to the polls was a statistic lost in the drama of Nixon's overwhelming reelection; Watergate was in the background, Vietnam was a major issue. Two days later, an exclusive interview with Garnett D. Horner of Washington's *Evening Star and Daily News* was published, in which Nixon said he was "completely confident we are going to have a settlement" there. "You can bank on it."

There were signs in different parts of the world that the peace talks would soon be resumed. On November 10, Xuan Thuy told Agence France-Presse that Le Duc Tho would be returning to the French capital; he indicated that another meeting with Kissinger was possible if the United States did not plan to seek a "radical" change in the nine-point draft agreement. From Hanoi, AFP reported that American POWs were being readied for release. In Manila, a U.S. minesweeping flotilla was being assembled to clear North Vietnamese harbors. In Vientiane, Premier Souvanna Phouma met with Phoumi Vongvichit, Secretary-General of the Neo Lao Hak Xat, the political arm of the Communist-led Pathet Lao; it was their first significant effort to settle the sputtering war in Laos. From Saigon came word that General Haig had arrived, carrying a Nixon letter cataloging the new American negotiating position. The outcome of Haig's mission was of vital significance to Kissinger; it would determine his negotiating range during the upcoming talks with Tho.

Haig, accompanied by Ambassador Bunker, met with Thieu and Nha at the presidential palace for more than two hours on Friday, November 10. The urgency of their discussions was underscored by a second meeting held later in the day between Haig and Nha. The next day, the four principals conferred again for almost four hours. Conveying the views of the President, Haig pointed to the American airlift then under way as evidence of Nixon's friendship for Thieu and his commitment to an honorable settlement. Thieu expressed appreciation for the incoming matériel and congratulated the President on his reelection, but he predictably refused to compromise his own negotiating position. He insisted not on a token but a total pullout of North Vietnamese troops from the south, and he rejected any notion of private understandings as substitutes for written commitments. He was also unyielding in his demand that Hanoi recognize the DMZ as a clear line of demarcation between North and South Vietnam, and he ruled out the possibility of Saigon's ceding sovereignty over any portion of South Vietnam. All in all, it was an attempt to strengthen his own bargaining position at a time when the Americans seemed so eager to press ahead with a deal.

Haig once again emphasized Nixon's own determination to accept nothing less than an agreement that was worthy of the vast sacrifices made by both South Vietnam and the United States; then, in his soft-spoken way, he suggested that if such an agreement were reached with Hanoi, the United States would feel justified in signing it, with or without Saigon's approval. "The iceberg is marching on its way," one Embassy official later said, "and all this talk here in Saigon is not going to stop anything." By then, Haig had so endeared himself to the Saigon establishment that some Vietnamese officials were privately referring to him as "the little tyrant."

While these critical talks were under way in Saigon, Kissinger spent the weekend at Key Biscayne, where the President was relaxing at his bay-front home. One day, Kissinger told Robert C. Toth of the *Los Angeles Times* that he was growing impatient with Thieu's "minimum demand" for a total North Vietnamese withdrawal. Thieu knew that the United States had abandoned that position in October, 1970. If he had not been able to force the NVA out of the south even with massive U.S. air and ground support, Kissinger argued, how could he insist on their withdrawal now, when a cease-fire was imminent? It seemed clear that Kissinger intended to wrap up the agreement by the end of the month — or by early December, at the latest.

Haig departed from Saigon that same weekend, leaving the U.S. Embassy to announce that his talks with the South Vietnamese President had been "cordial and constructive" — which meant there were still problems — and leaving Foreign Minister Lam to tell a news conference that the U.S. and Saigon positions had come "closer together" — which meant there was still a considerable gap. After brief stops in Phnom Penh and Seoul, Haig arrived at Andrews Air Force Base at about five in the afternoon. Kissinger welcomed Haig as he descended from the ramp of his jet; together, they boarded a waiting helicopter and whirled up to Camp David, the mountaintop retreat to which Nixon had repaired after the seclusion of Key Biscayne. The essence of Haig's report was that Thieu was still "not on board." Nixon was not really surprised, but he reaffirmed his intention to place Thieu's demands before Tho — without allowing those demands to obstruct an agreement.

On November 14, Hanoi Radio announced that Le Duc Tho had left Hanoi for Paris. "Recently the U.S. side proposed another private meeting between the United States and the Democratic Republic of Vietnam to solve the question of signing the Agreement on Ending the War and Restoring Peace in Vietnam," the broadcast said. "Once again, to show its goodwill and seriousness, the DRVN has agreed with the above proposal of the U.S. side. The Vietnamese people want the U.S. Government to negotiate seriously, sincerely and frankly, because only in this way will the war be ended early and peace restored."

Kissinger showed the text of the broadcast to a reporter. "Tell your friend McGovern that we're going to have a peace agreement, probably in a few weeks." Kissinger's contempt was showing: "McGovern and Thieu," he said. "What a ticket to contend with!"

Tho arrived in Paris on November 17, after his usual one-day stopovers in Peking and Moscow. His working smile, so familiar to reporters and cameramen, was missing. His message to assembled diplomats at Le Bourget Airport echoed the continuing Hanoi propaganda campaign centering on criticism of the United States. He questioned U.S. "sincerity," citing the massive American airlift to South Vietnam; he charged that the United States had "failed to keep its commitment" to sign the draft agreement on October 31; he demanded that the United States sign that agreement and "abide by the provisions agreed upon" — or be faced with diplomatic disaster and renewed warfare.

At the White House, Ziegler announced that Kissinger would return to Paris to resume negotiations the following morning. "If the other side enters into these negotiations with the same spirit of goodwill that has characterized the sessions since October 8," he volunteered, "we would expect a successful outcome." The negotiations should last "several days, perhaps longer."

That afternoon, Kissinger, the one authoritative source on Vietnam, told a reporter that the agreement was already "ninety percent completed." The other "ten percent" could be settled quickly, he added, "if Tho shows goodwill."

Kissinger returned to Paris on Sunday evening, November 19, for another round of secret talks with Le Duc Tho.

"The President has sent me here for what he hopes will be the final phase of the negotiations to end the war in Indochina," Kissinger told a gathering of diplomats and reporters in the oval VIP lounge at Orly Airport. "My instructions are to stay for as long as it is useful and to conduct the talks in a spirit of conciliation, moderation and goodwill."

Under heavy police escort, Kissinger was driven to the U.S. Ambassador's luxurious residence on the Faubourg St. Honoré.

"Where will tomorrow morning's meeting take place?" a reporter asked. Kissinger smiled. "I've seen to it that it will be impossible to have me followed. I am determined not to let this turn into a circus."

Peter Kalischer, the CBS News bureau chief in Paris, who had been covering the peace talks since May, 1968, picked up the challenge. At dawn, on November 20, he assigned two cameramen to the task of tracking Kissinger and Tho to their secret rendezvous. One cameraman took up a strategic position on a side street off the Faubourg St. Honoré. When the green iron door of the Ambassador's residence swung open, French police stopped the traffic so that Kissinger's white sedan, driven by an Air Force colonel, could cut into the fashionable shopping street and speed off to the secret rendezvous point. Other official cars tailed behind. The cameraman pursued his prestigious quarry through Parisian traffic — no small feat — and out into the French countryside. Despite persistent efforts by Parisian *flics* to shake him off the trail, he managed to stay behind the official motorcade for the forty-five-minute dash to the Léger villa at Gif-sur-Yvette.

The other cameraman, meanwhile, parked his motorbike inconspicuously near the North Vietnamese compound at Choisy-le-Roi. At 9:30 A.M., he spotted a convoy of black Citroëns snaking out of the compound and into the traffic. The police tried to shake him, too; when they failed, they forced him to the side of the road and threatened to shoot him on the spot unless he abandoned his pursuit. One policeman actually drew his revolver. The cameraman explained that he was no assassin, only a television reporter. Once the policemen left, he followed — but at a respectable distance. When he arrived, his colleague was already on the scene. Thus was the cover of Gif blown. For the remainder of the negotiations at this suburban villa, through drizzle, cloudbursts, and snow, there was always to be a small army of newsmen and cameramen waiting outside the two-story building — some perched in the treetops, waving and shouting, "Allo, Kiki, allo, Kiki," whenever they caught sight of Kissinger.

The first negotiating session began at 10:30 A.M. After a polite preliminary exchange of statements, Kissinger put Thieu's minimum demands on the table, noting that these were *Thieu's* demands, before Tho had the chance to reject them. Kissinger then presented Nixon's demands, pointing out that these were the *President's* minimum demands. Kissinger wanted to be sure that the envoy from Hanoi saw the distinction between the two.

Kissinger first raised the "linguistic problems." These had arisen because Tho had submitted his original draft in English. Both sides had worked from this draft, amending it to their mutual satisfaction. Each change in the English draft was then supposed to be transferred by Tho's aides to an identically worded Vietnamese draft. However, when Kissinger's Vietnamese-language specialist, David Engel, checked the Vietnamese draft, he found that the changes had not always been made. The result was that the two drafts differed meaningfully — a fact that Nha had spotted quickly when Kissinger had first showed him the Vietnamese-language draft in Saigon.

Kissinger was particularly determined to eliminate any ambiguities about the National Council of Reconciliation and Concord. Kissinger reminded Tho that they had agreed that the proper Vietnamese term was "administrative structure," not "governmental structure." Tho remembered. Dong, he suggested, had spoken imprecisely during his interview with de Borchgrave in Hanoi. The council was indeed an "administrative structure," never to be interpreted as a "coalition."

Next, Kissinger raised what he considered at the time to be "a largely technical matter." He presented Tho with a long list of "protocols" — the diplomatic term for the manner in which the principles of the agreement were to be implemented. For example, the basic agreement established the principle of a "standstill cease-fire," but only the protocols could determine how the cease-fire was to be arranged and safeguarded. In other words, how many peacekeeping troops? Checkpoints? Where would they be based? Operating under whose authority? Having what protection? Forewarned of the probability of a North Vietnamese land-grabbing operation the moment the cease-fire went into effect, Kissinger pushed for the establishment of an international police force that would be "on station" and "in sufficient strength" in plenty of time to minimize any such violations. This was the first time Kissinger had ever submitted a list of protocols to the North Vietnamese — a remarkable fact considering that only a month earlier he had been ready to sign an agreement with the North Vietnamese without any real backup mechanism to ensure the cease-fire. He had assumed at the time that the "technicians" — Sullivan, Aldrich, and company — would handle the details.

Tho offered no specific response to Kissinger's list of protocols.

Finally, as Kissinger was later to explain, "we wanted some reference in the agreement, however vague, however allusive, however indirect, that would make clear that the two parts of Vietnam would live in peace with each other and that neither side would impose its solution on the other by force." By any other name, this was an appeal for recognition of the original 1954 DMZ as a dividing line between the south and the north — one of Thieu's demands that Nixon had embraced but which Kissinger apparently had not considered significant enough to raise during the October negotiations. This was clearly a new addition to the draft. Tho offered no specific response to this proposal, either.

"My dear Henry," Tho said, as the sixth hour of their meeting was drawing to a close, "when our talks are concluded, can you arrange a position for me as a visiting Professor of Marxism at Harvard?" The question — a running joke between the two negotiators — seemed to be a signal of conciliation.

"With pleasure," Kissinger responded. "But of course I must be permitted to teach a course in political science in Hanoi."

They agreed to meet again on Tuesday, November 21, at 3 P.M. Gif was as good a "secret" place as any.

When Kissinger returned to the Ambassador's residence in Paris, he quickly drafted a cable to Nixon, itemizing the day's results, and he telephoned Haldeman with such nonsubstantive information as the length and mood of the meeting. Then, in a new show of solidarity with an anxious ally whose views would not determine the outcome of the negotiations, he briefed Saigon's Ambassador Pham Dang Lam, placing heavy emphasis on Tho's assurance that the council would not become a coalition. He was to develop a practice of briefing Lam after every session with Tho. Likewise, Tho and Xuan Thuy briefed the PRG's Foreign Minister, Madame Nguyen Thi Binh.

Kissinger spent most of Tuesday morning at the residence, conferring with aides and telephoning Washington. He emerged shortly after noon to escort a slim, pretty blond to Chez Tante Louise, a restaurant on the Rue Boissy d'Anglais. The restaurant had never earned a star in the *Guide Michelin;* but on that day it gained worldwide recognition because Kissinger chose to lunch there with Mrs. Jan Rose Cushing — wife of a Paris-based American lawyer — whom he had known before her marriage. Kissinger's reputation was such that he drew quite a crowd to the narrow street, and police had to be summoned to keep photographers and curious Parisians out of their *salade niçoise* and *foie de veau.*

After a well-photographed lunch, Kissinger drove off to Gif for the resumption of the negotiations. Things seemed to go well. At 5:45 P.M., Kissinger and Tho emerged for a head-clearing walk through the garden. "Allo, Kiki, allo, Kiki," the cameramen shouted from their aeries in the trees across the road. Kissinger beamed. Tho raised his finger to make a point. "Don't point your finger at me," Kissinger joked. "They'll think you're lecturing me." Tho replied: "I always point when I am about to smile." Tho then smiled, Kissinger smiled, and the cameras clicked.

At 7:30 P.M., both negotiators emerged, Tho escorting Kissinger to his car. They shook hands warmly, having agreed to reconvene Wednesday afternoon, and paused again for another cycle of pictures.

Later that night, after drafting his summary cable to the President, calling Haldeman, and briefing Lam, Kissinger flew to Brussels. He wanted to confer the next morning with visiting Indonesian President Suharto about his country's participation in a four-nation commission to help supervise the cease-fire once it took effect. Indonesia — along with Canada, Hungary, and Poland — had already agreed in principle to join such a force, but Hanoi was protesting Indonesia's participation on the grounds that it was an anti-Communist state allied to America. Kissinger believed that Hanoi's objection could be overcome, and he wanted to make sure that Indonesia remained one of the four countries on the force. He received such assurances from Suharto and his Foreign Minister, Adam Malik, during a seventy-five-minute breakfast in the Belgian capital.

In Paris once again, Kissinger arrived at the Gif villa, where Tho was already waiting for their third session to get under way. That afternoon, there were to be no joint appearances for pictures. Although Kissinger tossed off his usual wave for the cameramen on his departure three and a half hours later, Tho emerged looking glum. No smile. No wave.

News correspondents covering the talks had a tough time that night writing their stories; since they were not briefed on the talks, they had been basing their dispatches mostly on the width of Kissinger's and Tho's daily smiles. On a day when one negotiator smiled and the other did not, it made for a highly uncertain lead.

Kissinger's cabled report to Nixon remained basically optimistic, but there were signs of trouble. Kissinger thought Tho looked preoccupied. A 10 A.M. meeting was set for Thursday, Thanksgiving Day; maybe there would be an explanation then.

From Saigon, that day, there were other signs of trouble. Thieu's foreign policy adviser, Nguyen Phu Duc, was on his way to Paris and then Washington to convey Saigon's growing apprehensions about a cease-fire agreement and to try to extract last-minute assurances from the United States on Saigon's three basic demands: that there be no coalition; that all North Vietnamese troops be withdrawn from the south; and that the DMZ be clearly specified as a boundary between the two Vietnams.

More disturbing to Kissinger was a sudden barrage of criticism against him in Saigon's controlled press. A Saigon Radio commentary, describing Kissinger as "an ambitious person," accused him of "haste," "mistakes," "overconfidence" and "ambition." "It is very difficult for genuine Vietnamese to believe," the commentary said, obviously reflecting the views of the palace, "that a famous intellectual employed with confidence by the President of a powerful country, such as Mr. Kissinger, could be deceived by the Communists." In an obvious attempt to drive a wedge between Kissinger and Nixon, the commentary continued: "Perhaps he overplayed his hand as an assistant to the U.S. President. . . . One had the impression that Mr. Kissinger took one or two steps beyond his power to the point of overlapping that of the President whom he is serving. . . . One has good reason to believe that the time has come for Mr. Kissinger to gain some wisdom by abstaining from too conspicuously airing his ambition to create a legend for himself. . . . Hoping that the U.S. Ph.D. adviser realizes that no lesson is better than a lesson drawn from failure and abandons his illusion about an enemy whom he himself recognized as a miser who always tries to use petty and perfidious tricks to gain maximum profits, the South Vietnamese people resolutely express their determination to oppose any more hasty moves in the coming period."

Kissinger deeply resented Saigon's efforts to depict him as an unprincipled upstart who was deceiving the President. The same condemnatory description of Kissinger was reiterated in the local press, run by Saigon's wealthy elite, who were alarmed by a U.S. withdrawal. Several officials pointedly referred to Kissinger as "that Jew."

The gossip in Saigon's cafés even added Thieu to the list of those leveling anti-Semitic attacks against Kissinger. Thieu was quoted as saying: "The Jew professor comes to Saigon to try to win a Nobel Peace Prize." When this unconfirmed report got around town, one reporter said he asked Nha whether the quote was accurate and Nha denied it — with a playful jab in the reporter's ribs.

According to South Vietnamese accounts, Kissinger dispatched a cable to Nha, asking for an explanation of these attacks. Nha, as Thieu's closest adviser, denied any government connection with the sudden spate of anti-Kissinger denunciations, claiming that Saigon's press and radio were unfettered by government censorship. In a capital where the government regularly either suspends or closes down newspapers that deviate from the official line, this defense was hardly tenable. Nha later blamed it all on Saigon newspapers. "In government circles, we know better than that," he said. "We're not stupid."

Curiously, Saigon's allegations that Kissinger was operating on his own found an echo in Washington. The conservative biweekly *Human Events,* quoting unidentified sources in "the highest councils of the government," reported on November 25 that "the President is irritated with Dr. Kissinger for having virtually concluded an agreement that the Communists — in the words of one critical observer — 'can drive several thousand tanks through.' "

Haldeman and Ehrlichman had just learned about an extraordinary interview Kissinger had given to Oriana Fallaci on November 4, and they were outraged. The interview, published in Italy, created a worldwide sensation. Kissinger talked to Miss Fallaci at great length about himself. "The main point . . . in the mechanics of my success," he said, "comes from the fact that I have acted alone. The Americans love this immensely. The Americans love the cowboy, who leads the convoy, alone on his horse, the cowboy who comes into town all alone on his horse, and nothing else. Perhaps not even with a gun, because he does not shoot. He acts, and that is enough, being in the right place, at the right time. In sum, a Western. This romantic and surprising character suits me because being alone has always been part of my style, or, if you wish, of my technique."

Kissinger's suggestion that he was trotting around the world on his own sent the top cowhands at the White House corral into an uproar. "It was high noon in the old West Wing," one aide said. "At least half a dozen people who matter here in the White House hit the ceiling when they read that story. They called it the biggest ego trip anyone has ever taken." Another aide said that the interview was regarded as just "a blunder — Henry talking to a pretty girl; the whole thing had gone to his head."

Later, Kissinger would wonder about the interview and sigh, "I couldn't have said those things, it's impossible." But he never denied it.

November 23, a day of Thanksgiving for most Americans, turned out to be a day of puzzlement for Kissinger. He and Tho met for six hours, but it was as though someone in Hanoi had suddenly pulled the switch. The tone and content of the negotiations changed radically. The "goodwill" of the first three days turned to petty bickering, threats and outbursts of ill temper — according to one American diplomat, "a form of shoddy negotiation."

Tho suddenly revived his discarded demand for the ouster of the Thieu regime. Kissinger was stunned. Tho then went on to blast Saigon's specific demands. Denouncing Thieu's insistence on "two Vietnams" — south and north — Tho demanded "three Vietnamese states" — the north, and the south split into what Thieu held and what the Communist side held. Moreover, he emphasized that "the Vietnamese people are one" — a statement that ruled out the DMZ as a boundary line and left Hanoi with the right to move through it at will. Finally, Tho withdrew an earlier concession: a token pullout of North Vietnamese troops — a sign of goodwill to facilitate an agreement — was now "out of the question," he said.

Kissinger asked why Tho had changed his position. He received no satisfactory reply. It was as though the October breakthrough had been a hallucination. Kissinger warned Tho that the President had suspended the bombing of North Vietnam above the twentieth parallel in the expectation that the negotiations would proceed "seriously," implying that the bombing could be resumed at any time. Tho countered that the North Vietnamese were negotiating "seriously," and insisted that the Americans had introduced a whole new set of demands.

For the first time in the negotiations, Tho shouted at Kissinger and pounded the table. "The October 31 deadline is past," he said angrily, "the election is over, and, from our point of view, the war can indeed continue." Kissinger did not brush aside Tho's counterwarning as an empty threat. It instantly conjured up the depressing vision of a new Communist offensive, new American bombing, new Saigon bluster, and a new congressional drive to end the war by legislation rather than by "an act of diplomacy," which had always been Kissinger's goal.

The negotiations, for the moment, looked hopeless. Kissinger had assumed that a final document could be agreed on by week's end — another day or so. At this point, it seemed that a speedy agreement was out of the question; and he feared that he might be open to the charge that his October 26 promise — "peace is at hand" — was nothing more than a gigantic preelection hoax. It was clear that Kissinger needed new instructions, and so did Tho. They agreed, in their only agreement of the day, that it would be pointless to schedule another formal session at Gif for the next day. Perhaps an informal get-together might help resolve matters.

Kissinger's report to Nixon that night did little to improve the President's appetite for his Thanksgiving feast.

"We don't know what decisions were made in Hanoi at that point," Kissinger later explained, "but from that point on, the negotiations have had the character where a settlement was always just within our reach, and was always pulled just beyond our reach when we attempted to grasp it."

Kissinger theorized that there might have been a shift in position by one or two members of Hanoi's ten-man Politburo. The summertime decision to opt for a deal had not had the leadership's full support. It had been, Kissinger felt, a six-to-four or, at best, a seven-to-three decision. When Nixon resisted meeting the October 31 deadline; when he seemed to decelerate the rush for an agreement; when he pumped a year's worth of military matériel into South Vietnam in a matter of weeks; when he yielded to Thieu's mid-October revolt against the original timetable; and, finally, when Kissinger suddenly presented Thieu's minimum demands at this latest session, the Politburo — perhaps suspecting Nixon of a grand deception aimed at throwing the NVA off guard for a sudden ARVN offensive — began to pull back. Perhaps Hanoi, Kissinger hypothesized, had decided to wait for Congress to vote the United States out of the war, either by banning the bombing or cutting off funds for Thieu, or both.

The official North Vietnamese explanation of the Thanksgiving Day switch was simpler. Hanoi charged that Kissinger had changed the basic character of the October 8 deal by presenting new and far-reaching proposals.

Once again, on November 24, it was a CBS-TV crew, led by correspondent Tom Fenton, that pursued Kissinger to his meeting place with
Le Duc Tho. This time they met at Tho's residence, a modest North Vietnamese house on Rue Darthe in Choisy-le-Roi. Kissinger had hoped his
informal meeting with Tho could be kept a secret. Only Haig accompanied Kissinger, and they conferred with Tho for two hours. When
Kissinger emerged, he walked briskly toward the iron gate and turned
the handle. It wouldn't give. He pushed the gate but couldn't open it.
"How do I get out of here?" he pleaded, a question that summed up his
predicament on all levels. At last, a guard opened the gate. Kissinger
walked past Fenton with a "no comment."

In Paris that morning, there were rumors of another impasse. The
South Vietnamese had spread them; the North Vietnamese did not deny
them.

That afternoon, Kissinger spent forty-five minutes with French Foreign
Minister Maurice Schumann, enlisting his support to knock down the
rumors of despair. By early evening, AFP was quoting "authorized
circles" as saying that the "pessimistic rumors circulating about Vietnam
appear highly exaggerated." Kissinger smiled whenever he saw newsmen,
but the rumors persisted.

On Saturday, November 25, Kissinger returned to Choisy-le-Roi and,
during an almost two-hour meeting with Tho, proposed that the negotiations be recessed until December 4. Tho agreed. Tho said he would
remain in Paris to await Kissinger's return. The American envoy left the
North Vietnamese residence sporting his usual smile. Tho left, a few
minutes later, poker-faced.

In New York, where the President was spending a weekend shopping
and theatergoing with his family, Ziegler was instructed to say, "Both
sides are negotiating seriously," a signal to North Vietnam that the bombing would not yet be resumed.

In Hanoi, *Nhan Dan*, in an editorial signed "Commentator," a *nom de
plume* for the Politburo, questioned the entire basis of Kissinger's stance
at the Paris talks. "Is this a one-hundred-eighty-degree turn? A demand
that the whole problem be considered all over again? Is this a trick to
prolong the talks in hopes of covering up the acts of intensification and
prolongation of the war and continuing to pursue an evasive military
victory?"

In Paris, Nguyen Phu Duc and his South Vietnamese colleagues savored the unexpected recess in the Kissinger-Tho talks. It was an interesting omen; perhaps the recess might even be extended.

Kissinger flew directly to New York, arriving at 9:45 P.M. at JFK International Airport. He drove to the Waldorf-Astoria Towers in downtown Manhattan and immediately conferred with the President in his hotel apartment. An official "photo opportunity" allowed cameramen into the living room for pictures of both men seated in soft chairs, with loose-leaf notebooks and manila file folders in their laps. They spoke in whispers. Ziegler anxiously alerted the President to the possibility that the cameramen might overhear state secrets. One cameraman quickly reassured the President's spokesman that "not enough" had been overheard. Nixon scowled and continued his hushed discussion with Kissinger. Ziegler promptly ushered the photographers out of the room.

The President and his Vietnam negotiator talked privately for more than an hour. Normally, in such cases, Kissinger would later brief Ziegler on what to tell newsmen; this time, Nixon did the briefing. "President Nixon is confident that we will achieve the right kind of settlement," the spokesman said with assurance, "and that is the objective we are shooting for. President Nixon feels that the important thing is to achieve a settlement that will last, not just for the short term but for the long term. He is prepared to take the time that is necessary to achieve that kind of settlement, a settlement that will last."

Peace was not at hand. The timetable was slipping.

It so happened that Kissinger returned to the United States on the weekend of the Harvard-Yale football game — a fact that might have escaped his notice if not for an "extra" edition of "the *Harvard Crimson*." It reported that the former Harvard professor would be abandoning the White House and returning to Harvard in January. WBZ-TV, Channel 4 in Boston, broadcast the "exclusive" on its 11:30 A.M. newscast; some radio stations and news agencies picked up the lead. Hours later, the whole affair turned out to be a football-weekend prank — a bogus edition of the *Harvard Crimson* published by the *Yale Daily News.* Kissinger was not amused.

On November 28, Nguyen Phu Duc arrived in Washington. Thieu's original scenario had called for him to fly to Washington while Kissinger was tied up in negotiations with Le Duc Tho in Paris. The objective was a private meeting between Duc and the President; Saigon still sensed a split between Nixon and Kissinger, with Nixon taking the harder line on negotiations. Although Nixon may have had a few second thoughts about Kissinger during this tense period, the President rejected Thieu's attempt to drive a wedge between himself and Kissinger. He refused to see Duc alone. It was only after the Paris talks were suspended and Kissinger had flown back to the President's side that Duc got the message that he would be welcome in Washington.

The following day, he had a two-and-a-half-hour meeting with the President, Kissinger and Haig, shortly after Nixon had gone through the ritual of obtaining the JCS's approval for a Vietnam cease-fire. The President conferred with Duc a second time, the next day. These meetings were, to quote the spokesman, "very detailed," "very constructive" and "very frank." It took no genius to recognize that this was diplomatic balderdash.

At one point during this round of meetings, Duc delivered a personal letter from his President to President Nixon, demanding an urgent summit meeting before the signing of any cease-fire agreement. The last time the two Presidents had met was almost four years before, in the summer of 1969, when Nixon visited Saigon during a round-the-world trip. Nixon ruled out any summit with Thieu until after an agreement was signed.

He carefully explained to Thieu's emissary that the United States was going to sign an agreement — "with or without you" — as soon as he was convinced that the agreement was "right." Nixon, in outlining his intended course, apparently took into account the possibility that Thieu's outspoken resistance was pure bluff and that, in the end, he would go along with the United States. Nixon warned Duc that if Thieu opted to continue the war on his own, he would be running the risk of losing U.S. aid, either through a presidential decision or through congressional legislation. U.S. aid, Nixon said, was "essential" to South Vietnam's survival; as Kissinger put it, "If you don't sign, you'll destroy yourself." Nixon repeated the warning Haig had given Thieu: if Kissinger could complete the negotiations by December 15, the United States would sign the agreement. Tho had assured Kissinger that the "first group of American POWs" would be released "within ten days" after the cease-fire began — in other words, during the Christmas holidays. The vision of the release of these prisoners, the first of them shot down over North Vietnam in 1964, had an understandably powerful appeal for the President.

After Thieu received Duc's report, the South Vietnamese leaked a story claiming that Nixon had issued an "ultimatum" to the South Vietnamese — to sign or else. Saigon apparently assumed that an "ultimatum" story would encourage America's right wing to apply pressure on the White House not to abandon a beleaguered ally threatened by Communism. It turned out to be a gross and embarrassing overestimation. The story caused barely a ripple.

On November 30, Nha proposed that North and South Vietnam conduct their own negotiations, thus eliminating the need for "go-betweens": a clear reference to Kissinger. "Go-betweens were only significant during the first period of the peace talks," Nha's newspaper, *Tin Song,* editorialized. "Intermediaries only waste time, and they have the disadvantage of misunderstandings. The Communists want to retain these intermediaries, and if they reach a vague, unclear agreement, they can take advantage of it much more easily. The Communists must understand that they cannot reach any cease-fire accord without the agreement of the Republic of Vietnam." Implied in the editorial was Thieu's leverage over Nixon: the South Vietnamese could always ignore a cease-fire appeal, continue fighting, and destroy the chance of a cease-fire ever taking hold.

On December 2, Kissinger confided to James Reston: "I had the illusion that maybe we could get through these peace negotiations without heartbreak, but that was probably expecting too much. The war has been heartbreaking from the beginning."

Denounced by the left for "deceit," sniped at by the right for a "sell-out," caught in the vortex of Vietnamese arguments and counterarguments, Kissinger seemed suddenly tired. It was at this point that Nixon came through with a much-needed psychological boost. The President announced that his Assistant for National Security Affairs would be staying on at the White House into the second term — a show of confidence in Kissinger that he hoped would be fully appreciated in Saigon. As for the negotiations, scheduled for resumption in Paris on December 4, Nixon said through Ziegler: "The President is certain that the negotiations will be carried out with the same distinction that has marked the entire series of negotiations in which Dr. Kissinger has represented the United States." Asked if Kissinger's credibility had been impaired by Saigon's distrust of him, Ziegler added: "Dr. Kissinger not only represents the President fully, but follows the instructions provided to him by the President."

On December 3, as Kissinger was preparing to fly to Paris, he received some disquieting intelligence. In Hanoi, schoolchildren were being evacuated from the capital — apparently in anticipation of renewed American bombing.

On Monday, December 4, at 10 A.M., Kissinger and Haig drove to Tho's residence at Choisy-le-Roi for still another try at ending the war. Behind the shuttered windows of the two-story fieldstone house, the envoy from Hanoi began the meeting by reiterating the hard-line position he had taken at the close of the last one. By now, Tho could recite his demands in virtually one breath: Thieu had to go, there was only one Vietnamese people, there was no obligation on Hanoi's part to withdraw any troops, much less all of them; and Tho emphasized that the political prisoners in the south had to be released immediately or else the entire agreement might be jeopardized. This amounted to an implied threat once again to hold up the release of the American POWs. All in all, it was a head-on collision between the two sides. Kissinger felt drained. Nevertheless, after two and a half hours of deadlock, another session was planned for the afternoon, and still another for the next day. When Kissinger left the villa, he discovered a cat perched on top of his car — a black cat with white paws. Bad luck? Or good? "Who's the wise guy?" Kissinger asked, as an army of television cameramen recorded the scene.

At three o'clock that afternoon, the two sides continued their confrontation in a new setting — a luxurious country estate at Sainte Gemme, nineteen miles west of Paris. Tho, according to Kissinger, withdrew "every change that had been agreed to two weeks previously." This shattered Kissinger's earlier estimate that this session could be concluded "in two to three days." It was clear that he needed new negotiating instructions from the President; Kissinger was working on a tight leash. He recommended that Tuesday's meeting be canceled and that both sides meet instead on Wednesday, December 6.

The Tuesday between sessions produced a good deal of communication between the negotiator in Paris and the President in Washington. Nixon's instructions were: keep cool, try again to narrow the differences.

Followed by the platoons of photographers in crash helmets and brightly colored parkas, Kissinger and Tho met Wednesday in the fashionable suburb of Neuilly-sur-Seine at the home of Arnaud Clerc, an

American-born jeweler. A giant antenna was quickly set up on the grounds, presumably for instantaneous communications with the U.S. Embassy, just a couple of miles away at the Place de la Concorde. Against an expensive backdrop of Flemish paintings and tapestries, Kissinger and Tho began to inch back toward the level of agreement that had been reached on November 22, before Hanoi seemed to have a sudden change of heart. Kissinger was encouraged; his humor began to surface. Pointing to one of the chandeliers, he said: "When the light bulb starts blinking, it means we have to change the tape."

Clerc had divulged to the waiting reporters that the two sides had reached an agreement: they would share a leisurely French lunch; but it turned out that they settled for a quick snack of sandwiches, Coca-Cola, and 7-Up. For the Francophile diehards, there was red wine.

The next day, Kissinger breakfasted with Charles Collingwood, chief foreign correspondent for CBS News, an old hand at the Paris talks, who had made many trips to Saigon and had visited Hanoi in March, 1968. Kissinger did not go into specific detail, but suggested that the talks were on track. That night, Collingwood broadcast an optimistic report, implying that Kissinger expected a successful windup of the negotiations within a few days. That day, other reporters got different signals. "The mood at the negotiations," one of them said, "oscillates from deepest optimism to soaring pessimism."

The fact that the significant negotiations were taking place in secret between Kissinger and Tho did not interrupt the regular weekly rhythm of the Thursday semipublic peace talks by all four sides at the Hotel Majestic; the United States, South and North Vietnam and the Provisional Revolutionary Government went through their own form of negotiations. After the meeting that Thursday, Nguyen Minh Vy, a North Vietnamese official, charged that the United States had "threatened to escalate the war"; the talks, he said, were "deadlocked." Heyward Isham, the acting American chief, was more circumspect. "We should not permit disappointments and setbacks in the pace of the final negotiations to prevent us from displaying an unchanged and unchangeable intention to achieve peace," he said. Reporters thought that perhaps these gloomy comments reflected what was taking place at the secret talks.

In Washington, at the State Department's noon briefing, it was revealed that one hundred Foreign Service officers who had served in Vietnam had been alerted to prepare to return. A cease-fire was close, and they had to be in-country soon, to be in position to check on the cease-fire and report on postwar political developments. "We wouldn't alert all those officers and cause them problems with their wives and children right before Christmas," a spokesman said, "unless it was absolutely necessary."

In Vietnam, the war continued without letup. The VC carried out its fiercest rocket attack on Tan Son Nhut Airport in four years, and American warplanes continued their heavy bombing of Communist supply routes and positions.

That afternoon, Kissinger and Tho met for four hours at Gif. They continued to make modest progress. Tho dropped his off-again-on-again demand for Thieu's ouster. The "linguistic problem" relating to the National Council was again clarified to rule out a coalition. The probability of a token NVA troop withdrawal was again affirmed. Altogether, it represented an easing of Tho's position during the last few meetings, bringing him back on several points to his original commitments in the October 8 agreement.

That night, Kissinger cabled Nixon that agreement might be reached by Saturday and that if Secretary of State Rogers was to sign the final document — Rogers was then in Brussels attending a ministerial meeting of NATO — he should be told to be in Paris by late Friday.

On Friday, December 8, Kissinger and Tho shifted the site of their talks back to Neuilly-sur-Seine. There was further progress, but clearly not enough to conclude an agreement. Once again, Kissinger had misread the signals, his optimism outdistancing his judgment. Rogers was told to fly home and forget about Paris for the time being.

On Saturday, December 9 — a bright, chilly day in Paris — Kissinger walked through the Place de la Concorde and visited two of his favorite museums — the Jeu de Paume and the Orangerie. He relaxed for a while before Monet's *Waterlilies*.

At 3 P.M., he drove to Gif for a three-and-a-half-hour meeting with Tho. Once again, there was progress. "We thought we had narrowed the issues" to a point, Kissinger later explained, "where, if the other side had accepted again one section they already had agreed to two weeks previously, the agreement could have been completed." The "one section" concerned the integrity of the DMZ, and all it implied as a noninfiltratable boundary between North and South Vietnam.

Kissinger recommended that the "principals" — namely, he and Tho — reconvene on the following Monday, but that their experts meet on Sunday to continue to work on the implementing protocols: for example, marking up maps to show which parts of South Vietnam were to be considered VC-controlled, which Saigon-controlled, and which were to remain ambiguous. The protocols also involved language. "We were sufficiently close," Kissinger later disclosed, "so that experts could meet to conform the texts so that we would not again encounter the linguistic difficulties which we had experienced previously, and so that we could make sure that the changes that had been negotiated in English would also be reflected in Vietnamese."

Before leaving Gif, Kissinger told Tho that Haig would be returning to Washington that night, prepared to go on to Saigon to insist on Thieu's endorsement of a "final draft agreement." Kissinger said he hoped that Haig could be in Saigon by Monday or Tuesday and a final agreement initialed in Paris a day or two later.

The experts — Sullivan on the U.S. side, Deputy Foreign Minister Nguyen Co Thach on the Vietnamese — met on December 10 at Clerc's home in Neuilly-sur-Seine. There was an unpleasant surprise. Thach gave Sullivan seventeen new changes; he called them "linguistic" but several clearly crossed the line into substantive. They could be managed, Sullivan believed, but it would require more time. He began to suspect that perhaps the North Vietnamese were "playing games." A U.S. official described the nature of the talks at the time as "a war of attrition at the negotiating table instead of on the battlefield; it's really a question of who has the solidest nerves."

That night, Sullivan briefed Kissinger, and Kissinger briefed South Vietnamese Ambassador Lam, and the South Vietnamese only too eagerly leaked a story that the talks were again deadlocked.

Monday, December 11, opened a week of extreme tension. Kissinger met with Tho at Neuilly-sur-Seine and immediately raised the question of the seventeen new "linguistic changes." Tho did not answer. He returned to one of his favorite themes — the release of all political prisoners in the south. Again there was an implied threat that their release might be linked to the release of the American POWs. Both sides recognized the stakes were high; such linkage could destroy the negotiations. Kissinger sidestepped this explosive issue for the moment by countering with one of Saturday's still-unresolved issues — the DMZ. Tho didn't even want to talk about it. Kissinger tried another tack to keep the negotiations from collapsing. He raised one of Thieu's more recent recommendations — that all four warring parties, including the PRG and Saigon, sign the cease-fire accords. Tho angrily rejected the idea, denying any claim to legitimacy by the President whom Hanoi derisively dismissed as an American *fantoche* — a puppet. It brought the negotiations back to the basic question of what the war was all about: the political control of the south.

There were few smiles for reporters that night.

Tuesday's meeting was essentially a replay of the previous day's stalemate. Tho declined to withdraw his suggestion of linkage between the prisoners — the political ones being held by Thieu in the south and the American ones being held by Hanoi in the north. And his resistance to firming up the DMZ as a boundary line remained as stubborn as ever. Stymied on the big issues, Kissinger suggested they take on the linguistic issues that Thach had raised with Sullivan the previous Sunday. After four and a half hours of bargaining, they succeeded in reducing the seventeen disputed points to two. They also agreed to meet again the following morning.

Early Wednesday morning, Kissinger met with James Reston. A reading of his column the next morning suggests that Kissinger told him that the meetings with Tho were drawing to an inconclusive close and that Thieu, in Kissinger's judgment, posed the greatest obstacle to a settlement by insisting, in effect, on a life-insurance policy for his regime. Kissinger said that the next big decision was Nixon's.

Later that morning, Kissinger and Tho met again at Neuilly-sur-Seine. It proved to be a maze of contradiction and conflict. When Sullivan sought to confirm that indeed only two "linguistic changes" remained, Thach presented him with sixteen new "linguistic changes," four of which were definitely "substantive." When Kissinger tried to focus on central issues, Tho unveiled an even bigger surprise. He presented Kissinger with Hanoi's "protocols" for implementing the cease-fire — as the

American diplomat impatiently noted, "six weeks after we had stated what our aim was, five weeks after the cease-fire was supposed to be signed." To complicate matters further, as Kissinger later explained, Tho's "perception of international machinery" was "at drastic variance" with his own. The North Vietnamese, he continued, were interested in a token force of two hundred and fifty troops, dependent for their logistics and communications upon either the VC or Saigon; in other words, upon whichever political-military side controlled the zone under investigation for possible violations of the cease-fire. Kissinger wanted a force of roughly five thousand men enjoying full freedom of mobility and controlling its own logistical base; in other words, independent of the contending Vietnamese parties. To Kissinger, this Communist position suggested one of two possibilities: either Tho was angling for concessions or Hanoi was planning only a brief battlefield respite before launching still another offensive in the south. Either way, Kissinger found it an unproductive confrontation, and he informed Tho that he was returning to Washington but that Sullivan would remain in Paris to continue trying to find some common ground with the North Vietnamese on the "protocols."

"It cannot do," Kissinger would later say, "that if every day an issue is settled, a new one is raised, that when an issue is settled in an agreement, it is raised again as an understanding and if it is settled as an understanding, it is raised again as a protocol."

The list of unresolved issues was clear: Kissinger could not get Tho to accept a firmed-up DMZ. He could not get Thieu to cede any trace of sovereignty to the PRG. He could not even convince the contending Vietnamese parties to compromise on a signing ceremony. Finally, he faced "total deadlock" on the "protocols."

The North Vietnamese view was quite different. According to their spokesmen, it was the Americans who had sabotaged the opportunity for peace; who had returned to Paris after the deadline had elapsed with a whole new set of demands. It was only after Kissinger tried to introduce a certain amount of specificity into an agreement that had been drafted in October with deliberate ambiguity, they maintained, that Le Duc Tho came up with new counterproposals of his own.

As the North Vietnamese saw it, to agree to Kissinger's demand for recognition of the DMZ as a borderline would have implied recognition of Thieu's regime, the political issue that the war was all about; to accept some of his other demands would have imperiled the objective of winning legitimacy for the PRG.

Still another factor was their memory of the last quarter-century of history. They believed that Ho Chi Minh had been tricked out of victory by the French in 1946, and then by the Geneva Accords in 1954; now they feared that Nixon was about to play the biggest trick of all by pretending to go along with the Paris talks for domestic political reasons, while preparing, after his reelection, to impose his will by renewed bombing if he couldn't get his way at the negotiating table. Even some American officials would later concede privately that Hanoi indeed had an arguable case.

Just before departing from Orly Airport Wednesday night, Kissinger declared: "I am returning to Washington and will exchange messages with Special Adviser Le Duc Tho as to whether a further meeting is necessary. In the meantime, Ambassador Sullivan and two members of my staff are staying here and will be meeting under the direction of Ambassador Porter with experts of the other side."

His statement carefully suggested continuity when in fact there was deadlock. But, better than anyone else, he knew that he was walking into a stormy national controversy.

The first challenge to Kissinger's integrity took the form of a question from a reporter. "Dr. Kissinger, do you think peace is at hand?" His jet had just touched down at Andrews Air Force Base. "That's a good phrase," Kissinger rejoined with a weak smile. "Wonder who used it?"

The next morning, Thursday, December 14, Kissinger provided the President with a firsthand report on the Paris negotiations; over the next two days, they would spend almost eight hours together. To end the war "by an act of diplomacy," Kissinger needed the full support of the President — "now more than ever," as the GOP campaign posters had once put it. Kissinger would give Haldeman no grounds whatever for detecting daylight between the President and his national security adviser on the issue of war and peace.

Their first big decision was reached late that morning. Nixon dispatched a strongly worded cable to Hanoi, warning that "serious negotiations" would have to be resumed within seventy-two hours — or else. Nixon, angry, was ready to resume the bombing; so was Kissinger.

The threat to Hanoi was coupled with a decision to warn Thieu that White House patience was not boundless. Any further opposition would produce a cutoff of aid — by the President, not the Congress. Kissinger concurred.

A third decision was to send Kissinger to brief the top officials in the bureaucracy. Within forty-eight hours, Kissinger shared his version of the Paris negotiations with Rogers, Laird, Helms, Admiral Moorer of the Joint Chiefs, Vice-President Agnew, and the immediate White House staff.

With Moorer, Kissinger raised an important question: how many B-52s were operational throughout the world? Moorer was not keen on using the eight-million-dollar giant eight-engine Stratofortresses over North Vietnam during heavy weather. The loss ratio could run as high as three or four percent. Moorer assumed the President was getting ready to use the B-52 in a new air assault against North Vietnam.

On Friday, the President decided that the public should be briefed on the breakdown in the Paris talks. A question arose as to who would carry the news to the nation. Kissinger proposed that the President ought to explain the situation; Nixon was the one who usually delivered the prime-time reports on Vietnam. Nixon, supported by Haldeman, argued that Kissinger should handle the assignment; after all, he had taken the credit for the good news at his October 26 news conference; now he had to take his lumps.

On Saturday, December 16, at 11:43 A.M., Kissinger stepped behind the podium in the White House Press Room to explain why peace was barely in view. By mentioning the President's name no fewer than fourteen times — on October 26, Nixon was mentioned only three times — Kissinger suggested that the key to a future settlement lay with Nixon. "We have not reached an agreement," Kissinger emphasized, "that the President considers just and fair." He added: "If we can get an agreement that the President considers just, we will proceed with it." He explained why he was going public, despite a pledge of secrecy to Le Duc Tho. "The President," he said, "decided that we could not engage in a charade with the American people." The North Vietnamese, he maintained, kept raising "one frivolous issue after another," unworthy of the pursuit of peace. "We will not be blackmailed into an agreement," Kissinger asserted. "We will not be stampeded into an agreement, and, if I may so say, we will not be charmed into an agreement until its conditions are right." Kissinger assured Hanoi that the United States still wanted peace, along the lines of the October 8 agreement, but he warned that time was running out. "No other party will have a veto over our actions," he observed in a parting signal to Saigon.

The news conference was focused so single-mindedly on the negotiations that the question of the possibility of renewed air attacks against North Vietnam was never raised. Kissinger volunteered nothing.

The annual White House Christmas party that evening was a drag. Originally, its theme was to have been "peace is *finally* at hand." It turned out to be a Fred Waring–conducted postmortem on the stalled peace talks. The President struck some of the guests as weary and preoccupied; so did Kissinger. "What went wrong?" was the question. "On one occasion, we thought we would have a final agreement the next day," Kissinger told a guest. "But these people have been fighting more than twenty years and it is difficult for them to reach an agreement."

By midafternoon Sunday, December 17, the time had run out on the President's seventy-two-hour ultimatum to Hanoi to start "serious negotiations." He reached for the B-52s. He ordered the resumption of massive and concentrated U.S. air attacks against North Vietnam, including the first-time-ever use of the giant bombers against the Hanoi and Haiphong areas. The first raids began late that evening, Washington time.

Nixon wanted not only to cripple the North Vietnamese capacity for more war-making but also to blast them back to the table; by his own logic, he was bombing for peace. This was the kind of logic that had led a U.S. Army officer, earlier in the war, to look out over the debris that had once been the South Vietnamese town of Ben Tre and say, "We had to destroy it in order to save it."

Kissinger supported Nixon's decision, despite subsequent hints, which he spread himself, that he disagreed with the President's bombing policy. "I was in favor of attacking the north," he told us.

He did not oppose the use of B-52s against military targets in or near North Vietnam's two biggest cities; but, according to a few informed sources, he did express reservations about B-52 bombing of congested population centers. The trouble was that, in Hanoi and Haiphong, the military targets were often side by side with residential areas.

He had additional reservations about springing such a massive bombing campaign on the North Vietnamese; he would have preferred warning Hanoi secretly, through Moscow and Peking, before the United States actually began bombing. But once his reservations, never seriously or persistently pressed, were overridden by the President, Kissinger stepped fully into line.

The bombing decision was, as Kissinger once put it, "absolutely agonizing and painful"; but he drew a clear distinction between what "pained" him and what he rejected. He did not reject the bombing; on the contrary, he considered it essential. He felt that the United States was being squeezed by both Hanoi and Saigon, and that the only way to break out of the pattern was to bomb the north and present Thieu with an ultimatum.

"It was an agony for me to think that at the very end — when I knew the end was in sight — that all the things we had tried to do . . . were all blowing again — but that didn't mean that I disagreed with the decision." It was, Kissinger later said, "the most painful, the most difficult, and certainly the most lonely that the President has had to make since he has been in office."

Shortly after the bombing began, Haig arrived in Saigon with a presidential ultimatum: if Thieu persisted in holding out against an agreement, the United States would sign a separate peace with North Vietnam, and all military and economic aid to South Vietnam would be cut off. Haig arrived in Saigon on Monday; by the time he left South Vietnam less than forty-eight hours later, much of North Vietnam's heartland was being destroyed, and Thieu, though overjoyed at the resumption of the bombing, found himself weakening in the face of Nixon's either-or challenge.

"You must not underrate Thieu's sense of realities," remarked one Saigon politician. "Nobody can say *nyet* forever." One of Kissinger's NSC staffers said, "Thieu had no hankering to be another Diem. He had a strong bent for survival." Thieu, in a detailed letter to Nixon, yielded on several critical points. He said he would agree to North Vietnamese troops remaining in the south; he would cede some sovereignty to the PRG; he would accept Kissinger's assurances that the National Council would not become a coalition; finally, he would take Kissinger's word that Russia and China might reduce their arms deliveries to North Vietnam.

Over the next twelve days, the bombing blitz built up in intensity. Flying in groups of three, the B-52s dropped their bombs at the same time, with the payload falling in a rectangular pattern about a mile long and half a mile wide. Each plane could carry about two dozen five-hundred-pound bombs and more than forty seven-hundred-and-fifty-pound bombs. About one hundred of the big strategic bombers and five hundred smaller Air Force, Navy and Marine fighter-bombers flew round-the-clock raids against what the Pentagon described as the "most heavily defended antiaircraft area in the world."

The United States rejected charges of "terror bombing," insisting that its air strikes had hit military targets in the Hanoi, Haiphong, and Thanh Hoa area.

During the first four days of bombing, the United States lost eight B-52s and four F-111 fighter-bombers. By the time the bombing ended, on December 30, the United States would acknowledge the loss of fifteen B-52s and eleven fighter-bombers. The official toll of American airmen reported missing during the entire bombing period of twelve days would stand at ninety-three, with thirty-one reported captured by the North Vietnamese. Hanoi claimed that U.S. losses were much higher.

Although a number of America's Asian allies supported the bombing, the reaction in most countries was one of shock and incredulity. "A form of torture and an outrage similar to those linked to names like Guernica, Lidice, Babi Yar, Sharpeville, and Treblinka," blasted Premier Olof Palme of Sweden. The U.S. Government bears "grave responsibility" for these "barbaric acts," warned Leonid Brezhnev; a day later, Soviet journalist Victor Louis speculated in a British newspaper that Brezhnev might delay his scheduled visit to the United States. Premier Chou En-lai warned that U.S.-Chinese relations were imperiled by the raids. Pope Paul VI said the "unforeseen worsening of events has intensified bitterness and anxiety in world opinion." The *Manchester Guardian* commented: "It is the action of a man blinded by fury or incapable of seeing the consequences of what he is doing." The reaction in the United States was equally negative. "He appears to have lost his senses," said William Saxbe of President Nixon. Saxbe was then a Republican Senator from Ohio; less than a year later, he was to become Nixon's fourth Attorney General. "TERROR BOMBING IN THE NAME OF PEACE," headlined the *Washington Post*. "War by tantrum," commented James Reston. "Stone Age strategy," said Senator Mike Mansfield.

This kind of criticism damaged Kissinger as much as Nixon. Columnist Joseph Kraft wrote that Kissinger "has been compromised and everybody in town knows it." Kenneth Crawford, a conservative columnist, said that Kissinger had been "had by the second-string Communists of Hanoi." Senator McGovern predicted that Kissinger would be fired, or resign, "in a very short time." Even Clayton Fritchey, an admirer of Kissinger, concluded: "If there is to be an Administration goat, it appears that Kissinger is in line for the honor." From the right and left wings of the political spectrum came blasts of criticism — for example, letters attacking "the Jewish Communist in the White House" — and from within the White House itself came whispers of doubt. Haldeman hinted to one reporter that Nixon had named Kissinger to his White House staff for the second term only as a diplomatic signal to Saigon and Hanoi. Don't bet on his longevity, Haldeman seemed to be saying. Ehrlichman told another reporter that Nixon might appoint John Connally to be Secretary of State, knowing that that appointment would drive Kissinger back to Harvard. Laird told still another reporter that Nixon had never authorized Kissinger to say that "peace is at hand."

"That was an extraordinary period," Kissinger later told us. "Extraordinary." He shook his head, as though he couldn't believe his own recollections. Hanoi was being bombed for a "peace" that Kissinger had promised but had been unable to deliver; Kissinger's enemies in the White House were trying to force him out in disgrace. Kissinger later told a columnist: "Haldeman nearly got me. He nearly got me." But getting rid of Kissinger at that agonizing moment of shattered American expectations for an end to the war and mounting American revulsion against the bombing would have been an embarrassment to the President; the two men were so inextricably meshed in the making of the country's foreign policy that repudiation of Kissinger would have been tantamount to admitting Nixon's own responsibility for the mess of the moment. That was too high a price to pay.

Throughout the twelve days of massive air raids against the north, the President had never explained his B-52 strategy to the American people and had in fact ordered a silence on the bombing throughout the bureaucracy. Kissinger reportedly urged the President more than once to go on the air and explain the reasons for the bombing, but Nixon declined. "The President decided," Kissinger later explained in a television interview, "that if this action succeeded, then the results would speak for themselves in terms of a settlement, and if a settlement was not reached, then he would have to give an accounting to the American people . . . of all the actions that led to the continuing stalemate."

For more than a week after the bombing began, Thach continued to meet with Sullivan in Paris, although the North Vietnamese negotiator walked out on several occasions. It was not until December 27 that Hanoi finally suspended the technical-level talks.

Early Saturday morning, December 30, the White House announced that there would be a special press briefing at 9 A.M. It obviously had to do with Vietnam, but *who* would brief? Kissinger had flown off to Palm Springs to visit with his Hollywood friends, who weren't likely to ask him about the bombing of Vietnam. The President was at Camp David. Ziegler was on a week's vacation in California. The briefer turned out to be Deputy White House Press Secretary Gerald Warren. To the mass of assembled reporters, Warren announced that the President had called a halt in the punishing bombing of the heartland of North Vietnam. "As soon as it was clear," the spokesman said, "that serious negotiations could be resumed at both the technical level and between the principals, the President ordered that all bombing be discontinued above the twentieth parallel."

Warren's announcement touched off a wave of relief at home and throughout the world. Hanoi wanted the bombing stopped, and Nixon wanted to stop the bombing before Congress reconvened on January 3, ready at long last to cut off funds for the war.

Sullivan was back in Paris on New Year's Day. He sensed a new seriousness on Thach's part. "How do you want to proceed?" the North Vietnamese diplomat asked his American counterpart. "We're going to meet every day," Sullivan replied, and "we're going to do a full day's work every day." "We don't have to work more than eight hours a day, do we?" Thach asked with a smile. Sullivan laughed. They got down to business at once.

Tho returned to Paris on Saturday, January 6, Kissinger the following day. Their final, final, final effort at a cease-fire, after years on a negotiating roller coaster, took place on the morning of January 8 at the Communist-owned villa at Gif. Kissinger arrived to a nonexistent welcome; not even the concierge was at the door to greet him. Kissinger hesitated for a moment, then pushed the door open and entered. The subsequent negotiation inside was not much warmer than the reception outside; when Kissinger finally left the villa, after four and a half hours of discussion, Tho did not see him to his limousine, as he had usually done in the past. Kissinger looked grim, and barely nodded to the newsmen waiting outside. Tho had opened the talks with a denunciation of the American bombing — but he had not closed the door to "serious" negotiations.

The next day, January 9, the two diplomats settled down to the task of completing the draft agreement. Issues that had been resolved, and then reopened, were resolved once again. There was forward movement. When Kissinger returned to the Ambassador's residence, he cabled the President that, in his opinion, there would be a breakthrough at last. "Happy birthday, Mr. President," Kissinger concluded. January 9 was Nixon's sixtieth.

Over the next three days, Kissinger and Tho continued to make progress. By the end of the week, they had completed the basic document. For seven and a half hours on Saturday, they reviewed every article, every sentence, every word. There were still minor difficulties on the protocols, but Kissinger was certain that Sullivan and Thach could handle them. By midafternoon, Kissinger invited a U.S. Embassy cameraman to photograph the negotiators around the table. Tho was told that Kissinger would carry their draft agreement to Nixon for his personal perusal and that Haig would then proceed to Saigon to obtain Thieu's approval. Tho bristled, but Kissinger assured him that the South Vietnamese President's position had undergone changes just as, he was relieved to note, Tho's had; Kissinger did not anticipate any difficulty in Saigon this time. Tho, for his part, assured Kissinger that he would remain in Paris and would remain "in *closest* contact." During the six final days of negotiations, they had conferred for a total of twenty-seven hours.

When Kissinger arrived at Orly Airport, shortly before 9 P.M., he cautiously suggested that there had been progress. "Special Adviser Le Duc Tho and I have just *completed* very useful negotiations," Kissinger added, choosing his words carefully. "I shall be returning to report to the President. The President will then decide what next steps should be taken to achieve a peace of justice and of reconciliation."

Minutes after Kissinger's jet headed out toward the Atlantic, the North Vietnamese mission released a statement, affirming that the "negotiations had made progress." It was the first time in three months that Hanoi had admitted "progress."

The final days before the almost anticlimactic cease-fire ticked off with precision.

January 14: Kissinger briefed Nixon shortly after his postmidnight arrival at Key Biscayne. They met again at midday. Ziegler said the negotiations had been "serious."

January 15: Nixon ordered a halt to all U.S. offensive military action against North Vietnam, including air strikes, shelling, and mining operations.

January 16: Haig arrived in Saigon and immediately conferred with Thieu.

January 17: Thieu reluctantly yielded to the terms of the Kissinger-Tho cease-fire agreement, but he expressed reservations about some of the protocols. Haig promised that Sullivan would *try* to satisfy them.

January 18: North Vietnam and the United States issued a brief joint statement. "Dr. Henry Kissinger will resume private briefings with Special Adviser Le Duc Tho and Minister Xuan Thuy on January 23, 1973," Ziegler announced, "for the purpose of completing the text of the agreement."

January 19: Sullivan and Thach managed to take care of some — but not all — of Thieu's reservations. Through Bunker in Saigon, Nixon told Thieu that the agreement could be improved no further and it would be initialed by Kissinger on January 23.

January 20: Nixon was inaugurated for the second time. He said the war was "coming to a close."

January 21: Bob Knudson, a White House photographer, was alerted to go to Paris the next day to take pictures of the initialing ceremony. At the same time, White House staffers were ordered to start compiling the various texts of the full agreement for release to newsmen later in the week.

January 22: Kissinger returned to Paris, and it was announced that his meeting with Tho would take place in the Hotel Majestic, site of the semipublic talks since May, 1968. It was to be the first time they would meet on neutral ground. The four-sided Majestic talks had been concluded on January 18 after four years of negotiations.

January 23: Kissinger and Tho settled the last few details in a final session lasting almost four hours. Then, at 12:30 P.M., they initialed the Agreement on Ending the War and Restoring Peace in Vietnam. America's longest, most divisive war was unofficially ended. Kissinger and Tho, smiling, emerged from the Majestic. It was a typical gray winter day in Paris. They shook hands warmly, again and again, providing every cameraman with a variety of good angles. All the members of both delegations shook hands with each other. Neither of the two principals made any formal announcement. That night, in a television report to the nation, Nixon provided the American people with some of the details of the agreement, adding, "To all of you who are listening . . . your steadfastness in supporting our insistence on peace with honor has made peace with honor possible."

"It was always clear that a lasting peace could come about only if neither side sought to achieve everything that it had wanted; indeed, that stability depended on the relative satisfaction and therefore on the relative dissatisfaction of all of the parties concerned."

That was vintage Kissinger, parsed with almost philosophical detachment at a January 24 news conference summing up the agreement. He had achieved not the optimum but the possible. Nixon got the prisoners back, Tho got the Americans out, Thieu got to keep his hold on power and the PRG got a degree of political legitimacy in South Vietnam. Everybody got something, but nobody got everything. That had been Kissinger's formula for diplomatic success ever since *A World Restored*, twenty years before the Vietnam cease-fire accord.

What did those three extra months of war accomplish — the three months between October 26 and January 23, including the massive raids against the north in December? Kissinger tried to make the interval seem worthwhile. Most important, he once told us, he had "removed any ambiguity about a coalition government." Next, "the specific identity of South Vietnam" had been "more sharply established," by the affirmation of the DMZ. Then, the international police force had been strengthened. The procedural wrangle over who would sign the final agreement, and when, had been resolved. Linguistic problems had been clarified.

Kissinger's official catalog of benefits stemming from an extra season of war is regarded with considerable skepticism by quite a few American specialists who followed the negotiations closely. "Peanuts," said one such official, when asked what those additional months of warfare had achieved. "That enormous bombing made little critical difference. What the B-52s did was to get the margin in January pretty much back to where it was in October, and by then that's all we wanted." There were some "modest" changes in the final agreement, but, he contended, the major breakthrough had already occurred in October.

Indeed, there are many who believe that it was not the bombing that brought Hanoi back to Paris but instead a U.S. readiness to sign an agreement that had essentially been outlined in October. "Look," one official said, in reviewing that crucial period, "we were in an embarrassing situation. Could we suddenly say we'll sign in January what we wouldn't in October? We had to do something. So the bombing began, to try to create the image of a defeated enemy crawling back to the peace table to accept terms demanded by the U.S. Maybe the bombing had some effect — there are differing perceptions on this — but the B-52s weren't critical, although the Administration has been able to sell that notion."

Most officials believed that the bombing was designed to be a massive show of psychological and military support for Saigon, an attempt to undercut Hanoi's future war-making potential, and a warning to the Communists in Moscow, Peking and Hanoi that Nixon was capable of strong action when he felt his interests threatened.

Months later, in a candid moment, Kissinger would suggest that the gains were marginal and that he would have urged the acceptance of a less precise agreement in October. But it was Nixon who was calling the shots in the concluding stages of the negotiations, and he had his reasons for delay. He did not want to sign an agreement without Thieu, an ally. He did not want to be stampeded into an agreement by Tho, an enemy. Kissinger had a bleaker vision of Saigon's future than Nixon. He believed that the most that could be salvaged from the U.S. involvement in Vietnam was a "decent interval" between an American pullout and the possibility of a Communist take-over. In the best of all Vietnamese worlds, nothing could be ensured for more than three or four years.

On January 27, Rogers signed the formal Vietnam agreement on behalf of the United States in Paris. Helen Thomas, a UPI correspondent who has covered the White House for many years, wanted to know what Kissinger was doing at the very moment Rogers put pen to paper in Paris. Because of the time difference, 11 A.M. in Paris was 6 A.M. in Washington. Kissinger's answer came through the press office. "Making love, not war," it said.

SIXTEEN

The Impact of Watergate

WITH THE END of America's longest involvement in a foreign war, Henry Kissinger believed that the country was on the threshold of one of the great creative periods in U.S. foreign policy. "Partly by luck, partly by design, partly by circumstance," he felt, the United States could now look forward to a period in which the accent would be on productive diplomacy rather than on the nightmare of Vietnam.

True, the opportunities for diplomatic spectaculars were shrinking — the doors to Moscow and Peking were already ajar — but, just as significant, the major nuclear powers seemed to share Kissinger's desire to preserve and expand these openings. The United States, he believed, could take advantage of this emergence of parallel foreign policy requirements to lead the world to an era of peace. "Oh, you can't say permanent peace," he conceded, shying away from eternity, "but at least you can help set the structure in place."

There were still loose ends to be tied up in Indochina; but, for the first time, Kissinger felt that he could move beyond the solution of immediate crises and concentrate on consolidating the progress already made in America's relations with Russia and China, and devote more attention to other parts of the world.

The Soviet Union: he wanted to solidify détente as an international habit and to achieve an historic SALT II agreement aimed at reducing the *offensive* nuclear stockpiles of the two superpowers.

China: he wanted to continue to expand U.S. relations with the world's most populous nation — his leverage over Russia.

Europe: he wanted to strengthen the Atlantic alliance, to revive Jean Monnet's vision of a "golden triangle" embracing all of Western Europe, Canada and the United States.

Japan: he wanted to restore the mutual trust that Washington and Tokyo had enjoyed prior to the 1971 "shocks" of the China opening and the dollar devaluation.

The Middle East: he wanted to defuse Arab-Israeli hostility, though in early 1973 he felt no acute sense of alarm about the situation.

Latin America: he wanted to chart a new beginning with a neighbor too long ignored.

To take on such an ambitious agenda required, in Kissinger's view, the healing of national wounds suffered through the long, divisive war in Vietnam and the re-creation of the bipartisan support that had strengthened U.S. foreign policy during the post–World War II period. He hoped that the way in which the Administration had ended the Vietnam war — by "not selling out the people with whom we had dealt," as he put it, and by achieving what he regarded as "decent objectives" — would help to usher in a "period of national reconciliation" — a blessed new beginning after a decade of foreign misadventures, domestic upheavals, and political assassinations.

Reconciliation would have to start with the bureaucracy — which had been excluded from every significant diplomatic development in the past four years. State Department officials complained, with some justification, that Kissinger had monopolized foreign affairs so completely that one of the great departments of government, with a staff of twelve thousand, had been reduced to mere paper-shuffling. Often its top officials would be called upon to explain policies about which they had not been fully briefed and which they did not fully support. Morale was nonexistent. Kissinger realized that virtuoso diplomacy — so invaluable in achieving the breakthroughs of Nixon's first term — would have to be replaced by more of a team effort. He planned to begin what he called the process of "institutionalizing" policy: involving the State Department in discussions and negotiations from which it had earlier been excluded.

Morale was low at the NSC, too.

Because of his one-man style of operation, Kissinger had become a kind of bottleneck in his own NSC system. Major decisions were often held up while he was away on his secret journeys. His diplomatic road shows may have left the audiences cheering in the aisles, but backstage at the NSC, the supporting cast waited restlessly for the return of the star. During these absences, his deputy, General Haig, and later, Haig's successor, Brigadier Brent Scowcroft, would pitch in, but everyone on the staff understood that Kissinger was the only one who could really make the decisions. Besides, important information was so closely held that many specialists in the outer reaches of the staff would be working on analyses without appreciating the full implications of their effort. "It was really a lonely place to work," said one NSC veteran. "Each man with his own piece of geography." Only belatedly did Kissinger recognize that the "wonderful machine" of the Administration's early years needed a tune-up.

Kissinger's new willingness to relinquish part of his control over policy-making was also motivated by personal reasons; in January, 1973, he did not plan to stay on at the White House through the second Nixon term. He was thinking of leaving toward the end of summer, perhaps in September. He felt that four years was enough time to serve in a job in which he was, as Senator Stuart Symington once put it, "Secretary of State in everything but name." There had been rumors during the past year or two that Kissinger might replace Rogers, but these rumors were always immediately spiked by the White House. Other rumors suggested that Nixon might name John Connally to replace Rogers — and Kissinger knew that he could not stay on with Connally as Secretary of State. Kissinger's relations with Nixon's other senior advisers had grown steadily worse, perhaps reaching their nadir in November and December, at the time of Kissinger's greatest vulnerability, when the "peace" that was "at hand" failed to materialize until several weeks later. At that time, he felt the palace guard was putting out totally misleading information, setting him up to be the "fall guy" in the event the Vietnam negotiations collapsed.

But Kissinger was not ready to leave just yet. He was reluctant to do anything that would embarrass the presidency; and if he waited another eight or nine months, he could leave at a time when everyone understood that he was departing voluntarily, when he could be fairly sure the policies he had initiated would be carried on. He would probably go to London for a period of decompression, leaving a career decision for a later date. Some of his close friends speculated that he would open an international consulting firm — "HAK, Inc.," for example. But this was all in the future. Before he left, he would try to institutionalize foreign policy and to create a bipartisan consensus of support.

But a funny thing happened to Kissinger on his way to his new objectives: Watergate. The discovery of one illegal scheme after another, linked to names at the highest levels of the Nixon Administration, resulted in the greatest political scandal of the century. By mid-April Kissinger had become moderately concerned about Watergate. By late May the scandal began to have a personal impact upon him. By the end of June he realized that it was jeopardizing the grand design of his foreign policy. As the acid of Watergate splashed around the world, corroding the international stature and credibility of the President, foreign chancelleries found themselves seriously pondering the question of whether the President himself would survive. Kissinger faced a simple fact of international life: the countries with which you are dealing have to believe in the validity of your commitments over a period of time; otherwise, they will tend to hedge their bets. For the rest of the year, as Watergate increasingly dominated the headlines, Kissinger tried desperately to keep the fabled, now imperiled "structure of peace" from toppling.

Europe: 1973, on the projected pre-Watergate calendar, was to have been the "Year of Europe."

The continent that had once been the political, cultural and economic center of the West had slipped out of Washington's range of vision during its long obsession with Vietnam. Relations with America's oldest allies were strained: attitudes, on both sides of the Atlantic, distorted. There were many reasons: Europe's growing economic competitiveness; America's increasing resentment about having to foot too large a bill for Europe's security; European concern about Nixon's unpredictable moves in foreign affairs. To many Europeans, America seemed to have lost its sense of priorities by getting bogged down in Vietnam; the country seemed deeply divided, caught up in a series of suicidal crises. To many Americans, Europe seemed to have lost *its* sense of priorities by putting selfish nationalism ahead of Atlantic unity; the Continent seemed to be engaged in egocentric babbling, confident that America would always bail her out in a crisis. Europe and America were going their separate ways — a drift that, if left unchecked, would be applauded as an act of statesmanship only by the Russians.

Kissinger was aware of all these emotional and intellectual crosscurrents; he had been concerned for years about the growing rift between the United States and Europe. During the Kennedy and Johnson years, when he was an outsider, he had criticized those in power —

McGeorge Bundy, George Ball, Walt Rostow — for alienating the Europeans by their high-handed treatment. Once in power, though, Kissinger began to sound exactly like them. He believed that most European leaders were politically weak and ambivalent about American policy. In the predétente days, they kept urging the United States to adopt a conciliatory attitude toward Moscow; now, with détente, they had begun to accuse the United States of forming a big-power condominium with the Soviet Union. Kissinger found their attitude illogical and exasperating. "I think any fair assessment has to blame the Europeans for ninety-five percent of what's gone wrong," he said. "What the hell did we do wrong?"

Nevertheless, Kissinger was determined to restore the Atlantic alliance with "a fresh act of creation, equal to that undertaken by the postwar generation of leaders of Europe and America." The goal of improving transatlantic relationships — apart from its obvious foreign policy benefits — was tailormade for Kissinger's plan to create a bipartisan spirit in the country. It was a goal no one, on either side of the aisle, could regard as controversial.

Kissinger began the effort by arranging a series of mini-summits between Nixon and the leaders of Western Europe for the spring and summer, and he projected a presidential swing through Western Europe in the fall.

And, with the help of a few close advisers — none from the State Department, despite his oft-stated desire to "institutionalize" policy — he drafted a speech, carefully seeded with references sure to evoke wartime memories of unity at home and abroad, in which he diagnosed the disarray in the alliance and proposed a cure: a "new Atlantic Charter."

The speech was delivered on April 23 at New York's Waldorf-Astoria before an audience that would quickly disseminate the message: a group of the nation's most influential publishers, editors, and television executives, invited by the Associated Press. Actually, Nixon had been asked to make the major address, but he had turned the assignment over to Kissinger, instructing him to "explain to Europe what we are all about." To ensure the most extensive coverage, the United States Information Service broadcast the Kissinger speech live to Europe and distributed texts to all U.S. embassies on the Continent.

Welcomed by a standing ovation as he approached the microphone, Kissinger began: "This year has been called the Year of Europe, but not because Europe was less important in 1972 or in 1969. The alliance between the United States and Europe has been the cornerstone of all postwar foreign policy. . . . 1973 is the Year of Europe because the era that was shaped by decisions of a generation ago is ending. The success of those policies has produced new realities that require new approaches." He went beyond generalities and frankly detailed some of the problems troubling the alliance. "There have been complaints in America," he observed, "that Europe ignores its wider responsibilities in pursuing economic self-interest too one-sidedly and that Europe is not carrying its fair share of the burden of the common defense. There have been complaints in Europe that America is out to divide Europe economically, or to desert Europe militarily, or to bypass Europe diplomatically. . . ."

He then made his key point: "The United States proposes to its Atlantic partners that, by the time the President travels to Europe toward the end of the year, we will have worked out a new Atlantic Charter setting the goals for the future — a blueprint that:

"Builds on the past without becoming its prisoner;

"Deals with the problems our success has created;

"Creates for the Atlantic nations a new relationship in whose progress Japan can share.

"We ask our friends in Europe, Canada and ultimately Japan to join us in this effort. This is what we mean by the Year of Europe."

Again, there was a standing ovation, as listeners began to compare Kissinger's speech to the famous Marshall Plan speech by Secretary of State George C. Marshall, at Harvard, almost twenty-six years earlier, dealing with the reconstruction of Europe after World War II.

Many written questions were passed up to the dais. Kissinger divided them into three categories: East-West relations, Indochina, and Watergate.

He launched into Watergate with a laugh.

Q: "Where were you the night they bugged Watergate?"

A: "I usually have excellent alibis for my evenings."

But then he turned serious. Acknowledging that the Watergate affair could affect the nation's foreign relations, he said, "A great deal will depend on how foreign countries will assess the degree of authority in this country, and the degree of dedication of the public to the objectives of its foreign policy. I have no question that the President will insist, as he has said publicly, on a full disclosure of the facts. When that is accomplished, and the human tragedies are complete, the country will go on."

"It is difficult," he said at another point, "to avoid a sense of the awfulness of events and the tragedy that has befallen so many people who

. . . for whatever reason, are alleged to have done certain things. So without prejudging anything, one should at least ask for compassion." He concluded by saying: "We have to ask ourselves whether we can afford an orgy of recrimination, or whether we should not keep in mind that the United States will be there for longer than any particular crisis, and whether all of us do not then have an obligation to remember that the faith in the country must be maintained and that the promise in the country should be eternal."

Again, there was applause, but applause can be terribly misleading. In this case, it led Kissinger to believe that he had placed Watergate in historical perspective and refocused national attention on the important challenge of the "Year of Europe." By the time he returned to Washington and turned on the evening television news shows, he realized that he had misjudged his audience. The network newscasts took note of the "new Atlantic Charter" but they featured his extemporaneous comments about Watergate. The next morning, only the *New York Times,* of all the country's leading newspapers, banner-headlined his prepared speech. The *Washington Post,* for instance, gave only passing notice to the Atlantic alliance, while it gave prominent play on the front page to his Watergate remarks.

Kissinger was astonished to find himself under attack because of his plea for "compassion" and his anxiety about "an orgy of recrimination." "Mr. Kissinger," editorialized the *Times,* "seems to be transferring guilt from those who instigated Watergate to those who have exposed it."

The European response to Kissinger's speech was even more disappointing. The phrase "new Atlantic Charter" offended many leaders on the Continent, to whom it suggested only a new form of Anglo-American hegemony. By early summer, the Administration quietly dropped the phrase. In its place came a new phrase: a "declaration of principles" — which Kissinger hoped would accomplish the same purpose. But a change of phrase was not enough; the differences between the United States and its European allies had become too deep to be bridged by good intentions or eloquent phraseology. Kissinger wanted a single charter, or declaration, linking military, political, and economic issues because he believed that it would enhance the bargaining power of the United States, which could then secure a better economic and political deal from the Europeans in exchange for maintaining three hundred thousand nuclear-equipped American troops in central Europe — the backbone of Atlantic defense. The Europeans, on the other hand, did not want to be tied down by new commitments to the United States.

They wanted America's nuclear protection against the possibility of a Soviet attack, but they did not want to support America's weakened economy. They wanted the freedom to make individual economic deals — for example, for Arab oil — without having to clear them with Washington. The Europeans decided it would be to their advantage to press for two separate declarations: a NATO declaration dealing with defense strategy, and a second declaration dealing with economic and political questions. After months of discussion, the Europeans refused to budge; and Kissinger was forced to accept their formula — with one condition: he insisted upon a third declaration that would spell out the relationship between Japan, Western Europe, and the United States.

In the meantime, Nixon had become so absorbed with Watergate that he was forced to postpone his grand tour of Europe.

Later, after the obituary of the "Year of Europe" had been published in newspapers on both sides of the Atlantic, Kissinger would look back on his efforts to reforge the unity of the alliance and wonder why he was having more trouble with America's allies than with her adversaries. Under normal conditions, he believed, the project would have generated a good deal of intellectual support at home, enough to overcome some of the very real problems dividing the United States and Europe. But because of the country's preoccupation with Watergate, Europe receded as an urgent item on the national agenda. The Europeans, for their part, became concerned about the stability of the Nixon Administration, and this made them even more reluctant to enter into any complicated new arrangements with the United States. The "Year of Europe," Kissinger concluded, had become an indirect casualty of Watergate.

Vietnam: In early February, 1973, before Watergate exploded, Kissinger flew off on his first trip to Hanoi. It was his way of shifting the postwar focus from "hostility to normalization." In nineteen hours of talks, he made it clear to Premier Pham Van Dong and Paris negotiator Le Duc Tho that the United States was ready, as pledged in the accords, to contribute to the reconstruction of North Vietnam and Indochina but that until the accords were "fully implemented," Congress might not be in the mood to appropriate any funds. Kissinger appealed to Hanoi to stop violating the cease-fire, and he agreed to press Saigon to observe the rules so painfully negotiated in Paris. He also used the occasion to remind Tho that during the Paris negotiations the North Vietnamese envoy had promised to use his influence to end the fighting in Laos and

Cambodia. Though the war in Laos was then just sputtering along, the one in Cambodia was raging.

After his return to Washington, Kissinger regularly checked the intelligence reports from Indochina to see if his appeal had had any effect. The reports were not encouraging. Violations of the cease-fire were continuing; no progress was being made toward organizing elections along the lines called for by the Paris Accords, and Saigon was proceeding with its own plans for nationwide balloting — without the participation of the National Liberation Front.

"It is a brutal fact," Kissinger said in April, "that . . . the important clauses of the agreement . . . have been systematically, if I may say, cynically violated by the other side." He then raised what he called "a profound problem" — whether the United States should "sign an agreement," which was "endorsed by an international conference," and then, as soon as the agreement was "violated," treat its signature as "irrelevant." Kissinger wanted the option to resume U.S. bombing of the north if Communist violations intensified.

Kissinger checked Congress's pulse almost as frequently as he checked the intelligence reports, and the reading was clear: Congress wanted "out." It had no interest in providing economic aid to North Vietnam — the "carrot" of the Administration's carrot-and-stick policy. Even the doves doubted that the aid would persuade Hanoi to preserve the cease-fire, and the hawks were aghast at the idea of contributing funds to Hanoi. What the Administration called "an investment in peace," they called "reparations"; and they wanted no part of it. As Senator Goldwater put it, "The North Vietnamese were the culprits in this. They could have ended the war before it caused any damage to their country. Their failure to do so caused many American deaths, and I don't think we should pay them for it."

In addition, Congress could see less and less reason to continue the bombing of Indochina — the "stick" part of Administration policy. All through March and April, Kissinger kept going to the Hill to argue that continued bombing of Cambodia would force Hanoi to comply with the Paris Accords and bring about a cease-fire there; but his efforts were regarded with increasing incredulity. He was fighting a losing battle. By the end of April, even the House of Representatives was beginning to swing against any further American military involvement in Indochina. The successive Watergate revelations that kept the President on the defensive emboldened a growing number of legislators to shed their silent frustration and speak out against the bombing in Cambodia. Overnight, the Watergate scandal created new allies for the Senators and Representatives who had been against the war for many years. Even former supporters of the war, such as Senator Norris Cotton of New Hampshire, suddenly began to favor a complete cutoff of funds for all military operations in or over Indochina. "As far as I'm concerned," the GOP conservative said, "I want to get the hell out."

Kissinger realized that Congress might soon limit the President's freedom of action and that he had better move quickly to secure a fresh affirmation of the Paris Accords from the North Vietnamese and negotiate a cease-fire in Cambodia. So, in an attempt to buy time to give Nixon's policy a chance to work, he asked for another Paris session with Le Duc Tho — "my old friend in the search for peace," to use Kissinger's sardonic phrase. Tho, who had read all about the debates in Congress, agreed. Their first meeting was set for May 17.

Watergate followed Kissinger to Paris. When he arrived, he was confronted by the headline in *France-Soir:* "THE SHADOW OF WATERGATE HOVERS OVER THE KISSINGER–LE DUC THO NEGOTIATIONS." The first session of Paris II, as it was soon called, lasted more than five hours, as the two men discussed ways of consolidating the shaky cease-fire agreement signed in January. There would be another forty hours of talks, and a second Kissinger trip to Paris in June, before the two negotiators came to an understanding.

They had smiles for the cameramen at the conclusion of each session, but this was hardly a clue as to what was taking place behind closed doors. At one session, the silver-haired envoy from Hanoi leaned across the negotiating table and looked directly at the envoy from the White House. "You know, Dr. Kissinger," he said, with mock seriousness, "I want to speak to you this time openly, sincerely, and honestly: you are a liar." Kissinger's reply has never been made public.

In a way, the entire effort seemed like a charade, even to a number of officials who were part of it. Kissinger no longer held the strong negotiating hand of earlier days, when there were more than five hundred thousand GIs in Vietnam and U.S. fighter-bombers and Stratofortresses ranged over the skies of the north. Kissinger knew it, and Tho knew it, too. Kissinger had always held in reserve the threat of renewed bombing if Hanoi did not live up to the cease-fire agreement. Now, as Watergate weakened the Administration and sentiment shifted on Capitol Hill, both sides realized that that threat was no longer credible.

The North Vietnamese themselves began to make what one high official described as "sly cracks" about Watergate. "You say we are sending equipment illegally into South Vietnam," they told Kissinger. "Well, that is just an effort to deceive public opinion, as you have done with Watergate. It is part of the same pattern." The negotiators were reflecting the line taken by Hanoi's official newspaper, *Nhan Dan:* "The Watergate affair can help many people . . . see clearly the nature of the present U.S. leaders." Watergate, it went on, "has exposed the viciousness and rottenness of those holding the highest positions in the United States."

On June 13, Kissinger and Tho finally completed their negotiations. Their twenty-five-hundred-word communiqué was essentially a reiteration of the original January 27 cease-fire agreement, with all of its ambiguities and weaknesses. The most important failure of the new accord was that it did not provide for an end to the fighting in Cambodia and Laos. At a farewell news conference in Paris, Kissinger indicated his own frustration with the talks when he said, "The art of compromise is not the most highly developed quality in Vietnam." He added that in the future he hoped to reduce his own participation in Indochina negotiations — "in order to preserve my emotional stability."

When Kissinger returned to Washington, he continued to court Congress, hoping to win more bombing time in Cambodia by sharing confidences about "diplomatic irons in the fire" and about the "probability" of a Cambodian cease-fire by early September. But Congress had heard it all before. On June 30, in an historic vote, weary hawks joined jubilant doves in overriding Administration protests and voting to cut off funds for all U.S. military activity in or over Indochina, effective August 15 — a compromise date that gave the White House a final six weeks to find a solution to the war in Cambodia.

It was in this time frame that Kissinger tried to get in touch with Prince Sihanouk, the deposed Cambodian ruler who was living in exile in Peking, to enlist his help in reaching a compromise; but the titular leader of the forces opposing the Lon Nol regime was then in no mood for discussion. "It is useless to talk to Kissinger," Sihanouk told reporters. "There is no time to talk. Now it is too late. We will continue our armed struggle." Perhaps Sihanouk recalled an occasion earlier in the year when he had sought a meeting with Kissinger, only to be told that Kissinger had no interest in seeing *him.*

Now, after Congress had acted to take the United States militarily out of the war, neither the North Vietnamese nor the Cambodian Khmer Rouge felt they had to do anything more than keep up the pressure and eventually Cambodia would fall into their hands. About the time the bombs stopped falling, Kissinger admitted to friends that he had "misjudged the effect of Watergate" on Communist policy. "It's a tragedy," he said, "a tragedy. We are tearing ourselves apart. I never realized how badly."

In Kissinger's view, the North Vietnamese were especially sensitive to the Administration's degree of authority. It took the United States "four years to teach them," he once explained, that the Administration possessed more authority than they thought. "Time and again, they had counted on a declining Administration position, and time and again they had been disappointed," he said. "But this time, they may well draw the conclusion that it is for real. It would be idle to say that the authority of the executive has not been impaired."

By the late summer of 1973, Kissinger was discouraged about the future of that corner of the world where the United States had invested so much. He had reluctantly come to the conclusion that Cambodia, once described by the President as "the Nixon Doctrine in its purest form," was lost. He assumed that the Lon Nol regime would survive for a while, but that ultimately it would not have the staying power to hold off the Khmer Rouge. A Cambodian collapse, he feared, would have a severe effect on the security of South Vietnam and Thailand.

By December, 1973, Communist attacks were on the upgrade throughout Cambodia and South Vietnam. Following an intensive round of negotiations in the Middle East, Kissinger stopped in Paris on December 20 to discuss the continuing warfare in Indochina with Le Duc Tho. Kissinger claimed Tho had requested the meeting; Tho insisted Kissinger had. In either case, by that time it was clear that Kissinger was determined that the United States would never again become enmeshed in Vietnam. "We are not going to make ourselves the principal party . . . to that whole mess," he told a small group of reporters that day. "We will not get into political discussions with both Vietnams. We spent four years trying to get out. We're not going to get back in."

The Kissinger-Tho talks took place several days after the Nobel Peace Prize Committee, on December 10, distributed its awards for 1973. Kissinger had earlier begged off the ceremonies in Oslo because of the press of business; he was in Brussels, attending a NATO council meeting, when his designated stand-in, U.S. Ambassador to Norway Thomas Byrne, evading snowballs and anti-American demonstrators, slipped through the rear entrance of an auditorium at the University of Oslo to accept Kissinger's award. The sixty thousand dollars that accompanied the prize was set aside by Kissinger for a scholarship fund for children of U.S. servicemen killed or missing in action in Indochina. Tho, who had been designated corecipient of the Nobel Peace Prize with Kissinger, had turned down the award because of what he described as "very serious violations" of the cease-fire by South Vietnam and the United States. "When the Paris agreement on Vietnam is respected, guns are silenced, and peace is really restored in South Vietnam, I will consider the acceptance of this prize," he said in his letter of rejection.

China: Kissinger visited China twice in 1973 — in February and again in November. On both occasions he had long talks with Mao Tse-tung and Chou En-lai — talks that advanced the cause of Chinese-American accommodation. But in the nine months between the two visits, there was a change of mood — subtle but unmistakable — that was caused as much by the political scandal in America as by new political strains within China.

Kissinger arrived in Peking on February 15, a couple of weeks after the Vietnam agreement was signed in Paris. On his third evening in China, at about eleven-fifteen, at the end of a long negotiating session, Chou looked across the table at Kissinger and said, rather casually, "Now I have something that may be a surprise for you. Chairman Mao would like to see you if it's convenient. And if it is convenient, I think you should go to your guesthouse and I'll pick you up there in ten minutes." The invitation was, as Chou suggested, a surprise; Mao normally met only with heads of state. Ten minutes later, Chou's limousine pulled into the circular driveway in front of Kissinger's guesthouse, and the two of them drove off to Mao's residence in Peking's Forbidden City.

The Chairman greeted Kissinger with a few words of English. "Please sit down. Make yourself comfortable." He did most of the talking, in broad, historical terms, about the past, present and future of the world. Kissinger contributed his observations. Kissinger sensed that Mao wanted to move toward closer relations with Washington, but he said nothing explicitly. At one point, Chinese cameramen appeared to record the scene, taking a photograph that would appear the next day in *Jenmin Jih Pao* and film that would be shown throughout China — a signal to the masses that their revered leader had continuing faith in the rapprochement with the United States. After almost two hours of talk, Mao escorted Kissinger to the door and they exchanged farewells.

Chou later confirmed what Kissinger had sensed: that Mao was willing to permit the United States to set up a "liaison office" in Peking — the highest form of diplomatic representation short of establishing an embassy. Kissinger had expected a lower form of representation — a trade or cultural mission; and he was pleased that Mao was prepared to go higher. But his real surprise came when Chou said that China would like to set up a "liaison office" in Washington — despite the fact that Chiang Kai-shek maintained a full-fledged embassy there. That was a sharp break from former Maoist practice of never coexisting in the same capital with Chiang's representatives.

In the middle of May, Ambassador David Bruce reached Peking to open the first United States liaison mission to the Chinese Communists since 1947; the last official American representation to the Communists had been at Yenan, Mao's capital in northwest China, between 1944 and 1947. The courteous welcome the seventy-five-year-old American diplomat received in Peking was a sign that China was ready to be politically flexible — without abandoning her belief that history, over the long term, was on her side. As Stanley Karnow, in Peking at the time, wrote: "They are currently citing an old line of Mao to the effect that American imperialism is sitting on a 'volcano' of 'irreconcilable domestic and international contradictions.'" This was not interpreted as a reference to Watergate, although the Chinese leader had begun to read about the scandal with interest.

In late May, Chinese Ambassador Huang Chen, who was then China's only ambassador belonging to the Communist Party's Central Committee, arrived in Washington. Less than twenty-four hours later, he was seated in a gold-upholstered armchair in the Oval Office. The swiftness of his first meeting with President Nixon was unusual; sometimes, ambassadors from countries with which the United States enjoys full diplomatic relations must wait for a month or more before setting foot in the White House. Nixon thanked Huang for the welcome Bruce had been given in Peking. "Ambassador Bruce has held more top assignments than any ambassador in the history of America," the President told Huang. He then expressed the hope that Huang would get comfortably settled in Washington. "If there are any slipups," he joked, "we will fire Dr. Kissinger."

The November visit — Kissinger's sixth to China but his first as Secretary of State — came after an exhausting swing through the Middle East in the wake of the Yom Kippur War. By contrast, China was relaxing and exhilarating — "Kissinger Country," as one reporter put it. "None of us who took this trip can ever forget the sense of excitement on entering China for the first time," Kissinger recalled in a toast to Chou at a banquet on November 10, the night of his arrival in Peking. "We thought it was a mysterious country until the Premier pointed out that it was more our ignorance than China's mystery." By then, he had mastered the art of using chopsticks.

"You have no idea how good it is," Kissinger said to Chou that night during the ritual of posing for photographs, "not to have to talk about two-forty-two" — a reference to the 1967 UN Security Council resolution calling for Israeli withdrawal from occupied Arab territory. The Chinese Premier laughed. At that point, Vice Foreign Minister Chiao Kuan-hua said, "What about resolutions three-thirty-eight and three-thirty-nine?" — the Middle East cease-fire resolutions that had been adopted by the Security Council in October. Kissinger replied that he had heard that Chiao had "pounded the table" during an argument with the Soviet Union's Jakob Malik at the time of the UN debate on the Middle East. "Not with my shoe, though," Chiao replied, in a jab at the Soviet Union; he was referring to the famous shoe-pounding by Nikita Khrushchev during a 1960 General Assembly meeting.

Kissinger's November session with Mao lasted two hours and forty-five minutes — an unusually long time. *Jenmin Jih Pao* featured pictures of them on its front page, as it had in February. This time, however, the newspaper stated that the talks had been held in a "friendly atmosphere." This was the first time the word "friendly" had been used to describe any of Kissinger's meetings with the Chinese leaders. It was interpreted as a signal of the importance that Peking placed on its relations with Washington.

After three and a half days of conferences, mixed with a bit of sightseeing, Kissinger and Chou agreed on the wording of a communiqué. It hinted that the two countries would soon establish full diplomatic relations. In response to speculation at the time that Kissinger was trying to entice Chou to visit the United States, Chou smiled. "As long as there is a representative of the Chiang Kai-shek clique, how can I go there?" he asked American newsmen.

Despite the photographs, the joking and the signals of goodwill, there was an undercurrent of uneasiness about this visit. The Chinese were concerned about *Shui men,* the Chinese word for Watergate: after all, Mao and Chou had bet on increasingly close ties with the United States as a counterweight against the Russians, and they feared that Watergate might undercut the President with whom they had negotiated. In an interview only a month before, Chou had told C. L. Sulzberger of the *New York Times* that he hoped President Nixon would be able to overcome his present difficulties. The Chinese Premier added that relations between the two countries had in no way been affected by Watergate. "You have had such things occur in your society before and undoubtedly will have them again," he said. "It is better not to talk about this issue." But Chinese officials speaking privately with American newsmen in the fall of 1973 were more explicit; they were concerned that any weakening of the President, as a result of Watergate, would be to the advantage of "a certain superpower" — the Soviet Union. "There are more important things in the world than Watergate," one of them put it.

At the final banquet in the Great Hall of the People, on November 13, Kissinger sought to reassure Premier Chou En-lai about the permanence of the American half of the Chinese-American relationship. "The progress that has been made in our relations will be continued in the years ahead, whatever happens in the future and whatever the Administration," he said.

American reporters traveling with Kissinger interpreted his pledge to mean that Watergate would not impede Washington's efforts to expand relations with China. The Secretary denied that his remarks were intended to reassure the Chinese about the possible impact of Watergate on Chinese-American relations. All he intended to say, he insisted, was that U.S. policy toward China had bipartisan support. He claimed that the Chinese were concerned that the Democrats were more isolationist than the Republicans.

After Kissinger's February trip to Peking, his spirits were soaring, and the surprise White House announcement about the opening of liaison offices dominated the headlines as still another bit of Kissinger magic. After the second trip, in November, his buoyant mood seemed tinged with uncertainty. He told reporters that he could not be sure when he would return. He wasn't sure what was going to happen in Peking, where new political rivalries seemed to be shaping up, and he certainly wasn't sure what was going to happen in a Washington stricken by Watergate.

The Brezhnev Summit: Soviet Party Chief Leonid Brezhnev's visit to America in June, 1973, came midway between Kissinger's two meetings with Mao in Peking. For the Chinese, Watergate that summer was just a rumble of distant thunder from the far side of the Pacific; but the Russians would see their leader flying into the center of the storm. Americans, that June, sat transfixed before their television sets, waiting for John W. Dean III to enter the Senate Caucus Room with a *j'accuse* against the President. Shortly after Brezhnev's arrival, the Senate Select Watergate Committee decided to postpone its hearings for a week so that Nixon could meet the Soviet leader without being embarrassed by what was expected to be extremely damaging testimony about his alleged involvement in the Watergate coverup. "I can see why the President's attention might be distracted by the Watergate investigation when he's trying to negotiate arms limitations agreements," Senator Sam Ervin, Jr., observed.

The summit had been in the works long before the Watergate scandal broke. In May, 1972, when Nixon was in Moscow, he had invited Brezhnev to pay a return visit to the United States. Kissinger had journeyed to Moscow to prepare for the first summit, and he returned to prepare for the second. He arrived in the Soviet capital on May 4, and was invited to join Brezhnev at the Soviet equivalent of Camp David — a guarded government compound near the Volga River village of Zavidovo, less than a hundred miles from Moscow. Kissinger was the first Westerner to visit this attractive rustic hideaway, complete with pool and sauna, deep in a birch forest, where the Russian leaders can get in a bit of hunting and hiking away from the tensions of Moscow. Not far from Zavidovo is an artificial lake, on which Brezhnev occasionally enjoys racing his motorboat. Kissinger was put up in a hunting lodge near Brezhnev's dacha, the site of their negotiations. Throughout his four-day stay, Kissinger found his host extremely solicitous — inquiring about the facilities, the service, the cuisine. He seemed eager to be reassured that everything was comfortable; he wanted to know whether Kissinger thought the President would enjoy Zavidovo. Once, Brezhnev invited Kissinger to join him in a boar hunt; the event called for Kissinger to don a quasi-military uniform. Kissinger refused to do any shooting. "I don't like to kill animals," he says. Despite his attitude, his host reserved for him one of the kills — a boar's head, sent to Washington weeks later, apparently in the Soviet diplomatic pouch, and presented to Kissinger by Ambassador Dobrynin.

During their talks at Zavidovo, Kissinger and Brezhnev concluded a series of agreements that would be unveiled during the summit meetings with Nixon. The two adversaries needed each other. Brezhnev had two concerns: he was in search of American assistance to help modernize Russia, and he was eager to firm up relations with the United States to offset the Sino-American honeymoon.

Nixon's problem could be summed up in a word: Watergate. Nixon had bailed Brezhnev out of a domestic crisis the year before with massive grain deliveries; Brezhnev could now help shore up Nixon's prestige.

Two days before he left for Washington, the Communist leader sought to cast a transatlantic image of a hail-fellow-well-met via American television and newspapers. He gave a news conference for eleven American reporters, and he spent more than three hours touring the Kremlin with them and talking about his forthcoming journey. It was the first time he referred publicly to the Watergate scandal. "It never entered my head whether President Nixon lost any influence as a result of the Watergate case," the veteran of Kremlin political infighting said in response to a question. "I am not going to the United States with any intention of bringing pressure to bear on the President because of the Watergate affair. It would be completely indecent for me to refer to it."

Brezhnev flew into Andrews Air Force Base on June 16 aboard an Ilyushin-62 four-engine jet. At Soviet insistence, his arrival at the airport was informal — and covered by only a small pool of newsmen, in contrast to the elaborate ceremonies, complete with President, dignitaries, honor guard, and massive press coverage, that had greeted Nikita Khrushchev on his visit to the United States in 1959. A light rain was falling. "This," said Secretary of State Rogers, heading the welcoming party at Andrews, "is a wheat rain, which in America is a very good omen." The visitor smiled. A light rain had fallen on Nixon's arrival in Moscow the year before, and the Russians had described it as "a mushroom rain." Brezhnev draped his coat over his shoulders, exchanged a few words with the waiting Russian diplomats and their families, and went off to Camp David. He would spend the weekend there and be welcomed formally at the White House Monday morning.

The Nixon-Brezhnev week in Washington went off smoothly, with the most serious known mishap being Brezhnev's spilling a glass of champagne at the State Department.

Brezhnev met with a group of American bankers and businessmen and made a pitch for expanded economic relations. He met with members of Congress and urged that they not let quarrels about Jewish emigration stand in the way of broadened cooperation. He sought to leave his listeners with the impression that he had made the journey not to "bury" capitalism — a word Khrushchev had used undiplomatically in 1959 — but rather to profit from it, in the form of trade, credits, and technology for the development of his country.

Throughout Brezhnev's stay in Washington — his itinerary was limited for reasons of security and concern over anti-Soviet and anti-Nixon demonstrations — the agreements that he had reached with Kissinger were signed, one day after another, in what amounted to a carefully orchestrated public relations campaign. These agreements included plans to:

- increase cooperation in developing the peaceful uses of atomic energy;
- exchange agricultural information;
- swap technology on transportation;
- expand cooperative research in oceanography;
- end the double taxation of private citizens and companies of one country based in the other;
- continue cultural exchanges for another six years;
- create a Soviet-U.S. Chamber of Commerce;
- expand commercial contacts;
- extend the routes of Aeroflot, the Soviet airline, beyond New York to Washington, and give an American airline a flight into Leningrad, in addition to Moscow.

Nixon and Brezhnev also pledged their countries to two agreements involving nuclear weapons. One set a target date — the end of 1974 — for completing SALT II negotiations, designed to limit offensive nuclear weapons; the other pledged both countries to avoid actions that could lead to a nuclear confrontation with each other or with a third nation, but carried no provision for enforcement.

For a finale, the two leaders flew to San Clemente for a weekend in the sun. The night before his departure from California, Brezhnev spoke on television, as Nixon had in Moscow. "Mankind has outgrown the Cold War armor which it was once forced to wear," the Soviet leader said. "It wants to breathe freely and peacefully." The two countries, he concluded, were only at the "beginning of a long road" that would require "constant care, tireless efforts, and patience."

Behind it all — the harvest of agreements and the show of camaraderie between Nixon and Brezhnev — was the hope that cooperation between these two huge nuclear powers on an increasingly broad range of subjects would diminish the chance of war. Kissinger believed that the pact to avoid nuclear confrontations was an historic achievement that would be hailed by Americans "as the beginning of a new period of international relations, a sort of formalization of the end of the Cold War." But America's mind was not on international diplomacy. It was on what Dean and Haldeman and Ehrlichman and Mitchell and the others would say once they entered the Senate Caucus Room and took the oath. The summit kept fighting for space on the front pages and on television; the bigger headlines were going to Watergate. Brezhnev, for his own reasons, lived up to his advance promise not to exploit the passions aroused by Watergate; indeed, there were times during the summit when Nixon, as one aide put it, "actually seemed to enjoy being President again."

"If the summit had occurred the way it was designed," Kissinger reflected, after the Soviet leader had departed, "that is, two or three months after the withdrawal of the last American troops from Indochina, it would have been seen by many as the beginning of an era of peace. When it occurred a week before the John Dean testimony, it was seen by many people as an attempt by the Administration to use foreign policy to escape from domestic difficulties."

After Brezhnev left, Administration critics on Capitol Hill, motivated either by the political desire to exploit the President's weakness or by genuine opposition to many aspects of Soviet policy, intensified their attacks against détente. They argued that Soviet Jews and other oppressed minorities should be able to emigrate freely; that Soviet dissidents, such as Solzhenitsyn and Sakharov, should be allowed to live and work without fear; and that Soviet leaders should be willing to gear their defense-heavy budget to the needs of their people. Russia could be forced to pay a higher price for American grain and Western technology, they argued. She could be forced to liberalize her society. If she refused, insisted these critics, in Congress and elsewhere, then there should be no credits, no lifting of trade restrictions, and if necessary, no détente.

Kissinger was appalled by this attitude toward Soviet-American relations. He rejected the notion that the purpose of American foreign policy was to reform the domestic policy of the Soviet Union. He felt that Watergate had contributed to the assault on détente.

Secretary at Last: For Kissinger, Watergate was a terribly complicated problem. He was not sorry to see Haldeman and Ehrlichman dismissed on April 30; although he had publicly urged "compassion" for those trapped in the Watergate mess, he privately condemned Haldeman and Ehrlichman as "men with a Gestapo mentality." The scandal began to touch Kissinger himself at the end of May, when his role in the wiretapping of thirteen officials and four newsmen between May, 1969, and February, 1971, was uncovered — a role that raised many moral and legal questions. In a climate of popular distrust of Administration practices, Kissinger's obsessive concern about leaks and secrecy was quickly associated with the mentality that had led to Watergate. His reputation suffered. Liberal columnist Shana Alexander wrote that he had "sunk from statesman to mere footman at the throne of power." Conservative columnist William S. White wrote: "The buildup of Henry Kissinger, able and useful though he is, into a Kissinger that never was had now come to a jarring halt." The iconoclastic columnist for the *Boston Globe*, Martin F. Nolan, speculated that Kissinger's resignation "before the summer is out would surprise no one who spends time at the White House."

Kissinger was stunned by the severity of the criticism. He feared that his "moral authority," as he often put it, would be damaged and he would lose credibility at home and abroad. The challenge became so acute that Haig began telephoning newsmen, appealing to their patriotism; he described Kissinger as a "national asset," and rejected the criticism of him as "terrible" and "very wrong." "Some reporters," Haig said, "have a commitment to destroy; they're on a crusade."

Kissinger, on a highly selective basis, personally sought to persuade some reporters — and through them, the public — that his role in the wiretapping had been peripheral. He acknowledged that he had provided Attorney General Mitchell and FBI Director J. Edgar Hoover with the names of those NSC staffers who might have handled classified information involved in the leaks or who might have talked with reporters. But he insisted that he had never "authorized, directed, or recommended" the taps. He had been told, he said, that "national security taps" were legal, merely a continuation of Kennedy and Johnson practices. If he had any doubts about those reassurances, he never expressed them. Occasionally, he admitted, he read summaries of raw wiretap information; most of the time, it was Haig who read them. By mid-1970, his story went, he had acquired enough clout with the President, and enough confidence in his position, to reject Mitchell's suggestion that the NSC play a bigger role in cases of domestic security. He detached himself and the NSC from all aspects of domestic security, turning away all wiretap reports, as well as requests for information about new wiretap suspects. He insisted that all domestic issues — security or otherwise — should fall properly under Ehrlichman's mandate.

Kissinger had always suspected that his own office phones at the White House and at San Clemente were tapped and that the wiretapping of the "seventeen" was really an indirect way of uncovering incriminating information against him.

His portrait of himself on this issue was that of an embattled good guy trying to hold off the bad guys and at the same time conduct an imaginative foreign policy that would serve the best interests of the American people.

Nor was wiretapping the only revelation that damaged Kissinger. Another was the "secret" bombing of Cambodia in 1969 and 1970. Critics of the Administration saw a parallel between the secret bombing and the secret operations connected with Watergate, and denounced them both as equally wrong. On this issue, Kissinger was not defensive. He found the critics' view too simplistic. Just because an action was secret, he explained, it was not necessarily illegal. He believed that a clear distinction ought to be drawn between the bombing — which he regarded as necessary, arguing that it had saved American lives during the initial stages of the withdrawal program and pointing out that Sihanouk had raised no major public outcry against the raids — and a wide range of Watergate-related activities — which he regarded as not only illegal but unnecessary and stupid.

Although Kissinger's defense on these two issues did not wholly restore his reputation among those who regarded wiretapping with distaste, or those who believed that the United States had no right to bomb a neutral country, there was a general feeling that in the long run his contributions to American foreign policy would far outweigh his complicity in the secret bombing or his involvement in the wiretapping. For this reason, he managed to escape direct association with the Watergate scandal. In fact, compared to the Nixon aides facing indictment, he stood out like a knight in shining armor — Lancelot among a band of brigands.

By early summer, Kissinger began to measure the damaging effect of Watergate upon the President's relations with Congress and upon America's relations with Western Europe, Indochina, China, and the Soviet Union; and he realized that he had to try to limit the damage. He joined Haig in recommending that the President cut all ties with Haldeman and Ehrlichman and release all relevant tapes demanded by the Special Prosecutor and the Senate Watergate Committee. At the same time, he made a determined effort to persuade columnists, commentators, and Congressmen to put Watergate into perspective; he urged them not to allow the scandal to distort the nation's priorities or interfere in a major way with its obligations around the globe. "History won't wait for us to sort ourselves out," he would often say in these private exchanges. And, as he had done at other critical junctures in his life, Kissinger would meet late into the night with his closest friends, including Rockefeller. In these conversations, he would emphasize one key point: that the world was at one of those unique moments when there was a real chance for ensuring peace, for another "world restored." If the United States continued to be consumed by Watergate without keeping an eye on the future, he warned, it could forfeit this historic opportunity. "Henry's views," a Harvard colleague of his once observed, "remind me of Goethe's old dictum that if he had to make a choice between disorder and injustice, he would choose injustice. The same is true of Henry — not because he favors injustice, but because he feels in his bones that there can be no justice without order."

Several friends left these sessions convinced that Kissinger should resign — for his own and the country's good. They felt Nixon could not survive the resignation of the only senior official who still commanded widespread respect, and that once Nixon fell, the country would begin a healing process and move forward. Other friends, such as Haig, shared many of Kissinger's concerns about the future; but Haig, as a military man, regarded any talk of resignation, particularly Kissinger's, as tantamount to desertion in wartime.

In a paradoxical way, it was Watergate that made Kissinger abandon the decision he had made earlier in the year to leave the White House in about September, 1973. "It tied me to the job," he told us, "because this was one area that hadn't been essentially touched by Watergate." There were other reasons for staying: his strong sense of public duty, his attachment to power, and, perhaps most of all, his determination to do whatever he could to preserve the laboriously constructed underpinnings of his "structure of peace."

He expressed his views publicly in an address on August 2 before the International Platform Association in Washington: "Our influence for good or ill will be measured by the world's judgment of our constancy and self-confidence. Our foreign policy will mean little if other nations see our actions as sporadic initiatives of a small group reflecting no coherent national purposes or consensus. No foreign policy — no matter how ingenious — has any chance of success if it is born in the minds of a few and carried in the hearts of none.

"Foreign policy must not become an alibi or a distraction from domestic ills. But, equally, domestic problems must not be used as an excuse for abandoning our international responsibilities. There can be no moratorium in the quest for a peaceful world. And as we pursue that quest we will need to draw upon the country's best minds, no matter what their partisan political persuasion — not on a bipartisan but on a nonpartisan basis. Especially at this moment of necessary self-examination, we must also reaffirm the basis of our national unity."

At about the same time, a ray of sunshine broke through Kissinger's gloom about Watergate. Haig informed Kissinger that the President might soon be naming a new Secretary of State; he hinted that Kissinger was to be Rogers's successor. A few days later, Nixon told Kissinger that Rogers "wanted" to resign. They discussed several possible successors. Kissinger mentioned to the President that he was planning to go to Europe in the near future to deliver a speech in London and to receive the *Goldener Bürger* award from his native town of Fürth. "You'd better not make any travel plans for the next month or so," Nixon suggested. "I'll need you close by." He did not elaborate.

Kissinger believed that he was finally going to get the title of the job he had been carrying out anyway.

On August 21, Kissinger was in San Clemente with his two children when Julie Eisenhower telephoned his cottage overlooking the Pacific. She wanted to know if Elizabeth and David would like to come over to the Nixon compound for a swim. In a little while, she was on the phone again. Would Kissinger like to join them? All three Kissingers got into their suits and within a half hour they were splashing in the presidential pool.

A few minutes later, Nixon came in for a dip. "Why don't you and I go down to the other end?" the President suggested to Kissinger. The two men drifted down to the shallow end of the pool; Nixon floated on his back while Kissinger, half in and half out of the water, sat on the pool steps. The President said, "I would like to nominate you for Secretary of State tomorrow."

Nixon opened his news conference on August 22 — his first meeting with reporters since March 15 — with the announcement of Kissinger's nomination. If he thought it would divert newsmen from Watergate, he was mistaken. It provoked not a single question. But later in the afternoon, the San Clemente switchboard lit up with congratulatory calls for Kissinger from friends and associates all over the country and the world.

The next day, it was Kissinger's turn to meet with reporters. Appearing relaxed, self-confident, squinting in the bright California sun at the outdoor news conference, he pledged that his conduct of foreign policy would be open — to the Congress, to the country, and of course, to the State Department. "We have to create a new consensus," he said, "which can give a new impetus and a new excitement to our foreign policy for the next decade or two."

He took pains to explain why he had conducted such a secretive policy during the first four years and how it would change during the next four. "In the first term of the President," he observed, "many important and some revolutionary changes were made. These required, to a considerable extent, secret diplomacy and they were conducted on a rather restricted basis. But now we are in a different phase. The foundations that have been laid must now lead to the building of a more permanent structure. What has been started is still very tender. . . . So what we are going to try to do is to solidify what has been started, to put more emphasis on our relationship with Europe and Japan, and to conclude during the term of the President the building of a structure that we can pass on to succeeding Administrations so that the world will be a safe place when they take over."

There were many questions — about the secret bombing of Cambodia, the wiretaps, the impact of Watergate on foreign policy, and, on a more personal level, about whether his "family heritage" might affect U.S. policy in the Middle East.

"I am asked to conduct the foreign policy of the United States," he replied, "and I will conduct the foreign policy of the United States regardless of religious and national heritage. There is no other country in the world in which a man of my background could be considered for an office such as the one for which I have been nominated, and that imposes on me a very grave responsibility which I will pursue in the national interest."

The very last question of the news conference was posed by a reporter who described it as "technical." "Do you prefer to be called Mr. Secretary or Dr. Secretary?"

Kissinger did not miss a beat. "I don't stand on protocol," he replied, with a smile. "If you just call me Excellency, it will be okay."

No one doubted that Kissinger would be confirmed as Secretary of

State, but his hearings before the Senate Foreign Relations Committee were not easy. For four long days, starting on September 7 in open session, and concluding on September 17 behind closed doors, committee members — Democrats and Republicans, hawks and doves — applauded Kissinger's brilliance and his contributions to American foreign policy; but they also questioned him closely about his secretive style of diplomacy and his acquiescence in the secret bombing of Cambodia and the wiretapping of NSC staffers and newsmen.

Chairman J. William Fulbright opened the hearings, which took place in the Caucus Room of the Old Senate Office Building, by expressing Congress's accumulated grievances about "policies made in secret and by executive fiat, policies which go against our national grain." The Chairman also condemned Kissinger's role in the wiretapping scandal, describing the issue as a "very serious matter of procedure and mutual trust." Other Senators, during their interrogation of the Secretary-designate, hit the same themes — secrecy, the bombing of Cambodia, and wiretapping.

Kissinger, under oath, meekly defended the use of wiretaps as one way of plugging unauthorized leaks of classified information, and he repeated his assertion that his role had been marginal: he had merely provided the names of people who had access to leaked information. The names, he said, went to Hoover and Mitchell. That, Kissinger added, was the "procedure believed to be legal at the time."

On a related subject, Kissinger denied any knowledge of the existence of activities of the "plumbers"; he told the committee he did not know that David Young, who was then working for Ehrlichman, had been a member of the "plumbers" engaged in internal security work. He did not mention the fact that he had listened to Young's taped interview with Admiral Welander — a fact that surfaced only four months later and raised more questions about Kissinger's credibility. And he promised that secrecy would no longer be the hallmark of his policy; he repeated his pledge of a new consensus with the Congress and a new dialogue with the American people about the content and direction of American foreign policy.

The committee was so concerned about Kissinger's possible involvement in illegal wiretapping that a special subcommittee was formed to meet with Attorney General Elliot Richardson and Deputy Attorney General William Ruckelshaus to be assured that Kissinger's hands were clean. The committee was so assured; and, on September 18, it recommended, by a vote of sixteen to one, that the Senate confirm Kissinger's nomination as Secretary of State. The lone dissenting vote was cast by Senator George McGovern as "symbolic testimony against Kissinger's role in the needless prolongation of the Indochina war, as well as the 1971 tragedy of Bangladesh." On September 21, the Senate accepted the committee's recommendation. By a vote of seventy-eight to seven, the Senate confirmed Kissinger's nomination.

The following morning, at a ceremony in the East Room of the White House, with President Nixon, the Cabinet, and his family looking on, Henry A. Kissinger was sworn in by Chief Justice Warren E. Burger as America's fifty-sixth Secretary of State.

SEVENTEEN

The Secretary at War

O PERATION BADR," code name for the Egyptian-Syrian attack against Israel, began at 2 P.M., Saturday, October 6, 1973, exactly two weeks after Henry Kissinger became Secretary of State. For Moslems, October 6 was a special day. It was the 1,350th anniversary of the Battle of Badr, which launched Mohammed's triumphant entry into Mecca and the subsequent spread of Islam. For Jews, October 6 was also a special day. It was Yom Kippur, the Day of Atonement, the holiest day in the Jewish calendar. For the new Secretary of State, October 6 was special, too. The coordinated Arab attack that started the fourth Middle East war in a single generation was his baptism of fire. It immediately posed a personal and diplomatic challenge to Kissinger. Could he, a Jewish Secretary of State, function effectively in this crisis? And could he somehow manage to salvage his policy of détente with Russia, the only country in the world that could have equipped Egypt and Syria for their attack?

The outbreak of war surprised Kissinger. Up until early Saturday morning, he had operated on the assumption that the situation in the Middle East, while always volatile, was still manageable. There had been clear signs of impending war for months, but most American officials, including Kissinger, misread the evidence.

In mid-November, 1972, a week after President Nixon's smashing reelection victory and four months after Egyptian President Anwar Sadat had expelled most of the Russian military advisers from Egypt, Sadat received a message from Leonid Brezhnev rejecting his request for more sophisticated hardware, the kind that would be needed to start a war. The Russian people, said Brezhnev, "wished to support the policy of détente," and therefore he advised Sadat "to accept the situation," meaning the status quo in the area. Brezhnev's meaning was clear: war in the Middle East could damage Soviet-American détente.

Sadat refused to accept this advice. War, to his way of thinking, was the only way to improve the Arab position. By involving the superpowers in the Middle East, he could force the United States to adopt a new policy toward Israel. On November 14, Sadat informed the Higher Council of the Arab Socialist Union, the only legal political party in the country, that Egypt would launch a war against Israel, perhaps within six months, certainly within a year.

Over the next few months, as Brezhnev picked up more information about Sadat's November 14 commitment, the Soviet leader shifted to a more adventuresome policy. Under pressure from hard-liners who contended that Russia could have both the benefits of détente with the United States *and* war in the Middle East, Brezhnev decided to increase the flow of sophisticated military equipment to Egypt. Soviet and Egyptian officials began shuttling between Moscow and Cairo, arranging the terms of the new arms program. Within weeks, additional Russian planes, tanks, bridge-building equipment, and electronic gear began arriving in Egypt. U.S. intelligence experts warned at the time that the flow was extremely heavy — too heavy, they sensed, if Egypt's intent was merely defensive. If these warnings ever reached Kissinger, they made no meaningful impression.

On February 23, 1973, Sadat's Kissinger, a tall, ascetic-looking man named Hafez Ismail, conferred with Nixon and Kissinger in Washington. The Egyptian's aim was to find out if the United States was willing to lean on Israel to relinquish occupied Arab lands. Ismail publicly described his talks as "warm, objective, and fruitful."

On March 1, Israeli Prime Minister Golda Meir came to Washington to find out if the United States intended to match recent Soviet arms deliveries to Egypt. Nixon, who had always pledged to maintain the military balance between Israel and the Arabs, promised to send Israel an additional forty-eight Phantom jets over the next four years.

That presidential decision — revealed in mid-March — confirmed Sadat's view that war was the only way to bring about a change in the American position toward Israel. He began to coordinate a common strategy with

two Arab leaders from opposite ends of the political spectrum: King
Faisal of Saudi Arabia on the right, and President Hafez Assad of Syria
on the left. Both had critical assets. Faisal had oil, an untested Arab
weapon. He was ready, for the first time, to commit oil to the battle to
recapture Arab land from Israel. Nothing was dearer to his heart than
the dream of praying in the Jerusalem mosque. Assad had manpower
and passion. He was always spoiling for a fight with Israel. The very
idea of war strengthened his political position in Damascus.

In early April, Sadat told *Newsweek*'s Arnaud de Borchgrave "the
time has come for a shock." Here is the relevant portion of their Q-and-A
session:

Q: "In other words, one has to fight in order to be able to talk?"

A: "At the very least. As you say, times have changed. And everything
is changing here, too — for the battle."

Q: "I can only conclude from what you say that you believe a
resumption of hostilities is the only way out?"

A: "You are quite right. Everything in this country is now being
mobilized in earnest for the resumption of the battle — which is now
inevitable."

"Words, just words," said American officials impatiently, after reading
the Sadat interview. They pointed out that back in 1971 Sadat had
issued a similar warning — that the "year of decision" had come. It came
and went, without an Egyptian offensive — and Sadat's warnings lost
currency.

On May 3, Assad returned from a twenty-four-hour visit to Moscow.
To fight, he needed more arms. Russia promised a massively accelerated
program of deliveries. Within a month, there were reports that Syria had
begun to receive a sizable number of Russia's latest T-62 tanks, plus
deadly new antitank missiles, another forty MIG-21 jet fighters, and a
complete air defense system for Damascus, including radar, SAM missiles,
and additional Soviet advisers.

Kissinger regarded this program of Soviet deliveries as "irresponsible,"
but he issued no formal complaints to the Russians. He was too absorbed
at the time with the fallout from Watergate, and besides he did not
believe that the Arabs, even freshly armed, would try to take on the
Israelis.

On June 12, Sadat flew to Damascus for urgent talks with Assad.
Earlier in their planning for the war, they had agreed on the advantages
of attacking Israel in the early fall, but there was still a major disagree-

ment between them about the purpose of the war. Was it, as Assad demanded, "to drive Israel into the sea," the slogan of all Arab extremists? Or was it, as Sadat preferred, to drive Israel out of some of the occupied Arab lands and then, using Faisal's oil as an economic weapon, to blackmail the United States into forcing the Israelis to go back to the 1967 borders? After lengthy deliberations, Sadat finally won Assad to his more limited objectives.

Throughout the summer, as more and more Soviet weapons flowed into Egypt and Syria, the military and political leaders of the two countries planned their campaign. D-Day was selected by General Ahmed Ismail, Egypt's fifty-five-year-old Minister of War, who reached into Moslem history for an inspiration and came up with October 6, the date of the famous Battle of Badr. The Egyptians later denied Israeli charges that the real reason they chose October 6 was to exploit the Day of Atonement, the holiest day in the year, when almost everything in Israel comes to a full stop.

In the final phase of preparation for war, Sadat won the limited cooperation of Jordan's King Hussein. On September 10, Hussein arrived in Cairo for a two-day summit meeting with Sadat and Assad. From the beginning, the Jordanian leader stressed that he wanted to restrict his country's role in the war. He would not join Egypt and Syria in attacking Israel, but he would pose the threat of a third front for Israel — thus tying down Israeli forces and preventing a flank attack through Jordan into southern Syria. Hussein and Assad deferred to Sadat to give the final order for the countdown.

On September 13, Israel provided Sadat with the pretext he needed. Four Israeli jets were patrolling — "routinely," the Israelis claimed — over the Mediterranean, extremely close to Syrian air space if not actually in it. Syrian MIGs scrambled to intercept them. Israel sent up reinforcements. Before the battle was over, at least eight and possibly thirteen MIGs were blasted out of the sky. Israel lost one plane. Assad immediately called Sadat and urged that "Operation Badr" be set in motion. Sadat gave the countdown order that night.

On September 22, Sadat informed Brezhnev that the war would begin on October 6. As far as one can tell, the Russian leader raised no objections. From his point of view, the scheme had obvious advantages. If cleverly manipulated, the war could damage the West, put the United States on the defensive, hurt the Israelis — and still not destroy détente.

On September 24, the CIA, which had kept a close check on the

Syrian and Egyptian maneuvers, spotted a few curious deviations from the usual pattern. For one thing, the Egyptians were maneuvering with formations as large as full divisions. For another, they were stockpiling more ammunition and overall logistical support than ever before. Finally, from a secret U.S. base in southern Iran, the National Security Agency, which specializes in electronic intelligence, picked up signals indicating that the Egyptians had set up a vastly more complicated field communications network than mere "maneuvers" warranted.

On September 25, Soviet transport ships entered the Mediterranean and headed for Egypt. They were carrying SCUD guided missiles, which can be rigged to fire nuclear warheads. The SCUD has a maximum range of a hundred and eighty-five miles, which means its warheads could hit Israel proper from positions west of the Suez Canal.

Later the same day, Syrian tanks began to break out of their usual defensive patterns. The CIA noted that there was "something seriously suspicious about the nature of the Syrian redeployment."

On September 26, Dayan visited the Golan front. He was the first Israeli leader to express concern about the Syrian movements. "Stationed along the Syrian border," he told Israeli troops, "are hundreds of Syrian tanks and cannons within effective range, as well as an antiaircraft system of a density similar to that of the Egyptians along the Suez Canal." Dayan still did not believe that the Arabs would dare to attack Israel, but he was sufficiently concerned about the Syrian movements to beef up Israeli patrols along the Golan front. He specifically ordered the 7th Armored Brigade, one of Israel's crack units, to leave its Beersheba headquarters and proceed to the front. It was to prove a critically important decision. If it were not for the skill and courage of the 7th Brigade, the Golan Heights would have fallen to the Syrians in the early days of the war.

On September 28, the third anniversary of Nasser's death, Sadat concluded a memorial speech with this passage: "Brothers and sisters, perhaps you have noticed there is a subject which I have not broached. This is the subject of battle. I have done this deliberately. We know our goal and we are determined to attain it. We shall spare no efforts or sacrifices to fulfill our objective. I promise nothing. I shall not discuss any details. However, I only say that the liberation of the land, as I have told you, is the first and main task facing us. God willing, we shall achieve this task."

On September 29, as Kissinger was reviewing a file of CIA reports, his attention was drawn to an unusual increase in Syrian tank movements near the Golan front. He asked his aide Lawrence Eagleburger to check with Israeli Ambassador Simcha Dinitz, a forty-five-year-old Tel Aviv–born diplomat with a degree in international law from Georgetown University, and ask for his assessment. In those days, Kissinger operated on the assumption that the Israelis had the best intelligence network in the Middle East and that if they were worried about a suspicious Arab tactic, they would not be shy about telling him. Dinitz called back in an hour. He said that the Syrian forces were still "in a defensive posture." The Syrians wouldn't go on the offensive, he said, unless they were taking part in a combined attack led by the Egyptians. So far, the Ambassador added, Israel had no conclusive proof that the Arabs were going to launch a coordinated, two-front attack. Kissinger told him that the United States would appreciate getting updated Israeli intelligence on this problem, as it became available.

Over the next week, there was a steady flow of intelligence indicating plans for an imminent Egyptian-Syrian attack; and yet the political leaders of Israel and the United States, incredibly, failed to recognize it.

They accepted the prevailing bureaucratic view that, while the Arabs had been carrying on extensive military maneuvers on their side of the cease-fire lines, they were not going to be so foolish as to start a war. Kissinger fully shared this view. He believed, at the time, that the Arabs were too disunited, their political leadership too undistinguished, to be able to coordinate an effective assault against Israel. Those were the days when Sadat was called a "clown" and Faisal a "religious fanatic."

Moreover, after several long talks at the UN with key Arab diplomats, Kissinger had concluded that what they wanted was a new round of negotiations, not a new round of war. They seemed eager to have him serve as an intermediary between the Arab world and Israel. Since he had negotiated an opening to China, begun a dialogue of conciliation with Russia, and contrived an arrangement of sorts between the North and South Vietnamese, they suggested it was time for him to apply his negotiating magic to the Middle East.

While the idea flattered Kissinger, he urged the Arabs not to expect "miracles." Kissinger wanted to help, but he still did not think the time was ripe for a settlement, and he did not want to create false expectations. At a luncheon he gave for thirteen Arab foreign ministers and ambassadors on September 25, he pledged an "open attitude" on the part of the United States, and explained that "emphasis must be put on the most practical means of finding accommodation in the area. We want to promote progress towards peace," he stated. "We will show understanding and we hope you, for your part, will do the same. . . . What is needed is to find ways to turn what is presently unacceptable to you into a situation with which you can live."

Mahmoud Riad, Secretary-General of the Arab League, struck an equally cautious, yet hopeful, note. While denying that the Arabs were expecting "miracles," he told reporters, "The U.S. wants to do its best to achieve a peaceful solution based on justice. . . . We hope something can be done in the future." He conveyed no sense of urgency to the reporters or to Kissinger.

There was still another reason why the Egyptian-Syrian attack against Israel took Kissinger completely by surprise. He had been focusing on the possibility that Israel, not the Arabs, might be planning an attack.

On September 28, a band of terrorists, calling themselves Eagles of the Palestine Revolution, ambushed a trainload of Soviet Jews heading for Schönau Castle, an overnight rest stop near Vienna on their journey to Israel. The Palestinians took five Jews and one Austrian customs official hostage, and demanded that Schönau be closed to Jewish emigrants. Austrian Chancellor Bruno Kreisky quickly capitulated to their demand. Mrs. Meir traveled to Vienna to try to persuade him to reverse his decision, but she failed. On October 3, the Israeli Cabinet met, in a mood of gloom and frustration, to hear Mrs. Meir's report on her unsuccessful mission to Vienna. No one had any ideas about how to respond to this kind of threat except by retaliating against the Palestinian camps throughout the Middle East and remaining firm against blackmail.

Kissinger, who had sensed the dimensions of Israeli outrage as conveyed by Dinitz a few days earlier, feared that Israel might feel compelled to launch a series of lightning strikes against the camps or even move against Egypt or Syria, in an attempt to stop the increasing terrorism. He had urged Dinitz to be patient, explaining that a new cycle of violence in the area could quickly escalate into a full-scale war, which would help neither Israel nor the United States. Even if, as he believed likely, Israel were to win another smashing victory, it would not bring a peace settlement any closer; the Arabs, he said, would never negotiate from a position of weakness and humiliation. Besides, the Soviet Union would not permit the Arabs to be clobbered once again; and if Russia intervened in any way to help the Arabs, the United States would have to intervene, on Israel's side, to protect its own position in the area; and the United States was in no mood to become involved in another military adventure so soon after Vietnam. Finally, Kissinger pointed out that another war, no matter who started it, might end up affecting the flow of Arab oil to the United States. Still, he was not sure if his arguments had convinced the Israeli Ambassador; and when his own intelligence officers brought him warnings about unusual Arab maneuvers, he tended to assume that the Arabs were merely bracing themselves for possible Israeli attacks.

On October 1, the Israeli government asked the United States to speed up the once-a-month delivery of Phantoms that had been promised in March. This request was prompted more by a desire to maintain the military balance of power in the area than by concern about an imminent outbreak of war.

On October 2, Syria mobilized her reserves. Egypt began intensive and, in some cases, obvious preparations for war along the whole length of the Suez Canal.

On October 4, forty-eight hours before the war began, Kissinger was at the UN discussing the Middle East and the growing energy problem with Foreign Minister Omar al-Saqqaf of Saudi Arabia. There was no hint of war, no threat of an oil cutoff.

That afternoon, Kissinger asked Israeli Foreign Minister Abba Eban if Israel would agree to hold "corridor conversations" with Egypt, with the United States — Kissinger or Sisco — serving as middleman, perhaps in November, after the Israeli elections. Eban said he would gladly return to New York to join in a new search for accommodation.

Late that night, hundreds of Russian dependents began to be evacuated — first from Cairo and then from Damascus. Kissinger's first thought was that Sadat had expelled another group of Soviet advisers; but none of the intelligence experts agreed with that line of speculation, and he dropped it. They believed that the evacuation was a sure sign of trouble. Kissinger was uneasy. He asked the experts: did the evacuation mean war? They gave him a quick tentative answer. War, they asserted, was always a possibility — but it was still "unlikely." The CIA promised a more considered judgment within forty-eight hours.

On October 5, D-Day minus one, the NSA in southern Iran picked up unmistakable signals of imminent war from the Suez front, and the Syrian tank formations, bolstered by scores of T-62s, suddenly swung into offensive formation.

At 11 A.M., the Israeli Chief of Staff, General David Elazar, canceled all military leaves, warning his staff that a call-up of reserves, meaning the bulk of the Israeli army and air force, was now possible. He recalled General Ariel "Arik" Sharon from retirement at his farm near Beersheba.

After looking at photographic intelligence of the Egyptian buildup, including canal-crossing equipment, the white-haired Sharon concluded: "I think there is going to be war in one or two days."

Elazar conferred with Mrs. Meir. He pleaded for permission to call up the reserves, and he urged her to consider "as a matter of highest priority" a preemptive air strike against Syrian and Egyptian positions.

In New York, Kissinger was testing the "corridor" idea with Egyptian Foreign Minister Mohammed al-Zayyat. The Egyptian official thought it was a good idea and, like Eban, promised to return to New York in November to discuss it. Still, Kissinger detected no hint of war.

At five-thirty that afternoon, Mordechai Shalev, the soft-spoken Chargé d'Affaires of the Israeli Embassy in Washington, delivered a message for Kissinger to Brigadier General Brent Scowcroft, Kissinger's deputy on the NSC staff. It was from Prime Minister Golda Meir.

"Information that has been accumulating," she noted carefully, "obliges us to take into consideration the military preparations in Syria and Egypt, the battle deployment and state of alert of their armed forces, and in particular, the increased military concentration at the front lines that may be motivated by one of the following two possibilities:

"A) a bona-fide assessment by one or both of these countries, for whatever reason, that Israel intends to carry out an offensive military operation against one or both of them;

"B) an intention on their part to initiate an offensive military operation against Israel.

"Should Syria or Egypt launch an offensive military operation, it would be important to make it clear to them in advance that Israel will react militarily with firmness and with great strength."

Kissinger received Mrs. Meir's message at 8 P.M. He attached no special urgency to it. He did not call Egyptian or Syrian officials. He made a note to call them on Saturday morning.

By 9 P.M., Ray Cline, then head of the State Department's Bureau of Intelligence and Research, reviewed the latest signals, and concluded that war would start the following day, or even sooner. Others at the State Department shared his sense of alarm, but somehow they couldn't communicate their acute apprehensions to the Kissinger cocoon at the Waldorf Towers. The two hundred and forty miles from Foggy Bottom to midtown Manhattan proved to be unbridgeable. No one wanted to take the responsibility for disturbing the Secretary in New York on a Friday evening, after hours.

Later that night, the CIA completed the report promised the day before. It was put in a pouch and sent to the Secretary's suite in New York. Although it cited all of the evidence pointing toward war, it still concluded that war was "unlikely."

Months later, one of Kissinger's aides was to concede: "Maybe if we were in Washington, we would have gotten Cline's message. We would have picked up the proper vibrations. But after the Secretary's talk with al-Zayyat, Sisco made plans to play golf on Saturday, and McCloskey made plans to spend the weekend in Connecticut. Everything was calm at the Waldorf. The Secretary was sure, as we all were, that there wouldn't be a war."

Saturday, October 6, began early for Kissinger. At 10 A.M. in Jerusalem — 4 A.M. in New York — Mrs. Meir summoned U.S. Ambassador Kenneth Keating to an urgent meeting in her Knesset office. She told him that she had just received word that Egypt and Syria were in the final hours of a countdown for war. There was no longer any doubt that war was imminent. She asked Keating to urge Kissinger to use all his influence to try to head off the outbreak of war. She suggested appeals to Egypt, Syria and the Soviet Union, and she assured the U.S. envoy that Israel would not launch a preemptive attack against either Egypt or Syria — something Kissinger had repeatedly warned Israel not to do.

Keating's cable reached the Waldorf Towers at 6 A.M. Kissinger was awakened immediately. He called Nixon, who was spending the weekend at Key Biscayne, with the alarming news. After hearing the Secretary's report, the President told him to telephone the foreign ministers of Egypt and Israel and to urge "restraint." Kissinger called and exhorted them to "avoid undermining . . . the cease-fire." With Eban, he added the extra warning: "Don't preempt!"

He then converted his hotel suite — 35A at the Waldorf Towers — into a command post, and he summoned Sisco, McCloskey and Eagleburger to work. In quick order, Kissinger called Soviet Ambassador Dobrynin in Washington and urged him to do what he could to head off war. The Russian envoy said he would try to help. Kissinger cabled King Faisal of Saudi Arabia and King Hussein of Jordan, two of the friendlier Arab leaders, and asked them to "use their good offices" to stop the outbreak of war. Kissinger called UN Secretary-General Kurt Waldheim, alerting him to the danger.

The Secretary then asked for the latest intelligence. It revealed that

Egyptian and Syrian armies had in fact swung into offensive formations, but that Israeli military units on both fronts had reacted to this clear-cut threat in an odd way. For the most part, they remained in static positions. Kissinger assumed, despite Mrs. Meir's messages, that Israel was really seeking to lull her Arab neighbors into a false sense of security and then, at just the right moment, planned to deal them a punishing preemptive blow.

At 7 A.M., there was more bad news. The Situation Room at the White House, operating under Scowcroft's control, had monitored a garbled report from Israel, which was interpreted as meaning that the Jewish state planned to launch a preemptive military strike against Egypt and Syria "in six hours." Kissinger, puzzled by the crisscrossing signals, angrily called Shalev and warned again against any preemptive action.

Kissinger's warning was not new. It had been his constant refrain for months. Shalev knew it by heart. So did Ambassador Dinitz, who was then in Israel to attend his father's funeral. "Don't ever start the war," Kissinger would admonish them. "Don't ever preempt!" He would then forecast absolute disaster if Israel ignored his counsel. "If you fire the first shot, you won't have a dogcatcher in this country supporting you. You won't have presidential support. You'll be alone, all alone. We wouldn't be able to help you. Don't preempt." It was the kind of warning no Israeli leader could ignore. Shalev assured Kissinger that Israel was not planning any preemptive action. Mrs. Meir had given her word. Besides, the Israeli diplomat said, there was overwhelming evidence that the Arabs were going to attack. Kissinger remained dubious.

As a double check, he instructed Keating to repeat his warning against preemptive action to Mrs. Meir. According to one Israeli source, Keating heightened the general warning with an implied threat. "If Israel refrained from a preemptive strike, allowing the Arabs to provide irrefutable proof that *they* were the aggressors," Keating was quoted as saying, "then America would feel morally obliged to help" Israel. No translation was needed. If Israel struck first, then the United States would feel *no* moral obligation to help. Israel would be alone.

As it turned out, Keating's warning was unnecessary. Mrs. Meir at just that moment was convening her "kitchen Cabinet," which actually met in her kitchen. She conferred with Deputy Prime Minister Yigal Allon, Defense Minister Moshe Dayan, and Minister Without Portfolio Israel Galili. She rejected the urgent pleading of Chief of Staff, Elazar, who argued for a preemptive strike against Egyptian and Syrian troop concentrations to disrupt what he now regarded as a certainty — an Arab attack. The Prime Minister decided that Israel would accept the first blows.

Her decision proved to be historic. By reversing twenty-five years of Israeli strategy — a strategy based on quick, bold surprises that invariably carried the battle to the enemy — she placed Israel on the defensive. She assumed, as did so many others, that Israel, even if attacked first, could rapidly repulse and rout the enemy. Mrs. Meir instructed Elazar to alert some units, but she refused to put the country on full alert. She refused even to call up the reserves. She didn't want to disrupt Yom Kippur; she didn't want to provoke the Arabs; she didn't want to spend about eleven million dollars, which a full alert would have cost (there had been two expensive false alarms earlier in the year); but, perhaps most important, she didn't want to go against Kissinger's injunctions.

Keating informed Kissinger about Mrs. Meir's decision. Kissinger informed al-Zayyat and Dobrynin. Then he called Shalev one more time, apparently even then harboring some doubts about Mrs. Meir's assurances. "We took the responsibility upon ourselves," he told the Israeli diplomat, "that you will really act accordingly." Shalev repeated his earlier assurances.

At 8 A.M., Egypt and Syria attacked. The war began. Within minutes, al-Zayyat was on the phone, accusing Israel of having provoked the Arab military moves by sending her naval force against the Syrian port of Latakia. This struck Kissinger as odd. If Israel were to start a war, he was absolutely sure that it would begin with an air strike, not a naval attack. At 8:25 A.M., Shalev called. "Egyptian and Syrian forces have commenced military action against Israel," he announced solemnly. Kissinger told him about al-Zayyat's accusation. Shalev denied it.

"What are you going to do now?" Kissinger asked.

"We'll take care of ourselves," Shalev replied.

Kissinger returned to Washington by midafternoon, convinced that the Arabs had started the war. Al-Zayyat's claim — that Israel had struck first — made a few converts at the Pentagon. But by evening, when WSAG, the Washington Special Actions Group, reconvened in a crisis atmosphere, additional information had convinced the top U.S. officials that Egypt and Syria had broken the cease-fire and that Israel had merely responded to their aggression. Joining the Secretary at this meeting were Deputy Secretary of State Kenneth Rush, Sisco, Defense Secretary James Schlesinger, CIA Director William Colby and JCS Chairman Admiral Thomas Moorer. This was the same group that was to make most of the basic decisions throughout the war.

That evening, they ordered the commander of the U.S. Sixth Fleet to move four ships — the attack aircraft carrier *Independence* and three destroyers — from Athens to Crete, five hundred miles from the coast of Israel. They ordered all U.S. embassies in the Middle East area to prepare for an evacuation of dependents. They considered calling for an emergency meeting of the UN Security Council, but they made no decision at that time.

After the meeting, Kissinger called Dobrynin and Lord Cromer, the British Ambassador, to find out if their governments would oppose a Security Council meeting. Lord Cromer hedged. Dobrynin seemed negative.

On Sunday, October 7, Kissinger got permission from the President to push for a Security Council meeting; but, because of Soviet reservations, the United States did not immediately appeal for a cease-fire. Sir Laurence McIntyre of Australia, President of the Security Council that month, began a quick round of consultations to find out if the big powers could agree on an agenda.

Kissinger, who had never been noted for his enthusiasm about the UN, concentrated instead on the battlefield situation, which he knew would determine his diplomatic tactics. He checked the latest intelligence. Israeli reservists, he learned, had broken away from Yom Kippur religious services and rushed to assembly points all over the country and then, depending on their units, to the Golan or Suez fronts. But their impact would not be felt for another day or two. In the war's early hours, the Israelis, once considered militarily invincible, were on the defensive; the Arabs, once ridiculed as militarily incompetent, were on the attack. Syrian tanks blasted big holes through the undermanned Israeli lines on the Golan Heights; were it not for the 7th Brigade, they would have smashed into Israel, pre-1967 Israel. Syrian guns lobbed heavy shells into Israeli farm settlements near the Sea of Galilee. Although the Israeli air force controlled the skies, and Syrian jets kept a respectful distance, Russia's newly installed air defense system began to take a heavy toll, heavier than the Israelis had ever considered likely. On the southern front, there was even more dramatic news. Thousands of Egyptian troops, supported by hundreds of tanks and armored vehicles, crossed the Suez Canal in a surprise move that caught the Israelis completely off guard, and established bridgeheads on the eastern bank for the first time since 1967. The famed Bar-Lev line began to crack under Egyptian pressure as the bridgeheads expanded, despite Israeli counterattacks.

Overnight, this well-coordinated Arab assault on the Jewish state shook Kissinger's cherished assumption that the spirit of détente would encourage the Soviet Union to use its influence in Egypt and Syria to head off war. Instead, it turned out that the Russians not only had known about the war in advance and alerted no one to the "threat to the peace"; but, in addition, they had contributed directly to the initial Arab successes by shipping massive quantities of ammunition to Cairo and Damascus in the two or three weeks immediately preceding the outbreak of hostilities. Kissinger was angry and disappointed: angry at the Russians, disappointed in himself. Years before, he had written: "the test of statesmanship is the adequacy of its evaluation *before* the event." He took another look at the prewar intelligence and concluded belatedly that the Russians must have calculated that they could have both détente and war. To what degree Watergate influenced their judgment, Kissinger could not be sure.

Although he was angry at the Russians, he realized that he needed their cooperation to contain the fighting and to establish a framework for negotiations. The Soviet Union was a major factor in the Middle East. For several years it had been his hope that one day the two superpowers would cooperate in stimulating a peace agreement between the Arabs and the Jews. Now he sensed that time was approaching. He resisted political pressures to denounce the Russians, and he kept open his channel of communication to Dobrynin.

He talked with the Soviet envoy several times that day. On one occasion, he gave him a personal letter from the President to Brezhnev, appealing for a cease-fire and a commitment to contain the fighting. Nixon reminded the Soviet leader that they had signed two special communiqués — in May, 1972, in Moscow, and in June, 1973, in Washington — pledging "to do everything in their power so that conflicts or situations will not arise which would serve to increase international tensions." Later that night, Dobrynin returned with a letter from Brezhnev to the President, agreeing to consider a cease-fire at the UN and expressing the hope that the fighting could be contained. Kissinger was moderately pleased with this exchange, because it seemed to suggest that Russia's aims in the Middle East were modest; and if Russia's aims were modest, then Arab aims might be, too.

Despite initial Arab successes in the first two days of the war, Kissinger retained his earlier confidence that Israel, even if attacked first, would quickly gather her resources and throw back her enemies. He expected a quick Israeli victory — in three or four days, at the most.

At 6 P.M., he met with Dinitz at the State Department. The Israeli envoy had just returned to Washington with a modest arms request from Mrs. Meir — essentially, an update of her plea of the week before to expedite the delivery of the forty-eight Phantom jet fighters, as well as tanks and electronic equipment.

Dinitz explained that Israel faced two thousand tanks on the Egyptian front, one thousand on the Syrian. He told Kissinger in some detail about Mrs. Meir's decision to reject Elazar's recommendation for a preemptive strike, and about Dayan's support for the Prime Minister's decision. The Defense Minister had agreed with Elazar that a preemptive strike made sense from a military point of view, but from a political point of view, he had opposed it. "That was the right decision," Kissinger acknowledged. Yes, Dinitz replied, but "that decision bestows a special responsibility on America not to leave us alone, as far as equipment is concerned."

Kissinger responded sympathetically to Dinitz's plea, and promised to help. It was clear, after all, that Israel was the victim of aggression, and that she needed a visible show of American support. Besides, if the Administration seemed too reluctant to help, the Ambassador could always appeal to a large group of Congressmen and columnists, most of them not Jewish, whose sympathy for Israel's fight for survival could easily be aroused. Dinitz used to laugh when Kissinger referred to them as his "shock troops," but the Israeli diplomat was fully aware of the pressure Israel's supporters could exert. Kissinger was eager to hold off an explosion of pro-Israeli sentiment on Capitol Hill that could complicate his dealings with the Russians. Moreover, Kissinger expected a quick Israeli victory — an expectation that was encouraged by Dinitz's upbeat report about the plans for Israeli counterattacks, then in the final stages of preparation — and he did not feel that it would be necessary to open a massive emergency pipeline of supplies to Israel. He did not want to be provocative. He did not want to antagonize the Russians, or the Arabs. The Administration was under heavy pressure from the oil lobby to give the Arabs a chance to recover their occupied territories or, at the very least, to take no pro-Israeli action that could goad the Arabs into imposing an oil embargo on the United States at a time of increasing energy shortages. If the Israelis were successful, as he fully expected, he did not believe that he would have to change his overall strategy.

Early on the morning of Monday, October 8, as the war picked up momentum on both fronts, Schlesinger met with his top aides and, according to reliable sources, rejected a request that Israeli planes be allowed to land in the United States to pick up ammunition and spare parts. Elazar had predicted that morning that Israeli forces would soon go on the offensive. His prediction was based, in part, on the expectation of increased American supplies. When Dinitz learned about Schlesinger's rejection, he was puzzled. He called Kissinger and pointed out that Russia was not embarrassed about helping her friends; why did the United States appear to be so reluctant about helping Israel? Kissinger said he would check. After an exchange with the Pentagon, he called back and announced that permission had been granted for "a limited number of Israeli planes" to land at U.S. bases and pick up supplies, "provided they paint their tails," that is, paint over the identifying six-pointed Jewish star. Clearly the Administration was trying not to offend the Arabs or the oil lobby.

At 1:15 P.M., Kissinger called Dinitz again. He had good news. He said the President had given his "approval in principle" to replace Israeli plane losses, which were running quite high. Dinitz expressed his gratitude and then repeated his question about the transport of ammunition and spare parts.

At 3:15 P.M., Dinitz called Kissinger to ask *when* the United States would start sending additional Phantoms to Israel. Plane losses were running much higher than expected. Kissinger said that was a sensitive problem, which he personally was negotiating with the Pentagon.

At 5 P.M., Dinitz called again. He had just been on the phone with Mrs. Meir, who pleaded that "top priority" be placed not only on the delivery of planes and tanks already requested but also on a new shopping list, necessitated by the intensified fighting and Israel's heavy losses. Kissinger said he would consider the new list; meantime, he disclosed that he had been able to get two planes out of the Pentagon, no more. Tanks, he said, presented an even more complicated problem. It would take "many weeks" to spring them from the U.S. inventory. What about transferring the tanks from an American base in Western Europe? suggested Dinitz. Kissinger said he would check. Why was it so difficult to get the planes, asked Dinitz, if the President had given his "approval in principle"? Kissinger hinted that he was having "bureaucratic difficulties at the Pentagon." Dinitz requested a meeting with Kissinger.

At 6:40 P.M., he was ushered into Kissinger's White House office. He told the Secretary of State that Senators Henry Jackson, Walter Mondale, Birch Bayh, Charles Percy, and other presidential aspirants had volunteered to help Israel get weapons. Dinitz said he didn't know how long he could hold off a public outcry. Israel needed planes and tanks, and she needed them immediately. There was no debating that point. Intelligence had poured into Kissinger's office all day indicating that Israel was having a rough time seizing the offensive. He revised his estimate that the Israelis would need no more than three days to defeat the Arabs; now, he thought, they would need five days. The Secretary told Dinitz, at last, that Israel would be getting the two Phantoms within twenty-four hours. Two? Dinitz exclaimed. Israel needed dozens! Kissinger claimed that if it weren't for his personal intercession, Israel would not even have gotten those two planes. The Pentagon opposed any Phantom deliveries at this stage of the war. Kissinger implied that he was fighting Dinitz's battles in the American bureaucracy.

In between these calls and meetings with Dinitz, Kissinger was carrying on a similar series of calls and meetings with Dobrynin; but with Dobrynin, he took a different line. Citing the demands from Capitol Hill for quick American aid to Israel and a reappraisal of the Administration policy of détente with Russia, he told the Russian envoy that he was holding back a rush of pro-Israeli actions. He appealed for Soviet cooperation in restraining the advancing Arab armies and in fostering a cease-fire in the Middle East. He cited with satisfaction the toast that Brezhnev had just proposed at a Moscow luncheon for visiting Japanese Prime Minister Kakuei Tanaka; Brezhnev had said that the Soviet Union supported "a fair and lasting peace . . . and guaranteed security for *all* countries and peoples of the area which is so close to our frontiers." Dobrynin echoed Brezhnev's line, word for word, and Kissinger assumed that this meant the Russians were taking "a conciliatory posture and urging restraint on the Arabs."

Still, that evening, in an address at the Pacem in Terris conference, he issued an indirect warning to the Russians. "We shall resist aggressive foreign policies," he said firmly. "Détente cannot survive irresponsibility in any area, including the Middle East." Kissinger had no doubt that Dobrynin would be filing his carefully worded warning to the Kremlin that night.

The Kissinger warning had no effect on Soviet policy. On Tuesday, October 9, the Secretary received a series of disturbing reports. One cited an increase in the number of Soviet supply ships steaming toward Syrian and Egyptian ports. Another focused on a big boost in the number of Soviet warships in the Mediterranean. Still another suggested that Brezhnev had changed his mild tone. In a message to President Houari Boumedienne, the militant leader of Algeria, the Soviet Party Chief urged the Algerian people to "use all means at their disposal and take all the required steps with a view to supporting Syria and Egypt in the difficult struggle imposed by the Israeli aggressors." Brezhnev seemed to be encouraging Algeria to join the Arab war against Israel. In Kissinger's mind, that was a far cry from urging restraint.

Kissinger and Dinitz met for the first time that day at 8:15 A.M. The Israeli diplomat was back in the Secretary's White House office, repeating his urgent demand for planes and tanks. Israel, he pleaded, had already lost at least fifteen Phantoms and forty-five A-4 Skyhawks, a light attack bomber. That amounted to a loss of twenty percent of all the planes Israel had ever received from the U.S. The new mobile SAM-6 missile, supplied by the Russians to Egypt and Syria, had been deadly accurate. Electronic jamming equipment, similar to that used by U.S. fighters against other SAM missiles over North Vietnam, was desperately needed. What was holding up deliveries? Kissinger again struck a note of sympathy. He cut short the meeting, explaining that he would deal with the entire problem on an urgent basis.

At 11:45 A.M., Kissinger called Dinitz, complaining again about his difficulties with the bureaucracy, implying that he was engaged in a one-man fight with the Pentagon to fulfill the Israeli requests. By this time, to facilitate communication, Kissinger had a private, secure line put into Dinitz's office at the Israeli Embassy. The Secretary asked the Ambassador to return to the White House at six-fifteen that evening.

That afternoon, Kissinger conferred with Nixon about the problem of Israeli supplies, and that evening, Kissinger was able to tell Dinitz that the President had approved "all" the Israeli requests. All plane and tank losses would be replaced. All electronic equipment, including jamming devices, would be furnished, and Israeli transport planes would be permitted to land at the Oceana Naval Air Station at Virginia Beach, Virginia, to pick up Sparrow and Sidewinder air-to-air missiles and other sophisticated hardware. Kissinger still expected the Israelis to wrap up the war by Thursday, but he thought the President's promise to replace "all" losses would provide a solid morale boost for Israel.

There had been increasing congressional pressure on the Administration all day to send more military supplies to Israel — Jackson taking the lead — and Dinitz wondered if it was this pressure that had produced the presidential decision.

At 8:45 P.M., Kissinger called Dinitz to say that Schlesinger would be available on Wednesday to discuss logistical details with the Israelis. Apparently there had been some presidential arm-twisting.

By dawn, Wednesday, October 10, American and Israeli intelligence picked up the first clear signals of a Soviet airlift into Damascus and Cairo. Its full dimensions were not yet known.

At 10:45 A.M., Kissinger called Dinitz to discuss the airlift. Both diplomats were obviously concerned: Kissinger, because the airlift was hardly an example of Soviet "restraint"; Dinitz, because his enemies had no trouble getting help, while he, as he put it, had to spend his time "painting Jewish stars off Israeli planes." The Secretary switched subjects. How was the war going? He was beginning to question his own rosy assumptions about a quick Israeli counterattack and victory. Dinitz provided the latest intelligence. On the Golan front, the Syrians had been stopped, but there was still heavy fighting. Israel was sustaining very heavy tank losses, largely because Syria had been equipped with an unusually effective antitank missile, the latest in the Soviet arsenal. On the Sinai front, the Egyptians had smashed or encircled the Bar-Lev line of Israeli defense on the east bank of the canal. More than twenty thousand Egyptian troops, four hundred tanks, and other armored vehicles had crossed the canal, and they were digging in. Again, Israeli losses were extremely heavy, in men and matériel. Elazar's promised counteroffensive could not yet get rolling. One major reason was the dwindling stockpile of Israeli ordnance. What about supplies? Dinitz asked with increasing exasperation. Hadn't the President given his approval? Israel, said Dinitz, needed the supplies immediately. Kissinger again promised rapid results.

He called Schlesinger and asked him to organize civilian charters to carry American military aid to Israel as quickly as possible. The Defense Secretary showed little enthusiasm for the idea, but he offered no opposition. Kissinger wasn't sure, at that point, if Schlesinger intended to help.

At 11:20 A.M., Scowcroft called Dinitz. There was intelligence from Amman that King Hussein had decided to send a limited Jordanian force into Syria to help the Arab cause. Scowcroft expressed Kissinger's hope that Israel would not respond with an attack against Jordan, and

he asked Dinitz to come to the White House at three-thirty that afternoon.

At the Pentagon, Schlesinger was well aware that Dinitz wanted to
see him to discuss military supplies for Israel. A tentative noontime
date had been set. At the last minute, the Defense Chief canceled the
meeting. His deputy, William Clements, a wealthy Texas drilling con-
tractor with close ties to the oil industry, had apparently persuaded
him that he needed more information about American inventories before
he could provide the Israelis with an exact timetable for deliveries. No
new appointment with Dinitz was set.

At the State Department, spokesman McCloskey said he could not
confirm "for the record" that Russia had opened an airlift into Syria and
Egypt, but he added pointedly that "any *massive* airlift . . . would
tend to put a new face on the situation." The United States was anxious
to find out how "massive" the airlift would become before committing
itself publicly to a response.

At the White House, Nixon and Kissinger briefed ten Senators and
nine Congressmen about the Mideast war. Mansfield, before the hour-
and-a-half meeting, told reporters that the United States must not get
involved in the war. "I want no more Vietnams," he said.

From Beirut, there were reports that Brezhnev was exhorting all Arab
leaders to join the fight against Israel.

That afternoon, the Administration's attention was suddenly absorbed
by still another major political crisis. Spiro Agnew resigned as Vice-
President, pleading no contest to a charge of tax evasion in Maryland,
his home state. His resignation, on top of the growing Watergate scandal,
weakened the Administration even more. Its effect was to increase the
pressure on Kissinger to avoid a foreign policy disaster that could end
up toppling the President from power.

Dinitz returned to the White House at 3:30 P.M., as scheduled. It was
a beehive of frantic activity. Kissinger was in the Oval Office. Scowcroft,
in his absence, told Dinitz that the Russians had just switched tactics
on a UN cease-fire. UN Ambassador John Scali reported that Moscow

was now proposing an immediate end to the fighting. The Russian move was clearly an attempt to freeze the battlefield situation at a point at which the Arabs had the initiative and the Israelis had not yet been able to mount a counteroffensive. Dinitz angrily rejected the proposal. Israel, he said, would never accept a cease-fire until Syrian and Egyptian forces had been driven back to the prewar lines. He urged the United States to open an immediate airlift of supplies to Israel to match the Soviet airlift to Syria and Egypt. Scowcroft promised to convey his appeal to Kissinger.

Late that afternoon, the NSA and the CIA received urgent reports from the Middle East that Russia's largest transport plane — the Antonov-22 — was spearheading the Soviet airlift and that these lumbering giants were coming into Damascus and Cairo at farily regular intervals, suggesting the airlift was becoming "massive." The intelligence reports graphed the Antonov-22's course from Kiev to Budapest and from there on a line over Belgrade to either Damascus or Cairo. Already twenty-one Antonov-22s had reached Syria, and two large Soviet transport ships had steamed through the Bosporus heading toward the war zone. It was estimated that each of them carried thirty-six hundred tons of military equipment. When these reports reached Kissinger's attention, he quickly called Dinitz. Could the Israeli Ambassador come to the White House at 8 P.M.?

The meeting that evening lasted for an hour and fifteen minutes. It focused on Russia's call for a cease-fire. Dinitz repeated his opposition. "The Russians are hardly in a position to appear now as the pacifists," the Israeli Ambassador stated, with some annoyance. "They are the ones who caused the war. They knew of the impending attack and didn't warn you and didn't prevent it. Now they are coaxing other Arab governments to join the fight against Israel, and they are sending a big airlift. And, after all this, they dare to ask to freeze the situation!" Kissinger did not argue against the Ambassador's logic. He had been making the same points to himself. After Dinitz left, Kissinger called Dobrynin and persuaded him to delay his cease-fire call.

Late that night, Kissinger received some disturbing intelligence. The CIA had learned that three Soviet airborne divisions in Eastern Europe had been put on alert. Since there was no crisis in Europe, Kissinger could only assume that they were being readied for possible deployment to the Middle East. But why? Russia's clients were fighting well; better than anyone had anticipated, in fact. And direct Soviet intervention could only trigger American counteraction, which could spiral into a nuclear war. Why? It was, as Kissinger would later put it, "a murderously dangerous situation, much worse, much more dangerous than the 1970 Jordan crisis." He called Dinitz and recommended a seven forty-five meeting on Thursday morning. He did not tell him about the Soviet alert.

Dinitz's car pulled into the circular drive at the diplomatic entrance of the State Department at 7:40 A.M. The Ambassador and Shalev, both bleary-eyed from fatigue, hurried through the quiet lobby, past the giant, rotating globe and a few reporters too surprised to get in a question. The elevator ride to the Secretary's seventh-floor suite took only a moment. Then, for over an hour, Dinitz and Kissinger focused on one problem — getting the Pentagon to supply Israel with planes, tanks, and electronic equipment on an emergency basis.

During the night, Kissinger had reached a major decision: Russia had to be stopped — not only to save Israel, but, in his mind, to spare the world from the possibility of a big-power confrontation. The Soviet airlift and alert had changed his attitude about Israel's capacity to win a quick victory. Just as he had misjudged prewar intelligence, so too had he misjudged the will and capability of the Arabs and the duplicity of the Russians. He was now determined to open a massive airlift of American military supplies to Israel. The United States had to match the Soviet airlift to demonstrate that American power in the area was still considerable, and to ensure that its ally could launch a successful counteroffensive. Kissinger had no doubt that with a major infusion of American arms and encouragement the Israelis could turn the tide of battle and restore a military balance in the area, thus presenting the United States with the diplomatic leverage to shape the postwar negotiations. Another major element of Kissinger's strategy at that point was to convince the Arabs that they could never win a victory with Soviet arms and that, in the long run, they would have to deal with the United States if they wanted to achieve any of their aims.

"We tried to talk in the first week," Kissinger later explained. "When that didn't work, we said, fine, we'll start pouring in equipment until we create a new reality."

Kissinger told Dinitz to see Schlesinger about getting the equipment. He implied that this time Schlesinger would be more accommodating.

Later in the afternoon, Kissinger argued forcefully with Schlesinger about the need to correct the military imbalance in the Middle East. He again urged his colleague to charter twenty American transport planes to fly emergency supplies to Israel. Schlesinger resisted Kissinger's appeal. The Defense chief argued just as forcefully that even a limited American airlift to Israel would so infuriate the Arabs that they would impose an oil embargo on the United States. The argument was resolved only after Kissinger had won the President to his point of view. Nixon ordered Schlesinger to charter twenty transport planes.

Early in the evening, Kissinger called Dinitz with the news about the charters. Dinitz then reminded the Secretary about Israel's daily, almost hourly, appeals for more warplanes, especially Phantoms. In the first five days of the war, Israel had already lost an estimated seventy-five planes, including perhaps as many as twenty-eight Phantoms. On this issue, Kissinger said that two Phantoms would be leaving for Israel on Friday, two on Saturday, and two on Sunday for a grand total of six. Dinitz pointed out to Kissinger that Israel was talking about plane deliveries of a totally different magnitude. Kissinger said that he understood Israel's problems, but Israel should also understand his. Dinitz filed a gloomy report to Jerusalem. By then he had just about decided that if he didn't get a firm commitment on major plane and tank deliveries by Saturday, he would "go public" — that is, he would encourage Americans — particularly those with influence in Congress, business and the press — to pressure the Administration into action to help Israel.

By 9:45 A.M., Friday, October 12, Dinitz still had heard nothing about the twenty charters. A half-dozen Israeli planes had transported military equipment from the United States to Israel, but that was, as he put it, "a drop in the bucket." He called Kissinger. "These delays," he said, "are costing human lives. Who's playing games?" The Secretary seemed surprised and angry. He believed he was getting a runaround from the Pentagon. He told Dinitz to call him in an hour if the Embassy still had no word from the Pentagon about the charters. Kissinger immediately called Schlesinger and, in the President's name, instructed him to arrange for the charter of twenty civilian transport planes. Schlesinger said the Pentagon had tried to hire civilian charters but failed. Most companies, he explained, did not want to get involved in the Middle East war. In that case, Kissinger snapped, get military planes, and get them quickly. Schlesinger later insisted that it was his idea to resort to U.S. military planes. At 10:30 A.M., with fifteen minutes to spare, the Pentagon called the Israeli Embassy with the news that military planes would be assigned to take care of their transport problems.

At 11 A.M., Kissinger held his first news conference at the State Department. The International Conference Room, lit up like a stage set, was crowded with reporters, cameramen, and officials. Kissinger, sporting a blue shirt and a neat hair trim administered by the White House's favorite barber, Milton Pitts, focused for the better part of an hour on détente, in general, and Russia's role in the conflict, in particular. The Secretary stated that so far the Russians had not behaved irresponsibly but that the war had "the potentialities for getting out of hand."

"It is of course an extremely volatile situation," he said, "The Middle East may become in time what the Balkans were in Europe before 1914. That is to say, an area where local rivalries that have their own momentum will draw in the great nuclear powers into a confrontation that they do not necessarily seek or even necessarily start." He gave the Russians, in public, every benefit of the doubt, but he ended on a firm note. "We do not consider the [Soviet] airlift of military equipment helpful. We also do not consider that Soviet actions as of now constitute the irresponsibility that on Monday evening I pointed out would threaten détente. When that point is reached, we will in this crisis, as we have in other crises, not hesitate to make a firm stand. But, at this moment, we are still attempting to moderate the conflict."

Early in the afternoon, Kissinger called Dobrynin and Dinitz to explain his comments. With the Russian, he emphasized his moderation — his hope for restraint; with the Israelis, he emphasized his toughness — his promise "to make a firm stand." He was, given the requirements of diplomacy, all things to all men.

By midafternoon, Dinitz learned from Israeli intelligence that the Russians had mobilized three airborne divisions. He quickly called Kissinger, who said the CIA had just received the same intelligence. He did not tell Dinitz that the CIA had received that intelligence two days before.

At 6 P.M., Dinitz, accompanied by General Mordechai Gur, then Israeli Defense Attaché, finally got his meeting with Pentagon leaders. Schlesinger headed an all-star cast: Clements; Robert Hill, Assistant Secretary for International Security Affairs; Admiral Raymond E. Peet, Deputy Assistant Secretary for ISA; James H. Noyes, another Deputy Assistant Secretary for ISA; and Major General Gordon Sumner, Jr., Director of the Office of Near Eastern and South Asian Affairs.

Dinitz reviewed the massive Soviet contribution to the Arab cause and then lamented the "unbelievably slow response of the Americans." Schlesinger did not dispute the Ambassador's rundown, but he explained that "political considerations" had caused the United States to "slow down." The U.S. did not want to destroy its "position and image in the Arab world." Charter companies feared Arab terrorism or reprisals and therefore refused to help Israel. Insofar as U.S. military transports were concerned, Schlesinger carefully emphasized that they would be permitted to carry military supplies to the Azores Islands, but no further. Israel would have to make other arrangements to get the supplies from the Azores to Tel Aviv. Dinitz was flabbergasted. He said, in that case, the supplies wouldn't get to Israel "in time for this war."

Schlesinger moved on to other subjects, none more critical to Israel than the delivery of planes and tanks. Here he paused for a moment and then disclosed that the rate of delivery for Phantoms would be "one and a half per day"; but, after "a couple of days," the deliveries would be stopped so that, as Schlesinger explained, the United States could "read Arab reaction before we decide on further shipments." In any case, there would be no more than sixteen Phantoms earmarked for Israel. The United States, he continued, intended to do no more than replace Israeli losses. Dinitz pointed out that Israel had already lost more than sixteen Phantoms. Schlesinger did not dispute his statistics, but he explained that the United States had to "operate in low profile in order not to create an Arab reaction." Schlesinger was alluding to a possible cutoff of Arab oil, but in his comments he made no specific mention of it. "Mr. Secretary, with all due respect," Dinitz said, "you are not giving us an answer." Schlesinger stuck to his guns. The meeting with the Israeli Ambassador had turned into a confrontation. "Mr. Secretary," concluded Dinitz, "in the recent period, we have undergone two crises in the Middle East. One, the Syrian and Jordanian crisis of 1970, and the other one, we are going through now. In 1970, your country needed something from us. Now we need something from you. I must humbly say that we acted differently at the time of that crisis than you do now." The meeting ended with a cold handshake.

Shortly after eleven o'clock that same night, Dinitz was ushered into Kissinger's White House office for a brief but dramatic meeting. Dinitz began by filling in the Secretary on his talk with the Pentagon chief. He placed special emphasis upon Schlesinger's insistence on shipping what would amount to one and a half planes a day for only a couple of days and then pausing to gauge Arab reaction. One and a half Phantoms a day, for a couple of days, he told Kissinger, was "a mockery to the poor." He repeated Schlesinger's statement that, in any case, no more than sixteen Phantoms would be sent to Israel — even though Israeli losses in that one category alone had more than doubled the Pentagon ceiling, and Nixon had issued a specific order to replace "all" Israeli losses. Israel, he stated, needed a minimum of thirty-two Phantoms. For the Israeli diplomat, this was clearly a crucial test of America's will and word. "If a massive American airlift to Israel does not start immediately," Dinitz emphasized, "then I'll know that the United States is reneging on its promises and its policy, and we will have to draw very serious conclusions from all this."

Dinitz did not have to translate his message. Kissinger quickly understood that the Israelis would soon "go public" and that an upsurge of pro-Israeli sentiment could have a disastrous impact upon an already weakened Administration. As one NSC insider put it, bluntly, "The Congress was behind the Israelis. The press was behind them. And to judge from the polls, the public was behind them. If the Israelis had gone public at that time, it could have been the end of the Nixon Administration." A high State Department source expanded on that theme. "There were enough people in the country," he said, "just looking for a breach of confidence in *foreign* affairs, above and beyond Watergate. We had always told the Israelis, 'When the chips are down, we're with you.' Well, the chips were down, and it looked as though we were not with them. At least, that's what they thought. They had taken a terrible beating from the Arabs. They were the victims of aggression. No doubt about that. They held their hand, because Kissinger told them not to strike first. And after all that, we reneged. We didn't come through. That's all Jackson needed. If Dinitz had gone public with everything he knew, it could have toppled the Administration."

Kissinger promised Dinitz that he would do "everything in my power" to overcome "bureaucratic difficulties" and launch a massive American airlift to Israel.

Kissinger then summoned Scowcroft into his office and, according to one knowledgeable source, asked if the Pentagon had been dragging its feet. Yes, Scowcroft nodded, up until last night. The charter problem, however, was "real enough." Kissinger became very angry. He quickly got Schlesinger on the phone and warned that the President would "blow his top" when he learned about the delays. Accusing Clements, Hill, and Noyes by name, Kissinger admonished Schlesinger for not "taking charge" of the resupply effort. Kissinger described the charters as a "matter of urgent national security." "Every morning I come in and ask, 'What about the charters?' and I'm told everything is all right," Kissinger said. "But in the evening, I'm told nothing has moved. Now what is going on?" Schlesinger tried to defend his aides and refute the Secretary's charges, but Kissinger interrupted him with an order to get busy implementing the President's policy.

When Kissinger finished talking with Schlesinger, he immediately called Haig. "We must put the fear of God in Schlesinger and Clements," he was quoted as saying. "They are working against presidential orders." Kissinger demanded that the problem of Israeli "resupply" be solved "urgently." Haig was surprised to learn that the charter problem still had not been solved. He suggested that Scowcroft be put in personal charge of it.

Clements, for his part, has denied that he was even aware of a problem with charters or that he was in any way sabotaging U.S. policy. On the contrary, he has maintained that he followed White House orders during the crisis. But a high Defense official said that because of "poor communications" between Kissinger and the Pentagon — "he was five miles away, across the river, and we couldn't read his mind" — he often did not know exactly what Kissinger was going to do next. Another Pentagon official was less charitable in his explanation of the breakdown in communications between Kissinger and the Pentagon chiefs. "Henry tried running the government by telephone that week," he explained, "and it can't be done that way." The Pentagon defense, in short, was that Kissinger was attempting to run the war out of his vest pocket, controlling the flow of information even to the top civilian managers of the Pentagon, and that he never fully explained his tactics or strategy to them. The Pentagon maintained that the strain across the Potomac existed only during the first week of the war and then cooperation between the State and Defense departments improved considerably.

Later that night, Kissinger asked Haig to arrange a meeting with Nixon.

Kissinger reviewed the day's developments with the President, and it would have been extraordinary if he did not lay particular stress on the Pentagon's obstructionist tactics. Nixon took immediate action. He instructed Haig to order Schlesinger to send ten C-130 transport planes, loaded with military supplies, to the Azores at once; then to fly twenty C-130s directly to Israel; and finally to facilitate a quick Israeli pickup of the cargo left in the Azores. When Kissinger informed Dinitz about the President's latest order, aimed at breaking through all bureaucratic roadblocks, the Israeli envoy expressed his gratitude but asked if it was possible for all of the American planes to fly directly to Israel. He explained that Israeli pilots were needed for combat duty.

At 1:45 A.M., Kissinger called again. The President, he said, had issued still another order to Schlesinger: to make absolutely certain that ten Phantoms reached Israel by midnight Sunday. Nixon was aware of the danger of a strong Arab reaction, but he was equally aware of the danger of a Soviet miscalculation of American intentions. He felt he had to make a strong, visible show of support for Israel. Dinitz thanked Kissinger but warned that Israel needed more than ten Phantoms. The war had cut deeply into Israel's air force.

At ten-thirty Saturday morning, the President summoned all his top advisers to an emergency meeting at the White House. Kissinger had alerted Nixon to the need for an unambiguous presidential order launching an American airlift of supplies for Israel. Kissinger, in his dual capacity as national security adviser and Secretary of State, joined Schlesinger, Moorer, Haig, Colby, and other officials. They heard the President ask one key question: why had there been a delay in implementing his previous orders about supplies for Israel? Schlesinger tried to explain his difficulty in chartering civilian transport planes. "To hell with the charters," Nixon exploded, according to one eyewitness. "Get the supplies there with American military planes! Forget the Azores! Get moving! I want no further delays."

Nixon's sense of urgency was prompted by more than pique; it was prompted as well by his realization that further delay could severely undercut his strategy in the Middle East.

After the meeting with the President, Kissinger began to lean very hard on Schlesinger. The order had been given; it now had to be implemented. By 12:30 P.M., after numerous calls, Kissinger learned that the C-5, America's answer to the Antonov-22, would carry the burden of the airlift, and that the first of the C-5s would shortly be airborne for Israel, with a refueling stop in the Azores. In addition, the ten C-130s that had been flown to the Azores during the night would soon be ordered to proceed to Israel. How many more Phantoms could be spared? Kissinger asked. Schlesinger yielded another four out of the U.S. inventory, meaning that Israel would be getting an initial consignment of fourteen Phantoms by Monday morning.

Kissinger called the Israeli Ambassador at 12:40 P.M. with the latest news. After, the repeated disappointments of the past week, Dinitz remained skeptical. An hour later, he called Scowcroft with a clear message: if the transport planes were not airborne by sundown, Saturday, he would have to conclude that the United States, by failing to keep its word, had precipitated a "crisis in Israeli-American relations." Scowcroft assured the Ambassador that there would be no "crisis." At 3:30 P.M., Scowcroft called to inform Dinitz that a fleet of C-5s had just left the United States for Israel. The Ambassador immediately cabled Mrs. Meir that "a massive American airlift" had begun. Kissinger had won what one of his aides later called the "Battle of 1600 Pennsylvania Avenue."

EIGHTEEN

The Cease-fire Alert

REPRESENTATIVE GERALD R. FORD, the President's choice to succeed Spiro Agnew as Vice-President, had been briefed about the airlift of military equipment to Israel before the prayer breakfast at the White House on Sunday, October 14. Striking a new image as a global strategist to go along with his new position as the man one heartbeat, or one impeachment vote, away from the presidency, Ford reflected the Kissinger approach to the Middle East crisis in his remarks to reporters: "I hope we get a military solution quickly, and then we can work on a diplomatic solution. You cannot have a diplomatic solution until you get a military solution."

The "military solution" Kissinger wished to bring about was a stalemate. From the very beginning, he believed that the airlift had to be finely tuned: on the one hand, to help Israel regain the military initiative, but not much more; and, on the other hand, to prod the Russians into accepting a sensible cease-fire plan that would open negotiations leading toward an overall settlement of the Middle East crisis. With these goals in mind, the Secretary urged the Pentagon to send ten more Phantoms to Israel, bringing the total up to twenty-four, and to dig further into its inventories to make sure that the American airlift not only matched the Soviet airlift — in volume and sophistication — but exceeded it.

Within a few days, as one C-5 after another rumbled into Tel Aviv, each one a signal of U.S. determination, the Kissinger strategy began to affect both the military and diplomatic sides of the war.

In the dead of night on October 15, Israeli commandos, their faces darkened to avoid detection, crossed over on rafts to the western bank of the Suez Canal just north of Great Bitter Lake. On October 16, Israeli armored units drove an iron wedge through Egyptian lines on the east bank and then built a pontoon bridge across the canal to the west bank — to "Africa," as the Israelis called it. Hundreds of Israeli troops and dozens of tanks and other armored vehicles crossed into "Africa" in a dramatic move that turned the tide of battle on the Suez front.

This cross-canal operation had been under intensive study since the fourth day of the war, but it had been put temporarily on a back burner. Dayan and Elazar, worried about a growing shortage of ammunition and equipment, had restrained General Sharon, commander of Israeli forces in the Sinai, from launching this daring mission. Only when Dinitz's cable announcing the airlift reached Mrs. Meir's desk on Saturday night did final preparations begin.

At first, the Egyptians tried to destroy the Israeli bridgehead, or to belittle its significance. But as the bridgehead widened and deepened, and as Israeli troops drove north toward the Cairo-Ismailia road and south toward the Cairo-Suez road, destroying dozens of SAM sites in the process, Sadat began to realize that his armies on the east bank could be cut off from supplies and left vulnerable to a devastating Israeli blow. He tried desperately to hold up the steady Israeli advance; but he failed. Losses on both sides were extremely heavy, but the Israeli offensive still continued. After seventy-two hours in "Africa," the Israelis were forty miles west of the canal and only fifty miles east of Cairo.

The airlift, as Kissinger had expected, stimulated activity on the diplomatic front, too. On October 16, Soviet Prime Minister Alexei Kosygin flew secretly into Cairo for three days of urgent consultations with Sadat. He carried a four-point "peace" proposal, obviously conceived before the Israelis crossed the canal:

1. a cease-fire-in-place;
2. Israeli withdrawal to the 1967 boundaries, after some minor changes;
3. an international peace conference, at which the final agreement would be negotiated and ratified;
4. and, most important, a "guarantee" by the Soviet Union and the United States of the entire agreement, including the cease-fire.

From the moment Kosygin arrived in the Egyptian capital, it was clear that the Russians wanted the conflict to come to an end. Kissinger would later note that they did not press their call for a cease-fire when their allies were on the offensive and they were the only ones running an air and sea lift of supplies into the war zone; but once the United States opened its own airlift and the Israelis suddenly went on the attack, they began energetically to press for a cease-fire. In Cairo, Kosygin tried to convince his ally of the advantages of a cease-fire-in-place; in Washington, Dobrynin echoed the same line in his long talks with Kissinger. But just as Sadat was not eager for a cease-fire while Israeli forces remained on the west side of the canal, so Mrs. Meir was unwilling to call a halt to the fighting while Egyptian forces were dug in on the east bank. Both belligerents balked at the idea of a cease-fire; but there was little that they could do to block it, once Russia and the United States decided that a continuation of the conflict ran a high risk of endangering their mutually advantageous policy of détente and of embroiling them in war.

During the last of Kosygin's long and occasionally bitter talks with Sadat, the Egyptian leader raised a crucially important question: what would happen if Cairo agreed to a cease-fire and Israel didn't agree or, even worse, agreed to a cease-fire and then massively violated it? Kosygin, according to Egyptian sources, told Sadat that the Soviet Union stood ready to help enforce the cease-fire — alone, if necessary. Sadat knew that was not an empty assurance; three Soviet airborne divisions had been alerted for possible use in the Middle East. The Egyptian President then gave his reluctant endorsement to the Soviet proposal on condition that Russia guarantee its implementation, with or without American help. Kosygin left Cairo late on October 18. He realized that the Russians now needed the United States to press Israel into accepting a cease-fire proposal.

That night, in Washington, Dobrynin gave Kissinger the draft of a Soviet proposal for a UN-sponsored cease-fire. The Secretary was puzzled by its extreme demands, including a call for a total Israeli withdrawal from "all" occupied Arab lands, including the Old City of Jerusalem. It was such an obvious "nonstarter" that Kissinger quickly rejected it. He told Dobrynin that such draft proposals would accomplish nothing.

The following morning, at 10 A.M., Dobrynin presented an invitation to the Secretary from Brezhnev asking him to fly to Moscow for "urgent consultations on the Middle East." The Soviet Party Chief, after considering Kosygin's report, had concluded that Sadat's forces were in bad trouble, and Assad's were in worse shape. In his judgment, they needed an immediate cease-fire. If Kissinger had refused to accept his invitation, he would have been prepared to dispatch Gromyko to Washington. Time was critical. The Israelis were advancing on Damascus. Their big guns were a little more than twenty miles away, within firing range of the outskirts of the city. In the south, the Israelis were continuing to expand their bridgehead in the very heartland of Egypt, building up their fighting force there to more than three hundred tanks and thirteen thousand troops. The situation of Russia's allies was becoming intolerable. The Israelis had to be stopped — and then forced to withdraw.

Kissinger spent very little time debating whether to snap up Brezhnev's invitation — for a number of reasons. First, he thought a rejection would probably force the Russians to go directly to the UN Security Council and propose a cease-fire. He believed that such a proposal would have been adopted unanimously. Next, by going to Moscow, Kissinger purchased an additional seventy-two hours of time for Israel to improve her military position; he figured that he would be in Moscow for at least forty-eight hours, and that twenty-four hours would be consumed in travel. Another reason: Kissinger wanted to be in personal charge of the negotiations from the very beginning. Despite his assurances, less than a month old, that as Secretary of State he was going to "institutionalize policy," he could not shake his style of playing a commanding role in every negotiation, particularly in a crisis. And, finally, perhaps most important, Kissinger believed, according to one close aide, "that the Russians were getting very anxious and very upset" and might even be considering "unilateral military action to stop the fighting." The Secretary considered the overall situation "murderously dangerous," an assessment he was to repeat time and again.

After checking with Nixon, he told Dobrynin that he would leave for Moscow that night right after dinner — in this case, a date the Secretary did not wish to break. It was with Chinese Ambassador Huang Chen, Dobrynin's arch-rival on the Washington diplomatic circuit, who was hosting a party prior to Kissinger's visit to China scheduled for late October. Departure for Moscow was set for 1 A.M. There was to be no announcement until shortly before takeoff.

All afternoon, Kissinger prepared for his trip. He conferred with the President, who shared his apprehensions about Soviet intentions. He asked Ray Cline, the State Department's intelligence chief, to prepare a quick study of those intentions. He assembled his traveling team: Sisco, Atherton, Sonnenfeldt, Eagleburger, McCloskey, Lord and a few other aides. And he talked at length with Dinitz about a cease-fire scenario. In rough terms, Kissinger knew what the Russians were proposing, and what the Egyptians were willing to accept, however reluctantly: a cease-fire-in-place, linked to an Israeli withdrawal to the 1967 line. The Israeli Ambassador rejected this proposal as unrealistic. He recommended instead a cease-fire linked to direct negotiations between the two sides that could lead to withdrawal and peace. Kissinger set his sights on achieving a solution that accented direct negotiations. If Brezhnev really needed American cooperation to rescue his Arab clients and to preserve détente and its dividends, then the Russians might be made to pay a high price.

While Kissinger prepared for his journey, the President was sending a signal to Moscow — and to the Arab states, too. In a special message to Capitol Hill, Nixon asked Congress for 2.2 billion dollars in emergency military aid for Israel. For the first time in many years, the United States proposed giving, rather than selling, this military equipment to the Jewish state. "The magnitude of the current conflict, coupled with the scale of Soviet supply activities," Nixon said, "has created needs which exceed Israel's capacity." Noting that the Middle East had become "a flash point for potential world conflict," the President added: "The United States is making every effort to bring this conflict to a very swift and honorable conclusion, measured in days not weeks. But prudent planning also requires us to prepare for a longer struggle." The President's message seemed packaged to enhance Kissinger's bargaining position in Moscow.

The Huang Chen dinner was a relaxed affair at the Mayflower Hotel. All the American officials and newsmen who would be accompanying the Secretary to China were invited. So was a small congressional delegation, headed by Senate Majority Leader Mansfield, House Speaker Carl Albert, and Ford. Kissinger arrived only thirty minutes late — for him, a birdie on the dinner course. He quickly drew Huang Chen into a corner, presumably to inform him about his upcoming trip to Moscow. But during the toasts, neither Kissinger nor Huang Chen revealed anything about the surprise Moscow trip. After dinner, Kissinger met privately with Mansfield, Albert and Ford. Then the Secretary headed for his limousine. A reporter stopped him. "Anything new on the Middle East, sir?" Kissinger glanced at the reporter. "No," he said, poker-faced, "nothing at all." Exactly thirty minutes later, the White House announced that Kissinger was about to leave for Moscow.

Kissinger's plane landed at Vnukovo Airport, Moscow, at 7:30 P.M., Saturday, October 20. While he was airborne, the Secretary received two signals. One came from the White House; the other from Riyadh, Saudi Arabia. The signal from the White House was highly unusual. The President flashed Kissinger what amounted to a "power of attorney" to sign any agreement in Moscow in his name. Nixon knew that Kissinger was planning to bring any agreement reached in Moscow back to Washington for presidential perusal and approval: that was the standard operating procedure. The President, who was about to fire Archibald Cox, the first Watergate Special Prosecutor — an action that would also force the resignations of Elliot Richardson and William Ruckelshaus from the two top jobs at the Justice Department, in what came to be known as the "Saturday Night Massacre" — was either too preoccupied with his political problems to think about urgent diplomatic matters or so worried about the possibility of a world conflagration that he decided to dispense with normal diplomatic procedure and give Kissinger the power to take immediate, binding action in his name. The Secretary was surprised by the White House signal but didn't question it.

The second signal, from Riyadh, had the impact of an economic H-bomb, but Kissinger was too absorbed with the problems of war and cease-fire in the Middle East to give it more than a passing thought. The supposedly pro-American government of Saudi Arabia, denouncing the U.S. airlift of arms to Israel and the President's special aid message to Congress, slapped a punishing oil embargo on the United States. For months, Faisal had warned that he would use his oil weapon in the Arab struggle against Israel; besides, he had committed himself to use this weapon in secret prewar negotiations with Sadat. On October 17, the oil-producing states had voted to reduce their production by ten percent. On October 18, Abu Dhabi had imposed an oil embargo on the U.S. On October 19, Libya had acted. On October 20, it was Saudi Arabia's turn, and the following day Algeria and Kuwait followed suit. In the months ahead, the oil embargo was to have a damaging impact on the American economy and way of life. It would force Kissinger to accelerate his diplomatic peace-making efforts in an attempt to persuade the Arabs to lift the embargo. But that weekend in Moscow, Kissinger had a more immediate aim. He wanted to exploit Russia's nervousness about the Israeli offensive to arrange a cease-fire that would lead to direct talks between Egypt and Israel.

Less than two hours after his arrival in the Soviet capital, Kissinger was escorted into Brezhnev's Kremlin office, and the two men began to explore ways of ending the war and salvaging the policy of détente. At the same time they kept a close check on the battlefield. Brezhnev reviewed the results of Kosygin's visit to Cairo and emphasized the need for an immediate cease-fire. He warned that the situation was extremely grave. Kissinger agreed with his grim assessment and with the need for a cease-fire; but he insisted that a cease-fire had to be linked to peace talks, or else it was sure to break down all over again. Their meeting ended well past midnight. There was no deal, but Kissinger had the impression that Brezhnev was so eager to preserve at least the spirit of détente, which in Russia had come to be identified with his rule, that he would make a major concession at their next meeting, scheduled for Sunday afternoon. It was almost 3 A.M. Sunday when Kissinger finally got a chance to call Haig at the White House to check on a couple of annoying problems. He found Haig totally preoccupied with other problems. It was only then that Kissinger learned about the "Saturday Night Massacre."

On Sunday afternoon, Brezhnev and Kissinger met for four hours. In the intervening time, Israeli troops continued their advance on Damascus and their flanking operations west of the Suez Canal. The two negotiators hammered out the details of a cease-fire arrangement that would lead to direct talks between Egypt and Israel. It was, for the Secretary, an immensely satisfying result. He knew that the Israelis would not be happy about the cease-fire coming at a time when they needed only a few more days to defeat the Egyptian and Syrian armies, but he also knew that they would appreciate the opportunity, at long last, for direct talks with Egypt. In the President's name, he sent an urgent appeal to Mrs. Meir to accept the cease-fire.

"We were hardly in a position to say no," one high Israeli official said. "We had no real choice. Here was a personal appeal from the President of the United States at a time when Israel was more dependent than ever on the United States."

Brezhnev won Sadat's agreement to direct talks with Israel — an approach Egypt had never before accepted — only after sending his additional assurances that Russia would — if necessary, alone — guarantee the observance of the cease-fire.

After reaching agreement with Brezhnev on the exact wording of the joint Soviet-American call for a cease-fire, Kissinger conferred with Gromyko and then the Ambassadors of Great Britain, France and Australia, all members of the UN Security Council, and then sent special instructions to Ambassador Scali in New York to call for an emergency meeting of the Security Council. The council convened early Monday morning, October 22, and unanimously adopted the superpower call for a cease-fire-in-place. Resolution 338 was to go into effect within twelve hours or, at the latest, by 6:52 P.M., Middle East time.

Kissinger left Moscow at 10 A.M. On his way back to Washington, he stopped for five hours in Jerusalem and two hours in London. His stop in Jerusalem — designed to explain the terms of the cease-fire — proved to be an emotional experience for him. The crowds at the airport cheered his arrival. Kissinger had the feeling, after talking with Israel's political and military leaders, that they were really very anxious to end the war, but they needed someone — a stranger they could trust — to end it for them. Kissinger was fulfilling the role.

His stopover in London — to brief Sir Alec Douglas-Home, the British Foreign Secretary, about the Moscow negotiations — gave Kissinger his first insight into the political significance of the "Saturday Night Massacre." He picked up a couple of British newspapers, and the headlines stunned him. He had no idea, up to that moment, that Nixon was in such deep, deep trouble. The newspapers also ran headlines about the Middle East cease-fire, and he was gratified that, at a minimum, he was still able to come up with achievements in foreign policy that Americans could support — achievements that reminded the world that the United States, despite Nixon's Watergate difficulties, was still a major, influential power.

On his return flight to Washington, Kissinger kept track of the cease-fire. There were violations. He had expected them. But he believed that they were manageable and that the time might fast be approaching for him to take a direct hand in midwifing a settlement between Egypt and Israel. He returned to Washington at 3 A.M., Tuesday, October 23.

Kissinger, who thrives on little sleep and big challenges, had hardly finished his breakfast in his White House office later that morning when there was a frantic call from the Soviet Embassy complaining that the Israelis had massively violated the cease-fire. Kissinger called Dinitz. "What the hell is going on here?" he wanted to know. Kissinger had been given the Prime Minister's word that Israel would respect the cease-fire; he had communicated that word to the Russians. Now the Russians could suspect Kissinger of duplicity, which could have a detrimental effect on his role as a middleman. Dinitz argued that it was not Israel, but Egypt, that had broken the cease-fire. Kissinger urged Dinitz in the strongest terms to tell Mrs. Meir that the United States expected Israel to live up to the terms of the cease-fire — "scrupulously," he added.

The Secretary then checked with his own intelligence experts. They confirmed the essence of Dinitz's account but added one important fact — that the Israelis had taken full advantage of the initial Egyptian violation to extend their lines on the west bank of the canal. Apparently what happened was that the commander of the Egyptian 3rd Corps, trapped on the east bank of the canal opposite the Egyptian city of Suez, ignored specific cease-fire orders from Cairo and attempted to break out of Israeli encirclement. The Israelis, still smarting over Egypt's original aggression, beat back that attempt and then intensified their military pressure on both sides of the canal. On the west bank, in particular, the Israelis kept edging toward the strategic prize of Suez itself. If the city fell under Israeli control, then there would be no way for the Egyptians to resupply the 3rd Corps. After only a short while, the Israelis would be in a position to destroy the best fighting force in the Egyptian army.

Kissinger resolved that he would stop the Israelis and save the 3rd Corps and thus guarantee a military stalemate. The Israelis would be on the west bank, the Egyptians on the east bank, and each side would have leverage over the other. From the earliest days of the war, it had never been Kissinger's policy to encourage the Israelis to win another decisive victory, such as they had won in 1967. Such a victory would not buy peace, but rather create tensions that would trigger still another war. Besides, Kissinger believed that in the current diplomatic climate, a clear-cut Israeli victory would contribute to a further isolation of Israel, and, given America's close ties to the Jewish state, encourage a new wave of anti-Americanism in the Middle East. The oil embargo might then become a permanent feature of Arab policy, rather than a tactical weapon. Finally, if Kissinger was able to gain acceptance as a go-between in the Middle East, he would have to demonstrate his impartiality. Saving the 3rd Corps would be such a test — for him and his policy.

In a series of talks with Dinitz, Kissinger cajoled, pressured, urged, implored, warned, threatened and pleaded with the Israeli envoy to understand his logic and accept his policy. At the same time, he told Dobrynin that he expected the Soviet Union to restrain the Egyptians. Stating the obvious, the Secretary said that continued violations on either side could only end up hurting both sides — and the cause of détente.

Publicly, Administration spokesmen refused to point a finger at Israel or Egypt. "Realistically," one of them remarked, "it was always in our minds that full performance would not come into effect on the specific hour on the clock."

By dusk, the number of violations had gone down, but Kissinger's anxieties had gone up. He postponed his visit to China after his intelligence experts alerted him to two sudden developments. They had detected a sharp and sudden drop-off in the number of Soviet planes carrying military supplies to Egypt and Syria — from about seventy flights a day down to half a dozen. In addition, they had picked up signals from the Ukraine indicating that a number of Soviet army and logistical units had been put on alert.

That night, Kissinger and Dobrynin worked behind the scenes to arrange a second UN call for a cease-fire. The Security Council met in almost continuous session.

By 1 A.M., Washington time, Wednesday, October 24, the second cease-fire went into effect; but, moments before the guns were ordered silenced for the second time in forty-eight hours, the Israelis announced that their forces had reached the outskirts of Suez and the 3rd Corps was effectively surrounded. When Kissinger got the news, he was furious. This time, when he called Dinitz, his voice did not boom, as it often did; he spoke softly, very softly, and Dinitz knew he was seriously worried. He warned the Israeli diplomat that the cease-fire would have to be respected, and he urged Dinitz to allow humanitarian convoys — food, water, medical supplies — to reach the 3rd Corps.

Later Wednesday morning, after further talks with Dinitz and Dobrynin, Kissinger attended a WSAG meeting at the White House, where he learned about a series of Soviet military moves. Four more divisions of Soviet airborne troops had been put on alert, bringing the total to seven divisions, or roughly fifty thousand troops. Five or six Soviet transport ships had crossed into the Mediterranean, raising the Russian naval presence in that area to an unprecedented eighty-five ships. About a dozen Antonov-22 planes had been spotted flying toward Cairo. The analysts wondered if they might be carrying some of those airborne troops. An airborne command post had been established in southern Russia. And, finally, special military orders had been intercepted, suggesting the Russians might be preparing to intervene in the Middle East.

Kissinger and Dobrynin exchanged urgent calls. The Secretary wanted to see if Dobrynin had hardened his bargaining position. He detected no such sign.

At 3 P.M., Sadat radioed an urgent appeal to Brezhnev and Nixon to send a joint Soviet-American peacekeeping force to the Middle East, basically to police the Suez cease-fire. He accused Israel of continuing violations. Kissinger rejected his appeal. He opposed the idea of sending big-power troops to a volatile area, believing that their presence would only exacerbate existing tensions.

At 4:15 P.M., Dobrynin arrived at Kissinger's State Department office to discuss the organization of a Geneva peace conference following a cease-fire. In the course of their talk, Scali called twice from the UN: first, to inform the Secretary that the Security Council would be called into session that evening; and second, to say that the "nonaligned nations" had begun to echo Sadat's appeal. Kissinger immediately warned Dobrynin that the United States opposed a joint Soviet-American peacekeeping force. The Russian diplomat said that, so far as he knew, his colleague, UN Ambassador Jakob Malik, had no instructions to support such a force. Dobrynin left.

A little while later, at 7:05 P.M., Dobrynin called. He had unintentionally misled Kissinger, he said; Malik *did* have instructions to support a nonaligned nation proposal for a big-power police force. Kissinger suspected that the Russians were actively encouraging such a proposal, and, in fairly blunt language, he urged Dobrynin to tell Moscow that the United States vigorously opposed the idea.

Kissinger then informed the President that the Russians seemed to be switching signals. Nixon reiterated his personal opposition to a big-power peacekeeping force.

At 7:25 P.M., Kissinger called Dobrynin, principally to convey the President's views on the subject. The Soviet Ambassador then added a disquieting new note. He said that Malik might not wait for the nonaligned nations to introduce the proposal for a big-power force; he might introduce it himself. Dobrynin argued that the Israelis were continuing to violate the cease-fire, and that Russia and America were responsible for maintaining it. Kissinger repeated his opposition to the proposal and warned that their countries might be heading for trouble.

At 9:25 P.M., Dobrynin called Kissinger with a "very urgent" message from Brezhnev to Nixon. The message was, within hours, to bring the two superpowers into direct confrontation. Normally Dobrynin would not have read the message on the phone but, this time, he said it was "so urgent" that he would make an exception. Slowly he dictated the message to Kissinger; a secretary, listening in on an extension, took down the four-paragraph text in shorthand.

The message began with an unusually cool salutation: "Mr. President," rather than with the usual Brezhnev opener: "My dear Mr. President"; and its tone was unmistakably tough. Brezhnev denounced Israel for "brazenly challenging both the Soviet Union and the United States" and for "drastically" violating the cease-fire. Then, echoing Sadat's line, the Soviet Party Chief said: "Let us together . . . urgently dispatch Soviet and American contingents to Egypt." The cease-fire had to be observed "without delay." Brezhnev then dropped his diplomatic bombshell. "I will say it straight," he said, "that if you find it impossible to act together with us in this matter, we should be faced with the necessity urgently to consider the question of taking appropriate steps unilaterally. Israel cannot be allowed to get away with the violations."

Kissinger could see the hedge: "consider the question . . ." But he suspected Brezhnev meant business. The Russian leader had extracted Sadat's agreement to a cease-fire, linked to direct talks with Israel, only on condition that the two superpowers — or Russia alone — would guarantee the cease-fire. He had gotten Kissinger's word that Israel would respect the cease-fire. Now, four days later, Israel had blocked access to Suez City, effectively encircled the 3rd Corps, and threatened to destroy the cream of the Egyptian army and perhaps topple the Sadat regime in the process. Kissinger believed that Brezhnev could not "tolerate" another decisive Israeli victory over Egypt. Kissinger also knew that the United States could not tolerate unilateral Soviet intervention. The U.S. and the USSR were on a collision course.

Ten minutes later, just to double-check, Kissinger called Dobrynin and read the text of the Brezhnev note back to him. "Is it correct?" Kissinger asked. "It is correct," Dobrynin answered. The Russian added that he had to have an immediate response. The Secretary advised him respectfully not to "press" the United States.

Kissinger immediately called Nixon. The President at that time was upstairs at the White House. The Secretary gave him a complete fill-in and recommended that the United States might have to alert its military forces as one way of deterring any unilateral Soviet move. The President concurred and empowered Kissinger to take charge of the American response. He added that if there were any problems, he would be available immediately.

Kissinger·hastily assembled three panels of experts to study the Brezhnev note and to assess Soviet intentions. Sonnenfeldt met with a small group of Russian experts at the White House; Sisco with a group of Middle East specialists at the State Department; and David Popper, then

Assistant Secretary of State for International Organizations, with a group of UN experts. While these study panels quickly reviewed the accumulated intelligence, Kissinger, in his capacity as national security adviser, summoned an emergency meeting of the President's top advisers, a rump NSC gathering of Schlesinger, Colby, Moorer, Haig and Scowcroft. They met at the White House at 11 P.M.

By that time, Kissinger had the opinion of the experts. There was, in their view, a "high probability" of some kind of "unilateral Soviet move." He informed the President's top advisers about the experts' opinion. Then he distributed copies of all recent Brezhnev communications, plus the latest note, and asked everyone present to study the package. Without exception, they concluded that the tone of the note, received that night, was "totally different" from the earlier communications — "harsh," "blunt," "leaving nothing to the imagination."

While his colleagues continued to deliberate about a proper American response, Kissinger called Dobrynin and urged him to make sure that Moscow did nothing "rash or unilateral," at least not until the United States had composed an answer to the Brezhnev note.

The U.S. answer came in two parts.

The first part was a military alert. Since the experts had concluded that there was a "high probability" that Soviet airborne troops would soon be flown to the Middle East, the Secretary quickly decided that the United States had to alert its military forces — ground, sea and air, both conventional and nuclear units. Schlesinger agreed. Both men felt that the Soviet Union had to be made aware that the United States would resist its efforts to tilt the military balance against Israel.

At 11:30 P.M., Schlesinger instructed Moorer to tell the service chiefs to alert most but not all military commands. For example, the Coast Guard, with its key air-sea rescue system, was not alerted until the following morning; and Strategic Air Command tanker planes, operating over the mid-Atlantic along the U.S.-Israel air lanes, were not moved north to handle the possible refueling of B-52 bombers. Two hours later, at one-thirty in the morning, Schlesinger returned to the Pentagon and widened the alert. The Panama Command was included. The aircraft carrier *John F. Kennedy*, carrying dozens of A-4 attack jets, was dispatched toward the Mediterranean. Fifty to sixty B-52 bombers were ordered from Guam to the United States. The fifteen-thousand-troop 82nd Airborne Division, based at Fort Bragg, North Carolina, was added to the alert; it was told to be ready by 6 A.M., Thursday, if necessary.

Finally, the entire Strategic Air Command (SAC) was put on alert; SAC was a critical signal to the Russians, because it controls nuclear strike forces.

There are five degrees of military alert, ranging from Defense Condition, or DefCon, 5, which is least alarming, to Defense Condition 1, which is war. That night, during the various stages of the alert, most U.S. units were put on DefCon 3. In one case — the Pacific Command — that represented no change, because the Pacific Command is always on DefCon 3. SAC usually operates on DefCon 4; it was moved up one notch. The fleet of Polaris submarines, carrying nuclear-tipped missiles, ranges between DefCon 3 and 2; that night, it was put at 3. The Sixth Fleet, cruising the Mediterranean, was on DefCon 2, and it stayed at that level.

The second part of the U.S. answer to Brezhnev was diplomatic. The Secretary composed a presidential response. He checked it with Schlesinger and Haig and cleared it with Nixon. In the message, the U.S. reaffirmed the terms of the Kissinger-Brezhnev understanding that the two superpowers would cooperate in the search for peace in the Middle East. It disputed Brezhnev's claim that Israel was "brazenly" violating the cease-fire. By late Wednesday night, in fact, there were comparatively few violations, on either side. The situation, the note said, did not warrant sending Soviet or American forces to the Middle East. The idea of one superpower taking "unilateral" action would cause great concern throughout the world. The United States could not accept such action by the Soviet Union; it could not but jeopardize the entire pattern of Soviet-American détente. The Nixon message focused instead on UN observer and peacekeeping forces composed of nonveto, or nonnuclear, members of the U.N. In this respect, the United States promised to cooperate with the Soviet Union. The U.S. note did not refer to the alert of American military forces. That was not considered necessary. "The alert itself," one official said, "was a signal which we knew they would get through their own electronic intelligence."

It is curious that, considering the seriousness Kissinger ascribed to the crisis, the Secretary never saw the President that night. Nixon, who struck a number of his close advisers as "remote," remained in his living quarters, upstairs, while his advisers conferred downstairs. Kissinger talked with the Chief Executive only once — on the phone. All other messages were relayed through Haig. The last one, at about 2 A.M., set the stage for a 7:30 A.M. meeting with the President and Haig.

Before leaving the White House, Kissinger started the process of informing America's allies. He called Lord Cromer, who was apparently in a snippy mood. The British Ambassador reportedly responded: "Why tell us, Henry? Tell your friends — the Russians." Then Kissinger sent a cable to Brussels, headquarters for the North Atlantic Treaty Organization, instructing U.S. officials to inform all NATO allies about the alert of American forces. Because of a breakdown in the NATO communications system, it took hours before the allies actually got the word. Kissinger's final call was to Dinitz.

At 7 A.M., Kissinger turned on the television news. He was, he later said, "surprised as hell" to learn that the alert had already become public knowledge. His expectation was that the news would leak out slowly — one unit here, one unit there — but that the American people would not learn anything about a worldwide nuclear alert for another twenty-four hours. By that time, either there would have been a major crisis, in which case the alert would have been seen as justified, or the crisis would have blown over, in which case the alert would have been eased. Keeping such news from the public was not a new tactic for the Administration — or the Secretary.

By the time Kissinger got to the White House for his 7:30 A.M. meeting with the President, the CIA had come up with an alarming report from Egypt — that the Russians might have landed nuclear weapons there. For several days, U.S. reconnaissance planes had kept track of a Soviet ship carrying radioactive material and heading toward Port Said. In the early morning hours of October 25, the ship docked. It was presumed by intelligence experts that the radioactive material was a nuclear warhead or, more likely, several warheads, and that they had been sent to Egypt to be tipped to SCUD missiles, which had reached Egypt earlier in the year. The experts had no definitive information on whether the radioactive material had actually been unloaded. The CIA report tended to harden Kissinger's judgment that the Russians were going to send airborne troops to Egypt. Nuclear weapons could serve as backup protection for a sizable Soviet force. On the other hand, Kissinger could not dismiss the possibility that the Russians were moving nuclear weapons into Egypt because they believed that the Israelis had nuclear weapons and intended to use them against Egypt. In the U.S. Government, there was no hard intelligence that the Israelis had nuclear weapons. Kissinger immediately ordered a study of Israeli nuclear capabilities.

With the President and Haig, Kissinger reviewed the military and diplomatic situation. After a few hours, they reached several conclusions:
first, that the United States would continue its efforts at the UN to set
up a peacekeeping force that excluded the major powers (early that
morning, the Security Council had considered a resolution that, while
not including the major powers, did not exclude them either); second,
that Israel would have to be persuaded to observe the cease-fire; third,
that the U.S. airlift of supplies to Israel would continue until all of her
losses were replaced; and, finally, that Kissinger would hold a news conference to explain the alert and Nixon would postpone, for at least one
day, the news conference he had scheduled to explain his firing of Cox.

When America went to work that morning, it was aware from news
reports that U.S. nuclear forces, on a worldwide basis, had been put on
standby alert, apparently in a dramatic move to dissuade Russia from
taking "unilateral action" in the Middle East. The news of the alert came
like a bolt of lightning out of a sky darkened by Watergate suspicion and
upheaval. For many people, still stunned by the "Saturday Night Massacre," it was impossible not to connect the alert to Watergate. After all,
only one day before, spokesmen had asserted that the number of violations was dropping and the crisis seemed to be passing. There was instant
speculation on Capitol Hill, in news offices and at political party headquarters — both Republican and Democratic — that the alert must have
been caused, at least to some degree, by the President's desire to deflect
attention from Watergate and talk of impeachment.

Kissinger has always claimed that the Watergate connection never
entered his mind as he planned and ordered the alert; that only the
urgent requirements of diplomacy governed his actions. That was why his
news conference so shocked him. One of the first questions focused on
Watergate.

"Mr. Secretary," the question began, "could you tell us whether the
United States received a specific warning from the Soviet Union that it
would send its forces unilaterally into the Middle East? Do you have
intelligence that the Russians are preparing for such an action? The
reason I raise these questions — as you know, there has been some line
of speculation this morning that the American alert might have been
prompted as much perhaps by American domestic requirements as by
the real requirements of diplomacy in the Middle East. And I wonder if
you could provide some additional information on that."

Kissinger answered slowly — as columnist Elizabeth Drew later put it

— "in a tone" that was "more in sorrow." "Marvin," he said, "we are attempting to conduct the foreign policy of the United States with regard for what we owe not just to the electorate but to future generations. And it is a symptom of what is happening to our country that it could even be suggested that the United States would alert its forces for domestic reasons. We do not think it is wise at this moment to go into the details of the diplomatic exchanges that prompted this decision. Upon the conclusion of the present diplomatic efforts, one way or the other, we will make the record available, and we will be able to go into greater detail. And I am absolutely confident that it will be seen that the President had no other choice as a responsible national leader." When the same question surfaced in different ways, Kissinger at one point lost his cool and began to lecture the press. "We are attempting to preserve the peace," he asserted, "in very difficult circumstances. It is up to you, ladies and gentlemen, to determine whether this is the moment *to try to create* a crisis of confidence in the field of foreign policy *as well*." (Italics added by the authors.)

It was clear from his response that Kissinger had adopted — perhaps only in the heat of the moment — Nixon's belief that the press was trying "to create" a "crisis of confidence" in domestic policy, meaning Watergate.

That day, reporters were asking the obvious questions, but they were not getting all of the answers. Kissinger recognized this failing himself. "We will be prepared . . . I am certain, within a week," he said, "to put the facts before you. . . . After that you will be able to judge whether the decisions were taken hastily or improperly." He later reneged on that promise because he did not wish to embarrass the Russians, whose support he still needed.

The news conference ran from noon to one o'clock, during which time the Secretary tried to be tough and conciliatory at the same time. Having confirmed the American alert, he warned the Russians not to send their troops into the Middle East and not to expect the United States to join them in a Big Two peacekeeping force for the area. Such an arrangement would only "transplant the great-power rivalry into the Middle East" — to him, an "inconceivable" proposition that could lead to a nuclear clash.

"We possess, each of us, nuclear arsenals capable of annihilating humanity. We, both of us, have a special duty to see to it that confrontations are kept within bounds that do not threaten civilized life. Both of us, sooner or later, will have to come to realize that the issues that divide the world today, and foreseeable issues, do not justify the unparalleled catastrophe that a nuclear war would represent."

Kissinger's remarks were being carried "live" on nationwide TV and radio. At the UN, where Scali and Malik were sparring with one another about whether the peacekeeping force should or should not exclude the big powers, delegates paused to listen to the news conference, delaying Security Council deliberations still longer. The delay proved to be important. It gave Malik extra time to call Moscow and get new instructions.

The Secretary, having brandished the hard line, then extended his olive branch. "We do not consider ourselves in a confrontation with the Soviet Union," he assured everyone. "We do not believe it is necessary at this moment to have a confrontation." Neither country had made any threats against the other, he said. "We are not talking of a missile-crisis-type situation." He even expressed the hope that his treasured policy of détente could survive the crisis. "If the Soviet Union and we can work cooperatively — first, towards establishing the cease-fire, and then towards promoting a durable settlement in the Middle East, then détente will have proved itself."

Kissinger, during his news conference, followed a clear two-track policy: soft-talking the Russians out of a confrontation, after having alerted American military forces to get ready for one. That was classic Kissinger. "We need a combination of extreme toughness, when we're challenged," he once said, but with enough flexibility "to give them the option of going to a more responsible course" without losing face. "It's in their nature" to probe any soft spot, but the United States "must be willing to face them down when they step across the line."

Malik's new instructions became evident just after Kissinger returned to his Foggy Bottom office from his encounter with the press. Persuaded no doubt that the influence game in the Middle East was getting too expensive for the Soviet Union, Brezhnev sought a face-saving compromise at the UN. He told Malik to stop pushing for the inclusion of the superpowers in the peacekeeping force and instead to yield to American insistence that they be specifically excluded from the UN force. Malik told Scali. Scali told Kissinger. Kissinger told the President. Although there was not yet any sign that Russian airborne units had been returned to their prealert status, Kissinger interpreted Malik's message as a signal that Russia had abandoned its go-it-alone tactic. The fifteen-hour crisis then eased considerably. The Security Council, swayed by Kissinger's warnings and apprised of the Soviet switch, passed Resolution

340 setting up a UN emergency force "composed of personnel drawn from states members of the United Nations except permanent members of the Security Council." The vote was fourteen to nothing, with China abstaining.

The two superpowers, to use Murrey Marder's phrase, "passed through the shadows of high crisis"; after a frightening exercise in nuclear muscle-flexing, they returned to the twilight zone of détente. The following day, October 26, Schlesinger, after conferring with Nixon and Kissinger, pulled the Southern Command in Panama and the Alaskan Command off alert status. Later in the day, he also relaxed the alert for the Strategic Air Command and the North American Air Defense Command. That meant that America's nuclear sword had again been sheathed.

The speed with which Washington cranked up the alert, and then cranked it down, gave rise to postmortem speculation that Kissinger, for one, had overreacted to the Soviet warning about "unilateral action." NATO allies, who had not alerted their forces, shared little of the Secretary's anxiety about Russian intervention in the Middle East, and they protested "a lack of advance consultations." They accused Kissinger of being "high-handed," and Kissinger accused them of being "craven." The Secretary also came in for criticism from sources closer to home. Schlesinger, to take only one example, publicly disputed Kissinger's version of the events. At a Pentagon news conference, the Defense chief asserted that there were "mixed reactions and different assessments of the probability" of Soviet intervention. Although Kissinger described the President's top advisers as being "unanimous" in their judgment that there was a "high probability" of a "unilateral Soviet move," Schlesinger said: "I think the probability of Soviet forces being en route was considered by some to be low." Later, when queried about the possibility that the Soviet transport planes spotted flying toward Cairo could have been carrying troops, Schlesinger added: "Nobody under those circumstances could dismiss that as a possibility, no matter how low he placed the probability."

The Pentagon leader also contested Kissinger's assertion that Watergate had nothing to do with the decision to put American forces on alert. "I think it was important," Schlesinger said, at another point in his news conference, "in view of the circumstances that have raised a question or may have raised a question about the ability of the United States to react appropriately, firmly and quickly, that this [the alert] certainly scotched whatever myths may have developed with regard to that possibility."

But if Schlesinger had trouble with parts of Kissinger's explanations of the alert, everyone — Kissinger, Schlesinger and many others — had trouble with Nixon's explanation. On the following evening of October 26, when the danger of a Soviet-American confrontation had passed, the President held one of his prime-time TV news conferences, devoted to an emotional defense of his Watergate actions. His defense, as usual, was coupled with a combative assault on the press. Of special interest to Nixon-Kissinger watchers was the markedly different tone both men took in discussing the alert.

For example, Kissinger asserted, publicly, that there were "ambiguities" in Soviet conduct. To Nixon, the Soviet position was unambiguous. "We obtained information," he said, "which led us to believe that the Soviet Union was planning to send a very substantial force into the Mideast — a military force."

Kissinger maintained that there had been no "threats" made by either side against the other. Nixon implied that there had been.

Kissinger stated that there had been no "missile-crisis-type of situation"; Nixon described it as "the most difficult crisis we had since the Cuban missile crisis of 1962."

These differences led some observers, including Thomas L. Hughes, President of the Carnegie Endowment for International Peace, to speculate that the two men were operating on "seriously different wavelengths."

Actually, the President and the Secretary were on the same "wavelength" in their private judgments about Soviet conduct and motivation in the Middle East: they both regarded the possibility of a unilateral Soviet military move as a very real threat. But they spoke at different times in the crisis — and clearly with different motivations. Nixon spoke that night as a politician under attack, trying desperately to keep one step ahead of impeachment. He knew that the crisis was over by then, and that his more extreme comments would cost little diplomatically — but they might help him with the American public. Kissinger had spoken as the nation's number one diplomat at the height of the crisis; he had to speak cautiously because he was trying to head off a big-power confrontation that could have led to a world war. There is no disputing Hughes on another point, however. Kissinger's "anguish as he listened to Nixon that Friday," as Hughes wrote, was "deep and mortifying." In conversations with a number of people that day, Kissinger said that it had been a "rough week" for the President.

With the benefit of hindsight, not even Kissinger has given Kissinger a straight "A" for crisis-management on the night of October 24–25. The Secretary has privately acknowledged, for one thing, that the consultation process with allies was "inadequate" and, for another, that the global, nuclear nature of the alert was too extreme. The Southern Command in Panama, for example, did not have to be alerted; nor did the Alaskan Command.

More important, he miscalculated the reaction of the American people to the sudden alert. But, unlike his critics at home and abroad, Kissinger has consistently maintained that the alert was "vital" to American security and that it was not prompted by Watergate. In his opinion, "if we had not reacted violently," the Russians would almost certainly have put their airborne troops into Egypt "to force the Israelis back to the October twenty-second line," thus liberating the trapped 3rd Corps and saving the Sadat regime from humiliation and a likely coup d'etat. There was, he said, a "three out of four chance" that the Russians could have intervened; and the United States could not have allowed such a substantial shift in the balance of power in the Middle East. It would have led not only to the destruction of Israel but also to an extremely destabilizing situation that in time could have led to another world war.

Kissinger assumed that if the Russians had managed to establish themselves in the Middle East as the saviors of the Arabs, it would have been very difficult to get them out. Their influence over future oil shipments would have increased. The United States could have survived, but Western Europe and Japan could not have gotten along without an expanding flow of oil. At his most pessimistic, Kissinger could imagine a situation in which Soviet domination of the Middle East might lead to the communization of Western Europe and Japan in five to ten years.

The alert was clearly not Kissinger's finest hour, but he has insisted that it was one of those necessary exercises in big-power politics, which firmed up the U.S. position in the Middle East and opened the door to a direct U.S. role in mediating the dangerous Arab-Israeli conflict. As he saw it, the cease-fire imposed by the two superpowers produced a military stalemate. The alert produced the crisis atmosphere so necessary in the Secretary's scenario to scare the belligerents off dead center. The timing — always a crucial element — seemed right, at long last, for Kissinger, as Secretary of State, to plunge into the politics of the Middle East. As Omar Saqqaf, the Saudi Arabian Foreign Minister had remarked the week before: "We think the man who could solve the Vietnam war . . . can easily play a good role . . . in our area."

NINETEEN

Henry of Arabia

The Launching of "101"

The part called for someone taller, slimmer, more adept at reviewing Arab honor guards, more traditional in his diplomatic style, a connoisseur of couscous and casbah conventions, a WASP. No producer had ever dreamed of Henry of Arabia.

And yet, after several months of flying into, among other places, Rabat, Tunis, Algiers, Cairo, Luxor, Aswan, Aqaba, Amman, Rayak, Damascus and Riyadh — yes, and Tel Aviv and Jerusalem, too — Kissinger would be the hero of the Middle East. Sadat would be kissing him and calling him "brother"; Fahmy would be embracing him; Saqqaf would be holding his hand; Faisal would be talking with him; Hussein would be taking him on joyrides in the royal helicopter; Assad would be swapping one-liners with him; Dayan would be praising his efforts to get Israel to withdraw from Arab territory; and *Al-Ahram*, Cairo's semiofficial newspaper, would be referring to him as "Superman" while *Al-Jazerah*, Riyadh's equally semiofficial newspaper, would be calling him a "mediator of peace."

Against stiff odds, Kissinger, in November, 1973, launched an extraordinary diplomatic effort to bring peace to the Middle East — step by difficult step. He seized the right historical moment in the aftermath of the Yom Kippur War to throw his energy, reputation, and skill into the nearly impossible task of midwifing a settlement between Arabs and Jews, and, in the process, persuading King Faisal and his friends to lift their oil embargo against the United States. He aimed for Israeli withdrawal but within the context of Israeli security. He encouraged the reemergence of Arab pride, but within a context of realism and responsibility. Kissinger's fame, already considerable, expanded still further until some Americans began to think of him as "Secretary of the World" and Chou En-lai, in a light moment, remarked that the Japanese were calling him the "Mideast cyclone."

When Kissinger reviewed the wreckage of the sixteen-day war — the zigzagging cease-fire lines that were fertile ground for new fighting — he knew that he was involved in a race against time. Israel seemed intent on having the victory Kissinger had aborted with his October 22 call for a cease-fire: Israeli troops were tightening their noose around the Egyptian 3rd Corps. Only after the Secretary warned Mrs. Meir that there might be a slowdown in American aid did Israel allow a convoy of a hundred and twenty-five trucks carrying humanitarian supplies to cross the cease-fire lines and reach the city of Suez. One convoy and no more, General Elazar insisted. As the Israelis resisted American pressure to open a permanent corridor to Suez and the 3rd Corps, Sadat threatened "to act" — if, as he put it, "my children" were harmed. Unlike the United States, which quickly deactivated its alert, Russia kept about fifty thousand airborne troops on alert, and the Egyptian leader always had the option of calling for their help.

Kissinger wasted little time organizing his first safari through the Arab world. On October 27, as *Al-Ahram* took the unprecedented step of publishing the full text of Kissinger's October 25 news conference, the Secretary learned that Sadat had accepted his offer to fly to Cairo on November 6 for a full day of meetings. The following day, Sadat cabled Kissinger that he was sending a high-ranking envoy, Ismail Fahmy, to Washington for a round of preliminary talks. Kissinger told Sadat that the Fahmy mission was "premature." Sadat replied, in effect, too bad, he's already on his way.

Kissinger was reluctant to receive Fahmy at that time because he had already invited Mrs. Meir to visit Washington at the same time. He understood from Dinitz that she needed reassurances from President Nixon about American support of Israel. As it turned out, the fact that the Egyptian and Israeli schedules overlapped proved to be fortuitous. It provided the Secretary with his first opportunity to act as a go-between in a crash effort to save the cease-fire and to encourage a diplomatic exchange between Egypt and Israel. Exhausted by the war and fearful of becoming merely the tools of the big powers, both belligerents welcomed Kissinger's effort.

Sadat had read Kissinger's notices. He believed that the Secretary could accomplish miracles. He felt that because Kissinger did not have to worry about charges of anti-Semitism, he would be the first Secretary of State who could persuade Israel to give up occupied Arab lands.

For her part, Mrs. Meir, recognizing Israel's enormous dependence upon the United States, said that Israel neither could nor would stand in the way of a sincere U.S. mediation effort. It was clear that the strategy Israel had followed since the 1967 war had backfired. Sadat had not come hat in hand, asking for negotiations with Israel; he had come gun in hand, crossing the canal, in a move that drastically altered the military and psychological balance in the Middle East. Mrs. Meir recalled Kissinger's decisive role in the Jordan crisis of September, 1970. She wanted to believe that, as Secretary of State, he could persuade the Arabs to live in peace with Israel. Four times in one generation, they had failed in their attempt to drive her country into the sea.

Fahmy, a suave Egyptian diplomat with a fondness for Cuban cigars, who was soon to replace al-Zayyat as Foreign Minister, flew into Washington on October 29, shortly after Kissinger appeared before a closed-door session of the House Foreign Affairs Committee. "Why is Fahmy coming here?" one Congressman wanted to know, pointing to Egypt's close relationship to Russia. "Because," the Secretary was quoted as answering, "he can get weapons from the Soviet Union. But he can get territory only from us." That simple fact was to become Kissinger's greatest leverage throughout the negotiations.

Mrs. Meir flew into Washington on October 31, shortly after Fahmy was received by the President. She met with Nixon the following day and got his assurance that, as she later put it, "the security and well-being of Israel are a major concern to the United States." The President, who always admired Israel's "moxie," enjoyed Mrs. Meir's company. "You know, Madame Prime Minister," the President smiled, "we have something in common — we both have Jewish foreign secretaries." "Yes," Mrs. Meir replied, "but mine speaks English without an accent."

For the next three days, Kissinger darted back and forth between Fahmy and Mrs. Meir, often well into the night, trying to narrow differences between the two sides. The essence of the problem related to the terms of the Brezhnev-Kissinger call for a cease-fire on October 22.

Egypt demanded that Israel return to the cease-fire lines of October 22. If not, Fahmy warned, Egypt could not agree to an exchange of prisoners of war. Such an exchange — within seventy-two hours after the cease-fire went into effect — was one of the unwritten understandings Kissinger had reached in Moscow. Nor, Fahmy added, would Egypt engage in direct talks with Israel. Such talks were an explicit condition of the cease-fire call.

Mrs. Meir argued that "no one alive" knew where the October 22 lines had actually been. Besides, she insisted, without an exchange of prisoners, an emotional issue in Israel, and without direct talks with Egypt, a long-standing diplomatic requirement for Israel, there would be no Israeli withdrawal.

These exchanges were interrupted only long enough for Kissinger to welcome Mohammed Z. Ismail, a Syrian Deputy Foreign Minister, to the State Department on the evening of November 2. Ismail, who had been at the UN, journeyed to Washington at the Secretary's invitation — a small sign that maybe even Syria, a militant Arab state, wished to join Kissinger's widening effort to start negotiations among the three main warring parties.

"We're in a three-ring circus now," one American official noted. "The Secretary sees Fahmy, then he talks to Golda, and now he's seeing the Syrian."

In all of these exchanges, the Secretary did not submit a U.S. "plan" for an Israeli-Egyptian accommodation; but he did suggest a number of U.S. "ideas" for bridging the big gaps between the two sides. For example, he suggested that Fahmy's call for an Israeli pullback to the October 22 lines be subsumed in a more ambitious negotiation aimed at a staged Israeli withdrawal across the canal and into the Sinai. Such a withdrawal, by definition, would lift the siege of the trapped 3rd Corps and remove the embarrassment of an Israeli force camped on the west bank of the canal. Of course, Kissinger implied, there would be a price, but only a modest one. Egyptian officials would have to meet and talk with Israeli officials and exchange prisoners of war.

When these "ideas" were first suggested to Mrs. Meir, she reacted with a vigorous negative. Why should Israel reward Egyptian aggression by withdrawing her troops from the west bank of the canal, she asked, while Egyptian troops would be allowed to remain on the east bank? Who, after all, was the victim of aggression; who the aggressor? And, as a result of the war, who sat with a dagger at the throat of the Egyptian army? Who was in "Africa"? Why, in other words, should Israel have to pay the higher price for accommodation? Although Kissinger could appreciate her logic, he still believed that ultimately Israel would have to withdraw from the west bank of the canal; after four increasingly costly wars in twenty-five years, he explained, Israel would have to break this cyclical pattern of warfare and run a risk for peace. Kissinger never argued that the nature of this negotiation — at least, in its early phases — was fair; he knew that it was not. Israel would be giving, and Egypt getting. But in the long run, he hoped that a balance between giving and getting could be created — a balance measured not just by territory but by shared experience across the negotiating table and later in the market-place — that would in time give both countries the feeling that there might be an alternative to endless war.

Understandably, Mrs. Meir resisted Kissinger's arguments. He was urging her to bargain away Israel's tactical military advantages, gained during a war Israel did not start — partly because of his own warnings against preemptive action — and to adjust Israel's military and diplomatic strategy to his concept of a fair negotiation. That called for a great deal of trust and confidence, and, in early November, there wasn't much of either. Nevertheless, Kissinger felt he had made some progress in persuading Mrs. Meir to consider the possibility of opening a humanitarian supply corridor through Israeli lines to the city of Suez and, across the canal, to the trapped 3rd Corps. One day, the *New York Times* carried an AP photograph showing Kissinger and Mrs. Meir at Blair House. The picture caught them both looking tired and grim. "Was it that bad?" a reporter asked Kissinger. He nodded slowly but said nothing. One of his aides later remarked: "That's the way it was with them most of the time."

With Fahmy, Kissinger had much better luck. Although the Secretary couldn't get Fahmy to drop his insistence upon an Israeli pullback to the October 22 lines, he was able to make progress on an interim arrangement that would result in an exchange of prisoners following Israeli agreement to open a supply corridor to the city of Suez. Kissinger hoped that when he went to Cairo he would be able to persuade Sadat to take a more farsighted view of the Egyptian call for an Israeli return to the October 22 lines.

By the time Mrs. Meir and Fahmy left Washington on Sunday, November 4, Kissinger had managed to draft an unofficial six-point proposal that took both Egyptian and Israeli views into account, and that he hoped he could use as the basis for negotiations between the two countries. Shuttling between Mrs. Meir and Fahmy had been a rather rough entrée to Middle East diplomacy for the Secretary. "How are you enjoying it?" a reporter asked innocently. "I didn't know how good I had it when I was negotiating with the Vietnamese," he grinned. "Then there were only three Vietnamese parties. Now there are four Arab parties, and one Jewish party, and I think that's a script worthy of Dante's *Inferno!*"

At 9:40 P.M., November 5, 1973, Kissinger's blue and white jet slipped out of the clouds and landed at Rabat International Airport, his first stop on a four-day, five-nation swing through the Arab world on his way to China and Japan. Two klieg lights turned the darkness into high noon as the Secretary stepped onto Moroccan soil and scored three quick firsts: his first time in Africa, his first time in an Arab country, and the first time he had ever been called on to review a guard of honor. Tall Berber troops in flowing red and white cloaks and black kaffiyehs stood on either side of the red carpet that stretched from the plane to the VIP lounge. They carried rifles and stood at rigid attention as the new Secretary of State ambled past them in self-conscious conversation with Foreign Minister Ahmed Taibi Benhima. He seemed distinctly out of place. After a few opening remarks, Kissinger and Benhima got into a long black limousine for the twenty-minute ride to King Hassan's palace, located behind tall sandstone walls on the outskirts of the city.

In conversations that night and again the following morning, the Secretary explained his role in the Middle East negotiations — "think of me as a catalyst," he said — and expressed his hopes for the future. "For the first time," he stated, "we have a chance for a real dialogue with the Arab world and a serious dialogue with Israel." Rabat's leading newspaper described him as a "pilgrim of peace."

Before his departure from the palace, Kissinger formally reviewed the Royal Guard. It was a very funny sight. The army band played a marching song, but Kissinger had terrible trouble keeping step with the music and with his escort — a tall, mustachioed sergeant-major carrying, upright, a glistening saber. When the review was over, Kissinger stopped, looked around for instructions, and then tentatively extended his right hand to the sergeant-major, whose right hand was then otherwise occupied in maintaining the sword at attention not two inches from his nose. There was an awkward pause. The sergeant-major, recovering quickly, sheathed his saber, saluted, and then shook the Secretary's hand. Kissinger at that moment must have made a mental note: find out how to review an honor guard!

Kissinger's plane had to fly north to Gibraltar and then over the Mediterranean before it could settle down at its second destination — a two-hour stop in Tunis. The more direct route, over Algeria, was off-limits. U.S.-Algerian relations had been broken after the 1967 war. Tunisia was a last-minute addition to the Secretary's itinerary — essentially a courtesy call on President Habib Bourguiba, who had often said that he favored negotiations with Israel. Kissinger wanted to encourage that kind of thinking in the Arab world. Since Kissinger and Bourguiba had very little business to discuss, they finished their private chat in twenty minutes.

Twice during the four-hour flight from Tunis to Cairo, the key stop on Kissinger's initial trip, he wandered into the rear compartment of the plane to chat with the fourteen reporters he had allowed on board to cover his trip. (It should be explained that the Secretary's plane is not an ordinary one. It is a specially configured Boeing-707, outfitted as a combination hotel and office, and electronically linked through the Pentagon switchboard to any phone in the world. The plane is divided into four compartments. The front compartment, housing the cockpit, the telex machines and a Buck Rogers console of phones and gadgets, is for the Air Force crews that fly and maintain the aircraft, one of a half-dozen in a special presidential fleet. The next compartment is subdivided into two rooms: one, a private bedroom with adjoining bath for the Secretary; the other his private office, featuring one high-backed armchair facing an L-shaped table and bench. The third compartment has four comfortable armchairs and a work table on each side of the center aisle. This area is for Kissinger's closest aides: Sisco, Atherton, Eagleburger, McCloskey, Bunker and Vest. The rear compartment, containing two dozen standard airplane seats, is reserved for reporters, security men and secretaries. The last three compartments are separated from one another by floor-to-ceiling partitions, so that the Secretary can have complete privacy from the traveling press corps and, on occasion, from his own aides. His predecessor, William Rogers, had initiated the practice of allowing newsmen to buy a seat on his plane and cover his travels. But, after the first few journeys, their interest waned, as they became more interested in Kissinger. Now, as Secretary of State, Kissinger has often had to turn reporters away. He always made it a practice of briefing the press at least once on every flight.) Kissinger was in an upbeat mood. His talks with King Hassan and Bourguiba had persuaded him that at least some of the Arab leaders favored "movement" toward a permanent settlement with Israel.

But it was Sadat who held the key. He could accept a compromise on the question of Israel's withdrawal to the October 22 cease-fire lines, thus opening the door to a step-by-step accommodation with Israel; and he could agree to reestablish diplomatic relations with the United States, which would have a salutary effect on America's position throughout the Arab world. Or, on the other hand, he could press for a series of UN resolutions demanding an Israeli pullback to the October 22 lines; and if Israel refused, then he could ask for UN sanctions. Such actions would further isolate Israel in the diplomatic community and diminish her support in the United States, which was beginning to feel the oil squeeze; they would also weaken America's position throughout the Arab world.

Kissinger refused to make any predictions. He carefully deflated the expectations of the press, and revealed very little about what he knew had already been accomplished in his talks with Fahmy and Mrs. Meir in Washington. "The U.S. won't huckster any plan now," he said flatly. "We're not going to be shot at by everyone." The situation, he explained, was extremely dangerous. The cease-fire line was "crazy." Imagine a war ending in such a way that the Israelis trap the 3rd Corps by encircling Suez City on the west bank of the canal and, at the same time, find their own encircling force gradually being trapped by a bigger Egyptian force (with or without Soviet troop assistance) operating closer to its main line of supplies in Cairo. "Weird!" Kissinger exclaimed.

What about diplomatic relations? he was asked. "I don't exclude it," he replied cautiously, "it might come up. We don't really have a fixed agenda." A Kissinger aide then explained that Fahmy had "linked" the reestablishment of relations to a resolution of the plight of the 3rd Corps.

Ismail Fahmy, the new Foreign Minister, who had returned to Cairo only the night before, led a small group of Egyptian officials out of the darkened airport terminal, down a long ramp, and then across the tarmac; Kissinger's plane was coming to a slow stop. Cameramen and reporters rushed to the foot of the stairs, and after the engine whine subsided, they flicked on their television lights, suddenly illuminating the chaotic scene with an unnatural brightness. Kissinger emerged, peered down at the lights, and then spotted Fahmy at the foot of the stairs. His face broke into a broad smile. He quickly bounded down the steps and approached his Egyptian colleague. He put his left arm around Fahmy's shoulder and pumped his right hand, exchanging pleasantries about midnight arrivals. The Secretary was all charm. It was as though he regarded Fahmy as a long-lost brother, and Cairo as Palm Springs.

Kissinger and Fahmy got into a black Mercedes limousine and drove to the Hilton Hotel in downtown Cairo. The ride took twenty minutes, enough time for Kissinger to catch glimpses of a capital anxious about a resumption of war. All automobile headlights were painted dark blue, or black. There were only occasional streetlights. Government buildings were protected by army troops, even in the dead of night, and by sand-bagged machine-gun nests. Convoys of army trucks rumbled through the city, heading east toward the front. Except for security men and newsmen, the hotel lobby was deserted, its windows painted dark blue and crisscrossed with heavy tape. Kissinger was escorted by plainclothes-men to a suite on the top floor. From there he could see the Nile, the life force of Egyptian culture for thousands of years.

"I want to see the pyramids tomorrow," Kissinger announced.

"You can't avoid them," Fahmy responded.

The two foreign ministers then conferred for about an hour, arranging and then rearranging the program for the Secretary's big day in Cairo.

"Welcome! Welcome!"

Sadat's deep baritone echoed through the reception room of the Tahra Palace, a heavily guarded villa in Cairo that had once belonged to one of King Farouk's wives; Kissinger, beaming, his right hand extended, approached the Egyptian leader, who was dressed in a military uniform. They shook hands for a full minute and then sat down on a sofa while the cameramen took their pictures and the reporters tried to listen in on tidbits of conversation.

"How was your trip?"

"Excellent, Mr. President."

"You are welcome here."

"Thank you, Mr. President."

For most of their three-and-a-half-hour talk, which started shortly after 10 A.M., the two statesmen were alone. That was always Kissinger's style. All of the other top Egyptian and American officials — Sisco, Fahmy, Atherton, Ashraf Ghorbal, a close Sadat aide — were invited into the garden. After spending a little while admiring the sprinkling fountains and spreading willows, they drew their wicker chairs into a large circle and discussed the general problems of the Middle East. Reporters and cameramen formed a larger concentric circle, thirty to forty feet away. Everyone waited, listening to the birds and the occasional barking of a dog. Every now and then, someone would glance up at the second floor of the palace, where Sadat and Kissinger were bargaining about war and peace.

At about 1:30 P.M., there was a sudden stir. One security man, then another, walked into the palace. Others moved toward the large center hallway. Everyone stood up. Then, at last, Sadat escorted Kissinger into the garden, the press approached, the officials retreated, and a mini–news conference began. Kissinger was unusually diffident. He deferred to Sadat. He spoke in low tones. Sadat, on the other hand, was smiling and expansive.

"Good talk, Dr. Kissinger?" a reporter asked.

"It was a constructive meeting," he replied softly.

"Will you be coming back to Cairo, Dr. Kissinger?"

"Yes, as the occasion requires."

An awkward pause.

"Mr. President," an American newsman asked, "will the U.S. now curtail its airlift of military supplies to Israel?"

"You should ask this question of Dr. Kissinger," Sadat answered, with a smile.

"Luckily," Kissinger interjected, "I didn't hear it."

There was laughter, much more than the line deserved. Another awkward pause.

"Dr. Kissinger, will there be a reestablishment of diplomatic relations between Egypt and the United States?" Kissinger smiled, squirmed, and said nothing. "We will have news for you later in the day, be patient," Sadat volunteered.

Later in the day, as promised, McCloskey announced, at a crowded news conference in a Hilton ballroom, that relations "in principle" had been reestablished and ambassadors would be exchanged within two weeks. Dr. Ashraf Ghorbal would represent Cairo. Hermann F. Eilts, a career Arab specialist in the State Department, would represent Washington. With this announcement, Sadat showed the Russians that he could make his own deal with the Americans. McCloskey had a second announcement — that Sisco and Harold Saunders, a Middle East expert on the NSC staff, had flown to Jerusalem. An Egyptian plane had taken them as far as Cyprus; an Israeli plane would take them the rest of the way.

McCloskey did not reveal any of the inside details of the Kissinger-Sadat meeting; but what happened at the Tahra Palace was that Kissinger had scored a quick success. He had persuaded Sadat to defer his demand for an immediate Israeli withdrawal to the October 22 lines — and to put this narrow issue into the broader context of a general disengagement of Israeli and Egyptian troops. The negotiation was, on occasion, quite tough. Sadat insisted that the disengagement could be accomplished only by the withdrawal of Israeli forces from *both* banks of the canal — not, as Mrs. Meir had proposed in Washington, by a return to the prewar lines: Egyptian forces returning to the west bank and Israeli forces to the east bank. Sadat told Kissinger that Egyptian forces would never abandon the east bank, that, if necessary, they would resume the war to liberate the 3rd Corps and that Russia would help them.

Kissinger urged patience and praised Sadat's willingness to give diplomacy a chance. At no time did Kissinger dispute Sadat's argument. Deep down, he accepted its logic — he too believed that Israel would have to withdraw from both banks of the canal. Besides, diplomacy was often a game of keeping one step ahead of catastrophe. By postponing a showdown on an Israeli withdrawal to the October 22 lines, he had gained time to strengthen the cease-fire and to prepare the way for a disengagement of forces.

In retrospect, Kissinger was to look back upon this first long exchange with Sadat as one of the "dramatic breakthroughs" of his diplomacy. "It brought about," he said, "a major turn in the foreign policy of Egypt and therefore in the whole orientation of the area." Kissinger was full of praise for the Egyptian leader. Sadat showed "great wisdom," he said. "You have to give him a lot of credit."

After his meeting with Sadat, Kissinger drove to the pyramids at Giza, on the outskirts of Cairo, at the very edge of the desert. He was followed by a convoy of reporters and cameramen. Henry and the Sphinx!

Hands behind his back, Prince Philip style, Kissinger walked slowly toward the largest pyramid, built in honor of Cheops, an Egyptian Pharaoh who ruled over fifty-five hundred years ago. Kissinger stared at this architectural wonder while his guide explained its history. One of his aides wisecracked: "He's looking it over because he wants to build one for himself." Kissinger expressed appropriate awe and amazement. "They did it without wheels, didn't they?" Or, "It seems incredible to me that they could do this." The Egyptian reporters were flattered by his interest. "Do you know much about our history, Dr. Kissinger?" one of them asked. The Secretary responded diplomatically, "I've always been fascinated by Egyptian history — its sense of permanence." The reporters scribbled down every one of his lines. He climbed the stone steps to the entrance to the pyramid and peered inside, into the gloom. "It would make a pretty good State Department press room, wouldn't it?" The State Department reporters laughed. Kissinger looked down the steps. "This is good training for a heart attack." More laughter.

Back once again at sand level, he watched a performance of Bedouin horsemanship from a Hollywood director's chair. Afterward, as he approached the Sphinx for closer scrutiny, cameramen battled for the best angle. "Do you feel like the Sheik of Araby?" a reporter asked. "Feel?" snapped Kissinger. "I am!" He looked at the Sphinx. "Which of us is the *real* Sphinx?" he mused. More pictures and pushing. "Just wait till I get into the movies. What I am looking for now is a leading lady."

Kissinger always enjoyed this banter with newsmen. He was good copy, and he knew it. His amusing lines shared space with his more serious endeavors on the front pages of most newspapers in the Middle East, and he was very conscious of the diplomatic value of this coverage. Here was an American Secretary of State, a Jew, visibly immersed in Arab culture, and devoted to the resolution of Arab problems.

It has always been Kissinger's special style to flatter and charm an adversary. Mohammed Hassanein Heikal, then editor of *Al-Ahram*, who spent the evening with Kissinger at a dinner hosted by Fahmy, later recalled Kissinger's remarks in an article for a French magazine.

The Secretary, he said, placed the Middle East in the context of his global negotiations. "I know that here I am touching upon a complex problem which is difficult to deal with," he judged; "more difficult than establishing an understanding with the Soviet Union." Yet Kissinger, alluding to his fabled ego, indicated that he intended to solve the problem. "I have a failing," he remarked disarmingly. "I have accumulated a small amount of the asset of success which I do not want to lose. My reputation is at stake."

Kissinger conceded that he was a bit concerned about "Arab romanticism." "Peace is not just around the corner," he cautioned. "It will take time: some six months or so or even a year before we see anything concrete emerge. World politics is not a conjurer's business."

Kissinger disparaged U.S. intelligence in a gesture to Arab pride. "Our calculations on the size of your concentrations were wrong," he admitted. "Our forecasts as regards your combat capability were also wrong."

At the same time, he disputed the common Arab claim that the U.S. airlift had "saved" Israel. "Even if the Israelis had not had the arms we sent them," he asserted, "they would not have been in the powerless position you imagine. They had prepared their counterattack across the Suez Canal before even receiving our aid."

On one point Kissinger was extremely blunt: the United States would never allow Russia to win a victory-by-arms in the Middle East. "Do not deceive yourself," he told Heikal directly, "the United States could not — either today or tomorrow — allow Soviet arms to win a big victory, even if it was not decisive, against U.S. arms. This has nothing to do with Israel or with you."

On Thursday morning, November 8, after a warm farewell embrace from Fahmy, Kissinger flew toward Amman for a brief stopover on his way to Riyadh. In accordance with his planned itinerary, he did not stop in Israel. The swing through the Middle East was designed, in part, to establish Kissinger's credentials as an "evenhanded" mediator. During the flight, he told newsmen that Sisco would rejoin the group in the Jordanian capital — "that is," he added, "if we ever see Joe again."

Kissinger was concerned about Israel's reaction to the six-point proposal. He assumed that Mrs. Meir would run a risk for peace — but not too large a risk. She had been persuaded in Washington to consider the possibility of allowing food and medical supplies through Israeli lines to the civilian inhabitants of Suez City and to the trapped Egyptian troops across the canal. For Israel, that would mean the abandonment of any plan to force the capitulation of the 3rd Corps. Even assuming that Israel was ready to drop such a plan, there was another problem. Dayan and the generals were worried that such a corridor could split Israeli forces on the west bank of the canal and leave them vulnerable to a punishing Egyptian attack.

"Are you going to call it the 'Kissinger Plan'?" a reporter asked, harking back to the Rogers Plan of December, 1969, which got nowhere. "Only if the Israelis buy it," Kissinger replied, with a broad grin. "And if not," the reporter continued, "would it then be called the 'Sisco Plan'?" Kissinger's grin widened.

Kissinger carried his uncertainty about Israel's reaction into Amman's International Airport, where he was greeted by one of his former Harvard students, Prime Minister Zaid al-Rifai. Across the tarmac was the Jordanian guard of honor, a snappy contingent of khaki-clad troops sporting red-and-white checked kaffiyehs. Beyond them, on the rooftop of the airport terminal building, were heavily armed troops manning machine guns. They were on alert for any possible Palestinian terrorism. If Kissinger spotted the extraordinary security, he paid no attention to it. He had all he could handle merely trying to maintain a degree of dignity as he reviewed his second guard of honor in three days. The Jordanian army band, playing bagpipes and drums, struck up a sprightly British marching song, as Rifai led his former professor past the cream of the Jordanian Legion, the best Arab troops in the Middle East. Once again, it was evident that Kissinger couldn't keep time to the beat, or to the sergeant-major's magnificent strut.

After a brief airport statement, Kissinger was whisked off to one of King Hussein's palaces in the hills overlooking Amman. He conferred with the King for about an hour about his peace-making effort, after which the two official parties sat down to a nine-course meal. It was then that the Secretary got word that Sisco had run into a snag in Jerusalem, and that he would not be able to join the group in Amman. Maybe he would catch up in Riyadh.

Everyone headed back to the airport by limousine except for Kissinger, who went by helicopter. The King was his pilot. They zoomed low over the city and finally settled on the tarmac about fifty feet from Kissinger's jet. The Secretary alighted from the helicopter looking green. Later, on the flight to Riyadh, he told reporters: "If it weren't for the honor, I would rather have walked."

Sisco had already had a four-and-a-half-hour meeting with Mrs. Meir the night before, shortly after his arrival from Cairo via Cyprus. He thought he had won her approval for the corridor proposal. But, that morning, the Prime Minister conferred with the leaders of the conservative Likud opposition party, and some of them balked. They had a number of hard questions, which Mrs. Meir had to check out with her own Cabinet and then with Sisco. That took extra time. By midafternoon, Mrs. Meir and Sisco conferred once again. This time, their meeting lasted almost two hours. Dayan and Allon joined their discussion. After a while, Sisco managed to allay some of their fears. UN checkpoints would be set up along the corridor to keep an eye on the flow of nonmilitary supplies to Suez City, but the corridor itself would still be controlled by Israeli forces. In addition, when the supplies reached the city, Israeli officers would have the right to inspect them — just to make certain no military supplies were smuggled into the convoy before it reached Suez. Mrs. Meir gave Sisco the green light to nail down the final details with the Egyptians. When the U.S. negotiator emerged from Mrs. Meir's study, he smiled at waiting newsmen. "I am optimistic," he volunteered. Then he sped off to the airport.

A U.S. Army plane was standing by to fly Sisco to Riyadh, but the pilot was informed that he would not have permission to land. Riyadh's explanation was that Saudi Arabia refused to give landing rights to *any* plane taking off from Israel. It took a few hours of haggling before someone in Kissinger's entourage persuaded someone in King Faisal's court to make an exception just this once.

On the flight from Amman to Riyadh, Kissinger kept popping into the press compartment and tossing off one-liners, apparently to relieve his own anxiety about what kind of a reception he would get in Faisal's rampantly anti-Jewish kingdom. One time, he pointed to three reporters who he knew were Jewish and announced in mock seriousness: "You three get off the plane last." Another time, he half-jested: "Only Wasps can disembark here." His eyes darted across the group. "Aren't there any Wasps among you?" Several hands went up. "Good," he decided, "you go first." There was some nervous laughter. "Henry," one of the reporters said, "if you can get off here, so can we." In fact, the Saudi Arabian government had waived all visa restrictions for the entire Kissinger party.

The Secretary didn't want to talk substance on this leg of the flight. He wasn't sure about the outcome of Sisco's mission to Jerusalem, and he wasn't sure how Faisal would react to him — or to his plea for a lifting of the oil embargo. So, once again, he tried to parry questions with humor. "I'd like to enjoy a little night life with you fellows in Riyadh," he smiled, "but I understand it starts at four in the afternoon and ends an hour later."

It was dusk over the desert as Kissinger's plane dipped low over primitive mud huts — there wasn't an oil well in sight — and landed at Riyadh's sand-swept airport. Foreign Minister Omar Saqqaf, wearing a flowing white robe with a black kaffiyeh and gold band, welcomed Kissinger with full honors. He shook his hand warmly, introduced him to several other Saudi officials, and then escorted him to the lounge. Reporters noticed that Saqqaf was holding Kissinger's hand. In Moslem countries, that is not unusual: one Moslem holding another Moslem's hand; but, in this case, the gesture seemed to be a special courtesy, a signal perhaps to other Saudis that Kissinger was acceptable. Even when Saqqaf and Kissinger sat down on a low, soft sofa to sip black coffee and exchange platitudes with the press, the Foreign Minister often reached for Kissinger's hand. "I'm beginning to wonder about myself, really," the Secretary later remarked. "In Riyadh, the Foreign Minister holds my hand, and once at Camp David, Brezhnev kissed me on the mouth."

After a brief stop at a royal guesthouse, Kissinger was driven to the Red Palace for his first meeting with King Faisal. The Secretary was escorted into a long rectangular room with dark drapes. Through the incense, Kissinger could see the King seated on his throne at the far end of the room. Two tall guards in black robes and black and white kaffiyehs, each carrying a Saracen sword, led Kissinger toward Faisal. The Secretary shook his hand. The King smiled, faintly. Kissinger sat down next to Faisal. He then noticed that, on both sides of the room, there were dozens of Royal Princes, all in black robes, many wearing sunglasses, some sipping coffee. Kissinger, at the King's request, got up and shook hands with every single Prince. Then Kissinger and the King agreed to meet privately after dinner. The meeting lasted two hours.

The Secretary tried to impress the King with his seriousness and sincerity. He began by telling Faisal that he had read all of the King's correspondence with Presidents Kennedy, Johnson and Nixon. He said he believed that, on the basis of that record, Faisal had good grounds for being disappointed in American policy. Johnson had promised the King that Israel would withdraw from occupied Arab lands; UN Resolution 242 had urged such a withdrawal; even Nixon had urged it. Yet nothing happened. In addition, when the Yom Kippur War erupted, the United States rushed military supplies to Israel — an action that coincided with Faisal's final decision to impose an oil embargo on the U.S. Kissinger expressed sympathy with the King's position, but he drew the King's attention to certain "new realities."

He described Nixon as "committed" to Israeli withdrawal, and he said that he was personally convinced that a settlement was now possible. He told the King what he had told Heikal — that his ego was large enough for him to believe that he could peacefully resolve Arab-Israeli differences. He appealed for Faisal's cooperation. For example, would the King support a peace conference? Yes, Faisal replied. Would the King support a lifting of the oil embargo? This was critically important, Kissinger explained, because a continuation of the embargo would serve to generate anti-Arab sentiment in the United States and complicate his diplomatic efforts to induce a gradual Israeli withdrawal from occupied Arab lands.

Faisal then explained his own position. He was, he said, fiercely anti-Communist and anti-Zionist. He opposed Russia and Israel and, ignoring most of recent history, he drew no clear distinction between their policies. For Faisal, Communists and Jews were peas in the same pod. The Jews, he said, took over the Communist movement in Russia, then led the 1917 revolution and finally established the Soviet Union. Then the Jews set up the state of Israel and furthered its policy of "aggression and expansionism." And now, "all over the world," Faisal said, looking directly at Kissinger, the Jews were "putting themselves into positions of authority." He told Kissinger that the Jews were trying to run the world, but that he would stop them with his oil weapon. It was no accident, he added, that the Jews were the only people mentioned unfavorably in the Koran.

Kissinger listened in silence. The Jews would have to give up all Arab lands, including Jerusalem, Faisal continued. For him, that was the key. He wanted to pray in the Jerusalem mosque before he died, and he warned that, after so many disappointments in the past, he would use his oil weapon until he compelled an Israeli withdrawal from Jerusalem. Did that mean that the oil embargo would not be lifted until Jerusalem had been recovered by the Arabs? Faisal's answer was elliptical enough to leave Kissinger with the impression that the embargo might be lifted once the Israelis began to withdraw.

Their conference was coming to an end. The King was tiring. Kissinger, as a prelude to departure, peered through "a cloud of incense" to admire a painting on the wall. "Is that the Arabian Desert, Your Majesty?" he asked. The King's generally dour face tightened into a grimace. "No," he answered. "That is our holy oasis." Kissinger apologized for his inadvertent mistake. Later, he said, "I guess I set back the lifting of the oil embargo by at least one month with that one comment."

After his unusually long meeting with King Faisal, Kissinger returned to his guesthouse. Sisco had just arrived. The Secretary wanted to review the six-point agreement, but there was not enough time. Three Saudi ministers arrived for more conferences and then dinner. It was past midnight before Kissinger and Sisco could sit down and pull all the loose ends together. That involved cables to Washington, Cairo, Jerusalem and Moscow — until finally, shortly before dawn, everything was in order except final approval by the Israeli Cabinet. That came as Kissinger was already airborne for Teheran and Islamabad, two brief stops on his way to China.

The six-point agreement, which set up the Kilometer 101 talks between Egyptian and Israeli generals on the Cairo-Suez road, took the form of a letter from Kissinger to UN Secretary-General Waldheim, which stipulated:

— that both sides would "observe scrupulously" the cease-fire;

— that they would "immediately" begin talks on settling "the question of the return to the October 22 positions in the framework of agreement on the disengagement and separation of forces under the auspices of the UN";

— that Suez would receive "daily supplies of food, water and medicine";

— that there would be "no impediment" to the transfer of nonmilitary supplies to the east bank;

— that UN checkpoints would be set up along the Cairo-Suez road and Israeli officers would enjoy the right to check on cargoes going to the east bank;

— and, finally, that as soon as the checkpoints were established, there would be "an exchange of all POWs, including wounded."

Though the agreement was a considerable achievement, it was still only a small, beginning step. It was worded vaguely, so that each side could claim a diplomatic victory, but it was precise enough to launch a process of direct diplomatic contact between Egypt and Israel and to overcome a few immediate problems that could have erupted into a new war at any time. More important, Egypt seemed ready to lead the Arab world in a process of accommodation with Israel. No one, least of all Kissinger, underestimated the difficulties or the dangers; but everyone appreciated the opportunity. Kissinger had won a little more time to focus on the next step — a peace conference between Arabs and Israelis.

On the Road to Geneva

On November 11, at Kilometer 101, then an Israeli-held checkpoint on the Cairo-Suez road, an Israeli general and an Egyptian general met in a UN tent for the purpose of implementing Kissinger's six-point agreement. Aharon Yariv, a brilliant Israeli intelligence officer, and Mohammed Abdel Ghany el Gamazy, one of Egypt's top military strategists, almost immediately ran into a deadlock. Israel wanted to check "nonmilitary" supplies entering Suez. The Egyptians argued that the agreement gave the Israelis no such right. Egypt, for its part, wanted to limit Israel's control over the Cairo-Suez road. The Israelis argued that, while the agreement called for UN checkpoints along the road, the road itself was to be left under Israeli control.

It took three days of long-distance backstage maneuvering by Kissinger, who was then visiting China and Japan, to break the deadlock. On November 15, the two generals agreed to a procedure for bridging their differences. As the UN set up checkpoints along the road, Egypt and Israel exchanged POWs: Egypt releasing two hundred and thirty-eight Israelis; Israel releasing over eight thousand Egyptians. This arrangement opened the way for a Geneva peace conference in late December.

Yariv and Gamazy then continued their deliberations, focusing on rival disengagement plans. That was a highly complicated endeavor. By early December, it was clear that the two generals could not reach agreement, and the "101" talks were suspended. The Egyptians began to complain that Kissinger had misled Sadat into believing that the Israelis were going to pull back to the October 22 lines. Kissinger argued that, on the contrary, he had always maintained that Israel would be unable to make any major moves until after the December 31 elections. This misunderstanding prompted Kissinger to pack his bags for another Middle East swing, his second in five weeks.

The Secretary wanted to maintain the diplomatic momentum. He believed that it was critically important, at this stage of the negotiations, to provide Egypt and Israel with new and acceptable alternatives to war. December's alternative was the peace conference. Kissinger envisaged a businesslike conference, consisting of the four principal belligerents — Egypt, Syria, Jordan and Israel — and their two big backers — the United States and Russia. The UN, serving as a kind of bureaucratic umbrella, would be represented by Secretary-General Waldheim, the conference's official host.

When Kissinger left Washington on December 8, en route to a NATO way-stop in Brussels, the conference was not yet a sure thing. No formal invitations had been extended. No agenda had been fixed. Kissinger's first task was obvious: to make certain that the conference would open on or about December 18, a working target date. In addition, he assigned himself two other interrelated tasks: first, to persuade the leaders of Israel that it was time to begin the process of withdrawal from most occupied Arab territory; and second, to persuade the leader of Saudi Arabia that it was time to lift the oil embargo.

On his first trip to the Middle East, Kissinger could not even fly over Algeria. On this trip, he was invited to fly *to* Algeria for a meeting with President Houari Boumedienne, the Algerian revolutionary leader who has been described as a "pragmatic fanatic." The meeting, which took place on December 13 in a Mediterranean villa on a high hill overlooking the Bay of Algiers, was a sign of the changing Arab attitude toward the new U.S. role as an intermediary in the Arab-Israeli conflict. Boumedienne, wearing a black cloak, greeted the Secretary in a dim, sparsely furnished room.

"Do you speak French, Mr. Secretary?" the President asked in French.

"I understand it. I read it," the Secretary replied in English. "But I don't speak it well."

After a few minutes for picture-taking, reporters and cameramen were quickly eased out of the room. Except for a notetaker and an interpreter, the two men were alone for two hours. They discussed bilateral relations, and they decided to open a "new dialogue" leading to a resumption of full diplomatic relations. Since 1967, when relations were broken, the two countries had maintained a lower form of diplomatic contact — "interests sections" — in one another's capitals. They also discussed peace prospects in the Middle East, and Kissinger won Boumedienne's endorsement of a Geneva peace conference.

At the airport, Foreign Minister Abdul Aziz Bouteflika said that the

Secretary's talk with Boumedienne had marked a "turning point" in Algerian-American relations, and that Algeria supported his peace-making efforts in the Middle East. So far so good, Kissinger felt, as he left Algiers for Cairo.

During the four-hour flight, Kissinger learned that *Al-Ahram* had taken an editorial swipe at his use of ambiguous diplomatic formulas. Apparently, the newspaper was reflecting Sadat's disappointment that the "101" talks had not yet produced any Israeli withdrawal. "The solution does not lie in clever diplomatic formulas couched in double meanings which each party can interpret in its own way to suit its purposes," it said. "Restricting the use of Arab oil or any other weapon," *Al-Ahram* continued, underscoring the link between oil and peace, "should be paralleled by Israeli withdrawal from occupied Arab territories on the way to a general settlement." Kissinger was miffed by the editorial, because it suggested that he was telling one thing to the Arabs and another thing to the Israelis. "That won't work," the Secretary told reporters. "It would be stupid Machiavellianism to tell different stories to different parties."

Kissinger landed in Cairo late in the evening of the same day. "I am delighted to be back," he told Fahmy, after a warm embrace. The two diplomats then drove off to the Barrages, a spacious villa eighteen miles north of Cairo. "Welcome, welcome," beamed Sadat, as Kissinger was escorted into a large reception room. "I hope you're in good shape." The Secretary, smiling, grasped Sadat's right hand — and held it, while cameramen snapped their pictures. "Excellent," Kissinger replied. "It's so good to see you." Sadat, wearing a military uniform, invited Kissinger to take a seat on a low sofa. The security men then beckoned reporters to leave the room.

Sadat and Kissinger conferred for two and a half hours, until well past midnight. They resumed at ten the next morning. Once again they were alone. Their aides — Sisco, Fahmy and the others — whiled away their time in a beautiful garden fragrant with jasmine shrubs and shaded by ancient banyan trees. They resumed their wicker-chair vigil in the sun.

After four hours, the security men, as usual, stirred first, then the cameramen, finally the officials, and once again Sadat and Kissinger made their grand entrance. Both were smiling, and they seemed relaxed. This time, Kissinger spoke first, and he reflected Sadat's eagerness for an Israeli withdrawal. "We agreed that disengagement of forces — separation of forces — should be the principal subject of the first phase of the peace conference," Kissinger announced, "and I will go to other countries to discuss with them their views on how to proceed." In Sadat's presence, Kissinger was still careful not to mention "Israel" by name. Sadat added: "I am really satisfied after the long, fruitful discussions we have had."

"Do you expect progress on disengagement before Christmas?" a reporter asked.

"Let us hope," replied Sadat. "Let us hope."

"Is it realistic to expect progress before the Israeli elections?" another reporter wanted to know. Kissinger shifted uncomfortably. Sadat fielded the question. "The Israeli election is not our problem but theirs. We are going to a peace conference. Let us hope that we can go on in a spirit of peace."

"Will you engage in direct talks with Israel?"

Sadat said that Egyptian representatives would "gather in the same room" with the Israeli representatives. "But," he added, "if you mean direct negotiations, no."

Did Sadat think the Arabs should lift their oil embargo, while Kissinger's peace-making mission continued? Before Sadat had a chance to answer, Kissinger interrupted with a jocular comment about the "persistence" of American reporters, and the news conference ended.

Kissinger then sped off to the airport with Fahmy. He was already two hours late for his departure for Riyadh. To reporters who accompanied him on the long flight to the Saudi Arabian capital, it was clear that the Secretary felt good about his extended talks with Sadat. He had obtained Egyptian agreement to attend the conference, Egyptian proposals on a disengagement of forces, Egyptian willingness to help persuade Syria to send representatives to Geneva, and Egyptian readiness to discuss a possible lifting of the oil embargo with other Arab states. Because Syria's participation was still a question mark, the opening of the conference might be delayed "a day or two," the Secretary acknowledged. But he added, with a broad grin, "It is my judgment that a conference is at hand." Every reporter remembered his October 26, 1972, comment that "peace is at hand" in Vietnam — it took another three months before the American guns were silenced — and they groaned. "Are we doomed to fly forever from one Arab capital to another?" "No," Kissinger responded, turning serious. "Just a day or two."

His hopes rested on Sadat. The Egyptian leader, Kissinger said, had a "sense of long-range objectives, a sense of reality. He could have taken the demagogic route, as some Egyptian newspapers did. But he chose to listen to an argument about what could reasonably be expected. He is very intelligent."

Kissinger had hardly left Cairo when Sadat dispatched Ashraf Marawan, one of his top assistants, to Damascus and to the oil-producing sheikdoms along the Persian Gulf to inform his allies about his lengthy talks with the Secretary of State.

It was early evening, December 14, when Kissinger returned to Riyadh. Saqqaf was at the airport to greet him. One again, the Saudi official held his hand during a brief news conference, and then the two ministers drove off to the royal guesthouse. Later in the evening, the Secretary conferred with Faisal in the King's *diwan*, his personal study. The carpets were thick. The room smelled of incense. Faisal was, as usual, dour. Kissinger tried to brighten the atmosphere with a few light comments, but the King's face remained impassive.

Their private talks, which lasted for two hours, must have made some progress toward lifting the oil embargo; a short time later one American official speculated that the chances were "better than fifty-fifty" that the embargo would be lifted early in 1974. Another official put the odds higher. Even Saqqaf, bidding Kissinger farewell the next morning, contributed to the generally rising optimism: "We think we are able to remove *every* stumbling block in our relations," adding, "I appreciated this meeting with my friend, Dr. Kissinger, whom I call Henry."

After his second meeting with Faisal, Kissinger began to refer to the King as a "very serious man, a man of his word." The Secretary, who needed the King's help, said that he appreciated Faisal's position: running a backward country that possessed a major percentage of the world's oil resources. He was, Kissinger added, "very savvy, once you understand the world in which he lives and in which he has to operate."

Despite the expected delay in the opening of the peace conference, Kissinger got word from Moscow that Soviet Foreign Minister Gromyko still planned to arrive in Geneva over the weekend; he also got word from the UN that Waldheim had delayed his departure for Geneva but promised to be there in time for the opening. Waldheim was at that time in the middle of a minor Arab-Israeli squabble. The Arabs wanted the UN to play a strong role at the conference; the Israelis wanted the UN to play only a symbolic role. Kissinger, in diplomatic messages to both sides, ended this squabble by telling the Arabs that Waldheim would extend the invitations to the conference and he would preside over its opening and by telling the Israelis that, no matter who sent the invitations and who presided over the opening, he and Gromyko would really run everything.

"Syria is going to be tough." That was Kissinger's judgment, as he flew into Damascus. He was the first Secretary of State to visit the Syrian capital since John Foster Dulles stopped there in 1953. Even before the Secretary's plane had come to a full stop, it was surrounded by tall, tough-looking Syrian troops carrying Kalashnikov machine guns. Kissinger emerged into a stiff breeze to be greeted by a small group of Syrian officials, who quickly whisked him off to the presidential compound in downtown Damascus. Along the way he might have caught a glimpse of a Palestinian refugee camp on the outskirts of the capital or of a few of the buildings, including the Soviet cultural office, which, according to the Syrians, had been bombed during the war.

Hafez Assad, a former air force commander who had seized power in 1970, gave the Secretary a correct welcome. Assad, considered a moderate in a murky coalition of religious fanatics, Baathist extremists and Communists, espoused a militant line against Israel and, by extension, against the United States. The picture-taking session was brief. A tall man with dark hair and narrow mustache, Assad sat in one corner of a sofa; Kissinger in the other. Neither tried very hard to make small talk.

After the reporters had been shooed out of the room, Kissinger and Assad talked for six hours, four hours longer than scheduled. The Secretary took a disarming, unorthodox approach to the Syrian strong man. "I've been traveling around the Middle East," he said, "and everyone tells me the Syrians are impossible. Tell me, Mr. President, why are the Syrians impossible?" Assad, astonished for a moment, burst into laughter. The ice was broken. And yet, according to one eyewitness, the meeting had a "Mad Hatter tea party quality" to it. Assad seemed to phase in, and then phase out, of the mainstream of the discussion: on occasion, he was sharp; at other times, he seemed to drift off into a dreamy reverie, twiddling his thumbs, closing his eyes and humming an Arab tune. Somehow the two men managed to discuss a wide range of problems. They agreed to improve communications between their countries by setting up "interests sections" in one another's capital. Since 1967, when diplomatic relations were broken, there had been no contact or representation of any kind. They reviewed the course of peace-making in the Middle East. Assad, as expected, affirmed a hard line against Israel, demanding a total withdrawal from the Golan. Kissinger focused on the peace conference. He wanted to be certain that Assad was committed to sending a delegation. Kissinger showed him a draft invitation. Assad raised no objections. Kissinger assumed then that Assad accepted the invitation. To be polite, he asked Assad if he had any comment to make about the invitation.

"Well, yes," replied Assad. "The invitation is fine except for one line."

"Oh," Kissinger said. "Which line?"

"The one that says the parties have agreed to come to the conference in Geneva. We have agreed to no such thing."

Kissinger was flabbergasted. During a brief break, he asked Sisco to contact Sadat and Gromyko immediately. Was this a new Syrian position? Or had the old one been misunderstood?

The hours passed. Most of the American officials and reporters had stayed on the Secretary's plane. Few of them had had any contact with Kissinger for quite some time. Their hunger and weariness increased. They speculated about what had happened to the Secretary. "He's just become the hundred and twenty-eighth Israeli prisoner." "He's off seeing Arafat." "The Syrians kidnapped him." "Maybe he's been assassinated." It was well past 11 P.M. when motorcycle sirens could be heard in the distance. "Well," one exhausted reporter remarked, "either he's finally coming, or they're finally coming for us." In a few minutes, Kissinger emerged from a limousine and told reporters that he and Assad had had "extensive and useful talks" and that "views" had been exchanged "very frankly indeed." He waved to the Syrian reporters. "It won't be another twenty years before the Secretary of State returns."

Kissinger visited three countries in the next eighteen hours: Jordan, where he obtained King Hussein's assurances that Prime Minister Rifai would be present at the conference, even if Syria chose not to attend; Lebanon, where he got the government's blessings for his peace-making efforts — at a secure air force base near Rayak, four miles west of the Syrian border, rather than in Beirut, which had been turned into a security man's nightmare by anti-Kissinger demonstrations; and finally Israel, where he used all his personal and diplomatic charm to win Mrs. Meir's approval of the peace conference and the disengagement talks that he had promised Sadat would follow on the heels of the conference.

Israel posed a special problem for Kissinger. He knew that he could not conduct an Israeli policy at the State Department. But he also knew that, as a Jew, he could not conduct a policy that could lead to Israel's defeat. If he were ever forced into that position, he told friends, then he would quit. In 1947, as a Harvard freshman, he had shared the Establishment view that the creation of a separate Jewish state in the Middle East would be, as he later put it, "a potentially historic disaster." He believed, at the time, that the Zionists would have been "better off forming a federal state with Jordan." Once he visited Israel, he changed his mind. The Jews had established a state "against all probability." They had performed a miracle. Privately and professionally, he was determined to help it survive.

But ever since the Yom Kippur War shattered so many illusions, including several of his own, Kissinger felt a growing conviction that Israel was pursuing a foolish, shortsighted policy, clinging to Arab lands that brought little security and tremendous resentment. The Arabs kept getting more sophisticated Soviet weapons, and they seemed to be riding a new crest of self-assurance and pride, more determined than ever to recapture their lands. Kissinger believed that their use of the oil weapon, which could destroy the Western economies, was driving an increasing number of oil-consuming nations into a reluctant anti-Israeli policy. He was convinced that no matter how often the United States corrected the arms balance in the Middle East, Israel would become increasingly isolated. "It is a tragedy," he once told a friend, "but these are a people who have come out of a ghetto, only to set up a state which has become a ghetto itself." Even in the United States, support for Israel would shrink, Kissinger believed, as more Americans shunned any foreign entanglements in the disillusioning aftermath of Vietnam. Kissinger thought that the time had come for Israel to make a good peace with the Arabs, affording her new, recognized, secure and guaranteed boundaries for the first time; if this opportunity was missed, then the big powers would more than likely be compelled to impose a solution.

It was late Sunday afternoon when Kissinger flew into David Ben Gurion Airport on the outskirts of Tel Aviv. On October 22, when he came to Israel with a cease-fire agreement, the Secretary had been cheered by most Israelis. By December 16, their mood had changed radically. They had been "traumatized" by the events of the previous two months. In early October, they lived in a world they considered secure — far from ideal, but at least secure. By mid-December, though their forces had moved into "Africa" and had even extended their control beyond the Golan Heights toward Damascus, they felt alone and terribly vulnerable. Even their friend, Kissinger, was flitting in and out of Arab capitals, embracing Arab leaders, engaged, they feared, in a shameless sellout of Israeli interests. The Israeli press became so hostile toward the Secretary of State that Mrs. Meir, in early December, felt obliged to chastise newsmen and editors for their tendency "to single out some personality and to take him apart." Kissinger, she asserted, was "being done an injustice." In the United States, a number of Jewish intellectuals harbored deep suspicions about Kissinger. Norman Podhoretz, editor of *Commentary*, told the Secretary on December 6 that he joined some Israelis in wondering whether he was "a Churchill disguised as a Chamberlain, or a Chamberlain disguised as a Churchill." *

When Kissinger stepped down from his aircraft, he was warmly welcomed by Eban, Dinitz and other top Israeli officials. Newsmen were kept behind barricades. A few hundred yards away, demonstrators were kept behind other barricades. Eighteen of them were arrested when they tried to push through. A couple of their placards read: "America — You Too, Brutus?" and "Kissinger Abandoned Formosa — Us Next?" The newspaper *Maariv* reflected Israel's muted sense of uneasiness about the Secretary's policy. "The Geneva conference has not yet begun," it said, in a lead editorial; "yet already the trust we put in the Americans has been severely torn. We cannot rely on their promises. . . . We can only ask ourselves whether, in the new conditions, there is any point to a conference." Kissinger, Eban and other top officials quickly boarded two army helicopters for the twenty-minute flight to Jerusalem. For twelve of the next twenty-two hours — the time Kissinger allotted to Israel — he engaged the Israelis in intense, passionate, difficult but, in the end, rewarding talks. Later, he was to describe the talks as "a breakthrough" that opened the way to the disengagement talks that would evolve out of the Geneva conference.

At 6 P.M., Kissinger arrived at Mrs. Meir's Knesset office, where he

---

* That was the day Kissinger invited a group of American Jewish intellectuals to his office in an effort to persuade them that he was not abandoning Israel; quite the contrary, that he was trying to save Israel from a coalition of "craven" Europeans, fanatical Arabs, and isolationist Congressmen.

conferred with the Prime Minister, most of the time alone, for the next three hours. At 9:30 P.M., Kissinger, Mrs. Meir, Sisco, Eban and other important American and Israeli officials began a three-and-a-half-hour dinner, remembered more for its stimulating repartee than for its Israeli cuisine. ("How one million Jewish mothers collectively can cook such awful food is an historical wonder worthy of a good Ph.D. study!" Kissinger later remarked.) The Secretary dissected his own policy, laying special stress on Israel's increasing isolation and vulnerability and yet expressing his deep concern about Israel's capacity to meet her current challenges. This was a unique moment to reach for peace, he said, even if the price was withdrawal from Arab territory. Occupation had not assured security. The Yom Kippur War disproved that hypothesis. Negotiate, he urged. Exchange land for new and guaranteed borders. Dinitz took the lead in disputing one of the Secretary's key points — that Israel was losing support even in the United States. Not so, the Ambassador claimed, citing some of the latest polls. Still, Kissinger was articulate and persuasive, and he seemed to win a majority of the Israeli Cabinet to his view.

At 1 A.M., Kissinger returned to the King David Hotel and told reporters and tourists in the lobby: "I am optimistic." For the next three hours, while the Cabinet met in Mrs. Meir's kitchen, Kissinger checked on whether Syria's objections to the conference had been overcome. Fahmy had flown to Damascus to confer with Assad. There was still no report on that meeting. The Soviet Ambassador in Damascus had also conferred with Assad. There was no report on that meeting, either. At 4 A.M., Allon and Dinitz came to Sisco's hotel suite to announce that Israel would attend the Geneva conference and that, immediately after the Israeli elections, Israel would engage in serious and substantive talks with Egypt about a disengagement of forces along the Suez front. Sisco quickly reported the good news to Kissinger, who then slept contentedly for all of two hours. He had overcome Israeli suspicions about his middleman role, an essential precondition to any successful negotiation.

Later in the morning, the Secretary discussed the conference with Eban and disengagement with Dayan and both subjects with Mrs. Meir. Then, before returning to the airport, Kissinger stopped briefly at Yad Va'shem, a gripping memorial to the six million Jews who were slaughtered in Europe during World War II. His aides detoured the press to the airport so his visit could be completely private. Only Keating accompanied him. The Secretary wore a yarmulke, and he lit a memorial candle for those Jews who were not as lucky as the Kissingers. He spent a half hour there, in silent meditation, gazing at the names of the Nazi death camps carved into the dark stone. Kissinger left Yad Va'shem "heartbroken" about Israel's lonely position and determined to avoid the need for other such memorials. He then understood more clearly Mrs. Meir's obsession about security. "With agony, goodwill, luck and patience — don't underestimate luck," Kissinger later said, "maybe we can shape something" that would "turn swords into plowshares."

At the airport, Kissinger and Eban told reporters that "complete agreement" had been achieved on "the procedures and terms of reference" for the "opening of the conference" and "the problems of a separation of forces." Kissinger and Eban shook hands, assuring one another that they would meet again in Geneva on December 21, the day the conference was then tentatively scheduled to open, and that Dayan would come to Washington soon after the Israeli elections to discuss disengagement in a more concrete way.

At 3 A.M., Tuesday, December 18, Kissinger was awakened by Sisco with the news that both Egypt and Russia had confirmed his impression of last Saturday that Syria would not be attending the Geneva conference. Fahmy had failed to change Assad's mind.

Late that afternoon, the Syrians formally announced that they would boycott the conference, and accused Israel and the United States of "maneuvers that would lead us into an endless wilderness." The Egyptians, on the other hand, formally announced that Fahmy would lead a high-level delegation to Geneva. Kissinger quickly moved to top both stories. On a stopover in Madrid, he had his spokesman, George Vest, announce that Waldheim had extended formal invitations to the Geneva conference and that subsequently the United States and Russia had been informed "by the parties concerned" that everyone except Syria had accepted and the conference would open on December 21 in Geneva. Privately, Kissinger encouraged the speculation that Syria's defection was actually a good thing because it eliminated the one Arab state that could make trouble at the opening session.

On December 21, the foreign ministers of Egypt, Jordan, Israel, the United States and Russia gathered at the Palais des Nations, once the headquarters of the League of Nations, under Secretary-General Waldheim's chairmanship to begin the long process of peace-making in the Middle East. There was minimum pomp and maximum security. For the first time in a quarter of a century of nonstop tension or war in the Middle East, Arab and Israeli ministers actually sat down in the same room, although they were not yet ready to shake hands or exchange a single informal word with one another. There was a forty-five-minute delay, caused by a seating problem; and there was a flare-up of propaganda between Fahmy and Eban; but a negotiating process had been started.

Kissinger, who organized the conference to give diplomacy a chance to work its occasional magic, emphasized his middleman role. "There is justice on all sides," he said. He spoke the Arabic words *"eli fat mat,"* which means "the past is dead" — and he quoted the Jewish sage Hillel, who had said, "If I am not for myself, who is for me? But if I am for myself alone, who am I?" Kissinger added the thought: "There is a greater justice . . . in finding a truth which merges all aspirations in the realization of a common humanity."

The following day, the conference adjourned after instructing Egypt and Israel to begin "forthwith" their talks on a disengagement of their forces. Early in the evening, Kissinger was driven to the airport on a dark back road to avoid any possibility of terrorist attack. Just a few days earlier, Palestinian extremists had attacked an American airplane at Rome's Fiumicino Airport, and there were rumors that they were heading toward Geneva. The Secretary stepped before microphones in a special VIP lounge, looking tired and striking a note of caution. "We have achieved substantially what we came here to do," he said in a soft voice. "Of course, the road to peace in the Middle East will be long and sometimes painful." He took no questions. Quickly, he was escorted past Swiss guards carrying submachine guns and he boarded his plane. He sneezed twice. "He's caught a cold," one reporter observed. "Good," another commented. "Good? Why good?" "Because it shows he's human."

The Aswan-Jerusalem Shuttle

Mrs. Meir's Labor Party suffered a setback in the December 31 elections. It lost seats in the Knesset, and its Likud opposition gained strength. But Labor remained the dominant political force in the country, and Mrs. Meir was asked to form a new government — a difficult task that ushered in a long period of political instability.

One of her first orders directed Dayan to go to Washington and talk to Kissinger about disengagement. The Defense Minister, a hawk who nevertheless believed in an Israeli pullback, left Israel on Thursday, January 3, 1974, and strode into the State Department lobby at 11 A.M. the next day. He discussed the concept of disengagement with Kissinger for four hours that day, four hours the next. The Secretary then told reporters, "The two positions have approached each other very substantially." Dayan added a note of restraint. "Everybody should realize that after such a long time of hostility and fighting, after bitter conflict between Egypt and Israel, it is very difficult to make even the first step towards an agreement. But I hope we are now in a position to achieve such a step eventually in Geneva."

Dayan based his hope on a private invitation he had just extended to Kissinger to return to the Middle East to spark the disengagement talks. The Secretary, who had had no intention of going back so soon, cabled Sadat, asking if the Egyptian government was also interested in such a mediation effort. Sadat's "yes" came back within forty-eight hours, and that persuaded Kissinger to make the effort. The Secretary decided to leave Washington midnight Thursday, January 10. His idea, at that time, was that he would try to help both sides frame their negotiating positions so that their representatives in Geneva would have a "fighting chance" to reach agreement — as Dayan had said, "eventually." Kissinger expected to be back in Washington by January 16, at the latest. One talk with Sadat, one with Mrs. Meir, perhaps a second with Sadat, one with King Hussein, one with Assad, a stopover in Brussels to brief NATO, and then home. "I want to grease the wheels at Geneva," he told reporters. "That's my goal."

After a refueling stop in Spain, Kissinger headed for Aswan, a winter resort city four hundred miles south of Cairo, for another meeting with Sadat. "Why Aswan?" came the obvious question. Kissinger explained that the Egyptian leader had contracted a bad bronchial cough and his doctors had advised that he go south to the subtropical warmth of the Upper Nile to recuperate. Aswan had a special connotation in Egyptian-American relations. In July, 1956, Dulles had abruptly canceled an American offer to join Britain and the World Bank in financing the four-hundred-million-dollar High Dam at Aswan that was President Nasser's great dream. As a result, the Egyptian leader shifted his country's diplomatic orientation. He asked Russia to help finance and build the dam, and Nikita Khrushchev jumped at the opportunity. That move opened the Middle East to Soviet economic and military penetration. When private citizen Richard Nixon visited the dam in the 1960s, he told Nasser: "Today I have seen America's greatest mistake."

Kissinger kept popping into the rear compartment of the plane to talk to the press. As the plane was approaching Egypt, he learned that Mrs. Meir had come down with a bad case of the shingles and she might not be able to join the deliberations. "The Arabs will never believe this," he exclaimed. "If we come out with anything on this trip," he said, "the sure sign for all of you will be when I start coughing and scratching at the same time."

Aswan I: The Secretary's jet came in over the desert and landed at 7:30 P.M. Friday on a bumpy runway at a military base near Aswan. Only a handful of reporters and cameramen had been permitted on the base, a secure area marked by antiaircraft missile sites, tanks, and troop concentrations. Their function, no doubt, was to protect the Aswan High Dam against possible Israeli air or commando attack. Fahmy, smoking a Cuban cigar, stepped out of the darkness near an apparently deserted terminal building and greeted the Secretary with a warm embrace. Then, after a few words to reporters, the two diplomats got into a cream-colored Mercedes limousine and drove to Sadat's villa on a hill overlooking the Aswan Low Dam, built by the British at the turn of the century.

The Egyptian leader, wearing a heavy military uniform, smiled broadly as Kissinger was escorted into the reception room. "Welcome, welcome," boomed Sadat, his deep voice carrying into the courtyard. This was to be a courtesy call, but Sadat and Kissinger turned it into an hour-and-a-half work session, which Vest later described as "useful and constructive."

Kissinger then returned to his hotel — the New Cataract Hotel, which looked as if it had been constructed by the Russians in the early 1960s. Fahmy joined him for a working dinner. Across the courtyard was the Cataract Hotel, an old sandstone architectural treasure that fronted on the Upper Nile and, with its tall ceilings, rotating fans and dingy bar, looked like a stage set for a Sydney Greenstreet movie. Both hotels were almost empty. The postwar jitters had sharply reduced the tourist traffic. For the next week, the Cataract Hotel became an unusual press center.

On Saturday morning, before Kissinger returned to Sadat's villa, he went sightseeing. The must stop on any tourist itinerary was the Aswan High Dam, a source of enormous pride to the Egyptians. Though the Russians had left, there were still Russian-language slogans on many billboards; "Welcome, President Sadat," one of them read, as if the Russians owned Aswan and were welcoming a foreigner to *their* project. The nationalist in Sadat clearly resented the overbearing attitude of many of the Russians, and he had resolved to strike a more independent policy. Kissinger's tour of the High Dam was proof of the success of Sadat's policy.

Later in the morning, Kissinger was taken by boat to the half-submerged ancient temple of Philae. One reporter, deeply impressed by this extraordinary example of ancient Egyptian architecture, told Kissinger, "Seeing this monument whets my appetite to come back as a tourist." "Don't worry," Kissinger replied, "we'll see them all before we're through with these negotiations."

By 11 A.M., Kissinger had seen Aswan's wonders, and he drove to Sadat's villa to resume the negotiations. "How did you enjoy the High Dam?" Sadat asked. "Very impressive," Kissinger responded. "It was not one of our more intelligent decisions." For the next three and a half hours, the Secretary and the President reviewed Dayan's "ideas" about disengagement — and Sadat's. For example, to what line in the Sinai would the Israelis be prepared to withdraw? What kind of armaments would be allowed in the evacuated territory? And how many? How large a UN force would be interposed between the two belligerents? Would Egypt agree to rebuild the cities along the Suez Canal and reopen the canal to international shipping? — for the Israelis, a guarantee of sorts that the canal would not again become a zone of combat operations. What would be the relationship between a disengagement agreement in the Sinai and one in the Golan? Or, between two such agreements and an overall peace settlement? The rival ideas had not yet been framed as formal proposals, but Sadat must have sensed that they could easily be converted into proposals, and that the differences between them could be narrowed and closed without too much trouble — as long as Kissinger could be persuaded to stay in the area. Sadat wanted a deal, but he wanted Kissinger to arrange it.

"Mr. Secretary," Sadat suggested, "why confine your objective merely to getting proposals? Why not try to finish the negotiation while you're out here?" After his talks with Dayan and Sadat, Kissinger felt that the two sides were "finally in the same ballpark." He would be pleased to complete the negotiation, he said, but he didn't know how quickly the Israelis wanted to move. He would soon find out.

Jerusalem I: On the nine-hundred-mile, two-hour flight from Aswan to Tel Aviv, Kissinger was unusually optimistic. Sadat, he said, had been "conciliatory and constructive." The negotiations "could come to a head fairly quickly." The talks with Sadat had been "more detailed and more useful" than Kissinger had originally thought possible. "We might get a serious negotiation started, maybe even settle a few issues," he said. He seemed to be revising his original goal.

Eban greeted the Secretary at the airport, and they immediately boarded helicopters for the ride to Jerusalem. "How's Golda?" Kissinger inquired. Eban said that she was too ill to take part in that night's working dinner.

After the Secretary paid a brief courtesy call on the Prime Minister, he went to dinner with Allon, Dayan, Eban, Dinitz and other top Israeli leaders. He told them that Sadat was suggesting a disengagement agreement, rather than simply an exchange of proposals for negotiation in Geneva. The Israelis liked Sadat's idea, and, late that night, the Israeli Cabinet authorized Kissinger to "present to Sadat an Israeli proposal on a disengagement of forces."

On Sunday morning, January 13, American and Israeli officials met in small groups to refine the proposal. They began working on maps, pinpointing the actual disposition of forces. For example, there were fifty thousand Egyptian troops, four hundred tanks, artillery and missiles on the east bank of the canal. The Israelis argued that the Egyptians would have to "thin out" that military force before they would agree to withdraw their troops to a line twenty miles east of the canal. These were complicated discussions. They continued over lunch and well into the afternoon.

In the early evening, Kissinger took a helicopter ride through a rainstorm to Dayan's home on the outskirts of Tel Aviv for a reception. Even there, it was business before pleasure. Elazar entered the crowded living room carrying a large portfolio. "Come, I have that map for you," he told Kissinger. "Careful," the Secretary replied, with a thin smile, "there are reporters here." For twenty-five minutes, Kissinger, Sisco, Dayan and Elazar closeted themselves in a small study. When they emerged, they looked pleased. "How is it going?" a reporter asked. "No comment," came the immediate reply from Kissinger, who then changed subjects and described how Arab leaders Fahmy and Saqqaf had respectively kissed him and held his hand. "The reason the Israelis don't get better treatment," the Secretary remarked, "is that Eban doesn't kiss me." In less than an hour, Kissinger was again airborne for Aswan. Suddenly Sisco appeared in the press compartment. "Welcome aboard the Egyptian-Israeli shuttle!" he said.

Aswan II: "The Israeli plan," Kissinger told reporters, "takes the Egyptian point of view into account, and I now think chances are pretty good that this Israeli proposal and the map will trigger a negotiation." Two hours and twenty minutes later, Kissinger's plane landed on the same bumpy runway at Aswan's military base. Fahmy welcomed him, and Kissinger told the Egyptian newsmen: "I hope that the plan that I am bringing from Israel will serve as a big step towards an agreement on the separation of forces."

Kissinger and Fahmy then proceeded to the New Cataract Hotel, where they conferred until well past midnight, reviewing the Israeli proposal in a very preliminary way. Only Sadat could make important decisions in Egypt, and everyone knew it. Fahmy asked if the Secretary would like to visit Luxor, site of some of Egypt's most impressive tombs. Kissinger declined. "I'm not going to Luxor until I've finished what I've come here to do," he said with an air of finality. Given no alternative, Fahmy arranged for another Kissinger-Sadat meeting for Monday morning, January 14.

At 10 A.M., under a brilliantly clear blue sky, Sadat greeted the Secretary in the shade of his garden gazebo. He was still clad in his heavy military uniform, though the temperature was over seventy degrees. After posing for pictures and bantering with newsmen, the two negotiators entered the villa for a four-hour session. Sisco, Fahmy and the others stayed in a nearby garden. Kissinger formally presented the Israeli proposal and map. He explained all of its provisions in great detail. This was a time for precision, not ambiguity. Sadat seriously pondered the proposal and then rejected it. Israel had requested explicit Egyptian assurances, for example, that the Suez Canal would be converted into a vibrant commercial waterway, stripped of military potential; that Israeli cargo and later Israeli flagships would be allowed to pass through the canal; and that the blockade of the Bab el-Mandeb Straits leading from the Red Sea into the Indian Ocean would be lifted. Sadat told Kissinger that while he might be prepared to extend private assurances to Israel on all three issues, he would not explicitly commit his government to such actions; in his view, they would appear to diminish his country's sovereignty.

Sadat also told Kissinger that he disagreed with the Israeli conception of a "thinned-out" Egyptian "presence" on the east bank of the canal. He said he would be prepared to reduce Egyptian manpower and fire-power on the east bank — but not to the same degree that Dayan had suggested. "Hellishly difficult" was Kissinger's description of the arms limitation problem.

Although Sadat seemed eager for a deal, Kissinger could sense that the Egyptian leader had great difficulty — politically and psychologically — in discussing "an Israeli proposal." The Secretary believed that the time had come for some innovative diplomacy. He asked Sadat to consider this proposition: that the United States, which earlier had flatly refused to "huckster" an "American plan," would come up with two documents: one would be an "American proposal" for troop disengagement along the Suez front, combining the most mutually acceptable features of the Egyptian and Israeli drafts; the other would be a "memorandum of understanding" containing a list of all of Sadat's private assurances to Kissinger. The "memorandum of understanding" would obviously but-tress the "American proposal"; together they would comprise the basis for a negotiation — what diplomats call "the terms of reference." Such an approach, in Kissinger's mind, would imply no binding American commitment of any kind, but it might help Egypt overcome the emo-tional hurdle of having to negotiate on the basis of an Israeli draft — and vice versa. Sadat accepted the Secretary's proposition, optimistically pre-dicting a breakthrough and an agreement within a few days. Kissinger said he hoped so, because he intended to drop the Aswan-Jerusalem shuttle on Thursday night. That time frame was a deliberate pressure tactic.

In the afternoon, Kissinger, Sisco, Sadat, Fahmy and Gamazy drew up "an American proposal" and "an American map." Late in the after-noon, Kissinger and Fahmy strolled out onto the sun-drenched veranda of the Cataract Hotel and, after swapping jokes with reporters, they sat down for the old British custom of "high tea." Across the Upper Nile, on a desert hill, stood the Aga Khan's mausoleum, glistening in its lonely opulence. "Get the dimensions of that," Kissinger said in an aside to one of his aides. "I may need one soon." Fahmy laughed. Kissinger peered at the sailboats on the Nile and the lengthening shadow of the mauso-leum. "I love the desert," he sighed.

In the early evening Kissinger and Fahmy reviewed the "American plan," which consisted of a disengagement proposal, a memorandum of understanding, and a map, and then drove to Sadat's villa for a final, detailed run-through before the Secretary's return to Jerusalem. The run-through was highly satisfactory, even though Kissinger knew that there were still major differences between Egypt and Israel. Though his role had changed — he was no longer simply a high-class messenger, carrying proposals and maps between Jerusalem and Aswan — he refused to become either side's lawyer in the negotiations. He told Sadat that he would accurately convey Egyptian views to Israel, but he would not bargain on behalf of Egypt. Nor, for that matter, when he returned to Aswan, probably within a day or two, would he do anything more than fairly present Israeli views. Otherwise his usefulness would be destroyed in a buzz saw of Middle East suspicion and distrust.

Jerusalem II: It was almost midnight, Monday, when Kissinger returned to Israel. The rainstorm had not subsided, and he was forced to drive from the airport to the King David Hotel in Jerusalem. It took almost two hours — enough time for him to give Eban a preliminary fill-in on his discussions with Sadat and on his new approach. When they reached the hotel, Kissinger and Sisco reviewed several of the main points of the "American plan" with Eban, Dinitz and Ephraim Evron, one of Israel's key diplomats, and they arranged a schedule of meetings for Tuesday, January 15.

No one had much sleep.

By 7 A.M., Dinitz was conferring with Mrs. Meir, and Mrs. Meir with Allon, Dayan, Eban and Galili. Their initial response to Kissinger's new approach was favorable, though the Prime Minister was aware that her Likud opposition would attack any agreement based, even in part, on unwritten understandings.

At 9 A.M., Dinitz reported the initial Israeli reaction to Kissinger. For the next three hours, American and Israeli officials reviewed the "plan" in detail. Kissinger conveyed his best judgment about what Sadat could, or could not, accept, but he didn't argue Sadat's case. At noon, Kissinger broke away from the formal negotiations to visit the contemporary Israeli Museum, which has an invaluable collection of archaeological artifacts and the Dead Sea Scrolls. Not only history but nostalgia awaited him there. The Director of the Museum's Education Department, Joel Shiftan, was one of Kissinger's former playmates from Fürth. The Secretary told Shiftan, as they examined several of the scrolls, that he had forgotten most of his Hebrew. It was, by then, 1:15 P.M., and Kissinger was already late for a "working lunch" at Eban's home, which lasted two and a half hours. At 4 P.M., Kissinger visited Mrs. Meir, whose recovery was slow but steady. For an hour and a half, he listened to her arguments about survival and security; and he in turn argued that the disengagement agreement was one good way of ensuring both. At 5:30 P.M., Mrs. Meir opened a critical five-hour meeting of her "kitchen Cabinet," while Kissinger returned to his hotel suite to await an Israeli decision. He knew that his progress had already surpassed his wildest expectations. Not only had he sparked a solid negotiation between Egypt and Israel, but he suspected that both sides wanted him to complete an agreement, rather than turn the negotiations over to lower-ranking officials in Geneva.

While the Cabinet met, Kissinger had a moment to consider the vast differences between the two sides. In Egypt, Kissinger negotiated with one man — Sadat. If he won Sadat's approval, then he needed no one else's. The negotiation, in this sense, was tidy. In Israel, Kissinger seemed at times to be negotiating with a whole country. He had to win Mrs. Meir's approval. That was essential — but it was not enough. Next he had to win the Cabinet to his point of view; and, to a lesser degree, the political opposition and the press. The negotiation was untidy and time-consuming. The differences between Egypt and Israel, in short, were the differences between an authoritarian regime and a freewheeling democracy. Kissinger's greatest successes have been with dictators or strong men; his greatest difficulties with popularly elected leaders.

At 10:30 P.M., the Israeli leaders, except for Mrs. Meir, came to Kissinger's suite to announce their latest concessions, one of the most important of which was the Cabinet's decision to drop its demand for a public Egyptian renunciation of the "state of belligerency" with Israel. They told the Secretary that the Cabinet would reach a "final decision" on a disengagement deal after Kissinger returned from his third visit to Aswan. It was past midnight when top American and Israeli officials returned to the job of refining and clarifying the disengagement package. Their formal negotiating session lasted until past 3 A.M.

That was when Kissinger decided, for the first time on this trip, to telephone the President. Normally, on his foreign travels, he limits his communication with Nixon to frequent cables. In this case, he made an exception, because the negotiation was moving so quickly and the United States was becoming, if not a guarantor of the agreement, at least a repository of the "understandings" on which the agreement was based. Kissinger, the high-flying diplomat, and Nixon, the isolated President, talked for thirty minutes.

The heavy rains continued on Wednesday, January 16, forcing Kissinger and Eban to drive rather than helicopter to the airport. First, however, they stopped at Mrs. Meir's residence to incorporate Israel's latest ideas into the "American proposal." The Secretary felt that Israel's position had become "moderate" and that he was close to a deal. On the drive, Eban, the diplomat turned tourist guide, pointed to the Latrun Monastery, outside of Jerusalem. "That's the place," he said, "where only one person is allowed to speak. Everyone else has to be quiet." The Secretary beamed. "Yes," he responded, "same as at the State Department." After they reached the airport and made a few comments to reporters, Kissinger invited Eban on board the "Aswan-Jerusalem Express," while they waited for Dayan to arrive from the Defense Ministry with a new map. "Eban thinks that an enemy of Israel," Kissinger told the traveling press corps, "is someone who supports Israel only ninety-nine percent of the time." Eban, smiling, added, "He's right."

Kissinger, turning serious, said that the "differences" between the two sides had been "substantially narrowed," and that they had been approaching the negotiations "with a spirit of fairness and justice." If that "spirit can be maintained," Kissinger remarked, then "we may at last find peace."

Dayan finally arrived with the map. After a brief private meeting in Kissinger's compartment, the Secretary escorted Dayan and Eban back to the reporters. "We've been wondering about whether to take Eban with us," Kissinger said. Eban and his wife had spent their honeymoon at the Cataract Hotel in 1948. "I've been spending so much time interpreting Eban to Sadat. Maybe it's now his turn to interpret me to Sadat." Everyone laughed, and Eban got off the plane.

Aswan III: Kissinger was airborne at 11:40 A.M. Two hours and twenty minutes later, the Secretary reached Aswan for the third time in five days. On the plane, he had told reporters that Jerusalem II had been "very fruitful." "We have already cleared up about seventy-five percent of all of the problems," he estimated. "We've got about twenty to twenty-five percent to go. I'm getting more ambitious all the time," he went on. "There are still problems, and some of them are tough. If we're on our way back to Israel in two hours, you'll know I presented the Israeli ideas to Sadat, he rejected them, and the negotiation has broken down. But if we go back tonight. . . ." He smiled.

Aswan was as warm and sunny as Jerusalem had been chilly and rainy. Fahmy was at the airport, and the two ministers, after their customary embrace, quickly drove off to Sadat's villa. The Egyptian President was in an excellent mood, welcoming Kissinger and joking about their diets. Kissinger, glancing down at his waistline, mumbled: "You're having better luck with yours." Kissinger and Sadat then followed the by now familiar routine. They went inside the villa to negotiate, while their aides remained in the sunny garden. They conferred for an hour and a half, during which time Kissinger managed to get Sadat to agree to scale down the Egyptian military presence on the east bank to a level he was sure Israel could accept: eight battalions, or roughly seven thousand troops; all missiles and all but thirty tanks out. Late in the afternoon, Kissinger and Fahmy conferred at the New Cataract Hotel, refining the arrangements reached earlier in the day. At 8 P.M., Kissinger was back at Sadat's villa for another hour of intensive talks. At 9:30 P.M., it was wheels up. The Secretary was winging his way back to Israel. "Only ten percent remains to be done," he told reporters. "It's unlikely that we can't go the rest of the way." "Did you have to do any arm-twisting with the Israelis?" a reporter asked. "Both parties feel their essential interests are being protected," Kissinger snapped. "There was no arm-twisting of any kind." But do you feel that you have now become "too evenhanded"? another reporter inquired. "Our friendship for Israel remains unimpaired," Kissinger maintained; and "if peace ever comes to this area, it will mean that friendship with one party does not have to be enmity towards the other."

Jerusalem III: The Secretary's plane landed once again in a heavy rainstorm. It was almost midnight. Kissinger had been gone for all of twelve hours. Once again he briefed Eban about his negotiation with Sadat as the two ministers drove to Jerusalem. The Secretary was bone-tired; but when he reached the King David Hotel, he immediately went into conference with Dinitz to arrange Thursday's schedule. After Dinitz left, he checked with Aswan, Washington, Moscow and the UN just to make certain that there would be no insurmountable problems about implementing the agreement.

At dawn, Thursday, January 17, the temperature in Jerusalem must have dropped sharply; because by the time Kissinger woke up after only three hours of sleep, an extraordinary snowfall had blanketed the city. Kissinger had been scheduled to drive to Mrs. Meir's residence at 9 A.M. for a conclusive meeting. It was canceled. Kissinger's limousine had neither snow tires nor chains. Dayan requisitioned an army jeep. With Allon and Eban, he drove first to the Prime Minister's home for final instructions and then, at 10:30 A.M., he managed to skid, buck, and slide to the hotel for a climactic session with Kissinger. It lasted two hours. Finally Eban emerged from the Secretary's suite. A broad but enigmatic smile on his face, he announced that there would be a statement in the early evening. An agreement? someone asked. A statement, Eban replied, without amplification.

Kissinger still wanted to visit Mrs. Meir. Fortunately, by lunchtime it had stopped snowing sufficiently for the army to clear a path from the hotel to her residence. The Secretary spent an hour and a half with her, trying to solve the remaining problems. Later in the afternoon, while Kissinger went to pay a courtesy call on President Ephraim Katzir, the Prime Minister presided over a two-and-a-half-hour Cabinet meeting in her kitchen. Because of the snow, five ministers could not even make it to Jerusalem. Those who did "unanimously" approved the terms of the disengagement agreement. At 7 P.M., Eban, Dinitz and Evron brought the good news to Kissinger's suite. The deal was still not complete. There were still a few points to be settled in Egypt. At 7:45 P.M., Saunders, whom Kissinger had left behind in Aswan, telephoned the Secretary to announce that Sadat had given his final clearance to the agreement. Kissinger plopped down into a soft armchair. "Joe," he said wearily to Sisco, "break open some champagne!"

At 9 P.M., Jerusalem time, or 3 P.M., Washington time, President Nixon appeared in the White House news room to read a special statement. On Friday, January 18, at Kilometer 101 along the Cairo-Suez road, he announced, General Elazar of Israel and General Gamazy of Egypt would sign an historic agreement on a disengagement of their forces along the Suez front. "This," the President said, "is the first significant step towards a permanent peace in the Mideast." There was, among some reporters, instant speculation that the President was again seeking to distract attention from Watergate; but most observers gave him high marks for backstopping an unusually successful mediation effort by the United States.

At 9:30 P.M., at the King David Hotel, Eban gave a small dinner party in honor of the weary Secretary of State. "An exemplary exercise in international conciliation," Eban said, referring to Kissinger's role. The Secretary, always conscious of history's fickle ways, responded cautiously. "In a few months," he said, in a voice scarcely above a whisper, "we will know whether this is an episode or a turning point in the Middle East." What he knew that night was that the disengagement agreement was unprecedented in Arab-Israeli relations, the first time Egypt and Israel would sign an agreement that advanced the cause of accommodation. "Two months ago," Kissinger later admitted, "I would have agreed with those who feared that Egypt was out to drive Israel into the sea. Now Egypt seems to be ready to give it a try."

The basic provision of the disengagement agreement called for an Israeli withdrawal from the west bank of the Suez Canal and from the east bank, too, as far south as the Gulf of Suez. The Israelis would pull their forces back approximately twenty miles into the Sinai. This strip of land would then be divided into three zones. The zone closest to the canal would be controlled by the Egyptians, who could keep seven thousand troops there; the middle buffer zone by the UN; the last zone by the Israelis, who would also be allowed to keep seven thousand troops there. All troops and arms dispositions would be symmetrical. The Israelis would retain control of the strategic Gidi and Mitla passes.

At 7:30 A.M., Friday, January 18, Kissinger drove through the snow-covered streets of Jerusalem to Mrs. Meir's residence. He watched while the Israeli Prime Minister signed the agreement on behalf of her country. Mrs. Meir then turned to the Secretary — "I sincerely and honestly believe," she said, "that you have made history this week." She paused. "There is no doubt in my mind about that." Outside, a group of Israeli cameramen waited in the snow. One of them hummed a variation on an old Israeli song about "David, King of Israel." He changed only one word. "Henry, King of Israel," he hummed, "live, live and flourish. Henry, King of Israel, live, live and flourish." Israel's deep suspicions of Kissinger seemed suddenly to have eased. The *Jerusalem Post* that morning ran a full-page cartoon, showing Kissinger dressed as an angel of peace sitting on top of a silenced cannon.

Aswan IV: By 10:30 A.M., Kissinger was again airborne for Aswan. The "last ten percent," the Secretary revealed, concerned "some definitions of arms limitations." Three hours later, the Secretary stood alongside Sadat, while the Egyptian leader signed the same copy of the disengagement agreement that already bore Mrs. Meir's signature. (Actually, Sadat had initialed his copy the night before, sealing the deal for Egypt.) Then, Kissinger and Sadat stepped into the sun, near the gazebo, so that the reporters could hear them publicly pledge their efforts to try to get a similar disengagement agreement between Syria and Israel. Sadat said solemnly that he was "committed for disengagement on the Syrian front." Kissinger added, just as solemnly, that he was "prepared to make the same effort on disengagement on the Syrian front" that he had made on the Egyptian front.

Sadat escorted the Secretary through the garden to his waiting limousine. There they stopped for a moment. Sadat put his hands on Kissinger's shoulders. "Mr. Secretary," he said slowly, "you are not only my friend; you are also my brother." The Egyptian President then kissed Kissinger on both cheeks.

In less than a month, Kissinger returned to the Middle East, his fourth visit in as many months, to launch the disengagement negotiations between Syria and Israel. During a rest stop in Cairo, Kissinger and Sadat held another one of their open-air news conferences. "Mr. President," a reporter asked, "what advice would you have for President Assad of Syria regarding disengagement?" Sadat put his arm around Kissinger. "Trust my friend, Henry," the Egyptian leader replied. "That's what I'd tell Assad. Trust my friend, Henry."

TWENTY

A Concluding Note

W HEN HENRY KISSINGER WROTE his Ph.D. study of Metternich and Castlereagh almost twenty-five years ago, he did more than draw a remarkable portrait of two statesmen who managed, in the upheaval of post-Napoleonic Europe, to balance competing forces and thereby provide a period of relative peace; at the same time, he unintentionally drew a portrait of himself.

"Both," wrote Kissinger in *A World Restored,* "dominated every negotiation in which they participated: Castlereagh by the ability to reconcile conflicting points of view and by the single-mindedness conferred by an empirical policy; Metternich through an almost uncanny faculty of achieving a personal dominance over his adversaries and the art of defining a moral framework which made concessions appear, not as surrenders, but as sacrifices to a common cause."

The strategy and style that have come to be associated with Kissinger's diplomacy first surfaced in this doctoral dissertation, and they have survived his conversion from scholar to statesman with striking consistency. Despite his reputation for excessive secrecy, mostly about tactics, his approach to global strategy, based upon a conservative's quest for balance, stability, and order, has been an open book for many years.

One central feature of his approach, from the very beginning, has been his belief in an interacting and nourishing link between domestic and foreign policy. A statesman has to understand this link. He must lead, but not too fast; he must remain anchored to the traditions of his society, but not too tightly. If Castlereagh and Metternich had any failing, in

Kissinger's view, it was their inability to strike the right balance between the requirements of diplomacy and politics. "A statesman who too far outruns the experience of his people will fail in achieving a domestic consensus, however wise his policies; witness Castlereagh," Kissinger wrote. "A statesman who limits his policy to the experience of his people will doom himself to sterility; witness Metternich."

Kissinger is too good a student of history to ignore the lesson of his own research. Recognizing that a successful foreign policy begins at home, he has encouraged the American people to adopt a new, post-Vietnam outlook on the world, and he is constantly seeking to broaden the base of domestic support for his policies. He courts Congress, woos the press, and dazzles the diplomatic corps. He has, to use the current jargon, "co-opted" many of his potential critics, giving them the cozy illusion that they are on the inside of policy-making. His mesmerizing of Chairman J. William Fulbright of the Senate Foreign Relations Committee is one of the wonders of Washington. The capital — the *world* — is his stage; a master performer, Kissinger dominates his environment, whether it is a closed-door hearing on Capitol Hill, a televised news conference at the State Department, or a midnight briefing about nuclear weapons in a Moscow nightclub.

Kissinger wields more power than any other presidential adviser or Secretary of State in the history of the Republic. He is not the conventional American diplomat. He is a professor who has been given the unique opportunity to put his theories into practice and to shape history. He has been called the first "European" Secretary of State — less a reference to his birthplace than to his style of diplomacy. He has tried to be detached, pragmatic, unromantic. He has drained the Utopian illusions from American foreign policy. Unlike John Foster Dulles, who refused even to shake Chou En-lai's hand, Kissinger will negotiate with anyone. Ideological labels do not deter him. This approach disturbs many Americans, who have been raised on idealistic standards of right and wrong in the conduct of American foreign policy. They do not understand his pragmatism or his willingness to deal with the devil, if necessary, to come up with the right agreement. Kissinger has seen America swinging between periods of isolationism and intervention, always cloaking her actions in morality; he has tried to steady the diplomatic pendulum. He has set aside idealism and does not seek perfection; a product of the Weimar Republic, he seeks only stability. For him, there is no higher form of international morality.

As the impresario of American foreign policy, he is extremely proud of his accomplishments; but he is not blinded by them. His ego coexists nicely with his realism. To reach the outer limits of the diplomatically possible — that has been his constant objective. He knows that the effort will be marked by unforeseeable complications. "Each success," he once remarked, "only buys an admission ticket to a more difficult problem."

He is particularly pleased that he negotiated the first strategic arms limitation agreement with the Soviet Union — an agreement that was part of a superpower effort to create a new détente — but he knows that the attainment of SALT II is going to be much more difficult; it involves more sophisticated weapons, and the policy of détente is now regarded with some suspicion in both Washington and Moscow.

The Chinese connection was a major diplomatic breakthrough. It in no way minimizes Kissinger's contribution to note that it was the Chinese, because they feared a possible Soviet attack, who made the first exploratory overture to the incoming Republican Administration less than a month after Nixon's election in November, 1968. Kissinger negotiated the opening to Peking with a pair of aging revolutionaries — Mao Tsetung, now past eighty; Chou En-lai, only a few years younger. Their successors are large question marks in Kissinger's future file.

In the Middle East, Kissinger scored the most unexpected of breakthroughs — the disengagement of Egyptian and Israeli forces along the Suez Canal in January, 1974, and, in the process, the beginning of new American relationships with the Arab world. It was a personal *tour de force;* yet its permanence is by no means assured. The Secretary needs no experts to tell him that Sadat's "Welcome, welcome!" is based on the premise that Kissinger will help the Egyptians achieve what they have not been able to achieve themselves, even with Soviet arms — namely, the pullback of Israeli troops from Arab territory. He knows that a Golan settlement between Syria and Israel will be more difficult to achieve; a deal on the west bank involving the Palestinians more difficult still; Jerusalem, perhaps impossible.

The American disengagement from Indochina was controversial. Kissinger was applauded by many people for his tenacity and skill in negotiating the terms of the ambiguous Vietnam accords signed in 1973, after three and a half years of negotiations; but at the same time that President Nixon spoke about "peace with honor," the war in Vietnam continued. The Administration's attempt to demonstrate America's will to the Communist world by resisting widespread demands for an earlier U.S. exit was unacceptably costly: thousands of additional lives were lost, and the integrity of the nation damaged still further. The "reasonable chance" that the United States gave Saigon remains untested. And as for Cambodia — the country that Kissinger once said would never become an American "tarbaby" — the fighting continues there, too, with the United States still picking up the tab for the war.

The Atlantic alliance poses a different kind of problem; new realities have emerged in the quarter of a century since NATO was established. But Kissinger's call in April, 1973, for a "fresh act of creation" to revitalize the alliance did not lead to a productive dialogue between the United States and Western Europe. The alliance is still in acute disarray, plagued by deepening political and economic differences. Kissinger seems frustrated in his attempt to deal effectively with the continent where he was born.

All these issues are complex. The days of the spectacular are over; now meticulous negotiation is needed to convert the breakthroughs into the routine of diplomacy. In the best of worlds, this would have required a major effort on Kissinger's part; but Watergate has compounded the difficulties. The break-in that presidential spokesman Ronald Ziegler once dismissed as a "caper" has mushroomed into the biggest political scandal in American history, and it has undercut the momentum of Administration foreign policy.

Even when the Secretary of State is involved in the most sensitive negotiations, he is pursued by Watergate. One night in January, 1974, as his jet plane was shuttling between Aswan and Jerusalem, a reporter asked Kissinger about a published story in Washington alleging that he was linked to the "plumbers." The Secretary vehemently denied the story. "Outrageous lie!" he exclaimed. Then, in a soft, almost plaintive voice, he added: "Must we discuss Watergate? Here? Now?"

Two months later, during his visit to Moscow — designed in part to set up a Nixon summit later in the year — Kissinger found that Brezhnev's attitude toward the Watergate issue had shifted somewhat since the previous summer, when the Soviet leader had played down the scandal. This time Brezhnev openly referred to Watergate in the course of their negotiations. "Four times, every hour," the Secretary was later to recall, with some exaggeration, the Soviet leader assured him that Moscow had no interest in exploiting Watergate. One such assurance would have been one too many. In a Kremlin corridor, a Soviet official jocularly asked an American reporter, "Are you looking forward to the visit of President Ford?" Helmut Sonnenfeldt, who was at Kissinger's side throughout the Moscow trip, later told Richard Valeriani of NBC News that the Russians seemed to be "biding their time and checking their bidding a bit" — stalling, in other words, while they waited for the outcome of legal and congressional moves against Nixon.

In addition to the foreign policy complications, the Watergate scandal has ended up distorting Kissinger's relationship with the President. At year's end, 1973, for the first time since Nixon moved into the White House, his name did not top the Gallup Poll listing of the men Americans most admired. The Secretary of State had displaced the President on the list. Quite often these days, at diplomatic dinners in Washington, it is not the President's health that is toasted; it is the Secretary of State's. Occasionally an ambassador will even congratulate Kissinger on his success in keeping foreign affairs safely outside the maelstrom of domestic political scandal. Increasingly, in recent months, he has been referred to as the President of American foreign policy.

But Kissinger is aware that he derives his constitutional authority from the President, and that he is Nixon's Secretary of State as much as he is America's. Before he was recruited from Harvard, Professor Kissinger had grave doubts about Nixon's suitability to lead the country, and he was outspoken in his criticism. "Not fit to be President," he was once quoted as saying. It would be extraordinary indeed if he did not regret the fate that tied him to a Nixon presidency, rather than a Rockefeller, or a Humphrey, one. He sees the irony of the situation: Richard Nixon, the President who gave him power, has now become his Achilles' heel; his leader — and at the same time his liability.

In the spring of 1974, Kissinger is solemn about Nixon, dutifully declaring that he does not expect the President either to resign or to be impeached, but adding that of course he is no specialist on the "domestic process." He knows that Watergate has crippled the President's capacity to lead the country, but he seems ambivalent about whether Nixon should resign; on the one hand, he admires the President's stated decision to fight for his job and thereby maintain the office of the presidency; on the other hand, he wonders whether the nation can sustain additional shocks, such as impeachment, without losing its capacity to cope with foreign challenges. The European in Kissinger has always believed that nations, like people, can suffer overwhelming tragedies — and fade from prominence.

Kissinger is a complicated man — moody, mercurial, with a melancholy streak. He may be depressed one minute, elated the next. He worries constantly. He is worried about the nation: specifically, about whether America will tear herself to pieces in a quest for political purity. Kissinger believes that nothing in politics is pure, and regards this quest, while understandable, as unrealistic. He is also worried about his own future. His reputation as a kind of superstar of statecraft has created expectations that may be unattainable, and he knows that some degree of disappointment is inevitable. He is haunted by the fear that somehow, someone will say something that links him directly to the Watergate scandal. Although he denies that he was involved in any way, he lives with the Kafkaesque nightmare that his former White House colleagues, jealous of his ongoing fame, will seek to drag him down into the mud.

Kissinger strikes many Americans these days as a solitary, troubled comet. A comet can blaze brightly; but once it begins to flicker, it loses its magic. There are critics, in Washington, and across the country, who believe they see the comet flickering. They charge that he has paid too high a price for SALT and détente with the Russians, alienated the West Europeans, antagonized the Japanese, begun the process of selling out Israel, failed to appreciate the intimate connection between foreign policy and international economics, and, despite repeated promises, continued to neglect the bureaucracy in favor of diplomatic showmanship. Kissinger, they say, has "institutionalized" himself, not his policies. At best, they see him as the expediter of the inevitable: in effect, simply capitalizing on the foreign policy requirements of America, Russia, and China during a time of transition. Kissinger, they sense, may be heading for a fall.

But for every critic of Kissinger, there are still at least a dozen defenders who see the comet burning brightly — in fact, against skies darkened by Watergate, more brightly than ever. There seems to be an almost desperate turning to Kissinger, in the hope that his achievements will help restore the nation's self-esteem. Even his personal life has been followed with intense curiosity by people all over the world. His marriage in March, 1974, to Nancy Maginnes and their secret departure for Acapulco was a front-page story; newsmen went flying off to Mexico in pursuit of a photograph of the honeymooners or perhaps an interview with the bride. The bridegroom beamed.

Kissinger has always said that when he leaves office, he wants to be able to look back and feel that he has "made a difference." Kissinger is still in mid-career; the Nixon Administration still in mid-crisis; the story is still not complete. Kissinger has made his share of mistakes, but he has also produced more than his share of successes. None is more meaningful to him than the launching of SALT — the effort to negotiate limitations on the development and deployment of strategic nuclear weapons. Others may be entranced by his achievements in Peking, Paris, or Jerusalem; indeed, Kissinger himself would be the first to applaud. But he knows that in a world stockpiled with nuclear weapons, the ultimate challenge is to defuse the future by tackling potentially explosive issues today. It is a simple matter of survival.

Henry Kissinger once quoted Metternich as saying: "Because I know what I want and what the others are capable of, I am completely prepared." Once again, perhaps unintentionally, he was talking about himself.

Sources

A Note on Sources

Our primary source was Henry Kissinger — a series of private interviews, plus his backgrounders, his news conferences, his writings, his speeches, coupled with the opportunities that the authors, as news correspondents, have had over the years to cover his diplomatic activities at the White House and at the State Department at home, from Peking to Moscow abroad. In researching his career, we have had extensive interviews with many of his friends and associates who have known him from his undergraduate days at Harvard to his occupancy of the Secretary's office at State. We have also talked with officials, scholars, journalists — in the United States, Asia, Europe, and the Middle East — who either have had firsthand dealings with Kissinger or have closely followed his policies.

Henry Kissinger's own writings were particularly useful for background in preparing this manuscript:

BOOKS

A World Restored: Metternich, Castlereagh, and the Problems of Peace, 1812–1822. Houghton Mifflin, 1957 (Paperback: *A World Restored: The Politics of Conservatism in a Revolutionary Age.* Grosset & Dunlap, 1964).

Nuclear Weapons and Foreign Policy. Harper & Row, 1957 (Paperback: Norton, 1969).

The Necessity for Choice: Prospects of American Foreign Policy. Harper & Row, 1961.

The Troubled Partnership: A Reappraisal of the Atlantic Alliance. McGraw-Hill, 1965.

Problems of National Strategy: A Book of Readings. Henry A. Kissinger, ed.,
    Praeger, 1965.
American Foreign Policy: Three Essays. Norton, 1969.

ARTICLES

"Military Policy and the Defense of the 'Grey Areas.'" *Foreign Affairs*, April,
    1955.
"Force and Diplomacy in the Nuclear Age." *Foreign Affairs*, October, 1956.
"Reflections on American Diplomacy." *Foreign Affairs*, October, 1956.
"Controls, Inspection and Limited War." *The Reporter*, June 13, 1957.
"The Policymaker and the Intellectual." *The Reporter*, March 5, 1959.
"The Khrushchev Visit — Dangers and Hopes." *New York Times Magazine*,
    September 6, 1959.
"Limited War: Nuclear or Conventional? A Reappraisal." *Daedalus*, Fall, 1960.
"For an Atlantic Confederacy." *The Reporter*, February 2, 1961.
"Reflections on Cuba." *The Reporter*, November 22, 1962.
"Domestic Structure and Foreign Policy." *Daedalus*, April, 1966.
"For a New Atlantic Alliance." *The Reporter*, July 14, 1966.
"The White Revolutionary: Reflections on Bismarck." *Daedalus*, Summer, 1968.
"Bureaucracy and Policymaking: The Effect of Insiders and Outsiders on the
    Policy Process, in Bureaucracy, Politics and Strategy." *Security Studies Paper
    No. 17*, University of California, Los Angeles, 1968.
"Central Issues of American Foreign Policy." *Agenda for the Nation*, Brookings
    Institution, 1968.
"The Vietnam Negotiations." *Foreign Affairs*, January, 1969.

Among the books by others used in the course of research:

Henry Brandon, *The Retreat of American Power*. Doubleday, 1973.
Allen Drury and Fred Maroon, *Courage and Hesitation*. Doubleday, 1971.
Daniel Ellsberg, *Papers on the War*. Simon & Schuster, 1972.
Stephen R. Graubard, *Kissinger, Portrait of a Mind*. Norton, 1973.
Roger Hilsman, *To Move a Nation*. Doubleday, 1967.
Harold C. Hinton, *China's Turbulent Quest*. Macmillan, 1972.
Marvin Kalb and Elie Abel, *Roots of Involvement*. Norton, 1971.
Stanley Karnow, *Mao and China, from Revolution to Revolution*. Viking, 1972.
David Landau, *Kissinger: The Uses of Power*. Houghton Mifflin, 1972.
John Osborne, *The Nixon Watch* series of books. Liveright.
Douglas Pike, *Viet Cong*. The MIT Press, 1966.
Robert Shaplen, *The Road from War, Vietnam 1965–1970*. Harper & Row,
    1970.
Edgar Snow, *Red Star over China*. Random House, 1938; *The Other Side of
    the River*. Random House, 1961.
Theodore H. White, *The Making of the President — 1968*. Atheneum, 1969;
    The Making of the President — 1972. Atheneum, 1973.
China and US Foreign Policy. Congressional Quarterly Service, 1971.

The Pentagon Papers, by the *New York Times,* based on investigative reporting by Neil Sheehan. Bantam Books, 1971.
The President's Trip to China, text by members of the American press corps. Bantam Books, 1972.

Also:

Hearings before the Committee on Foreign Relations. U.S. Senate, Ninety-third Congress, First Session, on Nomination of Henry A. Kissinger to be Secretary of State, Part 1 (September 7, 10, 11, and 14, 1973); Part 2 (September 16 and 17, 1973).

Transmittal of documents from the National Security Council to the Chairman of the Joint Chiefs of Staff: hearing before the Committee on Armed Services in the U.S. Senate, Ninety-third Congress, Second Session, Part 1 (February 6, 1974).

Also:

The *Boston Globe,* the *Christian Science Monitor,* the *Congressional Quarterly, Foreign Affairs, Foreign Policy,* the *Los Angeles Times,* the *New Republic, Newsweek,* the *New York Times, Time,* the *Wall Street Journal,* the *Washington Post,* the *Washington Star-News.*

In many cases, we have quoted from published interviews and accounts by individual journalists. Some of these quotations are identified fully in the text; the following chapter-by-chapter listing includes additional information about many published quotations that are not fully described in the text. It also provides specific page references for quotations drawn from Kissinger's published works. Finally, it lists published material that we have found most helpful on several specific subjects.

ONE: AN INTRODUCTION

"Opportunities cannot be . . ." (p. 4): Henry A. Kissinger speech at Pacem in Terris conference, Washington, D.C., October 8, 1973.
"you can assume . . ." (p. 7): "A Conversation with Henry Kissinger," with Barbara Walters, NBC, February 25, 1973.
"Are you shy . . ." (p. 11): Oriana Fallaci, "Kissinger." The *New Republic,* December 16, 1972.

TWO: THE HIRING OF HENRY

"That man Nixon . . . " (pp. 15–16): Barnard Law Collier, "The Road to Peking, or, How Does This Kissinger Do It?" The *New York Times Magazine,* November 14, 1971.

". . . the most dangerous" (p. 16): Chalmers Roberts, the *Washington Post*, August 23, 1972.

"Go see Henry . . ." (p. 16): Barnard Law Collier, op. cit.

"He really loved Miami Beach . . ." (p. 17): George Sherman, the *Evening Star* (Washington), June 22, 1969.

". . . outraged and offended" (p. 18): Nora Beloff, "Prof. Bismarck Goes to Washington." The *Atlantic Monthly*, December, 1969.

"For people of my generation" (p. 24): Joseph Kraft, "In Search of Kissinger." *Harper's*, January, 1971.

"A second-rate mind" (p. 25): Barnard Law Collier, op. cit.

THREE: THE GREENING OF A GREENHORN

". . . would cross the street . . ." (p. 31): Joseph Kraft, "In Search of Kissinger." *Harper's*, January, 1971.

Frau Wittenmayer's reminiscences (p. 32): Gaylord Shaw (of the Associated Press), a series of articles in the *Evening Star* (Washington), May 1–4, 1972.

Louis and Walter Kissinger's memories of Henry's childhood (p. 32): Lloyd Shearer and Henry Kissinger, "President Nixon's Brainchild." *Parade*, October 24, 1971.

Reminiscences by Israelis of Kissinger's boyhood (pp. 32–33): *Bamahaneh* (Israeli army magazine), September 5, 1973.

". . . difficult for Americans to visualize . . ." (p. 34): Henry Kissinger, *The Necessity for Choice* (Harper & Row, 1961), p. 6.

". . . man of great goodness . . ." (p. 34): Joseph Kraft, op. cit.

Paula and Louis Kissinger's memories of Fürth (pp. 34–35): Danielle Hunebelle, *Dear Henry* (Berkley Publishing Co., 1972), p. 36.

"It was my wife . . ." (p. 35): Lloyd Shearer, op. cit.

"My life in Fürth . . ." (p. 35): Gaylord Shaw, op. cit.

"That part of my childhood . . ." (p. 35): Barnard Law Collier, "The Road to Peking, or, How Does This Kissinger Do It?" The *New York Times Magazine*, November 14, 1971.

". . . For a refugee . . ." (p. 37): Gaylord Shaw, op. cit.

". . . working my way through high school . . ." (p. 37): Barnard Law Collier, op. cit.

"Becoming an accountant . . ." (p. 37): Joseph Kraft, op. cit.

Kissinger's parents on Henry's early Army career (p. 38): Danielle Hunebelle, op. cit., p. 39.

Kraemer's first appearance at Camp Claiborne (pp. 38–39): Barnard Law Collier, op. cit.

Frau Margerete Drink's reminiscences (p. 40): Gaylord Shaw, op. cit.

Mrs. Elizabeth Heid's reminiscences (p. 41): Milan J. Kubic, "Memories of 'Mr. Henry,'" *Newsweek*, October 8, 1973.

". . . shell-shock case . . ." (p. 42): Gaylord Shaw, op. cit.

"the moment when it became evident . . ." (p. 46): Henry Kissinger, *A World Restored: The Politics of Conservatism in a Revolutionary Age* (Grosset & Dunlap, 1964), pp. 4–5.

"What is surprising . . ." (p. 47): Ibid., p. 5.

". . . largest possible number of allies" (p. 47): Ibid., p. 19.

FOUR: ASCENT TO POWER

"In Greek mythology . . ." (p. 53): Henry Kissinger, *Nuclear Weapons and Foreign Policy* (Harper & Row, 1957), p. 3.

"In the long interval of peace . . ." (p. 53): Henry Kissinger, *A World Restored: The Politics of Conservatism in a Revolutionary Age* (Grosset & Dunlap, 1964), p. 6.

"The dilemma of the nuclear period . . ." (p. 53): Henry Kissinger, *Nuclear Weapons and Foreign Policy*, op. cit., p. 7.

"Limited nuclear war . . ." (p. 53): Ibid., p. 199.

"essentially a political act . . . an attempt . . ." (p. 54): Ibid., pp. 140–141.

"a spectrum of capabilities . . ." (p. 54): Ibid., p. 172.

"In terms of deterrence . . ." (p. 54): Henry Kissinger, *Nuclear Weapons and Foreign Policy* (Norton, 1969), p. 158.

"calamity far transcending . . ." (p. 54): Henry Kissinger, *Nuclear Weapons and Foreign Policy* (Harper & Row, 1957), p. 146.

"We are falling behind . . ." (p. 59): Henry Kissinger, *The Necessity for Choice* (Harper & Row, 1961), p. 98.

"Some years ago . . ." (p. 60): Ibid., p. 81.

"The years ahead . . ." (p. 60): Ibid., p. 85.

"It makes us overlook . . ." (p. 60): Ibid., pp. 199–200.

"Such attitudes . . ." (p. 60): Ibid., p. 97.

"The best method . . ." (p. 61): Ibid., p. 324.

the discussion of the interrelationship between the intellectual and the policy-maker (p. 61): Ibid., pp. 348–358.

"make concessions . . . a worsening of Berlin's position . . ." (p. 63): Ibid., p. 141.

Kissinger's recollections of his early 1960s experience in government (p. 64): from a speech at the Federal City Club in Washington on April 13, 1973, an excerpt from which was published in the *Washington Post*, April 15, 1973.

"The War in Vietnam . . ." (pp. 68–69): Henry Kissinger, "What Should We Do Now?" *Look*, August 9, 1966.

With reference to the "Pennsylvania" account (pp. 70–77): it was the unauthorized publication of the "Pentagon Papers" in 1971 that for the first time disclosed the full story of "Pennsylvania," although a variety of details had been revealed by two reporters, David Kraslow and Stuart H. Loory, in *The Secret Search for Peace in Vietnam* (Vintage Books, 1968), pp. 221–224; by one diplomat, Chester L. Cooper, in *The Lost Crusade* (Dodd, Mead, 1970), and by a president, Lyndon B. Johnson, in his memoirs, *The Vantage Point* (Holt, Rinehart & Winston, 1971). A comprehensive "Pennsylvania" account appeared under the by-line of Don Oberdorfer in the *Washington Post*, June 27, 1972, based on secret documents made available by columnist Jack Anderson.

Aubrac's conversation with Ho Chi Minh (pp. 72–73), and subsequent events: reported by Jack Anderson, the *Washington Post*, June 16, 1972, and later confirmed by White House officials.

FIVE: HENRY'S WONDERFUL MACHINE

Title of the chapter: from John Osborne's analysis of the NSC in the *New Republic*, January 31, 1970. His incisive reporting from the White House has been helpful.

"Forrestal's Revenge" (p. 79): Roger Hilsman, *To Move a Nation* (Doubleday, 1967), p. 19.

"He wanted to avoid . . ." (p. 80): Allen Drury and Fred Maroon, *Courage and Hesitation* (Doubleday, 1971), p. 74.

Kissinger's remarks on the Johnson NSC, and his own approach (p. 80): John P. Leacacos: "Kissinger's Apparat," *Foreign Policy Magazine* #5, Winter, 1971–1972.

"There are twenty thousand people . . ." (p. 90): Shana Alexander, "Kissinger by Candlelight," *Newsweek*, August 21, 1972.

SIX: SALT AND LINKAGE: MAKING THE RUSSIANS PAY

John Newhouse's *Cold Dawn, the Story of SALT* (Holt, Rinehart & Winston, 1973) was extremely useful for background on this chapter.

"Could a power achieve . . ." (p. 102): Henry Kissinger, *A World Restored: The Politics of Conservatism in a Revolutionary Age* (Grosset & Dunlap, 1964), pp. 144–145.

the information about the Soviet proposal for joint action with the U.S. against "provocative" attacks by third parties (p. 118): John Newhouse, op. cit.

SEVEN: RIDING THE VIETNAM ROLLER COASTER

Appeal to the Silent Majority

". . . the acid test . . ." (p. 142): Henry A. Kissinger, *A World Restored: The Politics of Conservatism in a Revolutionary Age* (Grosset & Dunlap, 1964), p. 326.

Sally Quinn story (p. 146): Sally Quinn, the *Washington Post*, October 10, 1969.

"If I'd known . . ." and "Seen one President . . ." (p. 147): Patrick Anderson, "Confidence of the President," the *New York Times Magazine*, June 1, 1969.

"the use of unbridled . . ." (p. 148): Jack Anderson, the *Washington Post*, August 18, 1972.

"Le Duc Tho is . . ." (p. 150): Marvin Kalb, "Conversation with Kissinger": a one-hour interview with Henry Kissinger on "CBS News," February 1, 1973.

Cambodia: The Doctrine of Force

"It was an upper-class coup . . ." (p. 153): T. D. Allman, "Anatomy of a Coup," *Far Eastern Economic Review;* reprinted in *Cambodia, the Widening War in Indochina* (Washington Square Press, 1971).

"officially winked" (p. 153): Norodom Sihanouk as related to Wilfred Burchett, *My War with the CIA* (Pantheon Books, 1972), p. 23.

Nixon's "pluses and minuses" list (p. 161): Stewart Alsop, "On the President's Yellow Pad," *Newsweek,* June 1, 1970.

"You have an order . . ." (p. 162): Laurence Stern, the *Washington Post,* November 28, 1973.

The encounter between Kissinger and the angry professors (pp. 165–167): based on an article by Michael E. Kinsley that appeared in the *Washington Monthly,* September, 1970, based on his *Harvard Crimson* accounts.

"He knew he was swimming . . ." (p. 168): Allen Drury and Fred Maroon, *Courage and Hesitation* (Doubleday, 1971), p. 77.

Frustration in Paris

text of Kissinger's private report to the President on ARVN (p. 177): Jack Anderson, the *Washington Post,* May 24, 1971; later confirmed by State Department sources.

Kissinger's appearance on "CBS Morning News" (p. 178): February 26, 1971.

"a little spring offensive . . ." (p. 178): Mary McGrory, the *Washington Star,* March 16, 1971.

Mary McGrory's report on the peace militants (p. 178): the *Washington Star,* March 12 and 16, 1971.

EIGHT: ON THE BRINK IN JORDAN AND CIENFUEGOS

"big-power recognition" (p. 186): recommended by Kissinger in the course of an appearance on "Face the Nation," CBS, July 27, 1958.

Dobrynin's turning "ashen" and other descriptions of this meeting (p. 211): Henry Brandon, *The Retreat of American Power* (Doubleday, 1973), p. 282.

Kissinger and Dobrynin joking about Alaska (pp. 214–215): John Newhouse, *Cold Dawn, the Story of SALT* (Holt, Rinehart & Winston, 1973), p. 218.

NINE: THE CHINA BREAKTHROUGH

Particularly useful for background on this chapter were:

Harold Hinton, *The Bear at the Gate.* American Enterprise Institute, 1971.
Donald W. Klein and Anne B. Clark, *Biographic Dictionary of Chinese Communism.* Harvard University Press, 1971.
Ross Terrill, *800,000,000 — The Real China.* Little, Brown, 1972.

Seymour Topping, *Journey Between Two Chinas.* Harper & Row, 1972.
China and US Far East Policy 1945–1966. Congressional Quarterly Service, 1967.
China and US Foreign Policy. Congressional Quarterly Service, 1971.

Also:

John Burns's dispatches from China in the *Christian Science Monitor.*

The Making of a New China Hand

"Enemy advances . . ." (p. 216): Henry Kissinger, *Nuclear Weapons and Foreign Policy* (Harper & Row, 1957), p. 347.
"All that we have to do . . ." (p. 217): from a speech by Richard M. Nixon during the California Senate campaign, September 18, 1950; excerpt reprinted in *China and US Foreign Policy* (Congressional Quarterly Service, 1971), p. 19.
". . . an unfortunate step . . ." (p. 222): *China and US Far East Policy 1945–1966,* op. cit., p. 133.
Hugh Sidey quote (p. 223): Hugh Sidey, "The Secret of Lincoln's Sitting Room," *Life,* July 30, 1971.
"It was not love of America . . ." (p. 229): testimony by Professor Allen Whiting during House Foreign Affairs Subcommittee Hearings on China, September 24, 1970.
Edgar Snow's conversation with Mao (p. 232): Edgar Snow, "What China Wants from Nixon's Visit," *Life,* July 30, 1971.
Edgar Snow's report of his conversation with Mao (p. 235) appeared in two articles in *Life:* "A Conversation with Mao Tse-tung," April 30, 1971; and "China Will Talk from a Position of Strength," October 1, 1971.
"We consider it highly unlikely . . ." (p. 236): Henry Kissinger interview on "CBS Morning News," February 26, 1971.
"an affair of a single evening . . ." (p. 236): Ross Terrill, op. cit., p. 165.

Over the Himalayas — and Beyond

Ross Terrill's discussions with the Chinese about Kissinger (p. 241): Ross Terrill, op. cit., p. 152.
"I am getting hell . . ." (p. 259): Jack Anderson, the *Washington Post,* January 3, 1972.
Truong Chinh's attack on Nixon-Kissinger (pp. 264–265): Robert Shaplen, "Letter from Saigon," the *New Yorker,* May 6, 1972.

TEN: "THE WEEK THAT CHANGED THE WORLD"

The President's Trip to China (Bantam Books, 1972).
"A sadder party . . ." (p. 274): Joseph Kraft, "Letter from Peking," the *New Yorker,* March 11, 1972.

"staggering capitulation" (p. 282): William F. Buckley's Shanghai column, February 28; it appeared in the *National Review* on March 17, 1972.
Particularly helpful in preparing this chapter were the reports from Peking during the President's trip by: Henry Bradsher, the *Washington Star-News;* Mel Elfin, *Newsweek;* Max Frankel, the *New York Times;* Stanley Karnow, the *Washington Post;* Robert L. Keatley, the *Wall Street Journal;* Jerrold Schecter, *Time;* R. H. Shackford, Scripps-Howard; Hugh Sidey, *Life;* Theodore H. White, National Public Affairs Center for Television.

ELEVEN: HAIPHONG HARBOR: A PLACE FOR JUGULAR DIPLOMACY

Kissinger's remarks to Reston (p. 288): James Reston, the *New York Times.*
"How he performs . . ." (p. 296): James Reston, the *New York Times,* April 26, 1972.

TWELVE: THE MOSCOW SUMMIT

Gromyko's apple-orange-microphone joke (p. 323): Henry Brandon, *The Retreat of American Power* (Doubleday, 1973), p. 290.

THIRTEEN: THE BEGINNING OF THE END

"third-rate burglary . . ." (p. 336): Ziegler news conference, Miami, Florida, June 19, 1972.
Nixon's comments on the dikes (p. 340): Nixon news conference, July 27, 1972.
Betty Beale (pp. 344–345): the *Evening Star and Daily News,* August 24, 1972.
Dorothy McCardle (p. 345): the *Washington Post,* August 24, 1972.
Mary McGrory (p. 345): the *Washington Star,* August 8, 1972.
Peter Lisagor (p. 345): the *Sunday Star* (Washington), June 18, 1972.

FOURTEEN: "PEACE IS AT HAND"

Arnaud de Borchgrave in Hanoi (pp. 362–363): account by Arnaud de Borchgrave, *Newsweek,* October 30, 1972.
Oriana Fallaci interview (pp. 374–375): "Thieu," *Newsweek,* January 20, 1973.
P. 384: U.S. military expenditures: Department of Defense, published in the *New York Times,* January 25, 1973; U.S. casualties: Department of Defense; South Vietnamese casualties: U.S. Senate Subcommittee on Refugees.

FIFTEEN: THE VIETNAM FINALE

Statistics on the air and sea lift to Saigon (pp. 388–389): William Beecher, the *New York Times,* November 3, 1972; Michael Getler, the *Washington Post,* November 8 and November 15, 1972; UPI, in the *New York Times,* November 21, 1972.

Garnett D. Horner's story (p. 391): Washington's *Evening Star and Daily News,* November 7, 1972.

Resumption of Kissinger-Tho talks (p. 394): Henry Hubbard, *Newsweek,* December 4, 1972. "Is Kissinger in Trouble?," *Newsweek,* January 1, 1973.

"the highest councils . . ." (p. 399): *Human Events,* November 25, 1972.

Oriana Fallaci interview (pp. 399–400): "Kissinger," the *New Republic,* December 16, 1972.

"it was high noon . . ." (pp. 399–400): *Time,* January 1, 1973.

Kissinger to Reston (p. 405): James Reston, the *New York Times,* December 2, 1972.

Kissinger to Reston (p. 410): James Reston, the *New York Times,* December 13, 1972.

"the most painful . . ." (p. 415), and "The President decided . . ." (p. 417): interview of Henry Kissinger by Marvin Kalb, CBS News, February 1, 1973.

Kraft quote (p. 416): Joseph Kraft, the *Washington Post,* January 4, 1973.

Crawford quote (p. 416): Kenneth Crawford, the *Washington Post,* December 23, 1972.

Fritchey quote (p. 417): Clayton Fritchey, *Philadelphia Evening Bulletin,* December 22, 1972.

Particularly helpful in preparing this chapter were the reports of: the CBS News bureaus in Paris and Saigon; Bernard Gwertzman and Flora Lewis, the *New York Times;* Marilyn Berger, Murrey Marder, and Jonathan C. Randall, the *Washington Post;* Darius Jhabvala, the *Boston Globe;* Robert C. Toth, the *Los Angeles Times.*

SIXTEEN: THE IMPACT OF WATERGATE

"Mr. Kissinger seems to be . . ." (p. 429): editorial in the *New York Times,* April 26, 1973.

"It is a brutal fact . . ." (p. 431): Kissinger's speech on April 23, 1973, at the Associated Press luncheon, in New York.

"They are currently citing . . ." (p. 436): Stanley Karnow and David Bruce in Peking, the *New Republic,* May 26, 1973.

"You have had such things occur . . ." (p. 438): C. L. Sulzberger's interview with Chou, the *New York Times,* October 27, 1973.

Leonid Brezhnev's news conference (p. 440): the *New York Times,* June 15, 1973.

Shana Alexander of *Newsweek;* William S. White, a syndicated columnist; and Martin F. Nolan of the *Boston Globe* were among many columnists and correspondents who reported at the time on the effect of Watergate on Kissinger (pp. 442–445).

material on the wiretapping issue (pp. 442–443) comes from newspaper and magazine accounts, plus interviews with officials on Capitol Hill, the Justice Department, the State Department, and the White House.

SEVENTEEN: THE SECRETARY AT WAR

Q-and-A session with Sadat (p. 452): Arnaud de Borchgrave, *Newsweek,* April 9, 1973.

Material on the prelude to the Israeli war (pp. 452–454) drawn in part from: *Insight on the Middle East War,* Insight Team of the *Sunday Times,* serialized beginning December 9, 1973. Published as a book by Andre Deutsch, 1974.

"The test of statesmanship . . ." (p. 463): Henry A. Kissinger, *The Necessity for Choice* (Harper & Row, 1961), p. 3.

EIGHTEEN: THE CEASE-FIRE ALERT

"More in sorrow" (p. 495): Elizabeth Drew, the *New Yorker,* March 11, 1974.

"passed through the shadows . . ." (p. 497): Murrey Marder, the *Washington Post,* October 26, 1973.

"Seriously different wavelengths" (p. 498): Thomas L. Hughes, "The Meeting of National and World Politics," a speech delivered on December 13, 1973, before the Women's National Democratic Club. Published as "Will Kissinger Topple Nixon?" in the *Washington Post,* December 23, 1973; and as "The Bismarck Connection: Why Kissinger Must Choose between Nixon and the Country," the *New York Times Magazine,* December 30, 1973.

For additional background on the U.S. military alert of October 24, 1973: James Reston, the *New York Times,* October 25, 1973; Michael Getler, the *Washington Post,* October 26, 1973; Joseph Alsop, the *Washington Post,* October 29, 1973; and David Binder, the *New York Times,* November 20 and November 25, 1973.

For additional assessments of the Middle East situation during the crisis period: from Moscow — Hedrick Smith, the *New York Times;* from Jerusalem — Terence Smith, the *New York Times;* from Washington — George Sherman, the *Washington Star-News.* Also, Walter Laqueur, *Confrontation: The Middle East and World Politics* (Quadrangle, 1974), a study of the 1973 war.

NINETEEN: HENRY OF ARABIA

The Launching of "101"

Heikal's recollections of Kissinger (pp. 511–512): Mohammed Hassanein Heikal, in *L'Express,* November 26, 1973, pp. 76–77.

Golda Meir's news conference (p. 526): published in the *Government Press Service Press Bulletin* of Israel, December 1, 1973, on the subject of Israeli press criticism of Kissinger.

the *Maariv* newspaper account about Israel's uneasiness with America (p. 526): appeared in early December, 1973. It was typical of a number of stories that were printed in the Israeli press during the same period.

TWENTY: A CONCLUDING NOTE

"Both dominated . . ." (p. 543): Henry Kissinger, *A World Restored: The Politics of Conservatism in a Revolutionary Age* (Grosset & Dunlap, 1964), p. 326.

"A statesman who . . ." (p. 544): Ibid., p. 329.

the Richard Valeriani interview with Helmut Sonnenfeldt (p. 547): the "Today" show, NBC, April 5, 1974.

"Because I know . . ." (p. 549): Henry Kissinger, *A World Restored: The Politics of Conservatism in a Revolutionary Age,* op. cit., p. 320.

Index